Bible Commentary

Bible Commentary

THE
MINOR PROPHETS

By

Theo. Laetsch, D. D.

Concordia Publishing House • Saint Louis, Missouri

To My Wife

Foreword

The study of Scripture must never lag. God speaks to each new generation through His Word, the Bible. The message of the Prophets is as significant for our day as it was to Israel of old. The Law of Sinai is as binding upon us as it was upon the Old Testament people under Moses, the Judges, and the kings. The Psalms express the heart cry of the ages and bring comfort to those who at the present moment sit in the valley of the shadow of death.

We still must know the Way, Christ Jesus of the Gospel, if we are to find peace and hope in a world which is in despair. We must go to the cross and look up to Him who was pierced for our transgressions. And to us still is given the challenging commission to preach the Gospel to the whole world with unrelinquishing zeal and undying fervor, as we have the pattern set for us in the Book of Acts and the epistles of the New Testament.

But no one will grow in grace, be filled with a burning desire to serve and share who keeps the sacred book closed and sealed. Jesus urges us to "search the Scriptures." Only then shall we know the truth which makes us wise unto salvation.

To create in Bible students an eager desire to increase their understanding of Scripture, *a new commentary* of the Bible is in the making by scholars of The Lutheran Church — Missouri Synod and is being published by Concordia Publishing House, St. Louis, Mo., under the direction of the Church's Literature Board.

The second of these volumes is herewith presented.

THE PUBLISHERS

Preface

The earliest known reference to the Book of the Twelve Prophets as a unit is found in Ecclesiasticus 49:10 (LXX, ed. Rahlfs, 49:12, Vulgate, ed. Hetzenauer), written about 180 B.C.: "And may the bones of the Twelve Prophets (τῶν δώδεκα προφητῶν, duodecim prophetarum) revive out of their place, for they comforted Jacob and delivered them with their confident hope." (Edgar J. Goodspeed in *The Complete Bible*, p. 134.) While this passage has been declared spurious by some former critics, it is found in the fragments of the original Hebrew text (about three fifths of the entire book) discovered in the genizah (a small room used as a repository for worn or damaged manuscripts) of an ancient synagog at Cairo, Egypt, 1896—1900. It appears quite certain that two or three centuries before the Christian era the writings of the Twelve Prophets were gathered in one volume. While Jewish and Greek writers referred to this book as the Twelve Prophets, the Latin writers used the term *Prophetae Minores*, MINOR PROPHETS; so the Vulgate, Augustine, etc.

Sequence and Chronological Order of the Twelve Prophetic Books

A. In the Masoretic Text

The Masoretes placed the three postexilic Prophets in exact chronological order: Haggai, Zechariah, Malachi. As preceding the postexilic era they placed the two Prophets of the Babylonian era, Habakkuk and Zephaniah, again in chronological order. The first group, the seven Prophets of the Assyrian era antedating the Babylonian era, is not arranged in strict chronological order. The various efforts to establish reasons for the present arrangement of the first Prophets lack convincing power.

B. In the Septuagint

The LXX arranged the twelve books in the following order: Hosea, Amos, Micah, Joel, Obadiah, Jonah, Nahum, Habakkuk, Zephaniah, Haggai, Zechariah, Malachi. As in the Masoretic Text the three postexilic Prophets are placed last; the three Prophets immediately preceding the exile were placed in the middle of the book; the remaining six were placed at the beginning, the three larger books first, Hosea, Amos, Micah, followed by three shorter books, Joel, Obadiah, Jonah.

Hence, while there is in general a chronological sequence insofar as the seven Prophets of the Assyrian era (Hosea, Joel, Amos, Obadiah, Jonah, Micah, Nahum) are followed by the two Prophets of the Babylonian, or Chaldean, era (Habakkuk and Zephaniah) and the three Prophets of the postexilic, or Persian, era (Haggai, Zechariah, Malachi), a chronological order is not observed in the sequence of the individual books of the Assyrian and Babylonian eras.

The Minor Prophets Are Inspired by God

The Minor Prophets are not inferior to the Major Prophets because of a minor degree of inspiration, authority, or reliability of their message. When the Son of God told the Jews to search the Scriptures, John 5: 39, He referred to the Old Testament in its entirety as it was known to the Jews of His time and is still known to us. Of these Scriptures Christ says that one may find eternal life in them, for they are they which testify of Him. Here the Savior asserts the divine power and authority of the Old Testament Scriptures and places them on the same high level that He ascribes to His own words, which are spirit and life, John 6: 63; cp. Luke 24: 27, 32, 44 f. When St. Paul wrote: "All Scripture is given by inspiration of God," etc., 2 Tim. 3: 16, he had in mind the Old Testament Scriptures in their entirety from Genesis to Malachi. In his sermon at Antioch he quotes or refers to the Pentateuch, to Joshua, to the Books of Samuel, to the Psalms, Acts 13: 17-41, as "the Word of God," v. 46. He bases his entire presentation of the doctrine of justification and its glorious fruits, Romans 3 ff., on one brief passage, "The just shall live by his faith"; three words in the Hebrew original, Habakkuk 2: 4, six in Greek, Rom. 1: 17. These words were written by a prophet of whose person and life we know nothing except that he was harassed by doubts as to the justice of God's government and was marvelously comforted by this divine statement. Yet the book of Habakkuk was one of the books of Holy Scripture given by inspiration of God; and this brief word spoken by God's prophet more than 2,400 years ago has not yet been fully fathomed, nor has it lost its power. Only in heaven, when we shall know even as we are known, 1 Cor. 13: 12, shall we fully understand the content and import of this brief oracle of God. Similarly, St. Peter quotes Amos 9: 11 as one of the words of the Prophets, Acts 15: 15 f. The Wise Men of the East were directed to

PREFACE

Bethlehem by a word of a Minor Prophet, Matt. 2:5-8; Micah 5:1. The Minor Prophets are indeed God's Word, the inspired oracles of the Lord. Therefore they are not only reliable sources for the political and religious history of Israel from the days of Amos to those of Malachi; they are also profitable for doctrine, for reproof, for correction, for instruction in righteousness, 2 Tim. 3:16 f. In these writings there is presented to us a faithful picture of man's abounding sin and of God's grace, much more abounding; of human fears and divine promises; of the believer's sorrows and God's comfort; of the child's weakness and the Father's strength. Jehovah's justice and His love, God's grace and His righteousness, God's threats and His promises, are presented not as mere attributes, not in dogmatic definition, but in practical application to man and their actual experience by the children of men. Let us be grateful for the writings of the Minor Prophets and diligently and prayerfully study these divinely inspired words.

THEO. LAETSCH

Table of Contents

NAHUM

HABAKKUK

ZEPHANIAH

HAGGAI

ZECHARIAH

MALACHI

The Minor Prophets

THE MINOR PROPHETS

Historical Background of Literary Prophecy

I. The Kingdom of Israel

The kingdom in Israel which had been promised to Abraham (Gen. 17:16), to Judah (Gen. 49:8), and for which a "King's Law" was incorporated in the Mosaic legislation (Deut. 17:14-20), had been prematurely desired by Israel (1 Sam. 8:1-9). God granted the wish and gave them Saul, a Benjamite, as king. He was anointed by Samuel (1 Sam. 10:1, 17-27) and ruled forty years (Acts 13:21), 1095—1056 B.C. Because of his disobedience the Lord rejected him (1 Sam. 13:13, 14; 15:23) and had David anointed in his stead (1 Sam. 16:1-13). When Saul was slain in battle, the tribe of Judah crowned David king, 1056 (2 Sam. 2:1-4), but Abner made Ishbosheth, the son of Saul, king over the other tribes (2 Sam. 2:8, 9). For seven and one-half years there was war between the house of David and the house of Saul. Then Abner made overtures of peace. Jealous Joab slew him (2 Sam. 3:1-39), and after the murder of Ishbosheth (4:1-12) the eleven tribes anointed David king over all Israel, 1048. David made Jerusalem the royal city and extended the kingdom of Israel from the boundary of Egypt in the southwest and Eziongeber, or Elath, on the Red Sea, on the southeast, to the Euphrates River in the north. Under Solomon, 1016—977, peace and prosperity reigned, until the king began to squander the public moneys on unnecessary buildings and imposed heavy taxes upon the people. As a result the rift between Judah and Israel, which had never quite healed (cp. 2 Sam. 20:1-22), broke open afresh when Rehoboam proudly and foolishly refused the petition of the northern tribes for a reduction of taxes (1 Kings 12: 1-20). For a period of 120 years, 1096—977, Judah and Israel had been united under the rule of Saul, David, and Solomon, with the exception of the seven and one-half years of warfare. The two houses were never again united politically, though for a short period, from 920 to 884, they were allied under the rule of Ahab, 918—897, Ahaziah, 897, and Jehoram, 892—885, who had married Ahab's daughter Athaliah, and Ahaziah, 885—884, of Judah; twenty-five to thirty-five years.

Jeroboam's policy of estranging the northern tribes completely from Judah and the Temple worship by placing two golden calves at

1

Bethel and Dan, inaugurating a feast of tabernacles in the eighth month, and permitting people of the lowest classes to become priests, was quite successful politically, but disastrous for the religious life of the Northern Kingdom (1 Kings 12:25-33). This idolatrous worship, called "the sin of Jeroboam, the son of Nebat" (1 Kings 14:16; 15:26, 30, 34; etc.), soon degenerated into the worship of Baal and other Canaanite and Phoenician deities. Therefore God "cut off" the house of Jeroboam and "destroyed it from off the face of the earth" (1 Kings 13:34; 14:7-11). Because all succeeding kings of Israel retained the calf worship, even Jehu, who eradicated the Baal worship (2 Kings 10:18-29), the Lord rejected one dynasty after another so that during the 250 years of Israel's kingdom not less than nineteen kings and nine dynasties ruled over Israel, one only seven days, Zimri (1 Kings 16:15). In the final verdict upon Israel's sins the "sin of Jeroboam" occupies a prominent place (2 Kings 17:16, 21-23). The royal cities of the Northern Kingdom were Shechem (1 Kings 12:1, 25; 977—ca. 975), Tirzah (975—923, 1 Kings 14:17; 15:21, 33; 16:6, 8, 15, 17, 23), Samaria (923—722, 1 Kings 16:24, 28), Jezreel (perhaps the summer residence of Ahab, 1 Kings 21:1, 23; 2 Kings 8:29; 9:10; etc.). Samaria was destroyed by Shalmaneser V, 722, and the inhabitants were deported to Assyria. (Tiglath-Pileser, 932; Sargon, 921; Ashurbanipal, cp. Ezra 4:10, 669—626.)

Judah survived Israel 136 years, because God remembered His oath given to David (cp. 1 Kings 11:13; 2 Kings 20:6; Jer. 33:15-26). Jerusalem was destroyed and the Temple burnt by Nebuchadnezzar and his captain, Nebuzaradan, 586, seventh to tenth day of Ab (2 Kings 25:8, 9; Jer. 52:6-13).

II. Egypt

The earliest history of Egypt is shrouded in darkness. The dynasties of Manetho, an Egyptian priest, ca. 250 B. C., who wrote a history of Egypt in the Greek language, begin with Menes or Mena, about 3400 B. C., who founded the First Dynasty.

Thotmes III, 1501—1477, of the Seventeenth Dynasty, extended his rule over Palestine, Phoenicia, and Syria to the Euphrates. This Empire Era continued in power till 1165, when Egypt lost its Asiatic empire, at the time of David. The Twenty-first Dynasty, 1095—945, was "a line of weak monarchs" (Barton, *Archaeology and the Bible*, p. 31). Foreign dynasties ruled 945—663. In 945 Sheshonk founded the Twenty-second Dynasty, lasting ca. 200 years. He gave asylum to Jeroboam (1 Kings 11:40, Shishak) and invaded Palestine in the days of Rehoboam (1 Kings 14:25-28). During Egypt's weakness, 850—750, Judah-Israel regained power. Tirhakah, an ally of Hezekiah, was defeated by Sennacherib of Assyria during the latter's siege of Jerusalem, 714 (2 Kings 19:9; Is. 37:9). In 670 Esarhaddon of Assyria invaded Egypt and made Egypt as far as Memphis an Assyrian province; while Ashurbanipal took Thebes, 661 (Nahum 3:8). In 663 a new dynasty, the twenty-sixth, had been formed by Psammetik, lasting till 525. His son, Pharaoh Necho, in an endeavor to regain an Asiatic empire after Nineveh was destroyed, 612, slew Josiah, king of Judah, at Megiddo in 609 (2 Kings 23:29), captured Syria, deposed Josiah's successor, Jehoahaz, and sent him captive to Egypt (2 Kings 23:33 f.). On a second campaign against Babylonia he was disastrously defeated by Nebuchadnezzar in 605 at Carchemish on the Euphrates (2 Kings 24:7; cp. Jer. 46). Hophra, a later king of Egypt, 588—569, tempted Zedekiah of Judah to rebel against Babylon, promised his aid, but suffered a decisive defeat (Jer. 37:4-17; 34:21, 22; Ezek. 29:1-21; 30:20-26).

Instead of trusting in the Lord and remaining loyal to Him, Judah vacillated between Assyria and Egypt (cp. Is. 30:1-7; Jer. 2:14-19); both countries contributed to the ruin of Judah.

III. Assyria

"And the beginning of his [Nimrod's] kingdom was Babel and Erech and Accad and Calneh, in the land of Shinar. Out of that land went forth Asshur and builded Nineveh and the city Rehoboth and Calah, and Resen between Nineveh and Calah; the same is a great city." (Gen. 10:10-12.)

Here we have the earliest Bible reference to Babel, or Babylon, and Asshur, or Assyria, kingdoms over which Nimrod, a Cushite, a descendant of Ham, ruled. V. 10 speaks of "the beginning" of Nimrod's kingdom; v. 11, of the next step of his empire building. Therefore it is better to regard Asshur not as the subject, but as the accusative of direction, and to translate the sentence: "Out of that land he [Nimrod] went forth to Asshur, Assyria." Nimrod built in Assyria a number of cities in close proximity, Nineveh, Rehoboth, Calah, and finally Resen between Nineveh and Calah. The same, i. e., Nineveh together with its adjacent cities, formed a huge complex united into one "great city."

Shinar (Gen. 10:10) may be related to Shumer, the land south of Babylon, from which the earliest civilization was introduced into Asshur (Olmstead, *History of Assyria*, p. 15). "The culture found in

3

Ashur is essentially the same as that of Babylonia or Elam, and everywhere the aristocracy have the same physical appearance. . . . Before entering Babylonia the Shumerians had invented a system of writing. . . . Ashur's own temple in his native city had a Shumerian name, as did the shrines of the mother goddess at Nineveh and Arbela respectively." (Olmstead, pp. 14, 16.)

The first names of Assyrian rulers may be traced to 2200 B. C. (Barton, *Archaeology,* p. 76). They were under the rule of Babylon. About 1430 Assyria became independent of Babylon, and by 1300, under Shalmaneser I, it had extended its boundaries west of the Euphrates, and under Tiglath-Pileser I to the shores of the Mediterranean, about 1100. Then its power rapidly declined, and since Egypt was ruled by weak kings at the same time, David and Solomon could extend their kingdom from Egypt and Elath to the Euphrates. Ashurbanipal, a very powerful ruler, 884—860, regained the countries up to the Mediterranean, shortly after the death of Jehoshaphat of Judah and Jehoram of Israel. Jehu paid tribute to Shalmaneser III, 860—825 (cp. Barton, pp. 77, 458), who also attacked Hazael of Syria, p. 459. Now came a period of decadence, 820—745, during which Uzziah of Judah, 810—758, and Jeroboam II of Israel, 825—773, established the boundaries of David's kingdom. This decadence of Assyria was contemporaneous with an era of weakness of Egypt, hence Judah and Israel were able to enlarge their borders. Menahem paid tribute to Pul of Assyria, 2 Kings 15:19, who is distinguished from Tiglath-Pileser. (2 Kings 15:29; 1 Chron. 5:26.) About 745 powerful Tiglath-Pileser III (745—727) began to rule Assyria. Pekah of Israel and Rezin of Damascus revolted against him, 735, and were defeated; Damascus was conquered, 732, the inhabitants of Galilee and East-jordanland were deported to Assyria (2 Kings 15:29, 30).

Shalmaneser V, 727—722, destroyed Samaria, and Sargon, 722 to 705, deported many Israelites (2 Kings 17). Under Sargon's rule, his son Sennacherib, later king of Assyria, 705—681, invaded Judah, besieged Jerusalem, 714, but his army was annihilated. Sennacherib was followed by Esarhaddon, 681—668, and the latter by Ashurbanipal, 668—626, who conquered Thebes in 661 (Nahum 3:8). Olmstead places Manasseh's captivity (2 Chron. 33:10ff.) in the reign of Esarhaddon (*History of Assyria,* p. 384); others in the reign of Ashurbanipal. Ashurbanipal was followed by his son, Ashuretililam, who was succeeded by Sinsharishkun. Assyria was in the throes of revolutions, and its power gradually waned until Nabopolassar of Babylon revolted against Assyria, 616, and destroyed Nineveh, 612, as had been foretold by Isaiah (ch. 10: 12-19; Nahum 2 and 3; Zeph. 2: 13-15).

A certain nobleman named Ashuruballit escaped from the Babylonian troops and established a new "Land of Assyria" with Harran as its captial, which was sacked by the Median allies of Babylonia in 610. With a great army of Egyptians sent to his aid by Pharaoh Necho II, Ashuruballit sought to regain Harran, but was defeated by Nabopolassar. Pharaoh Necho personally sought to conquer Assyria, was opposed by Josiah, whom he defeated at Megiddo, 610. Necho conquered Syria, swept on to the Euphrates, but in 605 was decisively defeated by Nebuchadnezzar, Nabopolassar's son, at Carchemish on the upper Euphrates, about 270 miles north of Damascus (cp. Jer. 46).

IV. Babylonia

This city is first mentioned in Gen. 10: 10; 11: 1-9.

Its beginnings are still doubtful. The earliest settlers seem to have been a people called Sumerians moving into Babylon from the south; founding a number of city empires. Hammurabi, 2104—2064? (2123 to 2083?), conquered all of Babylonia and extended his realm to the Mediterranean. About 1400 Assyria became independent and soon gained the ascendancy over Babylon, which was conquered about 1250 by Tukulti Ninurta, and for almost 800 years, 1400—612, Babylon did not succeed in retaining for any length of time the sovereignty over Assyria gained several times by energetic kings, e. g., when Merodach-Baladan in the time of King Hezekiah of Judah, 728—698 (2 Kings 20: 12), had successfully revolted against Assyria and ruled Babylonia for about twelve years; and for another year some time later, until Babylon was burnt by Sennacherib.

Nabopolassar, a Chaldean, viceroy of Babylon under Ashurbanipal of Assyria, revolted against Assyrian suzerainty immediately after Ashurbanipal's death, 626, gained his independence, and succeeded in establishing his power southward to the Persian Gulf and northward along the Euphrates River to Carchemish. About this time the Medes, who had been opposing the Assyrian forces with varying success, gradually gained control over the eastern border states of the vast Assyrian Empire. Nabopolassar shrewdly decided to make an alliance with this fast-growing nation. Together, the Babylonians and Medes attacked their veteran and weakening enemy and succeeded in completely destroying Nineveh, 612. Nebuchadnezzar, the son of Nabopolassar, conquered Syria, took Jerusalem, 606 (Dan. 1: 1, 2), and defeated Pharaoh Necho, the powerful rival of Babylon, at Carchemish,

605. Shortly after this battle he received word of his father's death, hurried to Babylon, and ascended the throne, ruling as the greatest of Babylonian monarchs, 604—562. He rebuilt Babylon in great magnificence, as the excavations by Koldewey show (cp. Dan. 3:1; 4:22, 30). He was a great builder, constructing temples, aqueducts, palaces, canals, etc., throughout his vast empire. In 597 he deported Jehoiachin of Judah together with a large portion of the population of the city and many sacred vessels to Babylon (2 Kings 24:8-16) and in 586 completely destroyed Jerusalem and burnt the Temple (2 Kings 25:1-21; Jer. 52:1-27).

Nebuchadnezzar died in 562. He was followed by his son, Evil-Merodach ("man of Merodach"), who liberated King Jehoiachin and placed him over all the kings held captive at Babylon (2 Kings 25: 27-30). After a brief reign of two years Evil-Merodach was killed by his brother-in-law, Nergalsharezer (also called Neriglissar), perhaps identical with the man of the same name, who is called "a prince of the king of Babylon" (Jer. 39:3) and who is named first among those who sat in the middle gate of captured Jerusalem. After a successful reign of four years he died, 555 B.C. His young son, Labashi-Merodach, succeeded him, but was murdered nine months later by a band of conspirators, led perhaps by Nabonidus, who then, as he states in his Stele, "was raised to the lordship of the land by the word of Merodach the lord," because Labashi-Merodach, "incapable of ruling, sat on the royal throne against the will of the gods."

This Nabonidus is the father of the Belshazzar of Dan. 5, where Nebuchadnezzar is called his father; it seems that Nabonidus was the son-in-law of Nebuchadnezzar, and hence the latter was Belshazzar's grandfather. Belshazzar ruled in Babylon as the *de facto* king during his father's absence.

V. Syria

Damascus is mentioned as early as Abraham's time (Gen. 14:15; 15:2). Saul fought against and defeated the king of Zobah (1 Sam. 14:47). David decisively defeated the Syrians, whose "kingdom" at that time seems to have been composed of a number of cities having their own kings. Hadadezer of Zobah, allied with the Syrians of Damascus, was defeated in a bloody battle in which 22,000 Syrians fell. Their land became tributary to David, who had placed a garrison at Damascus. Toi, king of Hamath, an opponent of Hadadezer, sent his son with gifts to David (2 Sam. 8:3-13; 1 Chron. 18:3-10; 19:6-19, the Syrian-Ammonite War). In penalty of Solomon's idolatry the Lord "stirred up" Rezon, a Syrian adventurer, who succeeded in gaining independence for Damascus (1 Kings 11:23-25). From this time until the conquest of Syria by Tiglath-Pileser ca. 730, about 200 years, the Syrians were the chief opponents of Israel and Judah. Asa (955—914) persuaded Benhadad, the successor of Tabrimmon and Hezion, to join him in war against Baasha of Israel (1 Kings 15:17-22). Benhadad II and his thirty-two royal allies attacked Ahab, besieged Samaria, and were defeated during a drunken carousal (1 Kings 20:1-21); a year later Benhadad returned, but again was defeated, Ahab sparing his life (ch. 20:22-43). Later Ahab, 918—897, and Jehoshaphat of Judah, 914—889, fought against the Syrians in an effort to regain Ramoth-Gilead. Ahab was slain in battle. In the rule of Jehoram of Israel, 896—884, Naaman, the Syrian, was cured of his leprosy (2 Kings 5). Samaria was again besieged by the Syrians but miraculously delivered by the Lord (2 Kings 6 and 7). Benhadad's successor was Hazael, an irreconcilable enemy of Israel (2 Kings 8:7-15). Jehoram of Israel and Ahaziah of Judah were decisively defeated by Hazael at Ramoth-Gilead, 885 (2 Kings 8:28, 29). Because of Jehu's (884—856) continuation of Jeroboam's calf worship, Israel was weakened by Hazael (2 Kings 10:32, 33; Amos 1:3) to such an extent that it became practically a vassal of Hazael and his son Benhadad III (2 Kings 13:3-7) during the last years of Jehu and the entire reign of Jehoahaz (856 to 841, fifteen years) and part of Jehoash's (841—825, sixteen years) rule. The latter succeeded in re-establishing Israel's independence, defeating Benhadad three times (2 Kings 13:14-25). His son Jeroboam II, 825—773, extended the boundaries of Israel to Damascus and Hamath (2 Kings 14:23-28).

A few decades after Jeroboam's death, Rezin, the Syrian king, allied himself with Pekah of Israel against Jotham of Judah, 758—743 (2 Kings 15:37), evidently for the purpose of forcing the latter to join them in a revolt against Assyria. They did not succeed, and when Ahaz of Judah, 743—727, adopted the pro-Assyrian policy of his father, they declared war upon him, the Syrian-Ephraimite War, 735—732. Rezin regained Elath, an important port on the Elanitic Gulf (2 Kings 16:6) which had belonged to Judah since Uzziah's time, about 810 (2 Kings 14:22). Together with Pekah, Rezin won a bloody battle against wicked Ahaz, who lost 120,000 killed and a huge number of captives, many of whom were deported to Syria, while Pekah released 200,000 Israelites taken captive by him (2 Chron. 28:5-15). Instead of trusting in the Lord, who through Isaiah had promised the early destruction of Israel and Syria (Is. 7:1-16), Ahaz appealed for help to Tiglath-Pileser of Assyria, who took Damascus, slew Rezin, and deported large numbers of Syrians to Kir (2 Kings 16:7-9), 732. Henceforth Syria became a vassal state of Assyria, later of Babylonia, Persia, and Alexander. After the death of Alexander, Syria and Mesopotamia were assigned to one of his generals, Seleucus Nicanor, who built Antioch ca. 300 B. C. and made it his capital city. Damascus was rebuilt in the Persian era (538—332) and again became a flourishing city. In 65 Pompey the Great put an end to the Seleucidian dynasty, and Syria became a Roman province.

HOSEA

Introductory Remarks

The Name of the Prophet

Hosea = help, deliverance, occurs five times as a proper name. Hoshea (Oshea), the servant and successor of Moses, later called Joshua (Ex. 24:13; Num. 13:8, 16; Deut. 32:44); an Ephraimite, one of the commanders appointed by David (1 Chron. 27:20); the last king of Israel, who was neither a help nor deliverer; the prophet Hosea (Hos. 1:1, 2); one of the signers of Nehemiah's covenant (Neh. 10:24; A. V., v. 23).

The Time of Hosea's Activity

Hosea prophesied in the days of Uzziah (810—758 *), Jotham (—742), Ahaz (—727), Hezekiah (—698), kings of Judah, and Jeroboam II (825—773), king of Israel. Uzziah and Jeroboam ruled contemporaneously 810—773. In his first prophecy, Hosea (ch. 1:4) foretells the collapse in the near future of Jehu's dynasty (cp. 2 Kings 10:30), which occurred when Zachariah was murdered six months after Jeroboam's death (2 Kings 15:8-12). Allowing five to ten years for the time elapsed between Hosea's prophecy and its fulfillment, we arrive at about 785—780 as the date of Hosea's call. Since he makes no mention of Samaria's destruction (722), he may have written his book before that event. His activity, therefore, extended from ca. 785 to 780 to ca. 725, a period of fifty-five to sixty years. Since early marriages were customary in Israel, the prophet may have attained an age of seventy-five to eighty years.

His Personal History

We know very little of the personal history of Hosea. His family is unknown. Early Jewish writers identified his father, Beeri (1:1), with Beerah, a prince of the tribe of Reuben, carried into exile by Tiglath-Pileser (1 Chron. 5:6). According to an ancient Christian tradition (Ephraem Syrus, Pseudo-Epiphanius) he was of the tribe of Issachar, from a place called Belemoth or Beleman; Jerome: Beth-shemesh.

---

* All dates according to Ussher.

9

Hosea's familiarity with the topography and history of the Northern Kingdom, the fact that he only rarely mentions Judah, and never names Jerusalem, that he calls the Northern Kingdom "the land" (ch. 1:2), and its king "our king" (7:5), that a large number of Aramaisms occur in his book, all combine to favor the opinion that Hosea is a native of the Northern Kingdom. "Every sentence of Hosea makes us feel that he had not merely once upon a time made this kingdom a passing visit, as Amos did, but knows it with the inmost consciousness of his heart, and follows all its deeds and efforts and fortunes with the emotions of such a profound sympathy as is only conceivable in the case of a native-born prophet of the country." (Ewald, *Die Propheten des Alten Bundes*, 1840, Vol. I, p. 172, quoted by Huxtable in *The Bible Commentary*, Hosea, p. 399.) We subscribe to the words of G. A. Smith: "The poetry of Hosea clings about his native soil like its trailing vines. . . . Hosea's love steals across his whole land like the dew, provoking every separate scent and color till all Galilee lies before us lustrous and fragrant." (*The Expositor's Bible*, Vol. IV, p. 499.)

Most of Hosea's symbols are connected with agriculture, rural life. He may have been a tiller of the soil before he was called as a prophet. His intimate knowledge of the history of his people and the political affairs of his day, the language, which, while terse, is beautiful, containing many similes, references, and figures which only a cultured man would employ, seem to point to the wealthier class of the rural communities.

Duhm's endeavor (*Theologie der Propheten*, pp. 130, 131) to prove that Hosea was a member of the priestly order lacks convincing proof. Hosea's frequent references to priests, to the Law, to uncleanness, to persecution in the Temple, do not warrant Duhm's conclusions.

A Jewish legend states that Hosea died in Babylon and that his body was buried at Safed, northwest of the Sea of Galilee, on the highest point in that region. According to another tradition he was a native of Gilead and was buried there. To this day the grave of Nebi Osha is shown near es-Salt, Ramoth-Gilead, south of the Jabbok River. (Eiselen, *The Prophetic Books*, II, p. 372.)

Political and Social Conditions

Hosea was called into office in those stirring times that ushered in the final catastrophe which swept away the Northern Kingdom, Ephraim, the ten tribes, into political extermination, 722. At the time that Hosea began to prophesy there appeared at least to the superficial observer no indication on the political horizon that the end was so near, so rapidly approaching. Jeroboam II ruled over Israel. Under Uzziah, or, as he is also called, Azariah (2 Kings 14:21; 15, throughout the chapter, except v. 13), Israel-Judah had regained the power and splendor which it had enjoyed in the days of Solomon, 1016—977, after having been at the mercy of the enemies for about 150 years, 977—825, the beginning of Jeroboam's rule according to Ussher. In 977 that unfortunate breach had occurred owing to Rehoboam's stubborn refusal to lighten the burden of taxation imposed by Solomon on Israel (1 Kings 12). This breach had been a divine punishment for king and people — for the royal house because of Solomon's shameful apostasy and idolatry (1 Kings 11:11-13); for the people because they also had forgotten God.

The political and commercial strength of the two kingdoms had been sapped for 150 years by intertribal warfare and oppression by foreign enemies. With the exception of a few years of peace, during the dynasty of Omri, there had been almost constant warfare between Judah and Israel. Asa had bribed the Syrian king Benhadad to worry Israel (1 Kings 15:20), who took Cinneroth and Naphtali, one of the most fertile regions, from Israel. Jehoshaphat and Jehoram of Judah were on friendly terms with Ahab, Ahaziah, and Joram of Israel, the royal houses intermarrying; but on the accession of Jehu hostilities again flared up between the two kingdoms.

Not only intertribal warfare weakened the kingdoms. Foreign enemies time and again invaded the land. The Philistines harassed Israel (1 Kings 15:27; 16:15). Syrian armies repeatedly invaded Israel (1 Kings 20—22; 2 Kings 5:2; 6:8—8:29; 10:32,33). Moab rebelled (2 Kings 1:1; 3:4-27; 13:20). Jehu's son Jehoahaz had only fifty horsemen, ten chariots, 10,000 footmen (2 Kings 13:7).

However, the Lord was not yet willing to reject Israel (2 Kings 13:5; 14:26 ff.). Better times dawned. Joash in the Northern Kingdom three times defeated the Syrians (13:25); Amaziah in the south defeated Edom (14:7). In unpardonable pride the old rivalry between Judah and Israel caused him to attack Joash, a course which brought him signal defeat (14:8-14).

Now came for the two kingdoms an almost unprecedented era of prosperity. Jeroboam II completed the good work begun by his father, Joash. He recovered Damascus, which had been part of David's and of Solomon's kingdom (2 Sam. 8:6). Advancing northward 200 miles, he conquered Hamath the Great (Amos 6:2), a city of the Hittites,

11

near Baalbek, on the Orontes, which had thrown off the yoke of Solomon.

At about the same time Uzziah subdued the Philistines and Arabians; made vassals of the Amorites; built strong outposts in the desert of Judah; fortified Jerusalem with towers (2 Chron. 26:9); had a standing army of 307,500 men fully equipped with the most modern armament, shields, spears, helmets, habergeons (coats of mail), bows, and slings. He was the first to introduce catapults and ballistae, powerful engines to throw missiles, stones, and arrows (2 Chron. 26:15). Elath, on the Gulf of Akabah, the northeastern arm of the Red Sea, was recaptured by either Judah or Israel; at least after the death of Jeroboam, Uzziah possessed it. Uzziah, having learned a lesson from Amaziah's defeat, seems to have lived in peace with Jeroboam, who in spite of his idolatry — his continuance, for political reasons, of the policy of Jeroboam I — was one of the ablest kings of Israel.

At the time of Hosea and his earlier contemporary Amos a generation had therefore grown up in Israel which knew not the bitterness of oppression by the enemy nor the shame of defeat, a generation which had little, if any, experience in actual warfare. Peace had ruled for many years, and consequently prosperity had returned to the poverty-stricken land. Not only had agriculture revived under the fostering care of Uzziah, who loved husbandry, agriculture, encouraging wherever possible the planting of orchards and vineyards (2 Chron. 26:10; Amos 5:11), the cultivation of farms and gardens; also in northern Israel the immensely fertile soil of Samaria was again being carefully and skillfully cultivated, once the danger of raids from surrounding enemies was past, and yielded rich harvests, thirty-, fifty-, hundredfold. Wealth came back to the impoverished people. Commerce assumed the proportions it had gained in the days of David and Solomon and the people began to flock to the cities.

Quite naturally, under such conditions, the building trades flourished. Amos refers to the building activity of his time. See also Hos. 8:14; ch. 3:11, 15; 5:11; 6:8, 11; Is. 9:10. Mark especially the proud and haughty spirit in the last passage. With increasing wealth more conveniences and luxuries were demanded. No longer a house built of unhewn stone seemed satisfactory; the latest style was to build homes of cedar wood and hewn stone squared and laid up in a manner more pleasing to the eye than the homes built from rough quarry stones. The homes became palaces. Amos constantly speaks- of *armonim*, high buildings, rivaling in size and beauty and grandeur of construction the palaces of the kings. For the proud owners were indeed princes of trade, kings of the money market. These nabobs were no longer satisfied with having a home in the city. As Ahab had built a summer residence in the cool hill country of Jezreel in order to escape the heat of summer, so the rich built their summer homes, vying with one another in point of splendor and convenience. Even hewn stones no longer satisfied their pampered tastes. Ahab built an "ivory house" (1 Kings 22:39), and Amos speaks of "houses of ivory" (Amos 3:15) whose walls and ceilings were embellished by plaques or small panels of ivory. Undoubtedly such palaces in city and country were among the "pleasant pictures" (Is. 2:16) show pieces, pointed out with pride to visitors from near and far. On the luxury and revelries in these homes, see notes on Amos 6:4-6, p. 170 f.

Side by side with this immense wealth and pomp was poverty, need, want, pauperism, poverty so great that people were sold into slavery because they could not pay a ransom sufficiently large to buy a pair of sandals (Amos 8:6), being absolutely penniless.

The immense wealth of the rich was not amassed by fair means. Says Hos. 12:7: He, Israel, is a merchant, a Canaanite; the balance of deceit is in his hand; he loveth to oppress, deceive, force to the wall every competitor. Isaiah pronounces a woe on them that join house to house and lay field to field till there be no place, that they may be placed alone in the midst of the earth (5:8). Amos draws a vivid picture of their great greed and filthy lucre (8:5,6); by a deft manipulation the scales were changed; for a small ephah an excessively large shekel was asked. Like Dives, these rich nabobs had no pity for the poor, were far from helping them, from alleviating at least in a measure their abject pauperism. It was the rich who swallowed up the needy (Amos 8:4) and made the poor of the land to fail; who took advantage of their poverty to rob them of what little they happened still to possess; who bought and sold them like cattle on the market (8:6). They panted after the dust of the earth on the head of the poor (2:7); they begrudged him the very dust which in sign and token of his poverty and misery he had placed on his head. Thus indeed did the rich store up violence and robbery in their palaces (3:10).

Was there no law and justice in the land? Could not the poor resort to the courts? Alas, that would have been as hopeless in those days as it often is in ours, worse than useless. (Is. 1:23; Amos 5:12.) Better to suffer in silence than look for justice, better to stay out of courts than to lose the last of your possessions and be condemned as a criminal.

The Religious Conditions

According to the clear command of God, Israel was permitted to erect altars only in "all places where I record My name" (Ex. 20:24), where either by special divine command (personally or through His prophets) an altar was to be erected (Deut. 27:4-6; Joshua 8:30; Judg. 6:19, 26; 1 Sam. 7:9, 17), or where God had appeared to an Israelite and thus had given him an occasion to sacrifice to the Lord (Judg. 2:5; 13:15 ff.; 21:4; 2 Sam. 24:21, 25). Altars built by the Israelites without such permission were regarded as idolatrous (Joshua 22:10 ff.), although the patriarchs seem to have erected altars wherever they pleased. In my opinion the altar built by Saul (1 Sam. 14:35) was built without such permission. In northern Israel, Elijah complained that the children of Israel had thrown down the altars of Jehovah (1 Kings 19:10), and he repaired the altar of the Lord on Mount Carmel (18:30). Whether all these altars had been erected by special divine command or in consequence of a divine manifestation, or were erected by pious Israelites who did not wish to take part in the syncretistic, idolatrous worship of the nation, yet for one or the other reason could not journey to Jerusalem, to the divinely appointed place of worship (Deut. 12:4, 5), is impossible to determine. These altars were erected in the honor and for the worship of the true God, in protest against the worship of the calves and other idols, and the worship at these altars by the believing children of God was pleasing to the Lord.

Israel had been absolutely forbidden to make any image of the Lord in connection with their worship (Ex. 20:4, 5; Lev. 26:1; Deut. 4:15-19) and to worship any other god. Yet worshiping the idols of the surrounding heathen nations was one of the besetting sins of Israel. Solomon built altars for the various idols of his wives and worshiped at these altars (1 Kings 11:1-11).

But it remained for Jeroboam I to make idolatry the official worship of the northern tribes. In direct transgression of Ex. 20:4, 5, he set up two golden calves as symbols of Jehovah (1 Kings 12:28-33). Political expediency directed his policy. In order to prevent a healing of the breach that had occurred (v. 27), he hit upon this wicked scheme (v. 26), which led to the ultimate ruin of the Northern Kingdom; "and this thing became a sin, for the people went to worship" (v. 30), the sin of Jeroboam, the son of Nebat, so frequently mentioned in the records. Not satisfied with having set up the golden calves, Jeroboam made priests of the lowest of the people who were not of the

14

sons of Levi, contrary to Ex. 28:1; Num. 16:17. He also made a house of "high places." Such high places are also mentioned by Hosea (10:8). Among the heathen it was quite the general custom to erect their altars on the summit of hills or mountains or to build artificial hills, or high places. It seemed to them that the summit of the hills was closer to heaven, the dwelling place of God. (Cp. Num. 23:13.) This custom of erecting altars on high places was not in itself sinful; for the Lord is everywhere and may be worshiped on hills and high places as well as in the valley (1 Sam. 9:12; 10:5; 1 Kings 3:4; 1 Chron. 16:39). Since, however, the Lord had (Ex. 20:24) permitted the erection of an altar only in the place where He would record His name, the indiscriminate building of high places was not in accord with God's will and is therefore censured (1 Kings 3:3). Jeroboam built high places not only without the command and sanction of God and therefore against His will, he built these high places in honor of forbidden images, the golden calves. Like king, like people. Not only did the people worship at Jeroboam's high places at Bethel and Dan, but in imitation of this worship and unhindered by the king they built altars and high places throughout the country, at first ostensibly to the honor of Jehovah, for the worship of the true God. Soon they erected beside these altars pillars, images (Hos. 3:4; 10:1, 2), *mazzeboth*. Pillars were originally not displeasing to God. They served as memorials of important events or special manifestations of God's grace (cp. Gen. 28:18, 22; 31:45; Ex. 24:4). Such memorial pillars, however, were erected also in honor of Baal (Hos. 3:4; 10:1, 2, A. V., images), just as "groves," *asherim*, were erected next to the altars of Baal, pillars in honor of Asherah, the Syrian form of Astarte, the Assyrian goddess of the star Venus. Figurines of Astarte have been found in large numbers throughout Palestine, usually presenting her as the goddess of fertility, with her hands touching her breasts. The worship of Baal and Astarte was connected with that most hideous form of immorality, "sacred" prostitution, which Herodotus calls the most atrocious law of the Babylonians (History I, 199), while the Hammurabi Code deals with it very leniently, § 178—182 (cp. Amos 2:7). This shameful worship was made the official religion of Israel by Ahab and Jezebel (1 Kings 16:30-33; 18:4, 18, 19; 19:1, 2, 10, 14; 22:6). Though Jehu exterminated Baalism as the official religion of Israel (2 Kings 10:18-28), he continued in the sin of Jeroboam, while the people persisted in Baalism under the guise of the true worship of Jehovah. Only the name Jehovah remained for a worship which was essentially Baalism (2 Kings 17:9-11).

15

In connection with some of these many sanctuaries, "ephods" (Hos. 3:4) were used for purposes of divination. These ephods seem to have been imitations, sometimes in gold (Judg. 8:27; 17:5), of the official garments of the high priest, described Ex. 28:4 ff., with its Urim and Thummim, the divine oracle (Ex. 28:30; Num. 27:21; 1 Sam. 21:9; 28:6; 30:7). Besides these ephods, soothsayers and wizards were in great demand (2 Kings 17:17). It seems that also the "teraphim" (Hos. 3:4), perhaps house gods similar to the Lares and Penates of the Romans, possibly little images of some deity, were used for purposes of divination. Wherever idolatry flourishes, there flourish superstition and witchcraft. Witness the many clairvoyants, spiritists, and similar agents of superstition and darkness in our highly enlightened age and country.

Sad to say, the land of Jehovah, the land wherein He dwelled (Num. 35:34), had become a land filled with idolatry, a land in which there was no truth nor mercy nor knowledge of God, but swearing, and lying, and killing, and stealing, and committing adultery, and blood touching blood, (Hos. 4:1 f.). Since Israel had defiled the land of Jehovah, this land was getting ready to spew them out as it had spewed out the wicked Canaanites (Lev. 18:28).

Such were the conditions when Hosea began to prophesy. Chapter 2 still presupposes a time of prosperity and plenty, though of increasing wickedness and crime. Jeroboam II still ruled (1:1). No one had listened to the warnings of Amos; his solemn pleadings had remained unsuccessful. Now once more a prophet raises his voice in warning, again threatening ruin, disaster, desolation, if this last word of warning would go unheeded. It remained unheeded, and within a few years the threatened judgment came over Israel.

As soon as Jeroboam II's strong hands no longer held the reins, a period of political unrest, rebellion, and anarchy followed. Jeroboam's son, Zachariah, was murdered after a reign of half a year by Shallum, who in turn after one month was slain by Menahem, ruler for eight or ten years. Pekahiah, his son, ruled two years and was murdered by Pekah, who was killed by Hoshea, the last king over Israel.

In the year 727 Shalmaneser IV, king of Assyria, overran the Northern Kingdom. Hoshea sought aid from Egypt, was summoned to appear before Shalmaneser, ca. 725, imprisoned (2 Kings 17:4), and henceforth the king of Israel disappears from our view "as a bubble upon the face of the waters" (Hos. 10:7). Samaria was destroyed after a siege lasting three years, 722, and the people were deported into Assyria (2 Kings 17:6).

During all this time of unrest and confusion, while the nation, without realizing it, was rushing headlong into ruin, Hosea preached and prophesied to his people, whom he loved so fervently. As Isaiah (Jehovah is my Salvation) was sent to preach to a rejected people to harden their hearts (Is. 6:9, 10), so Hosea (Salvation) was sent to preach to a nation doomed to be cast out forever. As Isaiah prophesied in language of exquisite beauty the coming glory of the Church of God in order to comfort the faithful remnant, so Hosea brings consolation to the hearts of the few believers still found in Ephraim by directing their faith and hope to that glorious day when again the number of the children of Israel, in a new covenant of grace and mercy, would be as the sand of the sea.

PART I

Hosea's Marriage
A Symbol of God's Relation to Israel

Chapters 1—3

CHAPTER 1

A. Superscription, V. 1

1 The word of the LORD that came to Hosea, the son of Beeri, in the days of Uzziah, Jotham, Ahaz, and Hezekiah, kings of Judah, and in the days of Jeroboam, the son of Joash, king of Israel.

Grammatical Note

V. 1. "Came unto." הָיָה אֶל is used of the evil spirit sent by the Lord upon Saul (1 Sam. 16:23; 19:9; with עַל: 1 Sam. 16:16; 19:20-23) in the sense of "took possession of him." The same phrase occurs Ezek. 45:16 (A. V., "shall give") in the sense "is under obligation, is bound to give."

V. 1. The word of the LORD, I AM THAT I AM, the Covenant God of justice and grace, holiness and mercy (Ex. 3:6-17; 34:5-8). This word "came" (Gr. N.) to Hosea, cp. Jer. 20:7 ff., taking possession of him, ruling him, making him willing to speak what the Lord told him, to do what the Lord commanded, obligating him to obedience and working that very obedience.

The kings of Judah are named first. The house of David had been chosen by the Lord Himself to be the ruling dynasty of His people and the ancestral family of King Messiah (Gen. 49:8-10; 2 Sam. 7:12-29). Jeroboam alone is named of the kings of northern Israel,

17

presumably because his ancestor Jehu had been anointed king over Israel by divine command (1 Kings 19:15,16; 2 Kings 9:1-6). He was a very able and successful ruler, the last "helper" of Israel (2 Kings 14:23-28). His son ruled only six months, and the last kings of Israel were usurpers, puppets of Assyria (2 Kings 15:8-31; 17:1-6).

B. Hosea's Marriage, Ch. 1:2-9

1. Hosea's wife, a symbol of faithless Israel, vv. 2, 3

2 When the LORD began to speak to Hosea, the LORD said to Hosea: Go, take unto yourself a harlotrous woman and children of harlotry, for the land has committed horrible harlotry, turning away from the 3 LORD. So he went and took Gomer, the daughter of Diblaim. Then she conceived and bare him a son.

Grammatical Notes

V. 2. "The beginning." Not infrequently a complete sentence takes the place of the genitive after a construct case (cp. Ex. 4:13; Num. 23:3; Jer. 48:36, etc. Gesenius-Kautzsch 130 d). This nominal clause serves as the protasis and is connected with its apodosis by ו. — "By Hoshea." ב does not necessarily denote an inner speaking or a speaking through the prophet. It may simply mean to talk with, to speak to, without denoting the manner of speaking (cp. Zech. 1:9,13,14; Num. 12:8). — "Take." The Hebrew term has the twofold sense of take (Gen. 18:7; 43:12, etc.) and receive, accept (Num. 23:20; Prov. 2:1; Ps. 6:10, A.V., 9; Jer. 9:19, A.V., 20, etc.). — "Wife of whoredoms." The idiom "man of," "woman of" some quality, is a common Hebrew idiom. It denotes not merely an inclination or propensity to the noun added, nor necessarily a profession, but invariably an inclination in action, a propensity manifesting itself. The contentious, or brawling, woman (woman of contention) (Prov. 21:19; 25:24; 27:15) is certainly not a woman merely inclined to this vice, but one who manifests her propensity. The man of bloods (Prov. 29:10; Ps. 5:7, A.V., 6; 2 Sam. 16:7) need not be a professional murderer, but certainly not a person who keeps his inclination shut up in his heart. Nor is the man of words (Ex. 4:10), of lips (Job 11:2), one who merely has the inclination to speak, but does not use it. "Children of whoredoms" here are children born in harlotry and who inherited a harlotrous spirit. Gesenius-Buhl, Luther: Hurenweib und Hurenkinder; *The Complete Bible:* a harlotrous wife and harlotrous children. This translation is borne out by the Lord's interpretation of this symbolic marriage (v. 2 b), the names given to the children (vv. 4, 6, 9), and by ch. 2:2-13: harlotry, adultery (vv. 2-5), lovers (vv. 5-13). — "Committed great whoredom." The absolute infinitive preceding the word "whoredom" emphasizes the magnitude and extent of the sin. — "Departing from," literally, from after, from behind, away from.

V. 2. "The beginning" (see Gr. N.). "By," rather, "with" or "to" (Gr. N.). Again Hosea stresses that he speaks not his own thoughts, but the Lord's word. The very first word addressed to Hosea imposed upon him an almost impossible task, yet by its almighty grace made him willing to submit to the Lord's will. As God later commanded Jeremiah not to marry nor to have children (Jer. 16:2 ff.), so here He commands Hosea to marry, yet to marry not a wife of his own choosing, but one chosen for him by the Lord. He was to take (Gr. N.) a woman of whoredoms and children of whoredoms (Gr. N.), a harlotrous woman and harlotrous children. Such a woman he was to marry and cherish in faithful marital love, and such children he was to acknowledge and love as if they were his own. The reason for this strange command is stated at once by the Lord: For the land hath committed great whoredom, departing from the Lord (Gr.N.). Hosea's matrimonial experience was to be a symbol of God's experience with His covenant people. Gomer's unfaithfulness to her loving husband was to picture to the people their unfaithfulness to their divine Spouse. The covenant relation between God and Israel is frequently compared to that of husband and wife or father and children. The former was already implied in Ex. 34:15 f. ("go a-whoring after their gods"; Num. 15:39, etc.) and brought out in full detail in the Song of Songs. (Cp. also Is. 50:1; 54:1, 5, 6; 62:4, 5; Jer. 2:2; 3:1 ff.; vv. 14, 20, etc.) On the relation of God as a father to His children, cp. Ex. 4:22; Deut. 32:5, 6, 19; Is. 63:16; 64:7 (A. V., 8); Jer. 3:4, 14, 22; Ps. 73:15; Mal. 1:6; 2:10, etc. The whole nation, regarded as a unit, is the wife, the mother, while the individual members constituting the nation are the children of God (the Husband of Israel and the Father of the Israelites) and of Israel (the legal wife of God and mother of the Israelites). This relation was to be one of mutual love and esteem. God had promised His grace and every blessing to His people (Ex. 19:5, 6; 20:6), and the nation, the wife, had vowed allegiance, loyalty, willing obedience (Ex. 19:8; 20:19). On this basis the covenant was established (Ex. 24:3-11). However, Israel had become a harlot, disloyal to her Husband and Lord, idolatrous (Hos. 1:2 b). By a strange symbolical act Hosea was to show to Israel the utter heinousness of her offense. Note the "for"; *for* the land hath committed whoredoms. The shameful whoredom of Israel, her unfaithfulness to her faithful Husband, her apostasy, her idolatry, her calf worship, her Baalism, motivated this command. Her former love toward God is not once mentioned as part of the symbolism, only her wicked apostasy.

V. 3. This command involved a fearful sacrifice on the part of the prophet. He was obliged to give up every hope of a happy marriage; to endure the agony of observing the adulteries of his wife; to expose himself to the suspicion of being as wicked as she. How unnatural it seems to us, and how difficult! Yet in obedience to God's will, ruled by His Word (see v. 1, p. 17), he took Gomer, the daughter of Diblaim. A remarkable example indeed of absolute submission to the Lord! "Only to do Thy will my will shall be!" — We note that there is not the slightest indication that the names Gomer and Diblaim are to be regarded as symbolical names, as are the names of the children (vv. 4, 6, 9). We have here the simple statement of these historical facts: Hosea married, Gomer conceived, she bare him a son. We might be inclined to regard this son as Hosea's legitimate child because of the pronoun "him." Yet in 1:4, 5 the name given to him — symbolizing judgment — and God's command, v. 2, demand that we regard him also as one of the "children of whoredoms" whom Gomer presented to Hosea as his son and whom he was to accept as if he were his own. On the part of Gomer that was indeed brazen impudence. Yet Israel was guilty of impudence even more shameful! She was the wife not of a human husband, but of the Lord! Against Him Israel, the nation, played the harlot, and her children, the individual Israelites, were, like her, steeped in idolatry and Baalism. Still Israel, the nation as such, demanded recognition as the spouse of Jehovah, and the individual Israelites claimed to be His children. As such they brazenly requested as their covenant right the protection and blessing of Him whose covenant they had broken long ago. What an impudence, worthy of their shameless adultery, to grieve Him with their sins, to cut Him to the quick with their wicked adulteries, to lay Him open to the suspicion as though He countenanced their idolatry (cp. Ps. 50:21; Rom. 2:24), and then calmly and with brazen impertinence to demand His help and aid because He was their Covenant God, Israel's Husband!

Objections Answered

The following objections have been raised against the view expressed above, that Hosea actually married a harlot:

1. Such a marriage would have been immoral. — An act is immoral, however, only if it violates a clear command of God. There is no divine commandment forbidding such a marriage, hence no reason to condemn it as immoral, particularly since God *commanded* this marriage. Only priests were forbidden to marry a harlot (Lev. 21:7), and Hengstenberg's contention that if such a marriage was sinful for a priest it was even more sinful for a prophet is neither Scriptural nor logical.

2. This view would not suit the symbolism. "It is the view of Hosea that Israel was pure at the beginning of her union with Yahweh and only corrupted herself at a later time. In order to have consistent symbolism, Gomer must have been pure when Hosea married her and must have become corrupt later." Eiselen, in *Proph. Books*, II, 374, states that this objection is generally made. Hosea's marriage, however, is nowhere said to symbolize the entire history of Israel, but her

apostasy (ch. 1:2, "for . . . committeth great whoredom") and her impending judgment (the names, vv. 4, 6, 9).

3. Such a marriage would not have accomplished its purpose. "Symbolical action, to be impressive, would require to be enacted in a brief space of time, so as to present a complete picture at one view, accompanied by its word of exposition." (*The Bible Commentary,* Hosea, p. 418.) Yet the symbolic bachelorhood of Jeremiah (Jer. 16:2, 3) extended through his lifetime. And there is no reason to assume that either Jeremiah or Hosea did not accompany his action by "its word of exposition." They even wrote it down for their contemporaries and posterity to read.

Other Interpretations

In order to save God from the charge of commanding an immoral act, many interpreters have regarded ch. 1:2-9 as an allegory, a parable (Calvin), or as a vision, a purely inner experience without external reality (Hengstenberg, Keil), or as a mere literary form in which the prophet presented his warnings and threats (Gressmann). Yet none of these explanations change the fact that God had commanded what is regarded as an "immoral" act, and they do not solve the difficulty. Moreover, as we have seen, the prophet presents the entire narrative as historical facts, actual events in his life. There is not the slightest indication that he is narrating a parable or allegory or vision. While the names of the children are clearly defined by the Lord Himself as symbolical, the names of Gomer and her mother, Diblaim, have defied every attempt at convincingly explaining them allegorically. This method of interpretation has been generally discarded now.

Another theory, widely accepted in our day, is that Gomer originally was a chaste wife, since "woman of whoredom" does not denote the harlot, but a woman inclined to harlotry. (See p. 18.) Gomer was a chaste wife until the birth of her first son (Wellhausen), or her third son (Budde, Bewer, *Lit. O. T.,* p. 94; Sellin, *Zwoelfprophetenbuch,* pp. 29—31; and others). According to this theory the promise, ch. 2:1-3 (A. V., 1:10—2:1), was displaced from its original position after ch. 3:5, "where it fits in beautifully," and was mistakenly inserted after ch. 1:9, "where it in an intolerable manner disrupts the threat ch. 1:9, which is continued ch. 2:3 ff." (A. V., 2:2 ff.), since it promises salvation without the slightest presumption of an inner return of the people to God or a change of mind toward the people on the part of God. The verses originally connecting 1:9 and 2:3 must have read somewhat on this order: And she weaned Lo-Ammi and ascended to (Bethel? Cp. 1 Sam. 1:23 f. on such journeys to sanctuary) and there played the harlot (cp. ch. 4:14, 15 f.). When this was told Hosea, he expelled her from her home (cp. 9:15) and said: She is neither my wife; nor am I her husband. And I will no longer love her children, for they are children of whoredom (ch. 2:3 b, 6)." (Sellin, loc. cit., p. 31.) "When Hosea after this experience wrote his book, he doubted the legitimacy of all three children and was convinced that her inclination to harlotry dated back to the day of his call." (Sellin, loc. cit., p. 32; cp. Bewer, *Lit. O. T.,* p. 94.) Ingenious? Perhaps. But interpretation? No! Eissfeldt calls this solution "highly artificial." (*Einleitung A. T.,* p. 432.) It is far worse! It is a perversion of Holy Writ, of God's Word! However, Th. Robinson's theory, adopted by Eissfeldt, is not any better: Chs. 1 and 3 are two versions of identical experiences by different authors, one, Hosea "I," ch. 3; the other, someone else, speaking of Hosea as "he," ch. 1. Pfeiffer dismisses this theory with a *mirabile dictu!* and proposes another solution, equally unsatisfactory: Gomer's "harlotry" was not physical, but "religious fornication," idolatry, "because the whole land is in such a state." (Pfeiffer, *Intr. O. T.,* pp. 567—569.) Yet whenever God speaks in these chapters of spiritual harlotry, he defines it as idolatry (ch. 1:2, "from after the Lord"; ch. 2:5, 7, 8, 10, 12, 13, 16, 17), while there is no such definition in God's command to marry a wife of whoredoms (ch. 1:2), as little as there is in ch. 3:1, 3, which latter passage Pfeiffer translates "a woman beloved by a paramour and adulterous" and interprets as "a common streetwalker." In both cases a harlot is denoted by the terms employed by Hosea. *The Complete Bible* translates "a harlotrous wife" and "harlotrous children." Revised Standard Version, "a wife of harlotry" and "children of harlotry."

21

2. The names of Hosea's children symbolic of God's judgments upon Israel, ch. 1:4-9

4 Then the LORD said to him: Call his name Jezreel, for in a short while I will avenge the bloodguilt of Jezreel upon the house of Jehu, and I will put an end to the king-
5 dom of the house of Israel. And it shall come to pass on that day that I will break the bow of Israel in the
6 valley of Jezreel. Then she again conceived and bore a daughter, and He said to him: Call her name "She Is Not Pitied." For I will no longer continue to have pity upon the house of Israel, that I should ever
7 pardon them. Yet I will have pity on the house of Judah, and I will save them by the LORD, their God, but I will not save them by bow, nor by sword, nor by warfare, nor
8 by horses and by horsemen. When she had weaned "She Is Not Pitied,"
9 she conceived and bare a son. Then He said: Call his name "Not My People," for they are not My people, and I will not be yours!

Grammatical Notes

V. 6. *"Lo-Ruchamah"* is not the participle, but third person feminine perfect of Puhal; She is not pitied.—"But I will utterly take them away." This translation would require the accusative, not the dative, לְ. נָשָׂא with dative in sense of "forgive" occurs, e. g., Gen. 18:24, 26; Num. 14:19; Is. 2:9. — "But," כִּי, = *that* I should forgive (cp. Gen. 20:9, 10; Ps. 8:4; 40:15; 44:20, A. V., 19). (G.-K. 166, 2.)

V. 9. "Then said God," "your God." In both instances the word "God" is not found in the original text.

Vv. 4, 5. Another historical fact. The Lord Himself chooses the names of the three children and in each instance states the reason for His choice. The names of the children of Gomer are symbolical of the fate which shall soon overtake Israel in penalty of her adulterous idolatry. Each one of the children of Gomer represents Israel in her entirety, only different phases of the judgment being emphasized by each one. Jezreel shall be the name of the first-born, for soon the Lord will avenge the blood of Jezreel upon the house of Jehu.

"The blood of Jezreel" is not the blood shed by Jehu in exterminating the house of Ahab and in seeking to eradicate Baalism from Israel. This extermination was commanded and commended by the Lord (2 Kings 9:1-10; 10:30). This term rather signifies the blood of Naboth shed at Jezreel by Ahab and Jezebel (1 Kings 21). This bloody atrocity stands out with special prominence in the long annals of crimes recorded against Israel and her royalty. The murder of Naboth was more than the judicial murder of an innocent man. It was the murder of a child of God who had placed loyalty to the Lord above obedience to royal covetousness and vanity. It was, in fact, the culminating crime in the long and bloody warfare of Baalism against the worship of the true God, revealing Baalism in its ugliness, its devilish opposition to the Law of the Lord. Therefore the curse of complete extermination was pronounced against the house of Ahab (1 Kings 21:19-24). Yet we must not forget that the atrocious wickedness of Ahab in introducing Baalism was traced by the Lord to the offense inaugurated by Jeroboam and continued by Baasha, who established calf worship as the official religion of Israel, which was threatened with the same penalty pronounced against Jeroboam (1 Kings 21:21, 22; cp. 1 Kings 12:26-33; 14:6-16; 16:1-3, 11). Baalism had been thoroughly suppressed by Jehu, but he retained the calf worship (2 Kings 10:31), the first step toward Baalism. In Hosea's days calf worship and Baalism were hardly distinguishable even though the first was blasphemously called the Lord's worship. Read chs. 4, 5, 8, which also speak of the disastrous moral disintegration following in the wake of idolatry. Since Jehu and Israel with him had nurtured calf worship, the root of Baalism, which fruited in the blood of Jezreel, therefore this blood of Jezreel, the result of calf worship and Baalism, would be avenged upon the house of Jehu and the nation (cp. 2 Kings 10:31-34; 15:8-12, 13-31; 17:1-41). "Israel shall be Jezreel." Note the alliteration, the sharp sibilants cutting the hearer to the very marrow. As in the final judgment upon Ahab the city of Jezreel played so prominent a part, so shall the bow of Israel be broken, Israel be shorn of its power in the Valley of Jezreel. While the exact location of the decisive battle fought before the siege of Samaria began is not named in the Bible, King Hoshea undoubtedly made his last stand in this valley, the scene of so many battles in ancient and modern times. Deborah, Gideon, Saul, Ahab, Josiah, Nebuchadnezzar, Vespasian, Justinian, Saladin, Napoleon, all fought here, the extensive plain offering an especially suitable battleground.

V. 6. This judgment upon Israel shall not be merely temporal like the seventy years of captivity of Judah. The name of the daughter which later was born to the prophet, *Lo-Ruchamah,* "She Is Not Pitied," symbolized the end of all mercy for Israel. "I will utterly take them away" (Gr. N.), rather, I will in no wise forgive them. They are rejected!

V. 7. Judah, on the contrary, was to find mercy and deliverance in a miraculous manner (cp. Zech. 4:6). There pious king Hezekiah (see 2 Chron. 31:20, 21) instituted his reformation (2 Chron. 29—31), and in response to his prayer Judah was saved by a special manifestation of God's grace and power from the Assyrians, who had hoped to annihilate Judah as they had destroyed the Northern Kingdom (2 Kings

18 and 19; 2 Chron. 32; Is. 36 and 37). When Hosea spoke these words, he could not possibly have foreseen their literal fulfillment decades later. We have here neither prophetical intuition nor political shrewdness, but the words of the Lord. The Covenant God interrupts His threat to call impenitent Israel back to Himself as her only Helper and to comfort the little faithful remnant with the assurance that in the greatest catastrophe He remained the almighty Savior.

Vv. 8, 9. The third child, a son, was to be called *Lo-Ammi*, that is, "Not My People," symbolizing the complete severance of covenant relations with the Northern Kingdom by the Lord of the covenant, because His people had persistently refused to fulfill the primary condition of this covenant: obedience (Ex. 19:5). The terrible judgment which came upon Judah only in the days of the Apostles (1 Thess. 2:16) now already was upon the Northern Kingdom. Ye are not My people, and I am not yours! Rejected by God, disowned by Jehovah, repudiated, rejected, forever! Verily, Israel shall be Jezreel!

CHAPTER 2

C. God's Compassion on Wicked Israel, Vv. 1-3 (A. V., 1:10—2:1)

1 (A.V., 1:10) Yet the number of the children of Israel shall be as the sands of the sea which can neither be measured nor numbered. And it shall come to pass that in the place where they were told: "You are not My people," they shall be called 2 (1:11) sons of the living God. Then the children of Judah and the children of Israel shall be gathered together, and they shall appoint for themselves one head and shall come up from the land; for great shall 3 (2:1) be the day of Jezreel. Say to your brothers: My people! and to your sisters: She has found pity!

Textual Note

V. 3 (A. V., 1). The LXX reads the singular, your brother; your sister. There is no reason to change the Masoretic text.

Ch. 2:1 (A. V., 1:10). Shall, then, the name of Israel perish from the earth? Did the unchanging Lord deliberately set at naught His promise given to the patriarchs (Gen. 12:3; 15:5; 22:18; 26:4; 28:14)? No, that promise, like all the promises of God, was still in Him yea and in Him Amen. Though Israel was faithless, the Lord God abideth faithful (2 Tim. 2:13). Though Israel is Jezreel, though the kingdom has been taken away, God's mercy withdrawn, the nation forever rejected, "yet the number of the children of Israel shall be as the sand of the sea, which cannot be measured or numbered." Here the Lord combines all the prophecies given to the patriarchs, taking various expressions from the various prophecies and combining them into one all-embracing promise in which all shall be fulfilled. There shall be countless children of Israel. How is that possible? "It shall come to pass," etc. V. 1 b (A. V., 1:10 b). God lives, and not one of His promises shall perish. He, the God of life, can (Luke 3:8), and He, the Lord of truth, will awaken children unto Abraham and Israel. Such as had not been His people, as had been children of wrath by nature, shall by His almighty grace be made children of the living God, who, like their Father, are possessed of life, spiritual life, life eternal. These sons of God, the true children of Israel, shall be found in the same place where it was said of them: "Ye are not My people." That name, of course, refers primarily to apostate Israelites. Yet they are not the only ones to whom this term applies. Even before Israel was so called, there were masses of such as were not God's people, the countless thousands of heathen of all nations and tongues and peoples, steeped in sin and vice (Eph. 2:1 ff.; Rom. 1:18 ff.). Out of this *massa perdita* of heathen with whom Israel according to the flesh had become amalgamated, the Lord will raise children unto Abraham, a true Israel according to the Spirit (Rom. 2:28, 29; 9:6-8; Gal. 4:28). Because of the admission and reception of these heathen into spiritual Israel, into the New Testament Church, God's promise given to Abraham shall indeed be fulfilled. Very clearly God here prophesies the admission of the heathen into covenant relations with God. So Peter (1 Peter 2:10) and Paul (Rom. 9:25, 26) interpret this prophecy.

V. 2 (A. V., 1:11). Then shall there be no more two kingdoms. That breach which for centuries had severed Judah and Israel shall have been healed. The true children of God out of Judah and Israel according to the flesh shall be gathered together and, with all the children of God among the Gentiles, shall form one people (Eph. 4:4-6), *una sancta catholica ecclesia.* And there shall be but one Lord. They shall "appoint themselves one head." Though the temporal kingdom was lost, alas! forever (v. 4), yet a kingdom, a spiritual kingdom, would be restored to Israel (cp. Acts 1:6). The King of the New Testament Israel is actually an Israelite according to the flesh, of the seed of Abraham, the house of David, Jesus of Nazareth. Under the leadership of this only Head "they shall come up out of the land." From wherever they have been called into the sonship of God, they shall come up into that spiritual kingdom of Christ, which knows no boundaries, no limits, which extends to the end of the world. Since they are in the world, yet not of it (John 17:11, 14), their conversation is in heaven (Phil. 3:20), to which they will finally come with songs and everlasting joy upon their head (Is. 35:8-10). Then "great shall be the day of Jezreel." The name of apostate Israel is here used of spiritual Israel insofar as it partook of the penalties inflicted upon Israel as a nation. Spiritual Israel, as part and parcel of the Northern Kingdom, was deeply affected and grieved by the loss of kingdom and power. It seemed indeed as though God had altogether rejected even spiritual Israel. Yet to the true Israel applies the blessed fact which the Lord through Isaiah revealed later to comfort Judah in her coming hour of sore distress (Is. 49:14-16; 54:4-10). Spiritual Israel, the Church of God, though feeling keenly the judgments of God visited upon the nations among which it dwells, was not rejected; in due time would come the great day of Jezreel.

V. 3 (A. V., v. 1). In true brotherliness shall all the members of God's people acknowledge one another as children of the one Father, all having experienced the same compassion. Read Rom. 15:7-13, which exactly describes the situation here pictured. Note that the three names Jezreel, Lo-Ammi, Lo-Ruchamah, mentioned as phases of the judgment of God, are here referred to in a manner which shows that every trace of wrath and punishment is gone.

D. Punishment and Reacceptance of Unfaithful Israel, Ch. 2:4-25 (A. V., 2-23)

1. The punishment of Israel, vv. 4-15 (A. V., 2-13)

4 (A. V., 2) Chide your mother, chide! For she is not My wife, neither am I her Husband. Let her remove her harlotry from her face and her adultery from her breasts 5 (3) lest I strip her naked and place her as on the day she was born and make her as the wilderness and set her like a dry land and 6 (4) slay her with thirst. And I will have no pity on her children because they are children of whore- 7 (5) dom; for their mother played the harlot; she who bore them lived in shame. For she said: I will run after my lovers who gave me my bread and my water, my wool and my flax, my oil and my drink. 8 (6) Therefore, lo, I am going to hedge up your way with thorns and build a wall for her so that she can-

9 (7) not find her paths. Then she shall run after her lovers but will not catch them. She will seek them but shall not find them. And she will say: I will go and return to my first husband, for then I fared bet- 10 (8) ter than now. And she had not considered that I had given her the grain and the wine and the oil and had given her much silver and gold, which she used for Baal. 11 (9) Therefore will I take back My grain in its season and My new wine in its appointed time, and I will wrest away My wool and My flax, which was to cover her naked- 12 (10) ness. And now I will lay bare her shame before the eyes of her lovers, and no man shall rescue 13 (11) her from My hand. And I will put an end to all her joy, her fes-

26

tivals, her new moons, her Sabbaths, and all her festival gather-
14 (12) ings. And I will lay waste her vines and her fig trees of which she said: These are my gifts which my lovers have given me. I will make a jungle out of them and the beasts of the field shall eat them.

15 (13) So will I visit upon her the days of the Baalim, to whom she offered sacrifices and decked herself with her rings and her jewels and ran after her lovers, while Me she forgot! — is the oracle of the LORD.

Grammatical Notes

V. 4 (A. V., 2). "Plead," רִיב, = quarrel, go to law (Ex. 21:18; Hos. 4:4); here = reproach, upbraid, reprimand (Gen. 26:21 f.; 31:36; Judg. 6:32, etc.). — "She," הִיא, this one. "I" = the emphatic אָנֹכִי, I, as far as I am concerned; stressing the contrast.

V. 7 (5). "Done shamefully." The Hiphil of בּוֹשׁ always = to put to shame. There is no reason to change this, with G.-B. and others, to = has done shameful things. — "She said." The perfect denotes an act which has become a habit (cp. Gen. 49:18; Ps. 31:17; Amos 5:21). G.-K. 106 g. We prefer the present. — "Give me." The participle = the donors.

V. 11 (9). "To cover her nakedness" modifies not "recover," but "wool and flax."

V. 12 (10). "Lewdness," nablut. The

form occurs only here, but, like the common form nebalah, denotes wicked folly, especially sexual depravity (cp. Gen. 34:7; Judg. 20:6,10).

V. 14 (12). "Rewards," אֶתְנָה, the hire paid for a harlot; only here; usually אֶתְנָן (cp. Hos. 9:1).

V. 15 (13). "Burn incense," the Hiph. הִקְטִיר is used of legitimate sacrifies, "to let an offering ascend in smoke," and nine times of illegitimate sacrifices, not restricted to incense (here; 1 Kings 3:3; 11:8; 12:33; 13:2; 2 Chron. 28:3; 34:25, K'tib; Jer. 48:35). — "Earrings," נֶזֶם, rings, either earrings (Gen. 35:4; Ex. 32:2, 3) or noserings (Gen. 24:22, 30, 47; Is. 3:21; Ezek. 16:12). Here without special notation = rings in general (Ex. 35:22; Judg. 8:24-26; Prov. 25:12; Job 42:11).

"In this second chapter the same cycle of events recurs as in the first, with this difference, that what is expressed by symbol in the one is simply narrated in the other" (The Pulpit Commentary).

V. 4 (A. V., 2). Turning to the few remaining faithful children of God (cp. 1 Kings 19:18), the Lord urges them to "plead" (Gr. N.) = chide, remonstrate with, their mother, the nation, in order to move at least some to repentance. "She" (Gr. N.), this one. God turns away from her in disgust. "She is not My wife, and I am not her Husband." She may still call herself My wife; but in reality we are parted, for as a harlot she has turned away from Me. "Out of her sight," literally, "her eyes," glowing with the fire of impure love (2 Peter 2:14); her breasts gleaming with jewels, see v. 15 (A. V. 13), amulets, idol figurines, etc.; her entire appearance and demeanor betray her true character. Away with that! Let her remove every trace of her adultery,

27

her idolatry; let her return in loving worship and faithful service to the Lord, her Husband, or she shall be put away forever.

V. 5 (3). As a commentary on this threat read Lev. 26:14-39, and note there the ever-growing severity of punishment, the ever-increasing stripping away of all her possessions (wilderness, foreigners, drought, wild beasts, war, exile), until she again is as castaway and helpless a babe as on the day she was born (Ezek. 16:3-5; Ex. 1:13-16; 2:23 b; 5:6-19, the lowly birth of the nation in Egypt).

Vv. 6, 7 (4, 5). See ch. 1:2, 6. "Not have mercy" (cp. Jer. 15:1-6; 16:5 b). "Hath done shamefully" (Gr. N.). Her own sins cry out against her, put her to shame, stamp her as a vile harlot, however proudly she may carry her head, however loudly she may boast of her deeds. Out of her own mouth she shall be condemned, for she says (Gr. N.): I will go after my lovers. Enviously she regarded the surrounding nations, Phoenicia, Egypt, Assyria, who did not worship the Lord, yet possessed far greater political power and prestige, worldwide commerce, huge riches, marvelous luxuries, and far greater freedom from moral restraints than God's people. Israel's religious, social, political life was not only governed by the Lord's Moral Law, but also regulated by innumerable rules, ceremonies, often concerning seemingly insignificant details. These laws were given by the loving Husband for wise and salutary purposes (cp. Gal. 3:23 ff.; 4:1 ff.). Yet how burdensome must many of them, e. g., Lev. 11:24-27; 15:1 ff., have been even to the faithful Israelites! (Cp. Acts 15:10.) What an unbearable yoke must they have seemed to such Israelites as had lost or never possessed true love for their God! To them God seemed no longer a loving Husband and Father, but a harsh taskmaster, who could only command and threaten and condemn. Once love to her Husband had waned, Israel cast about for other "lovers." She found them in the idols of the heathen nations (cp. vv. 15, 18, 19, A. V., 13, 16, 17) and such false gods as they themselves invented (1 Kings 14:9, calf worship). Clandestine trysts at first, secret visits to heathen temples and altars, where their lusts and passions could be gratified, and finally open rebellion against the form of worship commanded by the Lord, that was the history of Israel from the time of the Judges to the days of Hosea. And in the days of Jeroboam II idolatrous Israel suddenly gained power and riches rivaling those of David and Solomon. It seemed that idolatry paid better wages than service of the Lord. Their idols at least gave them (Gr. N.) "my bread," etc. They were the donors of the bread they looked for and regarded as their due for services rendered. Yet Israel had only heaped shame and reproach upon herself. Israel's whole national history had been the record of an unexampled love of God toward a nation by nature no better than others (Deut. 7:6 ff.; 9:4 ff.; Amos 9:7; Rom. 9:4-8). This God she had forsaken and, like many another unfaithful spouse, she longed and looked for other "lovers" and embraced them in the foolish hope, doomed to horrible disappointment, that the stagnant, foul waters of the stranger's love would prove sweeter than the running waters of her own well (Prov. 5:15 ff.).

Vv. 8, 9 (6, 7). Her way shall be like a labyrinth, surrounded by impenetrable hedges of thorns, by insurmountable walls erected by the Lord. She will follow after, literally, pursue, her lovers, the hot lust of her adultery driving her on. Yet she shall not find them. Note the change from "she" to "you" and back to "she." The Lord has withdrawn His hand from her. And her lovers, where are they? If they love her, why do they not hear her pitiful wail? If they are able to give bread and drink, why do they not help? Israel has left God, and not only has God left her, but even her very idols will not hear. She is lost, helplessly lost. How often have apostate Christians in time of need called to their idols only to experience the same thing! Worldliness, unionism, Modernism, are suicidal. (See Deut. 32:37 f.; Judg. 10:14; Jer. 2:28.)

The efforts of the loving Spouse to regain his unfaithful spouse shall not be in vain. His chastisements shall accomplish their purpose. As the Prodigal Son in misery and shame turned his thoughts back to the erstwhile despised home, so in the hour of her utter forsakenness apostate Israel will think of her former Husband. "I will go." The same word used v. 5; there the ungodly resolve to serve idols, here the blessed determination to return to God. I will "return to my Husband," for there, after all, I was better beloved, better taken care of, than by my lovers. (See Luke 15:17, 18.) That is ever the language of repentant sinners who have come to a knowledge of their folly in leaving God and running after idols.

V. 10 (8). At the moment God spoke these words, Israel was far from returning and submitting to her Husband in willing obedience. Therefore He must continue to show her the folly and wickedness of her way. V. 10 motivates God's action of v. 8 (6). In self-willed ignorance Israel refused to know that it was God who gave them all they needed. Yet they "made" their silver and gold into a Baal (cp. ch. 8:4). "Baal" is here used in the sense of the idol and his cult.

V. 11 (9) describes the manner of God's hedging in Israel (v. 8, A. V., 6). "Return." In order to teach her the simple lesson that He is the Giver of all gifts, He will return and take away what He has given, and take it away "in the time," "the season thereof," just at the time fields and vineyards promise a rich harvest. Suddenly there is nothing to gather into wine press or garner (cp. Hag. 1:9 f.; 2:16 f.). Likewise He will take away wool and flax, leave them nothing to cover their nakedness (Gr. N.). That is God's way of teaching ungrateful wretches the truth that every believer knows and confesses: "Naked was I and unswathed when on earth at my birth my first breath I breathed. . . . Naught, not e'en the life I'm living, is my own. God alone all to me is giving."

V. 12 (10). "Discover," uncover, reveal; lewdness (Gr. N.), her wicked folly. "In the sight of her lovers," in the very presence of her idols of whom she expected the blessings and freedom she craved for. Will they come to her help? There is no one to help the filthy, lewd hag, no one is willing, no one able, even if he should be willing. It is the Lord, whose grace she despised, who is now depriving her of all His gifts. Against Him man is helpless!

V. 13 (11). Her mirth, her joy, the chief joy of every believer, to worship in the Lord's Temple, shall be taken away from her. "Feast days" is the name of the three festivals recurring annually: Passover, Pentecost, Feast of Tabernacles (Ex. 23:14 ff.). New moons are monthly, Sabbaths, weekly festival days. "Solemn feasts" are enumerated Lev. 23 as follows: Sabbath, v. 3; Passover, v. 5 f.; Pentecost, v. 10 f.; Feast of Trumpets, v. 24 f.; Great Day of Atonement, v. 27 f.; Feast of Tabernacles, v. 33 f. The "new moons" did not belong to this latter class; cf. Num. 10:10. The distinguishing feature of the "solemn feasts" was the holy convocation (Lev. 23:2 ff.), the assembling of the congregation. All these various feasts were instituted by God to be days of rest and worship, memorials of His unbounded grace and merciful kindness and, for that very reason, days of joy and nation-wide rejoicing in the Lord (Num. 10:10; Ps. 122:1 ff.; 42:4). God says "her feasts," not "My feasts." Israel retained the formal celebration of these festivals, but had stamped them with a character altogether foreign to their intention. Israel regarded them merely as national holidays, occasions for social gatherings, for joyous merry-making, for grossly carnal enjoyments and pleasures. Since she had desecrated God's feasts, God will take away her feasts, even that outer shell to which she still clung after having thrown away the kernel. Alas, how often are the festivities of the Church of our day not so much memorials of God's grace as occasions for self-aggrandizement, spread-eagle orations, publicity for publicity's sake, etc.!

Vv. 14, 15 (12, 13). Israel had regarded her possessions as "rewards" (Gr. N.), as gifts paid to her by her paramours, the Baalim and calves, in reward of her faithful service. The Lord will convince her of the folly of her thoughts by removing not only the fruit, but also the plants. He will change their vineyards and orchards into a forest, jungle land. And the animals of the field will devour them, since there are no more people in the land (cp. Is. 7: 23 ff.; 13: 20 ff.; Micah 3: 12). This He will do in punishment of her idolatry, because she burnt incense (Gr. N.) to Baalim, and in their honor decked herself with earrings (Gr. N.), rings for ears and noses, and other "jewels," perhaps necklaces. So the Israelites served their idols, but the LORD, their Covenant God, their Creator, their Redeemer, their Husband, was forgotten!

---

2. God's reacceptance of Israel, vv. 16-25 (A. V., 14-23)

16 (A.V.,14) Therefore, behold, I Myself will allure her and lead her into the wilderness and speak to
17 (15) her heart. And I will give her vineyards to her from there, and the Valley of Achor as a door of hope; and there she shall answer Me as in the days of her youth, and as on the day she came up from the
18 (16) land of Egypt. On that day it shall come to pass — is the oracle of the LORD — you shall call "My Husband!" and no longer shall you
19 (17) call Me "My Baal!" And then I will remove the names of the Baalim from her mouth, and they shall no longer be remembered by
20 (18) their names. On that day I will make a covenant for them with the beasts of the field and with the birds of the sky and with the creeping things of the earth; and I will break the bow and the sword,

and war from the land; and I will make them dwell in safety.
21 (19) And I will betroth you to Me forever. I will betroth you to Me in righteousness, and in judgment, and in loving-kindness, and in
22 (20) mercies. I will betroth you to Me in faithfulness, and you shall
23 (21) know the LORD. And in that day it shall come to pass that I will answer — is the oracle of the LORD — I will answer the heavens,
24 (22) and they shall answer the earth, and the earth shall answer the grain and the wine and the oil, and they shall answer Jezreel.
25 (23) And I will sow her for Myself in the land; and I will have pity on "the Unpitied One"; and I will say to "Not My People": "My people are you!" And he will say: "My God!"

Grammatical and Textual Notes

V. 16 (A. V., 14). "Allure," פָּתָה, to be deceived; Pihel, to be persuaded, "lured," either in good sense, as Jer. 20:7 and here, or in evil sense = seduce (Ex. 22:15, A. V., 16; Judg. 14:15; Prov. 1:10; 16:29). The participle here = an allurer.

V. 17 (15). "Sing," עָנָה. Hengstenberg denies that this word ever means "sing," always "answer." Yet in such passages

31

as Ex. 15:21 (A. V., "answered them," rather "sang to them"; cp. vv. 1, 20); Num. 21:17; 1 Sam. 18:7; 21:11; 29:5, "to answer" would be altogether inadequate and unsuitable to the situation —

"There," שָׁמָּה, usually, thither; but in a number of passages a fuller form for שָׁם, there (cp. 2 Kings 23:8; Ps. 76:4, A. V., 3; Is. 34:15; Jer. 18:2; Ezek. 48:35).

V. 16 (14). "Behold" introduces an important announcement. "Allure" (Gr. N.). I Myself will be your Allurer, your Wooer. Baalism had lured Israel away from God. Now God seeks to win her back to Himself. The terrible curse proclaimed upon Israel is followed by the sweetest Gospel message. And again, like 1:9; 2:1, the transition is made without the slightest hint of any preparatory efforts on the part of Israel to gain God's favor. While Israel is still forgetting God, running away from Him to idols, the Lord woos her. Why? "Therefore" refers back to v. 15 (13). Because she has forgotten Me and I am Jehovah, the Covenant God (Ex. 33:19 b; 34:6, 7 a; Rom. 9:15, 16), who never retracts His promise (Micah 7:20; Rom. 11:29; 2 Tim. 2:19); therefore I will woo her. Here is the unfathomable mystery of divine grace. Here is mercy such as God alone is capable of. Our sin, our apostasy, our shameful ingratitude, our vile adultery, moves Him to pity, to love us. We bow in adoration before this incomprehensible God of mercy. "Bring her into the wilderness." It is the enemy who leads her into the wilderness, to humiliate, to annihilate her. Yet the enemy is only the instrument in God's hand to carry out His plans of regaining His wife's love. That is ever God's way of winning back His wayward children. He deprives them of their riches and pleasures which lured them away from Him (Luke 15:13 ff.). He leads the woman who shamefully abused His blessings and now is stripped of all her wealth and beauty (v. 5), destitute, despised, forsaken by her lovers (v. 9), into the wilderness, walks at her side, and "speaks comfortably unto her," literally, speaks upon her heart, lets His words of comfort, His reiterations of His everlasting love drop down upon her sorrowing heart like soothing, healing balm (Is. 61:1-3).

V. 17 (15). The very wilderness becomes to her a vineyard. She is once more safe in the arms and at the loving heart of her Lord and God! (Ps. 73:25 f.; Hab. 3:17, 18.) "And the valley of Achor for a door of hope." The vale of Achor symbolized the punishment there meted out to Achan (Joshua 7:25, 26). The very punishment of Israel shall be to her a door of hope. If He has kept His threats, if He has proved Himself Jehovah by sending this sorrow according to His word, then

He will be my Jehovah in keeping His promise of undying love and grace. "And she shall sing there" (Gr. N.), in the very wilderness shall she sing and shout, make even the howling wilderness resound with glad songs, "as in the days of her youth and as in the day when she came up out of the land of Egypt" (Ex. 15). For then she was delivered out of the hands of those who sought her destruction by oppression and cruelty. Now she is being delivered from the adultery of her idolatry, reconciled, restored, to the Lord, her God. It is a well-known fact that most of the glorious hymns of praise and adoration are the fruit of sorrow and tribulation, physical, mental, or spiritual agony, or a combination of them. See Psalms 3, 6, 7, 23, 27, 42, 46, 51, etc., and page through *The Lutheran Hymnal.*

V. 18 (16). "Thou shalt call Me" (Gr. N.), literally, Thou shalt call. Overwhelmed by the grace of her God, the Church calls, cries out, Ishi, O my Husband! This is a cry in which repentance and shame, joy and love and hope, are strangely intermingled. "And no longer shalt thou call Me 'My Lord.'" Such complete and perfect love will fill your heart that My relationship to you shall no longer seem to you, and be designated by you, as that of a mere owner, of a lord to his subject. No longer will you think of God as an owner who lords it over you, and of yourself as having no other right than to obey. No longer will your covenant relationship with God appear to you as a burdensome yoke, a state of bondage, slavery, from which you will seek every opportunity to escape in order to enjoy love and liberty by playing the harlot and running after other "lovers," vv. 7, 15 (A. V., 5, 13). Ah, no! At that day you will know Me, cp. v. 22 (A. V., 20), that I am now, ever was, and ever shall be Jehovah, your loving Husband.

V. 19 (17). "For" is not found in the original. The two statements are connected by the consecutive *waw*, "and so," introducing an intensifying consequence, "eine steigernde Konsequenz," Koenig, *Theol. A. T.,* p. 155. After addressing Israel v. 18 (16), He proceeds again in self-consultation: "I will take away," etc. He alone can, and He will remove every trace and vestige of idol worship out of Israel. All the names by which you called your Baalim, once so dear to you, shall be removed out of your mouth. No longer will you call your Baalim your helpers, your gods, your lovers, your trusted aids. So completely shall all idolatrous love be removed from your hearts, so thoroughly shall affection and love to the only God fill your soul and mind, that the very memory of the name of Baal shall have passed away. Even when you hear and use the word baal, this word shall not recall to your mind that idol whose name it was once upon a time. Every trace of idol worship shall be eradicated from hand and mouth and heart and memory.

V. 20 (18). The Lord is planning ways and means of proving to His Church His everlasting love. He had called upon the animal world to destroy Israel's crops vv. 11, 14 (9, 12 b) and upon the enemies to break her power (ch. 1: 4, 5). Now He will make a covenant with the animals for Israel's welfare. They shall no more destroy Israel's crops. And no longer will He permit her enemies to disturb her. Israel's portion henceforth shall be peace and plenty instead of warfare and famine, a promise which finds its partial fulfillment in this life and its full realization in the world to come. Here, as so often in O. T. prophecy, time and eternity merge into one grand picture. The perfect peace and riches of heaven will cause us to forget all trials of this life, however burdensome. Rom. 8: 18; 2 Cor. 4: 17.

While making His plans, the Lord once more turns to His Church, and out of the abundance of His heart His mouth speaks the sweetest words which human ears can hear, a declaration of unending love by the divine Bridegroom, a message which to this day fills our heart with joy and gratitude toward our God and Savior, who addresses these words to us also.

Vv. 21, 22 (19, 20). As God had become the Husband of Israel, the Church of the Old Testament (Jer. 2: 2; 3: 1, 14; Is. 54: 5; see also p. 19), so He will betroth unto Himself, establish His marriage with, the Church of the New Testament, composed of believers of all nations (Matt. 22: 2 ff.; 2 Cor. 11: 2). "Forever." This marriage covenant shall be an everlasting one, a union unaffected by the ravages of time, unsevered by the passing ages, unparted even by grim death (Rev. 19: 7-9; 21: 2, 9). This union remains eternally the same, that of the cordial, ardent, fervent love of the newly betrothed (cp. Jer. 31: 3). It is a betrothal based on righteousness and judgment. Righteousness was also the basis of the Old Testament covenant, a righteousness expressed in God's holy Law as given on Sinai and symbolized by those two tablets of stone which were laid into the Ark of the Covenant, over which dwelt Jehovah between cherubim as if sitting on a throne established on righteousness. This was, alas, a righteousness which no man could attain, which called every man into judgment, the inevitable outcome of which would be eternal damnation. Therefore already in the Old Testament the Lord revealed a different righteous-

34

ness, acknowledged by Him as perfect righteousness, the righteousness of faith in the promised Redeemer, the righteousness of forgiveness of sins, symbolized and foreshadowed in the Old Covenant by the shedding and sprinkling of sacrificial blood (Ex. 24:5-8; Lev. 16:14 ff.). This righteousness was procured in the New Testament by the Son of God, the Lord Our Righteousness (Jer. 23:5, 6). As man's substitute (Is. 53) He satisfied every demand of God's mandatory and punitive righteousness (Rom. 3:21-26; Heb. 9:11-28; 1 John 1:7; 2:2). On this judgment pronounced on our Substitute and this righteousness procured by Him is based God's betrothal, God's marriage covenant with His Church (cp. Eph. 5:25 ff.). Without this righteousness and judgment no betrothal would have been possible; but since Christ is our Righteousness, this betrothal, this covenant, is one based on "loving-kindness and mercies" (Gr. N.). "Loving-kindness" is the love of God toward the undeserving and unworthy, which assures us that in spite of our many shortcomings this betrothal shall not be annulled. "Mercies" are the yearning, pitying love of the parent toward their offspring whose very misery and helplessness rouses pity and commiseration (cf. Is. 49:15; Ps. 103:13). Grace and mercy. How often are these words used to describe the blessing of the New Testament Covenant! (Is. 54:4-10; John 1:14, 16, 17, etc.) This betrothal will not place on the bride such burdensome yokes as the thousand and one ceremonies and rules and regulations which hedged in the Israelite at every step, making the Old Covenant a heavy burden (Acts 15:10). Not the Law, but grace and mercy is the basis of the new betrothal, the sweet Gospel of redemption through judgment executed on Christ, of forgiveness of all our sins (Jer. 31:31-34; 50:20; Heb. 7:22 ff.; 8:6; 9:15; 2 Cor. 3:6-11). "In faithfulness" (Gr. N.). This betrothal is based on the unalterable faithfulness of Jehovah (Num. 23:19; 1 Cor. 1:8, 9; 10:13; 1 Thess. 5:24; 2 Thess. 3:3). "And thou shalt know the Lord." The Church shall, not only intellectually, but also with all her heart and soul and mind, know and love and joyfully, gratefully embrace Jehovah. His unchanging grace, His unending mercy, His never-failing faithfulness. What a precious wedding gift: the knowledge of the Lord (Jer. 9:23, 24; 31:34; John 17:3)! Luther compares this declaration to a wedding ring set with six precious jewels. (St. L. VI, 1157.) Three times the Lord announces His betrothal, reminding us of the tripartite blessing (Num. 6:24-26), in which, as here, He gives Himself to His Church. This is indeed a covenant granting far greater privileges than those promised in the Sinaitic Covenant. Yet for that very reason it involves far greater responsibilities and gratitude, and a greater measure of guilt incurred by breaking this covenant (Heb. 10:26-39).

Vv. 23, 24 (21, 22). Israel's prayers shall no longer remain unanswered. In his characteristically bold manner Hosea presents Israel's plea for food as addressed to corn and wine, by them relayed to the earth, by the earth to the heavens, by the heavens to God. The Lord hears the combined pleadings of His creatures and, answering them, commands the fructifying rains on the parched earth, so that it can bring forth corn and wine, and they in answer to man's prayers offer themselves to him for the satisfaction of his hunger and the quenching of his thirst. Paul's word that God is the Savior of all men, specially of those that believe, is applicable not only to His spiritual blessings, but also the gifts of the First Article and the Fourth Petition.

V. 25 (23). "I will sow," a play on Jezreel (Gr. N.). As the three children of Gomer, whose names symbolized God's judgment (ch. 1:4-9), were reaccepted by the Lord (ch. 2:1, 2; A. V., 1:10, 11), so the three names are mentioned here in a manner indicating that God's curse is lifted. God will sow "her," the Church, God's Spouse, "in the earth"; not Canaan only, for in the New Testament God's people are not restricted to Canaan. Throughout the world God will plant the seed of His Church, so that her branches will extend over all lands (Matt. 13:31, 32, 36-43; Rom. 10:18; also Is. 61:3 b, 11). In New Testament times there shall again be a great people of Israel, sown by God, having obtained mercy from Him, acknowledged by Him as His people, while they rejoice in Him who is indeed their God. Peace shall reign on earth again; for God in Christ reconciled the world unto Himself, magnifying His holy name, the Lord Jehovah of mercy and of truth.

CHAPTER 3

3. God's reacceptance of Israel is symbolized by Hosea's reacceptance of his unfaithful but penitent wife, vv. 1-5

1 Then the LORD said to me: Again go and love a woman such as is loved by paramours and is adulterous, even as the LORD loves the children of Israel, although they are turning to other gods and are lovers 2 of raisin cakes. So I in my interest provided her with fifteen shekels of silver and a homer and a half of 3 barley. Then I said to her: For many days you shall live quietly for me. You must not play the harlot nor offer yourself to a man; and I likewise will be for you. 4 For the children of Israel shall live a long time with no king, and no prince, and no sacrifice, and no sacred pillar, and no ephod, and no 5 teraphim. Afterward, the children of Israel shall turn and seek the LORD, their God, and David, their King, and they shall come tremblingly to the LORD and to His goodness in the end of days.

Grammatical Notes

V. 1. "Go," לֵךְ, an exhortatory interjection, Come! — "Yet," עוֹד, originally a substantive, then used adverbially, denoting (a) most frequently duration, "yet," "still" (Gen. 29:7; 43:27; Hab. 2:3); (b) addition, "besides" (Gen. 19:12; 37:9, etc.); (c) repetition (Gen. 8:12; 9:11; Jer. 3:1, etc.). Here the context demands "yet," "still" = continue to. — "A woman." The omission of the article stresses the qualitative aspect of the term, a woman of this kind (cp. Is. 28:2; 31:8; Amos 6:14; Ps. 77:16, A. V., 15, "arm"). G.-K. 125 c. — "Friend," רֵעַ, primarily a member of one's tribe or kin (1 Sam. 30:26), hence neighbor (Ex. 20:16), friend (Deut. 13:7; 2 Sam. 16:17); the bridegroom is called friend (Cant. 5:16), the husband (Jer. 3:20), the allies (Lam. 1:2), the illicit lovers, paramours (Jer. 3:1). — "Yet," ו. If "friend" = husband, ו is adversative (Gen. 2:20; 15:2; 17:21; Hos. 4:4); if "friend" = paramour, ו is explicative (Ex. 24:12; 25:12; 1 Sam. 17:40; Amos 3:11). Since either translation fits the situation, it may be hard to decide which is the intended sense. Personally we prefer "paramour." — "Look to," פָּנָה, turn, evidently a reference to Deut. 31:18. — "Flagons of wine," אֲשִׁישָׁה, from a stem = "to make firm," "press"; cakes of pressed raisins, used as luncheons (2 Sam. 6:19; 1 Chron. 16:3), at festival meals (Cant. 2:5).

V. 2. "Bought," כָּרָה, denotes (a) to dig (Gen. 26:25; Ex. 21:33; Ps. 40:7, etc.). That is impossible here. Hengstenberg regards ch. 3 as a vision and the woman as a bondslave whose ears Hosea pierced, bored, after having redeemed her, in order to obligate her to lifelong service. He appeals to Deut. 15:17; yet the situation there is entirely different from Hos. 3 (cp. Deut. 15:12-16); כרה never means to dig through, pierce, not even Ps. 40:7; A. V., v. 6; and while Hosea uses the word without "ear," Deut. 15:17 employs a different word and adds "ear." (b) כרה also means to buy, to conclude a bargain for (Job 6:27; 40:30; Deut. 2:6). This is the generally accepted meaning here, but presupposes that the woman, whether Gomer or another, had been reduced to slavery, while Hosea not once mentions slavery in connection with Gomer or the woman of ch. 3. Again, the price of a slave was 30 shekels (Ex. 21:32; cp. Zech. 11:12), while Hosea speaks of 15 shekels and a homer (about eleven bushels) and a *letech*, according to the Mishna, a half homer. A homer has 30 "measures," or seahs, hence the total amount of barley is 45 seahs at one-third shekel per seah = 15 shekels. Sellin computes the price of barley on the basis of 2 Kings 7:1, 16, 18, where the price is given as one-half shekel per seah. $\frac{1}{2} \times 45 = 22\frac{1}{2}$ shekels, quite a different sum! Sellin has the answer: While 2 Kings 7 speaks of a considerable falling of prices, yet even that may not have reached the low level of the normal price, one-third shekel per seah. "So the purchase price paid by Hosea would be exactly the price paid for redeeming a slave." (Sellin.) That is called scientific exegesis! — The lexicons list a third meaning of כרה. 2 Kings 6:23 the expression כָּרָה כֵּרָה occurs, "prepared provisions," A. V. This meaning fits the situation presented by Hosea exactly. Hosea provisioned his wife with fifteen shekels of silver and one and one-half homer of barley. — "To me," לִי, in my interest.

V. 3. "Abide," יָשַׁב, here = to sit quietly, remain inactive (Is. 30:7; Jer. 8:14); stay at home (Lev. 12:4; 2 Kings 14:10).

V. 4. "Image," מַצֵּבָה, an upright pillar used in worship (Hos. 10:1, 2; Ex. 23:24; 34:13). They are named together with Asherah statues (1 Kings 14:23; 2 Kings 17:10) as pillars of Baal (2 Kings 3:2; 10:26 f.). — "Ephod," a garment worn by the high priest (Ex. 25:7; 28:4-28), covering the upper part of the body, to which the breastplate with its Urim and Thummim was fastened. Later, a cult object, the exact nature of which is unknown (Judg. 17:5; 18:14-20).

Vv. 1-3. Hosea is told to love a woman who was "loved," the *inamorata,* the mistress of "friends" (Gr. N.), an adulteress. Was this woman Gomer (ch. 1:3)? This question ought to be settled by the fact that the Lord tells Hosea very definitely that the action commanded to him was to be symbolical of God's continuing love to, and reacceptance of, Israel. This love had been described at length in ch. 2. It was not a strange woman whom the Lord allured (2:16, A. V., 14) but idolatrous, adulterous Israel, whom He had led into the wilderness. To her He addressed that marvelous promise (2:17-25, A. V., 15-23) assuring her of His unfailing love, a love that disciplined only to win her back. This fact ought to be sufficient to establish the identity of the woman in ch. 3 and Gomer, ch. 1, unless text and context make this identification impossible. We shall see that instead of disproving the identity they support and demand it.

The supposition that the woman of ch. 3:1 was a common streetwalker whom Hosea married rests on the presumption that Hosea divorced Gomer, of which nothing is found in the text, and is opposed to the symbolism of God's command, ch. 3:1 b. The supposition that Gomer left Hosea and became a public harlot is equally untextual, so much so that Sellin assumes the loss of an original remark to that effect. Moreover, the arguments that the term "bought" (v. 2) necessitates the purchase of a bondslave and that "yet" (v. 1) denotes a second marriage are specious, since "yet" need not mean "again," but must mean "still," "continue to," according to the symbolism as explained by the Lord (v. 1), and since "bought," if translated "provision" (Gr. N.), solves the difficulty. Hosea in obedience to God's command did not divorce Gomer, but continued to love that adulterous woman, the paramour of illicit lovers. Yet Hosea's love was not a love that simply overlooked her wickedness, but was, like God's love to Israel, a faithful, and at the same time, a disciplinary, cleansing, training, sanctifying love. It was love. He did not put her away or have her put to death, though he had the legal right to do so (Lev. 20:10; Deut. 22:22). He continued to provide for her. He provisioned (Gr. N.) her with money and with food for a long time, about eleven bushels of barley. That was not the best of foods, yet it served the purpose (Joel 1:11; John 6:9, 12). Then he told her to remain quietly at home (Gr. N.) for a long time. No longer was she to play the harlot publicly, nor be for any man, neither as his wife nor mistress. This she was to do "for me," to show her changed attitude to her husband whom she had so shamefully betrayed, to prove her willingness to remain loyal to him. He promised her to remain her faithful husband, loving her as his own and only wife.

V. 4 explains the symbolism of vv. 1-3. "Abide many days"= a long time. Corresponds to same phrase, v. 3. Both the government and the religion of the Northern Kingdom were distinctively national-istic. The kingdom was established in rebellion against the divinely appointed house of David (1 Kings 12:19), and the religion, a peculiar mingling of worship of Jehovah with calf worship, also in rebellion against God's appointed place and manner of worship. The four items of Ephraimite worship date back to the time of the Judges. An Eph-raimite, Micah had established a sanctuary in his house with molten and carved images, an ephod, and teraphim (Gr. N.), and a Levite functioning as priest (Judg. 17:1-13). Later this sanctuary was re-moved to Dan (Judg. 18:1 ff.). Undoubtedly Jeroboam took over this sanctuary when he established Dan as one of the centers of his calf worship (1 Kings 12:28 f.). This was the worship characteristic of the Northern Kingdom and led to all the sins and atrocities of which the nation became guilty. Now Israel, who had drunk deep of the stolen waters seemingly so sweet and had fed on the sweetmeats of secret sins (Prov. 9:17), was put on a strict diet of barley bread. Deprived of her specific Ephraimite form of government and religion, Israel was to be exiled to foreign countries, ruled by foreign kings, surrounded by foreign worship, neither politically nor ecclesiastically an individual, independent nation. Ephraim was to be like a woman put away, for-saken, refused, barren (cp. Is. 50:1; 54:1, 6-8).

Hosea's threat, of course, has reference chiefly to the northern tribes. It is interesting, however, to read what Kimchi, a rabbinical author of the twelfth century, says on this passage. "These are the days of the captivity in which we now are at this day; we have no king or prince out of Israel; for we are in the power of the nations and of their kings and princes; and have no sacrifice for God, nor image for idols; no ephod for God that declares future things by Urim and Thummim; and no teraphim for idols, which show things to come, according to the mind of those that believe in them." Quoted in *The Bible Commentary*, Vol. VI, p. 428.

Yet even this severe punishment was intended for her eternal welfare. That exile was to be the wilderness into which God would lead Israel, not to destroy her, but to woo and win her (ch. 2:16-25, A. V., vv. 14-23).

V. 5. "Afterward," defined by Hosea himself as referring to "the latter days," the standing term for the days of the Messiah, the New Testament era (Is. 2:2; Micah 4:1; Jer. 23:20; 30:24; Ezek. 38:16; Dan. 10:14; Acts 2:17; 1 Cor. 10:11; Heb. 1:2; 9:26; 1 Peter 1:20; 2 Peter 3:3). Kimchi (on Is. 2:2) declares as a canon of interpretation that whenever this expression occurs, it is meant of "the days of the Messiah." The return of Israel is not a return of the nation to Palestine. Hosea never promises that. It is a return which is defined as seeking the Lord, the repentant return of the sinner to God. "And to David, their king," Hosea does not speak of the dynasty of David, of the return under Zerubbabel, a descendant of David, which included also members of the Northern Kingdom. David is here the name of David's Greater Son, Messiah (see Jer. 30:9; Ezek. 34:23, 24; 37:24 f.). The Babylonian *Talmud*, referring to this passage, says: "When Jerusalem is built, David comes." (*Megillah,* folio 18, 1.)

"They shall tremble toward Jehovah." Terrified by their sins, harassed by their enemies, "fighting and fears within, without," so they turn to God in the spirit of true repentance (Luke 15:18, 19; 18:13; Acts 2:37; 16:29, 30). Their trembling is not a sorrow of the world, working despair and death; it is rather a godly sorrow, a divinely created trembling, working repentance to salvation (2 Cor. 7:10). For it is a trembling unto Jehovah, the God of the covenant, and to His goodness and loving-kindness, a trembling pleasing to God (Ps. 51:17; Is. 66:2). It is a turning to God in trembling because of one's sin, yet trusting in that goodness and loving-kindness of God which is as changeless as God Himself. The knowledge of this goodness overcomes their fears and doubts, so that trustingly they cast themselves into the arms of Him who has loved them with an everlasting love, who therefore with loving-kindness hath drawn them (Jer. 31:3). Turning to God's goodness, conversion, is a work of God's grace alone. If His goodness would not awaken and engender faith in Him, our sorrow would be a sorrow unto everlasting death. That it is a sorrow unto life is the work of grace alone (Eph. 2:4-10).

With this gracious promise linking with the promises of ch. 2:1-3 (A. V., 1:10—2:1) and ch. 2:16-25 (A. V., vv. 14-23) Hosea closes the first part of his book.

PART II

The Lord's Lawsuit Against His Covenant People Based on Three Lethal Charges

Chapters 4—14

CHAPTER 4

A. The Lord's Summons, V. 1

1 Hear the word of the LORD, O children of Israel, for the LORD has instituted a lawsuit against the inhabitants of the land! For there is no faithfulness, and no loving-kindness, and no knowledge of God in the land.

V. 1. Hear the word of the Lord! The word of the prophet is the word of Jehovah, the Covenant God, addressed to His covenant people, the children of Israel. "For" motivates the admonition. The Lord is coming to His people to enforce the ancient Sinai Covenant. "Controversy," quarrel; here, a lawsuit. He is about to institute a court proceeding in which He, I AM THAT I AM (Ex. 3:14), is at the same time the Plaintiff, the Witness, the Prosecuting Attorney, the Judge, the Supreme Executive, Jehovah. Suicidal folly, not to hear and obey His word! He charges His people with the lack of the three basic requirements of His covenant with them, the lack of truth, of mercy, of the knowledge of the Lord. This charge is directed against the whole land, against all inhabitants of the land. In taking up and proving these charges, the Lord reverses their order, beginning with the last charge (4:2—5:14); then follows the second (ch. 6:4—11:11), and finally the first (ch. 12:1—13:16, M. T., 14:1). The first and last charges are followed by a glorious promise (ch. 5:15—6:3; 14:1-9, M. T., 14:2-10).

B. The Lord's First Charge: Lack and Rejection of Knowledge, Ch. 4:2—6:3

1. The charge preferred, proved, and punishment pronounced, ch. 4:2—5:14

a. The wickedness of rejecting the knowledge of God demands punishment, ch. 4:2-10

2 Perjury and lying and murder and theft have flooded the land, and bloodguilt is linked with blood-
3 guilt. Therefore the land mourns, and all that lives in it languishes: the beasts of the field as well as the birds of the air, and even the fish of the sea are swept away. Yet let no man chide and no one reprove!
4 And your people are like those that quarrel with the priest! And you
5 shall stumble by day, and also the prophet shall stumble together with you by night, and I will destroy

41

6 your mother! My people are destroyed for lack of knowledge. Because you have rejected knowledge, I will reject you so that you shall not serve Me as priests; and as you have forgotten the Law of your God, I also will forget your children.

7 The more they increased, the more they sinned against Me. Their glory

8 I will change to disgrace! They feed on the sin of My people, and they, every one of them, longingly

9 look for their iniquity. And so it has come to this, "Like people, like priest!" And I will punish them for their conduct, and their deeds will

10 I requite on them. And they shall eat but not be satisfied; they shall play the harlot, but not increase, because they have ceased to serve the LORD.

Grammatical Notes

V. 6. "Lack," בְּלִי = annihilation, nonexistence, cp. Is. 38:17; poetical for "not."

V. 10. "Commit whoredom." The Hiphil הִזְנוּ is used here, v. 18, and 5:3. We see no reason to deviate from the usual sense of the Hiphil, "to seduce to harlotry," found Ex. 34:16; Lev. 19:29; 2 Chron. 21:11, 13; particularly since the Hiphil occurs only in these passages and since Hosea uses the Qal so frequently (1:2; 2:7, A. V., 5; 3:3; 4:12, 13, 14, 15; 9:1). In v. 18 the absolute infinitive emphasizes the verbal idea = eagerly seducing to harlotry.

V. 2. The Lord looks at the land He called His own (Lev. 25:23; Deut. 32:43). Here He dwelt among His people (Ex. 25:8; 29:45, 46). Against defilement of this land He had so solemnly warned (Lev. 18:24-30). Now He sees floods of wickedness covering it; sees it desecrated by crime waves, mortal sins, crying to heaven for vengeance. "Swearing," the Hebrew words denote false swearing, perjury, blasphemy; "lying" = deceit, fraud, falsehood; murder, theft, adultery, which sins all are capital crimes. "They break out" may be either predicate of the five preceding infinitives or may be added as a new charge, the brazen-faced, unashamed violations of God's Law, yet publicly and openly committed, arrogantly flaunted by men defying the laws of God and men, and all going unpunished. "Blood toucheth blood," here not merely in sense of murder, but in general, bloodguilt, mortal crimes (cp. Lev. 17:4; 20:9, 11 ff., 27; Is. 1:15; 4:4). The whole land is flooded with crime and rebellion.

V. 3. Already the consequences of this dreadful depravity are evident in the form of God's judgments. The earth mourns, because drought and locusts or warfare destroy its crops (cp. Is. 24:4, 7; 33:9; Jer. 12:4, 11; Joel 1:10). All the inhabitants of the land languish, are weakened, enfeebled from lack of proper nourishment. Not only the sinners, but all creation suffers for man's sin (Gen. 3:17; 5:29; Rom. 8:19-22). What a wicked thing is sin, so dear to man! What wickedness on the part of man to drag all nature, beasts, and birds, and fish, the inhabitants of earth and sky and sea, into his own well-deserved punishment!

V. 4 is addressed to Israel, a nation which the Lord had covenanted to accept as a kingdom of priests, both in its entirety (Ex. 19:6) and because of its special order of Levitical priests (Ex. 28—30), who were to serve as representatives of the people in the performance of the priestly functions of Israel (Ex. 28:1; Heb. 5:1). The fundamental requirement of God's covenant was willing, unfaltering obedience (Ex. 19:5; 23:20-22; cp. Deut. 6:1-25; 1 Sam. 15:22, etc.). Three times the people had solemnly pledged obedience (Ex. 19:8; 20:19; 24:3-7). Only forty days later this priestly nation and its divinely appointed high priest rebelled against God (Ex. 32:1-10). This spirit of rebellion, this inclination toward idolatry remained characteristic of Israel. God had sent prophets to warn against this apostasy. He had made it the special duty of every individual to rebuke idolatry and idolaters (Deut. 13:1-10; Hos. 2:4, A. V., v. 2). Yet God foresees the hopelessness of such rebukes even if they should be administered. In words of bitter irony, and at the same time of stern reproach, He says: "Let no man strive nor reprove another!" Why His reversal of Hos. 2:4? God answers, addressing the nation, the kingdom of priests: "Thy people," your entire nation, "are as those that strive with the priest." This refers to an ordinance given by the Covenant Lord to His covenant people (Deut. 17:8-13). Difficult cases of law were to be submitted to the priests as a court of appeals, who were to render a decision on the basis of God's Law. Refusal to accept the decision of this court, quarreling, "striving," with the priest, was a capital crime, rebellion against God, whose representatives these priests were. The priestly nation had turned into a rebellious people, traitors to their Covenant God, ripe for rejection. God no longer calls them My people, but thy, the nation's, people. He has disowned them (cp. Ex. 32:7, "thy," "thou"). The only time the term "that strive" recurs is 1 Sam. 2:10, translated "adversaries," and they meet with the same condemnation.

V. 5. The former kingdom of priests, now a nation of disgruntled, quarrelsome insurgents, will have to bear the punishment of revolutionists. "Stumble," fall, like drunkards bereft of reason, helplessly tottering along on their way to destruction. With the people the prophet, the singular without article, denotes whatever prophet they had. The true prophets had perished. Their "prophets" were deceivers, like themselves stumbling along, blind leaders of the blind (Luke

43

6:39). "In the day," "in the night." At all times they pursue the same course, every day and every night bringing them closer to destruction. "Your mother," the nation as giving birth to the individuals (cp. ch. 1:2). "I will destroy," rather annihilate, wipe out. The Northern Kingdom has disappeared completely. While the Jewish people are recognizable to this day, the identity of the ten tribes has been destroyed. We speak of the "lost ten tribes." Why? Again God answers.

V. 6. Once God's people, they are now wiped out as a nation "for lack of knowledge," literally, for the annihilation (Is. 38:17), the nonexistence, of the knowledge which alone is life, the knowledge of the God of salvation, without which no knowledge can avail (Jer. 9:23, 24; John 17:3). The fault of this lack of knowledge was not God's. He had given them ample opportunity to acquire this saving knowledge, but "because thou hast rejected knowledge," God had rejected them, had taken from them the honor of being a kingdom of priests and deprived them of the Levitical priesthood, the only one recognized by Him. The priest sent to the people settled in the depopulated territory of Israel was not a Levitical priest, but one of the priests serving the calves of Jeroboam (2 Kings 17:26, 27; cp. with 1 Kings 12:31). Israel had rejected God's priests. God rejected Israel from His priesthood, from His kingdom, from His grace and salvation. They were without God, without hope, without light, without life. They had forgotten the Law of their God. Now He will forget their children! Rejected! Forgotten! Horrors of horrors! Be not deceived, God is not mocked! (Gal. 6:7, 8.)

Vv. 7-10. Yet this horrible penalty was the just judgment of the Holy One for their horrible sins, which are enumerated once more. Not only by revealing His Word, Law and Gospel, to them, but by His abundant blessings had He shown His favor to Israel as a nation. Yet they repaid His grace with ingratitude. In proportion to the increase of their population, of their prosperity and power, the huge mass of sin daily committed increased. God's penalty? I will change their glory (cp. Ex. 19:5, 6; Deut. 4:7, 8; Rom. 3:2; 9:4, 5) to shame, that shocking shame described v. 6. Why? Another charge! Vv. 8-10. "The sin of My people they eat." The Hebrew word for sin denotes also the sin offering. The sin offerings at Bethel and Dan were actually sinful, since they were not offered at the divinely appointed place (Deut. 12:5-11) nor by the divinely appointed priests (1 Kings 12: 26-33), therefore called "sin," "the sin" or "way of Jeroboam"

44

(1 Kings 12:30; 13:34; 15:26, 30, 34; 16:19, 26, 31, etc.). Hence, the life's business of the priests and kings of Samaria was the perpetuation of a sin condemned and punished by the Lord in the severest manner. In addition to that, the heart, literally, the soul, i. e., the desire, the appetite, of the priest was set on the iniquity of the people. These priests looked upon sinners, conscience-stricken and terrified by their guilt, as easy victims, to be kept in a constant state of turmoil and terror, so that they would keep on bringing more and more sin offerings in a vain effort to unburden their conscience. Careless sinners were strengthened in their carefree spirit by being told that it was an easy matter to obtain God's favor for a small sum of money. Motivated by the hope of gain, these priests were belly servants of the lowest sort. Indeed, like people, like priests, the people as wicked as the priests, the priests as perverted as the people. And therefore both people and priests are alike in judgment. The just God, the Lord of the covenant brazenly broken by priests and people, will punish them according to their wicked principles and shameless doings. "Because they have left off to take heed of the LORD," God will withdraw His blessings. "Not have enough." Ill-gotten gain, riches acquired by fraud and deceit, can and will never satisfy the soul. The hunger for riches, power, fame, knows no bounds (cp. Is. 9:20), and quite frequently God punishes greed and covetousness in the manner described Hag. 1:6, 11; 2:16, 17. "Commit whoredom," literally, seduce to harlotry (see Gr. N. on v. 10), here, as the succeeding context shows, in the sense chiefly of spiritual harlotry, idolatry, although this was frequently connected with physical immoralities. The priests and the people were not only themselves active in idolatry, but also seduced others to join them in the lewd and immoral idol worship.

---

b. The ominous consequences of serving sin, ch. 4:11-19

11 Harlotry and wine and new wine
12 take away the understanding. My people inquire of wood, and a rod divines for them, for a spirit of harlotry has led them astray, and like whores they have left their
13 God. On the summit of the mountains they sacrifice, and on the hills they make their offerings under the oak and poplar and terebinth because their shade is pleasant. Therefore your daughters play the harlot, and your brides commit
14 adultery. I will not punish your daughters when they play the harlot, nor your brides when they commit adultery; for they themselves go aside with prostitutes and sacrifice together with sacred harlots. And a people who has no understanding rushes into ruin.
15 Though you are playing the harlot, Israel, let not Judah become guilty! Come neither to Gilgal, nor go up to Beth-Aven, and do not swear,
16 As the LORD liveth! For like a heifer running wild, Israel runs wild. Now the LORD will pasture

45

17 them as a lamb in a wide-open
18 space. Ephraim is in league with
idols: Let him alone! When their
wine gives out, they eagerly seduce

19 to harlotry. Her rulers dearly love
shame. A wind has bound her up
in its wings, and they shall be put
to shame by their sacrifices.

Grammatical Notes

V. 18. "Drink" = strong wine, Is. 1:22; Nah. 1:10. — "Is sour," קָר = third person sing. of סוּר, to depart, cease. Harkavy, *Students' Dictionary*, translates: after the carousal has ceased. — "Do love, Give ye," אָהֲבוּ הָבוּ. A.V. regards *hebu* as the imperative of *yahab*, but the imperative always reads *habu*, Ps. 29:1 f.; 96:7 f., etc. The phrase may have been intended as Pealal form, an intensifying stem, denoting quickly repeated actions or emotions, "they keep on dearly loving shame," G.-K. 55 e, *ahabhabu;* or *hebu* may be dittography.

Vv. 11-14. "Whoredom" here, spiritual harlotry, particularly Baalism — the fertility cult, inseparably connected with immorality — and calf worship, in itself unfaithfulness to the divine Spouse (Hos. 1:2; 1 Kings 12:29, 30). "Wine," not only the drunken carousals at the idol festivities, but in general drunkenness, so often reproved by the prophets (Hos. 7:5; Is. 5:11; 28:1, 3; Joel 1:5; Amos 2:8, 12; 6:6). "New wine," see ch. 2:8, may have been intoxicating when drunk to excess, but here, added to wine, refers particularly to drinking and feasting being made the chief objects of one's life, inordinate desire for enjoyment. "Take away the heart," the seat of life in its various forms and aspects. These sins will slowly but surely rob man of his understanding of God's will and word, enfeeble his will to serve God, vitiate his emotions so that they become passions no longer controlled by an intellect governed by God's Word and a will to fulfill God's Law. What crimes have been committed in the name of religion! What follies and nonsense and blasphemous doctrines are taught as the Word of God! (Russellism, Eddyism, and other "isms.") The destructive power of intoxicating drink is manifest everywhere. How many Christians have forgotten that God loves a cheerful giver and will give only if he gets something in return, a good dinner, or ice cream and cake. "Ask counsel, etc." (v. 12). The folly of idolatry. God's people worship their "stocks," wooden idols ridiculed by Isaiah, ch. 44:9-20; 45:20 (Luther: die Kloetze ihrer Goetzen); Jer. 10:3-11; the work of their own hands. "Staff," rods or sticks used for purpose of divination, the position of which after being cast to the ground, or the inscription turning up, was regarded as forecasting one's course to take, declared by the staff. How it was possible that God's people should sink to such depths of superstition is answered v. 12 b. Having refused to follow the Lord of holiness and mercy, they were possessed by the spirit of error leading them ever deeper into folly and shame. On every mountaintop (v. 13), on every hill, under oaks and poplars and "elms," rather terebinths, large trees affording pleasant, cool shade, they practiced their immoral idolatry (cp. Jer. 2:20; 3:6, 13; 2 Kings 16:4; 17:9-18). There were harlots plying their trade and sacred prostitutes luring the men, young and old, to "do their religion and enjoy it." (Cp. Amos 2:7, incest!) In retribution of their spiritual adultery, God will punish these ungrateful wretches (v. 14), "whoring away from under their God" (v. 12), by inflicting upon them the shame and sorrow of having their own daughters and brides become harlots and adulteresses (Deut. 22:24). Israel, once a priestly kingdom, was becoming a nation of harlots, fornicators, adulterers! And God will not punish the daughters and brides. That is not a relaxation of the Sixth Commandment, a more lenient view of the failings and foibles of the weaker sex (so Sellin); it is one of the most horrible judgments of God on an apostate nation (cp. Rom. 1:24 ff.), the judgment of hardening in the service of sin a self-hardening people. A nation, even God's own people, that does not and will not understand God's Word and will, shall fall! What a lesson for our nation, our Church!

Vv. 15-19. Judah is warned against following the example of her sister nation lest like judgment overtake her. Gilgal, hardly that of Joshua 4:19, 20, rather the northern Gilgal, named also Hos. 9:15; 12:12 (A. V., 11); Amos 4:4; 5:5 as a seat of idolatry. In the days of Elijah and Elisha a school of the prophets was located here (2 Kings 2:1; 4:38). Beth-Aven, cp. ch. 5:8; 10:5; house of nothingness, vanity, undoubtedly is Bethel (Amos 4:4; 5:5), because one of the golden calves was placed there (1 Kings 12:29). Judah should not "offend," become guilty, by participating in this idol worship in the hope of some advantage. Judah would only heap guilt and punishment upon itself, particularly if it would commit idolatry while swearing by the name of the Lord, i. e., under the pretext of worshiping Him. Israel will suffer the penalty of her guilt. She had become like an unruly (same word as Prov. 7:11, "stubborn," defined 11 b, 12) heifer (v. 16). "Now," under these circumstances, the Lord will put them to pasture like a lamb in a wide-open space where they can run wild as they please without feeling curbed by the stockade of God's Law, without His guidance and protection, as helpless lambs, an easy prey to any enemy. The next verse (v. 17) explains God's action. Because Ephraim (= Israel) is joined, mated, wedded (cp. Is. 44:11 "fellows," associates, Mal. 2:14 "companion"), to idols, God's patience is at an end. Let him alone! Let him shift for himself! "Their drink is sour" (Gr. N.), rather, their wine gives out." When the supply of wine is finished and their passions have been aroused, "they have committed adultery" (Gr. N. on v. 10), rather, they eagerly urge one another to adultery. Such drunken revelries occur not only among the people; the leaders of Israel even lead in this wickedness. "Her rulers," literally, shields (cp. Ps. 47:10), because they are to serve as guardians of God's people and shield them against seduction, dearly love (Gr. N.) shame, love what is shameful: oppression, fraud, venality, adultery, etc. (ch. 7:4-7). "In her wings" (v. 19) pictures the swiftness of the onrushing inescapable hurricane, catching them up, carrying them on its wings, and hurling them into destruction. Their sacrifices are of no avail, whether offered to idols, nonentities, unable to hear them, or offered to Jehovah, who will not accept the sacrifices of an unfaithful, rebellious people. Forsaken of their idols, forsaken by the Lord, left to their sin and guilt, they are helpless and hopeless indeed!

CHAPTER 5

c. Lack of knowledge of the Lord is the sure way to complete ruin, vv. 1-14

1 Hear this, O priests! Pay attention, O house of Israel! Listen, O royal house! For the judgment is upon you, because you have become a snare at Mizpah and a net spread
2 out on Mount Tabor. The apostates have gone to great lengths of depravity. Yet I shall be Chastise-
3 ment to all of them. I know Ephraim, and Israel is not hidden from Me. For now you have played the harlot, Ephraim; Israel is defiled.
4 Their deeds will not permit them to return to their God, for a spirit of harlotry is within them, and they
5 do not know the LORD. The pride of Israel shall testify to his face, and Israel and Ephraim shall stum-
6 ble by their guilt. Judah also shall stumble with them. Though they keep coming with their sheep and their cattle to seek the LORD, they
7 shall not find! He has withdrawn Himself from them. They practiced deceit against the LORD, for they have born illegitimate children. Now a month will consume them
8 and their portions. Blow the ram's horn in Gibeah, the trumpet in Ramah; sound the alarm at Beth-
9 Aven. After thee, Benjamin! Ephraim shall become desolate on the day of punishment! Among the tribes of Israel I make known what
10 is certain. The princes of Judah have become like those who move
11 the boundary lines. Upon them I will pour out My wrath like water. Ephraim is oppressed, crushed by judgment, for he was determined to follow (human) or-
12 dinances. And I am as a moth to Ephraim and like decay to the
13 house of Judah. When Ephraim realized his sickness and Judah her festering wound, Ephraim went to Assyria and sent to King Jareb. Yet he could not heal you, nor could he relieve you of your fester-
14 ing wound. For I am like a lion unto Ephraim and as a young lion to the house of Judah. I Myself will tear to pieces and go away. I will carry off, and there is none to deliver.

Grammatical Notes

V. 2. "Revolters." שֵׂטִים, a form occurring only here. A similar form occurs Ps. 40:5, on which Koenig (*Die Psalmen*, p. 524) has the following note: "Since שֵׂט with initial שׂ has its closest parallel in שֵׂט, 'apostate' (Hos. 5:2), it is better to regard it as a concrete noun rather than as the abstract μανίαι of LXX." G.-B.: "revolters"; others: "aberrations"; Sellin: "apostasy"; *Complete Bible*: "Shittim" (cp. Num. 25:1), changing the points. We agree with Koenig and A. V. — "Are profound," or "made deep" (cp. Hos. 9:9; Is. 29:15), gone to great depths; we would say, lengths. — "Make slaughter," שַׁחֲטָה, a verbal abstract (cp. סָרָה, Is. 31:6), "slaughtering." Others compare Hos. 9:9 and read שַׁחֲתָה, corruption, ruin. — "Rebuker," מוּסָר, rebuke, chastisement. The abstract for the concrete designates the certainty of judgment.

V. 4. "Frame," יִתְּנוּ, = "give," here = "permit, allow" (cp. Gen. 20:6; Ex. 3:19, etc.). The imperfect pictures crime following crime, making return ever more difficult.

V. 5. "Testify," עֲנה. LXX, Targum, Luther, etc., translate "humble." In this sense the verb is never construed with בְּ or בִּפְנֵים. In the sense of "testify" this construction is quite common (Deut. 19:16, 18; Is. 3:9; Prov. 25:18; Job 16:8).

V. 7. "Dealt treacherously." The root idea of בָּגַד is to clothe, cover; cp. בֶּגֶד, garment; to cover one's real purpose or nature = to act deceitfully. The perfects describe the whole life as one act of treachery and bringing forth children; the imperfect יֹאכְלֵם, the progressive consuming.

V. 8. "After thee, O Benjamin!" G.-B., Look behind you! G.-K., Behind you (is the enemy)! LXX, ἐξέστη, shud-dered; Wellhausen, Sellin, Shudder! Marti, Terrify Benjamin! Judg. 5:14 the phrase is used in a different sense.

V. 9. "Desolate," שַׁמָּה, astonishment to the point of horror (Jer. 8:21); object of horror (Jer. 19:8); cause of it (Ps. 73:19). — "Shall surely be," the Niphal part. fem.: that which is firm, trustworthy.

V. 10. "Wrath," from a root = to run over, of floodwaters (Job 6:15; Is. 8:8; Neh. 1:8), signifies wrath as an overflowing, irresistible flood (Gen. 49:7; Is. 14:6; Amos 1:11).

V. 11. "Broken in judgment." מִשְׁפָּט is adverbial accusative to רָצוּץ, broken with respect to judgment (cp. on this accusative Gen. 41:40; 2 Sam. 21:20; Job 1:5, etc. G.-K. 118 m). "Judgment" here = law and order (see Jer. 7:5; 22:15; 23:5, etc.). — "Willingly," הוֹאִיל, to undertake (Deut. 1:5), be pleased to do (2 Sam. 7:29), be determined to do, even if obstacles or difficulties arise (Joshua 17:12, "would dwell"; Judg. 1:27, 35; 1 Sam. 12:22). — "Commandment." צַו occurs only here and Is. 28:10, 13, where in v. 10 it is employed by the unbelieving Jews to voice their dissatisfaction and disgust with God's way of teaching. Through His spokesmen, the prophets, God stressed over and again two points, man's sin and God's grace. This constant repetition of the same truths was sneeringly referred to by the Jews as a teaching proper for little children (Is. 28:9 f.), who needed precept upon precept, etc. But as a philosophy of life for grown-up, intelligent people, who daily had to cope with the exigencies of life, this teaching seemed to them hopelessly inadequate as to its contents and equally unsuitable in its method. In this sense of inadequate and inefficient rules and ordinances the Lord in bitter irony employs the term

49

in the present passage. The singular צֵא without the article here is collective, as, e. g., מַקֵּל, branch, sing., Jer. 1:11; coll., Gen. 30:37; עֵץ, tree, Ps. 1:3; trees, Gen. 3:8; Is. 10:18; נֶפֶשׁ, soul, Gen. 2:7; souls, Ex. 1:5.

V. 13. "King Jareb." מֶלֶךְ יָרֵב. Quite generally this term is now regarded as a translation of the Assyrian *sar rab*, great king, and therefore pointed מַלְכִּי רָב, or, as Cheyne suggests, מַלְכִּי רָם. Yet, as Sellin observes, there is a serious objection to this change. The ʾ compaginis is found elsewhere only in the construct state and in participial forms (Sellin, loc. cit., p. 70). He suggests מֶלֶךְ כַּבִּיר. Yet neither the latter nor

any of the former suggested readings ever occur in the Hebrew translation of "great king," *sar rab*, where this term is used by Assyrians in designation of the Assyrian king. In 2 Kings 18:19, 28; Is. 36:4, 13 the translation of "great king" is מֶלֶךְ גָּדוֹל, and in the Aramaean letter Ezra 5:7-17 the writers speak of Solomon as a great king of Israel, מֶלֶךְ לְיִשְׂרָאֵל רַב (v. 11). Ps. 48:2 God is called מֶלֶךְ רַב. In no instance is the term מַלְכִּי רַב used. Therefore we are convinced that King Jareb is an appellative designating the Assyrian king as a king eager to fight. *Expositor's Bible*, King Combative, Pickquarrel; Vulgate, ultor, revenger. LXX transcribes Ἰαριμ.

V. 1. The "house of Israel," here the Northern Kingdom, placed in center, flanked by its spiritual and civic leaders. "Priests," here the illegal priesthood instituted by Jeroboam (1 Kings 12:31), the leaders in perpetuating the idolatrous worship (1 Kings 12:26-33). "House of the king," not only his immediate family, but all the various functionaries of the kingdom, his official family. "Hear," listen, hearken, pay close attention; "give ear," listen carefully and steadily. All are to take heed, for all are in like sin and like danger. "For judgment," here in sense of punitive judgment, sentence, as the following "because" proves. "Judgment" has the article in the original, referring to the specific punitive judgments threatened to the covenant breakers (cp. Lev. 26:14 ff.; Deut. 28:15 ff.). This judgment is unto you, relates to you, shall come to you, "because," etc. "Mizpah" hardly the Mizpah of Samuel's victory (1 Sam. 7:5 ff.); that belonged to the Southern Kingdom; rather Mizpah in Gilead, the Eastjordanland, part of the Northern Kingdom (Judg. 10:17; 11:8, 11, 29, 34, the home of Jephthah). Its identification with the Mizpah of Jacob and Laban (Gen. 31:49) is doubtful. The custom noted Judg. 11:39, 40 may have degenerated into idolatry and the erection of an illegal sanctuary there. Tabor, a mountain in Westjordanland, had been the scene of Balak's glorious victory over the heathen, idolatrous enemies. Now both Mizpah and Tabor were turned over to illegal, idolatrous worship, where Israel and its leaders (v. 1) set traps and placed nets to catch and enmesh God's people in shameful idolatry and licentiousness. Forsaking God and His Law breeds sins and crimes.

V. 2. The rebellious nations together with their priests and kings went to great lengths in their wickedness. "Are profound" (see Gr. N.). Murder was an everyday occurrence. Yet God is a rebuker (Gr. N.).

Vv. 3, 4. He, the Searcher of hearts (Jer. 17:10), knows them (Ps. 50:21; 90:8; 139:1 ff.; Amos 9:1-4). "Committest whoredom" (Gr. N.). On "whoredom" cp. ch. 1:2; 2:1 ff. Ephraim was the instigator of the calf worship: Jeroboam was an Ephraimite (1 Kings 11:26), and Bethel was its chief sanctuary, one of the important cities of Ephraim. Its seductive power had caused all Israel to become defiled, unclean. So deeply had the people become enmeshed in the toils of idolatry that they never gave a thought to returning to the true worship. Idolatry was so firmly imbedded in their social, political, religious life that it would not permit them to return to the Lord. Jehovah still calls Himself their God, ready to receive them back into His grace. The spirit of harlotry had killed all love to Him. They no longer knew the Lord and had no desire to turn back to Him. Again the basic sin of lack of knowledge (cp. 4:1, 6, 14) is repeated.

V. 5. "Pride" = the objects of the people's pride, no longer the Lord, but their own accomplishments, their wealth, their mansions and palaces, their fortresses, their military power (particularly under Jeroboam II, 2 Kings 14:25-28), their idolatry, calves, and Baalim. (Cp. Is. 9:9, 10; Hos. 2:13; 8:4; 9:4-7; 13:2; Amos 3:14; 4:4; 6:4-8, 13; 7:13.) All these objects of their pride are in fact so many witnesses testifying to their apostasy and treachery. Though they are called, and call themselves, Israel, "prevailers against God" (Gen. 32:28), and Ephraim, fruitful, prosperous (Gen. 49:22 ff.; Deut. 33:13-17), they shall "fall," stumble, reel, stagger, crash to the ground because of their guilt; and since Judah equals them in transgression (cp. Jer. 3:6-11), she likewise shall fall.

V. 6. Since Israel lacked and rejected knowledge, they did not realize that God had promised to accept their sacrifices and grant them His grace only if they would approach Him with a truly penitent heart, acknowledging their sin (ch. 5:15) and trusting in His grace (ch. 2:19-23; 11:4; 14:2, 4 ff.). Moreover, God had forbidden the erection of altars at any place not chosen by the Lord for the revelation of Himself (Ex. 20:24, 25; Deut. 12:11-14). In direct violation of God's will they worshiped in a manner and at places of their own choosing (Ex.

20:3 ff.; 23:24, Baalism; 1 Kings 12:27 ff., calf worship). Therefore the Lord had withdrawn His gracious presence from these apostates. No matter how often they would seek Him or how many sacrifices they would bring, not once would they find Him.

V. 7. "Dealt treacherously" (Gr. N.), because under the guise of worshiping Jehovah they had inaugurated a false worship (1 Kings 12:26 ff.); treacherous, because they covered their sinful, wicked heart with a garment of their own choosing rather than accept the robe of salvation offered to them by the Lord (Hos. 2:19, 20; Is. 61:10). Treacherous, unfaithful to their divine Husband, they had begotten strange children (cp. Hos. 1:2; 2:1), children of apostasy, reared not in keeping with God's command (Deut. 6:7) and Abraham's example (Gen. 18:19), but in Baalism and calf worship (cp. Jer. 7:17, 18; 17:2). "A month devour them." Month, here perhaps in the sense of a comparatively short time (cp. Zech. 11:8). Or it may denote the change of the month of the Passover (1 Kings 12:32), seemingly a minor matter, yet a flagrant disobedience of God's will in order to perpetuate a kingdom conceived in pride, begotten in rebellion, and doomed to destruction (2 Kings 17:7-11); or month = new moon (Hos. 2:11; Num. 28:11-15; Is. 1:13; Amos 8:5) used collectively (G.-K. 123 b) for all festivals connected with idolatry. Israel's sin (no matter to which particular transgression Hosea refers here) will devour them and "their portions," their allotted territories (Joshua 18:5-10). The people were deported, swallowed up by heathen nations, and large portions of the Northern Kingdom were never recovered by Israel.

Vv. 8, 9. The manner of "devouring" is now described. The prophet pictures the confusion and destruction caused by a sudden, swift campaign by hostile armies (cp. Jer. 4:5 ff.; Is. 10:28-34), which affects all "the tribes of Israel" (v. 9), the only time Hosea uses this expression. Ramah is about six miles north of Jerusalem, Gibeah midway between the two cities. Beth-Aven, either Bethel like 4:15; 10:5, or a town near Bethel (Joshua 7:2; 1 Sam. 13:5). Ramah and Gibeah were cities in Benjamin, taken by Baasha, recaptured by Asa (1 Kings 15:16-22). The cornet, ram's horn; the trumpet, the straight trumpet, both used to alarm the people (ch. 8:1; Amos 3:6; Jer. 4:5), are being sounded; loud cries are heard: "After thee, O Benjamin!" (Gr. N.), warning against the impending danger and rallying the soldiers round their standards. Yet all preparations will be futile! Ephraim, the fruitful, shall be desolate, (Gr. N.), an object of horrified astonishment because of its devastation coming in the day of rebuke (cp. Rebuker,

v. 2). Hosea is not voicing his own thoughts. He is announcing to all the tribes words of infallible truth (Gr. N.), placed into his mouth by the God of the Amen (Is. 65:16, margin). Cp. Luke 21:33; 2 Tim. 2:13.

V. 10. Turning first to Judah, Hosea charges the princes (Gr. N.) with being like them that remove the boundaries. To change the boundaries is like "claim jumping," one of the most despicable crimes, forbidden Deut. 19:14; Prov. 22:28, cursed Deut. 27:17; mentioned in connection with oppression of the defenseless, Prov. 23:10; Job 24:2. To be "like" them is to set aside ruthlessly the legal, vested rights of one's fellow man, whenever they conflict with one's selfish interests or desires, to tyrannize and take every possible advantage against the weaker neighbor. "Wrath" (Gr. N.). Like a mighty, unrestrainable flood, God's wrath will be poured out on Judah.

V. 11. Addressing Ephraim, the prophet again proclaims first the penalty, then the guilt. "Ephraim . . . judgment" (Gr. N.). Violence and oppression rule in Ephraim to such an extent that law and order have been broken, crushed, ground into the dust by the heel of despotic rulers. Why? Because Ephraim willingly walked after the "command-ment" (Gr. N.). Here the term refers to the many laws, and precepts, and schemes, and policies advocated and adopted by the nation and its rulers in order to preserve their existence as a state and to defend their commonwealth against the many dangers from within and with-out. All these regulations the Lord regards as entirely inadequate. Far from preserving the nation, they would only increase confusion, break down law and order, accelerate Israel's ruin. For all these rules and precepts left out of consideration the Lord and His Word and will, and substituted man's effort for the wisdom and counsel of the Covenant God. Now, oppressed and broken, they must learn by ex-perience the lesson so often dinned into their unwilling ears by the Lord's spokesmen, what an evil thing and bitter it is to forsake the Lord, their God.

V. 12. Having withdrawn His gracious presence from them (v. 6), only His just and holy wrath remains. He will be unto them as a moth and as rottenness. Moths do their destructive work silently, secretly. "Rottenness," decay; the verb is used of decaying wood (Is. 40:20; cp. Prov. 10:7). The noun occurs five times: here; three times of bone decay, caries (Prov. 12:4; 14:30; Hab. 3:16); Job uses the same com-bination of moth and decay in describing his wretched condition (Job 13:28). Bone decay was practically incurable except by amputation; it sapped the strength and joy of life, rendered its victim a helpless wreck. God, the all-powerful Preserver of His people (cp. Deut. 8: 4; 29: 5), has become to them like a destructive moth; the Healing Physician (Ex. 15: 26; Deut. 32: 39) like an incurable disease eating away at their very vitals.

Vv. 13, 14. When Israel finally realized its imminent political destruction, instead of returning to the Lord, it sought alliances with human helpers, mighty Assyria, King Jareb (Gr. N.). Yet even this powerful ally could not heal nor cure, for a Mightier One than the great king of Assyria was destroying Israel, tearing it to pieces like a lion. None can rescue those whose destruction the Lord has determined. Their very allies to whom they turned for help instead of returning to the Lord were used by the Lord to destroy Israel, deporting the ten tribes (2 Kings 15: 29; 17: 1-6), making their land an Assyrian province (2 Kings 17: 24-41), and devastating the land of Judah (2 Kings 18:13-16), being prevented from capturing Jerusalem only by a divine miracle in answer to Hezekiah's prayer (ch. 19: 1-37). To call Israel to like repentance and trust in the Lord was the purpose of the Lord's warning extending through chs. 4 and 5. That is the next thought brought out by Hosea.

---

2. The purpose of God's charge: a plea for Israel to return to their Covenant God, ch. 5:15—6:3

15 I will go and return to My place, until they acknowledge their guilt and seek My face. In their affliction they will long for Me.

CHAPTER 6

1 Come, let us return unto the LORD, for He has torn, and He will heal us.
2 Let Him smite, and He will bind us up. He will revive us after two days; on the third day He will raise us up that we may live before Him.

3 And let us know, and run after the knowledge of the LORD. He surely shall rise as the morning dawn and shall come to us like a shower, as the latter rain watering the land.

Grammatical Notes

V. 15. "Seek Me early," שׁחר is a denominative verb derived from the noun שַׁחַר (cf. G.-K. 38 c), "dawn." The Pihel, the primary idea of which is intensity, frequently expresses eager occupation with the object denoted by the verb, e. g., עָפָר, dust, Pi., throw dust; שׁחר, dawn, Pi., to occupy one's thoughts with the dawn, make use of the morning, i. e., to do something early and eagerly, Cp. G.-K. 52 h. See Prov. 1: 28; 13: 24; Is. 26: 9. LXX translates ὀρθρίζω, make use of dawn, be early.

Ch. 6: 1. "He hath torn." הוּא טָרָף, the emphatic הוּא = He, and none other (Gen. 15: 4; Deut. 3: 22, "He"; Is. 34: 16, "it"; 38: 19, "he"). The perfect "has torn" denotes the action as a unified whole, begun in the past and continuing in the present (cp. Gen. 32:11; 49:18; Ps. 10:11). — "He has smitten," יַ, jussive, literally, let Him smite. The jussive expresses a command (Gen. 1:3, 6, 9, 11) or a permission (Deut. 20:5, 6, 7; Is. 27:6; Hos. 14:5, 6, M. T., 6, 7). Hosea changes from the perfect to the jussive in order to indicate that Israel in submission to God's will permits Him to punish. — "Will heal . . . will bind up." The imperfects of progressive duration describe the entire process of healing from the first application of soothing balm to full recovery.

V. 2. "After," מִן, two days being the starting point "from" which one begins.

V. 3. "Shall we know," נֵדְעָה, and "if we follow," נִרְדְּפָה, are cohortatives, expressing inclination, desire, impulse. — "And former rain unto the earth." יוֹרֶה here is not a noun, but participle, Hiph. of ירה, to moisten (cp. ch. 10:12, send rain, and Prov. 11:25, Hoph., to be watered).

Ch. 5:15. The Lord repeats His threat. As the lion returns to his den after having pitilessly slain and killed, so the Lord will "return to His place," will withdraw His gracious presence so bountifully bestowed upon His people and so shamefully abused and prostituted by them. Yet while the lion does nothing to repair the damage he has caused or to alleviate the agony of his victims, the Lord even in turning away from His apostate nation has thoughts of peace toward them (Jer. 29:11). He will turn away not forever and finally, but only until they "acknowledge," become conscious of, realize, their "offense," their guilt, and seek His face, turn back to Him in repentance and faith, pleading with Him to make His face shine again upon them, once more to be gracious unto them. To effect such a return was the very purpose He had in mind when He wounded and tore them to such an extent that human aid was of no avail. "In their affliction," so He says, revealing His divine purpose, they will seek Me early (Gr. N.); they will long for Me, turn mind and heart and lips and hands and feet to Me, their Covenant LORD of infinite mercy (cp. Hos. 2:7 b).

Ch. 6:1. Opinions vary as to the speaker and to the character of this prayer (vv. 1-3. LXX inserts λέγοντες, "saying," after 5:15; so the Targum, Luther (und sagen, and say), and others. J. M. Powis Smith in *The Complete Bible* places a colon after 5:15 (as does the Vulgate), and quotation marks before 6:1 and after 6:3. These interpreters regard 6:1-3 as a prayer of the people when trouble would begin, or have come upon them. Yet there is no indication in the text that the people are speaking here. Hosea remains the speaker. As God's spokesman he had announced God's judgment and its purpose, and as God's spokesman Hosea teaches the people how to pray and does so in words which the Lord Himself puts into his mouth (cp. Jer. 1:9). As to the nature of this prayer, many interpreters regard it as a superficial prayer spoken by a people whose repentance was not deeply

55

rooted. George A. Smith: a repentance so shallow as to be futile . . . received by God with incredulity and impatience (*Expositor's Bible in loc.*). J. M. P. Smith heads ch. 5:15—6:11 a: "Israel's deep depravity belies her facile repentance" (*The Complete Bible*). Sellin calls it "a prayer of repentance composed by Hosea for his people using his own style, yet intentionally not reflecting the deepest repentance demanded by him and the Lord. The divine voice of God in answer to this prayer demands something far more sincere and thorough. Two factors are missing entirely: the confession of sin and the solemn promise of a moral change, of faithfulness. . . . Hosea has produced a masterpiece. He has idealized the piety of his contemporaries, has approximated it to his own, yet at the same time has implied that its conversion still lacks the perfection and deepest depth of true conversion (*'das Beste und Tiefste')*." Sellin proposes that Hosea in ch. 6:2 refers to the Canaanite Adonis myth, according to which Adonis was revived two or three days after his death. This miracle is to encourage them to express their hope of a speedy revival of Israel by the Lord. (Sellin, *Das Zwoelfprophetenbuch*, 1929, pp. 70, 71.) We shall see that Hosea's prayer is indeed a masterpiece, yet in a sense altogether different from Sellin's interpretation.

Hosea, whose loving heart is but the reflection of God's everlasting love (Jer. 31:3), at once falls in with God's purpose stated 5:15 b, and at once does all he can to effect the return of his people. He cannot convert them; that is God's work exclusively; but he can plead with his people and proclaim to them the life-giving Word of the God of grace. "Come!" he invites them. He realizes their urgent need of repentance. Yet he, the preacher of repentance, teaching them a prayer of true repentance, includes himself in their number, speaks as a sinner to his fellow sinners. "Come," he cries, "let us return unto the LORD!" Conscious of his and his fellow men's guilt, seeing the urgent need of a speedy and thorough change of their course, he himself starts out and urges them to join him. What gives him the courage and strength to do this? The very fact that this new course is a return to the Lord Jehovah, their Covenant God. True, as such He had made good His covenant threat. The Lord, and He alone (Gr. N.), has torn (ch. 5:14). The enemies were but instruments in executing his judgments. This very fact, that the Lord was manifesting Himself as the unchangeable God of righteousness and justice, fulfilling His covenant threat (Lev. 26:14-46; Deut. 28:15-68), gave Hosea the assurance that He, the everlasting I AM THAT I AM (Ex. 3:14), would graciously fulfill His covenant promises if with all their heart they would return to Him (Deut. 30:1-10). "Come, let us return to this LORD! He hath torn, and He will heal us. He hath smitten," rather, "Let Him smite" (Gr. N.). He has the power and the right to smite us. We have deserved His punishment. Let us humble ourselves under His mighty hand! He can and will bind us up, bandage our wounds (cp. Ezek. 34:4, 16). "He will heal . . . bind us up" (Gr. N.).

V. 2. Hosea is sure that the Lord will not delay His help if Israel returns to Him in true repentance. "After two days," etc. (Gr. N.). This is not the language of a shallow, hypocritical repentance; not the prayer of self-righteousness, which is in fact self-deception; least of all, the hope based on a heathen myth. It is the confident prayer which God's prophet teaches to his people in the words placed into his mouth by the Lord Himself (Jer. 1:9). It is the language of faith that trusts God and His Word and makes God's way of looking at things his own. The Lord assures His people (Is. 17:13, 14; 26:20; 54:7, 8). Even the seventy years of exile are but a "little displeasure" (Zech. 1:15; Ezek. 11:16, "little sanctuary," literally, "a sanctuary for a brief time," seventy years!). Moses says: Ps. 90:4, and in conformity with this fact pleads: Satisfy us early, v. 14; and David prays: Ps. 30:5. The beginning of God's help comes at once, even if noticeable only to the eyes of faith (Heb. 11:1). Even the penitent cry for help is a divine gift, an assurance that God has not rejected His people. In His own time and in His own manner He will gradually revive, raise up, strengthen, establish His trusting children (1 Peter 5:10; 2 Tim. 4:16-18). "And we shall live in His sight." A new life, a blessed life will begin, a life under His loving care and gracious providence. On "in His sight" cp. Gen. 17:18 and context, vv. 17-21.

V. 3. "Then shall we know," rather, "Let us know, learn to know" (Gr. N.). This knowledge is defined as the knowledge of the Lord (Jer. 9:23, 24; John 17:3). The apostate people had lost this only saving knowledge (4:1), were destroyed for lacking it (4:6, 14; 5:4-6). Now let us relearn this knowledge. "If we follow," rather, "Let us follow," pursue, as a hunter eagerly pursues his quarry. What is needed is not a feeble, hesitant effort of which one soon tires, but persistent, diligent search for knowledge (Prov. 2:1-9; Jer. 4:3, 4; John 5:39; 1 Peter 2:2). As an incentive to such diligent pursuit of knowledge as revealed in Holy Writ the prophet adds the promise: "His going forth" to your help "is prepared," firmly established, "as the morning." As surely as the dawn follows night according to divine decree (Gen. 8:22; Jer. 33:20, 25), so surely the Lord's going forth to their aid is established by His divine promise (Deut. 30:1 ff.). Cp. Is. 54:7-17; Mal. 4:2. As the "rain," the showers, "the latter rain" a few weeks before the harvest, so essential for maturing and proper filling out of the kernels of grain, "and former rain," rather, "moistens" (Gr. N.), the earth, so will the life-giving grace of God cause Israel to grow and flourish, spiritually and materially. On the idea cp. Is. 35:7; 55:10-13; 61:3, "trees of righteousness." God calls to repentance, works it by His Word, justifies, sanctifies, blesses with manifold gifts, preserves. Depravity is wholly mine, salvation altogether Thine.

This prayer which Hosea as God's spokesman teaches his people is indeed one of the most beautiful prayers of repentant faith. Here is no longer the language of a self-satisfied, self-confident people; no longer the dissatisfied grumblings of carping critics of the Lord's rule, impatient with His chastisements, revolting against His judgments. Here is penitent confession of their own guilt and unworthiness, humble submission to God's mighty hand. Here is firm confidence that the Covenant Lord can and will help, a faith that believes God's promise even where no help, no healing is visible. Here is the firm resolve to follow after knowledge of the Lord and in His strength walk in His ways. A model prayer indeed!

C. The Lord's Second Charge: Lack of the Love Demanded by the Lord, Chs. 6:4—11:11

1. The charge preferred and judgment pronounced, chs. 6:4—10:8

a. Israel's hypocrisy renders impossible his reacceptance by the Lord of grace, ch. 6:4-11

4 What shall I do with you, O Ephraim? What shall I do with you, O Judah? For your love is like the morning cloud, like the dew which
5 vanishes early. Therefore I hew them by the prophets and slay them by the words of My mouth, and My judgment goes forth like the light.
6 For I take pleasure in love and not in sacrifice and in the knowledge of God rather than in burnt offerings.
7 But they, like Adam, transgress the covenant. There they commit trea-
8 son against Me. Gilead is a city of evildoers, filled with bloody tracks.
9 And like a gangster lying in wait, bands of priests commit murders on the way to Shechem. Surely,
10 they perpetrate crimes. In the house of Israel I behold horrors! There Ephraim plays the harlot, Israel is defiled. Also Judah!
11 A harvest is appointed for you when I shall turn the misfortunes of My people.

Grammatical Notes

V. 4. "Early dew . . . goeth away," מַשְׁכִּים הֹלֵךְ. Early does not modify "dew," but "goeth away." Two participles are co-ordinated: "rising early, going away," while we would subordinate: going away early = swiftly disappearing (cp. Hos. 13:3). "Goodness," marginal reading, "mercy," חֶסֶד,

best defined as loving-kindness: warm-hearted, unselfish love that leaves one's own rights out of consideration and longs only to do good, to help another, friend or foe, worthy or unworthy. Used to denote (1) God's love to mankind (Ex. 34:6, "goodness"; v. 7, "mercy," note the circumstances, Ex. 32 f.; Ps. 36:6, A. V., v. 5, "mercy"; v. 8, A. V., v. 7, "loving-kindness"; Ps. 63:4, A. V., v. 3, "loving-kindness"); (2) man's love of God (Is. 57:1, literally, men of kindness; Jer. 2:2, love; 2 Chron. 32:32; 35:26, "goodness," Neh. 13:14, "good deeds"); (3) man's love of his fellow man (Gen. 21:23; 2 Sam. 3:8; 9:1,7). The context of our passage demands the sense of man's love to God, which, of course, manifests itself in keeping His Law, which demands love of God and fellow man. In *Quartalschrift — Theological Quarterly* (Wisconsin Synod), Vol. 50, July, 1953, to October, 1954, Dr. P. Peters has written a very thorough and instructive article on "The Old Testament Covenant Term *Chesed*."

V. 5. "Hewed them by the prophets." חָצַב is always construed with the accusative of the object, never with בְּ in the sense of hewing into. Sellin translates: I have lashed out among the prophets (dreingehauen unter die Propheten) and quotes Is. 10:15; 1 Kings 5:15 (M. T., 29) in support. Yet in Is. 10:15 בְּ is instrumental, A. V., correctly, "therewith"; and 1 Kings 5:15 it is בְּ loci, "hewers in the mountains" (cp. 2 Chron. 2:2, 18, M. T., 2:1,17); Job 19:24 it is בְּ loci.

V. 7. "Dealt treacherously." בָּגַד = to clothe, cover with a garment; wickedness with the garment of piety; here, idolatry with the garment of orthodoxy, worship of Jehovah.

V. 11. "He hath set," שָׁת. Since a change from third person to first in so brief a sentence would be very harsh, we prefer to translate "one has set" in the sense of passive "there is set." See on this usage G.-K. 144 d. Gen. 11:9; 16:14; 48:1, etc.

Sellin regards the reference to Judah here and in ch. 4:15; 8:14; 12:1 (A. V., 11:12) as a gloss, reads כְּשׁוּבִי instead of בְּשׁוּבִי, and regards the clause as the first clause of ch. 7:1: In the measure that I restored . . . (ch. 6:11), in the measure that I healed . . . (ch. 7:1), there was revealed, etc. That surely is taking unwarranted liberties with the text.

"Returned the captivity," שׁוּב שְׁבוּת. It seems best to regard the noun as a derivative of *shub*, a cognate accusative denoting the internal object: turn a turning; change a change. Cp. on this accusative 1 Sam. 1:6; Ps. 14:5; Prov. 15:27; Lam. 1:8. G.-K. 117 p. The phrase occurs for the first time Deut. 30:3, in parallelism with divine compassion, while the regathering and return of the Israelites, v. 3 b, is described as the consequence of the change of their state. Similarly, Job was not in captivity or exile, but his miserable state was turned, changed, Job 42:10. Sodom was overturned, not exiled or imprisoned, Ezek. 16:53. Joel 4:1 (A. V., 3:1) does not speak of the return of prisoners but of changing the sorrowful state of the Church, harassed by its enemies. Hence, while the return of exiles and captives is a change of their sorrowful state, the phrase "turn a turning" is more comprehensive, denoting any change, chiefly of a state of misery and sorrow. The Hiph. "turn back a turning" may be translated "restore the fortune"; cp. Jer. 32:44; 33:7, 11; Ezek. 39:25, etc.

V. 4. An anguished cry proceeding from the heart of the God of eternal love and mercy. In a bold, yet very effective anthropopathism the Lord is pictured as a father undecided what to do with his wayward children. Israel and Judah profess to worship and serve the true God, offer their sacrifices to Him, at the same time flagrantly transgressing His Law. Their love (Gr. N.) is as the morning cloud, an early fog, like dew, both short-lived, disappearing with the morning sun. It is not patterned after God's love to men (Ps. 36: 5, 7; 103:11, 12), nor after the believer's love of God (Ps. 73: 25, 26), but a selfish love, professing affection only in order to obtain something in heaven or on earth, and forgetting Him, neglecting His worship and service as soon as the need is past.

V. 5. All the efforts of God to train His people have been foiled by their stubbornness. He has hewn them as the stone mason hews the rock until it is fit to be used as a building stone (1 Chron. 22: 2), a pillar (Prov. 9: 1). We think of such noble reformers as Elijah, Elisha, Amos, the prophets concealed by Obadiah (1 Kings 18: 4). He had slain the wicked by the word of His mouth announced by His spokesmen (cp. 1 Kings 21: 19-24; 22: 15-37; 2 Kings 9: 1-10). "Thy judgments." His punitive judgment as in 2 Kings 25: 6; Jer. 1: 16, inflicted upon Israel, "have come to light," are manifest in the turbulent social and political conditions which overwhelmingly prove that God is fulfilling His threats pronounced Lev. 26: 14 ff.; Deut. 28: 15 ff.

V. 6 states the reason for His hewing and slaying. He desires, literally, delights, takes pleasure, in love and in the knowledge of the Lord, and has made every effort to engender this love and this knowledge in His people. Such loving knowledge of the Lord will prompt man willingly to offer sacrifices in keeping with His will (Lev. 1 ff.). Without such love and such knowledge God does not desire sacrifices or burnt offerings. Sacrifice, the shedding of an animal's blood, the burning of the carcass, such "sacrificing" can be done by heathen, by wicked and depraved people. Only if the sacrifice is the offering of a heart knowing and loving Jehovah, will it be pleasing to Him. That is the lesson taught in connection with the very first sacrifice recorded in the Bible (Gen. 4: 3-7). Before the sacrifice can please God, the offerer must be pleasing to Him, must know and love Him.

V. 7. "Like men," not "in Adam," or "in Adamah" (Joshua 3: 16), nor "in human manner," but like Adam, who forgot his obligation to love the Lord and yielded to his own desire, breaking the covenant God had made with him (Gen. 2: 16 f.; 3: 17). So they transgressed

60

the Sinaitic Covenant, summarized Deut. 6:5. "There," pointing to the land He gave them (cp. Gen. 12:7; Ex. 13:5, 11; 20:12), "have they dealt treacherously" (Gr. N.), calling themselves My people while transgressing My covenant; worshiping calves under the guise of worshiping Me (1 Kings 12:28-33; cp. Ex. 20:4, 5).

Vv. 8-10. Gilead, the Eastjordanland from the northern boundary of Moab to Lake Gennesaret, is called a city of evildoers; polluting, literally, heeling, tracking, the land with blood, murders, whose bloody tracks are seen throughout the country. "By consent" (v. 9), literally, to Shechem, a Levitical city and a city of refuge (Joshua 21:20, 21). The priests are so depraved that even these cities, set aside for God's special servants and to prevent the slaying of innocent people, no longer afford safety from the murderous sword of priests who like gangsters infest the city and its approaches. They commit lewdness, the word denoting particularly crimes of immorality (Lev. 18:17; 19:29; 20:14; Jer. 13:27). The road from Samaria to Bethel, the chief seat of the calf worship, led through Shechem, and pilgrims coming from or going to Bethel were murdered, raped, outraged by gangs of priests! Truly, a horrible thing, an abomination in Israel (v. 10), the offspring of the man who had clung to God until he received His blessing (Gen. 32:28, 29). There Ephraim, the blessed and fruitful one, became harlotry (Hos. 1:2; 2:2) and Israel, the victor over God, became defiled!

V. 11. Turning to Judah, the prophet speaks of a harvest in store for them, when also Judah will reap what they have sown, good or evil. Since He had threatened Israel with His judgments, the "also" addressed to Judah must speak of a like harvest of evil appointed for Judah. The nature of this judgment is indicated by the phrase "turn the captivity of My people." The judgment is the humiliation of Judah, the calamity coming upon them. A turning of this calamity is in store only for "My people." V. 11 is a warning addressed to Judah to examine themselves whether they are still His people; if not, to return, lest they harvest the evil fruits of their wickedness.

<hr>

CHAPTER 7

b. Israel's fatal domestic policy, vv. 1-7

1 When I was ready to heal Israel, the guilt of Ephraim became evident and the manifold wickedness of Samaria. For they commit deceit, and the thief enters, while 2 gangsters plunder in the streets.

Yet they do not consider that I take note of all their wickedness. And yet their deeds surround them; they 3 are before My face. They delight the king with their wickedness and 4 the princes with their deceits. They are all adulterers, like an oven heated by the baker, who ceases to stir the fire from the time he kneads 5 the dough until it is leavened. On the day of our king the princes become sick with the heat of wine. He stretches forth his hand with 6 scoffers. For they bring near their

heart like an oven, lying in wait. All the night their baker sleeps; in the morning he burns like a flam- 7 ing fire. They all are hot as an oven and devour their judges. All their kings fall! There is none among them that calls to Me!

Grammatical Notes

V. 1. "Cometh in," יָבוֹא, enter, here of the thief who breaks into the home. — "Spoileth," פָּשַׁט, to spread, to overrun a city or country in search of food or spoils (1 Chron. 14:9, 13, "spread themselves"; 2 Chron. 25:13, "fell upon"; 28:18, "had invaded").

V. 5. "He stretched out his hand." מָשַׁךְ, to draw out, stretch out, stretch forth, most likely denotes a familiar associa- tion, "handshaking," the hail-fellow- well-met spirit.

V. 6. "They have made ready their heart," קֵרְבוּ. Pi. to bring near (Ps. 65:5), to present (Is. 41:21), be ready (Ezek. 36:8); here with an object, make ready. They made ready their heart, their mind. Like the baker makes ready his oven for baking, so they made one another willing to accomplish their pur- pose "while they lie in wait," literally, by their intrigues encouraging, inciting, inflaming one another until they were ready to act.

Vv. 1, 2. Israel, Ephraim, Samaria. Israel, the victor over God; Ephraim, the fruitful; Samaria, the impregnable fortress! Yet Israel was sick, needed healing. And as the extent of the damage done by a cancer appears when the surgeon makes an exploratory incision, so when the Lord was about to heal Israel, the people He had called by this noble name, He found that sin had conquered them. Then it became evident that Ephraim was fruitful only in sin and guilt; that Samaria, the unconquerable fortress, was being dominated by manifold wicked- nesses (plural). They commit deceit, their whole life was a lie, posing as the people of the Lord, while they worshiped calves and Baal and followed their own lusts and passions. Thieves break into the houses, and gangsters loot and pillage in the streets and roadways. (See Gr. N.) And not once does the thought come to them that the Lord observes and stores up in His memory all their wickedness, every single item (v. 2; Ps. 14:2-4; 50:21 f.). And yet it is impossible not to see their wickedness, so completely do their deeds surround them. They are before My eyes, open sins, flagrant crimes!

Vv. 3-7. These gangsters, instead of being suppressed by the authorities, are used by kings and princes to carry out their wicked schemes, to terrorize or purge undesirable opponents of their regime; serve as informers, spies, conspirators, false witnesses, etc. "Adulterers" (v. 4), the term denotes one that is unfaithful to his spouse; then, one who is unfaithful to God and His ordinances and institutions; here, to the divine institution of government. Justice and righteousness, the essential virtues demanded of the rulers (Ex. 23:6-9; Lev. 19:15; Jer. 22:3-5, 15-17), were prostituted by the kings and rulers; while the people lacked that honor and respect toward their government demanded of them by the Lord (Ex. 22:28; Eccl. 10:20). All unfaithful, all like adulterers! Since God no longer ruled in their hearts, loyalty to the king was a matter of policy rather than duty, of self-interest rather than of public welfare. Conspiracies and revolutions were the order of the day. Hosea compares the scheming of revolutionaries to execute a *coup d' état* to a baker who kneads his dough, kindles a fire so that the dough will not be chilled during the cool of the night, then goes to sleep. Next morning the dough has raised sufficiently for baking; he stirs the fire up to blazing heat, bakes his bread, and accomplishes his purpose. So a band of wicked conspirators, tiring of the old regime, plan to "bake their bread," kill their king. They make all the necessary preparations, stir up dissatisfaction, etc. Their heart burns with fierce passion like an oven, "heated by the baker," kept at fever heat by their eager desire to assassinate the king. The opportune time comes, "the day of our king" (v. 5). Does Hosea wish to call the attention of his people to the atrocity of slaying "our," the people's, ruler? Or does he mean to picture the wicked hypocrisy of the conspirators in rendering him lip honor, calling him "our king," and themselves his friends and loyal supporters? An opportunity finally presents itself for carrying out their well-laid plans. The day of the king, his birthday, or anniversary, or a day singled out by them to honor him. "Stretched out his hand" (Gr. N.). "Made ready their heart" (v. 6, Gr. N.). Together with scorners, who make fun of the laws of God and man (Ps. 1:1), he sits at the banquet table where they gorge themselves with food and drink, until "the princes have made him sick with bottles of wine," rather, till they have become sick with the heat of wine, which has robbed them of their last fears, their last qualms of conscience. The royal feast turns into bloody butchery. The royal blood mingles with the wine pouring out of the overturned goblets (v. 7). Read the record of kings murdered by conspirators, gangsters, during the final years of the Northern Kingdom. Four of the last six kings were murdered. Indeed, the people devoured their judges, the kings as the administrators of justice; all their kings are fallen: Menahem, a vassal to the

Assyrians (2 Kings 15:19), Hoshea imprisoned (ch. 17:4). Their domestic policy was a total failure because they had left God and His Word out of consideration. And for the same reason their foreign policy was doomed to like failure.

---

c. Israel's ruinous foreign policy, ch. 7:8-16

8 Ephraim, he has mingled himself with the nations. Ephraim has be-
9 come a cake unturned. Foreigners have consumed his strength, and he does not know it! Also gray hair are sprinkled upon him, and he
10 does not know it! And the pride of Israel testifies against him. Yet they do not return to the LORD, their God, nor do they seek Him in
11 spite of all this. So Ephraim has become like a silly dove that has no understanding. To Egypt they call,
12 to Assyria they go. As they are going, I will cast My net over them. Like birds of the sky I will bring them down. I will chasten them in keeping with the proclamation
13 within their congregation. Woe to them, that they have strayed from Me! Destruction to them, that they have rebelled against Me! I have been redeeming them, and they
14 speak lies against Me! They do not cry to Me from their hearts when they howl upon their beds. Their only worry concerns grain and
15 wine. They desert Me! And I have kept on training them. I strengthened their arms. Yet against Me they have ever planned wickedness!
16 They turn — not upward! They are like an unreliable bow. Their princes shall fall by the sword for the ragings of their tongue. This shall be their reproach in the land of Egypt.

Grammatical Notes

V. 8. "Mixed himself," יִתְבּוֹלָל. The verb is a ritualistic term, stirring or mingling oil into the flour of the meal offering until every particle of flour was בָּלוּל (Ex. 29:2, 40; Lev. 2:4 f.; 7:10; Ps. 92:11, A. V., 10), translated "anointed"; oil = the symbol of the Holy Spirit. The Hithpolel is causative-reflexive, causing himself to mingle, deliberately mingling himself. The imperfect describes the gradually increasing measure of mingling. This mingling with oil, symbolizing the Holy Spirit, until the whole offering was saturated with it, consecrated and made it acceptable to God. Cp. Ps. 92:10 (M. T., 11), where the Psalmist uses this term of himself (translated anointed) to express his assurance that God has made Him acceptable (a different word from Ps. 23:5).

V. 12. "Chastise them," אֲיַסִּירֵם. Either the Massora suggests to read Pi. אֲיַסְּרֵם, or it is one of the rather infrequent examples of non-contraction (cp. G.-K. 25 f, 70 b). — "Congregation," here not קָהָל, but עֵדָה, etymologically stressing the meeting as an appointed one, a common term (Ex. 12:3, 19, 47; Lev. 4:13, etc.).

V. 14. "Howled," יְיֵלִילוּ. The usual form is יְיֵלִיל; here the prefix is added to the already contracted form (cp. G.-K. 70 d, where other such forms are listed: Job 24:21; Is. 15:2, 3; 16:7; Jer. 48:31). — "Assemble themselves," יִתְגּרְרוּ. The root idea denotes the violent, tumultuous attack of a hostile band (Ps. 56:7; 59:4; 140:3; Is. 54:15). In Jer. 30:23 the Hithpael is used of a violent windstorm.

Hence the meaning of the Hithpael evidently is to work oneself up into a violent rage. The Hithpael is causative-reflexive, the imperfect describing the ever-repeated ragings. The LXX translates κατετέμνοντο, and about twenty MSS. read יִתְגּוֹדָדוּ (Kittel), "cut themselves," a reading adopted by a number of commentators. This may have been the original reading, or it may have been an effort to remove a difficulty in the original text.

V. 16. "The Most High." עַל is used here in its etymological sense as a noun, that, or He, which is above, on high (cp. Hos. 11:7; 2 Sam. 23:1). The accusative is that of direction. — "This." זוֹ is a rare form for זֶה; only here and Ps. 132:12. Keil regards it as masculine; G.-K., as feminine (G.-K. 34 b).

Vv. 8, 9. Ephraim, who had the promise that he would be strong in God (Gen. 49:24-26; Deut. 33:17), had "mixed himself" (Gr. N.) among the nations. Israel's privilege had been to "dwell alone," "solitarily" (Num. 23:9; Deut. 33:28; Micah 7:14), trusting in the Lord, who had promised to be their God, their strong Ally and Helper. Instead of mingling, thoroughly imbuing himself, with the Spirit of God, Ephraim deliberately mingled himself with the nations. Eagerly he snatched at every opportunity to make alliances with the surrounding nations, gradually imbibing in ever-increasing measure their spirit. Cp. 1 Sam. 8:5, 20, "like all nations," and God's answer vv. 6-8; Solomon's marriage for "reasons of state," 1 Kings 11:1-13. And the result of this "statesmanship"? "Ephraim is a cake not turned," baked on hot stones or clay "ovens" placed over the fire, on which a thin layer of dough was placed and turned over so as to bake evenly on both sides. "Not turned," it burnt to a crisp; unfit for food, fit only to be thrown away. Foreigners devoured their strength (v. 9); their financial strength by ever-increasing taxes, their spiritual strength by idolatry, their physical strength by immorality and luxurious living. Israel was fast aging, becoming senile, ever-increasing sprinklings of gray hair manifested his waxing old and decaying; he was ready to vanish away (Heb. 8:13). "And he knoweth it not!" The loss of the knowledge of God deprives an individual and a nation of the ability to recognize their true nature and the impending judgment. They cannot understand the signs of the times, are unable to read the handwriting on the wall, because they do not realize that by turning away from God, from His Gospel, from His Law, they have cut themselves off from the Fountain of life and are on their death march (Jer. 2:12-19; Is. 9:9-21; 2 Kings 15:8-31).

Vv. 10-12. See ch. 5:5. And still they do not return to Jehovah, who is still their Covenant God; still they refuse to seek help of Him who alone can help and whose help, if ever, they sorely need "for all this" in their threatening ruin. And so, by refusing to return, the Ephraimites have become like a "silly dove" (v. 11), easily deceived and seduced, fluttering back and forth undecidedly between Egypt and Assyria (v. 12), cooing once toward the one and then to the other or to both at the same time, pursuing a weak and vacillating policy of nearsighted opportunism instead of relying with their whole heart and soul on God, the Lord of Hosts, who had promised and again reminds them that He is their God. They are without heart, lacking proper intellect, proper emotions, proper will, for they have cast God out of their heart, their life. God still rules and will thwart their plans. As often as they call to Egypt or go to Assyria for help, He will cast His net upon them, bring them down, spoil their highflying plans, enmesh them in their political intrigues, chastise, punish them. Every attempt to regain their power and prosperity will drag them deeper into bankruptcy and national ruin. And He does this in keeping with His "report," His solemn proclamation to their congregation, assembled at Sinai (Ex. 19 ff.), again in the land of the Moabites (Deut. 1—30), and to the present generation through His prophets.

Vv. 13-16. "Woe to them!" This is the only time Hosea uses this expression. Destruction to them! They have run away, they have rebelled against Him, and in order to justify their apostasy they speak lies against Him who is ready to redeem them! What black ingratitude! Yes, they cry to Him when they are in trouble, but "their heart is not turned to Me" (v. 14). They are concerned only about material matters. For these they ask, not in humble repentance, like beggars at the Throne of Grace, but howling in despair and violent demands. "They assemble" (Gr. N.). They whip themselves up into violent, tumultuous ravings and ragings, and their purpose is: corn and wine, food and drink, material aid. "They rebel against Me," literally, depart, go away against Me. That is God's view of their prayer. It is not approaching God. Their violent demand, their raging, rioting, roaring is not prayer, but departing from God, segregating themselves from Him, against Him, revolution! "I have bound," literally, instructed, trained them (v. 15); and I have strengthened their arm, time and again, so that they did not need foreign alliances (Ex. 14:13-31; Joshua 6; 10:12; Judges 4 and 7; 1 Sam. 7; 2 Kings 19:35). Yet they "imagine mischief," are planning wickedness against Jehovah! That was the thanks the foolish people and unwise rendered to the Lord (Deut. 32:6). They return (v. 16), but not to God on high (Gr. N.). Like a deceitful bow, which has lost its power, can no longer drive the arrow to its mark, all their efforts, religious, social, political, in business and at home, will lack success. The "rage," the boisterous, defiant tongue of the princes, their open disavowal of the Lord will ruin, slay them. "Their derision." For this they will be derided by the selfsame Egyptians whose aid they sought when Assyria opposed them and whom they opposed when that seemed better diplomacy. Serves them right, the turncoats!

CHAPTER 8

d. Israel's judgment is rapidly approaching, vv. 1-14

1 Set the trumpet to your lips! As an eagle upon the house of the LORD! For they have transgressed My covenant and rebelled against My Law.
2 To Me they shall cry: My God, we
3 know Thee! Israel! Israel abhors what is good; an enemy shall pursue
4 him. They make kings, but without Me; they make princes, but without My knowledge. With their silver and their gold they make idols for themselves, that they might be cut
5 off! Your calf is offensive, O Samaria! My wrath burns against them! How long will they be incapable of purity? For this also is
6 capable of purity? For this also is from Israel! A workman has made it, and it is not a god. Surely, the calf of Samaria shall become splin-
7 ters. For they sow wind, and they shall reap the whirlwind! Stalk it has none! The sprout does not produce flour. If perchance it should produce, foreigners would swallow
8 it up! Israel is swallowed up! Now

they are among the nations like an
9 unattractive vessel. For they go up to Assyria, a wild ass, alone, for himself! Ephraim gives out para-
10 mour's gifts. Even if they dispense gifts among the nations, I shall now gather them so that they shall begin to be small because of the burden
11 of the king of princes. Because Ephraim made many altars unto sin, altars shall be for him unto
12 sin. I have been writing for him the myriad things of My Law. As a strange matter they were re-
13 garded! Sacrifices of My gifts they sacrifice; meat, and they eat. The LORD has no delight in them. Now He shall remember their guilt, and punish their sins. They shall return
14 to Egypt! Israel has forgotten his Maker and built temples, and Judah has multiplied fortified cities. I will send fire into his cities, and it will consume his palaces.

Grammatical Notes

V. 2. "Israel" emphatically, boastingly, placed at the end, Israel are we!

V. 3. "Cast off," חֵן, literally, to stink, be offensive, so v. 5. Here = to regard as offensive, be disgusted with, cast off in loathing (Ps. 43:2; 44:10, 24). — "Good," without article, hence qualitative, all that has the quality of goodness.

V. 5. "Innocency," נִקָּיוֹן, cleanness, physically (Amos 4:6), morally (Gen. 20:5; Ps. 26:6; 73:13).

V. 6. "Was it also." וְהוּא. ן here = also, in addition (cp. 2 Sam. 1:23; Eccl. 5:6). "It" refers to calf, v. 5. — "Workman," any skilled workman in wood, stone, or iron; artisan.

V. 7. "Stalk," that which stands; cp. "standing corn." — "Bud." צֶמַח always denotes an individual growth or plant, never a mere branch or bud of a plant (Gen. 19:25; Jer. 23:5, etc.).

V. 9. "Wild ass," פֶּרֶא, play on Ephraim. — "Alone by himself," בּוֹדֵד, participle of בָּדַד, to be alone, isolated. The verb occurs here, Ps. 102:8; Is. 14:31, always participle; the adjective, Num. 23:9; Deut. 33:28; Micah 7:14, etc. According to God's will, Israel was to be separated, alone. — "Hired." הִתְנוּ, Hiph. of תָּנָה, occurs only here and Qal v. 10. Most probably connected with אֶתְנָה (Hos. 2:14), אֶתְנַן (Deut. 23:19; Ezek. 16:31, 34, 41, etc.), the "hire" paid to a harlot. Plural predicate with singular subject. — "Lovers," rather, loves, denotes faithful marital love, Prov. 5:19; here, illicit love, the plural intensive.

V. 10. "Sorrow a little." וַיָּחֵלּוּ מְעָט, Hiph. of חָלַל = to begin. "Sorrow" would require יָחִילוּ. The complement of a transitive verb is often an infinitive (Gen. 37:5; Deut. 3:24); at times, a second verb (Hos. 1:6; 5:2), or a participle (Is. 33:1; 1 Sam. 16:16), or even an adjective (1 Sam. 3:2 and here, מְעָט). We translate: So that they shall begin

(to be) small, insignificant. — "For," מִן = on account of, as Ex. 6:9; 15:23; Is. 53:5, etc. — "King of princes," *Melech sarim*, either a king (and) princes or "king of princes" as the Assyrian rulers styled themselves. In either case the oppressive rule and exorbitant taxation is the "burden." LXX, "They will 'cease' a little while from 'anointing' a king and princes." This requires changes of M. T.

V. 12. "Great things," רִבּוֹ. K'tib רִבּוֹ = ten thousand, a myriad. K'ri רַבֵּי = multitudes. The prosaic Masoretes did not like the poetic "myriads," which they regarded as numerical, and changed the seeming exaggeration to a prosaic "multitudes."

V. 13. "Mine offerings." הַבְהָבַי, only here, from יָהַב, "to give," occurring only in imperative (Gen. 29:21; Ps. 29:1, etc.). On reduplication of second and third consonants, see G.-K. 84 n.

V. 1. "To thy mouth," literally, the palate, here as the organ of speech (cp. Prov. 5:3; 8:7; Cant. 5:16). With clarion voice Hosea is to proclaim God's message. He is to serve as God's alarm trumpet. Judgment is near, is here! Swiftly, suddenly, inerrantly it comes, like an eagle, a griffon vulture, swooping down upon his victim (cp. Deut. 28:49). "Against the house of the LORD," here, not the Temple, which was not yet to be destroyed, but the land in which, or the people among whom, God had promised to dwell (Ex. 25:8; Lev. 26:12, cp. Hos. 9:15; Jer. 12:7; Zech 9:8; Num. 7:89). They had forfeited the blessing of His protection by transgressing His covenant, by revolting against His Law.

Vv. 2, 3. "Shall cry," rather, "is ever and again crying," professing their knowledge of the Lord and the fact that they were Israel (Gr. N.). They forgot that Jacob became Israel only when he clung to the Lord in unwavering faith, and then only by divine blessing (Gen. 32:24-30). They had cast off (Gr. N.) good, not only the Lord and His salvation, whose revelation was their choicest possession (Deut. 4:6 ff., 32 ff.; cp. Ps. 73:25, 26). They rejected and loathed everything that was good. Now the enemy shall pursue them (cp. Deut. 28:47 ff., in contrast to vv. 7-14).

V. 4 proves the godlessness and rejection of all good things on the part of Israel. In selecting their kings and princes they left God and His Law (Deut. 17:14-20) out of consideration; chose men whom the Lord "knew not" as kings qualified to rule His people (cp. 1 Kings 14:7-11; 21:20-25; 2 Kings 10:28-34; 15:8-31). Such kings God had given to Israel in His anger (Hos. 13:11), in punishment of their sins. The wicked, rebellious people, revolting against the Lord, deserved no better kings and rulers. Their silver and gold, God's gifts (Deut. 10:14; Ps. 50:12; 115:16; Hag. 2:9, A. V., 8), they have used for their idols, to make statues of Baal (Hos. 2:8, M. T., 10), golden or silver calves set up in various cities, and used them for the upkeep of the priesthood, the sacrifices, the ritual, the harlotry connected with these sanctuaries so abominable to Jehovah. And all their moneys and riches spent for idolatry in reality served only one purpose, to cut them off, to cause God's judgments to come upon them. The worship of the almighty dollar will be the ruin of America also.

Vv. 5, 6. "Hath cast thee off," rather, is offensive (Gr. N., v. 3), and therefore your sacrifice is not a sweet savor to Me (Gen. 8:21; Lev. 1:9, 13, 17; Eph. 5:2), but a stench (Lev. 26:31; Amos 5:21). Far from pleasing the Lord or serving as a means of attaining His favor, their worship kindled God's anger. Impatiently He asks: How long will they be unable to obtain cleanness? (Gr. N.) Purity, innocence before God can be obtained only from the Lord in answer to penitent prayer (Ps. 51:1, 2, 7, 9, 10; cp. Is. 1:18). And they persistently refuse to turn to the Lord, but cling to their self-chosen worship. "For" (v. 6) explains why the calf is offensive. For from Israel is this also! Beside other abominations (Book of Judges), Israel, the people honored of God (Gen. 32:28; Ex. 19:4-6), had sunk so low as to make a calf their god. From Israel was "it," the calf (Gr. N.). A workman, an artisan, has made it. The Lord has nothing to do with its origin, its ritual, its worship. It is not a god. As its origin, so its end will prove its vanity, for slivers, broken splinters, shall be the calf of Samaria. It is not even a living calf, but a dead image!

V. 7. The fate of their idol will be their own. In a bold yet highly effective figure the prophet pictures the folly of idolatry and sin service. Who would ever try to sow wind? After carefully plowing the soil and harrowing it, here is a man trying to grasp wind and sow it in expectation of a rich crop! Folly of follies! Yet the pleasures and treasures which man makes the sole object of his ambition, his labor, his life, which are his idols worshiped and served by him, are as elusive as wind. True, wind is boisterous, and sin also noisily proclaims its promises of wealth, honor, prestige, enjoyment. Yet all these are wind, vanity! The world's wisdom cannot satisfy (Eccl. 1:17; 2:12-17); its riches and honors and pleasures cannot give true peace (Eccl. 2:4-11; 6:2-9). Yet how much time and labor is spent in trying to obtain them; how many cares and worries does it cost to sow wind! And all these efforts are futile, disastrous! They shall reap the whirlwind! Ruin, destruction, eternal damnation is their harvest! All their efforts produce no "stalk" (Gr. N.), nothing that will stand the ravages of time. If there is an occasional "bud," a sprout, a growth (Gr. N.), it will yield no "meal," no food worthy of the name. And if perchance there should be some "yield" (Ps. 37:35; 92:7), strangers, foreigners will swallow it up (Luke 12:15-21). The idolatry and sin service of Israel was the direct cause of its disintegration and ruin (2 Kings 15—17).

V. 8. Not only will their possessions be swallowed and their land taken over by the enemy (2 Kings 17:5-41), but Israel as a nation will be swallowed up. Having mixed themselves among the nations (Hos. 7:8), they are to be swallowed up by them. While the Jews are to remain forever a distinct people (Matt. 24:34, 35), the ten tribes have completely lost their tribal, national, and racial distinction, have become unrecognizable, the lost tribes! Once they were a people honored by the Lord to be His own (Ex. 19:5, 6; Deut. 5:28, 29). They mingled with the nations, which, after they had "sucked them dry" *(Expositor's Bible),* cast them off as a vessel no longer pleasing to them, a despised, rejected people! God's words, how true they are!

V. 9. This national ruin was the direct outcome of their alliance with Assyria, which involved acceptance or at least toleration of Assyrian idolatry (2 Kings 16:10-16; 19:8-19). Assyria was the whirlwind (cp. Hos. 12:1; 13:15) that came upon Israel, who had sown the wind of sinful trust in man and man-made idols. "A wild ass" (Gr. N.), a stubborn, self-willed animal, untamable; a comparison not very complimentary, but very true! "Alone" (Gr. N.), obstinately refusing to go with God on the way of God's Law, as a separate people (Deut. 33:28). They rather hired lovers, "loves" (Gr. N.). The greatest Lover, the God of everlasting love (Ex. 34:6; Jer. 31:3), had offered Himself and all His grace to Israel (Ex. 29:45, 46; Lev. 26:12). Yet

they go out to hire illicit loves, such as their flesh desired and as they
hoped to gain from alliances with heathen nations: political power
and prestige, commercial advantages, riches, luxury, pleasure. In seeking these "loves," they were interested not in the spiritual or even
material welfare of their allies, but in the satisfaction of their own
desires. They were ready to abandon and betray their allies whenever some other lover offered them better advantages. For such
vanities they were willing to pay the highest price, their liberty, their
salvation, their God. Stupid, stubborn asses!

V. 10. The pernicious folly of their political schemes will soon
become manifest. God will foil their plans. Though they have time
and again paid out their harlot's hire to the surrounding nations, God
will now gather them before His judgment throne to pay out to them
the due reward of their wickedness. They shall "sorrow" (Gr. N.),
rather, become small and insignificant, impoverished because of the
"burden," the enormous taxes paid to their own king and princes and
to foreign rulers, who taxed them to death. (Cp. 1 Kings 9:15-19;
12:4-15; 2 Kings 15:19, 20.)

Vv. 11-13. "Altars to sins." Israel's altars were erected from
sinful motives (1 Kings 12:26-33). Therefore these altars, the out-
growths of sinful ambition and stubborn rejection of God's will, became the springheads of innumerable sins. Every sacrifice at these
altars was contrary to God's Law (Deut. 12:5-14; cp. 1 Kings 13:1 ff.).
False worship, no matter how elaborately and devotedly carried out,
is sin. Israel could not offer even the excuse of ignorance. God had
prescribed in minute detail the manner, time, and place of His worship
in the "great things" (v. 12), rather, the multitudes, or myriads
(Gr. N.), of details recorded in the writings of Moses and later
prophets. While God was eager to make His people acquainted with
His laws, they regarded them as a strange matter, as if they did
not concern Israel. Indeed, they brought many sacrifices (v. 13) and
piously called them "God's offerings." In bitter irony the Lord adopts
this designation, although to Him they were mere "flesh," because the
place and the priests of Israel's sacrifices were illegal. "They eat."
That was their chief concern. Their purpose was not to obtain forgiveness (Lev. 1:4; 16:6, 10 ff.) and to express their gratitude to God
(Lev. 7:12 ff.; 22:29), but to satisfy their appetites, their desires
(cp. Hos. 4:12-18). Their sacrifices served only to recall to God's
mind the wickedness and hypocrisy of an idolatrous people still calling

71

themselves His people. Instead of forgiving their sins, He will punish them. The people shall go to Egypt, here a symbol of captivity and exile (cp. ch. 9:3, 6; 11:5). Israel was deported not to Egypt, but to Assyria (2 Kings 15:29; 17:6).

V. 14. Israel and Judah are alike, are one, in their base ingratitude, forgetting their Maker to whom they owed all they had. Instead of trusting in Him, they built great buildings, temples, palaces, fortresses. Jehovah will put their proud self-exaltation to shame. Fire shall consume their palaces, their cities.

CHAPTER 9

e. The way of sin leads into exile, vv. 1-9

1 Do not rejoice, O Israel! Do not exult like the nations! For you have played the harlot against your God. You have loved the harlot's hire on all the threshing floors for
2 grain. The threshing floor and the wine vat shall not feed them, and the new wine shall deceive her.
3 They shall not remain in the LORD'S land. Ephraim shall return to Egypt, and in Assyria they
4 shall eat unclean food. They will not pour out a libation of wine to the LORD, nor will their sacrifices be pleasing to Him. Their offerings shall be as the bread of mourners. All that eat it shall become polluted. For their bread is for themselves only; it shall not come into
5 the LORD'S house. What will you do on the festival day and on the
6 day of the LORD'S feast? For behold, because of destruction they go away. Egypt will be gathering them; Memphis will be burying them. Their valuables in silver, thistles will inherit them; thorns
7 will be in their tents. Come are the days of punishment! Come are the days of recompense! Israel shall know: A fool is the prophet! Demented is the man of spirit, because of your manifold guilt and
8 your great enmity. The watchman of Ephraim is at the side of my God. The prophet is a fowler's snare on all his ways, enmity in the
9 house of his god. They have gone to extreme depths in their corruption as in the days of Gibeah. He will remember their guilt! He will punish their sins!

Grammatical Notes

V. 7. "Fool," אֱוִיל, from אוּל, to be at the front, a leader; used only in a derogatory sense to denote a person who places himself first, has too high an opinion of himself, a fool. (Cp. Prov. 10:8, 10; 12:15; 15:2; 24:7; 2 Cor. 10:12.)

V. 8. "Watchman" is nominative, "Ephraim" its genitive. Keil's translation: "Israel" is on the lookout for prophecies "at the side of the Lord" is a contradiction of the actual state of affairs. Instead of going to the Lord, they went to their lying prophets. Modern translators (Guthe, Sellin, and others) change "My God," *elohai*, to "tent," *ohel*: "Ephraim lies in wait at the tent of the prophet." There is no need of any textual change.

V. 9. "Deeply corrupted." הֶעְמִיקוּ, "they have made deep," takes a verbal complement: שִׁחֵתוּ "they have corrupted." (Cp. Gr. N. on ch. 5:2, p. 49.)

Vv. 1-4. It seems that Israel had been granted a bountiful harvest (cp. v. 2). This they regarded as a token of God's favor; proof positive that the prophets of doom had been mistaken. They rejoiced like "other people" = heathen; exulting not in a God-pleasing manner, promising to dedicate themselves and their possessions to the Giver of all good gifts, but in the manner of the surrounding nations. The Lord disillusions them. The very manner of their rejoicing proved their estrangement from God, their unfaithfulness to their Husband. In the light of ch. 2:5, 8; 4:12, we regard "whoring" as spiritual adultery, yet from ch. 4:13, 14 we may conclude that the harvest festivals also were occasions for boisterous festivities in honor of the fertility deities and that they committed at the threshing floors and the wine presses the shameful immoralities against which Hosea and Amos so vehemently protest. The rich harvest does not change the fact that judgment is near. It is rather a call to repentance (see Rom. 2:4 ff.). If they continue in their apostasy, the richest harvest in field and vineyard will not benefit them (v. 2); they will suffer famine and thirst. Their heathen rejoicing will be replaced by heathenish lamentation when they are carried off into exile far away from Jehovah's land (v. 3); back "to Egypt," here again, as in ch. 8:13, a symbol of captivity and oppression (cp. 11:5) as explained immediately: "eat unclean things in Assyria." All food which was not sanctified to the Lord by the presentation of the first fruits, was unclean food to Israel (Ex. 22:29; 23:19; 34:22, 26; Lev. 23:10-12, 15-17). In the heathen lands Levitically clean food could hardly be obtained. There they could no longer offer drink offerings (v. 4), *pars pro toto*, their unbloody offerings, or sacrifices, their bloody offerings, in a manner pleasing to the Lord, for there they would have no temple (cp. Deut. 12:5-14). "Bread of mourning," unclean food, unclean and polluting shall all their offerings become (cp. Deut. 26:13, 14; Num. 19:11-14).

V. 5. "Solemn day" and "day of the feast" are synonyms, applied to all festival days prescribed by the Lord. See Lev. 23:1-44 on "solemn day," literally, "day of convocation, assembling," and Lev. 23:39, 41; Ex. 32:5; 34:18, 22, 25; Judg. 21:19 on "day of the feast," or festival day (cp. ch. 12:9, Gr. N.). All these days of rest and rejoicing in the Lord with all their joyous memories and solemn inspirations will be a thing of the past.

V. 6 states the reason for vv. 4, 5. They are no longer in the Lord's land. "Because of destruction," their whole land will be desolate, depopulated. Egypt, Memphis, one of its capitals, are here, as in v. 3, symbols of captivity, exile personified. The exile shall assemble them, no longer the festivals of the Lord, which they had desecrated by changing the divine ordinances (1 Kings 12: 32 f.). Captivity shall bury them. No longer shall they find a last resting place in God's land. "The pleasant places," literally, the objects of their desire. "For their silver," their money (cp. Deut. 2: 28; 23: 20, A. V., 19; Amos 2: 6, etc.). "For" here expresses a relation of the silver to these objects. To obtain these objects was the purpose of their efforts to gain money. On these objects they gladly spent their money; hence "pleasant places" here = their splendid homes, palaces, and other objects that money could buy. Nettles, weeds shall possess, literally, inherit them. No children left to whom to bequeath their wealth, only nettles! And their tabernacles, tents, the lowlier homes of the poorer classes, shall be overgrown by thorns.

V. 7. "The days of visitation," of punishment, stressing the divine infliction, "of recompense," requital, emphasizing the punishment as well deserved, in keeping with the enormous guilt (see v. 9). Israel shall learn by bitter experience the truth of what God had vainly tried to teach them, that the prophet, here the false prophet in contrast to God's spokesman (v. 8 a), is a "fool," a conceited, self-seeking fool (Gr. N.). The self-styled "spiritual man," literally, man of spirit, is mad, a psychopath, suffering from illusions instigated by the father of lies. (Cp. 1 Kings 22: 21-23; Jer. 23: 11-17, 25-27, 31, 32.) The unbelieving people called God's prophets fools and madmen (2 Kings 9: 11; Jer. 29: 26). Israel shall learn that not God's prophets, but their self-chosen men of spirit were men whose spirit was controlled by an evil spirit (cp. 1 Kings 18: 26-28). "For the multitude," etc., connects with the threat v. 7 a, stating its cause: "hatred," occurring only here and v. 8. Its root meaning is "to be hostile, belligerent, to persecute." It undoubtedly refers to such hostilities and persecutions as narrated in 1 Kings 13: 4, 9 ff.; 18: 17; 19: 1-3; 22: 8, 18, 24-27.

V. 8, 9. "Watchman" (Gr. N.). Prophets are called "watchmen," placed on the walls of Zion not merely to proclaim the coming of deliverance (Is. 52: 8), but chiefly to warn against approaching danger (Jer. 6: 17; Ex. 3: 17; 33: 2-7; Micah 7: 4-13), anxiously awaiting God's word (Hab. 2: 1). The term is used Is. 56: 10 of false prophets, neglectful of their solemn duty. The true watchman of Ephraim is one whose chief concern is that Ephraim remain what his name implies: a fruitful and prosperous nation. Such a watchman "is with my God," clinging to the true God, obedient to God's word, going where he is sent, speaking what he is told (Jer. 1: 7), faithfully doing his duty, firmly trusting in God's protection (2 Chron. 15:2; Ps. 73:23, both passages using the same word "with"). The "prophet," in distinction to the "watchman," is the false prophet described v. 7, who sets his snares and traps "in all his ways." Wherever he goes, whatever he does, his object is to snare the people by his lying prophecies and the true prophets by his pernicious schemes. He sows "hatred," enmity, oppression against God's faithful children and prophets. In the house of "his god," (note the distinction to "my God," v. 8 a), he schemes with his fellow deceivers. Hosea indignantly calls them "fowlers' snares," "hatred." They are living snares, enmity personified. Noble prophets, indeed! Yet their lying prophecies meet with a warmer welcome than does the message of God's true prophets (cp. Micah 2:11). These false prophets are chiefly responsible for the deep depravity of Israel, compared by Hosea (v. 9) to the heinous wickedness of Gibeah (Judg. 19, 20), which led to the almost complete annihilation of the tribe of Benjamin. Solemnly the prophet repeats his threats pronounced ch. 8:13 b.

---

f. Israel's suicidal ingratitude, ch. 9:10-17

10 As grapes in the wilderness I found Israel; as the first fruit on the fig tree in its first season. They came to Baal-Peor and consecrated themselves to Shame and became objects of abomination like their 11 love. O Ephraim! Like a bird their glory is flown away. No more birth, no more pregnancy, no more 12 conception! Yes, if they raise their children, I will make them childless, without a man! For woe upon them also when I depart from them! 13 Ephraim, as I chose it as a Tyre, was planted in a pleasant place, but Ephraim is appointed to lead out to 14 the murderer his sons. Give them,

O LORD! What wilt Thou give them? Give them a womb that miscarries and breasts that are dry! 15 All their wickedness was in Gilgal, for there I hated them; for the wickedness of their deeds I will drive them from My house. No more will I love them. All their princes are revolters. Ephraim is 16 stricken! Their roots are dried up; no more do they bear fruit; even if they bring forth, I will slay the 17 darlings of their womb. My God has cast them off, for they did not obey Him, and they will be homeless wanderers among the nations.

Grammatical Notes

V. 10. "Separated themselves." This expresses the root idea of נזר. The verb occurs ten times; five times the Hiphil as a Levitical term for the "separation" of the Nazarites, who separated, consecrated, dedicated themselves "unto," ל,

God by refraining "from," מן, the use of wine and strong drink, from shaving and cutting their hair, from coming near a dead body (Num. 6:1 ff.). The Hiphil is also used of the separation from various defilements or uncleannesses (Lev. 15:22). The Niphal is used reflexively of the priests' "separation" at certain times from holy things, the usual food of the priests (Lev. 22:2); of separating from food by fasting (Zech. 7:3; cp. v. 5). Ezek. 14:7 the Niphal with

מֵאַחֲרַי denotes separation "from after" God, while in the present passage the Niphal with לְ means separate "unto," by devoting, dedicating oneself to Baal. — "Shame," הַבֹּשֶׁת. The article justifies the equation of Bosheth with Baal; cp. Jer. 3:24; 11:13, and the interchange of Bosheth and Baal in such proper names as Ishbosheth (2 Sam. 2:8; 4:8) and Eshbaal (1 Chron. 8:33; 9:39); Jerubbaal (Judg. 6:32; 7:1) and Jerubbesheth (2 Sam. 11:21). Cp. also τῇ Βάαλ, Rom. 11:4.

V. 10. "According as they loved." G.-B. derives אֲהָבָם from אָהֵב, illicit love, Prov. 7:18 ("loves"), but regards it as *abstractum pro concreto*, "paramours"; so also Luther, "Buhlen," Keil, and others. We prefer to retain the abstract sense; according to their illicit love.

V. 11. "Birth." לַדָה is the infinitive of יָלַד, usually לֶדֶת; but לַדָה, 2 Kings 19:3; Is. 37:3; Jer. 13:21, is used substantively. — "Fly away," Hithp. causative-reflexive, shall cause itself to fly away.

V. 13. "Ephraim as I saw Tyrus." רָאָה frequently is used in the sense of regarding with pleasure, cp. v. 10; Ps. 22:18; 1 Sam. 6:19; Obad. 12; with לְ, to regard one as suitable for a certain purpose, to select, or choose for that purpose. I chose Ephraim as a Tyre. — "As," "but," וַ . . . כַּאֲשֶׁר, in like manner as . . . so. . . .

V. 15. "Hated them," שְׂנֵאתִים. The perfect presents actions, events, or states, which in some manner extend to the present time although completed in the past. The English present best suits the sense; e. g., He has hidden His face and still hides it, Ps. 10:11; I have stretched out my hands and still do so, Ps. 143:6. Here, I have hated and still hate.

V. 10. Wandering in the parched desert, the weary, thirsty traveler suddenly happens on an oasis where a grapevine offers him luscious fruit pleasing to the eye, quenching his thirst, satisfying his hunger; the more welcome and pleasing because one does not expect grapes in the desert. The first early figs, with what joy are they welcomed, how highly prized! Such joy is a feeble picture of God's joy over Israel in the days of her youthful bridal love (cp. Ex. 19:8; 24:3, 7; Deut. 5:27-29; Jer. 2:2, 3). These people, how did they change! "Baal-Peor," see Num. 25. "Separated" (Gr. N.). They had dedicated themselves heart and soul to God at Horeb, but the allurement of immorality had caused them to dedicate themselves body and soul (Num. 25:6) to that "shame" (Gr. N.). Baalism, heathen idolatry, spiritual and physical adultery, remained the besetting sin of Israel (Judg. 2:11-19). In accordance with their illicit love (Gr. N.), they became abominations. The greater the fervency of their Baal worship, the more zealous and fanatic their devotion to idolatry, the more abominable and detestable they became to their God.

Vv. 11-13. Now the divine nemesis! Israel's glory, its fruitfulness (cp. 4:7; Ps. 127:3-5), shall fly away. By its idolatry and immorality

Israel is causing its own decay. No birth, no gestation, no conception! Absolute sterility! The magnificent tree, once so fruitful, has become sterile, useless, encumbering the land (Luke 13:7), fit only and ready to be cut down and burnt. Even should they succeed in rearing some children, the Lord will bereave them. Their sons shall be slain until no one is left, in horrible yet just penalty of their shameful apostasy (v. 12). "As I saw." (V. 13, Gr. N.) God had chosen Ephraim to be like Tyrus, planted in a pleasant place, a fertile land (on the glory of Tyre see Ezek. 27 and 28), to become a strong and powerful nation, a shining example of God's grace and power to the surrounding nations (cp. Jer. 4:2). In like manner they shall now feel the full extent of His holy wrath. Israel is now chosen to lead out their children to the killer.

V. 14. Hosea, though deeply affected, voices his full agreement with God's judgment of annihilation. As if debating with himself, he interrupts his thoughts with a question, yet he cannot find a more terrible and more appropriate penalty than that which the Lord had just pronounced. "Miscarrying," rather, a childless womb, and dry breasts, that could not give nourishment. Israel's mothers no longer deserve and no longer shall be granted the blessed privilege of bearing and rearing children, for they have committed harlotry against their divine Husband (Hos. 1:2; 2:2-5).

V. 15. Gilgal, mentioned ch. 4:15 beside Bethel (Beth-Aven) as the site of an idol sanctuary, was also the scene of Israel's rebellion against God in prematurely desiring and demanding a king in spite of divine and prophetic warning. See 1 Sam. 8:5-22, particularly "like all the nations," vv. 5, 20; "rejected Me," v. 7. Also 1 Sam. 11:14; 12:12-24. It was their "great wickedness" (12:17, 19, 20) that prompted their request for a king. "There I hated them," not "began to hate," Keil, Huxtable, Sellin, but the perfect simply states the fact, that for their wickedness He hated them, and still hates them (Gr. N.). His hatred had begun far earlier (Ex. 32:9-14). Gilgal was another source of His hatred, because there their wickedness had manifested itself in so glaring a manner by their obstinate request for a king and was still manifesting itself by their persistence in idol worship; for this two-fold rejection of God He has hated them, and still hates them, and will hate them if they do not repent. "Drive them out," same word used by Sarah (Gen. 21:10). The Israelites are not worthy to dwell in God's house and be heirs with God's children. The Lord has withdrawn His love (cp. Jer. 15:1; 16:5 b). There remains only hatred, wrath (cp. Heb. 10:26, 27, 30, 31). Their princes, the advisers and

77

associates of the kings, are rebels; rejecting God's Law, they let their own ambitions dictate their policies.

V. 16 repeats the threat of vv. 11-14. "Smitten," same word as Jonah 4:7 (by a worm), v. 8 (by the sun), Amos 4:9 (by a divine curse), Mal. 3:24, A. V., 4:6. Their very roots are dried up and can no longer furnish nourishment to the tree. Apostasy from God, particularly if connected with sins against the Sixth Commandment, fornication, abortions, the use of contraceptives, etc., will sap the vitality of a nation, amounts to national suicide. And even if they "bring forth" a child or two, the Lord Himself will slay these petted and pampered darlings, brought up not in the nurture and admonition of the Lord (Eph. 6:4), but in disrespect of God and His Word. Epidemics, bloody wars are His dread instruments of death.

V. 17. "My God," for the preaching of whose word Hosea was being ridiculed, will fulfill His and my word. He will cast them off, despise, reject them, because they refused to hear Him, obey His word spoken by the prophet (Luke 10:16). Wanderers, like birds driven out of their nest, fluttering about aimlessly (Prov. 27:8; Is. 16:2), like Cain, homeless vagabonds (Gen. 4:12), in fulfillment of God's covenant threat (Deut. 28:65 f.).

CHAPTER 10

g. Israel's calves and kingdom shall perish, vv. 1-8

1 A vine plunderer is Israel. He lays up fruit for himself. As his fruit is multiplied, so he multiplies his altars; as his land improves, he im-
2 proves his images. Their heart is treacherous. Now they shall bear their guilt. He shall break the necks of their images; He shall ruin
3 their idol statues. Yes, then they shall say: We have no king, for we did not fear the LORD! And the
4 king, what shall he profit us? They talk business; they perjure themselves when they make covenants; and like a poison weed judgment blossoms on the furrows of the
5 field. Anxiously concerned for the calf of Beth-Aven are the inhabitants of Samaria. Yes, his people mourn for him, and his priests dance for him, for his glory which
6 goes into exile away from him. He himself, too, shall be brought to Assyria, a tribute offering to King Jareb. Ephraim shall bear disgrace, and Israel shall be put to shame by
7 his counsel. Samaria, her king, annihilated like foam on the waters!
8 And destroyed are Aven's high places — the sin of Israel; thorn and thistle shall grow up on their altars. And they shall say to the mountains: "Cover us," and to the hills: "Fall upon us!"

Grammatical Notes

V. 1. "An empty vine," others, spreading vine. קקק never occurs in either sense; always, "plunder, despoil" (Qal, Is. 24:1; Jer. 19:7; Nah. 2:3, and here; Niph., Is. 19:3; 24:3; Polal, Jer. 51:2). — "Vine," גפן, always fem., hence בוקק, in better keeping with grammar, is to be regarded as predicative rather than at-

tributive. The participle = characteristic trait. — "Bringeth forth," שָׁוָה,
Pi., here = set, lay down, store (Ps.
16:8; 21:6; 89:20; 119:30). — "Fruit," result or product of one's activity; profit,
gain (Ps. 58:12, A. V., 11; Prov. 12:14;
31:16, 31).

V. 2. "Divided." חָלַק means to divide,
distribute, Joshua 14:5; 18:2; 1 Sam.
30:24; never to be divided. Another
stem = to be smooth, slippery, treacherous (Ps. 55:22, A. V., 23; Hiph., Ps. 5:10;
Prov. 2:16; 28:23). While this is the
only passage in which the verb is applied to the heart, there is no reason to
change the text. The tongue, the words,
would not be smooth — treacherous, if
the heart were not smooth — treacherous (cp. Jer. 17:9). One of Hosea's
bold yet true figures. "He shall break,"
הוּא, refers to the Lord, who calls
Himself הוּא אֲנִי (Deut. 32:39; Ps. 102:27;
2 Sam. 7:28), unalterably, eternally the
same, fulfilling His threats and promises in His own determined time and
manner (Is. 41:4; 43:10,13, etc.). "Break
down," עָרַף = to break the neck (cp.
Ex. 13:13; 34:20).

V. 3. "No king." מֶלֶךְ without the article emphasizes the qualitative force of
the term: "a king," v. 3 b; הַמֶּלֶךְ, points
to the king then ruling.

V. 4. "Spoken words." דִּבֵּר is often
used of any business, or legal, or private matter (Ex. 18:16; Joshua 20:4;
2 Sam. 19:29); with דִּבֶּר, to conduct or
carry on any business. — "Swearing
falsely," etc. The absolute infinitive
אָלוֹת (for אָלֹה, Hos. 4:2, G.-K. 75 n)
and כָּרֹת describe the manner, or nature, of their actions. — "Judgment,"
here in the sense of right, law and
order (cp. Deut. 16:19; 27:19, etc.).

V. 5. "Inhabitants," שָׁכֵן. Collective singular with plural predicate (cp. Hos. 4:4,
G.-K. 145 c, d). — "Shall fear because
of," לְ גּוּר as in Job 19:29 and לְ יָרֵא
in Joshua 9:24; Prov. 31:21 = be anxiously concerned for. — "The calves,"
עֶגְלוֹת; the plural fem., heifers, does not
prove that there were female calves at
Bethel or a number of calves, called
heifers ironically. The fem. plural is
used as an abstract noun, "calfhood,"
a usage found not only in formations of
feminine nouns: כְּלוּלוֹת, bridal state
(כַּלָּה, bride), but of masculine nouns:
בְּחוּרִים (state of youth, Eccl. 11:9; 12:1).
G.-K. 124 d. "Calfhood" = idolatrous
calf worship. — "Priests," כְּמָרִים, etymology uncertain, in Old Testament
a designation of idol priests exclusively,
here; 2 Kings 23:5; Zeph. 1:4. — "That
rejoiced." The omission of אֲשֶׁר would
be unusually harsh here. גִּיל = to move
in circles, dance. Kittel and others
suggest יְיֵלִילוּ = howl. Keil compares
חִיל, twist in pain, Ps. 96:9.

V. 6. "Shall be carried," יוּבָל אוֹתוֹ. The
active construction suddenly changes
into the passive. Cp. Ex. 10:8; 27:7; Is.
17:1, etc. G.-K. 121 b. — "Present." מִנְחָה
here in the sense of present or tribute
to gain the favor of a person, Gen. 32:14,
19, 21 (A. V., vv. 13, 18, 20); 1 Kings
10:25; Is. 39:1; Ps. 72:10).

V. 7. "Foam," קֶצֶף. Etymology uncertain. Some translate "splinter," tossed to
and fro on the waters, or carried away
by the stream. Others, "foam," caused
by the "anger" (קֶצֶף) of the water.
"Foam" is the more drastic figure and
suits the verb better; the sliver is carried off, the foam annihilated, dissolved
into nothingness.

V. 8. "Thistle." דַּרְדַּר occurs only here
and Gen. 3:18.

V. 1. "An empty vine," rather a plunderer, despoiler, of the vine (Gr. N.). A plunderer of the vine is not interested in the improvement and conservation of the vine; nor has he any consideration for others (cp. Deut. 24:21, 22). His only purpose is to "bring forth" (Gr. N.), to lay down, store up, "fruit" (Gr. N.), profit, gain, for himself. Recklessly he plunders the vine for himself to the last grape. Let others look out for themselves, let the mistreated vine die; his greed must be satisfied. Israel shamefully abused the many spiritual and material blessings granted to them. Without consideration for the Giver of these gifts, or for their own salvation and the welfare of their neighbor, each one looked out for himself, first, last, and all the time. Recklessly they plundered the resources of the land and the nation in self-aggrandizement, building huge fortresses, stately mansions, etc. Instead of bringing the wonderful news of God's revelation to all the world, they sought contact with other nations only with a view to their own financial and political benefit. For political reasons their kings married foreign, idolatrous wives (1 Kings 11:1-9), changed the order of worship (ch. 12:26-33), introduced rank heathen idolatry (ch. 16: 30-33; 18:22-29). For selfish reasons they plundered the vineyard of God's planting (Ps. 80:8-11), wantonly destroyed its blessings, impoverishing it materially, enfeebling it politically, depraving it socially, paganizing it spiritually. As their fruit, their wealth, increased, so increased the number of their idol altars; ever larger sanctuaries dotted the land, embellished with an ever-increasing number of ever costlier and more elaborate and beautiful idol images.

V. 2. "Divided" = smooth, trickish, treacherous (Gr. N.). Jeroboam simulated solicitous care for the convenience of his dear people; professed to worship their ancient Lord and Deliverer (1 Kings 12:28), merely in order to cover up his own selfish ambition (v. 27). Like king, like people (vv. 30 b-33). They had apostatized from the Lord and His Law (Ex. 20:4, 5; Deut. 12:13, 14); they were children of harlotry (Hos. 1:2; 2:2-5), and still they persisted in calling themselves God's people and expected and demanded His blessing, protection, and aid. "Now" (see Gr. N. on ch. 2:10). "Found faulty," be guilty, bear their guilt and punishment (Gr. N.). "He," either God Himself, or through His instruments, will break down, literally, break the neck of (Gr. N.), their altars and spoil, ruin their images, their pillars. Altars and idols are personified. Against God they are helpless (cp. 1 Sam. 5:1-7).

V. 3. "For," rather, "yes," "surely," "certainly"; "now," under these circumstances, when they see their sanctuaries and their idols destroyed by the enemies, they shall cry out in abject despair: We have no king worthy of the name, fit for his office. "We feared not the Lord" does not express true repentance. It is the repentance of Judas, of men with tricky hearts, incurably wicked (Jer. 17:9), still ruled by sin, still refusing wholeheartedly to turn to the Lord. The king we now have, what shall he do for us? If we had a king like the Jeroboams, we might hope for better times; but now? Blaming others for the consequence of their own fault is the old and ever new treacherous trick of sin and Satan and man's depraved heart. It will not turn to the Lord that healeth them!

V. 4. Their treacherous heart manifests itself in perfidious acts. They speak words, conduct their business, private, legal, political affairs, under guise of law and order. Yet they commit perjury, swear oaths they have no intention to keep; make solemn promises, inviolable pacts, sacrosanct covenants, which at their convenience they regard as mere scraps of paper. So judgment, law and order (Gr. N.), ceases to be right, sprouts like poison weeds, growing luxuriantly in the furrows of a field. Might is right. Power and wealth is the law of the land. Under the protection of the law the greatest crimes are committed. The state, the church (Israel was a church-state, a state-church), that neglects God and His Word, is doomed to perish.

Vv. 5, 6. Even the approaching disaster does not rouse Israel to turn back to God. The first thought of their tricky heart concerns their idols. Beth-Aven = Bethel, see ch. 4:15. "Fears because of" (Gr. N.). What will become of our national shrine (cp. Amos 7:13)? so the people moan. The priests, the idol priests (Gr. N.), "rejoice," rather, perform a ritual dance, imploring the idol to help them and himself. They hoped that their calf would save them from defeat and ruin, and all the glory and honor they had heaped upon it vanishes, departs. Not the calf, but Assyria, the enemy, is victorious. The calf is disgraced (v. 6), carried into Assyria as a present, a tribute to King Jareb (see ch. 5:13), not to be worshiped by him, but to be placed into the temple of Marduk as one of his captives. Cp. 2 Kings 18:33-35; 25:13-16; Ezra 1:7-11, and Cyrus' proclamation that all the "gods" that had been brought to Babylon by the former kings and placed into the temple of Marduk were restored to their original homes by Cyrus. (Barton, *Archaeology,* 6th ed., p. 483 f.) Ephraim has lost its God, lost its calf; its only take is shame, ridicule! And Israel is put to shame! Why? Because of its own counsel, its carefully planned and deliberately continued idolatry, inaugurated by Jeroboam and retained by his successors for political advantages, and eagerly adopted by the people because of its relaxations of the demands of God's holy Law. Their wise counsel turned out to be shameful folly!

V. 7. The glory of Samaria, her king = kingdom, has disappeared like foam, an evanescent glory, dissolved into nothingness (cp. v. 15).

V. 8. "Aven" = worthlessness, vileness, without the slightest trace of value and substance. "Aven" may be intended for Beth-Aven = Bethel (chs. 4:15; 5:8; 10:5), yet it seems preferable to refer it to all the idolatrous high places in Israel, not only to those erected to Baal, but chiefly to those erected to the worship of Jehovah (2 Kings 17:9-12; Amos 7:9) contrary to His will (Deut. 12:11-14), and particularly to the "house of high places" built by Jeroboam I at Bethel (1 Kings 12:31, 32). At Dan a high place may have existed since the days of the Judges (cp. Judg. 18:14-31). These high places constituted the "sin of Israel," were the symbols of their apostasy from Jehovah (1 Kings 14:9). In designating them "Aven," the prophet condemns them all as inane, worthless, a deception and a fraud. They shall be destroyed, covered by thorns and thistles (cp. Gen. 3:18, the only other passage where this term for "thistle" occurs), neglected, forsaken. And the deluded people, forsaken by their helpless gods, cast off by the Lord, stand in awe and terror as they see God's judgments coming upon them. Alas, instead of seeking His grace with penitent hearts, they implore the mountains and hills to cover them in their vain efforts to escape the wrath of the Lord (Amos 9:1-4; Luke 23:30; Rev. 6:16).

---

2. The purpose of God's action against Israel, ch. 10:9-15

9 Since the days of Gibeah you have sinned, O Israel! There they stand! The war against the reprobates did 10 not overtake them at Gibeah. When I please, I will chastise them, and nations shall be gathered against them because they have tied on to 11 their two iniquities. And Ephraim is a well-broken heifer loving to thresh; yet I Myself will pass over her fair neck. I will harness Ephraim, Judah will plow, Jacob 12 will harrow for himself. Sow for yourselves righteousness! Reap in accordance with love! Break up your fallow ground! And it is time to seek the LORD, until He come and rain righteousness upon you. 13 You have plowed wickedness, reaped perversion. You have eaten the fruit of deceit. For you have trusted in your way, in the multitude of your warriors. And there 14 shall arise the noise of war against your people, and all your fortifications will be destroyed, as Shalman destroyed Beth-Arbel on the day of battle. Mother and child shall be 15 dashed to pieces. So shall Bethel do unto you for your extreme wickedness! In the morning dawn the kingdom of Israel shall be completely annihilated.

Grammatical Notes

V. 9. "Hast sinned," "stood." The two perfects denote an action in its completion, even if it or its consequences extend to the present time. Gen. 49:18; 1 Sam. 2:1. The English present is the best translation. G.-K. 106 g. — "Iniquity," עֹלָה = עׂולָה as many MSS read.

V. 10. "In My desire," construed like a temporal clause with simple waw = When I desire, then. . . . Cp. Gen. 22:4; 40:9,16; Ex. 12:3, etc.—"Chastise them," וְאֶסֳּרֵם, stem יׇסׇר. Verbs פ"י, particularly with a sibilant as second consonant, frequently (like פ"נ verbs) assimilate the י (cp. Gen. 28:18; Is. 44:12; Jer. 1:5). The shwa mobile under the second consonant frequently takes the form of Chateph Qamez (cp. Is. 27:3; 62:2; Jer. 31:33). G.-K. 60 a, 71. — "Bind themselves," בְּאָסְרָם. The verbal suffix, except that of first person נׅי־, rarely, if ever, occurs with the infinitive, which takes the nominal suffix, hence: his binding, while he binds; not, while one binds them. G.-K. 61 a. Note the alliteration with וְאֶסֳּרֵם. — "Two furrows." עֵינֹתָם; K'tib demands a plural of עַיׅן = (a) eye, the plural of which is replaced by the dual; (b) wellspring, with feminine plural. Neither sense suits the passage. The rendering of the Targum and A. V., "furrows," cannot be established. Huxtable in the Bible Commentary suggests עׂונָה, cohabitation, occurring only Ex. 21:10. There, however, it denotes lawful duty of cohabitation,

a sense impossible here. Q'ri, LXX, Syrian, Vulg., read עֲוׂנֹתָם, their iniquities, an emendation almost universally adopted and rendering a sense suitable to context.

V. 11. "Loveth," אׇהַבְתּׅי, part. fem. with compaginis emphasizing the construct case, usually accented, except before a preposition or accented syllable (cp. Lam. 1:1). — "Passed over," here in inimical sense as, e. g., Nah. 3:19; Job 9:11; 13:13. — "Ride," אַרְכּׅיב, make him carry a rider, i. e., harness him, set him to work. — "Break his clods," יְשַׂדֶּד־לֹו. The etymology of שׇׂדַד, occurring only here, Is. 28:24; Job 39:10, is uncertain. Generally translated "to harrow." Guthe (ZAWB 34, 75 ff.) sought to prove that it denotes plowing the deep end furrow; yet Procksch (Jesaia I, Sellin's KAT, p. 365) points out that according to v. 25 the three verbs, "plow, open, break clods," in v. 24 serve to "make plain," to level, to smoothen out the field; that, therefore, שׇׂדַד is correctly translated "break the clods," by harrowing. — "His clods." לֹו is dative incommodi, to his sorrow and disgust.

V. 12. "To yourselves," לָכֶם, לְ commodi; "in righteousness," לְ of direction, aim, purpose (Gen. 31:30; Jer. 5:3; Job 10:6). — "In mercy." לְפׅי = in accordance with, in proportion to (Gen. 47:12; Ex. 12:4; 16:16, 18; 1 Kings 17:1, "no rain but in proportion to my word").

V. 9. Once more Gibeah is mentioned (cp. 5:8; 9:9), where the atrocious crime recorded Judges 19 and 20 was committed; characterized there as lewdness and folly, "a foul and carnal deed" (The Complete Bible), such as had not occurred before in Israel (Judg. 19:30; 20:6). Israel has not changed. As in the past they stood proud, defiant, so they still stand stubborn, self-confident transgressors. The "battle" in Gibeah = that bloody war (cp. the constant repetition of this term Judg. 20:14, 25, 29, 33 f., 36), in which Benjamin was reduced from 26,700 armed men to 600 (Judg. 20:15, 47, 48; 21:6). Such a war had not yet touched Israel and could not touch them, they boasted. That ancient battle was directed against the children of iniquity; they were God's favorites! Had not Jeroboam extended the limits of their kingdom (2 Kings 14:25, 28)? Had not Pekah disastrously defeated Judah (2 Chron. 28:6, 8)? Surely, the Lord was on their side! Only lying prophets could threaten them! Yet suddenly the end came!

V. 10. "In My desire" (Gr. N.), when My predetermined hour has come, I will punish them. Nations shall be assembled in fulfillment of the covenant threat (Lev. 26:14 ff.; Deut. 28:15 ff.), while Israel was persisting in its two transgressions: the apostasy from the house of David and from the true worship of the Lord (1 Kings 12:19, 27-33). Compare Hos. 3:5, where Israel's return is described as seeking the Lord, their God, and David, their king (cp. also 2 Kings 17:20-23). The reference is not to the two calves, for that was but one sin, idolatry.

V. 11. Ephraim had an able trainer, the best possible instructor: God and His Word, Law and Gospel (cp. Ps. 119:9-16, 43, 44, 97-105). Yet he had begun to demand blessings without obligations. Like a young heifer treading out the grain, walking leisurely over the corn, permitted to eat her fill (Deut. 25:4), growing fat and sleek, Ephraim loved to thresh, to do work which to him seemed pleasant, productive, profitable, neglecting and forgetting the training of his Master, resenting His instructions as soon as they ran counter to his own desires; shirking the arduous duty of self-discipline (Deut. 32:15-18) demanded by the Lord. Now the Lord was ready to fulfill His threat, Deut. 32:19-25. He will pass over her (the heifer's = Ephraim's) "fair neck," literally, the "beauty" of her neck, the objects of her pride, Ephraim's flourishing prosperity; will rise up against it, pass over it in His fury. No longer will Ephraim be treated like a petted heifer, but set to work. Ephraim, the Northern Kingdom, will be made to ride, to carry a rider; Judah, the Southern Kingdom, will have to draw the plow; Jacob, the twelve tribes (cp. 12:1, 2, on Ephraim — Judah — Jacob), no longer called by their honorable name (Gen. 32:28), will, like sinful, fugitive Jacob, be driven out of their homeland into exile, into hard labor of slavery. The three predicates are to be connected with each of the three subjects, as, e. g., Hos. 4:5; 6:10 b; 8:14.

84

V. 12. The admonition is vested in the language of agriculture. Fallow ground is woodland that is to be plowed for the first time. Such land, usually overgrown with weeds and brambles, must not be seeded after the first plowing, but must be worked and reworked until all or most of the weeds have been killed, else the faster growing weeds would choke the little seedlings. To obtain the best harvest, carefully selected seed must be sown, and the reaping must be done in proper manner. All three operations require strenuous, diligent, intelligent labor. The Lord tells the Israelites, all tribes, to sow for themselves, for their own benefit "in righteousness," and "reap in mercy" (Gr. N.), literally, to sow with a view to obtain righteousness and reap in proportion to, in keeping with, mercy. The Lord Himself explains the figurative language: It is time to seek the Lord; diligently, prayerfully, with all their heart to search for the Lord (cp. Deut. 4:29), until He comes and rains righteousness upon them. The Hebrew conjunction "until" frequently implies the arrival at the goal, the attainment of one's object (Is. 42:4; Ps. 57:2, A. V., 1; 94:13; 110:1). The underlying idea is that the Lord has withdrawn His gracious presence (cp. vv. 10, 11; ch. 5:6, 14, 15). Yet there is still time and opportunity to seek the Lord, and He is still willing to come and rain righteousness upon them if they seek Him untiringly and sincerely. This explains the righteousness which according to v. 12a is to be the aim and object of their sowing, their seeking. It is not a man-made righteousness, but that righteousness which the Lord is ready to grant abundantly as a gift of His grace to all that seek Him and His righteousness. It is that righteousness to which the Lord had pointed ch. 2:19 and which He again promises ch. 13:14; 14:1-8, which was to be procured for Adam and all his seed by the Woman's Seed (Gen. 3:15), of which Isaiah, Hosea's contemporary, spoke (Is. 4:2 ff.; 9:5, 6; ch. 53; cp. Jer. 23:5, 6). Hence, sow toward righteousness = seek the Lord and His righteousness, prepared for you without any merit on your part by the Lord and sent by Him as freely, graciously, and abundantly as the rain from heaven. Reap in proportion to, in keeping with, mercy = accept this righteousness in humble gratitude as a free gift of grace, and show your gratitude in loving and serving God and keeping His Commandments. To do this requires a change of your attitude, a new beginning. Break up your fallow ground! Turn over the hard and weed-infested soil of your sinful heart. In the power of your God and His word of grace destroy the seeds of sin and wickedness ever more thoroughly and diligently. And do not delay. (Is. 55:6, 7; Heb. 3:7-15.) From sowing to harvest, from beginning to end, the aim and purpose of our life's activity is to be the attainment of God's righteousness and of holy living in gratitude for His grace.

V. 13. Israel had not done that in the past and is not doing that now. It has been and is still plowing wickedness (cp. Job 4:8). The soil the people plowed, from which they hoped to reap rich blessings, was wickedness, their own sinful heart (Jer. 17:9). All they thought and spoke and wrought, all their life's activity was centered on wickedness. Consequently they ate the "fruit of lies" = deceitful fruit, pleasant to their depraved taste, but poisonous fruit. And their sin was self-reliance. They trusted in their own ways, their self-conceived plans and devices, and in their military strength, instead of placing their trust in the Lord, their God (Jer. 9:23, 24 and the preceding context, vv. 2-22).

V. 14. In spite of all their pride a "tumult," the noise and din of war, shall arise "among," rather, against their people; all their fortresses will be razed. "Shalman" has been identified with Shalmaneser (2 Kings 17:3-6), though no reason for this abbreviation is given. Others = Salmanu, mentioned in one of Tiglath-Pileser's inscriptions (see Schrader, *Keilinschriften*, p. 283 f.), as a king of Moab, otherwise unknown. "Beth-Arbel," very likely the modern Kirbeth Irbid, about six miles southwest of Magdala in Galilee. We do not know the details, evidently a notorious example of cruel butchery, sparing neither women nor children, whom the mother vainly seeks to protect. Such shall be Ephraim's ruin.

V. 15. The primary cause of this ruin is Bethel, the king's sanctuary (Amos 7:13), its calf worship, the sin of Jeroboam, frequently mentioned in the Books of Kings, called by Hosea their "great wickedness," literally, wickedness of wickedness, the Hebrew superlative, cp. Song of Songs (Cant. 1:1). "In a morning," or dawn, usually the symbol of hope, here denoting the unexpected suddenness of the destruction, shall be cut off the last king of Samaria and with him perish the kingdom of Samaria.

CHAPTER 11

3. The Lord of the Covenant stands ready to receive penitent Israel, vv. 1-11

1 When Israel was young, then I began to love him, and from Egypt
2 I called My Son. They called to them, and in like measure they walked away from My presence. To Baalim they sacrificed, to carved
3 images they brought offerings. And I Myself taught Ephraim to walk, taking them up in My arms. Yet they knew not that I healed them.
4 With cords of man I drew them, with bands of love. And I became to them like those who lift the yoke lying on their jaws, gently gave

86

5 food to them. He shall not return to the land of Egypt; but Assyria — he shall be his king, for they have
6 refused to return. And the sword shall make the rounds in their cities and put an end to his liars and
7 consume him for his counsels. But My people are impaled upon their apostasy from Me. And they call him to Him above, yet in spite of all efforts one does not lift him up.
8 How can I give you up, O Ephraim? Surrender you, O Israel? How can I give you up like Admah, make you like Zeboim? My heart is turned against Me. My compassions
9 are altogether inflamed. I will not carry out the fury of My anger! I will not again destroy Ephraim! For God I am and not man, in your midst the Holy One. And I will not
10 come in fury. They shall follow the LORD. He will roar like a lion, yes, He will roar. And trembling will come the children from the
11 west. Trembling like birds they come from Egypt, and like doves from the land of Assyria. And I will let them dwell in their homes — is the oracle of the LORD.

Grammatical Notes

V. 1. "Child," נַעַר, denotes a person from infancy (Ex. 2:6; Judg. 13:5, 7; 1 Sam. 1:22; 4:21) to early manhood (Gen. 34:19; Judg. 17:7, etc.), frequently stressing inexperience or helplessness (1 Sam. 17:34, 42). The LXX reads: I called his children, לְבָנָיו, instead of "My Son."

V. 2. "As they called them," קָרְאוּ. LXX: כְּקָרְאִי, as I called them. The M. T. is correct. The plural "they called" is the indefinite plural, the English "one," the German "man." Often the passive form is the best translation: They were called, so they went, i. e., as often as . . . so often they. . . . G.-K. 144 d-k.

V. 3. "Taught to go," stem רֶגֶל, "foot," Tiphel a rare conjugation, teach to walk, lead. G.-K. 55 h. — "Taking them." קָחָם is either an ancient scribal error or elision of the ל, the full form being לְקָחָם (G.-K. 19 i).

V. 4. "Take off," מְרִימֵי = lift up (Hiph. partic.) for the purpose of easing the burden of the heavy yoke by changing its position. — "I laid meat unto them." אַט may be the first person imperfect Hiph. of נָטָה, I inclined Myself to him, or אַט is used adverbially: gently, kindly (Gen. 33:14; 2 Sam. 18:5; Is. 8:6). Gently towards them I gave food. אוֹכִיל follows the analogy of פ"ו stems.

V. 6. "Abide," חוּל, turn in a circle, dance. Others: rush down upon (Jer. 23:19; Lam. 4:6). — "Branches," בַּד, branch, also staff, rod (Ex. 25:13-15, 27, 28, etc.). Here = crossbeams, bars to secure the city gates (cp. Job 17:16), comprising all means of defense.

V. 7. "Bent," תְּלוּאִים, ל"א instead of ל"ה, G.-K. 75 rr, impale, put to death by fixing upon a pale or pointed stake (Deut. 21:22, 23; Joshua 8:29, etc.). — "They called them." See note on v. 2. "The Most High," עָל, height, that which is on high, above (cp. 7:16; 2 Sam. 23:1). — "None at all," לֹא יַחַד, altogether not = not one at all. — "Exalt," יְרוֹמֵם, lift up, raise to a higher level.

V. 8. "How." אֵיךְ with imperfect denotes a reproach (Judg. 16:15; Jer. 2:23; 48:14, etc.) or, as here, an impossibility (Gen. 39:9; 44:8, 34; Is. 20:6; 48:11, etc.). — "In Me." עַל used in this sense also 1 Sam. 25:36, "within him."

V. 9. "Into the city," בָּעִיר, from עוּר, to excite; in excitement, passion, anger; cp. Jer. 15:8, the excitement of fear.

V. 1. God, the faithful Lover of Israel, graciously leading and training His people, is rewarded with unfaithfulness. — God's love of Israel did not begin only after Israel had become a great nation (cp. Deut. 7:7, 8). Israel's greatness was rather the result of His eternal love, which began to manifest itself already in the early youth (Gr. N.) of Israel, in its birth as a nation in Egypt and in its deliverance from the house of bondage. But Israel repaid God's love with ingratitude (v. 2).

Read in this context without taking into account Matt. 2:15, it seems certain, indeed, that the clause "And called My son out of Egypt" refers to Israel and its deliverance out of Egypt. Yet this interpretation, plausible as it seems, runs counter to the Lord's own interpretation as recorded by His inspired penman, who very definitely states that the words "I called My Son out of Egypt" refer to the Christ Child. Matt. 2:13, 14 the Holy Spirit tells us that because of Herod's plan to slay the holy Infant, Joseph took the young Child and His mother, departed into Egypt, and remained there until Herod's death, "that it might be fulfilled which was spoken by the prophet, saying: 'Out of Egypt have I called My Son.' " He restricts the fulfillment of a divine prophecy to the words quoted, not including any other parts of Hos. 11:1, 2.

Various efforts have been made to solve this difficulty. The literal sense, some say, speaks of Israel; the mystical sense, of Christ. This solution is contrary to the ancient principle of sound Biblical hermeneutics, that every passage of Scripture has but one intended sense. To deny this principle would undermine the very foundation of Scriptural interpretation and open wide the doors to fanciful speculations and to uncertainty. In our day the typical mode of interpretation is favored generally. Israel's history is regarded as the type of Christ's life, and therefore, as Israel took refuge in Egypt and later was brought back to the Promised Land, so Christ fled to Egypt and later returned to His own country. Yet Matthew does not say that a type was fulfilled. He says that what was spoken by the prophet was fulfilled by Christ's sojourn in Egypt. He speaks of the fulfillment of a historical fact prophesied by Hosea, the historical fact: Out of Egypt have I called My Son. On the fulfillment of types and figures of the Old Testament see Heb. 8:5 (example and shadow); 9:8 (the Holy Ghost *signifying*); v. 9 (figure); v. 23 ("patterns" = representations, figures, of better things); 10:1 (shadow). On the distinction between types and God's Word see Heb. 10:1-4 (types) and vv. 5-9, 15-18 (Scripture); ch. 7:1-3, "made like," similar, an image, a copy, figurative;

ch. 7:17, 21 (Scripture). Not God's "prophetic act," as Pusey calls Israel's deliverance, but the word spoken by the prophet, centuries later was fulfilled by the event narrated Matt. 2:14. Since the Holy Spirit calls the return of Christ out of Egypt a fulfillment of what the prophet foretold, we accept His interpretation as authentic. The eternal God speaking of His love toward Israel in the distant past, foretells in the same breath an act of love in the distant future, calling His Son, an Israelite concerning the flesh (Rom. 9:5), out of Egypt. To the Eternal past and future is today (Ps. 90:4; 2 Peter 3:8). Whether the prophet himself or his hearers and readers in the Old Testament grasped and understood the meaning of the Lord, is quite a different question (1 Peter 1:11; cp. also Ex. 12:46; Zech. 12:10, and John 19:32-37).

V. 2. No matter how often they called (Gr. N.) them, how often pious men, rulers, or prophets, or laymen, pleaded with Israel to return, Israel "went from them," literally, from their faces, hated the very sight of these well-meaning warners, preferring Baalim and carved images to their Creator and Redeemer. "Burned incense" (Gr. N. on ch. 2:13, M. T., 15).

Vv. 3, 4. As a mother with patient kindness teaches her child to walk, takes him by his arms, carefully leads him until he has learned to walk safely, so the Lord lovingly took Israel by his arms and taught him to walk on His ways. With infinite patience He overlooked their lapses, bore with their impatience, assuaged their doubts and fears (Ex. 5:19 ff.; 6:9; 13:17, 21, 22; 14:10-13). He healed them (Ex. 15:22-27). So He "drew" them (v. 4; same word as Jer. 31:3) with cords of a man, suitable for weak, sinful men, whom He endeavored to tie to Himself in faithful, loving service by kind, gentle, humane treatment. More than that, He drew them with bands of love, a love such as only God is capable of (cp. John 3:16; Rom. 5:8; Eph. 5:2, 25 ff.; Jer. 31:3). He placed upon them a yoke, His holy Law. Yet when this yoke began to chafe, He took it off (Gr. N.), rather, lifted it up, so that no sores, or galls, or festering wounds, would form. "I laid next unto them" (Gr. N.), literally, gently, kindly, I fed them with spiritual and material food. As to the latter, see Num. 13:24-28; 14:7, 8; as to spiritual food, we think of the many promises of grace and forgiveness found interspersed with the demands of the Law; the sacrifices appointed for the atonement of sin; His grace manifested by His miracles (Ex. 12:36; 14:19-31; 16:1-15; 17:8-16; cp. Deut. 29:5; 32:7-14).

Vv. 5-7. The penalty of Israel's unfaithfulness. Israel will not return unto Egypt, the house of bondage from which they were delivered. Theirs will be a punishment far more severe. Assyria shall be their ruler and hold them in a captivity from which there shall be no return, for they refused to turn back to the Lord, their only Deliverer. — The interchange of singular subjects, predicates, and suffixes found vv. 1-12 may be explained by regarding the singular as referring to the nation as a unit, the plural as referring to the individuals forming this unit. The nation as a whole never returned to the land of Canaan, though individuals and groups of northern Israelites returned and together with Judah formed the post-Exilic Israel. Zerubbabel offered sacrifices for "all Israel," these sacrifices including twelve he-goats "according to the number of the tribes of Israel," Ezra 6:17; cp. 8:35; Ezek. 47:13; Mal. 1:1, 2, 5; see also Mal. 2:4, 7; Levi being a member of the Jewish commonwealth, though not a descendant of Judah, Heb. 7:11-14. Such expressions as found Matt. 19:28; Luke 22:30; Acts 26:7; James 1:1 would not have been used if only Judah had returned. 2 Chron. 11:3, 13-17; 15:8-15; 30:25 definitely state that at various times before the Exile families of the Northern Kingdom settled in Judah, hence were deported later with the Southern Israelites and returned later to Judah; cp. Luke 2:36, Anna of the tribe of Aser = Asher, a Northern tribe, Judg. 1:31 f.; Joshua 19:24-34.

The sword (v. 6) = murderous warfare, will "abide" (Gr. N.), will dance its dance of death in Israel's cities, consume, literally, completely destroy its "branches" (Gr. N.), rather, the bars on the city gates, their defenses, and devour! No special object is named, for no object will be spared. "Because of their own counsels," their godless statesmanship, their treacherous machinations, as described v. 7: "Bent" (Gr. N.), impaled, helplessly, hopelessly condemned to a painful, shameful death in penalty for their apostasy. "Though they called" (Gr. N.). There were still some in Israel who called their fellow men to direct their thoughts to the Most High (Gr. N.), upward, to things on high (Col. 3:1, 2). Yet all these efforts were in vain. Not one in any wise succeeded to "exalt" (Gr. N.), to uplift, to put them on a higher moral plane. Israel preferred to grovel in the filthy mire of sin and shame.

V. 8. The ever faithful Lord once more declares His unfailing, saving love. In one of his bold figures Hosea presents the great I AM as a man battling with himself in order to reach a decision. How (Gr. N.) can He give up Ephraim, His first-born, His dear son, His pleasant child (Jer. 31:9, 20)? How can He deliver (Gr. N.), surrender, Israel, whose Father He is (Jer. 31:9)? God knows that Israel has deserved a judgment like that of Admah and Zeboim, twin sisters of Sodom and Gomorrah (Gen. 10:19; 19:24 f.; Deut. 29:23). Yet His heart turns in Him (Gr. N.). His compassions are kindled "together"; all of the compassions and mercies of the infinite God burst out into full flame, consuming the fierceness of His anger burning unto the lowest hell.

V. 9. The Lord who is the Lord of unchangeable holiness, who will by no means clear the guilty, Ex. 34:7 b., still remains eternally the Lord of unalterable grace, Ex. 34:6, 7 a. He will not execute the fierceness of His anger. He will not "return" to destroy Ephraim, not again destroy that son whom He called in infinite love, v. 1, as He had once before brought him to the brink of destruction (Judg. 12:1-6; cp. Num. 1:33; 26:37). The Lord states the reason for this determination: Not because of their own merit or goodness will He refuse to annihilate them. They had no merit. They had deserved destruction a thousandfold. But He is God, not a man. Man often is ruled by his passions, by favoritism, by whims and fancies, by a spineless love without regard to justice, or by stern justice untempered by proper mercy, by cruel passion riding roughshod over righteousness and justice. God is never ruled by passion, by favoritism, by hatred. The just and righteous God, who hates sin and the sinner (Ps. 5:5, 6; Hos. 9:15), whose wrath against sin and the sinner burns unto the lowest hell (Deut. 32:22), is at the same time a God who so loves these sinners that He gave His only-begotten Son for their salvation. Yet His love toward sinners did not move Him to set aside the demands of His righteousness and justice nor to cancel one iota of these demands. He is God, not a man! His love was the love of the just and righteous God and therefore took cognizance of the necessity of the fulfillment of His Law (Gal. 4:4, 5); of the need of removal of sin from the sinner (Is. 53:6; 2 Cor. 5:21); of the necessity of satisfying His punitive justice (Is. 53:4, 5; Gal. 3:13). His own Son became the Propitiation for our sin (1 John 2:2), Jehovah Our Righteousness (Jer. 23:6). He is God, not a man; forgiving sin, declaring the sinner righteous without violating one iota of His eternal justice and righteousness (Rom. 3:20-26). He is the Holy One, absolutely distinct and separate from every other being, exalted above all human understanding, in whom absolute justice and perfect love, flawless righteousness and purest grace, seemingly contradictory opposites, are united without the slightest conflict in one holy being. To whom, then, will ye liken Me, or shall I be equal? saith the Holy One (Is. 40:25; 6:3;

Ex. 15:11). This holy God is "in the midst of thee," He tells Ephraim. He is still the Covenant God, still calling His wayward people to return to Him whom they have forsaken. He will not "enter into the city" (Gr. N.), rather, come in excitement, in irritation. He will not act in a sudden fit of anger as did that human world ruler Alexander, who in a drunken outburst of rage slew his bosom friend Clitus only to mourn him later in unconsolable remorse. He is God, not a man. Even His punishment, severe as it is, Israel's exile, serves the purpose of wooing and winning him back to Himself (Hos. 2; Micah 7:18-20). Jehovah is God, not a man; the Holy One!

Vv. 10, 11. Suddenly the scene changes. The Lord of eternity, to whom the distant future is as today (2 Peter 3:8), sees the results of His compassion and faithful love. He sees Himself at the head of a large assembly, as the Leader and Commander of the people (Is. 55:4), the Captain of our salvation (Heb. 2:10). He sees people walking after Him, following His standards, no longer going after their "lovers," their idols (Hos. 2:5), but following Him who roars like a lion. It is, however, not the roar of the Law demanding perfect fulfillment and thundering damnation, like the roaring from Sinai, causing them to flee (Ex. 19:18 f.; 20:18, 19; Heb. 12:19-21). It is the roar of the Lion of the tribe of Judah (Rev. 5:5), who proclaims the sweetest Gospel with a voice as the sound of many waters (Rev. 1:15-18). The Lord's people, His elect, are scattered far and wide. He roars, so that the sound of His Gospel goes into all the earth (Rom. 10:18). And lo! as He roars, "sons," children of God, tremblingly come from all the four corners of the earth, trembling in sorrow for their sins, trembling with joy at hearing the good tidings of great joy penetrating the darkness and misery of sin and death, calling them to life and salvation. They come from the west, literally, from the sea, the vast Western Sea, beginning with the Mediterranean Sea and going on to the Atlantic, the sea washing the continents of Europe and America. Other children come trembling like birds from Egypt (v. 11), representing the Dark Continent, Africa. Still others come like doves from Assyria, including its hinterland, the vast regions of Asia (cp. Ps. 72:8 ff.; Is. 11:11). He will place them in their homes, cause them to dwell safely and securely under His divine protection. Nothing is said of a return to Palestine. In the age of the Messiah, Zion, the Church of God, the kingdom of God, will reach from pole to pole. Its homeland is wherever the Gospel is preached (Luke 24:46, 47; Acts 1:6-8; Heb. 12:22ff.). Among these children will be found many descendants of Israel after the flesh, constituting part of the true Israel of the New Testament

(Gal. 3: 7-14, 28, 29; 6: 14-16). In this Zion they shall have their homes, protected by their King and Lord (Is. 4: 3-6). — It is the Lord who calls; it is His Word that converts; it is He who keeps and preserves them unto life everlasting. That is not idle speculation. It is, as Hosea solemnly asserts, "the oracle of the LORD"; an expression used by Hosea only here and in God's promise, ch. 2: 15, 18, 23 (A. V., vv. 13, 16, 21).

D. The Lord's Third Charge: Lack of Loyal Faithfulness, Chs. 12:1—14:10 (A. V., 11:12—14:9)

1. Charges preferred and punishment pronounced, promises intermingled, chs. 12:1—14:1 (A. V., 11:12—13:16)

CHAPTER 12

a. Wicked Israel contrasted with his ancestor Jacob, vv. 1-15 (A. V., 11:12—12:14)

1 (A. V., 11:12) Ephraim surrounds Me with lying and the house of Israel with deceit. And Judah is unruly against God, even against the faithful Holy One.

2 (A. V., 12:1) Ephraim pastures wind and pursues the east wind, all the time he multiplies lies and destruction. They make covenants with Assyria, and he carries oil to

3 (2) Egypt. But the LORD calls Judah into court and has in mind to punish Jacob for his conduct and to requite him according to his

4 (3) deeds. In the womb he seized his brother's heel, and in his man's strength he fought with God,

5 (4) so that he fought with an angel and prevailed. He cried and pleaded for His mercy. He found Him in Bethel, and there He spoke

6 (5) to us. And the LORD is the LORD of Hosts, Jehovah is His

7 (6) memorial. But you — return to your God, and keep love and judgment, and trust in your God

8 (7) continually. A Canaanite *is he*, in his hand are false balances.

9 (8) He loves to oppress. So Ephraim says: Surely I am rich! I have found power for myself! In all my gains they shall not find against me one wrong, where I have

10 (9) missed the mark. Yet I Myself, the LORD your God from the land of Egypt, I will again make you dwell in tents as in the days of

11 (10) the assembly. I have spoken to the prophets, and I Myself gave many visions and through the

12 (11) prophets spoke parables. If Gilead is falsehood, surely vanity shall they become. In Gilgal they sacrifice bullocks; their altars also shall be like stone heaps on the

13 (12) furrows of the field. And Jacob fled to the fields of Aram, and Israel served for a wife, and for a wife he guarded sheep.

14 (13) And by a prophet the LORD brought Israel up from Egypt, and by a prophet he was guarded.

15 (14) Ephraim has provoked Him bitterly; but his Lord will hurl his blood upon him and requite his disgrace to him.

Grammatical Notes

V. 1 (11:12). "Yet," עד here = continually; cp. Gen. 46:29, "a good while"; Ps. 84:5 (4), "still." — "Ruleth," רד not derived from רדה, to rule, but participle Qal of רוד, to wander, rove unrestrained (cp. Jer. 2:31; Hiph., Gen. 27:40; Ps. 55:3). — "With God." עם expresses a relation favorable (Prov.

24:21; 29:24) or opposed to (Ps. 55:19, "with," rather, "against"; 94:16); here favorable. — "Faithful with the saints." נֶאֱמָן not predicate to Judah, but attribute to קְדוֹשִׁים, here = plur. maj., like Elohim (cp. Prov. 9:10 b; 30:3; Joshua 24:19), the Holy One; like Elohim (2 Kings 19:4,16; Ps. 7:10, A. V., 9), it is here connected with singular attribute, G.-K. 132 h. There is no need to accept Kittel's suggestion: "is yoked together with harlots," *kedeshim,* or Sellin's: "is faithful to harlots." LXX translates in evident misunderstanding: Now God knows them, and he shall be called God's people.

V. 2 (12:1). "Feedeth on." While רָעָה often occurs in this sense, "shepherds" is in better keeping with parallel "followeth after." — "Desolation," שֹׁד. LXX has μάταια = שָׁוְא, vanity, a needless and weakening correction, adopted by Sellin, J. M. Powis Smith in *The Complete Bible.*

V. 3 (2). "Will punish." לִפְקֹד = in order to punish, stating the purpose of the lawsuit.

V. 4 (3). "Took by the heel." עָקַב, the root word of Jacob's name (Gen. 25:26); it also denotes to deceive, to "heel," to follow the footsteps of a person with malicious intent (Gen. 27:36; Jer. 9:3; adjective, Jer. 17:9). — "By his strength," בְּאוֹנוֹ, in his strength, adult vigor, manhood. The same word in v. 9 = financial strength, riches. — "Had power." שָׂרָה occurs only here and Gen. 32:29; related to שָׂרַר, rule (Is. 32:1; Prov. 8:16; Hiph., Hos. 8:4, M. T., 5), and שׂוּר; apparently implies victorious battling.

V. 5 (4). "Found Him," יִמְצָאֶנּוּ. "Found" here in sense of "meet with" (Gen. 4:14; 1 Sam. 9:11; 10:3); in v. 9 it is used in the sense of "obtain, acquire" (Gen. 26:12; Prov. 3:13).

V. 7 (6). "Turn to," תָּשׁוּב, jussive; the verb usually construed with אֶל (ch. 5:4); עַד (Deut. 4:30; 30:2); here, with בְּ, to indicate the close union.

V. 8 (7). "Merchant," כְּנַעַן, the son of Ham and his descendants, a merchant people (cp. Ezek. 16:29; 17:4, "merchants"; Zeph. 1:11).

V. 9 (8). "Yet," אַךְ here = surely, yes, ah! (Judg. 20:39; 1 Kings 22:32; Job 14:22.) — "Found me out," see note on v. 5 (4). — "Substance," אוֹן, see note on v. 4 (3).

V. 10 (9). "Tabernacles," אֹהָלִים, not in the modern sense of stately houses of worship, but "tents," the shelters of canvas quickly set up and taken down, the typical homes of nomadic people, desert dwellers. — "Solemn feast," מוֹעֵד, appointment, denotes any appointed time or season, any convocation, festival or otherwise (Num. 10:10; Lev. 23:2; Hos. 2:13, A. V., 11). Here it designates the Feast of Tabernacles as the reference to the preceding clause clearly shows. On this festival the Israelites for eight days dwelt in "booths," סֻכּוֹת made of live branches (Lev. 23:39-43; Neh. 8:14-18). The term "booth" is defined Is. 4:6 ("tabernacle") as a place of refuge against heat, or storm, or rain. It denotes the coverts, shelters, tents, in which the Israelites lived during their sojourn in the wilderness (Lev. 23:43), called אֹהָלִים, tents, "tabernacles," by Hosea here; also military tents (2 Sam. 11:11; 1 Kings 20:12,16, "pavilions"); shelters for cattle (Gen. 33:17); a watchman's hut or shack (Is. 1:8); cp. also Jonah 4:5; Amos 9:11. The Festival of Tabernacles, called Succoth by modern Jews, was to be a season of joyful thanksgiving for the ingathered harvest of fruit, wine, and oil (Ex. 23:16; Lev. 23:39, 40; Deut. 16:13-15). At the same time it was to remind them of the long sojourn in the wilderness, where they were obliged to live in shelters, tents, lacking the comfort and convenience of a settled life in permanent homes enjoyed by the later generations. And, finally, it was to remind them of the grace of their Lord, who even in the wilderness caused them to dwell in booths (Lev. 23:43), lovingly provided for them, giving them shelter and food, protecting them against their enemies, and finally leading them to the Promised Land. Hosea links up with the two purposes last mentioned. He threatens impenitent Israel with another period of dwelling in tents, in the wilderness of captivity in foreign countries far from the homeland. And he comforts the believing remnant that the Lord would remain even in foreign countries their gracious Protector, causing them to dwell in homes, be they ever so humble, and leading them to their eternal home. (Cp. Ezek. 11:16 ff.; 36:16-38.)

V. 11 (10). "Used similitudes," אֲדַמֶּה, Pi. of דָּמָה, to be similar, Pi. to make

something similar, to compare (Is. 40:18, 25; 46:5); here, to speak or teach by means of comparisons, parables.

V. 12 (11). "Is there?" אִם not the interrogative, but conjunction introducing the protasis of a conditional sentence. The perfect הָיוּ in the apodosis denotes the certainty of the destruction. Driver, *Tenses*, 136 y. — "Gilgal" is chosen here most probably in order to introduce the play on "stones," v.12 b (11 b); *gallim*. Gilgal = heap or circle of stones.

V. 13 (12). "Kept," שָׁמַר is at times used in sense of "shepherd" (Gen. 30:31); the participle, 1 Sam. 17:20. Note the play on נִשְׁמָר, "was preserved" (v. 14, A. V., 13).

V. 15 (14). "Most bitterly," 'תַּמְרוּרִים literally, bitternesses, the plural copiae, used adverbially. G.-K. 124 e, 118 q.— "Leave," וַיִּטֹּשׁ = to hurl down upon, here with דָּמִים = bloodguiltiness (Lev. 17:4; Joshua 2:19, singular; Lev. 20:9; Deut. 19:10; 22:8, plural).

Vv. 1-3 (A. V., 11:12—12:2). The holy and faithful God will punish His deceitful, unruly people. — Ephraim compasses, surrounds God, not in the manner described Ps. 26:6-8; Jer. 31:22 b, but with lies and deceit. Like an unfaithful wife she still demands the Lord's protection and support, while her every profession of love is a lie, her every action, deceit. Judah is no better, "ruleth" (Gr. N.), runs loose, unbridled; follows only the dictates of her own unrestrained wantonness. Israel forgets that the Lord, whose covenant they are breaking, is the ever Holy (Lev. 19:2; 21:8; Is. 6:3) and Faithful One (Num. 23:19; 1 Sam. 15:29). Loyal to His covenant, He will fulfill His threats as well as His promises. Ephraim "feedeth on" (Gr. N.), rather, shepherds, bestows his time and labor (cp. Gen. 31:40) and his loving, solicitous care (Is. 40:11; Ezek. 34:11-16), on what? Wind and the east wind, Assyria, and Egypt! (A. V., v. 1.) Note the chiastic position of the four terms. East wind — Assyria in the center as the deadly, murderous enemy like the hot, blasting, killing eastern wind

95

from the desert, flanked on both sides by wind — Egypt, notoriously like wind, vanity, making promises only to break them (2 Kings 18:21; Is. 30:7), luring them into destruction by their pledges of support. With Assyria Israel makes covenants, while at the same time he carries oil to Egypt. Olive oil was one of the chief products of Palestine (Deut. 8:8; 1 Kings 5:11; Ezek. 16:19; 27:17), while Egypt had to import it. In order to keep up their alliances with these two bitter rivals for world supremacy, they daily resorted to a policy of lies and deceit which could not but end in their destruction and desolation. For their duplicity was not only a despicable betrayal of their allies, resented and swiftly punished by powerful Assyria (2 Kings 17:4-6). It was also open rebellion against God's Law, against the First Commandment, demanding trust in God above all things, and the Eighth Commandment, prohibiting lies and deceit. The holy, faithful God institutes legal proceedings for the purpose of punishing (Gr. N.) "Jacob," all the tribes of Israel, no longer worthy of being called by their honorable name (cp. Gen. 27:36; Hos. 10:11, see p. 84). He will repay them according to their wicked policies and deceitful deeds (A. V., 2).

Vv. 4-7 (A. V., 3-6). In order to escape divine judgment they are told to emulate their ancestor's zeal to appropriate God's promised blessing. Already in the womb he took his brother by the heel (Gen. 25:26) in his eagerness to obtain the blessing given to Abraham. The Lord had chosen him to be the ancestor of the Woman's Seed (cp. Mal. 1:2,3; Rom. 9:10-13). Luther correctly regards the action of unborn Jacob as an evidence of his faith wrought in him by the Holy Spirit and adduces Luke 1:41,44 (St. Louis, VI, 1067, 1320 ff.). "By his strength," literally, in his manhood (Gr. N.), he fought with God (A. V., v. 4). With tears of repentance, in humble faith he implored the Angel of the Lord, who fought with him in the form of a man, in whom he recognized his God. He persisted in the battle, "had power" (Gr. N.) over the Angel, obtained the blessing he sought (Gen. 32:24-30). Coming to Bethel, he complied with God's command (Gen. 35:1-7), and there he "found," met with (Gr. N.), God (vv. 9-15), who repeated His former blessings given to Jacob and Abraham (Gen. 17:5-8; 18:18; 28:13 ff.; 32:28 ff.). There God spoke not only to Jacob, but to "us," to all Israelites, who were in the loins of Jacob (cp. Heb. 7:9,10). The speaker was not a tribal god, but Jehovah (cp. Ex. 3:15), the everlasting Lord of grace and truth and power, the Lord of hosts, Jehovah is His memorial (A. V., v. 5). Sin-

ful Israel must, like Jacob, return to this Lord in true repentance
(A. V., v. 6). He is willing to remain their God, eager to receive them
and re-establish that loving union of Ex. 19:5, 6. But they must turn
to Him and like Jacob prove their faithfulness by keeping "mercy,"
unselfish love of God (Deut. 6:5 ff.) and of their neighbor (Lev.
19:18), and "judgment," what is right and proper according to His
Law (Ex. 21:1; Ps. 19:10, A. V., 9). "Wait" (same word as Gen.
49:18, Jacob's deathbed confession!), hope patiently and trustingly for
the Lord's help in every time of trouble instead of placing your hope
on yourselves or other nations! Faith, love, hope is to be at all times
the characteristic of God's people!

Vv. 8-10 (A. V., 7-9). Unfaithful to God and man in his business
transactions, hypocritical Israel shall go into exile! Instead of being
wholesome leaven for the heathen nations, the Israelites had imbibed
the spirit of the Canaanite (Gr. N.), not only in accepting their
idolatry, but also in adopting their business tactics. "In his hand the
scales." They were ever ready for business and profit. And their
scales, not in conformity with Lev. 19:35, 36, were balances of deceit.
Business before religion, gain before God, profit by hook or crook!
They loved to oppress, to drive hard bargains. Money, influence, might
came before right. Proud of their success, they boast: "Yet" = ah!
(Gr. N.) I have become rich! I have "found," acquired, "me" for
myself (what selfishness is revealed here!) "substance" (Gr. N.)
(A. V., v. 8). Israel boasts that he is no longer a feeble child among
the nations. At last by his own efforts he has achieved manhood, has
become a powerful kingdom, respected and feared by other nations.
This points to the era of Jeroboam and Uzziah (p. 1, 2). Self-righteously Israel regards all his actions as being beyond reproach. He need
not be ashamed of any of his efforts to reach so high a pinnacle. None
of his labors, his laborious efforts, can find, and therefore can charge
him with any iniquity, any guilt, which might be called sin, missing
the mark. Every one of his transactions was strictly legal, in full
accord with law. He forgot that man's laws and God's Law do not
always agree on what is right and wrong. The law of the land had been
so skillfully manipulated, contained so many loopholes, that under the
guise of lawfulness the greatest outrages against love of God and one's
neighbor could be committed (cp. ch. 10:4). They had forgotten the
Holy and Faithful One and His covenant threat (Lev. 26:14-39; Deut.
28:15-68).

The faithful Lord reminds His disloyal people once more of this
threat in order to call them back from their ways before it would be

too late (A. V., v. 9). Unless they change their ways, they will "yet" =
again, dwell in tents as they did during their sojourn in the wilderness.
The "days of the solemn feast" = the Feast of Tabernacles, the joyful
harvest festival during which they were to dwell in "booths" (Gr. N.)
constructed of green branches (Lev. 23:40; Neh. 8:14-18). This was to
be a joyous festival of thanksgiving (Lev. 23:39, 40); at the same time
it was to remind them of the forty years of sojourn in the wilderness
during which the Lord made them to dwell in booths (v. 43). Hosea
uses the word "tabernacle" (Gr. N.) = tents, here in order to stress
the inconvenience, the unsettled life, the constant fear and anxiety
under which they were to live in the captivity threatened to them
(Lev. 26:33, 36; Deut. 28:65-68). The same God who delivered them
out of Egypt could and would deliver them into the power of cruel
enemies. Yet even in the wilderness, in exile, He would remember
them. He will make them dwell, provide for them (cp. Hos. 2:14 ff.;
Ezek. 11:16 ff.; Jer. 29:8-14).

Vv. 11, 12 (A. V., 10, 11). Disloyal Israel rejects the teachings of
their faithful Lord and will be punished. Three methods of divine
instruction are named: the revelation transmitted to prophets by
divine speech, in the form of visions, and in "similitudes," parables
either of words or of actions real or visionary (*The Bible Commentary*). Cp. Num. 12:6-8; 24:3, 4; 2 Kings 17:13. Many in number and
varied in form were the revelations granted to the Lord's people by
the ministry of the prophets as a special favor (Deut. 4:6-8, 32-36;
Ps. 147:19, 20). In shameful disloyalty Israel rejected the Lord's instruction and chose dead idols as their advisers. "Is there," rather,
"if Gilead is iniquity" (Gr. N.) (A. V., v. 11). Gilead, the Eastjordanland, was called a city of evildoers (ch. 6:8), here directly "iniquity"
(same word as Aven, ch. 10:8), denoting the vanity of idolatry. If this
vanity prevails in Gilead — and there is no doubt that it does — then
the penalty of Aven will surely be paid out to them. The Hebrew term
Aven, applied to Bethel (ch. 4:15; 10:5), denotes trouble, injustice inflicted on others (cp. Is. 10:1; Hab. 1:3), and its consequence for the
troubling person (Job 4:8; Prov. 22:8); in general, sorrow, trouble,
pain (Gen. 35:18; Job 5:6; Ps. 90:10). It also denotes sin (the cause
of trouble), iniquity (Prov. 6:12; Is. 1:13; 31:2); particularly lying,
deceit, treachery (Ps. 36:4; Prov. 19:28; Is. 58:9). Very appropriately
it is used to denote idolatry (1 Sam. 15:23; an idol, Is. 41:29; 66:3).
Cp. Amos 5:5; Bethel, God's House, shall become Beth-Aven, a house

of idolatry, of an idol. For that very reason it is a house of deceit, of disappointment, of shattered hopes and final destruction, because an idol is nothing in this world and can do nothing to help his worshipers (Ps. 115: 4-8; 135: 15-18; Jer. 10: 1-16; 1 Cor. 8: 4; 10: 19 ff.). Communion with the Lord of life grants life in fullness of perfection (John 10: 10); communication with idols can bring only death and eternal sorrow and pain. The altars at Bethel, preferred by Israel to the altar of Jehovah, shall like the idols, the vanities they represent, be reduced to vanity and shame. They shall become as heaps of stones in the furrows of the field, particularly the boundary furrows. The stones which are still found in great number on the fields of Samaria and Galilee are thrown aside by the tiller irritated by them, are regarded as a nuisance. *Sic transit gloria mundi!*

Vv. 13-15 (A. V., 12-14). Once more Hosea refers to the ancestor of Israel to teach them an important lesson from his life and experience. Jacob, a fugitive from home by his own fault, had fled to the "country of Syria," literally, the fields of Aram, Padan-Aram (Gen. 25: 20; 28: 2). There he who later was honored by being called Israel, "Conqueror of God," was compelled to work for his wife under a greedy and hard taskmaster (cp. Gen. 31: 15, 16, 39, 41), "kept" sheep (Gr. N.), working like a slave (Gen. 31: 40 f.). The double reference to service for a wife points to Gen. 29: 16-28. Yet, the Lord, true to His promise (Gen. 28: 13 ff.), blessed his labors (30: 43; 32: 10), protected him from Esau, and brought him back to Canaan (32: 11—33: 20). In like divine faithfulness to His promise (Gen. 15: 13-21; 46: 1-4) the Lord delivered Israel from bondage in Egypt by sending His prophet Moses (Ex. 1—15), who "preserved" (Gr. N.) Israel, faithfully shepherding them throughout their long journey to the Promised Land, and on several occasions preserved them from destruction (Ex. 32: 7-14; Num. 14: 1-45; 16: 41-50; M. T., 17: 6-15). Cp. his faithful instructions Deut. 1—33. Yet Israel, made a fruitful Ephraim by the Covenant Lord, provoked the Lord (A. V., 14) in spite of all favors received, rebelled in the wilderness (Ps. 95: 8-11; Book of Judges; 2 Kings 17: 7-41). "Leave," literally, cast, hurl (Gr. N.), his sin upon him to bear the unforgiven iniquity as a heavy bloodguilt in time and eternity. His "reproach," his shameless, blasphemous conduct toward the Lord (cp. Ps. 79: 12; Prov. 14: 31; Is. 65: 7; Rom. 2: 24) He will "return," bring back, to him. Israel will be covered with eternal shame and reproach (Is. 66: 24; Dan. 12: 2 b).

CHAPTER 13

b. Neither Israel's idols nor his kings are able to save the nation, ch. 13:1—14:1
(A. V., 13:1-16)

1 Whenever Ephraim spoke, there was terror! He was exalted in Israel; but he incurred guilt through Baal
2 and died! And now they are sinning more and more and are making to the best of their skill molten images for themselves of their silver, idols, entirely the work of craftsmen. To these they speak! Sacrificing men — kissing calves!
3 Therefore they shall be as a morning cloud and as dew that passes away quickly, as the chaff that is whirled away from the threshing floor, and as smoke out of the chimney. Yet I myself am the
4 LORD your God from the land of Egypt, and a God beside Me you know not, and there is no Savior
5 but Me. I Myself knew you in the wilderness, in the land of drought.
6 The better pasture they had, the more they filled themselves; the more they were filled, the prouder their heart became. And so they
7 forgot Me! So I shall become to them as a lion, as a leopard I will
8 watch for them on the way. I will meet them like a bear robbed of her whelps, and I will tear to pieces the enclosure of their heart. And I will devour them there like a lioness, wild beasts shall tear
9 them to pieces. It has destroyed you, O Israel, that (you are) against
10 Me, against your Helper. Where is your king that he may help you in all your cities, and your rulers of whom you said: Give me a king
11 and princes? I have been giving you kings in My anger and have taken them away in My wrath.
12 Wrapped up is the guilt of Ephraim,
13 stored up his sin. Pangs of a travailing woman shall come to him. He is an unwise son, for at the appointed time he shall not stand in the place of breaking through of
14 children. From the power of hell I will ransom them; from death I will redeem them. I will be your plagues, O death! I will be thy pestilence, O hell! Repentance is
15 hid from My eyes. Even if he be fruitful among his brethren, there shall come an east wind! The LORD'S wind from the desert shall come up, and his fountain shall be drained and his wellspring dried up. He shall strip the treasury of all precious vessels.
14:1 (A. V., 13:16) Samaria has become guilty, for she has rebelled against her God. By the sword shall they fall! Their children shall be dashed to pieces, their pregnant women be ripped open.

Grammatical Notes

V. 1. "Trembling," רְתַת, Aramaic, only here; cp. רֶטֶט (Jer. 49:24), terror, apodosis to the כְּ clause. — "Exalted himself," נָשָׂא, here intrans., as Ps. 89:10 (A. V., v. 9, "arise"); Nah. 1:5; Hab. 1:3. Others point נִשָּׂא, Niph. reflexive.

V. 7. "Observe," שׁוּר, look down from a higher place (Cant. 4:8; Num. 23:9).

V. 9. "Destroyed thyself," שִׁחֶתְךָ. "It has destroyed you" is the predicate to the כִּי clause. כְּ here = against; cp. Gen. 16:12; 2 Sam. 24:17; Is. 19:2, etc.

V. 10. "I will be thy king." A. V. is impossible. It necessitates the unwarranted insertion "is any other" and the translation of the adverb אֵפוֹא as an interrogative. אֱהִי is to be regarded as a dialectic form of אֵי or אַיֵּה, "where?" The form אֱהִי occurs only here and v. 14, which see. — "That may save," the final clause after an interrogative clause is introduced by וְ as in 2 Sam. 9:1, 3; cp. G.-K. 165 a.

V. 11. "Gave," "took away," the imperfects denote ever-repeated action. We prefer the present tense.

V. 13. "Stay long," יַעֲמֹד, stands, places himself; cp. Ex. 33:9; Joshua 20:4; enter, Jer. 17:19. עֵת, the appointed, right time (Gen. 29:7; Ruth 2:14; Jer. 8:7, etc.). — "Breaking forth," מִשְׁבַּר, cp. 2 Kings 19:3; Is. 37:3.

V. 14. "Ransom," פָּדָה, to buy the freedom of any person by paying a stipulated price or ransom. — "Redeem," אָגְאַל, to liberate because of close kinship. — "Grave," שְׁאוֹל, sheol, occurs sixty-five times. A. V. translates "grave," thirty-one times; "hell," thirty-one times; "pit," three times. Luther, "Hoelle," hell, sixty-one times; "Grube," pit, four times. The etymology is uncertain and disputed.—"I will be," LXX, אֱהִי, που, where? So Luther and most modern interpreters. Like the Vulgate, A. V. regards אֱהִי as the jussive, first person. This translation cannot be rejected on grammatical grounds. While as a rule jussive is restricted to second and third person, G.-K. lists as examples of first person jussive Deut. 18:16; 1 Sam. 14:36; 2 Sam. 17:12; Is. 41:23 K'tib; Hos. 9:15, always with לֹא; without לֹא, Ezek. 5:16 (G.-K. 109 d). Driver (Tenses, p. 60, N. 1) adds Is. 41:28; 42:6, and compares Job 23:9, 11. Our passage, therefore, would not be an isolated example of the jussive expressing one's desire or intention, although the form would occur only here as jussive. There is no grammatical necessity here for translating אֱהִי "where?" as in v. 10, since there is no אֵפוֹא in v. 14, which decides for the interrogative in v. 10. St. Paul clothes his paean 1 Cor. 15:55 in words more closely approximating the LXX text than that of the Hebrew Bible. He evidently found no difference in meaning between M. T. and LXX. Though

personally we prefer the A. V. rendering, it is not necessary to insist on either version as the only correct one. "Plagues," דְּבָרֶיךָ, not "words," in sense of legal procedure or right, LXX, δίκη, but "pestilence" (cp. Ex. 5:3; Lev. 26:25, etc.). The plural is that of amplification, intensifying the qualities inherent in the term (G.-K. 124 d). "Destruction," קֶטֶב, literally, a cutting off, epidemic (Deut. 32:24). The two terms are combined Ps. 91:6, 7, vividly describing the irresistible ravages of plague and pestilence.

"Repentance," נֹחַם, ἅπαξ λεγόμενον, derived from נָחַם, the original meaning of which is "to be sorry," (a) for another, Niph., four times (Judg. 2:18; 21:6, 15; Ps. 90:13); hence to comfort, so Pi., fifty times; Pu. pass., twice; Hithp. passive of Pi., twice (Gen. 37:35; Ps. 119:52); to stir up one's compassion, twice (Deut. 32:36; Ps. 135:14); (b) for oneself, or one's words or actions, repent, change one's action. Niph., some thirty or more times, twenty-five times of God's "repentance." In this latter sense the noun is used here. Sellin translates "vengeance" and continues v. 15 a, "for it separated between brethren." He refers to Is. 1:24 (A. V., "I will ease Me"); Gen. 27:42 (A. V., "doth comfort himself"), in substantiation of his translation; G.-B. adds Ezek. 5:13 (A. V., "I will be comforted"). But even in these three passages the term does not directly denote "vengeance," but "to seek comfort, ease"; the A. V. brings out the accurate meaning. And it seems to be rather precarious to adopt a meaning for which only three doubtful passages out of more than 100 can be quoted. There is no valid reason to change the rendering of A. V. Luther's "Comfort is hid" supposes a sudden change of speakers.

V. 15. "Fruitful," יַפְרִיא. The ל"ה verbs

101

quite frequently follow the analogy of ל"א verbs (Ex. 1:10; Is. 21:12; Hos. 11:7; Zeph. 3:1). See G.-K. 75 rr. LXX reads διαστελεῖ, will separate, יַפְרִיד; Vulgate, dividet. Hosea evidently intended a play on Ephraim.

Ch. 14:1 (A. V., 13:16). "Become des-

olate." תֶּאְשַׁם is not to be derived from שָׁמֵם, but from אָשַׁם, to be guilty and bear the consequences of one's guilt (cp. Hos. 4:15; 5:15; 10:2). The imperfect denotes the progressive increase of guilt, the perfect מָרְתָה, the rebellion as a historical fact.

Vv. 1-3. Ephraim's pride leads to the folly of idolatry and to destruction. — "Trembling" (Gr. N.). Though numerically not so strong as other tribes (Num. 1:33; 26:37), Ephraim's word carried authority. The other tribes respected him, listened to his advice, feared to oppose him. Yet in proud self-exaltation he introduced calf worship (1 Kings 12:26 ff.), thereby signing his own death warrant. Calf worship was the first step toward Baalism (1 Kings 16:30-33) and other heathen abominations, mortal sins (Lev. 18:24-28). Sinking ever deeper into sin (v. 2) and shame, the Lord's people worship the work of mortal hands! Men, rational beings, professing to worship Jehovah, kiss, adore, worship, expect help from calves, irrational brutes, dead idols! What foolish, stupid wickedness! In four symbols Hosea describes Israel's rapid dissolution (v. 3). Like the morning cloud (Hos. 6:4; Job 7:9); like dew (Hos. 6:4); like worthless chaff (Job 21:18; Ps. 1:4); like irritating smoke passing through the "window," the lattice work placed on the ceiling or the roof, so Israel will vanish!

Vv. 4-8. Israel's ingratitude and disloyalty to his Savior God leads to his destruction. In contrast to the idols the Lord remains the I AM THAT I AM. From Egypt onward He had been the God and Lord of Israel (Ex. 19:4-6; Hos. 12:9). They shall know no other God, for there is no other Savior (Is. 45:5, 6, 20-22). On His provident love in the wilderness (v. 5), see Deut. 8:2-4, 15, 16; 32:7-12; Jer. 2:6. They repaid His faithfulness with ever-increasing disloyalty, forgot Him! (V. 6.) (Hos. 2:15, A. V., 13; Deut. 32:15-18; Jer. 2:7-13.) Now destruction comes! With the strength of the lion (v. 7), the swiftness and cunning of the leopard, the fury of a mother bear robbed of her cubs (v. 8), the eagerness of a lioness seeking food for her young, so the Lord will meet His apostate people. No escape from the mortal wounds He inflicts! He tears the caul, literally, the covering enclosure of their hearts, either the breast, or the pericardium, the membranous sac surrounding the heart. When a nation deliberately and persistently rejects God's mercies, there is left for it nothing but God's wrath (Deut. 32:21 f.; Heb. 10:31).

Vv. 9-13. Israel can blame only himself for his destruction. It destroys you (Gr. N.), O Israel, the honorable name (Gen. 32: 28), that you are opposed to Me, your only Helper. As long as Jacob, the individual and the nation, was faithful to God and clung to His word and promise, he was Israel. Opposition to God, faithless rejection of His Word, is running headlong into destruction. O Israel! Salvation is completely Mine, destruction altogether thine! (Ch. 1: 7; 2: 8, 14-23.) That He is the only Helper is proved by the inefficiency of their rulers whom they had preferred to God. "I will be your king" (v. 10) (Gr. N.), rather, Where is now your king? Ephraim had not been satisfied with the divinely appointed house of David. They desired kings and princes, rulers, of their own (1 Kings 12: 19, 20). Wicked King Jeroboam and all his successors who walked in the sin of Jeroboam were given to rebellious Israel in God's anger, and removed in His anger because of the wicked idolatry of rulers and nation (v. 11). God was displeased with the separatism of Northern Israel. This iniquity, this guilt, of Israel is "bound up" (v. 12), wrapped up, securely reserved (Deut. 32: 34; Job 14:17), "hid," carefully kept in store (Prov. 2: 7; 13: 22), until the great Day of Judgment (cp. Rev. 20: 12, 13). Sorrow like that of a woman in travail (v. 13) shall suddenly come upon Israel, who like an unwise child will not place himself at the proper time ("stay long," Gr. N.) in the opening of the womb. Again Israel is compared first to the mother, then to the child (cp. ch. 1: 2; 2: 2).

V. 14. While Israel cannot help himself, postpones his repentance, stands at the brink of physical and spiritual, temporal and eternal death, the Lord of life, the Savior God stands ready to deliver him and encourages him to immediate repentance and enduring loyalty in one of the most beautiful Gospel promises recorded in the Old Testament.

The faithful God once more promises everlasting salvation.

"Grave" (Gr. N.). In Biblical usage Sheol is that state into which all men, even the believing children of God, enter at the moment of their death (Gen. 37: 35; 42: 38; 44: 29, 31; Job 17: 16; 21: 13; Ps. 83: 4; Is. 38:18). Without the Gospel and its redemption this state is one of horror. Sheol is described not merely as a cessation of all activity (Eccl. 9: 10), it is not merely the beginning of the dissolution and decay of the body separated from the soul (Gen. 3: 19). That already is not a pleasant thought. That alone would make of death a gruesome matter, so gruesome that even Paul would rather be clothed upon by sudden transformation than be unclothed (2 Cor. 5: 2-4; 1 Cor.

15:51 ff.). But death is far more than that. If there were no Gospel of redemption, to die, to enter Sheol, would mean to be cast together with death and "hell" (Hades, the Greek term for Sheol) into the lake of fire, the second death (Rev. 20:14, 15; cp. Is. 66:24; Mark 9:43-48). Death and hell, no more awesome, horrible facts can be imagined by man's most lurid fancies than these two words describe, the inescapable doom of every sinful, mortal man if there were no redemption. Any Christian who has experienced times when he felt utterly forsaken can realize why such experiences are called the agonies of hell, Sheol (Ps. 18:5; 86:13; 116:3).

"I will ransom, redeem them" (Gr. N.). The speaker is not Hosea (Ps. 49:7-9), it is the same Lord who spoke vv. 4-11. Note the chiastic position of hell, death, death, hell. First and last is hell, the worst enemy, whose destruction involves the destruction of death. "From the power of hell." Hell is pictured as a powerful, cruel tyrant, whose hand is evermore grasping more victims to fill his hall of torments (Prov. 30:16). Into the power of this tyrant sin had surrendered every human being, a power from which no man could deliver (Ps. 49:7-9). The Lord Himself will free sinful mankind by paying the ransom, by fulfilling the entire Law (Matt. 3:15), by removing their guilt (John 1:29), by suffering all the penalties of man's sin, by fully satisfying the demands of the just and holy God, Himself! From whatever is called Sheol, hell, the Lord has ransomed man. "Redeem." Redemption was the duty of the kinsman, the nearest relative. The eternal Son of God (Prov. 8:23-30), whose delights were with the sons of men (v. 31), became the Woman's Seed (Gen. 3:15), an offspring of Eve, the mother of all the living (Gen. 3:19), and took on their flesh (Heb. 2:14-18) to become their brother (Heb. 2:11 ff.), their kinsman, their Redeemer (cp. Job 19:25 ff.). I will be thy plagues! (Gr. N.) Here is the Lord, stronger than thousands of deaths, the Lord and inexhaustible Fountain of life (Ps. 36:9). He will be the plagues (Gr. N.) of death. He will, like an unconquerable pestilence, overcome and slay death! Ah, Death, where is thy sting? I will be thy destruction, O Hell. One more powerful than all the forces of hell will, like an incurable epidemic conquer, destroy, slay hell. Where is, O Hell, thy victory? "Repentance" (Gr. N.). Even the all-seeing eye of God cannot detect the slightest sign or trace of changing His mind. Remorse for having made this statement — none to be discovered! Regret for having issued this challenge — nonexistent! Retract My solemn word? Not as long as I am the God of truth (Is. 65:16)! Look to Gethsemane and Calvary for the victorious battle; to the empty tomb for the indisputable evidence of the redeeming Ransomer's victory; to Mount Olivet (Luke 24:50 f.) for the glorious ascension and coronation of the victorious God-Man (Eph. 1:20 ff.; Phil. 2:9 ff.).

Calvin, followed by Grotius, translates v. 14 a: I would ransom, I would redeem . . . , and regards these clauses as conditional sentences, the fulfillment of which would depend on their repentance. "Repentance is hid," he interprets: There is nothing to quench My wrath, since I see no repentance. Yet there is not the slightest reference to repentance as the condition of this promise. It is a promise independent of man's reaction, to be accepted by faith, yet not occasioned by faith, just as little as Gen. 3:15 was occasioned by man's faith, but was spoken to impenitent sinners for the purpose of calling forth faith and return to God.

Nor is there any grammatical reason obliging us to accept the translation almost universally adopted by modern interpreters. They regard v. 14a as an interrogation: "Shall I ransom . . . redeem?" etc., and v. 14 b: "Where are your plagues?" etc., as a command addressed to Hell and Death to place their destructive power into God's service for the destruction of Israel. The chief reason for this translation is the alleged difficulty or impossibility to square the interpretation given above with the preceding and following context. A promise of redemption, they say, would be incompatible with the threats pronounced vv. 7-13 and repeated vv. 15, 16; would nullify their very intent; would not accomplish its purpose. Yet we have the same situation Gen. 3:8-19. God's Law and its curse, vv. 8-13, followed by the first Gospel, v. 15, and this Gospel followed by the curse of the Law, vv. 16-19. The Gospel is spoken to penitent sinners, to call them to faith. Adam's faith as evidenced by calling his wife Eve, because she was the mother of all living, v. 20; and Eve's faith, "I have the man, the Lord!" (ch. 4:1) were generated by the Gospel which wrought repentance in hearts terrified by the curse of the Law, preceding and following the promise of the Redeemer. After all, God knows best when to preach Law only, or Gospel only, or Gospel preceded by Law or followed by it.

Huxtable objects to the A. V. translation on the ground that "thy plagues" in the sense of "plagues destroying thee" is both an unnatural form of expression and also presents an uncouth image. (*The Bible Commentary; in loco.*) Yet it is no more unnatural or uncouth than Is. 25:8: "He will swallow up death in victory." It is a bold, striking figure of speech, typically Hosean, and, oh, how comforting! A pesti-

105

lence attacked grim death and changed it into a powerless form!
An epidemic invaded hell, robbing it of its terror! And that pestilence,
that epidemic, is Jesus Christ, our Redeemer, our Ransom, our Savior
(Job 19:25-27; Ps. 17:15; Is. 25:6-9; 26:19, 20; 35:10; 57:1, 2).

The above interpretation is corroborated by the New Testament.
St. Paul, writing by inspiration of the Holy Spirit, states very clearly
that this passage will find its fulfillment on the Last Day in the resurrection unto life of all believers in Christ, the Conqueror of death
(1 Cor. 15:54, 55). If the Holy Spirit had intended Hos. 13:14 to be
one of the most dreadful threats, a divine summons that death and
hell do their utmost in destroying Israel, St. Paul, or rather, the Spirit
of God speaking through Paul, would not have regarded this impreca-
tion as a suitable garb for the most jubilant songs of triumph over
death and hell. Nor would he have introduced this passage together
with Is. 25:8 as Holy Writ to be fulfilled on Resurrection Morn. The
words as they stand written by Hosea and the interpretation by the
Holy Spirit stamp this passage as glorious, triumphant Gospel. Even
the Jewish Church recognized it as such. Calov and Pusey quote
a passage from the *Bereshit Rabbah,* the ancient Jewish commentary
on Genesis, dating before the fifth Christian century, the following
note on Gen. 25: "Rabbi Joshua ben Levi [ca. A. D. 225] says: With
the angel of death I went down to the gates of hell, and with me went
Messiah, son of David. When the captives which were in hell saw
the light of Messiah, they rejoiced to receive Him, saying: This one
will lead us out of the darkness as it is spoken in Osee: 'I will redeem
them out of the hand of hell.' "

What makes this Gospel the more remarkable is the fact that it
is addressed to a nation which had for 250 years maintained an illegal
and idolatrous worship. To this people the Gospel is preached,
although God knows, as the following verse states, that Israel as
nation will reject this last appeal, as it had despised all preceding
pleas, and will run headstrong and headlong into its doom. Yet God
knows that there is no other means of saving at least a few members
of this wicked people than His life-giving Gospel. In order to induce
all that have heard this marvelous message of grace and salvation to
accept it in repentant faith, the Lord once more points out the dire
consequences of unbelief.

V. 15. "Though he be fruitful" (Gr. N.). This is a play on
Ephraim's name, the fruitful. Hosea may refer to the prosperity
enjoyed under Jeroboam II (see p. 10 ff.), or to the temporary revival
of their power under Pekah (2 Chron. 28:6 ff.), only ten or twelve

years before the final collapse of Samaria, 722. Unless Israel repents, an east wind shall come (cp. ch. 12:1), Assyria, a wind sent by the Lord as His irresistible avenger completely devastating the land, turning it into a barren desert; despoiling the people of all their cherished treasures, reducing them to paupery.

CHAPTER 14

Ch. 14:1 (A. V., 13:16). "Shall become desolate," rather "becomes ever more guilty" (Gr. N.). She has rebelled; that one word summarizes the past and present history of the Northern Kingdom: Rebellion (cp. 1 Kings 12:19; 2 Kings 17:14-17). Now they shall reap the whirlwind, destruction, ruin, bloody, cruel warfare which spares not even women and unborn children! Ephraim, devoid of every form of life!

---

2. The marvelous promise of life and salvation to repentant Israel, ch. 14:2-10 (A. V., 1-9)

2 (A. V., 1) Turn, O Israel, to the LORD, your God, for you have
3 (2) fallen by your guilt. Take with you words, and turn to the LORD. Say to Him: Take away completely our guilt and receive graciously, and we shall offer
4 (3) calves, our lips. Assyria will not save us. We will not ride on horses. We will no longer say: Our gods! to the work of our hands. For in Thee the fatherless finds com-
5 (4) passion. I will cure their apostasies. I love them freely. For My anger is turned away from him.
6 (5) I will be as the dew to Israel; he shall blossom as the lily and strike his roots as Lebanon.
7 (6) His branches shall spread, and his beauty shall be as the olive tree and his fragrance like that of Leb-
8 (7) anon. Again will such as dwell in his shadow raise corn; and they shall blossom like a vine. His memory shall be like the wine of
9 (8) Lebanon. What more has Ephraim to do with idols? I have answered, and I will regard him. I am as a green cypress. From Me
10 (9) is thy fruit found. Who is wise that he might understand these things? understanding, that he might know them? For the ways of the LORD are right, and the just walk in them, while sinners stumble in them.

Grammatical Notes

V. 2 (A. V., 1). "Unto the LORD. עַד frequently connotes arrival at the goal. Gen. 11:31; Is. 8:8; 9:12 (A. V., 13), etc.

V. 3 (2). "Render," שַׁלֵּם; Pi., to make complete, e. g., a vow, fulfill, pay; Deut. 23:22; 2 Sam. 15:7; Ps. 116:14, 18. — "Calves of our lips"; "our lips" is apposition to "calves"; hence "as," or "in place of" calves we will offer our lips in grateful songs of praise.

V. 6 (5). "Lily," shoshannah (Susannah). Our white lily is not indigenous to Palestine. It may be the yellow lily, or the iris, or may include anemones, gladioli, and other varicolored flowers. (Dalman, Orte u. Wege Jesu, p. 140 f.)

V. 8 (7). "Shall return." שׁוּב here denotes repetition, "again"; cp. ch. 11:9. — "Scent," זֵכֶר, rather, "memory." The restored people, walking in God's ways,

107

shall be remembered by future generations like the memory of good, invigorating wine, serving its purpose, Ps. 104:15. On the idea compare Ps. 112:6; Prov. 10:7; 31:28.

V. 9 (8). "I have heard," the added personal pronoun stresses the fact that He alone can hear and that He as the God of the Covenant, v. 1, "Jehovah," is

ready and willing to answer their prayer. — "Observed," cp. 13:7: Num. 23:9; 24:17; Job 35:5, 13 f., denotes attentive and interested regard, here as the consequence of God's hearing the prayer of His people. The perfect "heard" denotes the action in completion, the imperfect "observed" the ever-repeated attention to all the affairs of His believing children.

Vv. 2-4 (A. V., 1-3). In order to escape the judgment (v. 1), turn, O Israel! There is no other way of remaining Israel in truth and deed (Gen. 32:28) than that of quitting your present course and going back to the one and only Helper, your Covenant God, who still calls Himself and still is your God. And make a thorough job of it (Gr. N.). Do not stop halfway, go all the way until you are safely enclosed in the everlasting arms of your Savior God. Such return is imperative! You have fallen, victims of Satan, death, and hell (ch. 13:14), from whose power the Lord alone can deliver. Return to Him not with mere sacrifices (Micah 6:6-12; Jer. 7:8-11). Take words (A. V., v. 2) not of rebellion, of impertinent demands, of proud self-rightousness, but words of repentant faith (Jer. 3:21-25). In a masterly manner Hosea pictures the return of a sinner overwhelmed by guilt and shame, sobbing forth his plea for forgiveness. We hear no oratory, no well-formed sentences, but the broken sobs, the stammering of a contrite heart and a crushed spirit, of a sinner scarcely daring to lift up his eyes to the righteous God, yet pleading for what he needs above all: All — forgive — guilt? Receive graciously! All they bring is guilt, all they hope for is forgiveness, grace, unmerited love. (Cp. Toplady's "Rock of Ages," stanza 3.) Note the absence of personal pronouns, as if their own persons were not worthy of help, no, not even of being mentioned! "Render" (Gr. N.). "Calves of our lips" (Gr. N.). In one of the bold figures so characteristic of Hosea, the prophet speaks of the thankofferings repentant Israel is to bring to the Lord. No longer shall they be satisfied with offering animals, young oxen. As their calves they will "render," present in return for God's grace, their lips, overflowing with songs of gratitude welling forth from hearts truly thankful for God's grace and forgiveness. (Cp. Ps. 26:7; 71:8, 15, 22-24; 116:17-19.) True repentance manifests itself not only in words, but also in deeds and attitudes. No longer will Israel put his trust in human alliances with such powerful nations as Assyria (A. V., v. 3);

108

.

no longer take pride in horses, imported by Solomon from Egypt (1 Kings 10:28 f.; cp. Deut. 17:16; Micah 5:9, A. V., 10; Zech. 9:10); no longer commit the wicked folly of idolatry (Is. 44:9-20; Jer. 10:3-16). Israel has found a better Helper than man, or beast, or idol: one in whom the fatherless, forsaken of all human aid, finds mercy, loving compassion, such as is found only in the Covenant God Jehovah (cp. Ps. 27:10; Is. 49:15).

Vv. 5-9 (A. V., 4-8). With a Father's love the Lord turns to His children, promising His choicest blessings. He will heal their apostasy. He, their true Physician (Ex. 15:26), will cure the cancer of disloyalty and implant true faithfulness in their hearts and lives (cp. Deut. 30:6, *after* vv. 1-5; Jer. 31:33, 34; Ezek. 36:25-29). He will love them "freely," spontaneously, without the slightest resentment, in self-forgetting love, as unchanging as He Himself is unalterably the same. When the repentant sinner turns to the Lord, he finds a God who will not turn away from the sinner, but who has turned away from His anger, is a reconciled Father (Ex. 34:6, 7 a; Ps. 103:8-17). He will be like dew to Israel, (A. V., v. 5) "the night mist of the summer months in Palestine, which represents the condensed moisture brought by westerly winds from the Mediterranean and cooled by the night air. As rain does not fall from the beginning of May to the latter part of October, the night mist supplies to the parched vegetation moisture abundant enough to sustain the summer crops." (M. L. Margolis, *Micah,* p. 55 f.) Here it signifies the reviving, invigorating grace, granting and strengthening new life, a life of sanctification and loyalty to God. So God's Church will grow as the "lily" (Gr. N.), the emblem of beauty (Matt. 6:28). Once filthy with sin (Hos. 2:2-5), she is now decked with the glorious garments of her Redeemer's (ch. 13:14) righteousness and salvation (Cant. 2:1; Is. 61:10). Once weak and yielding to every temptation, easily seduced, she will become insuperably strong, her roots grounded firmly as Lebanon, which no human power nor satanic might can unsettle (Matt. 16:18; John 10:27 ff.; 2 Tim. 2:19). No longer shall she be like a withered, dying heath in the desert, but like a vigorous, flourishing plant spreading its shoots ever farther and farther (A. V., v. 6) (Luke 24:47; Acts 1:8). "Beauty" designates royal majesty, honor, splendor (Num. 27:20; Ps. 21:6 b (5 b); 45:4 f. (3 f.). The chief glory of the olive tree is its oil, fit symbol of the Holy Spirit and His gifts shed abundantly on the Church (cp. Zech. 4:3, 6, 12-14). Its smell no longer is abhorrent to the Lord (Lev. 26:31; Amos 5:21; cp. Is. 1:11-15) and an offense to man (Ezek. 36:23; 1 Cor. 10:32, 33). It is now like the spicy air of Lebanon, its fragrant cedars and innumerable flowers, a sweet odor to God (Rom. 14:17, 18; Phil. 4:18) and at the same time healing and invigorating to sinful mankind (1 Thess. 1:2-10; 1 Peter 2:12; cp. also the healing waters and leaves, Ezek. 47:1-12).

"Shall return," v. 8 (A. V., 7), (Gr. N.). "Dwell under his shadow," Ephraim's, Israel's shadow, for salvation is of Israel (cp. Rom. 9:4, 5; John 4:22). Again such as dwell under the shadow of God's Church as her blessed members shall bring "corn," grain to life. They shall aid in fulfilling God's promise, Ps. 72:16 ("handful" = abundance), which foretells the rich harvests of souls gathered into the Christian Church and finally into the heavenly garners (Matt. 13:30, 43). See John 4:28-30, 42; Acts 8:4; 11:19-26, etc. The Church of God is a missionary Church. "And grow as the vine." The individual members of the Church shall flourish as a grapevine bearing fruit abundantly (Matt. 13:23; Gal. 5:22, 23; Eph. 5:9; Phil. 4:8). Its scent (Gr. N.), literally, memory, renown, reputation, is as the wine of Lebanon, whose praises were sung far and wide. (Cp. Prov. 10:7; 31:28; Ps. 112:6; Rom. 1:8; 16:19; Phil. 1:12-14.)

As long as the believers live in this world, they are in constant need of admonition and exhortation. Therefore the Lord warns His people, who by His grace had become an Ephraim (A. V., v. 8), fruitful, powerful, prosperous, against yielding again to idolatry, their besetting sin. The Lord will no longer have anything to do with idols. This implies that He will no longer put up with a people that after tasting and seeing His grace and goodness (vv. 5-8) will again worship false gods in any manner or form. He motivates His warning by showing that there is no need of, no excuse for, returning to idols. In the Lord they have all they need or can require (Ps. 73:25-28). I Myself, none other, have answered (Gr. N.) and will answer their prayers, something impossible to idols (Ps. 115:4-8; 1 Kings 18:26-29). It is the Lord, and He alone, who responds to the pleas of His people (Jer. 3:23; 1 Kings 18:33-39); no one else keeps an observing (Gr. N.) eye on His Church, watches over her welfare with the most intense interest (Is. 49:15, 16). He, and He alone, is as a green "fir tree" = the cypress, an evergreen noted for the durability of its wood, practically immune against decay. Its wood was used for the floorings and doors of the Temple (1 Kings 5:22, 24; A. V., vv. 8, 10; 6:15, 34), a fit symbol of life and vigor. The Lord, and He alone, gives life and strength. From Him alone is our fruit found. If there is any good in me, O Lord, I owe it all to Thee! (John 15:4-6; Eph. 2:10; Col. 1:3-14.) Having such a Lord, what need is there of idols?

V. 10 (A. V., 9). "Who is wise." In a remarkable statement Moses had already defined wisdom and understanding as cleaving unto the Lord, the Covenant God, to His Word, Law and Gospel (Deut. 4:3-9). Compare also Ps. 111:10; Prov. 1:7; 9:10, particularly 30:3-5, where wisdom is defined as knowledge of the holy God, the Creator and His Son (cp. Prov. 8:22-36), as revealed in the pure Word of God. Whosoever is wise — and surely there is none who would regard himself unwise, a fool — let him not merely profess to be wise (Rom. 1:22; 12:16). Let him understand these things which have been preached and proclaimed by Hosea. Understand them! Come to a keen insight into the nature and import of these things by distinguishing them from mere human speculation and recognizing in them the infallible words of the Lord God of heaven and earth (ch. 1:1, 2). "Prudent," the Hebrew word derived from the same root as "understanding." If he has learned to differentiate these things from all human teachings, then let him know them. This knowledge is not to be a mere intellectual grasping of certain facts. No, let all the powers of intellect, emotion, and will be directed and ruled by this understanding, so that he passes through life as an intelligent, willing, active, faithful member of God's Church. And again Hosea adds a powerful motivation as his parting word. For the ways of the Lord, which He has laid down in His holy Word for our justification, sanctification, and everlasting salvation, on which He Himself leads us, are straight ways. They lead directly to the goal, for they are the ways of the unchanging God of truth and grace and power. On them the "just," declared righteous through the merits of their Savior, can confidently walk, sure of their salvation (1 Cor. 1:8, 9), while the rebellious will stumble, stagger, fall therein. The Word spoken by the messengers of God and neglected, rejected by them, will judge them on that Day and condemn them (Mark 16:16; John 12:48). As a commentary on this concluding word of Hosea, read chs. 30—33, 35 of the Book of Isaiah, Hosea's great contemporary.

J O E L

Introductory Remarks

Joel, that is "Jehovah is God," was the son of Pethuel. He was active in Judah, probably in Jerusalem, and very likely was a citizen of Judah. (Ch. 1:14; 2:1, 15; 2:23—3:2, 6-8, 16-21.)

There is a difference of opinion as to the age in which Joel lived, and it can be only approximately determined. He lived after the victory of Jehoshaphat over the Moabites and Ammonites (cp. ch. 3:2 with 2 Chron. 20:1-26), and he mentions the Phoenicians, Philistines, Egyptians, and Edomites as the enemies of Judah (ch. 3:4, 19). We know that the Edomites had revolted against Judah under Joram (2 Kings 8:20-22), and the Philistines and Arabians had invaded and plundered Judah. Cp. 2 Chron. 21:16, 17; 22:1 with Joel 3:4-6. The relations between Egypt and Judah were hostile only in the earlier period after the separation of the two kingdoms (1 Kings 14:25, 26), and the hostilities on the part of Tyre and Sidon against Judah can hardly have commenced prior to the dethronement of Athaliah. Cp. 1 Kings 16:31; 2 Kings 8:18; 10:1. On the other hand, we fail to find any reference in the book of Joel to oppression on the part of the Syrians, who were already at war with Judah while Joash was on the throne (2 Kings 12:17, 18; 2 Chron. 24:23-25; Amos 1:3-5); nor is there any mention made of hostilities on the part of the Assyrians (since the time of Ahaz); much less do we find any reference to the later world powers, Babylonia and Persia. From this it is evident that Joel is not one of the later prophets, but very likely one of the earliest of this group. He follows close upon Obadiah. Cp. the relations between these two, Joel 2:32 with Obad. 17; Joel 3:3 with Obad. 11; Joel 3:19 with Obad. 10. Joel was active probably during the first two decades of Joash's reign (877—837), while the latter was under the guidance of the priest Jehoiada (2 Kings 11:12) (Delitzsch, Hofmann, Keil, Orelli). His book constantly presupposes the correct form of divine worship (ch. 1:9, 13, 14, 16; 2:1, 14-17), and conditions under Joash and Jehoiada warranted this (2 Kings 11:12, 17; 12:2; 2 Chron. 23:16, 17; 24:14). Furthermore, Amos, who lived at a later time,

112

apparently is acquainted with Joel's prophecies and several times refers to them. Cp. Joel 3:16 with Amos 1:2; Joel 3:18 with Amos 9:13. It is true that some investigators believe that Joel lived at a much later time, in the days of Josiah (639—609) (Koenig and others), but they have less ground to support their claim. — L. Fuerbringer, *Introduction to O. T.*

PART I

The Lord's Judgment: Locusts and Drought

Chapters 1:2—2:17

CHAPTER 1

A. The Superscription, V. 1

1 The word of the LORD which came to Joel, the son of Pethuel

B. The Lamentable Devastation of the Land, Ch. 1:2-12

2 Hear this, O elders, and listen, all you inhabitants of the land! Has such a thing occurred in your days or in the days of your fathers?
3 Tell your sons of it, and their sons to their sons, and their sons to the
4 next generation. That which the gnawer left, the locust ate; and what the locust left, the licker ate; and what the licker left, the strip-
5 per ate. Awake, you drunkards, and weep! And howl, all you wine topers, because of the new wine, for
6 it is cut off from your mouth. For a nation has come up against My land, strong and innumerable. Its teeth are lion's teeth, the fangs of
7 a lioness are his. It has made My vine a waste and My fig trees sticks. He has barked them clean and thrown them down; their branches
8 are made white. Lament like a virgin girded with sackcloth for the
9 husband of her youth. Meat offerings and drink offerings are cut off from the LORD'S house. The priests, the servants of the LORD,
10 mourn. Devastated is the field, the ground mourns, for devastated is the grain, dried up the new wine;
11 the oil dies away. Stand abashed, you plowmen; wail, you vine-dressers, for the wheat and barley, because the harvest of the field is
12 lost. The vine is wilted, the fig tree withered. The pomegranate, also the palm and the apple tree, all the trees of the field are dried up; yes, joy has withered away from the children of men.

V. 1. See Introductory Remarks, p. 112.

Vv. 2, 3. The Lord through His prophet speaks of a calamity so terrible that the oldest men cannot remember having heard even the rumor of any plague equaling this one; so unexampled that by divine command it is to serve all future generations as a warning memorial of God's dreadful judgments upon a sinful nation. To this day, over a space of more than 2,500 years, the record of this plague has been preserved in Holy Writ. So faithful is Joel's account that even today

113

its accuracy and vividness is freely acknowledged. In the December, 1915, issue of *The National Geographic Magazine* (XXVIII, No. 6) John D. Whiting writes in an interesting manner an eyewitness account of a similar locust plague covering all of Palestine and Syria, from the border of Egypt to the Taurus Mountains. After quoting Joel 1: 2-6 he begins his article: "Thus Joel, writing some seven or eight hundred years B. C., begins his description of a locust plague, which then as now must have laid waste this land. We marvel how this ancient writer could have given so graphic and true a description of a devastation caused by locusts in so condensed a form" (p. 511). We shall refer frequently to this article.

V. 4. "Palmerworm." The English word according to the *New Standard Dictionary* denotes "any hairy caterpillar that comes as a devouring pest in moving swarms." The Hebrew term denotes a "gnawer," or "shearer." "Locust," perhaps "the multitudinous one," because of its innumerable masses, is the commonest name. "Cankerworm." The English word denotes a larval moth with wingless females destructive particularly to fruit trees *(New Standard Dictionary)*. The Hebrew word is derived either from a root "to lick, lap up," hence, the licker or lapper (so Keil, Sellin, and others), or "to hop," hence "hopper" *(Complete Bible)*. "Caterpillar." The Hebrew term = devourer, stripper. "Locust," *arbeh,* would emphasize the immense masses, the other three terms, their insatiable voracity. In ch. 2: 25 the order of the four terms differs. The four terms may denote four different species of locusts, or four stages in the development of the insects, or, since there are several more names for the locust, the prophet may simply have chosen four terms (four is the number of completeness) (cp. Is. 11: 12; Jer. 15: 3; 49: 36; Ezek. 1: 5, 6; Zech. 1: 18, 20; 6: 1, 5), to designate the completeness of the devastation effected. In 1915 the first swarms of adult locusts appeared in March, coming from the northeast, going toward southwest in such "thick clouds as to obscure the sun for the time being" (p. 513). The females, about two and one-half to three inches long, at once began to lay their eggs, sinking a hole about four inches deep into the hard soil and depositing about 100 eggs "neatly arranged in a cylindrical mass" (about one inch long and as thick as a slate pencil) "and enveloped in a sticky glutinous secretion." "It is estimated by competent authorities that as many as 65,000 to 75,000 locust eggs are concentrated in a square meter of soil" (pp. 516, 521). Such patches of egg-filled soil covered the entire land from north to south, from east to west. "Once the female

locust has laid the eggs, her life's mission is done. She flies away —
whereto no one can say — and soon dies" (p. 516). Within a few
weeks the young locusts are hatched. "They were quite black and
resembled large ants, having no signs of wings." A few days after
hatching "they would start their forward march of from 400 to 600
feet per day, clearing the ground of any vegetation before them"
(p. 522). "They seemed to hop much like fleas" (p. 525). At the end
of May they molted, issuing forth in the "pupa" state, still unable to
fly, because "the large wings of its future state are fully developed
but neatly folded up in four membranous cases" (p. 536), standing
upright. This may be the reason why the "licker" or "hopper," *yeleq,*
is called "rough," literally, bristled (Jer. 51:27). In this stage the
locusts "walk like ordinary insects, leaping only when frightened into
a quicker pace, which they readily accomplish by the use of their
two long and powerful posterior legs" (p. 525). Their bodies were
colored bright yellow. In the last molt the wings emerge from their
sacs so that the locust can now fly. "The colors of its body are the
most delicate hues, but after a couple of days of flying they deepen
into a pronounced red effect" (p. 538).

Vv. 5-7. The drunkards, whose God is their belly, could no longer
serve their idolized gullet with the wine it craved. Nor could any
drinker of wine obtain any longer this divine and wholesome gift
(Ps. 104:14, 15). "New wine," the wine within the grape (Is. 65:8),
and as it flowed from the wine press, was regarded as a precious gift
of the Lord. Now it was cut off! A powerful and innumerable
"nation" (v. 6) (cp. "people," Prov. 30:25, 26) has come, its teeth
though tiny yet as strong as a lion's teeth. My land, My vine, My fig
tree (v. 7), the prophet speaks as the spokesman of God, the Owner of
the land, the Giver of all gifts. Now land and gifts are destroyed,
taken away. Vineyards served also as orchards. To this day olive
trees, fig, pomegranate, and other trees are planted in the vineyard
among the grapevines. Whiting writes: "Once entering a vineyard
the sprawling vines would in the shortest time be nothing but bare
bark. — When the daintier morsels were gone, the bark was eaten
off the young topmost branches, which, after exposure to the sun,
bleached snow-white. Then, seemingly out of malice, they would gnaw
off small limbs, perhaps to get at the pith within." Quoting Joel 1:7,
he adds a footnote: " 'And cast it away,' no doubt referring to the
chipping off the twigs" (p. 529).

Vv. 8-12. Not only the drunkards, but the entire nation as well is urged to lament, not only because of the material losses and discomfort, but because of the disruption of the divinely instituted worship. "Virgin," "husband of her youth." Cp. Deut. 22:22-29, where the betrothed virgin is called the wife of the man, while here the betrothed man is called the husband of the virgin. "Lament." To be separated by death from the bridegroom is the severest blow a bride can suffer. Israel had been cut off from communication with her divine Spouse by means of sacrifice, for the ingredients of the meat offering (flour and oil, Lev. 2:1-16) and the drink offering (wine, Lev. 23:13) were cut off (v. 9). Without these offerings the daily morning and evening sacrifices could not be offered in keeping with divine prescription (Ex. 29:38-42) and would have to cease. Had God rejected His people? Fields and acres were devastated; "corn," or "grain," wine, and oil, the three food staples and sacrificial essentials, destroyed; even the barley harvest, the food of the poor class, a failure! (Vv. 10, 11.) The "apple tree" (v. 12), either apple, or apricot, or quince, an aromatic fruit. In 1915 the fully developed flying locusts appeared about June 10 and at once began to complete the destruction begun in the earlier stages. They attacked the olive trees, whose tough, bitter leaves had not been to the liking of the creepers. Food becoming scarcer, both creeping and flying locusts attacked the olive trees, and "between the two they stripped every leaf, berry, and even the tender bark. — Likewise every variety of tree was attacked with the sole exception of the Persian lilac and the oleander bushes." Of the cacti "they ate away layer after layer over the whole surface, giving the leaves the effect of having been jack-planed. Even on the scarce and prized palms they had no pity, gnawing off the tenderer ends of the swordlike branches, and, diving deep into the heart, they tunneled after the juicy pit" (p. 542 f.). Surely, joy is withered away from the sons of men!

C. The Priests Are Urged to Proclaim a Solemn Fast, Ch. 1:13-20

13 Gird yourselves and mourn, O priests! Wail, O altar servants! Come, spend the night in sackcloth, O servants of the LORD! For meal offering and drink offering are cut off from the house of your God!
14 Sanctify a fast! Call a solemn assembly! Call together the elders, all inhabitants of the land into the house of the LORD, your God, and
15 cry out to the LORD, Alas for the Day! For at hand is the Day of the LORD! And as devastation from
16 the Almighty it comes! Is not before our eyes food cut off, from the house of our God joy and gladness?
17 The seed corn is shriveled up under the clods. The garners are desolate, the granaries broken down,
18 for the grain is dried up. How the animals groan! The herds of cattle are bewildered, because there is no pasture for them. Also the flocks of
19 sheep must suffer. To Thee,

116

O LORD, I cry! For fire has eaten the pastures of the wilderness, and flame has consumed all the trees of 20 the field. Even the wild beasts yearn for Thee because the water brooks are dried up and fire has devoured the pastures of the wilderness.

Grammatical Notes

V. 17 a presents great difficulties, since the three words occur only here and their etymology is uncertain. עָבַשׁ may be related to an Aramaic root = to dry up, to rot; פְּרֻדוֹת, probably Syriac *ferda*, "corn," "kernel," "berry"; cp. Jewish Aram., gravel, berry: מְגְרָפֿה, from an Aram. root = to sweep (cp. Judg. 5:21, the stream swept away the corpses), the noun denoting either what is swept away, dirt, clods, or what sweeps, rakes, an instrument for raking, sweeping; rake, hoe. Sellin changes the text to read: "The mules jingle (tinkle) with their chains (cp. Is. 3:18) under them in their barns." *The Complete Bible* offers: "The mules stomp at their stalls."

V. 13. The priests are to wear garments of mourning and lament. — "Ministers," the Hebrew term denotes an honorary service, rendered to a king (1 Kings 10:5; Prov. 29:12); to a prophet (2 Kings 4:43); to Moses (Ex. 24:13; Joshua 1:1); frequently of priestly or Levitical service (Deut. 10:8; 17:12; Num. 3:6; 18:2).

Vv. 14-20. "Fast," an ancient custom (Judg. 20:26; 1 Sam. 7:6; 2 Sam. 12:16, 21-23) commanded for the Day of Atonement (Lev. 16:29-31; 23:27-29: "afflict your soul" = appetites). — "Sanctify," the Hebrew term denotes separation, a setting apart by solemn ceremonies for a solemn purpose. — "Solemn assembly," a festival gathering on various occasions (Lev. 23:36; Deut. 16:8). — "All the inhabitants," not only the men (Ex. 23:17). On "Day of the LORD" (v. 15) see Obad. 15, p. 203 f. The Lord, the Covenant God, is the Almighty One, all-powerful in destruction, as the present situation proves. He has cut off "meat" (v. 16), literally, "food," before the people, and joy from the house of God, to which Ps. 26:7 a; 27:6 b; 150:1 ff. no longer apply. On v. 17 see Gr. N. The seed rots in the soil, the first indication of the drought accompanying the locust plague, see v. 20; storehouses and barns are falling to pieces since the despairing people are no longer interested in repairing them. Vv. 18-20 prove the prophet's and the Lord's sympathy with the suffering animals. "Perplexed," bewildered, wandering about aimlessly (cp. Ex. 14:3: "are entangled"). In sincere sympathy with his fellow men and suffering creation the prophet himself does what he had urged his people to do. He cries to the Covenant God for help, telling Him of the terrible devastation and leaving the manner of His deliverance to His wisdom, power, and grace. "Fire," "flame" (v. 19), does not refer to the locusts destroying

117

the fields as thoroughly as fire, nor to the efforts of people to destroy the locusts by starting fires. V. 20 b obliges us to think of a severe drought drying up the very wellsprings. "Wilderness," not in absolute sense, but of the steppe or prairie covered with vegetation in rainy season, drying up in the heat of the summer.

CHAPTER 2

D. Repent! The Day of the Lord Is Heralded by the Double Plague
Vv. 1-11

1 Blow the trumpet in Zion, and sound an alarm on My holy mountain! Let all the inhabitants of the land tremble, for the Day of the
2 LORD is coming! It is near! A day of darkness and gloominess, a day of clouds and dense darkness! Like as the dawn spreading over the mountains, a people great and strong! Like it there was none from ancient time, nor will there be after it another to the years of genera-
3 tions and generations. Before them a fire devours, and after them a flame burns! As the garden of Eden was the land before them, but after them a desolate wilderness. And there is nothing that escapes them!
4 Their appearance resembles that of horses; and like horses, so they run!
5 Like the rattling of chariots on the tops of the mountains they leap, like the crackling of a flame of fire devouring stubble; like a mighty
6 people prepared for war. Before them peoples are in anguish. All
7 faces are blanched with fear. They run like warriors, like men of war they climb the wall. Everyone goes on his own way; they do not criss-
8 cross their paths. None jostles the other. Everyone walks on his way. If they fall by means of defensive measures, their ranks are not
9 breached. Against the city they rush; on the walls they run; into the houses they crawl; through the windows they come like a thief.
10 Before them the land quakes, heaven trembles, sun and moon grow dark, and the stars withdraw
11 their light. And the LORD lifts up His voice at the head of His army. For His host is very great, for strong are the executors of His word; for great is the Day of the LORD, and very terrible. Who can endure it?

Grammatical Note

V. 6. "Gather blackness," rather redness, ruddiness, either by assembling it = become flushed with fear, or better, by withdrawing it = become pale.

Vv. 1-3. "Blow the trumpet," the *shophar*, horn, also called the ram's horn (Judg. 6: 34). "Sound an alarm." From Num. 10: 5 ff. it is evident that the alarm was sounded by a continuous peal, while the "blowing" — when distinguished from the alarm — signified short, sharp tones or blasts. The alarm was to be blown at Zion, the only sanctuary of Jehovah recognized by the prophets. Bethel and Dan were sinful sanctuaries (1 Kings 12: 29, 30; 14: 9). All the inhabitants of the land, including the Northern Kingdom, are to be summoned to Jerusalem as in the days of Asa (2 Chron. 15: 8-17; 19:4 ff.), and later,

118

in Hezekiah's reign (2 Chron. 30:1—31:6). "The Day of the LORD" (cp. Obad. 15). The locust plague and the drought were forerunners of the Lord's Day, which was coming, was near. Compare the similar expressions Matt. 24:33; Phil. 4:5; James 5:8, 9; 1 Peter 4:7 and 2 Thess. 2:2, 3; 2 Peter 3:8. "A day of darkness," etc. (v. 2) (cp. Ex. 10:15). The first swarms of locusts in February, 1915, came "in such thick clouds as to obscure the sun for the time being" (*National Geographic Magazine,* 1915, p. 513). And later the newly developed fliers passed over the Jordan Valley "in clouds sufficiently dense to darken the sun" (p. 544). "The morning," literally, the dawn; picturing either their swift advance, as the morning light speeds from crag to crag; or their great number; or the semidarkness of the twilight, the dusk preceding the brightness of the day. Graetz, Sellin, and others change the vowels and translate: like soot; or it may be referred to the red color of the locusts, which in the bright light of the sun appears like the redness of dawn. "Great," "strong," both terms denote numerical or physical strength, their great number and their power to destroy. "Not been ever." This does not contradict Ex. 10:14 f. There Moses speaks of Egypt; cp. the many references to Egypt (vv. 12-15); here the prophet speaks of a plague visiting the Holy Land. "Fire," "flame" (v. 3), may refer to the drought (1:19, 20), or it may be a poetical description of the devastation that sweeps the land like a fire, overwhelming everything before it and leaving behind it ruin and desolation. "Nothing shall escape them"; literally, and deliverance there is not before him = the locust. In 1915 the sections where no eggs had been laid or where the eggs had been carefully removed by governmental orders did not suffer from the creepers, but later the full-grown locusts came and cleaned up every bit of vegetation (p. 544).

Vv. 4-6. "Their appearance." An old Arabian proverb is still being repeated by the natives: "The locust has the form of ten of the giants of the animal world, weak as he is — face of a mare, eyes of an elephant, neck of a bull, horns of a hart, chest of a lion, stomach of a scorpion, wings of an eagle, thighs of a camel, legs of an ostrich, and tail of a serpent" (p. 549 f.). "Horsemen," literally, horses. "Noise of chariots" (v. 5) (cp. Rev. 9:9). "Before they were seen, a loud noise, produced by the flapping of myriads of locust wings, was heard, described as resembling the distant rumble of waves" (p. 513). "In battle array," cp. "His army," v. 11. "Much pained" (v. 6), the verb used of women in travail (cp. Jer. 30:5-7). "Gather blackness," rather, be blanched with fear (see Gr. N.).

Vv. 7-11. "Disastrous as they were in the country, equally obnoxious they become about the homes, crawling up thick upon the walls and squeezing in through cracks of closed doors or windows, entering the very dwelling rooms. — Women frantically swept the walls and roofs of their homes, but to no avail. — They even fell into one's shirt collar from the walls above. — A lady, after being away from home for half a day, returned with 110 of them concealed within the skirts. Whenever touched, or especially when finding themselves caught within one's clothes, they exuded from their mouths a dark fluid, an irritant to the skin and soiling the garments in a most disgusting manner. Imagine the feeling (we speak from experience) with a dozen or two such creatures over an inch long, with sawlike legs and rough bodies, making a race course of your back!" (P. 553.) Once started on their course, nothing could stop them; walls were scaled, they rolled on like a mighty, unconquerable flood. Their ranks remain unbroken by obstacles. "Thrust another" (v. 8), push, jostle. Even the "sword," missiles, means of defense do not stop their onward march of destruction. The earth shall quake. "When anything neared their [the creepers'] thickened masses [hopping like fleas], it seemed as if the entire surface of the ground moved, producing a most curious effect upon one's vision and causing dizziness, which in some was so severe as to produce a sensation not unlike seasickness" (p. 525). The clouds of locusts cause the entire atmosphere to be in a state of commotion as if the very heavens trembled. A very vivid symbol of the Day of the Lord, whose harbingers they were! "The LORD'S army" (v. 11). To this day the nations speak of the locusts as *Yaish Allah*, Allah's army. This mighty army is marshaled by a Mighty Leader, who utters His voice, directs the course of this great "camp," here in the sense of host, army (cp. Ex. 14:24; Joshua 10:5; 11:4). He, the Lord of strength, now carries out His word, His threat pronounced even before His people entered His land (Deut. 28:38-40). Cp. 2 Chron. 6:26, 28; 7:13. If the heralding plague is so great and terrible, who can stand in the fullness of the fury of the Day of the Lord? Cp. Luke 21:26; Rev. 6:12-17.

E. Only Sincere Repentance May Cause God to Spare His Land and His People, Ch. 2:12-17

12 Yet even now, is the oracle of the LORD, turn to Me with all your heart, and with fasting, and with weeping, and with lamentation.
13 And rend your hearts and not your garments, and turn to the LORD, your God, for He is gracious and compassionate, slow to anger, and great in loving-kindness and re- 14 lenting of the evil. Who knows but

that He will again relent and leave behind Him a blessing, meal offering and drink offering, for the 15 LORD, your God. Blow the ram's horn in Zion! Consecrate a fast! 16 Call a solemn assembly! Assemble the people! Consecrate a convocation! Assemble the elders, gather the children, also those that suck the breasts. Let the bridegroom come forth from his room and the bride from her bridal chamber. 17 Let the priests, the ministers of the LORD, weep between the porch and the altar and say: Have mercy, O LORD, upon Thy people, and do not surrender Thine heritage to shame, that Gentiles might taunt them! Why should they say among the peoples: Where is their God?

Grammatical Note

V. 17. "Rule over them." Rule מֹשֵׁל, is to be taken in the sense of "rule," "govern," not "deride," "taunt," as in Ezek. 12: 22 f.; 16: 44, etc. If the locust plague and the drought were to continue, the nation would be impoverished and weakened to the extent that foreign nations would easily subdue them, rule over them.

Vv. 12-14. It is not the Last Day, the Final Judgment. Even from this horrible plague there is deliverance possible, says the Covenant God of grace and mercy, inviting them to repent, to turn to their God. Note the insistence on a thorough, sincere repentance. The preposition "to" used here connotes arrival at the goal. Do not go only halfway, but do not rest until you are again one with God. To that purpose turn with all your heart, your whole life and being; manifest the sincerity of your repentance by fasting, weeping, mourning. Yet be not satisfied with rending your garment, with outward symbols and actions; rend, tear, your heart (v. 13), that deceitful and desperately wicked thing (Jer. 17: 9); turn away from its evil thoughts and desires and temptations, and turn to the Lord, your God, in sincere desire to serve Him alone. As an incentive the Lord adds that age-old, oft-repeated promise recorded Ex. 34: 6 as His name. Cp. Ps. 103: 2-13; Micah 7: 18-20 for God's comments on His name. Evangelical preaching is the only means to work true repentance. That alone turns the heart to God in true faith and love and hope. "Who knoweth" (v. 14) (cp. 2 Sam. 12: 22; Esther 4: 14; Jonah 3: 9; and the similar expression "it may be," Is. 37: 4; Lam. 3: 29; Amos 5: 15) does not express doubt, or unbelief, but is an admonition to unwearying, continued thoroughness in turning to God in the hope of acceptance. We need such admonition lest we tire in our daily sanctification. Again it is the Lord's cause, His preparations for man's salvation, His spiritual gifts, the means of grace, which are uppermost in the prophet's mind. The Old Testament offerings were means of grace divinely instituted; rich, choice blessings of the Lord, granting His people a way to communicate with the God of their salvation. What a blessing the New Testament means of grace, Word and Sacraments! May God preserve to us these blessings uncontaminated! He will if we turn to Him with our whole heart and make diligent use of these means.

Vv. 15-17. On v. 15 see 1:14; 2:1. All people, from infants to old men, are to assemble (v. 16), all joyous festivities to cease, the priests as representatives of the nation to weep and pray (v. 17), as Moses did (Ex. 32:11,12; Num. 14:13-19). "Rule over them." See Gr. N. Impoverishment of the land would give the surrounding nations the opportunity to subdue Israel, and rule of foreign nations would increase the danger of idolatry, the characteristic tendency of Israel before the Exile. And the nations would scoff at the Lord as though He were unable to protect His own people from harm and defeat. His own honor should prompt Him to come to the rescue of His chosen nation! The "porch," or portico, a space thirty feet wide and fifteen feet deep (1 Kings 6:3), was the entrance to the Holy Place and faced the altar of burnt offering, thirty feet square, standing in the inner court, while the people assembled in the outer or great court (2 Chron. 4:9).

PART II

God's Zeal for the Salvation of His People

Chapters 2:18—3:21 (M. T., 2:18—4:21)

A. The Removal of the Plagues and the Restoration of God's Blessing, Ch. 2:18-22

18 Then the LORD zealously favored His land and spared His people.
19 And the LORD answered and said to His people: I am ready to send you the grain and the new wine and the new oil, and you shall be satisfied therewith; nor will I make you any longer a reproach among
20 the nations. And I will remove the northerner from you, and I will drive him away into an arid and desolate land, his vanguard to the eastern sea and his rear to the western sea. And his stench will ascend and his stink rise, for He
21 has done great things. Fear not, O land! Rejoice and be glad, for
22 the LORD does great things! Fear not, O beasts of the field! For the pastures of the wilderness shall become green; for the tree shall bear its fruit, fig tree and grapevine yield their wealth.

Grammatical Notes

V. 18. "Then will the LORD be jealous," וַיְקַנֵּא. The etymology of קָנָא is disputed. The most suitable suggestion is that of Hoffmann (*Literarisches Centralbl.*, 1882, 320), Harkavy, and others, which connects the word with an Aramaic and Arabic root = to be red, to glow; hence, be fiery, eager, zealous. This etymology is favored by such passages as compare God's zeal to consuming fire (Deut. 4:24; 29:20; Ezek. 36:5, 6; Zeph. 1:18; 3:8). In general, it denotes zealous

122

eagerness to defend and preserve the rights, privileges, possessions, etc., of oneself or another.

In its various grammatical forms the word is used

I. Of God:

A. Of His zeal in preserving the honor of His name (as defined Ex. 3:14; 34:5, 6, 7; Is. 42:8, etc.), which honor He guards zealously against every neglect of His Word and will, particularly against every form of idolatry (Ex. 20:5; 34:14; Deut. 4:24; 5:9; 6:15; 32:16, 21; 1 Kings 14:22; Ps. 78:58; Ezek. 8:3, by Jews; Is. 59:17; Zeph. 3:8, by Gentiles).

B. Of His zeal for His Church (Joel 2:18; Is. 9:6; 37:32; 42:13; Ezek. 39:25; Zech. 1:14; 8:2).

C. Of His zeal against His enemies and those of His Church (Deut. 29:20; Ezek. 35:11).

God's burning zeal in destroying the enemies of His Church is at the same time fiery zeal for the welfare of His people (2 Kings 19:31; Ezek. 36:5 f.; 38:19).

II. Of man:

A. Of his zeal for God, God's honor, Word, will (Num. 25:11; 2 Kings 10:16; Ps. 119:139; 69:10, A. V., 9, of the Messiah; cp. John 2:17).

B. Of his zeal for himself or his fellow men.

While God's zeal is at all times flawlessly holy, it is a remarkable fact that all derivatives of קּנא denoting man's zeal for himself and others mean either improper or sinful, harmful zeal, envy, jealousy; improper (Num. 11:29; 2 Sam. 21:2), sinful (Gen. 26:14; 37:11; Ps. 37:1; Eccl. 4:4; 9:6; Is. 11:13; Ezek. 31:9; 35:11), harmful (Job 5:2; Prov. 14:30; 27:4). In Num. 5:11 ff. the prescribed ritual would decide whether the husband's "spirit of jealousy" was justified or not by proving the wife's guilt or innocence. This passage and Prov. 6:34 are the only passages in which קּנְאָה may include justifiable zeal for one's honor.

The A. V. and Luther translate Joel 2:18 as referring to the future. While this is grammatically possible, it seems preferable to adopt the translation of the LXX and the Vulgate, which render the verbs as historical imperfects, describing the result of Joel's admonition and the nation's fasting and prayer. Most commentators follow the translation of the LXX; see Driver, *Tenses*, XV. Sellin regards the two verbs as jussives and changes the pointing, for which change there is no need.

V. 18 states the result of the congregation's returning to the Lord in humble repentance and confident faith. The Lord again accepts them as His people. "Then will the LORD be jealous." See Gr. N. "Jealous" is used of the Lord in the sense of zealously defending His own or His people's rights. The underlying idea is God's very nature as described in His name Jehovah, I AM THAT I AM (Ex. 3:13-15). He would cease to be what this name involves if He were to acknowledge any one as His equal whose will He would have to consider before He could act. Hence He is unalterably opposed to all who refuse to acknowledge His absolute sovereignty. See Ex. 20:5; Deut. 29:18-20; Zeph. 1:17, 18; 3:7, 8. Since He loves His people as the apple of His eye (Deut. 32:10; Zech. 2:8), He is equally zealous for their welfare and regards any harm done them as a violation of His sovereignty, to be punished by Him as such. Cp. Is. 9:7; 37:2 and preceding and following context; Ezek. 36:5,6; Zech. 1:14-16. "Pity" = spare (Ex. 2:6; Mal. 3:17). On the idea cp. Ps. 103:13,14 (different word).

In a vast panoramic view the Lord now reveals to His prophet the history of God's people from the days of Joel until the end of time. Throughout the ages the Lord will be the Protector and Deliverer of His people in every trouble. This will be manifested (1) by the removal of the locusts and drought, vv. 19-27; (2) by the coming of the Messiah, v. 23 b; (3) by the coming of the Spirit, vv. 28, 29; (4) by the coming of the Day of the Lord, ch. 2:30—3:21.

Vv. 19, 20. The immediate physical needs are supplied first. The food staples (cp. 1:10-12) will be restored in ample sufficiency. Then their reproach will be lifted (v. 19 b). His deliverance will prove to the heathen world that Israel is still the people of the Lord, who can do mighty things. Also the locusts will be removed (v. 20). "The northern." While usually the locusts in Palestine come from the south, the great army of locusts in 1915 came from the northeast. (*National Geographic Magazine,* p. 513.) Hence the allegorical interpretation of the "locusts" cannot be defended by this verse. They will be driven into a land barren and desolate, into the arid desert country to the east and south of Palestine. "His face," his vanguard of the "army" (vv. 2, 7, 11) to the east sea, the Salt Sea; "his hinder part," the rearguard to the "utmost sea," literally, the sea behind, the western sea, the Mediterranean Sea. Facing the rising sun, before you is east; behind, west; to the right (Teman, cp. Obad. 9), south; to the left, north. "His stench," "ill savor." Whiting writes: "In Nazareth, where so many were crushed to death in the narrow streets, actual observers state that the air for a while was so putrid and vile as to be almost unbearable" (p. 544). Stench is all that is left of the enemy once so powerful and so dreaded. That is the fate of all enemies of the Lord. "For He has done great things," wrought an enormous destruction, so great that nations doubted the Lord's power to help. These doubts which may have arisen also in the hearts of believing children of God (cp. v. 17) are to be silenced completely and forever.

Vv. 21, 22. The Lord addresses the "land," the soil, and the beasts, irrational creation personified. As the three admonitions vv. 21a, 22a are addressed to both classes, so the two causal clauses vv. 21b, 22b state the reasons why together they are to rejoice. The Lord can do great things, work marvelous deliverance. The removal of the locusts and the drought will enable the earth to fulfill her purpose (Gen. 1:11, 12) and her desire (Hos. 2:21, 22) to produce grass and grain and fruit trees for man and beast, so that all the creatures depending on the fertility of the soil will be fully supplied with good.

B. The Promise of the Coming of the Teacher of Righteousness, for Whose Sake God Pardons His People, Ch. 2:23-27

23 And you, children of Zion, rejoice and be glad in the LORD, your God, He will give to you the Teacher unto Righteousness. And He will send down to you rain, the early rain and the late rain, in the
24 first place. Then shall the threshing floors be full of grain, and the vats
25 overflow with wine and oil. So will I repay you for the years which the locust and the licker and the stripper and the gnawer have devoured,
26 My great army which I sent against you. Then you shall eat your fill and be satisfied, and you shall praise the name of the LORD, your God, who has dealt so wonderfully with you; and My people shall
27 never again be put to shame. So shall you know that I am in the midst of Israel and that I am the LORD, your God, and there is none else. And My people shall never again be put to shame.

Grammatical Notes

V. 23. "The former rain moderately." מוֹרֶה is to be derived from a stem יָרָה = to show, point out; occurring about fifty times in the sense of "instruct," "teach" (cp. Is. 9:14; 30:20; Job 36:22, etc.); while it is very doubtful that it ever denotes "to moisten." There are four interpretations of this phrase: (1) The Teacher of Righteousness; Targum (second Christian century), the "Zadokite Fragment" (first century B. C., found in Cairo 1910), Vulgate, church fathers, the ancient Christian Church. (2) The LXX translates "the foods for righteousness," τὰ βρώματα εἰς δικαιοσύνην, whatever that means. The Syriac translation follows the LXX. Duhm, Marti, and others adopt this translation on the theory that הַמּוֹרֶה in v. 23 a was transposed from v. 23 b to take the place of an original מָזוֹן, food, in v. 23 a. מָזוֹן occurs only two times in M. T. and is not translated βρῶμα, but ἄρτους in Gen. 45:23, and τροφαί, 2 Chron. 11:23; while βρῶμα occurs only in translation of בִּרְיָה,

food for the sick; found only 2 Sam. 13:5, 7, 10. As Sellin observes, a reference to food here would also quite unsuitably anticipate v. 24, and a promise of food for the sick would be a rather doubtful promise. (3) "Rain moderately," A. V.; but εἰς δικαιοσύνην never means "moderately," or "in rightful proper measure"; δικαιοσύνη is invariably an ethical attribute, and there is no such thing as ethical rain. Hence "rain unto righteousness" cannot be a correct translation, particularly since there is no reason why only the early rain should serve for justification. Moreover, this translation does not do justice to the article with moreh. Finally, moreh never means "rain," not even Ps. 84:7, the only passage besides Joel 2:23 adduced by G.-B., "The rain also filleth the pools." The translation "pools" would require a change of vocalization: בְּרֵכוֹת instead of בְּרָכוֹת, blessing; "filleth" does not mean to fill, but to cause to put on, enwrap in, clothe in; and מוֹרֶה here also = teacher, collective, teachers clothe (others) in

125

blessing. So LXX, Vulgate: "For a lawgiver will also give blessings"; Syriac: "With blessings will be covered a lawgiver." (4) Sellin, while translating "teaching righteousness," follows the suggestion of Ehrlich, substituting אוֹת for אֵת, and translates: and has given you "a sign" that teaches righteousness, "since an eschatological prophecy on the order of Mal. 3:1; Is. 42:1 ff., 49:1 ff., would not fit into the context." We shall see that it does.

V. 23. See Gr. N. Another gift is in store for God's people, the greatest gift, the source in fact, of all other gifts of God to sinful man and creation groaning under the curse (Rom. 8:19 ff.). The Covenant God "hath given," the prophetic perfect foretelling a historic fact, will give, or gives (cp. Gen. 12:7; 13:15, "will give"; 13:16, "will make," all perfects, the language of the timeless God). "The Teacher unto Righteousness," see Gr. N. above and marginal reading of A. V. The article demands "the" Teacher, that Prophet foretold Deut. 18:15-19. Hence not Joel (Budde, Orelli, Klostermann), who certainly would not have used such language of himself; nor a series of prophets, including the Messiah (Keil); that would conflict with the definite article and the context speaking of the marvelous result of this gift already promised to mankind in Gen. 3:15. "And He will cause to come down," etc., the imperfect denoting progressive duration, ever anew, the strong *waw* connecting it with the preceding "give" as the consequence or result of the gift. For the sake of Messiah the Lord is gracious and sends rain, *geshem,* the general term; "the former rain," or as thirty-four MSS read, *yoreh,* falling from October to December after the seed is sown, and "the latter rain," *malqosh,* March and April, before the maturing of the grain. If *moreh* is the correct reading, the holy writer may have been induced to use this form in conformity with *moreh,* v. 23 a. It may, however, simply be a copyist's error.

The Messiah teaches a righteousness which He Himself has vicariously procured for mankind by His life, His suffering, His death. And since His words are spirit and life (John 6:63), He appropriates to men by His Gospel His righteousness, and thus is made unto us our Righteousness and Sanctification and Redemption (1 Cor. 1:30). "In the first month," literally, "as the first" (Deut. 17:7; 1 Kings 17:13; Is. 60:9; Zech. 12:7) of all the gifts enumerated vv. 24-26, all prophetic perfects with strong waw connecting these gifts with the sending of the Teacher of Righteousness, whose merits are retroactive (Heb. 9:15), even as Adam and Eve were given also temporal gifts (family, food, and drink) for the sake of Messiah while living on the earth accursed for their sakes (Gen. 3:16-19).

126

Vv. 24-27. "Floors," literally, threshing floors. "Fats" (vats), the reservoir into which the juice of the grapes flowed from the wine press (Is. 5:2; Jer. 48:33); also the wine press (Is. 16:10; Job 24:11). Wheat, wine, oil, the three food staples (cp. 1:10). "Years" (v. 25), plural, because the vineyards and orchards were thoroughly destroyed, robbed of their fertility for years. Whiting writes: "The majority of the groves have been so severely injured as to render them fruitless for several years" (p. 543). This applied also to the grapevines. Since olive oil took the place of meat and butter for the poorer class, the danger of undernourishment and death was a stern reality.

"Eat in plenty" (v. 26), literally, eat an eating and a being satis- fied, not merely nibbling at a few crumbs. Instead of lamentations (1:11), songs of praises will be heard throughout the land in honor of the Lord, who had dealt wondrously with His people, wondrously in sending His righteous judgments, a devastation so sudden and com- plete as no human power could have effected it, and even more wondrously in His rapid and complete deliverance (cp. Is. 28:23-29). "My people." God's own people, chastised, seemingly forsaken, yet chastened and not killed (2 Cor. 6:9). Compare also Is. 40—46, and remember that in Isaiah, as in Joel's prophecy, the Messiah (ch. 53) is in the very center, is the Heart, the Life, of God's Church in the Old and New Testament. "Shall know" (v. 27) by experience. Their faith was strengthened by God's wondrous dealing, experience working hope that maketh not ashamed (Rom. 5:1-6). And, refrainlike, once more the glorious promise: My people shall never be ashamed.

C. The Coming of the Holy Ghost, Ch. 2:28-32 (M. T., 3:1-5)

28 (M. T., 1) It shall come to pass afterward that I will pour out My Spirit upon all flesh. Then shall your sons and daughters prophesy; your old men shall dream dreams; your young men see visions.
29 (M. T., 2) And also upon the slaves and bondwomen I will pour out My Spirit in those days.
30 (M. T., 3) And I will set signs in heaven and on earth, blood and fire
31 (M. T., 4) and clouds of smoke. The sun shall be turned into darkness and the moon into blood before the coming of the Day of the LORD,
32 (M. T., 5) great and terrible! And it shall be that every one who calls upon the name of the LORD shall be delivered. For on Mount Zion and in Jerusalem there shall be an escape, as the LORD has spoken, and among the escaped whom the LORD has called.

Vv. 28, 29 (M. T., 1, 2). "Afterward" points back to "at first" (2:23). The sending of the rain not only manifested the power of God to keep His promise of sending the Messiah, but was at the same time

127

the guarantee of a second promise, the sending of the Holy Ghost in the days of the Messiah. "My Spirit." Already in the Old Testament we are told of the Spirit's activity: in creation (Gen. 1:2); in the work of sanctification (Gen. 6:3), stubbornly resisted; given as a special gift to Moses and the seventy elders (Num. 11:17, 25f); to Joshua (Num. 27:18; Deut. 34:9); Elijah and Elisha (2 Kings 2:9, 15). In the days of the Messiah the Holy Spirit will be poured out "on all flesh," not only given to a few individuals, members of the commonwealth of Israel. While the kindling and preservation of faith in every believing child of God also in the pre-Messianic times was the work of the Spirit of God (Gen. 6:3; Ps. 51:11, 12; 143:10; Is. 63:10), the special gifts of the Spirit were given only to certain individual Israelites. In the days of the Messiah, Savior not only of Israel, but also of all mankind (Gen. 3:15; 12:3; 22:18), the Spirit will be poured out on "all flesh," all mankind. On this usage of "all flesh" cp. Gen. 6:12; Is. 40:6; Jer. 25:31; Zech. 2:13; Jews and Gentiles, Acts 2:8-11, 39, 41; 10:34-47; 11:20, 21; 15:7-12. This does not mean that all men will be filled with the Holy Spirit. A thirsty man may stand at the brink of Mammoth Springs and die of thirst if he refuses to drink water. A man may be offered the full measure of the Holy Spirit and His sanctifying power; he will remain in spiritual death and die eternal death if he refuses, rejects, this gift. "All flesh" is defined as including sons and daughters, young and old, servants and handmaids (v. 29; M. T., 3:2). Irrespective of race or sex or age or social standing (cp. Gal. 3:26-29), God gives His Spirit not in scanty portions, but pours it out in abundant measure, an overflowing supply. The imperfect of progressive duration denotes the ever-renewed outpouring on generation after generation. What a revelation of unknown truths would the story of Bethlehem, of Gethsemane, of Calvary, as told by a little child, be to Moses and Micah and Isaiah and Jeremiah! Cp. Luke 10:24; 1 Peter 1:10 f. Any Christian can prophesy, foretell, the events occurring before and on the great Day of the Lord in far greater detail than did any of the Old Testament prophets. The firm unwavering trust of a Christian child has taught many a Christian parent the nature of true faith and true humility (Matt. 18:3, 4, 6). Many an uncultured "savage" has put highly educated Christians to shame by his zeal to spread the Gospel in the face of persecution and death! Sweet dreams of the Savior's continued presence, glorious visions of the Father's home of many mansions, how often have these results of the Spirit's presence made the weary hours on the sickbed pass more speedily, or revived the drooping spirit of the child of

God harassed by doubts and anxieties and fears! This does not mean that every dream of a Christian is a gift of the Holy Spirit. If a dream or a vision is at variance with any revelation of Holy Writ, it cannot be a gift of the Spirit. While the Spirit guides us into all truth and shows us things to come (John 16:13), His guidance cannot be at variance with what He spoke by the prophets and apostles (1 Peter 1:11; 1 Cor. 2:10-13). This Spirit is poured out on all flesh, freely offered to all mankind. Yet if man rejects this gift, his refusal will not only rob him of the enjoyment of this gift, but even increase his guilt and magnify his punishment.

One more scene in that grand panoramic view of the world's history granted to the prophet is described vv. 30, 31 (M. T., 3:3, 4): the coming of the Day of the Lord and the signs ushering in its coming. His description reminds us of some of the features accompanying the Lord's judgment upon Pharaoh and Egypt ("blood," Ex. 7:17-21; "fire," 9:23-29), and His descent upon Mount Sinai (Ex. 19:16-18). "Wonders" = portents, terrifying omens in the realms of nature and history of great disasters to come. "In the heavens and on the earth." The latter signs are named first. Blood, fire, pillars of smoke, signify bloody wars, conflagrations, pillars of smoke rising to the skies from the cities reduced to ashes by the attacking armies. All the murderous wars and horrifying devastations of cities and whole countries are portents warning mankind of the approach of that Day of wrath (Zeph. 1:14-18). The sun shall turn into darkness (v. 31; M. T., 3:4); not a mere temporary, natural eclipse, but a loss of its illuminating power. "The moon turned into blood," how, we are not told (cp. 2 Peter 3:10; Rev. 6:12, 13). From Matt. 24:6-8, 29 ff. and Luke 21:9, 25-27 we learn the sequence of these portents.

V. 32 (M. T., 3:5). Yet even that Day will not be a day of absolute destruction. The Lord is greater than His Day and all its terrors. All who call on the Covenant God of grace and mercy in humble repentance and confident faith, as Israel did in the locust plague (ch. 2:12-17), shall be delivered, shall escape. "For in Mount Zion," etc., Joel quotes Obad. 17: "as the LORD hath said," not "is the oracle of the LORD," nor "says the LORD." "Deliverance," escape, may be abstract (as, e. g., ch. 2:3; Gen. 32:9; 45:7), but because of the synonymous "remnant" it is better to take it as concrete, "delivered ones," "escaped ones." In Mount Zion, the seat of the LORD's sanctuary, in Jerusalem, the city chosen by the Lord as His abode (Ps. 132:13; 135:21; Zech. 3:2), there will be such as shall escape the destruction of the Lord's Day. In order to avoid any misunderstanding as if the

129

physical Jerusalem and Zion would afford deliverance, the prophet adds a definition of these terms; "and" is the explanatory "and" (cp. Ex. 24:12; 1 Sam. 17:40, "even"; Amos 3:11, "even"). "In the remnant," the preposition stamps this as a synonym of Zion and Jerusalem. The term is derived from a root describing deliverance out of great danger, death, and destruction (see Deut. 2:34; Joshua 10:20, 28-40, "left none remaining," no remnant); then it is used of such as have escaped the judgments coming upon the wicked (Jer. 31:7; Is. 1:9), a synonym of the Hebrew *she'ar*, remnant (Is. 7:3; 10:20-22; 11:11, 16; 28:5), and *she'erit* (Micah 2:12; 5:6), cp. also Rom. 9:27; 11:5; hence the elect of God, plucked by Him as a brand out of the fire (Zech. 3:2); the Church of God, the communion of saints. In this Church, the heavenly Jerusalem (Gal. 4:26; Heb. 12:22), alone is found deliverance, for the Church is the whole number of escaped ones, all those whom the Lord shall call and by His mighty Gospel call make them living members of His Church (Eph. 1:19, 20; 2:4-10). Joel is certainly not a millennialist expecting a restoration of physical Jerusalem.

CHAPTER 3

D. The Coming of Judgment Day, Ch. 3:1-21 (M. T., 4:1-21)

1. The day of retribution for the wrongs done to the Church, ch. 3:1-8 (M. T., 4:1-8)

1 For, behold, in those days and at that time, when I shall turn the captivity of Judah and Jerusalem,
2 then I will assemble all the Gentiles and will lead them down into the Valley of Jehoshaphat and will enter into judgment with them there for My people and My heritage Israel, whom they have scattered among the Gentiles and have
3 divided My land. And they have cast lots for My people: they have given a boy for a harlot and sold a girl for wine that they might
4 drink. Moreover, what are you to Me, O Tyre and Sidon, and all the districts of Philistia? Are you wreaking your vengeance upon Me? If you are avenging your- selves, swiftly and speedily will I turn back your revenge upon
5 your own head, on you who have taken My silver and My gold and My precious treasures into your
6 palaces; and you have sold the peo- ple of Judah and the people of Jerusalem to the Greek people in order to remove them far from
7 their own country. Behold, I am going to rouse them from the place to which you have sold them, and I will turn back your revenge upon
8 your own head. And I will sell your sons and your daughters through the people of Judah, and they shall sell them to the Sabe- ans, to a far-off nation; for the LORD has spoken.

Vv. 1-3. "Those days," that time = the time of the Messiah, the outpouring of the Spirit, the New Testament era. "Bring again the

130

captivity," literally, turn a turning, change the status of Judah and Jerusalem, the people of God, the Church, so that it is no longer restricted to the children of Israel, but is a world-wide Church, "all flesh" (2:28; M. T., 3:1). Valley of Jehoshaphat (v. 2), in the wilderness of Tekoa, southeast of Jerusalem, where the Lord had annihilated the forces of Moab, Ammon, and Edom threatening Jerusalem (2 Chron. 20:1-30). It is also called Valley of Berachah (l. c., v. 26) and Valley of Decision (Joel 3:14). Besides these enemies on the east the prophet names enemies on the west, Phoenicia and Philistia. Phoenicia had been friendly to Israel in the days of David and Solomon, but later had joined hands with Philistia and Edom to harass Judah (2 Chron. 21:10, 16, 17; Obad. 10—16). See notes p. 202. Phoenicia, a trading people, had founded Utica in North Africa ca. 1100 B. C., Carthage ca. 850. Their mercenary spirit led them to the infamous practice of slave trade, buying war captives and selling them to other nations. The Edomites had cast lots for God's people, giving a boy for a harlot, a girl for wine, to satisfy their sordid passions (v. 3). These enemies had also "parted My land," encroaching upon the land given by the Lord to the seed of Abraham (Gen. 15:18-21), and had scattered the Jews among the nations by selling them into slavery. Another enemy is named v. 19, Egypt. All these enemies had had ample opportunity to know the Lord and acknowledge Him as the sovereign God of justice and mercy. Cp. Ex. 15:11-18; Joshua 2:9-11; 1 Sam. 4:5-8. Still they had never submitted to the Lord. Therefore they will be judged in the Valley of Jehoshaphat, will be punished for their arrogance and cruelty.

Vv. 4-8. Turning to Phoenicia and Philistia, the Lord scornfully asks them: What have ye to do with Me? Literally, What are you to Me? Three times the contrast between mortal man, dust and ashes in spite of all his vaunted power and riches, and Jehovah is brought out. What audacity, what presumption, blind, insane, wicked folly for man to oppose God! "Render a recompense," the Hebrew verb means to accomplish, to do something to one, either good (1 Sam. 24:17, 18) or evil (Gen. 50:15, 17; Is. 63:7). Are you requiting evil to Me? The participle denotes a characteristic trait. They sought to return evil to the Lord by opposing Him, harassing His people (vv. 2, 3), thinking to impoverish Him by looting His Temple and carrying its silver and gold and precious vessels to their own palaces and temples (v. 5). The Hebrew word means any great, magnificent house or temple. And if you are doing something against Me, to harm or spite Me, I will swiftly and speedily pay back your deeds, your accomplishments, upon your head. For them a Valley of Jehoshaphat worse than Waterloo!

"Grecians," *Yevanim* (v. 6), descendants of Javan, Ionians (Gen. 10:2, 4; cp. 1 Chron. 1:5, 7; Is. 66:19; Dan. 8:21, etc.), cruelly deported Israelites far from their homes, where they were in imminent contact with idolatry and in danger of joining in it. Yet the Lord will stir them up (cp. Ezra 1:5, same word) out of their heathen environment (v. 7), either physically or spiritually, and will repay the enemies an eye for an eye (Ex. 21:24; Lev. 24:20) by Himself selling their sons and daughters to the Jews (v. 8), who will sell them to the Sabeans in southern Arabia (Job 6:19; Ps. 72:10; Jer. 6:20), as far to the southeast as Javan was to the northwest, "afar off." For the Lord hath spoken!

A like judgment will be meted out to all opponents of the New Testament Church, the Church of Christ. That also will be surrounded by enemies; no longer by Moab and Philistia, but by foes far more powerful, far more resourceful! We think of imperial Rome, of Gnosticism, Arianism, Islam, papal Rome, Rationalism, atheistic Communism. Yet all these enemies of God's Church will have their Valley of Jehoshaphat, when God Himself will judge them either in time or on the Last Day. To this final Judgment the prophet now refers, vv. 9-21.

---

2. The battle of the enemies of the Lord and His Church will end in disastrous defeat, while the Church goes on from glory to glory, ch. 3:9-21 (M. T., 4:9-21)

9 Proclaim this among the Gentiles: Prepare war! Arouse the warriors! Let all the fighting men approach
10 and come up! Beat your plowshares into swords and your pruning hooks into lances! Let the weak
11 say, I am strong. Hurry and come, all you round about, and assemble yourselves! — Thither bring down
12 Thy mighty ones, O LORD! — Let the Gentiles be aroused and go up to the Valley of Jehoshaphat, for there will I sit to judge all Gentiles
13 round about. Put in the sickle, for the harvest is ripe; come, and tread, for the wine press is filled, the vats overflow; for great is their wicked-
14 ness. — Multitudes, multitudes in the valley of decision! For near is the Day of the LORD in the Valley
15 of Jehoshaphat. Sun and moon turn black, the stars withdraw their
16 light. And the LORD roars from Zion and sends His voice from Jerusalem. Then heaven and earth shall tremble. But the LORD is the Refuge of His people and Strength
17 to the children of Israel. And you shall know that I am the LORD, your God, dwelling in Zion, My holy mountain. And Jerusalem shall be holy, and foreigners shall
18 nevermore pass through here. And it shall be that on this day the mountains shall drip new wine, and the hills shall flow with milk, and all the river beds of Judah shall flow with water. And a wellspring shall go forth from the house of the LORD and shall water the Valley
19 of Shittim. Egypt shall be a waste, and Edom shall be a waste wilderness, for the violence done to the children of Judah, in that they shed

20 innocent blood in their land. But Judah shall abide forever and Jerusalem from generation to gen-
21 eration. And I will avenge their

blood which I have not avenged. And the LORD shall be dwelling in Zion!

Grammatical Notes

V. 21. "That I have not cleansed," נִקֵּיתִי, Qal occurs only Jer. 49:12. Niph. = to be free from guilt (Num. 5:31; Jer. 2:35), to be exempt from punishment (Ex. 21:19; Num. 5:19, 28). Pi. = to declare innocent (Job 9:28; Ps. 19:13), to absolve from punishment (Ex. 20:7; Deut. 5:11). Here "declare innocent." God will declare and establish the blood of His people, which was shed by their enemies, as innocent blood by requiring it from the enemies (cp. Gen. 4:10 f.; 9:5 f.; Matt. 23:35; 27:25; Acts 5:28), by punishing them for their murder of His children. — The demonstrative אֲשֶׁר is omitted, as frequently; cp. Gen. 39:4; Ex. 4:13; Job 29:16, etc. G.-K. 155 n. — Others suggest to read נִקַּמְתִּי, avenge, for the first "cleanse."

Vv. 9-11. The Lord issues a proclamation to the Gentiles, the enemies of God and His Church. It is the Lord that challenges them to do their utmost to destroy His Church, for He knows that the gates of hell shall not prevail against it. We hear the enemies encouraging themselves: rousing their mighty men, their leaders of atheism and hatred of God, their men of war, the seasoned antagonists of the Church, to draw near to what in their mind will be the final, victorious assault. Plowshares, pruning hooks (v. 10), the implements of peaceful and useful occupation, are to be used for their destructive purpose; "weak," "no release, no excuse, and no exemption from any cause would be allowed" (Deane, *Pulpit Commentary,* Joel, p. 50). The enemies are intent on using all their resources, bend all their efforts, summon all their strength and skill, for this final over-throw of the Church (Ps. 2:1-3; Rev. 20:7 b-9 a). Joel hears the vast hosts call out to all the heathen, "Assemble yourselves" (v. 11), literally, "Come to help us!" "Come . . . round about," from everywhere! On to victory! Yet the prophet knows that it is the Covenant God, the Lord of His Church, who issues His challenge (v. 9 ff.). He will not and cannot forsake His Church. Though startled at the huge army advancing against the Church, yet in confident faith he turns to the Lord in prayer: Thither, where Thou hast assembled the enemies of the Church, cause Thy mighty ones, Thy heavenly host, to come down, O Lord! (V. 11 b.) Cp. Matt. 13:39-42; 2 Thess. 1:6-10.

Vv. 12, 13. As the Moabites, Ammonites, Edomites had come to Engedi in certain anticipation of victory, only to be annihilated, so the enemies of the Lord in their final attack on His Church will come as far as the Valley of Jehoshaphat, and then the Lord shall say: Job 38:11. There in the valley I sit, I throne, to judge, to condemn, to punish forever My opponents. Their very fury spells their doom. The Lord calls His angels to "put in the sickle" (v. 13), to cut down the wicked as the ripe grain is cut down. "Come, get you down," descend from heaven to do My work of vengeance, tread the wine press filled to overflowing so that even the vats (see 2:24) overflow. So great is the wickedness of God's enemies. Cp. on treading the wine press of God's wrath, Is. 63:1-6; Jer. 25:30; on threshing, Micah 4:12, 13; also Rev. 14:14-20, where both figures are combined.

Vv. 14-18. "Multitudes, multitudes," the word signifies a noisy, vociferous, boisterous crowd; the doubled plural, the immensity of the gathering loudly boasting of their victory to be gained. But it will be the valley of the decision, where God will finally and forever render His decision on His Day, which has then arrived. Suddenly darkness will envelop the multitudes; sun, moon, stars will no more shine (v. 15). And through the blackness of night the Lord will roar with a mighty voice from Zion and Jerusalem (v. 16), His heavenly sanctuary, where He dwells among His people (Ex. 25:8; Joel 3:17). The Church on earth, *ecclesia militans,* and the Church above, *ecclesia triumphans,* are one community of saints. Ah, that Zion, that Church, which the enemies had so confidently hoped to wipe off the face of the earth, is God's own creation, God's own dwelling place, an unconquerable, divine institution! At His voice the heavens tremble; the very earth, on which the hostile hosts are gathered, shakes. Very significantly now a veil is drawn, not a word is stated as to their final punishment. Out of darkness into darkness (Is. 8:22), a darkness too horrible for words! Yet that same Lord, terrible in His just wrath, is the Hope, literally, the Shelter, Refuge Place (Ps. 14:6; Is. 25:4) of His people, the Strength or Fortress (cp. Prov. 14:26; 18:10) of all true Israelites (Rom. 2:28, 29; cp. Joel 2:12, 13). Then shall it become forever evident to all that God dwells in Zion (v. 17), that the Church, the communion of believers in the Savior, is indeed the bride, the wife of the Lamb (Rev. 21:2, 9), immaculately holy (Jer. 31:40; Rev. 7:9, 14, 15; 21:2, 3). No strangers, unbelievers, hypocrites, so often mingled with the visible Church, will be found there even temporarily (Rev. 21:27; 22:3). V. 18 presents a beautiful description of the joy and bliss of that city of God in terms of mundane glory, the foretaste of which God's people possess and enjoy already in this life (Ps. 36:9; Is. 35; Ezek. 47:1-12), the full fruition of which will be theirs in their Father's home above (Ps. 17:15; Rev. 21 and 22). "Valley of Shittim,"

of acacia trees, was the last encampment of Israel (Num. 25:1), from
which they started out to cross the Jordan and enter into the Promised
Land (Joshua 2:1; 3:1). It must have been an oasis of some size, else
the whole nation could not have camped there for several months
(cp. Num. 25:1; ch. 26, the census; ch. 31, war against Midian; Deut.
34:8, thirty days of mourning). This earth is for the Christian a way
station to life eternal (Heb. 13:14). Accursed of God (Gen. 3:17;
5:29), it is watered by the living waters of the Gospel of God's grace,
proceeding from the throne of God (Ezek. 47:1 ff.). Even in Paradise
this stream will be the fount of life and joy (Rev. 22:1, 2).

Vv. 19-21. Egypt, once a friend of Israel (Gen. 46 and 47), then
became an oppressor (Ex. 1—14); Shishak of Egypt was the first to
desecrate the Temple (1 Kings 14:25 ff.); it shall become a desert
(cp. Is. 19; Jer. 46). On Edom, see Obadiah, pp. 194 ff., Jer. 49:7-22.
Both are types of the enemies of the Church, to be punished in divine
avenging of their oppression and shedding of innocent blood. The fulfillment of this threat is to be to future generations the divine guarantee that all the promises of God to His people shall be fulfilled.
Judah and Jerusalem (v. 20), the Church of God, shall abide forever
(Matt. 16:18). On v. 21 see Gr. N. God does not always at once
avenge the blood of His Christians shed for their faithfulness to
Him, though declared to be criminals by the enemies of God (Acts
16:20; 17:6, 7; 1 Cor. 4:9-13). By placing these martyrs at His right
hand on Judgment Day and condemning their murderers the Lord
will declare their blood to be innocent blood, even though He had not
at once punished their murderers (cp. Rev. 6:10, 11). "Dwelleth," the
participle is used, denoting the continuous, uninterrupted, unending
dwelling of Jehovah in the midst of His Church Militant (Eph. 2:22)
and Triumphant (Rev. 21:3). So Joel's prophecy ends on the same
note of triumph as does Obadiah's.

Luther closes his commentary on Joel with a prayer: "O eternal
Father of our Lord and Liberator Jesus Christ, we know what is the
lot of Thy Church in this life and the manifold troubles she must
endure from Satan and the world. Therefore we pray Thee for the
sake of this Thine only-begotten Son that Thou wouldst above all
strengthen our minds by Thy Holy Spirit so that we shall not succumb
in so many dangers; and then, that Thou wouldst frustrate the plans
of the enemies and by Thy faithful and marvelous help wouldst declare
to all the world that Thou watchest over Thy Church and wilt rule,
protect, and save her, who livest and rulest, one eternal God, God the
Father, God the Son, God the Holy Spirit, forever and ever. Amen."

A M O S

God's Impending Judgment upon Israel — A Call to Repentance

PART I
Prophetic Proclamations
Chapters 1—6

A. General Prophetic Proclamations, Chapters 1 and 2

Swift destruction threatened to Israel because, like the surrounding nations and Judah, Israel has rebelled against the Lord.

CHAPTER 1

1. Superscription, v. 1

1 The words of Amos, who was among the shepherds at Tekoa, which he saw concerning Israel in the days of Uzziah, king of Judah, and in the days of Jeroboam, the son of Joash, king of Israel, two years before the earthquake.

On the historical and religious background, see pp. 10—17.

Amos, Hosea, Isaiah, Micah, four great stars in the galaxy of Old Testament prophets, truly noble men of God, trying — alas, vainly — to stem the flood of iniquity engulfing God's people, and their inevitable ruin. Never has the holy Law of God been preached with greater earnestness and intensity than it was proclaimed by these men, who spared neither rich nor poor, neither young nor old, neither vociferous rebel nor unctuous hypocrite. And in no other period of the Old Testament era has the Gospel been heralded in language clearer and sweeter than these men spoke by inspiration of God. Yet all their faithful efforts, all their fervent appeals to their countrymen, could not hold back the overwhelming floodwaters of God's judgment sweeping away a people highly favored but unspeakably wicked and ungrateful. Still they continued in their call to repentance and salvation to a hardened generation, seeing but little success, yet faithful to their high calling. Their message is as timely today as it was more than 2,500 years ago. It is God's Word, enduring forever!

V. 1. Amos, the only person in the Bible bearing this name, derived from a root "to bear," "to place a load upon," both meanings being highly significant and descriptive of the prophet's activity. He was among the herdsmen of Tekoa. The exact meaning of "herdsman," *noqed*, which occurs only once more, 2 Kings 3:4, was unknown already to the Greek translators, who simply transliterated the word νωκηδ, 2 Kings 3:4, ναχκαριμ, Amos 1:1. Lucian has χαριαϑιαριμ, whatever that means. The term is generally regarded to denote a breeder of sheep, since Mesa, the king of Moab (2 Kings 3:4), certainly was no shepherd. This translation does not prove that Amos was wealthy. If the term means sheep breeder, he had a herd of his own, but how large a flock we are not told. That he actually was a shepherd is evident from 7:15: "as I followed the flock," literally, from after the flock, the same phrase used of David, 2 Sam. 7:8, who certainly was a shepherd (cp. 1 Sam. 16:11, 19; 17:15, 20, 28). The fact that he was "an herdman," a cattleman, and a "cultivator of sycamore fruit," 7:14, the fig-mulberry, whose fruit had to be "cultivated," punctured, before being picked, to make it edible, argues neither for his wealth nor his poverty but proves his versatility and willingness to work. It seems, then, that he did not have to become a prophet to "eat bread," 7:12.

"Tekoa," the ruins of which still bear the name Takua, lay on the western slope of the highest ridge running through Judah from south to north. Its name occurs already in the early annals of Judah. It was either founded by Ashur, or Ashur's son was named for the city (1 Chron. 4:5). It lay about six miles southeast of Bethlehem, at the edge of the wilderness of Tekoa, where Jehoshaphat had been granted his miraculous victory (2 Chron. 20:1-30; Joel 3:2, 12, 14). Tekoa had been built on a high hill rising some 2,600 feet above sea level, 3,800 above the Salt Sea (1,275 feet below sea level), 15 to 18 miles eastward, and had been fortified by Rehoboam (2 Chron. 11:6; cp. Jer. 6:1). "On this long descent the first step, lying immediately below the hill of Tekoa, is a shelf of stony moorland with the ruins of vineyards. It is the lowest ledge of the settled life of Judaea. The eastern edge drops suddenly by broken rocks to slopes spotted with bushes of '*retem*,' the broom of the desert, and with patches of poor wheat. From the foot of the slopes the land rolls away in a maze of low hills and shallow dales that flush green in spring, but for the rest of the year are brown with withered grass and scrub. This is the 'Wilderness' or 'Pastureland of Tekoa.' . . ." (*The Expositor's Bible*, IV, 460.) East and south of this wilderness begins the Wilderness of Judah, a chaos of arid hills, a picture of dreary desolation, as its

137

Hebrew name, Jeshimon, indicates, extending along the Dead Sea, the blue waters of which and their red background formed by the hills of Moab can be seen from Tekoa. Here in "this unmitigated wilderness," where "nature excites the faculties of perception and curiosity" . . . Amos "heard the voice of God calling him to be a prophet, and gathered those symbols and figures in which his prophet's message still reaches us with so fresh and so austere an air." (*The Expositor's Bible*, IV, 461.)

---

2. General announcement of judgment, ch. 1:2

2 He said, The LORD shall roar from Zion, and from Jerusalem He shall lift up His voice so that the pastures of the shepherds shall mourn and the summit of Carmel shall wither.

V. 2. "Will roar." The lion roars when he is about to make his last leap so fatal to the victim (Amos 3:4; Is. 5:29). His roaring indicates his hunger and his eagerness to satisfy it (Ps. 22:13; 1 Peter 5:8), his joyful assurance of victory (Is. 5:29), his defiance of any intruder (Judg. 14:5). His roaring, heard far and wide, threatening immediate danger (Jer. 25:30, 31), strikes terror into the heart of man and beast (Amos 3:8).

The Lord roars, Jehovah, the God of the whole earth (Is. 54:5), the Covenant God of Israel (Ex. 19:3-6; Lev. 20:26; cp. Ex. 3:14 ff.; 34:6, 7). If Israel obeys, then Ex. 19:6; if it disobeys, Ex. 20:5.

"From Zion," "from Jerusalem." There stood His Temple, His dwelling place, the place of His revelation (Ex. 25:21, 22; 29:42, 43; 40:33-38; Num. 7:89; Lev. 1:1; 1 Kings 8:10, 11). In protest to the idolatrous sanctuaries of the Northern Kingdom, Amos at the very start calls the attention of Israel to the fact that Jerusalem is the only rightful sanctuary. Men may seek to change the laws of God, but Jehovah is the same forever (Ps. 102:27; Mal. 3:6). His Law does not change because man refuses to obey it. He alone can change or abolish what He has commanded (Jer. 31:31 ff.; Gal. 3 and 4; Col. 2:16 ff.). He still regards the Northern Kingdom as part of His covenant people, yet warns them that He is ready to destroy them.

In a loud voice to be heard in all the land He proclaims His intention, ready to fulfill it, assured of the accomplishment of His revelation. His proclamation is chiefly that of the Law, not merely, however, for the purpose of demanding, threatening, condemning, but for the purpose of bringing them to the knowledge of their transgression and the danger threatening them, in order to crush their hearts, so that the

Gospel may work saving faith in them. The closing words of Amos' prophecies are sweetest Gospel (9:11-15), and that also is included in the "roaring" of the Lord (cp. Hos. 11:10, 11; Rev. 1:10, 15-18).

The Lord's roaring voice at first is exclusively that of the avenging Judge, as the effects prove. The "habitations," the pastures, of the shepherds are naturally the first in the mind of Amos the shepherd, and the first to feel the drought. The steppe, the dry country affording not overly plentiful pasture in favorable seasons, will be parched by drought, will "mourn." The fresh green is the raiment of joyous growth, while the gray somberness of the parched vegetation is the garment of mourning, of lamenting the dying and dead. Creation groans under the curse (Gen. 3:17; Rom. 8:19 ff.).

"Carmel" = a garden, particularly, an orchard or park well cared for (Is. 37:24; 2 Kings 19:23). Here, the proper name of one of the most fruitful and parklike mountain ranges, whose perennial springs outlasted even the three years and six months of drought in Elijah's days (1 Kings 17 and 18). If even Carmel dries out, what will happen to the rest of the land? Ruin, disaster, complete, all-comprehensive. Jehovah is ready to reject His people! Repent before it is too late! That is the very first message of the prophet and remains the burden of his book with the exception of its conclusion.

After this majestic introduction (1:1, 2) Amos reveals the content of the prophecy which Jehovah roars out of Zion. In order to arouse the attention of the people to whom this message is primarily addressed, in order to show them how deeply they were steeped in sin and shame, the Lord begins by describing the wickedness of the surrounding nations and their consequent doom; and finally brings home the lesson that the northern tribes are no better than their sister nation, Judah; and both no less guilty than the despised Gentile nations.

The first nation named is Syria, from whose enmity Israel had suffered most, who was most hateful to them, so that they would gladly listen to a denunciation directed against their age-old rival.

Then comes Philistia, another inveterate opponent of Israel; then Phoenicia, with whom Israel had been more closely connected during the past centuries than with Syria and Philistia. Next in order are three nations related to Israel by kinship, Edom, the descendants of Jacob's brother, Esau, and Ammon and Moab, the descendants of Lot, Abraham's nephew. Still more closely united was Judah, the seventh nation mentioned. The judgment comes ever closer to the northern tribes and finally is pronounced in the eighth oracle (2:6 ff.).

139

The masterly manner in which the judgment coming ever nearer to Israel is pictured has been very properly likened to a thunderstorm approaching from the distant horizon, rolling successively over Syria, Philistia, Tyre, Edom, Ammon, Moab, hitting Judah hard, but bursting with all its force and destructive fury upon unsuspecting Israel, leaving in its wake destruction and utter ruin.

---

3. Against Damascus (Syria), ch. 1:3-5

3 Thus says the LORD: For three transgressions of Damascus, and for four, I will not revoke it, because they have threshed Gilead
4 with iron threshing rollers. So I will send fire into the house of Hazael, and it shall consume the
5 palaces of Ben-Hadad. And I will break the bars of Damascus and cut off the inhabitants from the Valley of Aven and him that holds the scepter from Beth Eden. And the people of Syria shall go into exile to Kir, says the LORD.

Grammatical Note

V. 3. "I will not turn away the punishment thereof," לֹא אֲשִׁיבֶנּוּ, will not cause it to turn = recall, revoke it.

V. 3. Every one of the eight brief oracles begins with "Thus says the LORD." It is not the prophet voicing his own views and desires. It is Jehovah, the just Judge, the Searcher of hearts (Jer. 17:10), that speaks. "For three transgressions and for four." "These words express not four transgressions added to the three, but an additional trangression added to the former; the last sin, whereby the measure of sin, which before was full, overflows, and God's wrath comes. So in other places where the like form of words occurs, the added number is one beyond, and mostly relates to something greater than all the rest." Pusey in loc. cit. (Cp. Job 5:19; 33:14; Eccl. 11:2; Prov. 30:15-31.) "Transgression," literally, revolt, rebellion against the Lord of all the earth (Is. 54:5), the Covenant God of Israel (Ex. 19:3-6). This term is most suitable for idolatry. Choosing an idol as one's god is an act of rebellion and really inexcusable (cp. Ps. 115:4 ff.; Is. 44:9-20; Rom. 1:19 ff.). The sins named here are actually rebellions, crimes of so revolting a nature as to shock everyone that still has a residue of human feelings, outrages against God's Law inscribed in the heart of man and against his own conscience. With the exception of one, these sins are all committed against the covenant people of God. They express the utter contempt in which Israel and Israel's God was held by these nations. They are not sins of ignorance, but conscious and willful disloyalties and opposition against Jehovah. Cp. the Canaanites (Joshua 2:10, 11; 11:19, 20), Philistines (1 Sam. 4:6-9; 6:1-18; 7:7), the blasphemies of Rabshakeh (2 Kings 18:29-35). Another phrase repeated in every oracle is "I will not turn away the punishment thereof" (Gr. N.), literally, I will not revoke, recall, retract it. "It" in a mysterious manner refers to a calamity announced only later and serves to excite the attention of the hearer.

Damascus, one of the oldest still-existing cities (Gen. 15:2), was the capital city of Aram, Syria (Is. 7:8); here it designates the entire nation. The country surrounding it was known for its fertility, watered by the rivers Amanah ("the never-failing") and Pharphar ("rushing") (2 Kings 5:12), fed by the perennial snows of Hermon and Antilebanon. Situated on one of the main trade routes from the Orient to the West and South, it carried on a munificent commerce. On its beauty see Jer. 49:25. This wealthy, proud, luxurious city had committed inhuman cruelties. The reference most likely is to the subjugation of Gilead (extending east of the Jordan from the Sea of Genezareth to the Arnon River) by Syria (cp. 2 Kings 8:12; 10:32 f.; 13:3, 7), reconquered by Jeroboam II. "Threshing instruments," carts with sharp iron teeth attached to rolls which passed over the sheaves to thresh the gain and crush and shred the straw. Syria had made use of such barbarously cruel treatment of the captive Gileadites.

Vv. 4, 5. The royal palaces were to be gutted by fire, left a heap of ruins. "The bolt," collective, the bars closing and fastening the huge city gates, here figuratively of all defensive measures, will be broken down, the city taken. Valley of Aven, perhaps a proper name, site unknown. "Beth Eden," house of pleasure, some beauty spot reserved by the ruling princes, the "scepter holders," as a pleasure resort. Subjects and rulers will be cut off by death, the survivors led into exile back to their former home, Kir (Amos 9:7), near Elam (Is. 22:6), east of the Persian Gulf. "Saith the LORD." Spoken has Jehovah, whose word is as unchangeable as Himself (Ex. 3:14; Is. 65:16).

---

4. Against Philistia, ch. 1:6-8

6 Thus says the LORD: For three transgressions of Gaza, and for four, I will not revoke it, for they have deported the people of entire districts in order to turn them over to 7 Edom. And I will send fire against the wall of Gaza, and it shall con-8 sume its palaces. And I will cut off the inhabitants of Ashdod and him that holds the scepter from Ascalon, and turn My hand against Ekron, and the remnant of the Philistines shall perish, says the Lord LORD.

Grammatical Note

V. 6. "Carried away — the whole captivity." Whole, שְׁלֵמָה, entire captivity, men, women, and children, the entire population, were taken prisoner in order to be sold to Edom as bondslaves. Love of money stifled every trace of human feelings.

Vv. 6-8. Gaza was the chief among the cities of Philistia (named in the inscriptions of Tiglath-Pileser III and Sargon, see Rogers, *Cuneiform Parallels*, pp. 321—331). The Philistines had invaded Israel and depopulated entire, "whole" (Gr. N.), cities and districts, selling the captives to the Edomites, the inveterate enemies of Israel (Amos 1:11; Obad. 10 ff.), who in turn sold them to other nations. Rulers and people of Philistia shall perish to the last man. National extinction! On Gaza see Acts 8:26, and cp. Zeph. 2:4 ff., p. 367.

---

5. Against Tyrus (Phoenicia), ch. 1:9, 10

9 Thus says the LORD: For three transgressions of Tyrus, and for four, I will not revoke it, because they have turned over the entire exiled population to Edom and did 10 not remember the covenant of brethren. And I will send fire upon the wall of Tyrus, and it shall consume her palaces.

Vv. 9, 10. Tyrus, representing Phoenicia, was guilty of the same cruelty as Philistia and increased its guilt by selling these captives in breach of a solemn covenant of brethren. Already David and Solomon had made solemn fraternal covenants with Phoenicia. (Cp. 2 Sam. 5:11, 12; 1 Kings 5, particularly v. 12; 7:13-51; 9:13 "my brother.") This "league" (1 Kings 5:12) or a similar one was violated by Phoenicia. The city shall be destroyed by fire. On the glory and destruction of Tyrus see Ezek. 26—28.

---

6. Against Edom, ch. 1:11, 12

11 Thus says the LORD: For three transgressions of Edom, and for four, I will not revoke it, because he has pursued his brother with the sword and has stifled his pity, and his anger forever kept on tearing 12 to pieces, and his fury he retained forever. And I will send fire upon Teman, and it shall consume the palaces of Bozrah.

Family feuds are often the most irremediable quarrels; the closer the bonds of relationship, the fiercer is the hatred and implacable enmity, once the bonds are severed. Edom, the brother nation of Israel, became the relentless enemy of Israel, stifling his pity, killing his tender feelings in order to kill his hated brother. "Tore asunder," like wild beasts in sheer lust of murder and bloodshed. "Kept forever," guarded, watched over his wrath lest it cease to burn, constantly adding fuel, deliberately seeking cause to feed his wrath. On Teman and Bozrah, see p. 194; Edom's destruction, pp. 299 f.

7. Against Ammon, ch.1:13-15

13 Thus says the LORD: For three transgressions of Ammon, and for four, I will not revoke it, for they have ripped open the pregnant women of Gilead in order to en- 14 large their own boundaries. And I will kindle a fire upon the wall of Rabbah, and it shall consume its palaces with shouting on the day of battle, in a storm on the day of 15 tempest. And their king shall be exiled, he together with his princes.

Vv. 13-15. The Ammonites, descendants of Lot (Gen. 19:30-38), were a seminomadic people occupying the low hills east of Gilead. Their capital, Rabbath-Ammon, was situated south of the headwaters of the Jabbok River. Their boundaries are rather indefinite, though, whenever possible, they sought to enlarge them (cp. Deut. 2:19 f., 37; 3:16) by sudden raids carried out with inhuman cruelties (Judg. 3:13; 10:7-18; 11:4-36; 1 Sam. 11:1 ff.; 14:47, etc.). Their raid against Gilead, when they committed the brutalities mentioned by Amos, occurred perhaps in conjunction with that of Hazael of Syria (2 Kings 10:32; cp. 8:12), whose allies they may have been. As they had raided the cities and cruelly murdered young and old, so their own city shall be suddenly attacked, overwhelmed as by a stormwind, destroyed completely, and king and princes carried into captivity.

CHAPTER 2

8. Against Moab, vv. 1-3

1 Thus says the LORD: For three transgressions of Moab, and for four, I will not revoke it, for they have burnt into lime the bones of 2 the king of Edom. And I will send fire into Moab, and it shall consume the palaces of Kerioth, and Moab shall die amidst tumult, amidst shouting, amidst the blast of 3 trumpets. So I will cut off the judge in her midst, and together with him will I slay all her princes, says the LORD.

The Moabites, also descendants of Lot (Gen. 19:30 ff.), occupied the territory east of the southern half of the Dead Sea, from the Arnon south to the boundary of Edom. They committed the outrage of burning the bones of the king of Edom into lime, to be used as mortar, an unspeakably shameful deed illustrating the depths of depravity to which a highly cultured people, such as the Moabites were, can descend if they reject the Lord and His Word. This outrage may have occurred after Jehoshaphat's campaign against Moab, when Edom, formerly an ally of Moab (2 Chron. 20:20, 22), had joined Judah against Moab (2 Kings 3:5 ff., 26, 27). Kerioth is named as the chief city of Moab (Jer. 48:24, 41). It shall be burned. The nation shall die amidst the "tumult" (cp. Num. 24:17; *Sheth* = tumult, Jer. 48:45) and "shouting" and trumpet blasts of war. The "judge," very likely a synonym for king, and all princes shall be cut off by death or exile (cp. Jer. 48; Ezek. 25:8 ff.).

9. Against Judah, ch. 2:4, 5

4 Thus says the LORD: For three transgressions of Judah, and for four, I will not revoke it, for they have violated the Law of the LORD and have not kept His statutes, and their falsehoods, which their fathers followed, have led them astray. 5 And I will send fire into Judah, and it shall consume the palaces of Jerusalem.

Judah is not charged with such outrages and abominations as are the neighboring states. To the inhabitants of Judah alone was revealed the holy and the gracious will of God, Law and Gospel. They alone were in possession of God's truth. Yet their whole history was the record of their disobedience and despising of God's Law and their following the lies, the falsehoods, the deceptions of lying prophets, who seduced them from God's truth to false doctrines, the inventions of sinful man. This unbelief, this contempt of God's truth was sufficient cause for a punishment like that meted out by the God of justice to the wicked heathen who had not been so highly favored by Him (Luke 12:47, 48; 13:34, 35; 19:41 ff.; Rom. 2:1-29). Only by following the true God and His Word of truth can man escape the wrath of God.

10. Against Israel, ch. 2:6-16

6 Thus says the LORD: For three transgressions of Israel, and for four, I will not revoke it, for they sell the righteous for silver and the 7 needy for a pair of sandals, they who gasp for the dust of the earth on the head of the poor and turn aside the way of the humble; and son and father go into the same maiden in order to desecrate My 8 holy name. At the side of every altar they stretch out on garments taken in pledge, and the wine of those who are fined they drink in 9 the house of their gods. Yet I Myself destroyed the Amorite before them, whose height was like the height of cedars, who were strong as oaks, and I destroyed his fruit 10 above and his roots below. And I Myself brought you up from the land of Egypt and led you forty

years in the wilderness, that you might take possession of the land
11 of the Amorites. I also raised up some of your sons to be prophets and some of your young men to be Nazarites. Is not this so, O children of Israel? is the oracle of the
12 LORD. But you gave wine to drink to the Nazarites, and you commanded the prophets and said,
13 Prophesy not! Behold, I am going to create a stoppage under you, as

the threshing cart stops when it
14 has filled itself with stalks. Then flight shall be lost to the swift, and the strong shall not display his power; and the mighty man shall
15 not save his own life. And the archer shall not stand fast, and the fleet-footed shall not escape nor
16 the horseman save his life. And the stronghearted among the warriors, naked shall he flee on this day, is the LORD's oracle.

Grammatical Notes

V. 7. "Pant," שָׁאַף = to gasp, eagerly (Jer. 2:24; 14:6) long for, desire (Job 5:5; 7:2; 36:20; Ps. 119:131); of a person exerting all his strength to do something (Is. 42:14); eagerness to do harm (Amos 8:4; Ps. 56:2, 3; 57:4). For these last passages some assume a different root meaning: crush, bruise. — "To profane," לְמַעַן חַלֵּל, in order to profane, for the purpose of profaning, deliberately to profane.

V. 13. "Pressed." מֵעִיק and תָּעִיק occur only here. LXX, κυλίω = to roll; Vulg., to groan; Luther, kirren, groan, squeak; Hitzig and Wellhausen change to מֵפִיק,

sway; Keil, עוק is Aramaic for צוק, to press. Wetzstein, ZAW 3, 278, suggests an Arabian root = to stop, hinder, obstruct, which is offered by G.-B. and adopted by Sellin and others: "I will cause a stoppage." — The "cart," הָעֲגָלָה (לְהּ dat. incommodi), denotes not only a wagon (Gen. 45:19, 21, 27, etc.), but the threshing cart or sledge (Is. 28:27, 28). This meaning suits the context better than any other. — "Sheaves," see Jer. 9:22 (handful); Micah 4:12; Zech. 12:6. — The cart is stopped by the sheaves which fill up the rollers under the platform.

Now the storm gathering ever closer breaks in full fury upon the Northern Kingdom. We hear the accusing thunder of Jehovah's accusations (vv. 6-12); we see the destructive lightning flashes of His holy wrath (vv. 13-18). Israel had rebelled against the Lord by instituting the calf worship (1 Kings 12:19, 26 ff.; 14:8 f.). In the course of years it had degenerated to such a degree that there was little difference between this nation and its heathen neighbors. Throughout His charge the Lord stresses the fact that Israel is guilty of transgression, revolt against the Lord's Law (social injustice, incest, riotous idolatry, vv. 6-8), against His people (righteous, v. 6; meek, v. 7), against His blessings (vv. 9-12).

Vv. 6, 7 a. The righteous were sold for silver. The special hatred of the people and their social and civic leaders was directed against the righteous still remaining in the country, whose very righteousness, expressed in their lives, their words, their practices, was a con-

145

stant thorn in the flesh of the wicked. Hardhearted Shylocks, greedy money lenders, venal judges, all alike, suffered from the accursed hunger for gold, for money, for even a few pennies. After they had impoverished the righteous man by their trickeries, they sold him into slavery for a pittance, for a few pieces of silver, for the price of a pair of sandals. What despicable contempt of the rights of their fellow man, what shameful greed! They "pant after" (v. 7 a, see Gr. N.), eagerly desire, do all they can to place dust on the head of the poor, a symbol of sorrow and distress (Joshua 7:6; Ezek. 27:30; Job 2:12; Lam. 2:10). For this purpose they seek every means of humbling others, "turn aside," bend, distort, the way of the "meek," those who are still submitting to God's will as His obedient servants. These wicked men rejoice at every opportunity to make the difficult way of God's children still harder by frustrating their plans, doing all in their power to bring the meek on the way to ruin. For themselves, silver and gold; for others, dust and ashes; for themselves, luxuries and enjoyment; for others, poverty and sorrow; for themselves, success; for others, ruin and disaster!

V. 7 b. We see son and father on their way to a maiden, not in order to teach her the Lord's will, but to satisfy their own carnal lust. Their sin is not to be restricted to intercourse with the Temple harlots, the *kedeshim,* since the Hebrew word means a girl, a maiden. She need not even have been a public harlot. Intercourse of father and son with one woman was incest (Lev. 18:7, 15; 20:11), a mortal sin. Yet in deliberate revolt against God's will, for the very purpose of profaning (Gr. N.), defiling God's holy name, they committed this outrage, defying God and man to punish them. "What do we care?"

V. 8. They stretch out garments on the ground in order to keep their own clothing clean and unspotted. They used their poor neighbor's clothes given as pawns for loans, which were to be restored to the owner before sundown (Ex. 22:26, 27), in flagrant disobedience, in rebellion against God's Law. "By every altar," regardless of whether it was nominally Jehovah's altar (1 Kings 12:28) or the altar of Baal or some other idol, wherever they could manage to attend one of the riotous festivities. There they sought to quench their insatiable thirst with wine of the condemned, wine bought by the fines assessed against those whom they had prosecuted or condemned. This is another proof of their contempt of their neighbor and their utter disregard of God's Law. The Lord disavows any connection with these idols and their worshipers by calling the idols "their gods," man-made gods, unworthy of the name. Pusey makes the following comment on this last clause, "they drink," etc.: "In five words He condemns their luxury, oppression, perversion of justice, cruelty, profaneness, unreal service, and real apostasy. What hardheartedness to the willfully forgotten poor is compensated by a little churchgoing!"

Vv. 9-12. Israel's rebellion against God's blessings. God had destroyed, annihilated the powerful Ammonites, whose measure of sin was full (Gen. 15:10; Lev. 18:24 ff.), in order to give their land to Israel, whom he had miraculously delivered out of Egypt and faithfully led through the wilderness into the land He had promised to their fathers. He had given them prophets, Moses, Joshua, Deborah (Judg. 4:4), Samuel, Elijah, Elisha, the hundred prophets hidden by Obadiah (1 Kings 18:13), etc., and Nazarites (Num. 6:1 ff.) from their own midst. Yet in open rebellion they had told the Nazarites to drink wine (Num. 6:3) and the prophets to cease prophesying. Disobedience, transgression, revolt!

Vv. 13-16. God's sentence upon the rebels. "I am pressed." (Gr. N.) I shall cause a stoppage, an obstruction, as a cart (Gr. N.), a threshing sledge, stops when it is full of sheaves. The threshing cart consisted of three or more rollers set in a heavy wooden frame surmounted by the driver's seat. These rollers were attached to wheels on the outside of the framework, and if either the wheels or the rollers were clogged by the sheaves of grain over which the sledge was drawn by oxen, the sledge was stopped from further progress until the obstructing sheaves had been removed. Israel's military machinery, running smoothly under God's blessing, rolling on to victory, crushing the most powerful enemy (cp. Ex. 17:8 ff.; 1 Sam. 7:7-14; 2 Chron. 14:6-15; 20:1-30), would suddenly be stopped by the Lord. There is the swift, to whom flight is lost; the strong, who no longer can strengthen his force, no longer muster up sufficient courage to fight against the enemy; the mighty man, the man of heroic deeds, who cannot save his own life; the bowmen, usually forming a solid phalanx, who no longer can stand in line to meet the attacking army; the swift of foot, who, so often outrunning and slaying the fleeing enemy, cannot deliver himself from death or captivity. The rider on a horse cannot save his life; and even the stoutest of heart among mighty heroes can escape only with his bare life; the bravest of the brave, naked will he flee! Disorder, confusion, panic, defeat, ruin, perdition on this day coming ever closer. That is not the fantastic nightmare of a timid, despairing soul. It is the oracle of the Lord, who is about to fulfill His threat (Deut. 28:15-68; Heb. 10:31).

B. Five Specific Prophetic Proclamations, Chapters 3 to 6

1. Three judgment oracles, each beginning with "Hear ye!" Ch. 3:1—5:17

CHAPTER 3

a. Hear ye! Your ingratitude hastens the approach of God's judgment! Vv. 1-15

1 Hear this word which the LORD speaks concerning you, O children of Israel, concerning all the tribes which I have brought up from the
2 land of Egypt, saying, Only you have I known of all the families of the earth; therefore will I punish
3 you for all your iniquities. Can two keep on walking together unless
4 they are agreed? Will the lion roar in the jungle unless he has a prey? Will a young lion let forth his voice from his lair unless he has caught
5 something? Does a bird fall into a snare to the ground when there is no trap for it? Does a snare rise from the ground without having
6 caught a catch? When a trumpet is blown in a city, do not the people begin to tremble? If an evil occurs in a city, has the LORD not
7 wrought it? Surely, the Lord LORD will not do a thing unless He reveals His counsel to His serv-
8 ants, the prophets. The lion does roar, who will not fear? The Lord LORD does speak, who will not
9 prophesy? Make a proclamation over the palaces in Ashdod and above the palaces in the land of Egypt, and say, Gather together on the mountains of Samaria, and behold the great restlessness within her and the oppression in her midst.
10 They do not know to do what is right, is the oracle of the LORD, amassing violence and oppression
11 in their palaces. Therefore thus says the Lord LORD, An enemy; And surrounding the land! And he will deprive you of your power and
12 pillage your palaces. Thus says the LORD, As the shepherd rescues out of the lion's jaws two shinbones and an ear lappet, so will the children of Israel be rescued that sit in Samaria on the corner of the divan and on damask couches.
13 Hear, and testify against the house of Jacob, is the oracle of the Lord
14 LORD, the God of Hosts! For on the day that I shall punish the transgressions of Israel, I will punish the altars of Bethel, and the horns of the altar shall be broken, and they shall fall to the ground.
15 And I will smite the winter house together with the summer house, and the ivory houses shall perish, and there shall be an end to many houses, is the oracle of the LORD.

Grammatical Notes

V. 3. "Walk together," יֵלְכוּ, progressive imperfect = keep on walking together. — "Be agreed," נוֹעָדוּ. The perfect here denotes an act completed in the past whose effects still continue; the agreement is still valid. יָעַד, to appoint (2 Sam. 20:5; Jer. 47:7; Micah 6:9); Niph., to meet at an appointed place (Ex. 25:22; 29:42, 43; Num. 10:4, "gather"; so also 14:35; 16:11; 27:3). It never denotes an accidental meeting, the meeting is always at an appointed place, by agreement.

V. 6. "Shall there be." The imperfect vividly pictures the progress of evil, from its beginning, through its gradual development, to its final accomplishment, and throughout the whole procedure the Lord "has done" every detail, עָשָׂה, perfect.

V. 12. "In Damascus in a couch." עֶרֶשׂ, bed, divan (cp. Amos 6:4; Ps. 6:7; Prov. 7:16, etc.), ‎. Damascus is always written with , and never with a simple shwa under ד. The rendering "damask," a silken fabric made at or imported from Damascus, is not provable, since it rests on barest assumption. The exact meaning of the clause remains uncertain; very likely some article of luxury is intended.

V. 13. "In" the house of Jacob, ‏ל‏ here = against. Sellin, who regards the Israelites as the testifiers, changes "Jacob" to "Jeroboam," since Israel could not testify against itself and since Amos never calls Israel "the house of Jacob." He calls Amos 9:8 b spurious, "since it disturbs the connection between v. 9 and v. 8 a." As we shall see, it does not do that.

Vv. 14, 15. "Altars" — "altar" — "winter house" — "summer house" — "houses of ivory" — "great houses." One plural and one collective singular is followed by two collective singulars and two plurals. Note the chiastic form; the three collective singulars between two groups of plurals.

Vv. 1, 2. Very definitely the term "children of Israel" (cp. 2:11; 4:5) is interpreted by the Lord as including the whole "family," the twelve tribes. While spoken primarily to Israel, Judah is included in the very address. This is evident also from v. 2, which cannot be restricted to the ten tribes. "Only," "you," "I knew," three words of equal emphasis. "Only" is emphasized by its position; "you," by the employment of the full personal pronoun instead of the mere suffix. "I knew," emphatic by position. No other nation but the children of Israel, the twelve tribes, was privileged to be the object of that affectionate and effective knowledge which the unchanging Lord granted to Israel and whereby He chose this one nation before all other nations to be His own peculiar people (Ex. 19:5, 6; Deut. 4:7; 32:34; Ps. 147:19, 20). On this sense of "know" cp. Ex. 33:12, 13, 17; John 10:13-15, 27 f.; Rom. 8:29; 1 Peter 1:2. This unique distinction implied a special obligation of love and obedience (Ex. 19:5), a greater responsibility, and the certainty of severest punishments if they despised this singular honor (Lev. 26:14 ff.); note the term "seven times," repeated four times (Lev. 26:18, 21, 24, 28; cp. Luke 12:48).

Vv. 3-7. In a series of seven questions the Lord teaches a lesson in clear logical thinking in matters pertaining to religion and salvation, and warns against self-delusion by being satisfied with hazy ideas, haphazard surmises, happy-go-lucky reliance on misunderstood and misinterpreted truths and half-truths. "Walk together," "agreed." (See Gr. N.) The Lord had appointed a meeting with Israel (Ex. 19—24). He had expressed His willingness to walk with them under certain conditions (Ex. 19:5; 20:1-17), which they had accepted (ch. 19:8; 24:3, 7, 8). Now God asks: How can we continue to walk together as we have through the centuries if you no longer are agreed

to walk with Me, loving Me, obeying Me, serving Me as you agreed
to do? Your disagreement with Me will be the cause of your irrevers-
ible destruction, your ruin, the inescapable effect of your refusal to
keep on walking with Me. I warn you before our ways will be definitely and forever parted! That day is fast approaching! Are not all
events pointing to the fact that we are close — perilously close for
you — to the parting of our ways? Can you not read the signs of
the times? Have you lost the ability to understand the interrelation
of cause and effect and to apply this relation to your present situation?
Will a lion roar in the forest (v. 4) unless his victim is doomed?
Will the young lion send out his triumphant voice if he has not taken
his prey to his lair and is ready for the feast? You know that well
enough! Now the Lord is roaring against you (ch. 1:2; 2:4-16)! He is
ready to destroy you! Why, then, are you so unconcerned, why so
callous against His warnings, as if no danger were threatening, no
harm could come to you? — I ask you: Does a bird ever fall into
a snare on the earth (v. 5) unless that snare is placed there by some·
one for the purpose of catching a bird? If you see a snare rising up
from the ground, must there not be a reason for such rising? You
know that a bird must have been caught, that the purpose of setting
the snare has been accomplished. Why, then, can you not understand
the handwriting on the wall? War, drought, famine, pestilence do not
come by accident! They are sent as snares, as instruments of your
destruction! Are you so blind as to be unable to reason from effect to
cause, that behind these calamities stands the Lord, who is now fulfilling His threats against His apostate people? When people going
about their business or amusement in the city suddenly hear the shrill
blasts of the watchman's trumpet (v. 6), will they not be gripped with
fear and terror? I am blowing the trumpet! Have you no ears to
hear? Israel might object: Drought, famine, losses, wars are to be
expected in the life of a nation. We cannot always have peace and
plenty! Why worry? Better days will come again! The Lord will not
and cannot forget His own people! The Lord tells them: Shall there
be (Gr. N.) an evil in the city and the Lord hath not done it? Local
and national calamities are not due merely to natural causes, are not
only the consequence of human mistakes, or faulty legislation, or
political folly, or inadequate statesmanship. These and other matters
may be contributory causes. The final Author of all evil (and all
good) is the *Lord*. He has done it! (Cp. Is. 45:7.) Yet this Lord is
not an arbitrary tyrant who destroys for the sheer lust of murder
(v. 7). Even when He does evil, He remains the same, unalterable

(Ex. 3:14) God of mercy and justice (Ex. 34:6, 7), who does what He does from a just cause and for a just and merciful purpose. The cause is man's sin, against which God has warned man time and again. The purpose is to warn man against rebelling against his Creator and call the sinner to repentance, back to his God, the highest Good, man's only Savior. This merciful God (Ezek. 33:11-20) assures His people that He will do nothing unless He has revealed His plans, conceived in His secret counsel, to His prophets, and they in turn have raised the word of warning to all people. In His sure Word of prophecy we have His revelation, given by inspiration of God for doctrine, for reproof, for correction, for instruction in righteousness (2 Tim. 3:16). If only all men would search these Scriptures! (Is. 8:13-22; 2 Peter 1:19-21.)

V. 8. The prophet makes the final application. The Lord has roared! The prophet is not merely a calamity howler, he is God's spokesman; merely an announcer of God's secrets revealed to him, to be transmitted by him to his people. Why blame the prophet for speaking as he does? Why tell him to remain silent (ch. 2:12 b)? God has spoken! Why should not His prophet speak? How can he remain silent? (Cp. Jer. 20:9.) And why should not the people hear his warnings? Why not incline their ear and hear so that their soul might live? (Is. 55:3.) Why will ye die, O house of Israel? (Ezek. 33:11.)

Vv. 9, 10. Israel was called to be a bright and shining example of godliness and righteousness to the surrounding nations (Deut. 4:5-8). Its light had changed to almost heathen darkness. And now God calls upon the Philistines and Egyptians to assemble round about Samaria in order to view the wickedness of Israel and witness its destruction. The city of Samaria was built on a high hill rising 300 feet from the surrounding fertile plain. Omri had bought this hill from its former owner, Shemer, and named the city for him (1 Kings 16:23 f.). This hill was encircled by mountains still higher, from which one could look into the city. The foreigners were to behold the "tumults," riotings, revolts, unrest (cp. 2 Chron. 15:5), "vexations." Scenes of violence, rioting mobs, cruel oppression, gangster rule, were everyday affairs. Such conditions were the result of rejecting the light of God's Word (v. 10). Idolatry leads into darkness and ignorance of what is right, as Modernism with its questionable morality plainly shows. Samaria seemed to prosper. Huge palaces, stately mansions, were built in which the rich enjoyed every available comfort and convenience. Amos calls these riches "violence," wrong, cruelty, and

151

"robbery," oppression (cp. Jer. 22:13), because they were obtained by violence and robbery.

Vv. 11, 12. The Lord's judgment. The Lord sees what is still invisible and unbelievable to these wicked nabobs: an enemy surrounding the city on all sides. The enemy is not yet named, not because the Lord does not know him, but in order to keep Israel in agonized uncertainty. Note the sudden dramatic change from riches and wickedness to the siege! The seemingly impregnable fortress will be taken, its palaces robbed of all the loot and plunder amassed there by oppression, the city completely destroyed. There is not much hope for the survival of a lamb of which only two legs, shinbones, and the tip of an ear remain undevoured by the bear (v. 12). So complete shall be the ruin of Samaria, the luxurious city, and the downfall of its wealthy inhabitants who sat in the corner of a bed, a divan, a soft couch, snug and cozy "and in Damascus in a couch" (Gr. N.), a phrase that defies exact translation, undoubtedly also referring to some elegant piece of furniture.

Vv. 13-15. Hear ye! The Lord still addresses the heathen foreigners whom He had summoned to behold Israel's wickedness and destruction. They are to hear, listen attentively to what the Lord has to say, and of course to apply it to themselves. Yet they are also to testify "in" (Gr. N.), rather, against the house of Jacob, the sinful nation, and pronounce God's judgment upon Israel (v. 14). They refused to hear their own prophets (ch. 2:12 b; 7:13). Now the Lord sends heathen messengers, the uncircumcised Philistines, the idolatrous Egyptians as His heralds of destruction! What a humiliation for proud, supercilious Israel! These foreigners, worshipers of idols, are to teach God's chosen people the wickedness and dire consequences of false worship; are to pronounce the Lord's judgment on the covenant breakers. God will visit the altars (Gr. N.) of Bethel. Evidently a number of altars had been erected there since Jeroboam had built the first one. The Lord will not come as the Lord of mercy and forgiveness to honor these altars with His gracious presence. He will come to destroy them. These altars are part of the transgressions, the revolts of Israel. Idolatry is rebellion against the Lord, and the fruitful mother of all transgressions and rebellions. The horns of the altar shall be cut off. The horn was a symbol of strength, dominion, honor (1 Sam. 2:1, 10; Ps. 89:18, A. V., 17; 92:11, A. V., 10; Amos 6:13); the four horns on the four corners of the altar of burnt offering (Ex. 27:2), to which the sacrificial blood was applied (Ex.

29:12; Lev. 4:25, 30, 34; 8:15), were symbolic of sure, reliable forgiveness and salvation, defending the sinner against the accusations of Satan and his own conscience. To these horns clung the guilty transgressors for safety (1 Kings 1:50 f.; 2:28-38; cp. Ex. 21:14). Even the symbols of salvation were to be struck off the altars of Bethel, which had neither God's permission nor promise, no right of existence, no authority to forgive sins, no power to save. Though nominally erected in honor of Jehovah, they were evidences of Israel's rebellion, an abomination to the Lord, ready to be destroyed. Together with these altars the stately mansions of the rich were to perish (v. 15). Winter house and summer house may refer to separate apartments in the same house (Judg. 3:20; Jer. 36:22), or to different residences, according to the season. Ahab's palace at Jezreel evidently was his summer home (1 Kings 21:1; 2 Kings 9:30 ff.). "Ivory houses," whose walls and furniture were embellished by ivory plaques or small panels attached to the furniture and inlaid in the walls (cp. 1 Kings 22:39; 10:18, Solomon's throne; Ps. 45:9). "Great houses," the stately mansions of the rich; others, many houses. Such is "the oracle of the LORD," to be transmitted to Israel by their heathen neighbors (cp. 2 Kings 18:25; 2 Chron. 35:21; Jer. 40:2 f.; 50:6, 7).

CHAPTER 4

b. Hear this word, ye kine of Bashan! Vv. 1—13

(1) Luxurious life changed to shameful captivity, vv. 1-3

1 Hear this word, you cows of Bashan, you who are on the mountain of Samaria, who oppress the poor, do violence to the needy; who tell their lords, Bring, that we may 2 drink! The Lord LORD has sworn by His holiness, Behold, days are coming upon you that they will drag you away with hooks, and the 3 last of you with fishhooks. And you will go through the breaches, each woman straight ahead; and you will be cast away toward Hermon, is the oracle of the LORD.

Grammatical Notes

V. 1. "Kine," פָּרוֹת is feminine; yet the suffixes and personal pronouns are partly feminine, partly masculine: oppress, masculine; crush, say, feminine; masters, upon you, take you, masculine; your posterity, feminine. This change in gender can hardly be due to relaxation in differentiation of the genders (G.-K. 135 a). Amos knew the difference between masculine and feminine forms. He used both forms in order to indicate that the "kine," while primarily women, included also the men. In a similar manner the term "daughters of Jerusalem" in the Song of Songs is with one exception (ch. 3:11) construed as a masculine (cp. 2:7; 3:5; 5:8; 8:4; "queens," ch. 6:8, 9; "flock," usually masculine, is feminine and masculine in ch. 4:2). We are to think of ideal personages, men and women, young and old. V. 2. "He will take you away," either

153

Jehovah, or the third person is used indefinitely, one will take you away, you shall be taken away (G.-K. 144 d). In neither case is the enemy, who of course is Jehovah's instrument, named. V. 3. "Cast into the palace," וְהִשְׁלַכְתֶּנָה. The fuller form of the second person plural feminine suffix occurs only here, although the personal pronoun occurs in the fuller form four times (Gen. 31:6; Ezek. 13:11, 20; 34:17); the simpler form only once (Ezek. 34:31). (G.-K. 32 i.) הַהַרְמוֹנָה. This statement has not found a satisfying solution. It seems best to read הַהֶרְמוֹנָה, toward the Hermon, the accusative of direction, and read the Hophal instead of Hiphil; you shall be cast toward the Hermon.

Vv. 1-3. The Lord compares the inhabitants of Samaria, particularly the women, to kine (Gr. N.), cows, of Bashan. Bashan was noted for the excellency of its cattle, luxuriating, growing fat and sleek on the rich pasture lands (cp. Deut. 32:14; Micah 7:14). The men of Samaria were habitual oppressors of the poor, the weak and lowly; the women, just as cruel, crushed the needy, destitute. Not a day passes but these petted, pampered society ladies cry to their lords for money. "Lords" they call their husbands, yet these husbands are the slaves of their wives, must obey their every whim or suffer the consequences. Give! Give! Money! Cash! In order to satisfy their insatiable lust for luxuries, drinking parties, riotous banquets, the men must furnish the money. And the men obtain the money by cruel, heartless oppression of the lower classes. Madam Nabob sits in luxury, dines and wines, and whines for money; her lowly sister together with her family must work — work — work; their labor never flags! And what are their wages? A bed of straw, a crust of bread, and rags. (Cp. Hood's "Song of the Shirt," st. 6.) These poor unfortunates have no human friend to plead their cause. The Lord rises up as their Vindicator (v. 2). He swears by His holiness, His exalted majesty, His separation from all that is sinful, His hatred of all that is evil and all that are evil (Ps. 5:4, 5; 11:5). "He will take you away." They will be dragged off into captivity "with hooks," and their posterity, their remnant = every last one of them (cp. Amos 9:1), with fishhooks. The *Senjirli stela*, discovered 1888 in northern Syria, commemorates Esarhaddon's victory over Taharka of Egypt. The Assyrian king is shown holding in his left hand ropes extending to the lips of two captive kings. Our text may refer to this Assyrian custom, or Amos may picture Samaria as a fishpond round which the enemy sits on the encircling mountains and draws out one captive fish after the other, until none are left.

"At the breaches" (v. 3), through the broken-down walls and

gates the women are led away, every woman walking straight ahead. No longer as in her heyday does she look around to see whether she and her fineries are duly observed. No, bowed down in shame, she looks neither to the right nor left, stares straight ahead, hoping no one will see her. "Ye shall cast them into the palace" (Gr. N.), rather, you shall be cast out toward Hermon, the mountain range north of Palestine. As the Lord does not name the enemy, so He does not reveal the exact location of the place of their exile (cp. 3:11; "beyond Damascus," 5:27; "in a polluted land, forth of his land," 7:17). Hermon lay on the northern boundary of Bashan, hence a proper place for the kine of Bashan, who were out of place in God's land.

---

(2) The Lord's call to rebellious Israel: Prepare to meet thy God! Ch. 4:4-13

4 Come to Bethel and trespass! At Gilgal multiply trespasses! And bring your sacrifices every morning and your tithes every third day.

5 Burn a thankoffering of leavened bread, and noise abroad your vows, proclaim them! For so you love it, O children of Israel! is the oracle

6 of the Lord LORD. And I also, I have given you cleanness of teeth in all your cities, and lack of food in all your places. Yet you did not return to Me, is the oracle of the

7 LORD. And I Myself also withheld the rain from you, while there were still three months till harvest. And I let rain fall upon one city, and upon another I did not let rain fall. One section was rained upon, while a section on which it did not rain

8 dried up, so that two or three cities staggered to one city in order to drink water, but were not satisfied. Yet you did not return to Me, is the

9 oracle of the LORD. I smote you with blight and with mildew repeatedly. Your gardens, your vineyards, your fig trees, and your

olive trees the locust devoured. Yet you did not return to Me, is the

10 oracle of the LORD. I have sent a pestilence among you in the manner of Egypt; I have slain your young men with the sword, while at the same time your horses were carried off, and I brought up the stench of your camps even into your noses. Yet you did not return unto Me, is the oracle of the LORD.

11 I have overturned some of you as God overturned Sodom and Gomorrah, and you were like a brand plucked out of the fire. Yet you did not return unto Me, is the

12 oracle of the LORD. Therefore, thus will I do to you, O Israel! Because I will do this to you, prepare to meet your God, Israel!

13 For behold, He who formed the mountains and created the wind, and reveals to man what His plan is; who makes dawn darkness and treads on the heights of the earth: Jehovah, the God of Hosts, is His name.

Grammatical Notes

V. 4. "Every morning," "after three years." לְ is distributive in both phrases (cp. Gen. 49:27; Ps. 30:6; 59:17). — "Years," יָמִים, days, every triad of days = every third day.

V. 5. "Offer," קַטֵּר. The inf. abs. may be used for any form of the verb, here plural imperative. The Qal = to smoke, is not used. Pi. = to cause to smoke, to burn (of illegitimate sacrifices, 2 Kings 18:4; 22:17, etc.).

V. 6. "Returned unto." עַד implies arrival at this goal (Gen. 11:31; 50:11).

V. 10. "Manner," דֶּרֶךְ, literally, way, here in sense of custom, manner (cp. Gen. 19:31; 31:35; Is. 10:24, 26). — "Have

taken away, עִם שְׁבִי סוּסֵיכֶם, together with the captivity of horses = together with the captured horses.

V. 13. "Thought," שֵׂחַ, derived from שִׂיחַ, to think, meditate (Ps. 119:15, 23, 48, etc.); never used of God's plans.

Vv. 4, 5. Gilgal, near Shechem (cp. Hos. 4:15; 9:15; Amos 5:5). Israel's sacrificial cult, the calf worship, so zealously observed, is actually a revolt against the Lord; a "multiplying," a constant repetition of the sin of Jeroboam (1 Kings 12:26 ff.; 14:9 f.; 15:26, 30, 34, etc.). God tells the people to continue in their "transgression," rebellion (see Gr. N. on "transgression," ch. 1:3). They are to bring their sacrifices every morning (Gr. N.), and their tithes, which were to be paid annually (Lev. 27:30) and a second tithe triennially (Deut. 14:28), "after three years" (Gr. N.), rather, every third day. They are to continue to "offer" (v. 5) (Gr. N.), to burn, leavened bread or cakes contrary to God's command (Lev. 2:11; 7:12, 13); to give their freewill offerings (Lev. 7:16; 22:18-23) in the spirit of self-glorification, of flamboyant proclamation and boastful publication (cp. Matt. 6:1-18). Such worship they liked, because it pleased their self-righteous spirit (cp. Luke 18:11, 12). Yet they are not to make the mistake of thinking that the very frequency and the volume of their gifts and sacrifices and tithings were pleasing to God. He saw only the rebellious spirit which made the people and their offerings an abomination to Him. He speaks to them in bitter irony, commanding them to keep on in their rebellion. When the heathen deliberately disregarded the Law of God written in their hearts and in the book of nature, God surrendered them to unnatural lusts and sins before finally destroying them (Rom. 1:20 ff.). So God announces to highly favored Israel, who knew His Law by special revelation, that He is now ready to surrender them to their rebellion and stubborn refusal to return to Him. He turns them over to sin and Satan. No longer will He restrain them from heaping revolt upon revolt, so that His judgments may be heaped upon them in the day of His reckoning with these ungrateful rebels.

Vv. 6-11. Already His judgments had begun. Five judgments are named, and five times the charge is repeated that they had refused to heed His warning, had continued in their rebellious state. Sellin remarks that it is not necessary to assume that the calamities occurred within a short time, perhaps during Jeroboam's rule, although that is not impossible. God is dealing here with the life not of an individual, but of a nation. The events may have been separated by decades and centuries. Nor is the sequence necessarily that of time; some of the judgments may have been repeated a number of times. The sequence, rather, is climactic, from lesser to greater. "Cleanness of teeth" is defined as want of bread; lack of anything to put between the teeth. This want was not confined to the crowded cities; it was nation-wide. Yet Israel ignored the warning. They did not return "unto" God. If they made an attempt at repentance, it stopped before it reached its goal, true union with God. God withheld rain at the time it was needed for the proper maturing of the crops (v. 7). In order to prove that He had not lost His power, He sent rain to some fields and cities, while others lacked rain completely, so that the rivers dried out and people had to go long distances for a scanty supply of water. And still they did not return to God! (V. 8.) The Lord sent "blasting" (v. 9) caused by hot winds, drying up, burning up, killing all vegetation. (Cp. Gen. 41:6, 27; Deut. 28:22.) "Mildew," blight (Deut. 28:22), spoiling what little survived or revived after the hot winds. When gardens, vineyards, and orchards promised rich harvests, God sent the "palmer worm," the locust, literally, gnawer (Joel 1:4; 2:25; Deut. 28:39). Yet stubbornly Israel clung to its rebellion, seeking help from its calves instead of the Lord.

God sent pestilence (v. 10), epidemics, after the "manner" (Gr. N.) of Egypt, which was, as the Roman historian Pliny calls it, the mother of contagious diseases. He sent war, so often accompanied by epidemics in the crowded, unsanitary camps, so that sword and sickness slew the young men, the hope of the nation, "and have taken away" (Gr. N.), rather, together with the horses you had captured. Initial victories were followed by defeat and disastrous epidemics, so that the stink of their camps came up to their nostrils. But even this stench did not remind them of their sin and the great need of repentance. Obstinately they retained their false worship, refused to turn back to the Lord. God had sent earthquakes among them (v. 11), overthrowing (same word as Gen. 19:25, 29; Deut. 29:23; Jer. 20:16) "some of you," literally, "among you." Earthquakes are among the most dreadful visitations of God, suddenly, unexpectedly, in a few moments destroying whole cities, slaying thousands of men, women, children, leaving the survivors like brands plucked out of the fire (Is. 7:4; Zech. 3:2), deprived of all of their possessions. So Israel had been brought to the verge of ruin. "Yet have ye not returned unto Me, saith the LORD." Incurable stubbornness! Unpardonable revolt!

157

Vv. 12, 13. Therefore, because of your persistent refusal to return to Me, thus, so, will I do unto you. The Covenant God, unchangeably faithful to His Word, will now deal with them as He had threatened to do with covenant breakers (Lev. 26:14 ff.; Deut. 28:15 ff.). "Prepare," stand firm, be ready, "to meet thy God, O Israel!" These words remind us of Israel's first meeting with the Covenant God ("Be ready," Ex. 19:15, 16; God's meeting His people, vv. 16-25; the covenant, chs. 20—24). Israel's Covenant God is not a weak, man-made god unable to fulfill His covenant promises or threats. He is the omnipotent Creator, who has formed the immovable mountains (v. 13), emblems of eternal strength; He has also created the wind, invisible, intangible, evasive, yet highly destructive. He is the omniscient Lord (Ps. 139), who as the Searcher of hearts (1 Sam. 16:7; Jer. 17:10) knows and declares to man what is his thought (Gr. N.). Witness His revelation of the real nature of their worship, having its source in their wicked heart and being essentially rebellion against God, although it was so highly esteemed by them. He is the Ruler of the universe, who can change the light of the morning to darkest night, hope and joy and prosperity to bitter woe and despair. He treads upon the high places of the earth (cp. Deut. 33:29; Micah 1:3). To tread upon is to be the victorious conqueror (Job 9:8; Ps. 91:13; Is. 63:3). He is Jehovah, the unchanging LORD (Ex. 3:14), the sovereign God of the mighty hosts of heaven (Ps. 103:20 f.). This is His name, and as such He will reveal Himself now. Prepare to meet thy God, O Israel! Israel, conqueror of God, so their ancestor, sinful Jacob, had been called (Gen. 32:28). The nation can once more become Israel, conquerors of God, by turning in their hour of utmost need to the Lord, their Helper, and, like their ancestor, cling to Him in humble, repentant faith and confident trust that in the Lord, their God, is the salvation of Israel (Jer. 3:23). In order to encourage them to such return, He calls them Israel, and Himself "thy God." Refusal to heed this final appeal will deprive them of every hope of escape from His final Judgment — rejection.

CHAPTER 5

c. Hear ye! Seek Me, or perish! Vv. 1-17

1 Hear this word that I am uttering against you, a dirge, O house of
2 Israel! Fallen, no more to rise, is the virgin Israel! Bowed down to the earth! None to raise her up!
3 For thus says the Lord LORD: The city that went forth a thousand strong shall have a hundred remaining, and she that went forth a hundred strong, shall have ten
4 remaining. For thus says the LORD to the house of Israel: Seek

158

5 Me, and live! Do not seek Bethel, and do not go to Gilgal, nor pass over to Beersheba! For Gilgal shall surely be exiled, and Bethel shall
6 become falsehood. Seek the LORD and live; lest He break out as a fire upon the house of Joseph and consume it, and there be none to
7 quench it for Bethel; you who are turning judgment to wormwood and hurling righteousness to the
8 ground! He who has made the Pleiades and Orion, who turns to morning light the shadow of death and darkens day to night; He that calls to the water of the sea and pours them out over the surface of the earth, His name is the LORD,
9 who causes destruction to break forth on the strong, and destruc-
10 tion comes upon the fortress. They hate the reprover in the gates and detest him who speaks the truth.
11 Therefore, because you trample on the poor and exact from him a toll of grain, you have built houses of hewn stones but shall not live in them; you have planted vineyards, yet shall not drink their wine.
12 I know your manifold transgressions and your monstrous sins, you who oppress the righteous, take bribes. And they thwart the needy
13 in the gate. Therefore the prudent man is stricken dumb at this time,
14 for this is an evil time. Seek good, and not evil, in order that you may live and that the LORD God of Hosts may thus be with you, as
15 you say. Hate evil, and love good, and establish judgment in the gate. It may be that the LORD God of Hosts will be gracious to the rem-
16 nant of Joseph. Therefore, thus says the LORD God of Hosts, the Lord: In all squares there shall be lamentation, and in all streets they shall say, Woe, woe! And they shall call the plowman to mourning, and lamentation to those who know
17 how to wail. And in all vineyards there will be lamentation, for I am passing through the midst of you, says the LORD.

Grammatical Notes

V. 1. Lamentation," קִינָה, a song expressing grief, particularly at the death of an individual (Amos 8:10), sung by professional mourning women (Amos 5:16; Jer. 9:16, A. V., 17), by relatives and friends (2 Sam. 1:17; 3:33; Jer. 9:19, 20, A. V., 20, 21); also at the death of a nation (Ezek. 19:14; 27:32; 28:12; 32:2, 16). They were often composed in the "Qinah" or elegiac meter. "The two parts of the verse are of unequal length: the first has four accents, the second three; more accurately, a rest replaces the last foot of the verse. The oldest and best example of this Qinah meter is found in Amos 5:2. . . . The elegies of David (2 Sam. 1:17-27; 3:33 f.), earliest of all, are not in the elegiac, but in ordinary measure." (Pfeiffer, *Introduction*, p. 270 f.)

V. 5. "Gilgal shall surely, etc." A play on words, *Gilgal, galoh, yigleh.*

V. 9. "Strengthens the spoiled," הַמַּבְלִיג שֹׁד. Qal does not occur in Hebrew; Arabic, to shine; Hiph., to cause to shine, flash forth; "He flashes forth destruction against the mighty." Hiph. occurs Ps. 39:14; Job 9:27; 10:20 = to shine, flash forth joy. The second "spoiled" also שֹׁד, destruction.

V. 11. "Burden," מַשְׂאַת, a lifting up (Ps. 141:2), burden (Zeph. 3:18), collection (2 Chron. 24:6, 9), oblations (Ezek. 20:40), also a portion of food placed before an honored guest (Gen. 43:34) or sent to him (2 Sam. 11:8). — "Dwell in them," "drink," imperfects, either inchoative, begin to dwell, or preferably, durative, continue.

V. 13. "Prudent," מַשְׂכִּיל, Hiph. participle, to pay attention, to have insight, understanding, to accomplish understandingly and successfully (Deut. 29:8;

159

A. V., 9; 1 Kings 2:3; Jer. 23:5; Prov. 10:19). Never used in an evil sense, of a time-serving schemer. Sellin translates in sense of "Maschil," in superscription of Psalms (Pss. 32, 42, 44, 45, etc.). "The Maschil will be silent, no longer sung." No need for such farfetched guesswork. — "Keep silence," to be stricken dumb with horror and anguish (Lev. 10:3; Lam. 2:10; 3:28; Ezek. 24:17), petrified (Ex. 15:16, "as a stone"). The secondary meaning of "patiently waiting, hoping" (Ps. 37:7; 62:6, A. V., 5) does not suit the context here.

V. 16. "Streets," רחבות, the open spaces or squares at the city gates, in larger cities also elsewhere (Jer. 5:1; 9:20), where people, young and old, met for pleasure, business, community meetings, etc. (Gen. 19:2; Judg. 19:15-20; Prov. 1:20; Is. 15:13; Jer. 48:18; Zech. 8:4f.) — "Highways," חוצות = outdoors, streets, the narrow city streets.

Vv. 1-3. Israel's death song. — The prophet, God's spokesman, composes a "lamentation" (Gr. N.) over Israel (cp. Micah 2:4 f.; Jer. 9:10, 17-22). While Israel was at the zenith of its power, Amos by divine inspiration chants the nation's death song, "as if a living man in the midst of his pride and luxury and buoyant recklessness could see his own funeral procession and hear, as it were, over himself 'earth to earth, ashes to ashes, dust to dust.' It would give solemn thoughts, even though he should impatiently put them from him." (Pusey.) "The virgin" (v. 2), one that has not yet submitted to anyone, unconquered (cp. Is. 47:1). By the gracious power of God the little nation of Israel had retained its independent kingdom. Now, several decades before the actual destruction, Amos sees her fallen, "is forsaken," lies prostrate on her soil, in ruins, without the slightest hope of being raised up. No one, neither she herself, nor another human deliverer, nor God, will ever restore her to her former glory. Israel is not only decimated (v. 3), but nine tenths of her military force has perished in war (on "go forth" = march to war, see 1 Sam. 8:20; Is. 42:13; Zech. 14:3), the remainder were exiled (cp. 2 Kings 17:6, 23, 24).

Vv. 4-15. Seek the Lord, or perish! "For" introduces the entire paragraph, vv. 4-17, which states the reason why Israel must die. It has left the Lord and become guilty of idolatry, social and judicial injustice and oppression. — Israel's death can be averted if it obeys the Lord's call: Seek the Lord, the Fountainhead of life (Ps. 36:10, A. V., 9; Jer. 2:13). He has no pleasure in the death of the wicked, therefore the two imperatives Seek! Live! are repeated v. 6. — Seek not Bethel (v. 5; cp. 3:14), the chief seat of Jeroboam's calf worship; ch. 4:4 Gilgal is added; here a third illegal sanctuary is added, Beersheba, in southern Judah. There Abraham had erected an altar (Gen. 21:31-33); God had appeared there to Isaac and Jacob (Gen. 26:24;

46:1; cp. also 1 Sam. 8:2; 1 Kings 19:3). Later it became an illegitimate sanctuary frequented by Israel (see also ch. 8:14) and by Judah (see 2 Kings 23:8). Gilgal shall "surely go into captivity" (Gr. N.), and Bethel shall "come to nought," become a house of vanity, a Beth-Aven (cp. Hos. 4:15; 5:8; 10:5). The fate of the idol is the fate of its worshipers.

The Lord repeats His call, Seek! Live! (v. 6), but then goes on to pronounce inescapable destruction upon the house of Joseph (cp. 5:15; 6:6), the Northern Kingdom. He will kindle a fire which no one in Bethel, neither people, nor priest, nor idol, could extinguish. This shall be the punishment for their perversion of justice, turning it into wormwood (v. 7), bitterness, for the oppressed people, and "leaving off righteousness in the earth," literally, casting it on the ground, trampling it under foot (cp. Is. 28:2; Ezek. 22:20). Again this is, like 4:13, the word of the Creator and Ruler of the universe, with whom nothing is impossible. "Seven stars" (v. 8), generally regarded as the constellation known as Pleiades (cp. Job 9:9; 38:31); others, Sirius, or Scorpion. Orion is also named in the Job passages. The Lord can easily turn the shadow of death (Ps. 23:4) to brightest morning if you seek Him; He will turn day into darkest night if you refuse to seek Him. He in whose hands are the waters of the vast ocean is also the Ruler of the nations, and He can pour them like a destructive flood over Israel (cp. Jer. 1:13, 14). "The LORD is His name"; see notes on ch. 4:13. As such He reveals Himself when He "strengthens the spoiled," etc. (v. 9) (Gr. N.), rather, when like a flash of lightning suddenly He sends desolation, ruin, to the strong, cruel oppressors, and destruction, ruin, unfailingly comes to fortresses, those powerful defenses, alliances, trusts, political machines they have built to fortify and safeguard their position. Such men hate anyone who dares to rebuke them (v. 10), be he prophet, priest, prince, commoner. "In the gates," the large open space at the city gates, the judges tried their cases (Deut. 21:19; 2 Sam. 15:2 f.; Is. 29:21), legal business was transacted (Ruth 4:1, 11), matters of public interest discussed (1 Kings 22:10). Whenever anyone opposed the wicked schemes proposed by the ruling party, the perversion of justice so often perpetrated by venal judges (cp. Jer. 17:19-27; 19:2 ff.), they sought to silence him by bribery or force (Is. 29:21; Jer. 38:1-6). With equal loathing these men, steeped in deception and treachery, regarded anyone who was still honest, who spoke the truth, who dared to lay bare and fight against the machinations of the greedy oppressors. Now (v. 11) the Lord Himself exposes their wickedness, their ignoring the sacred

161

rights of their fellow men, exacting from them "burdens" (Gr. N.) of gain to pay their debts, depriving the poor and needy of their little food in order that they themselves might live in luxury; a brazen defiance of such divine commands as Lev. 25:37; Deut. 23:19. Of course, they did not call it "usury," or interest, but they graciously received it as a gift, presented to them by the poor man in gratitude for favors bestowed upon him by noble Mr. Richman. Shameful hypocrisy! The greedy vampires shall not enjoy their ill-gotten gain. They had built houses of hewn stone such as only the rich could afford, others were satisfied with brick or unhewn stone (Is. 9:10). Yet they shall not dwell (Gr. N.) in them for any length of time. The Lord will fulfill His threat (Deut. 28:30 b; cp. Micah 6:15; Zeph. 1:13), for He knows (v. 12) and will punish their manifold revolts against God's Law, their "mighty," flagrant, outrageous sins, their oppression of the just, their venality, their favoritism (cp. 1 Sam. 12:3).

"Therefore" (v. 13), because of this general wickedness, the prudent (Gr. N.) shall keep silence (Gr. N.). The nation in its vast majority goes through life like dumb, driven cattle, or in that spirit of rashness "After us the deluge," unable and unwilling to discern the signs of the times. But the man of understanding, viewing all things in the light of God's Word, will be stricken dumb with horror and anguish when he sees sin and rebellion against all laws, human or divine, sweeping like a tidal wave over all the land, engulfing the nation in its embrace of death, leaving disaster and desolation in its wake. Such a time is, indeed, evil time; evil in its upheaval against God's Word, evil in its horrifying consequences.

Once more (v. 14) the Lord urges them to turn back to Him, and at the same time He defines His demand to seek Him. That involves seeking good and not evil, the unalterable requirement if you are looking for life, physical and spiritual, as individuals or as a nation. Only so, and surely so, will their ancient battle cry "The Lord is with us!" be justified.

To seek good and not evil means to hate, detest, all that is evil (v. 15) and to love all that is good, all that God, who is Good (Ps. 34:8; 73:1; 100:5), commands to man (Ps. 19:7 ff.; Prov. 3:1 ff.), namely, to establish, uphold, in the gate (see v. 10), judgment, justice, such as is in keeping with God's norm, His holy Law proclaimed by Him in His covenant. It may be that the Lord will be gracious to the remnant, what is left, of Israel. It seems as if the longer Amos meditates on the wickedness of Israel, the less hope he has for Israel's repentance and restoration. "Ye shall live!" he had hopefully, confidently exclaimed vv. 4, 6; then, "that ye may live," v. 14; now, "it may be," perhaps a remnant will escape the total extinction of the nation. Perhaps a remnant will be saved (Is. 10:21, 22)! Joseph, once two flourishing tribes (Gen. 48:1-5; Deut. 33:13-17), will be a remnant, a small band, and that only "perhaps"! How sad! (Prov. 14:34.)

Vv. 16, 17. Wailing throughout the land! In all "streets" (Gr. N.), rather "squares," and in all "highways" (Gr. N.), the narrow streets of the city, is heard the cry of despair, Ho! Ho! War! War! Pestilence, epidemic, stalks through the city (ch. 4:10) and spreads throughout the rural sections. The farmer is called from his work to lament over a member of the family. Even the wailing women (Gr. N. on v. 1) succumb to the grim enemy, and lamentations are chanted to those who were so proficient in wailing over others. Alas, Israel is no longer God's people! The covenant nation, redeemed out of the bondage of Egypt, has become an Egypt, rebels against God and oppressors of God's people. Therefore He who regardeth not persons (Deut. 10:17; cp. context vv. 15-22) will treat Israel as Egypt was treated. The angel of death passes through the land (Ex. 12:12) and spares no house, for Israel rejects the atoning blood of the Redeeming Lamb (Ex. 12:7; 23:20, 21).

---

2. Two woes pronounced against impenitent Israel, ch. 5:18—6:14

a. First woe: Inescapable captivity beyond Damascus, ch. 5:18-27

18 Woe to them that long for the Day of the LORD! What good shall the Day of the LORD do you? It is
19 darkness and not light! As if a man flees from a lion and a bear meets him; and when he comes to his home and rests his hand on the
20 wall, a serpent bites him! Is not the Day of the LORD darkness without light? And dense darkness
21 without brightness? I hate, I loathe your festivals and will not smell
22 your festival assemblies! Even though you offer your burnt offerings and meal offerings, I am not pleased! Nor will I regard your thankofferings of fatted oxen! Re-
23 move from Me the noise of your songs, and to the music of your
24 harps I will not listen! But let justice roll on as water and righteousness as everlasting streams.
25 Have you brought sacrifices and meal offerings to Me in the wil-
26 derness for forty years? But you carried the booth of your king and the framework of your images, the star of your god whom you have
27 made for yourselves. And I will deport you beyond Damascus, says the LORD, whose name is the God of Hosts.

Grammatical Notes

V. 18. "Desire." Hithp. is causative-reflexive, to cause or urge oneself to desire, to stir up, nourish one's desires.

(Cp. Deut. 5:18 b, A. V., 21 b, "covet"; Num. 11:34; 2 Sam. 23:15.)
V. 25. "Unto Me." "Me" is emphasized

by its position. The M. T. very properly has placed a makkeph between "brought" and "unto Me," combining the two words into a unit, of which only the last word is accented. (G.-K. 16.)

V. 26. "But," ‫ו‬, "and" here adversative (cp. Gen. 17:5; 42:10; Ex. 5:18). — "Ye have borne." Geo. A. Smith, in *Expositor's Bible,* Sellin, and others translate "Ye shall bear," since both grammar and the argument oblige us to take it as future (Smith). Sellin: "To assume that Amos here charges Israel with having worshiped Assyrian astral deities would be imputing to him an incredible ignorance of history." He strikes "the star" and "your images" and refers the verse to processions in which an image of Jehovah covered by a baldachin, or canopy, was carried about on the annual festival of Jehovah's throne ascension — a pure fiction. We hold that neither grammar nor history makes the rendering of our Bible incorrect or impossible. Driver, *Tenses,* 119 a, favors the future but adds in a note: "The perf. with simple waw, giving a past sense, meets us occasionally unexpectedly, e. g., Amos 7:2, 4; Ezek. 20:22; Job 16:12." And G.-B. lists

12 perf. with waw as frequentatives, e. g., Gen. 21:25; 49:23; Ex. 36:38; 2 Kings 23:12, and seven as denoting a continuous remaining in a past state, e. g., Gen. 15:6; Num. 21:20; Judg. 3:9, and leaves the future or the past rendering in Amos 6:26 to the choice of the reader. (G.-B. 112 rr, ss.) Nor is the A. V. impossible on historical grounds; see exposition, p. 165 f.—"Tabernacle," ‫סָכּוּת‬, the Assyrian-Babylonian Sakkut, cp. Sukkoth-Benoth (2 Kings 17:30), here pointed with the vowels of ‫שִׁקּוּץ‬, abomination, idol. This was the name of the planet Saturn as an astral deity. — "Moloch," ‫מַלְכְּכָם‬, your king, here your god; cp. Deut. 33:5; Jer. 10:7, etc., where God is called king. — "Chiun," ‫כִּיּוּן‬, the Assyrian Kaimanu, or Kaiwanu, identified with Saturn; the LXX misread this name Raiphan; cf. Remphan, Acts 7:43; Aquila, Symmachus: Chion.—"Your images," apposition to the preceding proper nouns. — "The star of your god." God, here plural, your gods; ‫כּוֹכַב‬, the construct in apposition to gods, describing the nature or character of these gods as star gods, astral deities. (G.-K. 128, 1.)

The prophet joins in the universal lamentation in two woe songs, ch. 5:18-27 and 6:1-14. Unlike the people, however, he sorrows not only for the destruction, but also for its cause, and calls the people back to the Lord.

Vv. 18-20. The Day of the Lord, so eagerly desired by the people, shall be to them a day of darkness. — Israel "desired" (Gr. N.), eagerly longed for the Day of the Lord (see Obad. 15, pp. 203 f.) as a day of salvation, peace, and prosperity. The prophet asks: To what end is it for you? What will its purpose be for you? For you who refuse to seek the Lord (vv. 4, 6, 14), rebel against Him (v. 11 f.), this day is a day of darkness without the least light (vv. 18, 20), of inescapable ruin and death. In a vivid manner he pictures the impossibility of escape. A man having barely escaped a roaring lion is suddenly confronted by a vicious bear (v. 19). He eludes this second danger. He reaches the safety of his home. Rejoicing over his good fortune, he leans, totally exhausted, against the wall, where, alas! a venomous serpent hidden in a crevice of the wall inflicts a mortal wound. Though Israel has escaped many dangers, there is not the least glimmer of light to brighten the black night of death about to encompass the nation (v. 20). Their constant rebellion against the God of the Covenant and their foolish revolt against the kings to whom they had pledged loyalty brought on their national death and destruction (2 Kings 17:4-6; 24:20; 25:1-11).

Vv. 21-24. Israel's hypocritical worship will not save them. — Israel's "feast days," the three chief festivals (Ex. 23:14-17), their solemn assemblies, the gatherings on these festival days, or on other occasions (Lev. 23:36; Deut. 16:8; Is. 1:13; Joel 1:14), were an abomination to the Lord. Their offerings and sacrifices (v. 22) were not a sweet savor to the Lord (Gen. 8:21; Lev. 1:9). The stench of the people's sins, their hypocrisy, their rebellion, make the people as well as their offerings nauseating to Him (Gen. 4:5-7). He will not accept these offerings, not even regard them, look at them, so offensive to Him are the offerings of this rebellious people. Their festival songs are to Him a hideous noise (v. 23). He closes His ears against the music of their "viols," harps. He looks not for mere external worship and sacrifice. Rather let judgment (v. 24), God's norm, His Law and His Gospel, run down as water, spreading throughout the country, and righteousness, good works demanded by the Law and wrought in the lives of the believers by the power of the Gospel, fill the nation like a mighty stream (Ps. 85:7-13). Alas, the nation refused to return to God!

Vv. 25-27. Israel's long-continued idolatry will lead to its final rejection. The Northern Kingdom had from its very origin adopted the idolatrous worship of calves as its national religion (1 Kings 12:26-28), a device of Jeroboam's own heart (v. 28), a making of other gods, rank idolatry (1 Kings 14:9 ff.), and the history of the twelve tribes is a record of ever-repeated idolatry and rebellion against God. This tendency, this morbid hankering after false gods, dated back to the early days of Israel's acceptance as God's covenant nation. Only forty days after the solemn declaration of this covenant, Israel asked Aaron to make gods for them to go before them, and worshiped the golden calf (Ex. 32:1-6). Israel would have been exterminated then and there had not Moses so unselfishly and powerfully interceded for them (Ex. 32:7—34:11). Israel, however, did not cease to worship idols. They remained a stiff-necked people as God had called them

165

(Ex. 32:9). Forty years later Moses tells them Deut. 9:6-24 and finds it necessary to warn them time and again against idolatry, and twice in particular against that special form of idolatry with which the Lord here charges the nation: the worship of the host of heaven, of sun, moon, and stars, individually or collectively (v. 26; see Deut. 4:19; 17:2,3). Throughout the history of Israel from its earliest beginnings it was constantly exposed to its insidious influences. Star worship was one of the earliest and most widespread forms of idolatry. At Mari, an ancient powerful city on the middle Euphrates, about 250 miles north-west of Babylon, excavations in 1933 uncovered a temple of Ishtar, the goddess of the planet Venus. This temple dates from the third millennium before Christ. The royal palace of Mari was adorned with mural paintings, one of which represented the king of Mari receiving from Ishtar the staff and ring which were the emblems of his authority. (Finegan, *Light from the Ancient Past,* p. 46, quoting A. Parrot, the French leader of the excavation.) Mari was an ancient city of the Amorites, a Semitic nation extending its rule from Babylonia to the Mediterranean lands. They made the Babylonian language and religion (star worship) the language of these countries for many centuries. Abraham made a covenant with Amorite princes (Gen. 14:13; see also v. 7; 15:16, 21; 48:22). They were still a powerful nation in the days of Moses and Joshua (see Ex. 3:8, 17; 33:2; 34:11; Num. 21:13-34; Joshua 24:8).

The false gods worshiped by Abraham's ancestors in Ur of the Chaldees (Joshua 24:2), were astral deities venerated by Chaldeans. The "images" which Rachel had taken from her father (Gen. 31:30 ff.), and which later were buried by Jacob (Gen. 35:2 ff.), were *teraphim* (ch. 31:34), small statuettes of Ishtar. In Egypt, Israel was exposed to the danger of various forms of idolatry, among them solar worship. The chief god of Egypt, Ra, also called Amon, was the god of the sun. As late as the end of Joshua's life, Israel still possessed and worshiped such gods as had been worshiped by their fathers in Chaldea and in Egypt (Joshua 24:14, cp. v. 2). Hence by ancestry, by environment in Egypt, by the proximity to the Amorites and other nations addicted to star worship during their sojourn in the wilderness, and by their rebellious spirit (Ex. 32:9; Deut. 9:6; Ps. 95:10, 11) the Israelites were inclined to star worship. The translation of v. 25 in our Bible does not impute to Amos an unbelievable historical ignorance, but is in full keeping with grammar and the facts as they are known to us. Amos also supplies the names of two of these star gods. In the wilderness Israel carried the "tabernacle" (Gr. N.), the image of the Babylonian-

Assyrian Sakkuth, the god identified with the planet Saturn. Him they regarded as their "Moloch" (Gr. N.), their king or god. Another idol was Chiun (Gr. N.), the Assyrian Kaimanu, another deity identified with Saturn. Israel aped the heathen festival processions in which the "images" (Gr. N.) of "the star of your gods" (Gr. N.), their star gods, were carried about. These idols they worshiped in the wilderness (v. 25), in which they had experienced so many manifestations of Jehovah's power and love (Ex. 15: 23 ff.; 16: 1-35; 17: 1-16; chs. 19—24; Deut. 8: 3, 4; 29: 5, 6). Him they rejected and worshiped the work of their own hands! Folly supreme! Abominable ingratitude! Damnable wickedness! The names used by Amos may be as ancient as the idols, or Amos may call the ancient idols by the names current at his time. The sin remains the same, star worship. In quoting this passage, Stephen adds another truth (Acts 7: 41 ff.). Because Israel refused to acknowledge and serve the true God as He had revealed Himself to them, God surrendered them in divine judgment to their self-chosen ways which could end only in ruin and damnation. (See Rom. 1: 17 ff.; Ex. 5 to 15, Pharaoh's hardening; Matt. 12: 32 ff.; 1 Thess. 2: 14-16; Heb. 10: 26 ff.) Naturally, He has in mind only the stubbornly impenitent. There was even in the wilderness a remnant. (See Ex. 34:10-27; Num. 11: 25-29; 14: 24, 30 f.; 22: 12; Deut. 4: 1-9.)

In Amos' time Israel's day of grace was fast coming to an end. Both kingdoms will go into captivity beyond Damascus (v. 27). The exact location is not yet revealed (cp. 6: 14). Hosea was the first prophet to name Assyria as the land of exile (Hos. 9: 3; 10: 6; 11: 15). That is the word of the world Ruler, whose name is the Lord, the God of Hosts. The ten tribes were deported to Assyria 722 B. C., never to return as a nation (2 Kings 17: 1-6). Judah's captivity (606—536) was a temporary punishment. Amos' proclamation was a warning addressed to both kingdoms, a call to repentance, a call to return in faith and loving loyalty to the Lord, the Covenant God, "whose name is the God of Hosts," the Ruler of the universe.

CHAPTER 6

b. Second woe: Complete destruction by a nation coming from the north, vv. 1-14

1 Woe to them that are at ease in Zion and to them that put their trust in the mount of Samaria, men of mark of the choicest of the nations, to whom the house of Israel
2 comes! Pass over to Calneh, and see; and from there go to Hamath the Great, and go down to Gath of the Philistines. Are they better than these kingdoms? Or is their territory larger than your terri-
3 tory? O you who put far off the evil day and bring close the seat of
4 violence; who are lying on ivory couches and are sprawling on divans, and eating the lambs from

the flock and calves from the midst
5 of the stall; who are crooning to
the tune of the harp, and like David
devise for themselves musical in-
6 struments; who are drinking wine
by bowlfuls and anoint themselves
with the finest ointments, yet do
not grieve for the ruin of Joseph!
7 Therefore now they shall go into
exile at the head of the exiles, and
gone is the riotous shout of the
8 sprawlers! The Lord LORD has
sworn by Himself, is the oracle of
the LORD God of Hosts, I abhor
the pride of Jacob and hate his
palaces! And I will surrender the
9 city and all that is in it! Then it
shall be that if ten men are left in
10 one house, they shall die! And a
man's uncle and the man to burn
him shall lift him to bring the bones
out of the house. And one shall
call to whoever is in the inner part

of the house, Is there anyone still
with you? and he shall say, Not
one! and he shall say, Hush! For
one may not mention the name of
11 the LORD! For, behold, the LORD
commands, and He will smite the
great house into ruins and the small
12 house into splinters. Do horses run
on cliffs? Or does one plow the sea
with oxen? For you have turned
judgment into poison and the fruit
of rightousness into wormwood,
13 you who rejoice in a thing of
nought and are always saying, Have
we not by our strength acquired
14 power for ourselves? For, behold,
I am about to raise up against you,
O house of Israel, is the oracle of
the LORD, the God of Hosts, a nation, and they shall oppress you
from the entrance of Hamath to the
brook of the wilderness.

Grammatical Notes

V. 1. "Named," part. pass. of נָקַב,
to pierce (2 Kings 2:10; Hab. 3:14), to
mark (by piercing), to specify, designate, e. g., wages (Gen. 30:28), a name
(Is. 62:2); here, the noted people, no-
bility, aristocracy. — "Chief," literally,
the beginning (Gen. 10:10), the first
fruit (Ex. 23:19), the best, choicest
(Deut. 33:21; Jer. 2:3; 49:35).

V. 3. "Put far away," מְנַדִּים, Pi. of נָדָה =
to remove, cast out (Is. 66:5), reject
with disdain. — "Seat," שֶׁבֶת, the sitting,
dwelling, throning (Ps. 27:4; 127:2).

V. 5. "Chant," פָּרַט, only here; to separate, pluck, cut off. Cp. the noun, only
Lev. 19:10, "every grape" = the grapes
separated from the vine and falling to
the ground while picking. To break, or
cut off, the voice while singing = to
croon, to sing in an unnatural manner.

V. 6. "Bowls," the noun derived from
a stem = to sprinkle, water (Ezek.
36:25), blood (Lev. 1:5, 11; 3:2, etc.);
hence a vessel or bowl from which

blood was sprinkled (Ex. 27:3; Num.
7:13-85, "basons," sacred vessels, usually quite large).

V. 7. "Banquet," literally, loud shouting,
clamor, only Jer. 16:5 (lamentation)
and here of riotous joy.

V. 10. "Make mention," the Hiph. of
זכר, here = to call upon God's name in
prayer of supplication (Ex. 23:13;
Joshua 23:7; Ps. 20:8, A. V., 7; Is. 48:1).

V. 12. "There" is not found in the original. One must either supply "there"
or read with Michaelis, Kittel, Bibl.
Hebr., and others, בַּבָּקָר יָם, which involves no change of consonants and
offers a suitable sense: the height of
impossibility. Sellin's בְּבָקָר רָם: Does
a wild ox plow like an ox? requires a
greater change of the text.

V. 14. "Afflict," לָחַץ, to press, oppress,
crush (Ex. 3:9; Judg. 2:18; 4:3, etc.);
cp. Num. 22:25, where Niph. = thrust
herself, pressed herself, and Qal =
crushed, occur.

V. 1. This chapter is directed primarily against the social and political leaders of Judah and Israel. Note that here Zion, i. e., Jerusalem-Judah is named first. Amos rebukes not only the Northern Kingdom, but addresses first of all the Southern Kingdom. Both kingdoms, the entire nation from Dan to Beersheba, are equally guilty and will meet with like destruction. "At ease." The flourishing condition of the two kingdoms during the long reigns of Uzziah and Jeroboam II (see pp. 10 ff.) had lulled them into false and foolish security. They trusted in their strong fortifications, in Zion, the impregnable city, and in Samaria, just as inaccessible. Above all, they were confident that God would never forsake His own chosen people (cp. Jer. 7:4 ff.). They forgot that God's mercy (see 2 Kings 14:26 f.) was calling them to repentance (Rom. 2:4 ff.). An occasional reversal served only to increase their self-assertive haughtiness (Is. 9:8-10, 13). Their leaders were "named" (Gr. N.), noted, renowned men, leaders of the "chief of the nations" (Gr. N.), Israel, a nation highly honored by the Lord, called Israel, conquerors of God, Gen. 32:28 f., the first fruits of all nations (Jer. 2:3; cp. Ex. 19:5; 2 Sam. 7:23 f.; Amos 3:2). To these leaders came the house of Israel for advice, for leadership in matters pertaining to civil, social, or political affairs. Their advice, their example, whether good or bad, was eagerly followed by the people.

V. 2. The prophet names three cities quite powerful at that time: Calneh, Hamath, Gath. Calneh here is not the city named Gen. 10:10, in Babylonia, but Kullani, frequently mentioned in Assyrian inscriptions, some distance above Hamath. The Assyrian king, quoted Is. 10:9, boasts that he had conquered such powerful cities as Carchemish, on the Euphrates, Calneh, or Calno (Kullani), Arpad, Hamath, Damascus, and Samaria. The territory of Hamath formed the northern boundary of Israel (Num. 13:21; 34:8; 2 Kings 14:25-28). Hamath is called "the Great" by Amos (6:2). Calneh and Hamath were two of the 19 city-states that rebelled against mighty King Tiglath-Pileser of Assyria (745—727 B. C.) and were subdued only after several campaigns. (Rogers, *Cuneiform Parallels to the Old Testament*, pp. 309 ff.) Gath, the third city named by Amos, was one of the five royal cities of Philistia (Joshua 13:3; Judg. 3:3; 1 Sam. 6:4, 16, 18), destroyed by Uzziah (2 Chron. 26:6).

The prophet selects these three cities in order to teach Israel its ingratitude toward the Lord. These three cities were powerful city states, yet none of them was "better" or occupied more territory than "these kingdoms," Judah and Israel. The past history of Israel was one of small beginnings, Abraham's son Isaac was born when Abraham was 100 years old (Gen. 21:5); Isaac's son Jacob, 60 years later (Gen. 25:26); 130 years later the children of Israel numbered 70 souls (Gen. 46:27; 47:9). In Egypt they grew into a large nation (Ex. 1:7; 12:37); were enslaved and marvelously delivered and brought to the Land of Promise, because God loved them (Deut. 7:6 ff.; 10:21, 22). The small family had grown into a nation as powerful and large as Calneh and Hamath and Gath. More than that, the Lord had honored them by making them the chief of the nations, v. 1. In spite of all these unmerited blessings Israel remained an ungrateful people, unmindful of the Rock that begat them (Deut. 32:6-18).

V. 3. They "put far away" (Gr. N.), scornfully rejected the warning prophecies of God's messengers. Evil days? Hard times? Decay and destruction? Perish the thought! Their great prosperity (2 Chron. 26:5), their success against their enemies (vv. 6-8), their well-planned agricultural and farming policy under state supervision (v. 10), their fortifications and immense war machinery comprising the latest weapons of offense and defense (vv. 9, 11-15), their wise statesmanship and vast resources — all this guaranteed to them like success for the future. Instead of gratefully, loyally serving the Lord, to whom they really owed what success they had attained, they shamefully abused his gifts, pressed them into the service of the selfish ambition of their sinful flesh. Thus, instead of putting away, staving off, the evil day even for a while, they actually hasten its coming; "they cause the seat of violence to come near." On "seat," see Gr. N. They brought on the enthronement of violence and oppression, where justice and equity ought to have ruled. Already the poor in the land were groaning under heartless oppression by the rich, the venality of the judges (ch. 1:6-8; 5:7, 11, 12; 6:12 b; 8:4-6), and before long the harsh, oppressive tyranny of a heartlessly cruel enemy would crush all the nation underfoot.

Vv. 4-6 describe in vivid language the luxurious, riotous, selfish life of the people. In the homes of the rich were found all the conveniences and luxuries of the day. There were "beds," or divans, of ivory, richly decorated with ivory plaques and panels (see ch. 3:15 on "ivory houses"), on which Mr. Richman sprawled; luxuriant couches, on which the lady of the house stretched out her weary limbs after having returned from a stroll through the avenues of the city where she had exhibited her beauty, enhanced by many an artificial means (Is. 3:18-23). The less fortunate sisters, the common rabble, the dames of the underworld, the flappers of 750 B. C., admired their richly attired sisters and ran to the next bazaar to buy some cheap bauble, some of the latest beauty helps, in order to look like their more favored sisters. In the elegant homes of the rich and in the temples of their idols (ch. 2:7, 8) riotous feasts and banquets were held. Only the most dainty meats were served, lambs selected from carefully tended flocks, calves from the midst of the stall (cp. Mal. 4:2), kept in special stalls, fed with special feed. At these banquets men and women idled away their time by "chanting" (Gr. N.), crooning to the sound of the "viol," the harp (v. 5). They also invented for themselves, not to God's glory, instruments of music. The better such noisemakers suited the intention of their inventors, to affect the nerves, create excitement, stir up passions, the higher was the inventor honored. He was likened to David, who had introduced many musical instruments in the Temple service (1 Chron. 23:5; 2 Chron. 29:25, 26). There may even be a grain of truth in the statement of Josephus that David "made instruments of music," which are then described (*Ant.* VII, 12, 3). Amos, of course, uses these words in bitter irony. Such crooning, accompanied by jazzy instrumental music, was regarded as the highest "superart" by the delighted audiences. The heads and bodies of the assembled guests were anointed with "the chief ointments," the finest and most expensive perfumeries, filling the hall with their intoxicating odors. The passions kindled by the voluptuous music and suggestive dress were nourished by the rich food and fanned into irrepressive ardor by large bowlfuls of wine freely making the rounds (v. 6). The term used here for "bowls" in all other passages denotes ritual bowls used in the Temple for sprinkling the sacrificial blood upon the altar (see Gr. N.). Were they used at these banquets in the homes and the idol temples in order to give a semblance of piety to these orgiastic festivals, as the saying of grace before modern family dinners ending in drinking bouts? We are reminded of Belshazzar's feast (Dan. 5:1-5).

Such people of course were "not grieved for the affliction of Joseph." "Affliction," here = ruin, smashing destruction; "grieved" = sick, ill at ease. They may often have returned feeling sick and ill at ease because of the overindulgence in food and drink; but they were always ready for another bout. Yet never did they grieve for the ruin of Israel, the spiritual downfall of the nation, their utter lack of trust and faith in the God of salvation, the total absence of loving obedience to His will (Jer. 3:1 ff.; Hos. 4:1; cp. Hab. 1:4 b). This rejection of God, of His Law and His Gospel, was the real affliction of Joseph, the nation of Israel, especially the Northern Kingdom. Very clearly God had foretold that (Lev. 26; Deut. 28), and Israel's history had proved it (Judg. 2:10-23). Yet this spiritual downfall did not

171

worry these people. They were perfectly satisfied as long as they had food and drink and were rich enough to satisfy their desires.

V. 7. God pronounces His judgment upon these "leaders" (v. 1) of the people. They shall be the first to go into captivity, leaders on the long journey into foreign countries, where no longer they shall join in the "banquet" (Gr. N.), the riotous shoutings of those stretched out on their divans; for all that shall be removed, gone, past forever.

V. 8. In an especially solemn manner the Lord impresses upon these dissolute belly servants His abhorrence of "the excellency of Jacob." Israel is called by the name of its sinful father, who selfishly sought his own advantage by fair means or foul. "Excellency" includes all that the nation boasted of, pointed to with pride. One item only is mentioned as an example of their fleeting pomp and parade: the palaces, the mansions, the show places, built by the blood and sweat of the poor and filled with the gain of violence and treachery (Amos 3:10). All these excellencies, the entire city and everything in it, will be delivered up, surrendered to the enemy, not because the enemy was so powerful (cp. Lev. 26:7, 8; Deut. 28:7), but because Israel had so flagrantly transgressed God's covenant and thereby provoked His vengeance (cp. Deut. 28:45 ff.). This threat concerns both Zion and Samaria (v. 1). "City" is used collectively, referring to both capital cities.

Vv. 9, 10. Pestilence, the grim companion of war and famine, will stalk through the country and slay not only the first-born (Ex. 12:29, 30), but also young and old. Nor will this unwelcome guest visit only the hovels of the poor. The palaces of the rich, where ten men still remain after the ravages of war and siege and famine, will not be spared. The ten also shall die. "A man's uncle" (v. 10), all closer relatives having died, will have to render the final service to the dead. Together with a helper he will have to carry out the bones, here (as Ex. 13:19; Joshua 24:32; 2 Kings 13:21) the corpse, in order to burn it. So many have died that it will be impossible to grant anyone an honorable burial. The bodies must be burnt in order to clear the city from the horrible stench and the danger of spreading contagion among the survivors. Only extreme emergencies made it necessary to burn a corpse, which in Israel was a penalty for extreme wickedness (Lev. 20:14; 21:9). The only exception is recorded here and 1 Sam. 31:11-13. The "burning" mentioned 2 Chron. 16:14; 21:19; Jer. 34:5 refers to the burning of fragrant spices at the burial of the king, an honor not granted to wicked Jehoram (2 Chron. 21:19, 20).

The gruesome task is completed. The uncle calls to one "by the sides" (cp. Jonah 1:5), in the interior of the palace, either a survivor hiding in the farthest corner, or the uncle's assistant, Is anyone with you? In answer to his No! the uncle says, Hush! Silence! For it is not permitted, not proper, not possible to mention (Gr. N.) the name of the Lord. This is not, as Keil suggests, a warning lest by mentioning the name Jehovah the attention of the Lord would be directed to the speaker and he also would be slain. The Lord needs no such reminder. The expression is rather one of hopeless despair. The God of life has forsaken the city and has surrendered it to bloody warfare, famine, epidemics, horror, despair, death!

V. 11 repeats the reason (cp. v. 8) for the horrors of vv. 9, 10. The Lord has commanded them, war, epidemics, death (vv. 9, 10), as well as the enemy forces (v. 14). He retains full command until His will is carried out. He shatters the great houses of the rich into ruins, the little houses of the poor into "clefts," broken, severed particles. Rich and poor alike are guilty and are punished alike by the Chief Commander.

Vv. 12-14. It cannot be otherwise. It would be ridiculous to try to change the purpose for which horses and oxen were created, their very nature. It would be folly to expect horses to race along steep cliffs accessible only to goats and chamois; or to demand oxen to plow "there" (Gr. N.), rather, the sea. That would be folly on the part of man and disastrous for both the beasts and their owners. We seem to hear Israel inquire, Why do you ask this question? The Lord states the reason. "For ye have turned," etc. "Judgment" here denotes the norm, the standard. In Israel the norm of judgment was to be God's will as revealed in His Law and His Gospel. This norm, if properly applied, produced as its "fruit" (Gr. N.), its product, its result, that righteousness which the Lord demands in His Law and generates by His Gospel. Yet Israel changed God's Law — which demanded as righteousness true love of God and the fellow man (Deut. 6:5; Lev. 19:18; Matt. 22:36-40) — into its very opposite. Their norm of action was self-love, interest in their own welfare. And their righteousness was not that of faith and trust in the Lord their Righteousness (Jer. 23:6) and of loving obedience to His will. It was a righteousness proceeding from selfishness. Every thought, word, and deed had as its ultimate object their own personal profit, by fair means or foul. Such judgment was "gall" (cp. Deut. 29:17; 32:32 f.; Jer. 8:14), deadly poison, to the people, ruinous to the state. The "fruit," the product, the result, of such righteousness was not happiness, peace, contentment, but "hemlock," rather, wormwood, bitter, offensive, repulsive, causing bitter tears, hard feelings, discontentment among the people. Examples of such judgment and righteousness are given ch. 2: 6-8; 3: 10; 4: 1; 5: 10 ff., 15.

Another example of a somewhat different nature is given in v. 13. "Horns" are the symbol of power. In self-satisfaction they rejoiced and placed their trust not in the God of their salvation. Rejecting Him, they regarded their own "strength," their military skill and prowess, their statesmanship, as the sole cause of their power and prosperity. The Lord assures them that their confidence is based on sinking sand; they rejoice in a thing of naught, that has no real existence, that cannot endure. And He tells them that all their judgment and righteousness will turn for themselves also into poisonous, deadly gall and bitter, noisome wormwood. He, the Lord, the God of Hosts, the Covenant God of Israel, the Ruler of the world, will fulfill the threats of His covenant (Deut. 28: 49 ff.). He will send a nation (v. 14) which could not accomplish anything against Israel without His will (Amos 3: 6 b; Deut. 28: 7). Yet now they are His instruments of punishing His wicked people. They will "afflict" (Gr. N.) Israel, oppress the nation, devastate their territory from the "entering in," the way leading to Hamath (see p. 169), unto the river of the "wilderness," the Arabah, the desert along the eastern shore of the Salt Sea (cp. 2 Kings 14: 28). This river may be the Arnon, which separated Israel from Moab, or some other river flowing into the Dead Sea on its eastern shore.

PART II

The Lessons of Part I Are Taught in Five Visions
Chapters 7—9

CHAPTER 7
A. The Lord Forming Locusts, but Relenting, Vv. 1-3

1 Thus the Lord LORD caused me to see: Behold, He was forming locusts when the aftermath began to sprout, and, behold, it was the second growth after the king's mow-
2 ing. And when they had finished consuming the vegetation of the land, I said, Lord LORD, oh, forgive! How can Jacob stand? For
3 he is so small! The LORD relented of this. It shall not happen! said the LORD.

Grammatical Note

V. 2. "Grass," greens, herbage, vegetables, including grass. — "By whom," מִי, as who, i. e., in what state, how, will Jacob stand? Cp. Ruth 3:16, as who = how, are you?

Vv. 1-3. The Lord forming grasshoppers. — These visions were shown to the prophet by the Lord Himself. They are not merely the result of his own reflections, but divine revelations. The Lord God, the Creator and Ruler of the universe, the mighty mountains, the wide sea, the huge canopy of heaven (ch. 4:13; 5:8; 9:6), creates with equal power and wisdom the small and smallest creatures, and "forms," shapes, fashions them so that they can carry out the purpose for which He made them. Grasshoppers, small, weak, easily killed individually, seemingly harmless, yet what havoc can they create! (Joel 1 and 2.) It was the beginning of the "shooting up," the sprouting, of the "latter growth," literally, the later mowing, the aftermath. The first mowing, at least the greatest part of it, was claimed by the king (cp. 1 Sam. 8:12-15; 1 Kings 18:5, 6) for feeding the army horses. If the second growth was destroyed by locusts, there was little, if any, hope of raising sufficient fodder for the cattle. — The locusts had finished the destruction of the grass (Gr. N.), the vegetation of the land, when the prophet interceded for his people (v. 2). That was one of the functions of the prophets (Gen. 20:7; Ex. 32:11 ff.; Num. 14:13 ff.; 1 Sam. 7:8; Jer. 14:8 f., 13, 19 ff.; 15:1). Forgive! If God will send a locust plague, "by whom" (Gr. N.) shall Jacob arise? He is small, too small to survive so terrible a plague! That will bring the nation to the verge of ruin! Already it is weakened by heavy taxation in order to finance the ever-increasing national expenses (cp. 1 Kings 14:25-28; 2 Chron. 26:6-15). War and public improvements at all times were expensive and could easily sap the resources of nations even larger than Israel. The Lord heard the plea of His prophet and relented (v. 3). He did not send the locust plague. One man's prayer saved the nation!

B. The Lord Ready to Send Drought, but Relents, Ch. 7:4-6

4 Thus the Lord LORD caused me to see: And, behold, the Lord LORD was calling in order to punish with fire; and it began to consume the great deep, and it consumed the 5 land. Then I said, Lord LORD, oh, stop! How shall Jacob stand, for 6 he is so small! The LORD relented of this. Also this shall not happen! said the Lord LORD.

Grammatical Note

V. 4. "A part," חֵלֶק, the portion allotted to one, here to Israel = the land of Israel. LXX reads "the portion of the Lord," allotted to His people. "Did eat," the perfect at times denotes the determination to do a thing (cp. Ruth 4:3, "selleth," Gen. 23:11, 13, "give," though the money was only given, v. 16). — If the prophet's plea had not been heard, the whole land would have been devastated.

Vv. 4-6. The first vision presented God doing a work seemingly unworthy of the Lord of the universe, shaping insignificant creepers. The second vision shows this same God having at His beck the mighty forces of nature. He "called to contend by fire." He summons fire into His controversy with Israel; intense, burning heat, drought. He is the Lord who can make the heaven like brass (Deut. 28: 23, 24, dust and sandstorms; cp. ch. 11: 10-17; 1 Kings 17: 1, 7; 18: 2, 5; Jer. 14: 1-6). Even the great deep, which poured out its waters in the Deluge (Gen. 7: 11; 8: 2), the underground waters, feeding the wellsprings of the land, were "devoured," were beginning to dry up, so that the rivers and streams no longer furnished the necessary supply of water. "Did eat up a part" (Gr. N.). "The part," the land allotted to Israel was parched, burnt, like an arid desert. Again the prophet beseeches the Lord to halt the plague, and again the Lord relents (vv. 5, 6; see vv. 2, 3).

C. The Lord Setting the Plumb Line to Israel, Which Had Rejected All Warnings, Ch. 7:7-17

7 Thus He caused me to see: And, behold, the Lord was standing on a wall built according to the plumb line, and in His hand was a plumb 8 line. Then the LORD said to me, What do you see, Amos? And I said, A plumb line. Then the Lord said, Behold, I am setting a plumb line in the midst of My people Israel. I will no longer pass 9 them by! The high places of Isaac shall be desolate and the sanctuaries of Israel laid waste, and I will arise against the house of Jero- 10 boam with the sword. Then Amaziah, the priest of Bethel, sent a messenger to Jeroboam, king of Israel, telling him, Amos has conspired against you in the midst of the house of Israel. The land cannot endure all his words. For so 11 Amos has spoken, Jeroboam shall die by the sword, and Israel shall surely be deported from his land. 12 Then Amaziah told Amos, Seer, go, flee into the land of Judah, and eat bread there, and there prophesy! 13 And at Bethel you shall no longer continue to prophesy, for this is the king's sanctuary, and the royal 14 house is here. Then Amos replied and said to Amaziah, I am not a prophet, nor am I a son of a prophet; for I am a herdsman and 15 a cultivator of sycamores. And the LORD took me away from the flock, and the LORD said to me, Go, prophesy to My people Israel! 16 So now hear the word of the LORD! You are saying, Do not prophesy against Israel, and do not drop a word against the house of 17 Isaac. Therefore thus says the LORD, Your wife shall play the harlot in the city, and your sons and daughters shall fall by the sword, and your land shall be divided by a measuring rope, and you shall die in an unclean land, and Israel shall surely be deported from its land.

Grammatical Note

V. 7. "Plumb line." The Hebrew word denotes a metal, most probably lead (Latin, plumbum), fastened to the end of the line.

Vv. 7-9. The third vision: No more leniency shown to Israel. — Amos sees the Lord standing upon a wall, "made by a plumb line" (Gr. N.), rather, ready for a plumb line, in need of a plumb line. This plumb line in the hand of the Lord is the object of Amos' attention (v. 8). As a wall which the plumb line shows to be completely out of plumb is ready for condemnation, so the Lord will no longer pass by this crooked and perverse people. The plumb line of God's revelation applied to Israel shows that God's people are no longer true to their covenant promise of loyal obedience (Ex. 19:7, 8; 24:3, 7). Instead, they make it their practice to be out of line with God's norm, disregarding His Law, which demands holiness, and rejecting His Gospel, which promises a Redeemer. Such a nation is ripe for judgment, for destruction. Vv. 8, 9 enumerate the chief irregularities and their chief instigators: the high places of "Isaac," here as the parallelism shows = Israel, and their sanctuaries devoted to the calf worship and other forms of idolatry. They shall be desolated, laid waste. Since the house of Jeroboam II had followed in the footsteps of Jeroboam I, the instigator of calf worship (1 Kings 12:26 ff.; 2 Kings 14:23, 24), the Lord would rise up against the royal house of Israel with the sword and annihilate it in bloody warfare.

Vv. 10, 11. Immediately after hearing Amos' prophecy, Amaziah, apparently the high priest of Bethel, sent a delegation to Jeroboam and charged Amos with stirring up a conspiracy against the king in the very heart of his land. Amaziah very shrewdly does not stress Amos' denunciation of Israel's apostasy from the Lord, does not mention his pleas for repentance, nor his pleadings with God (vv. 2, 5). He deliberately changes the general threat (v. 9 b) into a personal threat against Jeroboam (v. 11). As a good politician he mentions not his own interest in the deportation of Amos, but only his patriotic concern for the welfare of the community: "The land is not able to bear all his word." Evidently Amos' courageous testimony had not been altogether futile. People were beginning to listen to him, perhaps even daring to criticize prevailing conditions, to speak of the need of reform. Such action, of course, seemed like high treason to the priest of Bethel. To allow a man like Amos to continue his activity would endanger the welfare of the state, would spell ruin and disaster to the kingdom. Amaziah, a blind leader of the blind!

Vv. 12, 13. It is impossible to tell whether Amaziah summoned Amos before or after the return of the delegation, whether he acted with or without the command or sanction of the king, of whose reaction to the charge we are not informed. Amaziah was determined to rid the

177

country of this calamity howler. "O thou seer," you gazer, you man of such horrible visions, "flee to Judah!" Go back where you came from! "Eat bread," a nasty slur, as if Amos' chief concern was to put something into his mouth (Micah 3:5, 11). You have no business here at Bethel (v. 13). This is the king's chapel, the royal sanctuary, where only those can officiate that are appointed or sanctioned by the king. Moreover, this is the king's court (Gr. N.), a kingdom house, the place where our nation worships, and we do not need any men from Judah to prophesy at our national shrine. We note again the close connection in which Bethel and its calf worship was regarded to stand with the very life and independence of the Northern Kingdom (cp. 1 Kings 12:26 ff.).

Vv. 14, 15. Calmly Amos refutes Amaziah's insinuation that he was in the business of prophesying for the sake of money. He was not a prophet of the king that had chosen this profession for selfish reasons (cp. Jer. 23:9-32; Micah 2:11; 3:5, 11). He had been engaged in a profession which provided sufficient income, a herdsman, a gatherer of sycamore fruit (see p. 137). Nor was he a prophet's son, trained in a special school for prophets such as had been instituted by Samuel (1 Sam. 19:19f.) and later by Elijah and Elisha (2 Kings 2—6). He had not been commissioned to preach by human teachers or superiors. In fact, he had never thought of becoming a prophet. He was, like Samuel (1 Sam. 3:1-21), like Elijah (1 Kings 17:1ff.; 18:1ff.; 19:15ff.), a prophet by divine appointment, commanded to leave his chosen profession and to be the Lord's spokesman to Israel (v. 15). Who was he to disobey the Lord, merely because a human priest disliked his proclamations?

Vv. 16, 17. Since Amaziah had rebelled against the word of the Lord spoken by the Lord's messenger, Amos pronounces in the name of the Lord God's judgment upon Amaziah. His wife was to become unfaithful to him (v. 17), as he had become unfaithful to the Lord (cp. Hos. 1:2; 4:14; 1 Kings 12:28-31); his children would be slain, his land, allotted to him (cp. Joshua 21:1 ff.), would be taken over by strangers; he himself would die in exile in an unclean, "polluted," idolatrous land; his exile shared by the entire surviving nation.

CHAPTER 8

D. The Basket of Summer Fruit, Vv. 1-14

1 Thus the Lord LORD caused me to see: And, behold, a basket of
2 summer fruit. Then He said, What are you seeing, Amos? I answered, A basket of summer fruit. And the LORD said to me: The end has come to My people Israel! I will no more continue to pass them by.

178

3 And the songs of the palace shall lament loudly on that day, is the oracle of the Lord LORD. Many are the corpses He throws down
4 everywhere. Hush! Hear this, you who are trampling on the needy in order to destroy the meek in the
5 land, saying: when will the new moon pass that we may sell wheat, and the Sabbath, so that we may open wheat? to make the ephah small and the shekel large, and to manipulate the fraudulent scales?
6 to buy the poor for silver and the needy for a pair of sandals and to
7 sell the refuse of the wheat? The LORD has sworn by the pride of Jacob: I will never forget all your
8 deeds! Shall not the earth tremble because of this, and all that dwell therein lament, and all of it rise up as the Nile, and mount and sink
9 as the Nile of Egypt? And on that day it shall come to pass, is the oracle of the Lord LORD, that

I will cause the sun to set at noon and will send darkness to the earth
10 on the day of light. And I will change your festivals into mourning and all your songs to a dirge; and I will put sackcloth on every loin and on every head baldness; and I will make it as the mourning for an only child and its end like
11 a bitter day. Behold, days are coming, is the oracle of the Lord LORD, that I shall send hunger into the land, not a hunger for bread nor a thirst for water, but for hearing
12 the words of the LORD. And they shall wander from sea to sea and run from north to east to seek the Word of the LORD, but shall not
13 find it. On that day the fair maidens and the young men shall faint
14 for thirst. And they that swear by the guilt of Samaria and say, As your god lives, Dan! and, As your cult lives, Beersheba! shall fall and not rise again.

Grammatical Notes

V. 3. "Cast them forth." Literally translated: A multitude of corpses He flings down in every place. The verb is singular, not plural as A. V.

V. 4. "Poor," עָנָו. The K'tib demands עֲנָוִי = the meek, subjecting themselves to the Lord and His will (cp.

Ps. 10:17; 22:27, A. V., 26; 25:9; Is. 61:1). The K'ri derives it from עָנִי, having no property, poor, humble; frequently designates the pious Israelites (cp. Is. 41:17; 49:13; 54:11; Hab. 3:14, etc.). In v. 6 "poor" = אֶבְיוֹן, the weak, lowly, underprivileged (cf. ch. 5:11).

Vv. 1-3. Like other persecutors of God's Church and His prophets, Amaziah had imagined a vain thing (Ps. 2:1). His raging against Amos had not accomplished its purpose. Far from being silenced, the prophet with undaunted courage continues to carry on his divine mission as if nothing had happened. He knows that he is the spokesman of the Lord Jehovah, who is undisturbed by the ravings of His enemies. As the Lord's representative he must be equally calm and composed, undisturbed by opposition and persecution. God is with him and will not forsake His servant (Ps. 56:12, A. V., 11; 118:6). He does not even change the manner of introducing his message (cp. v. 1 with 7:1, 4, 7). Nor does he tone down his words. In frank, straightforward, unmistakable language he goes on to castigate the wickedness of Israel.

179

There can be no doubt that this term includes the twelve tribes, the two kingdoms, Judah and Israel, for neither the one nor the other was exclusively "My people of Israel." Only after the final rejection of the northern tribes (722 B. C.) did they cease to be God's people of Israel; and thereafter this term designates Judah. The Lord had shown him a basket of fruit (v. 1). Amos recognizes the contents, and the Lord turns the term "summer fruit" *(kayits),* used by the prophet, into a very effective play on words. "The end *(qets)* is come upon My people Israel!" (V. 2.) As long as the fruit still hangs on the tree, there is the opportunity to grow and develop. The faithful gardener during this time will bend every effort to bring the fruit to the highest possible perfection. Once the fruit is picked, the opportunity for growth is past, irrevocably ended. God, who still regards the nation as His people and calls it by its honorable name, Israel (Gen. 32:28), had as the Covenant God done everything to make Israel a nation worthy of its high distinction (Ex. 19:5, 6; Deut. 4:5ff.; 33:26-29). Now the end has come, the end threatened so long ago (Deut. 28:15 ff.), the end which Israel had brought upon itself by rejecting its Covenant God. The people of Israel had become like the heathen nations. Now He will no longer spare them, but punish them as their iniquitous ingratitude deserved (Amos 3:1, 2). Their Temple songs, their congregational hymns, "shall be howlings" (v. 3). The Hebrew is still more impressive. The songs are personified; the very songs howl, shriek, on that day, the Last Day (cp. Obad. 15, p. 203). The Lord is speaking! He will "cast forth" (Gr. N.) many dead bodies. "With silence," rather, an admonition: Silence, hush! The majesty of the Lord's avenging justice and holiness will strike men dumb (cp. ch. 6:10; Zeph. 1:7).

Vv. 4-6. Israel a nation of greedy profiteers. The rich and prominent men, the social and commercial leaders of Israel, abused their position to harass and suppress the poor and needy. They "swallowed up," panted for (See Gr. N. on ch. 2:7, p. 145), the poverty-stricken people, as a wild beast pants for its victim. They harassed the "poor" (Gr. N.), the meek, submissive people, who committed their cause to God in patient prayer, knowing only too well that it was futile to try to obtain justice in the venal courts against these leeches. These people were an easy prey to the greedy oppressors, who "made them to fail," destroyed them without pity. Outwardly they observed the Sabbath (v. 5) as a divinely appointed day of rest on which no business was permitted (Ex. 20:9, 10), and the new moon, a day of worship

(Num. 28:11) on which business seems to have ceased (2 Kings 4:23; Is. 1:13; Hos. 2:13, A. V., 11), though there is no such divine command on record. Neither Sabbath nor new moon could end fast enough for these money-mad men, who disliked to be deprived even for one whole day of the opportunity to make money. Their insatiable lust for gold impelled them to resort to shamefully fraudulent tricks. Even the barest necessities of life, wheat and "corn," grain in general, were to them welcome means of squeezing profits out of the needy brethren. The "ephah," the bushel measure used in selling grain, was deliberately made small, while the shekel, the weights of stone or metal used in weighing the money of the buyer, were made heavier, so that beside the legal profit they procured even larger profits by illegal means. A third trick were the false scales used by them. Debtors unable to pay were sold into slavery for a few shekels, the needy for a pair of shoes (v. 6), either sold because they could not pay for the shoes they had bought, or for a price just sufficient to buy a pair of sandals. Regard for the poor brother was dead!

Vv. 7-10. Suddenly the scene changes from earthly, human injustice to heavenly, divine justice and vengeance. The Lord has sworn by the excellency of Jacob, by all that Jacob regards as excellent and glorious. He will never forget any of their works (Ps. 50:21 f.; 90:8; Eccl. 12:14). This widespread injustice and uncurbed wickedness spells the ruin of the land. Trembling, abject terror will seize the land, the inhabitants, and heart-piercing sorrow all that dwell therein (v. 8). "It shall rise up wholly as a flood," literally, the Nile, it will be "cast out" = swollen with floodwaters, and "drowned" = sink, as the flood of Egypt. The rising and sinking of the floodwaters of the Nile, spreading ruin and disaster, are emblems of earthquakes which shall spread destruction throughout the land (cp. ch. 1:1, 2). To the horrors of the earthquake will be added an eclipse (v. 9), frequently mentioned in connection with God's judgments, and both as harbingers of the Last Judgment (cp. Is. 13:10; 24:21-23; Joel 2:10, 31; 3:15; Zeph. 1:15). Then there will be no more gay festivities (v. 10) for which the money was pressed out of the poor, no more songs, nor gaudy clothes, nor marvelous hairdos, but mourning, and lamentation, and sackcloth, and baldness, the hair having been torn out in despairing grief, and bitter woe on a bitter day!

Vv. 11-13. The Lord threatens a judgment far more horrible than the worst physical drought or famine. He will withdraw His Word from them! They had despised, rejected, trampled under foot His

181

Word. They had forbidden His prophets to prophesy (Amos 2:12); they had persecuted and slain them. In just judgment the Lord sends a famine of His Word, takes it away from them. In their dreadful political ruin, in the downfall of their nation, they shall run to and fro, totter like drunk men (Is. 24:20) or blind (Lam. 4:14 f.), from sea to sea (v. 12), from north to east, in all directions, seeking God's Word, one word of comfort and consolation. They shall not find it! No bread of life to nurture their starving soul, no drop of Gospel water to quench their awful thirst. Even the fairest maidens and the youth in the prime of life must perish (v. 13). Neither beauty nor strength can save them from famishing. They are hopelessly, helplessly, eternally lost, victims of everlasting death. That judgment of the God of unalterable holiness has been fulfilled time and again in the lives of individuals and in the lives of nations.

V. 14. Once more the Lord names the underlying cause of this judgment: false worship. On "the sin of Samaria" cp. Hos. 8:5 f.; Micah 1:5; "Dan," 1 Kings 12:29 f.; on "the manner," or cult, of Beersheba, Amos 5:5. Thinking oneself wiser than God, tampering with God's revelation, changing, contaminating, falsifying His holy Word, substituting man's ideas, man's philosophy, for the eternal wisdom of the Lord is ruinous, suicidal. Here their judgment is pronounced by the Lord, from whose tribunal there is no appeal: they shall fall and never rise up again. He that hath an ear, let him hear!

CHAPTER 9

E. The Lord Rejects the Apostate Nation, Vv. 1-10

1. The Lord smites the Temple and His sinful people, vv. 1-6

1 I saw the Lord standing at the altar, and He said, Smite the capital, and the thresholds shall shake! And smash them on the heads of all of them! And I will slay the last one of them with the sword. Not a fugitive of them shall flee away, and not a survivor of them shall 2 escape. If they break through to hell, from there My hand shall take them; and if they go up to heaven, from there I shall bring them down. 3 If they hide themselves on the top of Carmel, I will search for them and take them from there. If they hide themselves from Mine eyes in the bottom of the sea, there will I command the serpent, and it shall 4 bite them. And if they go into exile before their enemies, there will I command the sword, and it shall slay them. So will I set Mine eye upon them for evil and not for 5 good. And the Lord LORD of Hosts — when He touches the earth, it melts, and all who live in it mourn; and it rises, all of it, like the Nile, and it sinks like the Nile 6 of Egypt. He builds His stairs in the heavens and forms His arch above the earth. He calls the waters of the sea and pours them out over the surface of the earth. His name is JEHOVAH!

Grammatical Notes

V. 1. "Upon the altar." עַל is very frequently used in the sense of "at the side," "beside." Cp. Gen. 16:7; 18:2; 45:14 f.; Ex. 14:2,9; Judg. 3:19, etc. This seems to be more suitable here. — "Lintel of the door," כַּפְתּוֹר, denotes the ornaments on the golden candlestick (Ex. 25:31-36; 37:17-22); here and Zeph. 2:14 the ornamental capital of a pillar. — "Posts" = the sill, threshold (Judg. 19:27; Is. 6:4; Zeph. 2:14, etc.).

V. 3. "Serpent." Amos 5:19 the serpent was named as the final slayer. Is. 27:1 the mighty streams Euphrates and Tigris are compared to serpents, because many a person met his death in their mighty waters. In like manner the Lord has His "serpent," his slayers in the sea, either its waters or the sea monsters inhabiting the sea.

V. 6. "Stories," מַעֲלוֹת. The noun denotes either the act of ascending (Ezra 7:9), or the thoughts ascending (Ezek. 11:5), or, usually, the means of ascent, steps, stairs (Ex. 20:26; 1 Kings 10:19 f.; Neh. 3:15; 12:37; Ezek. 40:6, 22, 26, 31-37, etc.). It is never used in the sense of upper room, story, chamber. — "Troop," אֲגֻדָּה, that which ties, band (Is. 58:6); a bundle (Ex. 12:22); a band of men (2 Sam. 2:25); here evidently the firmament of heaven, firmly bound together and held together by the mighty hand of God. The word occurs only these four times. — "In the earth," עַל, here, over the earth, rather than "in" or "on," because the sky seems to rest on the earth. "Over the earth" is in keeping with the facts and presents a far more effective picture of God's marvelous power.

V. 1 a. In the fifth and last vision Amos sees the Lord standing "upon" (Gr. N.), rather, beside the altar. The prophet does not use the term Jehovah, but Adonai, denoting one possessing power, authority, designating God as the God of absolute authority and power to do as He pleases with His subjects. Very significantly God is not called Jehovah, the Covenant God. He is about to sever covenant relations with Israel, because the nation has broken His covenant times without number, contemptuously refusing to honor, obey, love Him. The Lord is standing beside the altar. This is not the altar at Bethel, as many presume. At Bethel there were a number of altars (cp. 3:14). Nor does ch. 8:14 warrant a reference to the altar at Bethel here, since neither Bethel nor the altar at Bethel is mentioned in ch. 8:14. That verse speaks of the "sin of Samaria," comprising Israel's entire idolatrous cult, practiced from Dan in the extreme north of Israel to Beersheba in southern Judah. Cp. ch. 5:5, pp. 160 f. At Beersheba undoubtedly also members of the Southern Kingdom participated in the idolatrous worship, the exact nature of which is not known. Moreover, in this chapter the Lord addresses not only Samaria, but Judah as well, the latter being an integral part of Israel, or the children of Israel brought up out of Egypt (v. 7); called the house of Jacob, the house of Israel (vv. 8, 9). See also ch. 2:10 ff.; 3:1, 2; 6:1 (where Zion is named before Samaria). From Zion and Jerusalem the Lord roars against all the eight nations (ch. 1:3, 6, 9, 11, 13; 2:1, 4, 6). For Amos, the prophet of the Lord, there was only one altar deserving to be called "the altar," that at Jerusalem; nor would the Lord have honored the temple and altar at Bethel with His presence.

The Lord speaks, but we are not told whom He addresses. Not the agent, but the shattering destruction is the important matter. The reason why no smiter is named may be that the final rejection came to the two kingdoms at separate times and by different enemies. For the Northern Kingdom it came 722 B. C. by the Assyrians from the north. For Judah the final judgment came for the wicked apostates, the bad figs (Jer. 24:8 ff.), in the Babylonian Captivity, 606—536, which came for the good figs as a warning chastisement (Jer. 24:5-7). When the Jews after the Exile had fulfilled the sins of their fathers (Matt. 23:32), their house was left to them desolate (v. 38; cp. 1 Thess. 2:16). From this Final Judgment no unbeliever shall escape.

Vv. 1b-4. "Smite the lintel of the door" (Gr. N.), rather, the ornamental capitals, the upper members of the two huge pillars erected by Solomon in the Temple (1 Kings 7:21), called Jachin ("He establishes") and Boaz ("In Him is help"). Neither their size nor their beauty shall save them from destruction. So forceful shall the stroke coming from above be that the "posts" (Gr. N.), the thresholds, shall shake. Like a sudden whirlwind dipping from the clouds, destruction shall strike and smash the building from roof to foundation. Nor is only the Temple to be destroyed. A huge festival assembly, representing the entire nation (cp. Ex. 23:14, "thou," the nation, with v. 17, "all thy males" representing the nation), is gathered at the Temple and buried under its ruins. "All of them," "the last of them," will be slain. In the strongest terms possible the impossibility of escape is described. The fugitive will accomplish his flight as little as any survivor in the awful calamity will find deliverance. On v. 2 cp. Ps. 139:8-10. Neither the deepest depth of hell nor the highest height of heaven will offer them a place of escape. Neither the thickets on the top of Mount Carmel (v. 3), nor the bottom of the sea shall hide them from the eye of the all-seeing, avenging God. "The serpent" (Gr. N.), the sea monsters, will devour them. Even exile will not deliver them from judgment; the sword will consume them (v. 4). It is not a human detective, not an employee of the FBI, that pursues them relentlessly. It is God who commands His sword, that God whose hand is all-powerful and whose eye is all-seeing. He has set His eye upon them and stretches out His hand toward them not for good, but for evil. His destruction of His own Temple, His visible dwelling place among His people, is the incontrovertible proof that He no longer acknowledges them as His own peculiar people, His covenant nation, among whom He dwells with His mercy and forgiveness (Ex. 34:6). He has rejected them. Cp. Jer. 14:11 f.; 15:1 ff.; 16:3-6. His sword is not the sword of man, killing the body only, it is the sword of the righteous and holy Lord, who is able to destroy both body and soul in hell (Matt. 10:28; Luke 12:5). Him they did not fear! Him they refused to love and obey!

Vv. 5, 6. If anyone is able to carry out His threat, it is the Lord God of Hosts, the omnipotent Ruler of the universe. If He touches the earth, its very rocks melt and pour their burning lava, turning into solid rock, over flowering landscapes, fruitful fields, and teeming cities. Nothing strikes despairing fear deeper into man's heart than feeling the very ground under his feet quake, rising and sinking as if it were no longer solid earth, but had turned into the waters of the Nile at flood and ebb. The Lord is the Ruler not only of the earth, it is He that is the absolute Lord of heaven also. He builds His "stories" (Gr. N.), His stairs, or steps, to His throne in heaven (v. 6). As Solomon's throne had six steps (1 Kings 10:19 f.; 2 Chron. 9:18 f.), so here the prophet speaks of steps, or stairs, leading to God's throne of glory. Scripture frequently speaks of the "heaven of heavens" (Deut. 10:14; 2 Chron. 6:18; Neh. 9:6; Ps. 68:33; 148:4). Paul speaks of a third heaven (2 Cor. 12:2); the Letter to the Hebrews states that Christ passed into the heavens, literally, through the heavens (Heb. 4:14). Paul says that Christ ascended up far above all heavens in order to sit at the right hand of God in the heavenly places. These created heavens through which, and far above which, Christ ascended to God's eternal, uncreated dwelling place into "heaven itself," "the presence of God" (Heb. 9:24), are compared by the prophet to steps, or stairs, to God's throne. And God Himself has built these steps in the heaven. What a powerful, majestic God, whom even the heaven and the heaven of heavens cannot contain, but are merely the steps leading up to His eternal throne of glory! "He has founded His troop" (Gr. N.), His arch, His vault, "in the earth" (Gr. N.), over the earth. This arch is the grand firmament with its innumerable host of stars, its glorious sun, its beautiful moon (Gen. 1:7, 8, 14-19), daily running their courses, declaring the glory of their Creator. This firmament, humanly speaking, is the gorgeous floor from which ascend the heavens like marvelous steps to the very throne of Jehovah. He it is who "calleth for the waters," etc. See ch. 5:8 b. This Lord had condescended to choose Israel as His people, a kingdom of priests, a holy nation! To have this Lord as one's Ruler, the reconciled Father in heaven, what an honor! To serve Him, what a joy! To be protected by Him, what safety! To be opposed by this Lord, to be rejected by Him, to be objects of His wrath, what unutterable woe! Israel, the covenant nation, had contemptuously rejected the Lord. Now the Lord is ready to reject His people.

2. The sinners shall perish, the just shall live by faith, ch. 9:7-10

7 Are you not like the Cushites to Me, O children of Israel? is the oracle of the LORD. Did I not bring up Israel from the land of Egypt and the Philistines from Caphtor and the Syrians from Kir?

8 Behold, the eyes of the Lord LORD are upon the sinful kingdom, and I will destroy it from off the face of the earth! Nevertheless I will not entirely destroy the house of Jacob, is the oracle of the LORD,

9 For, behold, I am giving command, and I will sift the house of Israel among all the nations, as one sifts with a sieve, but not a bundle shall

10 fall to the ground. By the sword shall die all the sinners of My people, they that say, There shall no evil come near us or overtake us.

Grammatical Notes

V. 7. "Caphtor," named Deut. 2:23 as the home of the Caphtorim, here = the Philistines (cp. Gen. 10:6, 13 f.), who already in Abraham's day (Gen. 21:32, 34; cp. Gen. 26:1-8) had migrated to the eastern coastlands of the Mediterranean Sea, which derived the name Palestine from them. Caphtor is identified by LXX and ancient interpeters with Cappadocia in Asia Minor; now generally with the islands of the Aegean Sea, particularly Crete (cp. Cherethites, 1 Sam. 30:14; Ezek. 25:16; Zeph. 2:5). Some of them may have migrated to Palestine via Egypt, where there seem to have been colonies established by them in the Delta country. The pottery found in ancient Philistian cities was "quite unlike the traditional form of Canaan," . . . "patterned after styles well known in the Greek world, whence the people came." (*Westminster Historical Atlas*, p. 45 b.) "Kir," see notes on Amos 1:5.

V. 8. "Saving that," כִּי אֶפֶס, only that, in the sense of but, yet (cp. Num. 13:28; Deut. 15:4).

V. 9. "Sift" is connected with "I will command" by strong וֹ, as the result of His command He will sift, וַהֲנִעוֹתִי. The Qal = to move, reel, tremble, shake. Hiph. = causative, I will shake Israel, "like as corn is sifted"; "corn" is not named; the passive form יִנּוֹעַ = to be shaken, as if one, that is, Israel, were shaken in a sieve. — "Least" is not in the original. — "Grain," צְרוֹר, never occurs in this sense. The word is derived from צָרַר, which, used transitively, always means "to bind up" for the purpose of safekeeping or guarding. The verb occurs nine times (Ex. 12:34, dough; 1 Sam. 25:29, soul bound up, kept securely; 2 Sam. 20:3, concubines "shut up" under guard; Job 26:8, waters bound up; Prov. 26:8, a stone which is not to be tied to a sling; Prov. 30:4, waters; Is. 8:16, testimony bound up and sealed in the heart; Hos. 4:19, Ephraim; Hos. 13:12, Ephraim's iniquity). — The noun צְרוֹר occurs eight times, denoting that which is bound, connected, or wrapped up chiefly for safekeeping, also the wrapper or bag (Gen. 42:35, twice, "bundle," "bundles"; Job 14:17, bag; Prov. 7:20, a bag of money; Cant. 1:13, bundle, sprigs of myrrh tied together into a bundle and placed for safekeeping close to the heart; Hag. 1:6, "bag with holes." 2 Sam. 17:13, for which interpreters claim the meaning "small stone" or "pebble" as the only suitable one, is just as suitably translated "bound together," "connected," "a coherent part." Not a coherent part shall be left of the city.) These passages already would warrant the translation of our passage "bound up," namely, in God's grace, safely guarded by Him, rather than "grain" (A. V.), "Koernlein," kernel (Luther), or pebble, preferred by most commentators. There is, besides, another passage in which both a verbal and the noun form of this stem occur, which brings out very clearly the two thoughts expressed in Amos 9:9, that of scattering the wicked and preserving the believing children of God. 1 Sam. 25:29: "The soul of my lord [David] shall be bound (צְרוּרָה) in the bundle (בִּצְרוֹר) of life with the LORD, thy God." This passage is the more convincing since it was spoken not by a poet or prophet, but by a woman, Abigail, in the course of a conversation, proving that the phrase must have been current among the people. She adds:

"and the souls of thine enemies, them shall He sling out as out of the middle of a sling." The idea of the believers forming a "bundle" tied together in a unity of life "in the Lord God," tied up in whom, hidden in whom, they are safe, must have been quite common, we might say, proverbial. What is bound up shall not fall to the ground, says the Lord. This "bundle," the elect of God, the chosen remnant, may be hidden among the dirt and chaff, as the 7,000 at the time of Elijah (1 Kings 19:10, 14, 18), yet the Lord knows them and will deliver the godly out of temptations (2 Tim. 2:19; 2 Peter 2:9). The objection that "a bundle" does not suit the figure of a sieve is answered by a reference to 1 Sam. 25:29, where a similar mixing of metaphors occurs, bundle, stone in a sling. — Sellin translates צְרוֹר "pebble"; regards the sieve as a mason's sieve, the sand to be used for the mortar falling to the ground, while the stones are thrown to the side as unfit for use, not one stone falling to the ground. He regards the sifting as God's punitive judgment, which none of the sinners shall escape. The sudden Gospel promise is to him also a stumbling block. He eliminates "among the nations" (v. 9), and "saving that I will not," etc. (v. 8 b). Do not the stones cast aside fall to the ground? Changing the text is not interpreting it, but doing violence to it.

Vv. 7-10. The self-confidence of apostate Israel will not save them from rejection and destruction. — This paragraph is directed against the sinful kingdom. Text and context compel us to regard the singular "kingdom" as comprising both the Southern and the Northern Kingdom. Cp. remarks on v. 1. The twelve tribes are still regarded as one kingdom, Israel. "Sinful," literally, a kingdom of sin, i. e., of missing the mark (see Judges 20:16, "miss"). The Lord can find no more suitable word in describing the actual state of Israel. They had missed the high mark of their divine calling to be God's chosen people (Gen.

12: 1 ff., 17: 7-10; Ex. 3: 16, 17), His first-born son (Ex. 4: 22 f.), a holy kingdom of priests (Ex. 19: 5, 6); missed it so completely that "sin," missing of the mark, is the characteristic of this nation so highly honored. They are "sinners" (v. 10), the Hebrew participle denoting continuity, custom, habitual practice. They were covenant breakers, had mixed with the nations (Hos. 7: 8), had sold their birthright for a mess of pottage. Therefore the Covenant God could no longer regard them as His people, although they still boasted of their high distinction.

In righteous reproof the Lord takes up four stock phrases current among apostate Israel. "We are children of Israel" (v. 7 a), participating by inheritance in the glorious name and blessing bestowed upon our illustrious ancestor (Gen. 32: 28-30). The Lord tells them that a nation constantly rebelling against Him is no better than the despised "children of the Ethiopians," literally, of the Cushites, the descendants of Cush, the son of wicked Ham, brethren of the accursed Canaan (Gen. 9: 18 ff.; 10: 6; Zeph. 2: 12, p. 371).

A second boast: "The Lord has brought us up out of the land of Egypt" (v. 7 b). The Lord tells them that by their neglect of the very purpose for which He had brought them to the Land of Promise, by their persistent refusal to keep their covenant promise of obedient service, they had lost all their high privileges. Their revolt against the Covenant God had deprived them of all covenant blessings, left only covenant threats, changed the very character of the nation. No longer were they the covenant people, but simply a nation among nations. And no longer was the Lord their Covenant God, but simply their sovereign Ruler as He was the Ruler of all nations, shaping their history and destiny. He had brought the Philistines from Caphtor and the Syrians from Kir (Gr. N.). He had caused these nations, neighbors to Israel, to travel from afar to their present homes. Israel's revolt had changed the very nature and character of their migration from Egypt to Canaan. No longer did God view that as a redemption in keeping with His promise to Abraham, Isaac, and Jacob, no longer as a guarantee of deliverance from all enemies (Lev. 26: 1-13; Deut. 28: 1-14). No, Israel had no more claim on special covenant favors, no more claim on blessings promised to their ancestors. A sinful nation among sinful nations, under God's majestic rule of His unchanging justice and holiness. His grace they had cast aside, rejected! Now God had withdrawn His grace from them.

A third boast, "The eyes of the Lord are upon us" (v. 8), was based on Deut. 11: 12; Ps. 33: 18 f.; 34: 16, A. V., 15; 101: 6, forgetting Deut. 11: 16 f.; Ps. 34: 17, A. V., 16. Therefore the Lord tells them that

His eyes indeed were on them and their land, and since He saw only a kingdom of sin, He would in keeping with His covenant threat destroy kingdom and people.

A fourth boast, "The evil shall not overtake nor prevent, anticipate, surprise us" (v.10), summarizing the three former boasts, is summarily dealt with by pronouncing the sentence of death by the sword, warfare and its accompanying famine and epidemics upon all sinners who persist in missing their mark.

In the midst of these dreadful threats we read a marvelous promise (vv. 8 c, 9), revealing the wonderful truth that there is no conflict between God's holy and righteous wrath and His merciful lovingkindness. Neither of these attributes, contradictory though they may seem to man's reason, cancels or disagrees with the other. Both God's justice and God's grace remain forever in harmony in the one, indivisible, unalterable Essence of God. To whom, then, will ye liken Me, or shall I be equal? saith the Holy One (Is. 40: 25).

The Lord had used a very emphatic expression, announcing His intention to destroy the sinful kingdom of Israel from off the face of the earth. In the same breath He continues with what seems entirely incompatible with the preceding words, so incompatible that Geo. A. Smith asks: "Can we believe the same prophet to have uttered at the same time these two statements?" (*Expositor's Bible,* loc. cit.) He finally concludes that the entire passage, v. 8 c and vv. 11-15, "prospects of the future restoration of Israel . . . absolutely without a moral feature," a "change to hope coming suddenly, without preparation and without statement of reason," are one of the numerous signs contained in the prophetic books "that later generations wove their own brighter hopes into the abrupt and hopeless conclusions of prophetic judgments." Smith and other critics voicing similar sentiments do not understand the Gospel of the free grace of God in the promised Redeemer. The Gospel of Christ crucified made unto us wisdom, and righteousness, and sanctification, and redemption (1 Cor. 1: 30; cp. Rom. 3: 19-31), is and will remain to the Jews a stumbling block and to the Greeks foolishness, until God Himself by this very Gospel shines in their hearts to give the light of the knowledge of the glory of God in the face of Jesus Christ, the Lord our Righteousness (2 Cor. 4: 6; Jer. 23: 6).

"Saving that" (v. 8 c., see Gr. N.) = only I will not utterly destroy the house of Jacob! The next verse explains the seemingly contradictory statements. Both are true. The Lord is now ready to command and Himself carry out His determination. He will "sift" (Gr. N.), cause to move, will disperse, scatter, Israel among all nations, like as corn is sifted in a sieve (Gr. N.), literally, as a sieve is shaken. The prophet has in mind the grain sieve, large or small, which was shaken to and fro in order to separate the chaff, and dust, and broken kernels from whole, sound kernels, which remained in the sieve. Israel will be shaken in the sieve of the Exile, by trials and tribulations. The chaff and dirt, the sinners mixed among God's people, will fall to the ground, perish, die, be eternally separated from the congregation of the righteous (Ps. 1:4-6). "Yet shall not the least grain" (Gr. N.), literally, a bundle, shall not fall to the ground. Not one of those whose soul, like David's, was bound in the bundle of life with the Lord (1 Sam. 25:29) shall fall to the ground, be counted worthless, swept away like chaff by the blast of God's judgment. V. 10, see above, p. 170f.

CONCLUSION, CH. 9:11-15

The Restoration of the Falling Hut of David in the Days of the Messiah

11 On that day I shall raise up the falling tabernacle of David. I will wall up its breaches; I will restore its ruins, and I will build it as in 12 the days of old, so that they shall possess the remnant of Edom and all the nations on which My name is called, is the oracle of the LORD 13 who does this. Behold, days are coming, is the oracle of the LORD, that the plowman shall crowd the reaper, and the treader of grapes him that sows the seed; and the mountains shall drip with new wine, and all the hills shall be dis- 14 solved. And I will reverse the fortune of My people Israel, and they will build the waste cities and inhabit them, and they will plant vineyards and drink their own wine and make gardens and eat 15 their own fruit. And I will plant them in their own soil, and they shall never again be rooted up from their land which I have given them, says the LORD, your God.

V. 11. "In that day," when the events announced vv. 8-10 shall have occurred, when Israel shall be scattered among all nations (cp. Acts 2:9 ff.) in the New Testament era, God will raise up the tabernacle of David. On the meaning of tabernacle see note on Hos. 12:10, A. V., 9, p. 94. The royal dynasty of David was called the house of David by the Lord (2 Sam. 7:11, 13, 16; 1 Kings 12:19, 20, 26, etc.). This dynasty will no longer be worthy of being called a house. It is "fallen," falling; the participle denotes a characteristic state. From its very beginning David's kingdom seemed doomed to fall. Judah alone accepted him as its king. He failed to gain any of the other tribes (2 Sam. 2:2-9). Only after seven years of warfare was he crowned king of all Israel (ch. 5:1-5). Already in David's time the kingdom

190

showed signs of disintegration. Absalom's revolt (2 Sam. 15—19) and
Sheba's rebellion (ch. 20) threatened to reopen the rift between south
and north (cp. 19:40 ff.). A lasting breach was effected by the revolt
of Jeroboam (1 Kings 12:19). Frequently the Davidic kingdom was in
grave danger (1 Kings 14:25-28), once hanging on the slender thread
of a baby's life (2 Kings 11:1-3). See also 2 Kings 14:11-14; 16:5-8;
18:13—19:37; 21:10-16; 2 Chron. 33:11; ch. 36. After the Exile the
Jews were subject to foreign nations. Hand in hand with this political
decadence went the spiritual downfall of the house of David; in fact,
this latter was the real cause of the former (2 Kings 23:26). In the
time of Jesus the civic rule was exercised by Rome, and the spiritual
leadership by legalistic, self-righteous Pharisees and unbelieving,
worldly Sadducees. The house of David seemed destined to be ex-
tinguished. The once magnificent mansion was like a miserable shack,
its foundation crumbling, its roof sagging, its walls cracked, the whole
building ready to collapse. Yet the Lord Himself will do the humanly
impossible. He will raise up the fallen hut, and raise it to glory far
surpassing that of its highest former splendor. He will wall up its
breaches. The restored house of David will not be a house divided
against itself, engaged in internecine strife. There will be one King
and one kingdom (Hos. 2:11; Ezek. 37:22). He will raise its ruins,
the parts fallen to the ground. Restored to strength and beauty, it
will stand before all the world, a holy temple of God (1 Cor. 3:17; Eph.
2:20 ff.; 5:27; Rev. 21:2 ff.). Not only will it regain all its glory as in
the days of old (cp. 1 Kings 10:4-9), it will extend to the end of the
world, as prophesied by Ps. 22:26 ff.; 45:3 ff.; 72:7 ff.; 89:13-37.

This was fulfilled in the days of Messiah. Jesus and the Apostles
began their work by calling to repentance the lost sheep of the house
of Israel (Matt. 10:6; 15:24; Luke 24:47; Acts 1:8; 2:5 ff.; 13:46; 14:1).
Among these converts from the Jews there were undoubtedly a number of members of the ten tribes (cp. Matt. 4:12-25; Luke 2:36). In the
Church of the New Testament the breach separating the Northern
and the Southern Kingdom of Israel will be healed.

V. 12. Another enmity will be changed to harmony, another line
of demarcation wiped out, that existing between Israel and the surrounding nations. (Acts 8:5 ff., 27 ff.; 9:15; 10:1 ff.; Eph. 2:11-22.)
Edom is named first, the inveterate enemy of Israel (ch. 1:11 ff.;
Obad. 1, p. 194). Even David had not succeeded in uniting these two
nations, descended from a common ancestor, Isaac (Gen. 25:20 ff.).
The "remnant," here in the sense of Is. 1:9; 10:22 f.; Rom. 9:27 ff.;
11:4-7, the elect, chosen children of God, those "heathen" to whom God

191

has given the honor to be called by His name. The conquered city is called by the name of the conqueror (2 Sam. 12:28), becomes his property; the wife is called by the name of the husband, because she is his own (Is. 4:1); so the prophet (Jer. 15:16), Jerusalem (Dan. 9:18 f.), Israel (Deut. 28:10; Is. 63:19), are God's own prophet, God's own city, God's own people, because God Himself has called His name upon them (Num. 6:27). This honor shall no longer be restricted to one nation as in the Old Covenant (Ex. 19:5, 6; Deut. 7:6; 14:2; Amos 3:2 a). In the New Testament this honor is granted to the believers from every nation and race and tongue (Gal. 3:26-29). This is not the fantastic dream of an overenthusiastic visionary. This is the unalterable oracle, the unfailing decree of the Lord, who alone can, who alone will, accomplish this, just because He is I AM THAT I AM (Ex. 3:14).

V. 13. The plowman preparing the soil for a new seeding shall overtake the reaper busily gathering in the harvest from the seed sown by the sower into soil prepared by the plower. On the other hand, the treader of grapes will overtake the man diligently sowing seed for future crops. In other words, in the Church of Christ there will be incessant preparation and seeding, and never-ceasing reaping and harvesting. In the Church of Christ the work of preparing and sending out missionaries and that of preaching the Word will go on forever, and just as continuous will be the joyful gathering of sheaves into the garners, the bringing of converts into the Church, the growth and expansion of God's kingdom until the end of time. Throughout the ages, Christian homes (Gen. 18:19; Deut. 6:6-9; Eph. 6:1 ff.) will be established, and Christian congregations organized, and daily the Lord of the Church will add to it such as should be saved (Acts 2:47). "And they shall plant vineyards," etc. See Joel 3:18, pp. 134 f.

V. 14. Since Amos prophesies here of the New Testament era, these words refer not to the return of Israel out of the Exile, but to the restoration of God's Church to its greatest glory after the advent of great David's greater Son. Cities and countries wasted by sin and unbelief, superstition and vice, are rebuilt by the preaching of God's Gospel, as the history of the Church during the past twenty centuries proves. Drinking wine and eating the fruit of the Gospel: cp. Is. 55:1f.; Matt. 11:28 ff.; Rom. 5:1 ff.; Gal. 5:22; Eph. 5:9 ff.; Col. 3:1 ff.; Rev. 22:1 ff.

V. 15 is the Old Testament language for such N. T. promises as John 10:27 f.; Rom. 8:28-39; Eph. 1:3 ff.; Phil. 1:6; Rev. 21:1 ff. "He which testifieth these things saith, Surely I come quickly! Amen. Even so, come, Lord Jesus!" (Rev. 22:20.)

O B A D I A H

The Glory of Jehovah as the Everlasting King

A. The Lord Calls upon the Nations to Attack Edom, V. 1

1 The vision of Obadiah. Thus saith the Lord God concerning Edom, We have heard a rumor from the LORD, and an ambassador is sent among the heathen, Arise ye, and let us rise up against her in battle.

V. 1. The superscription: The Vision of Obadiah. Obadiah = Serving Jehovah, was a fairly common name. Of only three persons called Obadiah do we know more than their name. (See 1 Kings 18: 3-16; 2 Chron. 17: 7 ff.; Neh. 10: 5; 12: 25.) "The silence of Holy Scripture as to the prophet Obadiah stands in remarkable contrast to the anxiety of men to know something of him." Pusey. Delitzsch presumes that he may be identical with the prince of like name who was sent out by Jehoshaphat as a member of the royal commission on popular education (2 Chron. 17: 7-9). Since he was a prince, he may have participated in the unsuccessful effort of King Jehoram to quell the revolt of the Edomites (2 Chron. 21: 8-10; cp. "his princes"). This would lend some plausibility to Delitzsch's suggestion that God later chose this pious prince as His prophet to announce His judgment upon Edom. Quite evidently, as we shall see, the oracle was written by an eyewitness of Edom's cruelty.

"Vision"; the Hebrew term is used (1) of visual revelations (Dan. 8: 1, 2, 13, 15, 17, a number of which were audio-visual; Is. 29: 7); (2) of purely oral revelations, "seen," "perceived" by the ear (1 Chron. 17: 15; Ps. 89: 19; Hab. 2: 2, 3); (3) the written record of the revelation (Obad. 1; 2 Chron. 32: 32; Is. 1: 1; Nah. 1: 1). What Obadiah wrote was not the product of his own reflection, of his keen insight into the political and religious conditions of his day; nor was it merely the application of God's Word to a given situation. It was a vision, a divine revelation of God's purpose. To avoid any misconception as to the true character of his message, he adds, "Thus says the Lord God." He is God's spokesman (cp. Jer. 1: 5-9) and, like Jeremiah (Jer. 36:1-6), God's penman. (Cp. 2 Tim. 3: 15, 16; 2 Peter 1: 20, 21.) "The Lord

God," *Adonai Jehovah,* the Lord Jehovah. *Adon* = lord, ruler, one possessing authority. (Cp. Gen. 45: 8, 9.) *Adonai,* my Lord, is used in human or divine speech exclusively as a designation of the true God, proclaiming the absolute authority of God, the Creator and Ruler of the universe. On *Yahweh* see Ex. 3: 13 ff.; 34: 5-7, and p. 203.

"Concerning Edom." Edom embraced a tract of very mountainous country about 110 miles long and 30 miles wide. It was bounded on the north by the land of Moab and the southern shore of the Dead Sea; on the east by the Midianites, and on the south by the Gulf of Akabah, an arm of the Red Sea on the east side of the Sinaitic Peninsula. The western boundary was formed by the southern section of the Arabah, that deep depression through which the Jordan flows, 685 feet below sea level at the Sea of Galilee, 1,275 feet at the Great Salt Sea. From the southern shore of the Salt Sea the depression slowly rises back to sea level at the Gulf of Akabah. Edom derived its name from Esau (hairy), also called Edom (red; see Gen. 25: 25, 30). Esau established his dwelling place in Edom, formerly called Mount Seir ("shaggy, rugged," well describing the character of the land), after driving out the Horites (cave dwellers), named for Hori, the grandson of Seir (Gen. 14: 6; 32: 3; 36: 8, 9; Deut. 2:12-22; 2 Chron. 20:10-23; Is. 21:11; Ezek. 35: 2-7). Edom is also called Teman, from Teman, a grandson of Esau (Gen. 36: 11, 15, 42; Jer. 49: 7, 20; Obad. 9). Teman = lying on the right side as one faces the sun, south (Joshua 15: 1, etc.); the southern section, or the southern chief city standing for the whole country. Edom's two chief cities were Bozrah and Teman: Bozrah in the north was an almost impregnable fortress; Teman, identified with modern Tawilan, in the southern part, was protected by the mighty fortress of Petra (cf. v. 3).

Edom was the inveterate enemy of Israel (cp. Num. 20:14-21; Judg. 11: 16 ff.; 1 Sam. 14: 47, 48; 2 Sam. 8: 14; 1 Kings 11:14-25; 2 Chron. 20:10-30; Amos 1: 6, 9, 11), proud, vengeful, cruel. Against this enemy the first oracle of literary prophecy is directed.

"We" = the prophet and all who hear or read his prophecy. He assures them again that this message comes from the Lord. "Rumor," not in the sense of a vague, unreliable rumor that might well be ignored. Literally, "that which is heard," a message, news, that demands to be heard, obeyed; used of divine proclamations (e. g., Is. 28: 9, 19; 53:1, etc.). A pronouncement of the Lord LORD certainly demands attention. "An ambassador," left undefined. We might think of the ambassadors of some human king who is sending them to the surrounding kingdoms, urging them to join him in a campaign against

Edom. It may, however, be preferable to regard the "ambassador" in the light of 1 Kings 22:19-38, where the Lord, in order to destroy Ahab, sends a lying spirit, who through the prophets promises success to Ahab's campaign. So the Lord now sends His spirits, who through the ambassadors persuade the nations to join Him in a united attack upon Edom. The conspiring nations, of course, had their own ambitious interests in mind, but unknown to themselves they were only pawns in the hands of the Lord. It is the Lord who places Himself at the head of this undertaking, who urges the nations, "Arise! Let us arise against Edom in battle!"

B. Cruel, Proud Edom Shall Be Destroyed Completely, Vv. 2-9

2 Behold, I have made you small among the nations. Utterly despised

3 are you! The arrogance of your heart has misled you, you who dwell in the clefts of the rock, who dwell safely on high, who say in your heart, Who shall bring me

4 down to earth? Though you build high as the eagle and your nest had been set among stars, thence will I bring you down, is the oracle

5 of the LORD. If robbers had come to you or plunderers by night — how complete is your destruction! — would they not have stolen until satisfied? If grape gatherers had come to you, would they not

6 have left gleanings? How thoroughly is Esau ransacked, their

7 hidden things searched out! Back to the border will send you all the men that had made covenants with you. They with whom you were at peace will deceive and overpower you. Your bread they have made a wound under you! There is no

8 understanding in him. Shall I not on this day, is the oracle of the LORD, cause wise men to perish from Edom and understanding from

9 the Mount of Esau? And your warriors, O Teman, shall be dismayed, so that every man might be cut off from Mount Esau by slaughter.

Grammatical Notes

V. 4. "Though thou set," etc. אִם with the perfect denotes the condition as fulfilled in the past. Yet in imprecatory statements the speaker sometimes posits as actually fulfilled what he regards as impossible (G.-K. 159 m. Cp. Ps. 7:4 ff.; Job 31:5, 9, 21, 39). "Set," שִׂים, is passive participle. (See Num. 24:21; 1 Sam. 9:24.)

V. 7. "They that eat thy bread have laid a wound under thee." This statement has puzzled interpreters. LXX translates: "They placed ambushes (nets, traps), ἐνέδρα, under you." Vulgate: "Those who ate together with you" = your friends, associates, "shall place ambushes under you." Kittel in *Biblia Hebraica* leaves the choice between deleting with LXX לחמך as a parallel to שלמך or reading לְחָמֶיךָ. He suggests to read מָצוֹר (cp. Job 19:6, "net") for מָזוֹר. The change from "wound" to "net," "ambush," is adopted by a number of interpreters. R. S. V.: "your trusted friends have set a trap under you." J. Powis Smith in *The Complete Bible:* "Your associates have put a foreign people in your place." Similarly Halevy, Sellin, and others.

Yet there is no need to change the M. T., which, literally translated, reads,

"Your bread they have placed as a boil under you." Nor is it necessary to supply with the A. V.: "They that eat." The text demands the rendering: Thy bread they shall place as a boil under you. G.-B. regards the translation "trap" as uncertain and its connection with Assyrian "*mazuru*" = "The fuller's rod," used in stirring clothes or cloth for cleaning or shrinking, as questionable. The translation of מָזוֹר as trap, ambush, is supported by no other passage and is not demanded in the present passage, as we shall see; while "wound," "boil," from a root = "to squeeze or press out" (Judg. 6:38; Job 39:15), hence, what must be pressed out = a festering wound, a boil, is found Jer. 30:13; Hos. 5:13. — Moreover, the translation "trap," "ambush," creates a real difficulty. No one sets a trap, lays a net, or places an ambush *under* the object to be caught. It would be dangerous folly to try to place a trap or net under a lion or tiger in order to catch him; and who would think of placing an ambush under a hostile army? Nets, etc., are placed *for* others. (Cp. Ps. 31:4; 35:7; 57:6; Prov. 1:17 f.; 29:5.) . . . "Bread" quite commonly denotes that which nourishes and promotes the health and strength of an individual or a nation; financially = income, wealth, riches; politically, statesmanship, power, etc. The rich copper and iron deposits in Edom's territory were bread and butter for the Edomites financially and politically. Yet this very bread would be placed under them as a festering wound, a bold metaphor, but very appropriate; see interpretation, p. 197 ff.

V. 2. While the plotters took every precaution to avoid any possible failure, they could have had no positive assurance of final success. But the Lord knows the outcome because He Himself willed it. He states it even before the enemies attack Edom. "I have made thee small," "thou art greatly despised"; both verbs are perfects, describing the facts as already accomplished. The Lord is sure of the success of His plans. He already sees Edom shorn of all its power and glory, covered with contempt and shame, although the enemies are still preparing their plans.

The Lord, the just Judge, vindicates the justice of His severe judgment. The Edomites have brought divine judgment upon themselves by their overweening pride, described in vv. 3-9, their heartless cruelty, vv. 10-15, their open, contemptuous rejection of Jehovah, v. 16.

Vv. 3, 4. Edom's pride shall be humbled. The prophet names four items on which the pride of Edom was based: its power, its wealth, its alliances, its wisdom. But not one of these advantages, nor all of them combined, could prevent its ignominious ruin.

Edom prided itself on its military strength and superiority (vv. 3, 4). The very character of its land, the high hills, the lofty mountains, the steep crags, the tropical heat, the scarcity of water, all combined to make a campaign against Edom exceedingly difficult and its success problematical, if not impossible. The innumerable caves, natural and artificial, offered refuge for the people of the land and vantage points for the soldiers from which surprise attacks, sudden raids, could be made upon the enemy. While the invaders plodded their weary way in the fierce heat, without adequate food and water supply, the Edomites enjoyed the coolness of the caves, where they had not only hidden their treasures, but had also stored ample food supplies, while huge cisterns filled in the rainy seasons furnished the needed water during the dry summer. In addition to these natural military advantages, "practically every site throughout the length and breadth of the land consisted either of a great fortress or a strong blockhouse." (N. Glueck, *The Other Side of the Jordan,* 1939, p. 140.) The northern boundary was protected by a strongly fortified hill, about one-half mile northwest of Busaireh, the Biblical Bozra, the "jagged precipitous hill of Sela, with the ancient site of the same name on top of it. . . . A narrow cleft down this hillside, widening at the bottom of the slope, was formerly dammed up by a strong masonry wall thrown across its outlet. At one time thus a considerable amount of water was impounded. Most of Sela on the hill is given over to catchment basins, cisterns. . . . Dominating the entire site is a small, prominent, cone-shaped projection, . . . in the center of which a deep cistern had been sunk." (Loc. cit., pp. 166, 168.) Near the southern boundary was the strong fortress of Petra (2 Kings 14: 7, "Selah," the Rock; 2 Chron. 25: 11, 12, "the rock"), situated on the center of a sandstone cliff several miles long, one mile wide, separated from the adjoining table by a canyon running from east to west, formed by erosion. This canyon is from twelve to twenty feet wide, with perpendicular or overhanging walls from 200 to 250 feet high, and affords the only entrance to the city. (*The Sarcophagus of an Ancient Civilization,* Geo. Robinson, 1930, p. 54.) Glueck shows photographs of Petra (loc. cit., p. 22) and Bozrah (pp. 166—168), and Jeremiah speaks of Edom's "terribleness" (ch. 49: 16), that feeling of terror and hopelessness which must have overcome the attacking forces at the sight of these formidable fortresses. Yet even though Edom had built its nest high as the eagle (v. 4), so that it would feel perfectly safe against any attack; yea, though it had actually accomplished the impossible (Gr. N.) and had placed its nest among the stars, neither the one nor the other would avail against the Lord. "From there will I bring you down, says the LORD."

Vv. 5, 6. Edom's pride in its wealth. Edom was by no means a desert country. Fertile valleys were watered by rain and irrigation; "terracing, soil conservation, water economy, preservation of forests,

197

seem to have been the self-understood rote and rule of the former inhabitants of Transjordania from the earliest agricultural history of the region to and through the Byzantine period." (N. Glueck, loc. cit., p. 116.) The soil supplied ample foodstuffs for home consumption and export (cp. Is. 63:1; Micah 2:12). The Edomite pottery sherds bespeak a wealthy, highly cultured people (Glueck, loc. cit., p. 145). The rich copper and iron mines near Ezion-Geber were the source of great wealth. Edom also controlled the great trade routes from Ezion-Geber, one leading to Egypt, the other, the King's Highway (Num. 20:17), portions of which are still traceable (Glueck, loc. cit., p. 15), running from that port through the length of Edom and Transjordania north to Damascus. At Ezion-Geber trading vessels assembled from Arabia, India, Africa, with wares for Egypt, Syria, Assyria, and to return home laden with goods from these latter countries. Edom served as the broker of this world-wide trade, exacting duties, tolls, and other taxes, buying and selling at great profit. Now all these riches, piled up in the course of centuries, would be taken from the Edomites, no matter how carefully they had hidden them. Thieves and robbers usually leave at least something untouched. Grape gatherers overlook a few grapes. Rich Edom, how poor it will become! (V. 6.) Its most secret hiding places ransacked, not an iota of its riches left to it. Beggars!

V. 7. Edom's alliances will prove to be a deception. Since Edom controlled the main trade routes to the surrounding countries and had grown prosperous and powerful, the neighboring states naturally were eager to win and retain the good will of a nation controlling their life line. Edom had succeeded in making trade pacts and defense agreements and other covenants with not a few nations. Again Jehovah was left out of consideration, and again Edom's self-satisfied pride was its own undoing (Prov. 11:2; 16:18). The selfsame allies in whom the Edomites proudly placed their trust will turn against them or disappoint them. Fugitive Edomites, looking for safety and refuge in the neighboring countries, shall be turned back to their own "borders," their own land, by their former allies. No one welcomed displaced people. Like men without a country, the Edomites had to flee from city to city, fugitives and vagabonds like Cain (Gen. 4:12), because Edom, the brother of Israel (cp. Num. 20:14 ff.), hated and cruelly oppressed his brother nation (Obad. 11-14).

"The men that were at peace with thee," their allies, shall "deceive" Edom, deliberately betray their associates by refusing to come to their aid, but rather joining the enemy forces and "prevailing" against them, fighting against them, and contributing to Edom's down-fall and ruin. "They that eat" is to be omitted (see Gr. N.), rather, "Thy bread they have laid as a festering wound under thee." Recent explorations have thrown light on these enigmatic words.

At Ezion-Geber was found "an elaborate complex of industrial plants . . . devoted to smelting and refining of copper, of which, as we have seen, great quantities abound in the immediate vicinity and along most of the length of the Wadi Arabah [a rift or valley extending from Ezion-Geber northward to the Dead Sea]. . . . Iron also was treated in this plant. . . . Ezion-Geber was the Pittsburgh of Palestine." (Glueck, loc. cit., p. 94.) This industry, besides the marvelous fer-tility of the soil, was one of the chief sources of Edom's wealth and political influence, so that it might well be called the bread of Edom. And this bread, the copper and iron they had exported to the neighboring countries, will come back to them in the form of swords and spears and chariots and other instruments of war used in attacking Edom, and will be laid under proud Edom like a festering wound sapping its very life. While we have here a very bold figure, it is highly appropriate to the actual situation. History repeats itself. The metals and materials furnished to Asiatic and European nations by American industrialists and politicians seeking their own aggran-dizement are already beginning to be like a festering wound laid under our youths to sap their lives.

"There is no understanding in him." This sudden change from the second to the third person is not unusual. The Lord, turning away from Edom in righteous wrath, announces to all the world His judg-ment upon Edom. (Cp. Hos. 2: 2-5, third person; v. 6, second; vv. 7-15, third; v. 16, second; v. 17, third; v. 18, third plural; vv. 19, 20, second; v. 23, third.) "Understanding," the power of discrimination, of dis-tinguishing between right and wrong, profitable and harmful.

Vv. 8, 9. Edom must have been known for its wisdom and intel-ligence and must have been proud of these natural endowments, else the Lord would not have named these qualities among the items of its pride. "Wise men" not only, but also "understanding," the very faculty of making right decisions will be destroyed by Him who alone is the Giver of all good gifts. In their utmost need, when they saw their fortresses fall, their riches vanish, and even their allies and trusted friends prove unfaithful, in the hour when they needed wisdom and understanding more than ever, even these were blotted out. Their statesmanship, their political finesse, their business acumen, their mili-tary judgment — all gone, all vanished (v. 9). They do only the wrong thing. Its mighty men, its social and civic and military leaders are confused, seized by paniclike fear, held in the grip of blank despair, and so all perish. Proud, boastful, rich, powerful, wise Edom lies not only prostrate, but is exterminated to the last man! What a price to pay for pride!

C. As the Just Judge of the World the Lord Pronounces His Judgment Against Edom, Vv. 10-16

10 For the outraging of your brother Jacob shame shall cover you, and
11 you shall be cut off forever. In the day when you stood aloof, in the day when foreigners carried off his substance and aliens entered his gates and cast lots on Jerusalem,
12 you were as one of them. Do not gloat over the day of your brother, the day of his calamity! Do not rejoice over the sons of Judah on the day of their destruction! Do not open your mouth wide on the day
13 of distress! Enter not into the gates of My people on the day of their disaster! Do not also you gloat over his affliction on the day of his disaster! Do not stretch out your hand toward his substance in the
14 day of his disaster! And do not stand at the crossroads in order to cut off his escaped ones, and do not deliver into captivity those of his
15 that did remain! For near is the Day of the LORD upon all the nations! As you have done, it shall be done to you! Your deed shall
16 come back upon your head! For as you have drunk upon My holy mount, so shall all the nations keep on drinking continually and shall drink and gulp down and shall be as if they had not been.

Vv. 9, 10 repeat and intensify the threat of v. 2. "Greatly despised" (v. 2), "covered with shame" (v. 10), "made small" (v. 2; cp. "cut off," v. 9), now "cut off forever" (v. 10). V. 3, "pride," here another characteristic sin of Edom, violence. The Hebrew word denotes every kind of wrongful, hurtful action against another, particularly oppression, cruelty. Cp. Amos 1:11 on Edom's cruelty against his brother, also Num. 20:14 ff.

Vv. 11-14, the prophet describes in climactic form the violence of Edom toward his brother nation in distress. "Stoodest aloof," literally, on the other side, opposite, aloof, making no effort to aid his brother nation, when "strangers," aliens, carried away his "forces," literally, "strength," used of military or financial strength. "Cast lots," only here, Joel 4:3 (A. V., 3:3); Nah. 3:10; allot, apportion the city for plunder. Thus the Edomites proved that they were "as one of them," actually taking sides with the enemy. The next step, "looked on" (v. 12) with satisfaction, gloat over (see Ps. 22:17; 37:34; 54:7; 112:8). "Became a stranger," was treated like a stranger, harassed, maltreated. Next, they "rejoiced," laughed at their misery. Then they proceeded to "speak proudly," literally, make one's mouth large or wide, with loud and boisterous voice jeering, mocking, maliciously haranguing the captives. Not satisfied with this, they entered Jerusalem to feast their eyes on its affliction and calamity (v. 13); then they took to plundering the homes and enriched themselves with the "substance" (same word as "forces," v. 11), the belongings of their brethren, while others stood at the "crossways" (v. 14), or, as the word may be translated, the narrow defiles, passes (literally, something cutting off), through which the fugitives sought to escape. Mercilessly the Edomites cut off their escape and turned them over to the enemies, or bought captives to resell them into slavery afar off. (Cp. Joel 3: 6; Amos 1: 6, 9.) They even entered the Temple, whose silver and gold had been carried off by the Philistines and their allies (Joel 3: 5) and made the sanctuary of the Lord the scene of riotous orgies (Obad. 16 a).

To what day of distress does the prophet refer? Opinions vary. Some interpreters regard the book as a prophecy of the future destruction of Jerusalem, 586. W. Moeller places Obadiah between Amos and Hosea (Einleitung in d. A. T.); Pusey in his Commentary, a little later. Modern commentators almost unanimously regard Obadiah as post-Exilic. Marti, in Kautzsch, Die Heil. Schr. des A. T.'s, dates vv. 1-15 ca. 500—475 B. C., and regards vv. 16-21, ca. 135—108; vv. 8, 9, 15 a as eschatological revisions. Sellin dates vv. 1-10 before 586, "because Jeremiah quotes them ch. 49: 11-14, 15 b., ca. 500; vv. 15 a, 16, 17 a, 21, ca. 400; vv. 17 b, 19, 20, several decades later." Geo. Adam Smith in The Expositor's Bible regards vv. 1-6 as written by an Exilic author, starting from an earlier prophecy already utilized by Jeremiah, while vv. 10-21 are post-Exilic and descriptive in vv. 11-14 of Nebuchadnezzar's sack of Jerusalem. In a footnote we read: "That the verses of Obad. 10 ff. refer to this event will always remain the most natural supposition, for the description they give so completely suits that time that it is not possible to take any other explanation into consideration."

In spite of these confident assertions of many critics we hold that Obadiah is not speaking of the destruction in 586; neither prophetically nor restrospectively. While he enumerates a number of harrowing details of a great calamity, with not a syllable does he mention the six characteristic marks of 586: (1) the razing of the walls (2 Kings 25: 10; Jer. 52: 14; Neh. 2: 13-17); (2) the burning of the royal palace and all houses (2 Kings 25: 9; Jer. 52: 13); (3) the burning of the Temple (2 Kings 25: 9; Jer. 52: 13); (4) the capture and deportation to Babylon of the king (2 Kings 25: 7); (5) the deportation to Babylon of the entire nation with a few exceptions (2 Kings 25: 11, 12); (6) the

emigration of the Jews to Egypt (2 Kings 25:26; Jer. 41:16—43:22).
Moreover the A. V. rendering of vv. 12-14, "thou shouldest not . . ."
is not only contrary to grammar, since waw with the jussive never
refers to the past; it is also strange, to say the least, to warn a nation
against a sin long past. Just as unsuitable is it to regard this warning
as pertaining to a future sin. To regard the last clause of v. 11 as
prophetic, "Thou shalt be as one of them," asserting a future fact, and
then warning against that very fact in order to prevent its accomplishment, is utterly illogical. God never speaks in that manner. Neither
the prophetic nor the retrospective interpretation is acceptable in view
of the actual situation it is to describe.

The solution of this problem is to regard the prophet as an eyewitness of a calamitous destruction of Jerusalem. We can point to such
a destruction in the time of Jehoram, the successor to Jehoshaphat on
the Jewish throne. Edom had been subjugated by David (2 Sam. 8:14;
1 Kings 11:14-16), Solomon (1 Kings 9:26-28), and Jehoshaphat
(2 Chron. 20:1-26, 35 ff.; 1 Kings 22:47; 2 Kings 3:9). But under the
latter's son, Jehoram, Edom revolted and, though defeated, maintained
its independence (2 Kings 8:20-22; 2 Chron. 21:8-10). Libnah, near
the Philistian boundary, also revolted at this time (2 Kings 8:22). The
Philistines and Arabian tribes from southern Arabia attacked Judah,
destroyed Jerusalem, pillaged the royal palace and the city (cp. cast
lots, Obad. 11), took Jehoram's wives and children captive, leaving
only one son (2 Chron. 21:16,17). Joel, prophesying only a few years
later than Obadiah, charges Phoenicians and Philistines with having
cast lots (cp. Obad. 11) for God's people (Joel 3:3-6). Here we have
a historical situation which exactly fits the calamity that Obadiah
describes. This interpretation does not violate the text. The verb
forms beside the jussives employed by the prophet are two infinitives
(stoodest, carried away captive) which per se do not indicate the time
of occurrence, and two perfects (cast, come). "The Hebrew perfect
serves to describe actions, events, or conditions which the speaker
desires to present as actually existing (faktisch vorliegend; Driver:
the act in completion) irrespective of whether they have occurred in
a definitely closed past, or still extend into the present, or are regarded
as already completed, although still future." (G.-K. 106 a. Cp. Gen.
49:18; Ps. 10:11; 31:7; 141:1.) If we regard vv. 11-14 as a reference
not to the past nor to the future, but to the present, and Obadiah as
an eyewitness, then the warning vv. 12-14 is entirely in place. The
Edomites had stood by and were still standing by (inf.); they were
still looking with satisfaction as they had done for some time, etc.

(perfects). Hence the dating of this book in the time of Jehoram is in full keeping with Biblical facts, with grammar and logic.

The calamity described vv. 11-14 certainly did not last only one day. The "day" of their distress might have been going on for weeks and months and might continue for months and years to come, until Judah had fully recovered from the ravages described 2 Chron. 21: 16, 17. God had not yet rejected Edom although the mills of God's judgment were beginning to grind and the end would be total ruin. The Lord of everlasting mercy seeks to save Edom from destruction by warning them to discontinue their violence. Through His prophet He cries to the malicious enemies of His people: Do not stand aloof! Do not gloat! etc.

V. 15 adds the reason for His warning: The Day of the Lord is coming! Just what does this term signify?

A. It is the Day of Jehovah. Jehovah is:

1. The great I AM THAT I AM (Ex. 3:14, 15), the Absolute Being, self-existent, self-determining, the omnipotent sovereign Creator and Ruler of the universe (Is. 40:12-28; chs. 44, 45, 48); the one and only God (Is. 42:8; 44:6, 8); the God of all the earth (Ex. 19:5; Joshua 3:11; Zech. 6:5); the Judge of all the world (Gen. 18:25; Ps. 94:2).

2. The God of unchanging justice and mercy (Ex. 34:5-7).

3. The God of the Covenant, who established His covenant with Israel (Ex. 19—24), graciously ruling, guiding, and protecting His people; who has promised to establish a covenant embracing all nations (Jer. 31:31 ff.); who will destroy all opponents of His covenant, all unbelievers, be they heathen or apostates (Ex. 20:5; Lev. 18:24-30; Deut. 32:20-42).

B. It is the Day of the Lord. The phrase, the day of someone or something, occurring no fewer than ten times vv. 11-15, denotes a definite time in the past, present, or future when the person or object named, or something in connection with this person or object, comes into prominence or manifests itself in a special manner or degree. Cp. beside Obad. 11-14, e. g., the day of trouble (Ps. 20:1), of temptation in the wilderness (Ps. 95:8), of battle (Prov. 21:31), of pride (Ezek. 16:56), of the wicked prince (Ezek. 21:25), of Jezreel (Hos. 1:11), of Gibeah (Hos. 9:9), of Midian (Is. 9:4).

In v. 15 Obadiah connects the fulfillment of his prophecy with the approach of the Day of the Lord. This is the first time that this term is used in Old Testament literature, though its content was known before. The Day of the Lord is that day appointed by the Lord as the

Day of Judgment, a day of vengeance unto all unbelievers, of everlasting salvation unto all that have accepted Him as their Redeemer. (Cp. Matt. 25:31-46; Acts 17:31; Rom. 2:5-10; 2 Thess. 1:7-10.) This term comprises not only this one day, but also all its manifold heralds and forerunners and the eternities following upon the Last Day. Every visitation, every judgment of the Lord, be that a just penalty for the enemies of His kingdom or a gracious visitation for the members of His Church on earth, is a forerunner of, and a guarantee for, the final Day of the Lord. These individual harbingers of the Last Day form as it were the rays diverging from the focal point, the Last Day, towards which they at the same time converge. Therefore every judgment of God upon the wicked world is in a certain sense and to a certain extent a Day of the Lord, presaging the great Day of the Lord, whether it be the destruction of Jerusalem in 586, or the annihilation of Edom, or the fall of Babylon, or the Civil War, or World War I or II.

Picture to yourself a huge active volcano, towering over the entire landscape, its fiery, blood-red glow illuminating the darkest night and reflected even in daytime in the dark-black smoke billows constantly issuing forth from its crater. Incessant rumblings manifest the immense power of the forces at work in that huge sea of fire confined in underground caverns, as if waiting only for an opportunity to burst forth in ruinous devastation. Stretched out for many hundreds of miles before that monstrous giant are volcanic foothills, some of the mounds of which seem so far distant as to preclude the possibility of any connection with the far-off monster volcano. Yet underneath all the region lies the same sea of fire, feeding not only the giant mountain, but the foothills as well as the most distant knolls. As one of these lesser volcanoes in the foreground goes into action, sending its fiery streams of lava down its side, belching forth flames and smoke sky-high, it may seem to the distant observer as if the monster volcano had erupted, as in fact it sometimes does, at the same time. Yet every outburst of every volcano, great or small, in that range is caused by that vast underground sea of fire bursting forth through the crater of the pygmy or the monster volcano.

That sea of fire is an emblem of the fire which the holy Lord God has kindled in His wrath against the sin of man, a fire which burns to the lowest hell (Deut. 32:22). This wrath bursts forth volcanolike in the judgments of God preceding and foreshadowing the great Judgment Day of God, whose rumblings, whose fiery smoke already mingle with the noise and destruction produced by the outbursts of the lesser volcanoes, all of which are connected and linked up with the great *dies irae, dies illa,* and, like that volcano which shall completely destroy heaven and earth, are fed by the same fire of God's wrath.

It is therefore not mere poetic license nor a misconception on the part of the prophet when he speaks of the Day of the Lord as coming upon all the nations or upon Israel. The judgments visited upon the nations during the centuries of history are an integral part of the Day of the Lord, which extends like a volcanic range throughout the history of sinful mankind and will reach its final consummation on the Last Day, when time shall be swallowed up by eternity.

The same applies, of course, to all manifestations of God's grace, every one of which flows from that unfathomable sea of divine goodness and love which shall be revealed in its full perfection on that great Day of the Lord.

The Day is near! In an endeavor to save Edom, Israel's brother nation, the prophet warns it of the impending judgment descending surely, swiftly on all nations, none excepted, not even Edom basking in its imagined strength and security. Then the Lord will demand an eye for an eye (Ex. 21:24; Matt. 5:38). Their "reward," literally, what is given to one as his deserts, good or evil. Edom is the type of all enemies of the Lord, whose hatred against Him is manifested in various ways, from standing aloof, in more or less polite refusal to have anything to do with God's Church, to mockery, persecution, and blasphemous desecration of God's holy institutions (v. 16). As Edom has despised and rejected God and His revelation, so will He despise and reject Edom and all His enemies. As Edom has drunk wine in God's sanctuary to the point of intoxication, so God will force His enemies to drink the wine cup of His furious wrath (Ps. 75:8; Is. 51: 17, 22; Jer. 25:15; Rev. 14:10), until, like irrational brutes, bereft of all reason, they totter to their own destruction. *Quem deus vult perdere, prius dementat.*

Is there any possibility of escape? The answer is given vv. 17-21. Yes! But only in the Zion they despise, and hate, and seek to destroy!

D. As the God of Unchanging Grace the Lord Has Established an Escape and Holiness on Mount Zion, Vv. 17-21

17 But on Zion there shall be escape, so that there shall be holiness and the house of Jacob possess their
18 possessions. Therefore the house of Jacob shall be fire and the house of Joseph a flame, and the house of Esau as stubble, so that they shall kindle them and consume them. But there shall not be one left over of the house of Esau; for
19 the LORD has spoken! Then shall the Negeb possess the Mount of Esau, and the Shephelah the Philistines, and they shall possess the

field of Ephraim and the field of Samaria, and Benjamin (shall pos-
20 sess) Gilead. And the captivity of this host of the children of Israel that are among the Canaanites, even unto Zarephath, and the cap-

tivity of Jerusalem, which is in Sepharad, shall possess the cities of
21 the Negeb. Then shall deliverers ascend the Mount of Zion and shall judge the Mount of Esau; and Jehovah's shall be the Kingdom.

Grammatical and Textual Notes

V. 20 has proved quite troublesome to translators and critics. LXX: And the beginning of the deportation is this: For the children of Israel the land of the Canaanites as far as Sarepta, and the deportation of Jerusalem as far as Ephratha; and they shall possess the cities of the Negeb. Marti, Kittel (Bibl. Hebr.), Sellin, The Complete Bible, regard "Mount of Esau," "the Philistines," "the fields of Samaria," "Benjamin" (for which Sellin and Kittel suggest "children of Ammon"), as glosses. The Complete Bible substitutes "Halach and Haber" (cp. 2 Kings 17:6; 18:11) for "this host," הַחֵל הַזֶּה; Sellin reads, "that is Halach," and regards it as a gloss. Kittel proposes to accept either the LXX rendering or to read "Halach." Sellin regards also "which are in Sepharad" as a gloss.

The A. V. supplies "shall possess," not found in M. T. Its marginal reading supplies a second "shall possess that." I know of none that supports this latter reading. The A. V. is favored by Jerome, Kimchi, Hengstenberg, Keil, and others. There is a third rendering adopted by the ancient Targum, Jarchi, Luther, Pusey, and others: "The deportation of this host of the children of Israel that is among the Canaanites as far as Zarephath, and the deportation of Jerusalem, which is in Sepharad, shall possess the cities of the South."

This rendering regards "the Canaanites" as an accusative loci (as, e. g., Num. 10:36; Judg. 11:29; 1 Sam. 13:20; Prov. 10:24; 28:22; Job 15:21, etc. See G.-K. 118 f.). It does not add anything to the Hebrew text; follows the M. T., which placed an athnach under Sepharad, regarding the two deportations 19 a as the subjects of "shall possess," 19 b. Since it does not alter the Hebrew text and is in full keeping with Hebrew grammar, we prefer this rendering. The changes in the text are unnecessary as we shall see.

"Sepharad" has not definitely been identified. G.-B. makes no effort to do so. LXX "Ephratha" seems a mere guess. Targum, Syrian, most Jewish interpreters suggest Spain; Vulgate, Bosporus; Keil-Delitzsch, Sparta (cp. 1 Macc. 12:2, 5, 6; 14:16, 20, 23). Inscriptions from the time of Sargon and Esarhaddon mention a district in Media bearing this name. The identification generally adopted is that of Sardis in Asia Minor, which is called Saparada in a number of Persian inscriptions, connected with Yauna (Ionians). Since this view agrees with Joel 3:6, it seems to be the best solution of this difficult problem.

V. 21. "Saviors." LXX evidently read Hophal, passive, those delivered, saved, instead of moshiyim. There is no valid reason to change the text.

Vv. 17-21. This section consists of three subdivisions, each introduced by an imperfect of progressive duration followed by perfects with strong waws establishing a relation with the preceding imperfect.

The three imperfects announce three promises in their progressive fulfillment throughout the ages, while the perfects announce blessings resulting from the promises in their fulfillment. Briefly stated, we have here the future history of Judah-Jerusalem, the Church of God (vv. 17, 18a), of its enemies (vv. 18b, 19), of those members of the Church who are oppressed, held captive by the enemies (v. 20).

Vv. 17, 18a. "Mount Zion," the eastern hill of Jerusalem, on which the stronghold of Jebus (Jerusalem) was built, captured by David and called David's city (2 Sam. 5: 6-9; 1 Chron. 11: 4-7). On the northern spur, called Moriah (2 Chron. 3:1), separated from the southern half by a shallow valley later filled up, Solomon built the Temple, God's dwelling place among Israel (1 Kings 8: 10-13; cp. Ex. 25: 8; 29: 45). Because of the presence of God, Mount Zion was the very life center of Jerusalem, of Israel, the Church of God of the Old Covenant, and is therefore a very fitting symbol of the New Testament Church, Jerusalem above (Gal. 4: 25f.; Heb. 12:22-24), and the Church Triumphant (Rev. 21 and 22). On Mount Zion, within the Church of God, "shall be deliverance." The imperfect describes the successive flow of this stream of salvation. Generation upon generation may come and go, and each will find salvation on Mount Zion (Is. 33: 20-24; Lam. 3: 22 f.). "Deliverance," literally, escape; that escape from the old evil Foe promised already in Paradise (Gen. 3:15), and then throughout the centuries, the hope of all believers in life and death (Gen. 5: 29; 48: 16; 49: 10, 18), foreshadowed by the sacrifices for the atonement of the sinner (Lev. 1: 4; 16: 1-34) prefiguring the substitutionary sacrifice to be accomplished by the Deliverer (2 Cor. 5: 19-21; Heb. 9 and 10). As a result of this deliverance, there is holiness, a holiness perfect in every detail, such as is demanded by the Lord of holiness (Lev. 19:2; 20: 7, 8) and promised by Him to His covenant people as one of the blessings of the Sinaitic Covenant (Ex. 19: 6), a holiness not of man's making, but procured by the promised Messiah (Gen. 3: 15; Is. 53), offered to all mankind (Ps. 22: 22-31; Is. 61: 1-3), appropriated to all who accept it by faith (Gen. 15: 6; Is. 61: 10). Where there is deliverance, there are also delivered people; and where there is holiness, there are holy people, for the Word of this deliverance, the Gospel, is not preached in vain (Is. 55: 10, 11; John 6: 63). Both "deliverance" and "holiness" are used as abstract (2 Sam. 15: 14; Joel 2: 3. — Ps. 93: 5; Amos 4: 2) and concrete nouns (2 Kings 19: 30 f.; Is. 4:2. — Ex. 28: 36; Jer. 2: 3).

Another result of this deliverance and its resultant holiness is stated in the next clause, introduced by strong waw. "The house of

Jacob" designates Israel as the descendant of sinful, weak, vacillating Jacob, who by God's grace became an Israel (Gen. 32: 24-30). "Possess their possessions." In the Old Testament God's people had the promise of a land to be their own (Gen. 12: 7; 15: 18-21; Ex. 3: 16, 17; Deut. 1: 8; 6: 3, 23). This promise had been given to sinful Jacob fleeing from his home (Gen. 28: 13), and in addition the promise of unlimited "spreading abroad" to the west and east and north and south (Gen. 28: 14). Even if the Israelites in punishment for their sins would be deported from their homeland, the Lord had solemnly promised a return to the Holy Land if His people would return to Him in true repentance (Deut. 30: 1-5). For the duration of the Sinaitic Covenant the Lord had obligated Himself to such a return of His repentant people to His land. And He kept His promise (Ezra 1: 1-5). Yet, returning from the Babylonian Exile, they did not repossess all their former land. A great portion of the Land of Promise (Gen. 15: 18-21) was possessed by other nations and never regained by the Jews. Obadiah, however, prophesies a time when the house of Jacob shall possess their possessions, and proceeds with a promise of complete victory over the house of Esau, their inveterate enemy. In this victorious conquest Jacob will be aided by "the house of Joseph," here the Northern Kingdom, "Israel." Joseph's sons, Manasseh and Ephraim, were adopted by Jacob on his deathbed as his own sons (Gen. 48: 1-6) and blessed by him (vv. 8-20; cp. Deut. 33: 17, last clause). Manasseh and Ephraim were the strongest tribes of the ten forming the Northern Kingdom; hence it is here called the house of Joseph. Obadiah speaks of a time when the two kingdoms shall be reunited. (Cp. Hos. 1: 11; Is. 11: 12-14.) The reunited brethren shall conquer Edom, who shall become as stubble before Judah and Israel, who shall consume him as fire and flame devours (v. 18 a). Therefore the history of the house of Jacob, of Mount Zion, of Israel, of the Church of God, as Obadiah prophesies it here, shall be a history of deliverance, of holiness, of possession of their promised possessions, and victory over their inveterate enemy. The fulfillment of this prophecy will be discussed at the end of this prophecy (v. 21).

V. 18 b. V. 18 b might have been added by another perfect with waw. The prophet changes the tense to indicate that a new thought is to be introduced. The devouring of Edom shall be a total extinction, so that there shall not ever, at any time, be a remnant. Edom as a nation and as individuals shall vanish completely. And this complete extermination of the ancient foe shall have marvelous consequences for God's people, which are brought out by the two perfects with

strong waw (v. 19), describing the repossession of land never occupied
by the Church of God or lost to the forces of idolatry and wickedness.
"For the LORD hath spoken it." Edom, the type of all enemies of
the Church, surely shall be exterminated; God's people shall conquer
the land.

The fulfillment of this prophecy began when the Edomites were
expelled from their homeland some time between 550 and 400 B. C. by
the Nabataeans, a highly civilized nation, who conquered Edom and
Transjordania until they in turn were subdued by the Romans
ca. A. D. 105. The Edomites occupied the Negeb, which was called
Idumaea, and harassed Judah, temporarily even occupying Hebron
(1 Macc. 4: 61; 5: 65), until Judas Maccabaeus defeated them ca.
185 B. C., slaying 20,000 (cp. 1 Macc. 5: 3, 65; 2 Macc. 10: 15-23;
Josephus, *Ant.*, XII, 8.1). Fifty years later John Hyrcanus Judaized
them by compelling them to adopt circumcision and to obey the Mosaic
Laws. Antipater, an Idumaean, was appointed procurator of Judea by
Julius Caesar 47 B. C., and his son Herod, later called "the Great,"
succeeded in having himself appointed king by the Roman Senate.
He captured Jerusalem 37 B. C. and began his bloody rule, ending only
with his death. Almost seventy years later, John of Gischala, the
leader of one of the factions bitterly fighting one another for the
sovereignty of Jerusalem, called the Idumaeans to his assistance. Some
20,000 responded and at once began their work of plundering and
murdering until they were finally somehow persuaded to leave the
city. (Josephus, *War,* IV, ch. IV, 1—6.) Simon of Gerasa attacked
Idumaea, "and did not only ravage the cities and villages, but laid waste
the whole country, . . . so that there was nothing left behind Simon's
army but a desert." (Jos., *War,* IV, ch. IX, 7.) By promising them the
liberty to plunder and murder at will, he succeeded with their aid to
enter Jerusalem, where he at once engaged in bloody battle against
the other leaders, inflicting and sustaining great losses. At the beginning of the siege by Titus he had, besides 5,000 Jews, as many
Idumaeans under his command. Seeing the hopelessness of resisting
the Romans any longer, the commanders of the Idumaeans sent five
delegates to Titus asking him to spare them if they would surrender.
Their plea was granted, but when they were about to leave the city,
Simon killed the delegates, imprisoned the commanders, and forced
the remaining Idumaeans to fight on. (Jos., op. cit., VI, ch. VIII, 2.)
The few survivors took refuge among the desert tribes and were ab-
sorbed in their communities. Thus ended the proud and cruel nation
of Edom.

In vv. 19, 20 various enemies of Judah are named. Edom and Philistia, the two inveterate opponents; the Canaanites "unto" = as far as, Zarephath, Sarepta in New Testament (cp. 1 Kings 17:9; Luke 4:26), about halfway between Tyre and Sidon. Hence, Canaanites here = Phoenicians, who had joined the enemies (Joel 3:4-6; Amos 1:9). Not only Gentile nations were inimical to Judah, but the Northern Kingdom was since its founding opposed to its sister nation. Jeroboam had introduced the worship of Jehovah under the form of a golden calf, contrary to God's will and an abomination to Him (1 Kings 12:26-33; 14:7-16), leading to Baalism, which Ahab made the official religion (ch. 16:29-33; 18:20 ff.). The prophets of the Lord were persecuted and killed (ch. 18:7-14, 22; 19:1-14). "The fields of Ephraim," "of Samaria," designate the western half of the Northern Kingdom. The territory of Ephraim constituted the southern section of the western half. Ephraim always was proud of its prowess (cp. Joshua 17:14 ff.; Judg. 8:1 ff.; 12:1 ff., and notes on Hos. 13:1) and played an important part in the history of the Northern Kingdom. Joshua (1 Chron. 7:20-27), Abimelech (Judg. 8:31; 9:1-3, 22), Samuel (1 Sam. 1:1), Jeroboam (1 Kings 11:26), all were Ephraimites. Shiloh, where the Tabernacle stood for a long time (Joshua 18:1; Jer. 7:12), was an Ephraimite city. Hence Ephraim often was used as a designation of the Northern Kingdom. Hosea prefers this name, using it thirty-six times. About thirty years before Jehoram of Judah ascended the throne, Omri had built Samaria, in the thirty-seventh year of Asa of Judah (1 Kings 16:23, 24), who ruled four years longer (ch. 15:10), followed by Jehoshaphat, ruling twenty-five years (ch. 22:42), succeeded by his son Jehoram. Samaria then became the name of the Northern Kingdom. At a time when the name of the royal city was becoming to be used as a designation of the entire kingdom, Obadiah regarded it necessary to name both "the fields of Ephraim" and "the fields of Samaria," in order to make it clear that he was speaking of the entire kingdom, not only of either the tribe of Ephraim or the city of Samaria. This again points to this early age as the date of Obadiah's prophecy. After the fall of Samaria (722) the Israelites were deported to Assyria and the land was repopulated by heathen nations (2 Kings 17:24 ff.), who opposed and harassed the Jews, the Church of God (Ezra 4:1-24; 6:1-10; Neh. 4). Later they were known as the Samaritans (Luke 9:52 f.; John 4:9). "Gilead," the hilly Transjordanland from the northern boundary of Moab to the Sea of Galilee, or to the Sea of Merom, given to idolatry, opposed to the true religion, was deported by the Assyrians (2 Kings 15:27-29; 1 Chron. 5:26). Syrians took Elath, near Ezion-Geber on the Gulf of Akabah, and evidently subdued the entire Westjordanland (2 Kings 16:6), which later was Hellenized.

Obadiah prophesies a time when all these territories would again be possessed by God's people, having returned to the Lord in repentance and faith (cp. Deut. 30:1 ff.). "The South," the Negeb = the southern section of the territory of the tribe of Judah from Beersheba to Kadesh-Barnea, a semiarid region, capable, however, of supporting quite a large population by proper conservation of water supply. "The Plain," the Shephelah = the broken foothills up to and including the coastal plain, separated from the "hill country" of Judah by several deep valleys. Others restrict this term to the fertile coastlands, including Philistia and the Plain of Sharon. "Benjamin," the northeastern section of the Kingdom of Judah (cp. 1 Kings 12:21, 23; 2 Chron. 11:12). And all this as the result of the extinction of the house of Esau according to the infallible word of the Lord.

Vv. 20, 21. On v. 20 see Gr. N. — What about the captives dragged out of their homeland (vv. 11, 14)? The Lord of the Covenant has not forgotten them! Again a new thought is indicated by an imperfect (v. 20) and its result by a perfect with strong waw (v. 21). Pointing to a band of captives being dragged out of their homeland to Phoenicia, and calling to mind another company of Jerusalemites being deported to distant Sepharad (Gr. N.), he holds out for them a cheering promise of return to their homeland. "The children of Israel" here are the same called "children of Judah" (v. 12), "Jacob," or "house of Jacob" (vv. 10, 17), because they are in truth and fact "children of Israel," God's own, whom He never forgets. They shall possess the cities of the Southland, the Negeb (v. 20).

What a marvelous promise vv. 19, 20! Not only shall God's people repossess the districts of their own land which they had lost to the enemy, or from which they had been deported, but even Philistia, which they had never possessed, yea, and Edom, which had never been promised to them (cp. Deut. 2:5), shall in time come to be their possession!

Vv. 19, 20 do not mean to say that every district named shall possess only that territory named in the predicate. We meet here, rather, with a quite common Hebrew idiom. A number of subjects and a corresponding number of predicates are listed, each of the predicates being connected with one of the subjects. In reality all the subjects are but parts of one body which carries out the work described by the predicates. Israel, God's people, shall again possess or take possession of the various districts and countries named, so that the land occupied by them shall exceed by far the territory they possessed in the days of Obadiah.

When and how were the promises of vv. 19, 20 fulfilled? We need not resort to guesswork. The Lord Himself has indicated the time as well as the manner of fulfillment. As long as the Old Covenant continued, He had promised a return to repentant Israel (Deut. 30: 1-5, note the twofold "possessed," "possess," same word as Obad. 19). The Lord kept His promise (Ezra 1: 1-5, and note the reference to repentance, "all whose spirit God had raised," v. 5). In the course of the Old Testament many others returned (cp. Ezra 7 and 8; Neh. 2). Yet already Balaam had prophesied that Edom, Seir, was to be a possession for his enemies in the time of Messiah (Num. 24: 17, 18), while Amos reveals that the restored hut of David would possess the remnant of Edom, namely, all which are called by the Lord's name (Amos 9: 11, 12). Acts 15: 13-18 James applies this latter prophecy to the Church's victorious conquest of all the Gentiles by the preaching of the Gospel. Matthew and Mark tell us that people from Jerusalem, Judea, Galilee, from beyond Jordan, Decapolis, Idumaea, Tyre, and Sidon were gained for Christ's kingdom by Christ's preaching. The Book of Acts records the fulfillment of Obad. 17-20; the conquest of the countries and districts named by Obadiah by the Church of the New Testament, the true Mount Zion: Philistia (Obad. 19), Acts 8: 40; 9: 32-43; Samaria (v. 19), Acts 8: 5-17; Zarephath in Phoenicia (v. 20), Acts 11: 19; Sepharad (v. 20), in Asia Minor, Rev. 3: 1, and Paul's activity. Paul was a Benjamite, and Benjamin is named as possessing Gilead, at Paul's time having a mixed population of Jews and Gentiles, representative of conditions under which Paul labored in the world at large.

V. 21. But what about Edom? Are they hopelessly doomed to eternal damnation? No! Obadiah had spoken stern words of judgment against the relentless enemies of God's people. Yet he closes his prophecy with a glorious promise. By the gracious power of God, who grants a return even to captives in distant countries, there is deliverance also for Edom! Edom, indeed, will be "judged," yet not by such as come to execute God's punitive judgment, to preach eternal damnation, but as "saviors," deliverers. This term was applied to the "judges" of the early history of Israel in the Holy Land, who were called by the Lord primarily to be deliverers of His people, to save them from their oppressors (Judg. 2: 16, 18; 3: 9, 10, 15; 6: 15); and then to govern them and lead them in the ways of the Lord. Their efforts were blessed with success at least while they lived (Judg. 2:18,19; 3:11, 12, etc.). In similar manner deliverers will be sent to Edom. And this is the result of the deliverance recorded v. 20. Gratitude for their own salvation will prompt the delivered children of God to ascend Mount Zion and proclaim salvation to Edom, their enemy and oppressor (cp. Is. 40:9; 63:1 ff.). Salvation for Gentiles comes from no other source than the salvation of the Jews, from Zion, where God has revealed Himself as the God of grace, from the Jews (John 4:22), of whom as concerning the flesh Christ came (Rom. 9:5). By their efforts there will be delivered ones, a remnant (Amos 9:12), also in Edom, for Jehovah is the Lord of unfathomable grace (Ex. 34:6, 7).

Vv. 16, 18 the complete extinction of Esau is foretold. In v. 21 Edom is still existent. Old Testament prophecy does not always proceed in a strictly chronological manner. The future is revealed to the prophet in perspective, in a panoramalike manner. Events lying decades and centuries apart chronologically are revealed to them as essential parts of the picture without any reference to their exact chronological sequence (cp. 1 Peter 1:11). It pleased God not to reveal all facts to His prophets.

And again Edom is a type and symbol of the grace of God evidenced in the preaching of the Gospel of salvation unto all people. Though this Gospel is at all times to many a savor of death unto death, yet there are always some to whom it is the savor of life unto life (2 Cor. 2:14-16; Mark 6:6; John 8:24).

Thus by the faithful co-operation of the members of God's Church, be they clergy or laymen, the Kingdom shall be the Lord's. "Kingdom," the Hebrew term used here denotes particularly the honor, dignity, and power of royalty. The Hebrew perfect "shall be" denotes an established fact. Jehovah is and remains King Supreme in His kingdom of power governing the affairs of the world, in His kingdom of grace ruling, blessing, extending, protecting His Church and all its individual members, and leading them finally into His kingdom of glory (Rev. 21 and 22). In spite of all opposition of the forces of hell (Ps. 2:1-3), Jehovah is and remains King of Kings and Lord of Lords! In time and eternity Jehovah's is the Kingdom!

J O N A H

The Universality of God's Grace Versus Man's Proud Particularism

Introductory Remarks

1. Historical Background

After the death of Jeroboam II of Israel and toward the end of Uzziah's long reign over Judah a new period in the history of the two kingdoms began, the Assyrio-Babylonian ascendancy over Israel. Already in Ahab's time Shalmaneser III, king of Assyria, had fought a bloody battle at Karkar on the Orontes River in Syria in order to quell a revolt of a number of Syrian kings whom Ahab had joined. This battle evidently was not as decisive as the extravagant boastings of Shalmaneser on his obelisk — the only known reference to this battle — indicate. In 1846 another obelisk of black limestone recording the military achievements of Shalmaneser was found in his palace. Five rows of reliefs extend round its four sides, each row picturing a king kneeling before Shalmaneser and paying tribute to him. On the second row the lower inscription reads: "Tribute of Jehu, son [or as Rogers prefers 'of the land'] of Omri, silver, gold," etc.; Jehu is shown kneeling before Shalmaneser. (Rogers, *Cuneiform Parallels*, p. 304.) "The land of Omri" is generally identified with Israel, whose powerful King Omri was known far and wide. Jehu is called the "son," or successor, of this mighty king. This identification may be correct, even if there is no other mention of such tribute being personally paid by Jehu. Be that as it may, before Menahem's rule (2 Kings 15:14 ff.) no Assyrian king had invaded Israel. Some 80 years after Shalmaneser's death the power of Assyria declined for a period of half a century, coincident with the rules of Jeroboam II and Uzziah. Then Pul, usually identified with Tiglath-Pileser III, usurped the throne. He was a great warrior and an able statesman. He invaded Israel during Menahem's rule (2 Kings 15:17 ff.). That was the beginning of the downfall of the Northern Kingdom. (Cp. 2 Kings 15:29; 16:5, 6;

17:1-6, 24ff.) Before this crisis the Lord had sent Jonah to Jeroboam with the promise of the restoration of the ancient boundaries of Israel. This same prophet was then sent to Nineveh, perhaps during the year of its greatest decline, when the king was stripped of his power and the real rulers were the "turtanues," the highest officials, combining military and civil powers. These men wasted the strength of the nation in their efforts to conquer western Asia, while neglecting the affairs at home. Olmstead speaks of a decline of the Assyrian dynasty, of a breakdown of the central power, of constant encroachments on the part of Haldia, of defections in the south, of revolts which disturbed the country at this time (Olmstead, *Hist. of Assyria,* pp. 166, 169). That may be the reason why the name of the king of Nineveh is not mentioned by Jonah, although we must not forget that Jonah was not a professor of history carefully recording every detail. He was a prophet, whose interest was a religious one, and the mere name of a king was irrelevant to his purpose.

2. Jonah's Person

We see no valid reason to reject the uniform tradition of the ancient Jewish and early Christian Church which identified our prophet with "Jonah, the son of Amittai, the prophet which was of Gath-hepher" (2 Kings 14:25), who foretold the re-establishment by Jeroboam II of the ancient boundaries of Israel by the recovery of territory lost to the enemy. Gath-hepher, also called Gittah-hepher (cp. Joshua 19:13), lay about 2½ miles northeast of Nazareth, in the territory assigned to Zebulun, in central Galilee. The threefold identity, that of the prophet's name, that of the father's name, that of office, make the identity of the Jonah who fled before the Lord and later went to Nineveh and the Jonah of 2 Kings 14:25 practically certain.

Jonah, therefore, prophesied at a time of critical periods in the history both of Assyria and Israel. God's gracious promise to Israel (2 Kings 14:25) was fulfilled by Jeroboam, but since Israel did not repent of its wickedness (2 Kings 17:7-18), it rushed headlong into ruin. God's threat against Nineveh, pronounced by the same prophet during the period of Assyria's temporary decadence, caused Nineveh to repent, so that God spared the city (Jonah 3:10; 4:11) and restored it to its power, which led ultimately to Israel's destruction. Nineveh's conversion at Jonah's preaching in a time of threatening national ruin is therefore — aside from God's grace — quite reasonable also from a purely psychological point of view. See also notes on Jonah 3:5 ff.

We know nothing more of Jonah's person and his history than what we learn from his book and 2 Kings 14:25.

3. Historicity of the Book

"The story of Jonah is neither an account of actual happenings, nor an allegory of the destiny of Israel or of the Messiah (cp. Matt. 12:40); it is fiction — a short story with a moral — like the book of Ruth . . . or the stories about Daniel." — "As with Oriental fiction in general (cp. Daniel, Tobit, the *Arabian Nights*, etc.), the supernatural is the *piece de resistance* of the narrative." — "The author of the story utilized ancient myths and folk tales in his story of the fish." — "Out of such miscellaneous materials the author has composed a charming story intended to teach the lesson clearly expressed at the end of the book, namely, that Jehovah's loving-kindness and compassion are not restricted to the Jews, but extend to the heathen as well." (Pfeiffer, *Introduction to the Old Testament*, pp. 587 f.) Kautsch-Bertholet informs his readers: "Every effort to interpret the book literally and the miracles as historical happenings misunderstands completely the real purpose of the author and leads to absurdities altogether foreign to him." (Kautzsch-Bertholet, *Die Heiligen Schriften des Alten Testaments*, II, 49.) And Sellin declares: "Silly polemics against the miracle narrated in ch. 2, no less than a silly defense of the historical fact of this miracle for a long while actually blinded theology with regard to the unique significance of this splendid booklet." — "The book is a really charming adaptation of the ancient Jonah legend by an author whose purpose it was to teach his particularistic contemporaries in the age of Nehemiah that Jehovah's mercy is universal." (Sellin, *Zwoelfprophetenbuch*, p. 288.)

Pfeiffer lists some of the arguments usually advanced against the historical credibility of Jonah's book. "The storm at sea, the big fish, the gourd, and the worm are all explicitly said to have been divine miracles. — A man's survival for three days in the belly of a fish, or even a whale, which is the only marine animal of sufficient size, is physiologically improbable, to say the least, even if alleged modern parallels are taken into account. The instantaneous and general conversion of Nineveh to the religion of Jehovah could not be taken seriously for a moment by historians of antiquity. They also know perfectly well that no Assyrian king was ever called King of Nineveh"

216

(ch. 3:6), a title no less absurd than "King of London," and that Nineveh never was "an exceeding great city of three days' journey" (3:3), for the circuit of its walls in the time of Sennacherib measured about eight miles." (Pfeiffer, *Intr. to O. Test.*, p. 588.) Eiselen also urges the startling number of miracles in a book of such small compass as an argument against the historicity of the book. "Here are twelve miracles in a book of forty-eight verses. Is there anything like it anywhere in sacred writ?" (Eiselen, *The Proph. Books of the O. Test.*, pp. 454 f.)

We shall take up some of these "arguments" in the course of exposition. In general we may say that Christians do not believe in a God cut to proper shape to satisfy man's reason. We believe in a God who has revealed Himself in the Bible, which according to Christ — who calls Himself the Way, the Truth, and the Life (John 14:6) — cannot be broken (John 10:35), is the truth (John 17:17). In this revelation of Himself God tells us that He is a God whose understanding is past searching out (Is. 40:28; Ps. 147:5; Rom. 11:33); that with Him nothing shall be impossible (Matt. 19:26; Luke 1:37; Rom. 4:21). What is man to limit God's wisdom and power to such matters as man can grasp and understand? We are not to exalt ourselves against the knowledge of God, but to bring into captivity every thought to the obedience of Christ and His Word.

"But these miracles are so incredible!" we are told. More incredible than Israel's clothes and shoes not wearing out in 40 years (Deut. 8:4; 29:5)? than manna falling every morning in the desert and ceasing in Canaan (Ex. 16:14-35; Joshua 5:12)? than Peter walking on the water (Matt. 14:29)? than Lazarus coming from the grave four days after his burial (John 11:17, 44)? A miracle is an occurrence past human understanding. The degree in which it surpasses human reason is for God to determine, not for man's reason. "But twelve miracles in 48 verses! Who can believe that?" Read Acts 2 and Acts 10, dealing with two critical periods in the history of the New Testament Church. There we find in the 47 and 48 verses of each chapter as many miracles and references to supernatural occurrences as there are in the 48 verses of Jonah's book, narrating the mission of the Jewish prophet to a Gentile nation in a critical period for both kingdoms.

Even the fact that the story of Jonah's miraculous delivery out of the belly of the fish is absolutely unique in the history of miracles does not argue against its historicity. This unique miracle may have

217

been and, as we shall see, has actually been, performed for a very special, unique purpose. It was to prophesy and typify the greatest miracle on earth, that miracle on which our entire Christian faith, the certainty of our redemption, our hope of resurrection and eternal life is founded. In fact, Christ Himself connects His unique rest of three days and three nights in the grave before His resurrection with Jonah's being three days and three nights in the belly of the fish, "as Jonas — so the Son of Man." Christ evidently regarded Jonah 1:17 not as a parable or fiction, but as a historical fact, as historical as His resurrection.

Modern critics seek to weaken the force of Matt. 12:40 by saying that Jesus refers to Jonah only by way of illustration, which makes it of no special consequence whether Jonah belongs to the realms of fiction or fact (Eiselen, *The Proph. Books,* II, p. 446), or as Geo. A. Smith puts it: "Suppose we tell slothful people that theirs will be the fate of the man who buried his talent; is this to commit us to the belief that the personages of Christ's parables actually existed? Or take the homiletic use of Shakespeare's dramas — 'as Macbeth did,' or 'as Hamlet said.' Does it commit us to the historical reality of Macbeth or Hamlet?" (*The Expositor's Bible,* Vol. 4, p. 683, footnote.) Yet the examples quoted are not pertinent. (1) There is not the slightest indication in Matt. 12:39-42 that Jesus is referring to a parable or quoting from a drama or that the Pharisees regarded the story of Jonah as an allegory or novel. (2) There is not the slightest indication that Jesus or His opponents regarded Jonah (vv. 39, 40, 41) or the repenting Ninevites as in any manner less historical persons than Solomon, or the queen of the South (v. 42), or Jesus Himself, a greater than Solomon and Jonah (v. 41f.). (3) Jesus had been challenged to give His enemies a sign authenticating His claim to a divine mission. He will give them only one sign. As Jonah was in the belly of the fish, and was delivered, so Christ. As — so, in like manner. If Jonah's sojourn in the belly of the fish was mythical, then Jesus' burial and three days' rest in the grave would, according to His own logic, be a myth; His "resurrection" not a resurrection, but a myth, and His claim to be the divinely sent Redeemer would be — the pen refuses to write it. As Jesus lay in the grave three days, as Jesus rose again, as these are historical facts, so is the three-day captivity of Jonah in the fish's belly and his deliverance not a legendary story, a mere parable, but irrefutable fact, historical truth. Else Christ would never have regarded it as a sign and prophecy of His own burial and resurrection after three days.

JONAH

4. Authorship, Date

"The opening words of the book, 'Now the word of Jehovah came unto Jonah, the son of Amittai,' would point to its having been written in the reign of Jeroboam II (788—747 B. C.), since, according to 2 Kings 14:25, the prosperous years of this king were foretold by 'Jonah, the son of Amittai, which was of Gath-hepher.' For it is evident that we are to understand by the Jonah of this book the prophet mentioned in 2 Kings 14:25. This would indicate a date for the book soon after 800 B. C." (Oesterley and Robinson, *An Introduction to the Books of the Old Testament*, p. 372.) This has been the traditional view of the ancient Jewish Synagog and the ancient Christian Church.

Oesterley-Robinson, however, continue: "The arguments against such an early date are, however, overwhelming." These "overwhelming" arguments are based on the occurrence of certain words and phrases, of which "a few illustrations," 14 all told, are offered: "Like to be" (1:4); "mariners," "ship" (1:5); "think upon" (1:6); "for whose cause" (1:7); "be calm" (1:11f.); "prepare" (1:17; 4:6, 8); "preaching" (3:2); "decree" (3:7); "in a night," "labor" (4:10); "thousand" (4:11). These words and phrases "constitute a strong argument for the late date of the book of Jonah especially on account of the approximation to Aramaic which they exhibit. . . . They date the book approximately 350 B. C. or thereabouts; some scholars would put it a little later." (Op. cit., p. 374.)

Even if we grant that all these forms are Aramaic, they cannot prove the post-Exilic authorship of the book. As early as Hezekiah's reign, Aramaic was the language of diplomats, which even the political and military rulers of Judah understood (2 Kings 18:26; Is. 36:11, "Syrian" = Aramaic). In the native land of Jonah, Northern Israel, the early presence of Aramaic forms and expressions is readily explained by the close proximity of Syria and Phoenicia, and particularly by the thirty years of Syrian domination before the rule of Jeroboam II (2 Kings 13:1-7, 14-25). This "bitter oppression," together with the years of warfare for the deliverance of Israel (2 Kings 13:25; 14:23-28), certainly tinged not only the political, military, and business language with Aramaisms, but affected also the literary and religious language of Northern Israel. Therefore, the presence of Aramaic forms would rather be a strong argument for identifying the author of our book with the Jonah of 2 Kings 14:25 and dating his book in Jeroboam's reign.

219

From other points of view the argument for post-Exilic authorship based on Aramaisms is rendered uncertain and invalid. It is a well-known fact that Israel was not a seafaring nation. That was part of God's plan to keep Israel "alone" (Deut. 33:28; cp. pp. 238 f.). The port of Ezion-geber on the Gulf of Akabah (1 Kings 9:26; 22:48) was available only as long as Edom was subjugated by, or allied with, Israel. On the Mediterranean shore Accho and Dor had harbors of a sort, but not safe enough to encourage commercial navigation. Even Joppa rendered only mediocre service as a fair-weather port. Hence Israel could never develop a maritime people (*Westminster Atlas*, p. 18 f.). When Solomon and Jehoshaphat undertook to build navies, both had to depend on Phoenician shipbuilders and mariners in building and manning these ships (1 Kings 9:26; 10:11; 2 Chron. 8:17 f.; 9:10). A number of the Aramaic terms and expressions in our book were used by such foreigners, the captain and sailors, and are quoted ch. 1:6, 7, 8, 11 (Gr. N., p. 223); or adopted for emphasis' sake by Jonah (Gr. N. on 1:12, pp. 226 f); just as he adopted the official Assyrian term for "decree," 3:7 (Gr. N., p. 233). A number of the alleged late Aramaisms are found in classical Hebrew: "like to be," 1:4 (Gr. N., p. 222); "prepared" — appointed, 1:17, M. T., 2:1 (Gr. N., p. 228); "in a night," 4:10 (Gr. N., p. 242); and are of indisputably early usage; "for whose cause," "for my sake," 1:7, 12 (Gr. N., p. 223); "thousand," 4:11 (Gr. N., p. 225). "Preaching," 3:2 (Gr. N., p. 233), and "labor," 4:10 (Gr. N., p. 238), if Aramaic forms, are sufficiently explained by the Syrian-Aramaic oppression of Northern Israel. The available facts point to the identity of the prophet sent to Nineveh with the Jonah of 2 Kings 14:25 and to the dating of his book at about 850—825 B. C.

PART I

Jonah's Commission, Disobedience, and Punishment

Chapter 1:1-16

CHAPTER 1

A. Jonah's Commission and Flight, Vv. 1-3

1 And the word of the LORD came to Jonah, the son of Amittai, say-
2 ing, Arise, go to Nineveh, that great city, and preach against it; for their wickedness has come up before Me.
3 But Jonah rose up to flee to Tarshish from the presence of the LORD and went down to Joppa; and he found a ship bound for Tarshish. So he paid his fare and went aboard to go with them to Tarshish from the presence of the LORD.

220

Grammatical Notes

V. 2. "Against it." עַל denotes direction toward a person or object, here "against." (Cp. Judg. 9:18; 16:12; 2 Sam. 18:32; Ezek. 5:8; 26:3.)

V. 3. "Fare thereof," literally, its fare = the ship's fare, not as Ehrlich and Sellin suppose, the rental price for the entire ship, but the fare charged a passenger for the use of the ship; cp. railroad fare, bus fare.

V. 1. On Jonah's person, the date and authorship of his book, see Introductory Remarks, pp. 214 ff. On Nineveh, see Nah. 1:1, pp. 294 f.; Zeph. 2:13, pp. 372 f.; on its size, see remarks on Jonah 3:3, pp. 234 f.; 242 f.

V. 2. Jonah is told to cry "against" Nineveh (Gr. N.). Nineveh's wickedness comprised, besides her idolatry, her inordinate pride (cp. Is. 10:5-19; 36:18-20), and her cruel oppression of the conquered nations in deporting the entire populace to distant lands (2 Kings 15:29; 17:6; Is. 36:16, 17), her inhuman warfare. "The merciless cruelty of his campaigns is the constant boast of Ashur-nasirpal II. 'I stormed the mountain peaks and took them. In the midst of the mighty mountains I slaughtered them; with their blood I dyed the mountain red like wool. With the rest of them I darkened the gullies and precipices of the mountains. I carried off their spoil and their possessions. The heads of their warriors I cut off, and I formed them into a pillar over against their city; their young men and their maidens I burned in the fire!' — 'I built a pillar over against the city gates, and I flayed all the chief men who had revolted, and I covered the pillar with their skins; some I walled up within the pillar, some I impaled upon the pillar on stakes, and others I bound to stakes round about the pillar!' " (Luckenbill, *Ancient Records of Assyria and Babylonia,* pars. 447, 443; quoted by J. Finegan, *Light from the Ancient Past,* p. 170.)

This wickedness had "come up before" God, cried to Him for punishment. (Cp. the similar expressions Gen. 4:10; 6:11, 12; 18:20, 21; Rev. 16:19.)

V. 3. Jonah "rose up," made preparations for a long journey. But in direct opposition to the will of the Lord he went not east, toward Nineveh, but west. His intention was to flee to Tarshish, an ancient Phoenician colony on the southwest coast of Spain, the farthest city to the west known at that time, "out of the world." To the Greeks it was known as Tartessus, or, as the historian Polybius calls it, Tarseion. (Cp. Gen. 10:4; Is. 23:1-25; Jer. 10:9; Ezek. 27:25.) He himself states the reason for his flight (ch. 4:2), his intense Jewish nationalism and

221

religious isolationism. He fled "from the presence of the LORD."
To stand in the presence of someone is often used in the sense of acting
as one's official minister. (Cp. Gen. 41:46; Deut. 1:38; 10:8; 1 Sam.
16:21 f.; 1 Kings 17:1; 18:15; 2 Kings 3:14, etc.) To flee from His
presence = to refuse to serve Him in this office. Others regard the
face of the Lord as the Holy Land, where God dwells in the Temple.
Luther: "God has two manners of presence, one natural, the other
spiritual. In the natural manner He is present everywhere. Spiritually,
He is only where His Word, faith, Spirit, and worship is present. —
Therefore, we can actually flee from God by fleeing to a place where
there is no Word, faith, Spirit, and knowledge of God. So Jonah fled
from God." Two paragraphs later he says, "Jonah manifestly was disobedient to God's positive command, since he fled and would not go
to Nineveh" (St. L. XIV, 848 f.). By fleeing to Tartessus in the extreme
West he hoped to make it impossible to serve God as His prophet, as
His official minister in the far East. His flight certainly was not due
to a superstitious belief that God's omnipresence was confined to the
land of Palestine. (Cp. ch. 1:9ff.)

B. The Storm, Vv. 4-10

4 But the LORD hurled a great wind upon the sea, so that there was a great storm on the sea, and the
5 ship thought to be broken up. And the sailors became frightened, and everyone cried to his god. Then they hurled the ship's cargo into the sea in order to lighten it. But Jonah had gone down into the lower part of the ship, and had lain down, and was lying in a deep
6 sleep. So the captain approached him and said to him, How can you sleep so soundly? Get up, and call to your God! Maybe God will be mindful of us, so that we shall not
7 perish. Then they said one to another, Come, let us cast lots to find out for whose sake this evil has come to us. So they cast lots, and
8 the lot fell on Jonah. Then they said to him, Now tell us on whose account this evil has come to us. What is your business? Where do you come from? What is your country? And from which nation
9 are you? And he told them, A He-brew am I, and I fear Jehovah, the God of heaven who has made the
10 sea and the dry land. Then the men were stricken with great fear and said to him, How could you do this? For the men knew that he was fleeing from Jehovah, for he had told them.

Grammatical Notes

V. 4. "Sent out." טוּל, to move forward, Hiph., to hurl; same word as vv. 5, 12, 15, "cast forth." — "Was like to," חָשַׁב, Qal, to think (1 Sam. 18:25; 2 Sam. 14:14; Jer. 23:28; 26:3; 36:3; Pi., Prov. 24:8, here used of an inanimate object. Such personifications of inanimate creation are not at all infrequent in sacred literature. (Cp. Is. 14:8; 35:1; 44:23; 49:13; 52:9; 55:12; Ezek. 6:1ff.; Micah 6:1ff.; Ps. 19:2-7; 96:11-13; 98:8; Rom. 8:19ff.) Hence this expression cannot

be regarded as an Aramaic form, nor as post-Exilic.

V. 5. "Mariners." מַלָּחִים (see Ezek. 27:9, 27, 29) is usually connected with מֶלַח salt, like our colloquial "salt" for sailor. G.-B. prefers a connection with Assyrian "malachu" (cp. Ezek. 27:9 a), "mariners," which LXX translates κωπηλάται, oarsmen. It seems that the term denotes the sailors, perhaps including the oarsmen; while חֹבֵל (Jonah 1:6; Ezek. 27:8, 27–29, "pilots," A. V., κυβερνήτης, LXX; cp. Acts 27:11; Rev. 18:17) denotes the steersman, helmsman, the officers; and the "shipmaster," v. 6, רַב הַחֹבֵל, is the chief steersman, the highest officer, the captain.

"Ship." סְפִינָה "is usual word for ship in Arabic and Aramaic." (Keil-Delitzsch.) אֳנִיָּה is the general term, comprehending all classes of ships or boats, from large seagoing vessels (Ps. 104:26; Prov. 31:14; Ezek. 27:9, 29) to rowboats (Job 9:26, "swift," literally, reed, papyrus, used in constructing small Nile boats). Jonah uses this term in ch. 1:3, 4, 5 a, while he uses סְפִינָה, in v. 5 b, either for the sake of variety or in order to define the type of ship more accurately. The root סָפַן means to cover, panel. (Cp. 1 Kings 6:9; 7:3,7, the "paneling" in the Temple covering walls, ceiling, and floor; Jer. 22:14; Hag. 1:4, "ceiled.") Hence it may denote a covered, or decked, ship, in whose "inner parts," יַרְכְּתֵי, its holds where the cargo was stored, Jonah sought to hide himself. The "sides," יַרְכְּתִים, translated "sides," Ex. 26:27; "from the sides,"

Jer. 6:22; "in the sides," Ezek. 32:23. — "Fast asleep," used only in Niphal, denotes lying in deep, stuporlike sleep (Jonah 1:5, 6; Ps. 76:7, A. V., 6), "dead sleep" (Judg. 4:21; Dan. 8:18; 10:9); the noun occurs in Gen. 2:21; 15:12; Prov. 19:15, etc.

V. 6. What meanest thou?" מַה־לְּךָ = What to you? What is the matter with you? — "O sleeper," same form as "fast asleep" (v. 5); participle: Sleeping?! Astonishment mingled with anger and resentment. — "If so be that God." "God" has the article in the original and refers to "thy God," the Lord Jehovah, from whose presence Jonah was fleeing (vv. 3, 10). — "Think upon us." יִתְעַשֵּׁת, an Egyptian-Aramaic term, occurring only here in Biblical language; used by the captain speaking the Aramaic language, quoted verbatim by Jonah.

V. 7. "For whose cause," בְּשֶׁלְּמִי. The Aramaean sailors here use the short form of the pronoun שֶׁ; in v. 8, the longer form, אֲשֶׁר; while Jonah uses the short form in v. 12; both forms being used by Aramaeans and Israelites in Jeroboam's time, p. 219. The shorter form cannot be used to prove post-Exilic authorship, since it occurs as early as Gen. 6:3; Judg. 5:7; 6:17; 7:12; 8:26; 2 Kings 6:11. אֲשֶׁר לְ and שֶׁל "frequently circumscribe the genitive, particularly when two genitives are dependent on a noun. (Cp. 1 Sam. 17:40; 2 Sam. 2:8; 1 Kings 15:20; and Cant. 1:1, where otherwise suffixes are used. Even בַּאֲשֶׁר לְמִי, Jonah 1:8." G.-B. sub אֲשֶׁר, p. 73; A 4 d.)

Casting Lots

Not only heathen have made and still make it a practice to arrive at a definite decision by casting lots; we also read that individual Israelites and the entire nation made use quite frequently of some sort of lot. H. Speckhard calls attention to the fact that in the Old Testament, the era of nonage, of minority (Gal. 4:1 ff.), God graciously condescended to declare His will through visible, external means (Synodical Report, Michigan District, 1910, p. 24 ff.; translated by R. Herrmann,

The Book of Jonah. Concordia Publishing House, 1942). The Urim and Thummim, placed into the breastplate fastened to the ephod worn by the high priest in his official duties (Ex. 28:30; Num. 27:21), served to reveal God's will, the exact manner of such revelation being unknown to us. (See Joshua 9:14; 1 Sam. 22:10, 13, 15; 23:6-13; 30:7 ff.; Neh. 7:65.) As far as the Biblical records go, the Lord commanded to cast lots only in matters of importance (Lev. 16:8; Num. 26:53 ff.; 33:54; 34:13; Joshua 7:13 ff.; chs. 14—21); or God's appointed representatives issued the command (1 Sam. 10:18 ff.; only *after* 9:15 ff.; 10:1). Saul's use of the lot (1 Sam. 14:37-45) was an act of a king rejected by God (1 Sam. 13:13 f.), an example illustrating Prov. 16:33, without giving permission to resort to casting the lot.

In the New Testament there is no divine command to cast lots in order to find out God's will. The only instance on record of resorting to a decision by means of casting lots was on a unique occasion, when an apostle of the Lord was to be chosen to take the place of Judas, whose office was to be taken over by another according to divine prophecy (Acts 1:20; Ps. 69:25; 109:8). Under the guidance of the representatives of Christ, the apostles, who were appointed by the Lord Himself, the congregation took steps to fill the vacancy. They were well aware of the special requirements for the apostolic office (Acts 1:21, 22). Apparently the two men appointed as candidates were the only ones to be found among the 120 souls (Acts 1:15) having the necessary qualifications. Yet the congregation was equally aware that an apostle of Jesus Christ could be appointed only by the Lord Jesus Himself (Matt. 10:1 ff.; Mark 3:14 ff.; Luke 6:13 ff.; Gal. 1:1; 2:8; 1 Tim. 1:1; Titus 1:3). Therefore they did not dare to choose either one, but left the matter entirely to God's will by casting lots to ascertain whom the Lord would choose. And the Lord chose by directing the lot to fall upon Matthias (v. 26).

This is the only example recorded in the New Testament of casting lots by apostles or congregations. Neither the deacons (Acts 6:1-6), nor Paul and Barnabas as missionaries to the heathen (Acts 13:1 ff.), nor the delegation sent to Antioch by the congregation at Jerusalem (Acts 15:22 ff.), nor the pastors placed in the newly planted congregations (1 Tim. 4:14; Titus 1:5) were chosen by lot.

In order to prevent confusion and quarrels, the lot was quite frequently resorted to in Israel without divine command in matters of minor importance; e. g., in establishing the order in which the priests and Levites were to serve (1 Chron. 24:1-19, see vv. 5, 7; 20-31, see v. 31), the singers (1 Chron. 25:1-31, see vv. 8, 9), the gatekeepers (ch. 26:1-19, see v. 13 f.), etc. It would not be sinful if a congregation or individual Christians resorted to the lot in order to decide certain details in carrying out a work in which they are agreed in general. But the outcome of the lot is not to be regarded as a divine decree. A congregation may, after all, decide to change plans favored by the lot. (Cp. Prov. 18:18.) Prov. 16:33 teaches the simple truth that it is God who rules and governs the most important as well as the most insignificant matters, the falling of a hair (Matt. 10:29, 30) as well as the rise and fall of mighty kingdoms (Jer. 18:6 ff.). He governs also the falling of a lot, yet without revealing whether our choice on the basis of the lot will work out for our weal or woe.

Vv. 4, 5. The Lord "sent out" (Gr. N.), hurled, a great wind upon the sea; and, humanly speaking, the winds obeyed their Creator, who had hurled them with all His power, and blew with all their might into the sea. And the waters in like obedience raised their waves and billows higher and higher, tossing the ship to and fro. One moment it hung perilously trembling on the crest of a huge wave, only to be hurled into the yawning abyss until it was covered with water. "It was like to" (Gr. N.), literally, it thought. In a vivid personification thoughts of fear are ascribed to an inanimate object. Such personifications are not at all uncommon. (Cp. Is. 23:1, 14; Zech. 11:2; Ps. 98:8; Is. 55:12.)

Even the experienced sailors were stricken with fear at the unusual vehemence of the storm (v. 5; cp. Matt. 8: 24 ff.). They tried every available means of saving their ship and their lives. When prayer addressed by each of them to his chosen deity did not help, they hurled the "wares," the cargo, overboard. Yet these efforts were as futile as their prayers had been ineffectual.

Vv. 6-8. Finally the captain remembered the Israelite who had professed to flee from the presence of his God, Jehovah. Where was he? Jonah had "gone down into the sides" (Gr. N.) of the ship, into some obscure corner, where he hoped to remain unobserved. Like the chosen disciples of Christ (Matt. 26: 40, 43), the divinely chosen prophet was sound asleep (Gr. N.) under circumstances which ordinarily would have made sleep impossible. Yet the long journey from Gath-hepher to Joppa, some 60 miles or more, the mental and spiritual agony he had endured, robbing him of his sleep, had left him in a state of such complete physical exhaustion that he had sunk into a death-like stupor. The captain awakes him. What meanest thou, what is the matter with you, "O sleeper" (Gr. N.)? Hoping against hope, he calls on him to pray. The heathen reminds God's prophet to do his duty! Call on your God, Jehovah, perhaps that God (Gr. N.) can and will help where his gods had failed. We are not told that the prophet prayed. How could he approach God in prayer while determined to flee from Him? The sailors resort to another means to allay the storm (v. 7). Convinced that someone must have roused the anger of the sea god, they cast lots to detect the guilty person. Jonah knows he is the culprit, yet will not confess. He was the sole cause of the storm which had caused physical and mental anguish and financial losses to the sailors. Yet he is perfectly willing to let them suffer greater losses, to let them die, rather than to confess. Undoubtedly he hoped that the lot would not reveal him; at least he was willing to take a chance. Was he better than these ignorant heathen? The cords of sin (Prov. 5: 22) had enmeshed him and held him fast. Jonah gambled, and lost! God Himself so directed the lot that it fell upon Jonah. This is the finger of God! his conscience told him. The sailors, convinced of his guilt, now ply him with questions as to his occupation, his country, his people (v. 8). Perhaps one or the other regarded him as offensive to the sea god. (Cp. Acts 28: 4.)

Vv. 9, 10. Now, at last, Jonah frankly confesses. "I am a Hebrew," the usual term by which Israelites were known to foreigners (Gen. 14: 13; 39: 14, 17; 1 Sam. 29: 3; Acts 6: 1). He also confesses his faith in the Lord, the Creator of heaven and earth and sea. He had already

225

told them that he was fleeing from the presence of the Lord. Yet they
had regarded Jehovah as one of the many local gods whose wrath one
could escape by leaving the country over which he ruled. Now for the
first time they were being told that the Lord, the God of Israel, was
not a local god, that He was the Creator of the universe, the Ruler of
wind and waves. Jonah had unintentionally, contrary to his national-
istic and isolationistic prejudices, brought these Gentiles to the knowledge of the true God. Such is the power of God's Word, a power
altogether independent of the speaker's will and intention. The sailors
express their amazement at Jonah's folly to escape such a God (v. 10).
They are God's instrument in chiding the prophet. Why hast thou
done this? The prophet's answer is not recorded. Very likely he could
not answer. There he stands, hanging his head in silent shame, a sorry
spectacle!

C. The Miraculous Calming of the Storm After Jonah's Voluntary Self-Sacrifice, Vv. 11-15

11 Then they said to him, What shall
we do with you, so that the sea
may calm down for us? For the
sea was surging higher and higher.
12 So he told them, Take me and hurl
me into the sea! Then the sea will
calm down for you. For I know
that this great storm has come upon
13 you because of me. And the men
tried to break through in order to
get back to the land, but they
could not, for the sea surged higher
14 and higher. Then they cried to the
LORD and said, Ah, LORD, let us
not perish for the life of this man,
and do not bring innocent blood
upon us, for Thou, O LORD, doest
15 as Thou pleasest. So they took
Jonah and hurled him into the sea,
and the sea ceased from its raging.

Grammatical Notes

V. 13. "Rowed hard." חָתַר occurs seven
times and denotes digging into, or
through, an object, the heavy wall of
the Temple (Ezek. 8:8), the stone wall
of a house (Ezek. 12:5, 7, 12; Job 24:16),
into hell (Amos 9:2). The noun occurs
Ex. 22:2, "breaking up"; Jer. 2:34, "secret search," literally, digging through
a wall. It always implies hard work,
here that of breaking through the walls
of water. The imperfect describes the
repeated, continued efforts.

V. 14. "We beseech Thee." In the original two different interjections, the first
the stronger one, אָנָּה, Ah! Oh! the second, נָא, Now! Pray! The A. V. reading
is very suitable.

Vv. 11, 12. In spite of Jonah's frank confession, the first evidence
of his repentance, the storm continued to rage in ever-increasing fury.
Now the sailors apply their newly acquired knowledge of God by
appealing to His messenger for information as to what they should do.
Since the Lord had sent the storm, He alone could still it. And since

Jonah's resolve to flee from the Lord had caused the storm, they reason that something must be done with him to quiet the storm. Yet they do not take this matter into their own hand. The Lord through His prophet is to decide. Jonah shows that his repentance is sincere. No longer shall these men suffer for his disobedience. He offers himself as the victim to be sacrificed in order that they might be saved (v. 12). As the prophet of God he tells the sailors to cast him into the sea and promises them that this act would cause the storm to cease, the sea to be calm. No longer does he flee from the Lord! He commits himself, body and soul, to the will of His Lord. Here he shows heroic faith! He is still God's confiding child, even though he has sinned grievously.

Vv. 13-15. The prophet's answer does not appeal to the sailors. Is there no other way to save their lives except by depriving a fellow man of his life? "They rowed hard" (Gr. N.), tried to break through waves and wind in another effort to regain the shore. But the waves were against them! And what is puny man against the unleashed elements, against the Lord, at whose command storm and sea battled against the ship! To this Lord they appealed when all their efforts to save Jonah's life had proved unsuccessful (v. 14). "We beseech Thee" (Gr. N.). Ah, Lord, may we not perish for taking the soul, the life, of this man! Lay not upon us innocent blood! On this expression cp. Gen. 4:10 f.; 9:4 ff.; Deut. 19:10 ff.; Matt. 27:24, 25. These Gentiles had the Fifth Commandment written in their hearts and revolted from slaying a man who had, as far as they knew, done nothing worthy of death. Compare their action with that of "God's people," the Jews (Luke 23:13-25). Yet they are willing to submit to God's will even though they do not understand it, even against their own inclination: "Thou, O Lord, doest as it pleases Thee!" Here we have a confession by newly converted Gentiles which is actually the human reflex of the Lord's explanation of His name Jehovah, I AM THAT I AM (Ex. 3:14 a; 33:19 b; cp. Rom. 9:15 ff.). Thou, O Lord, hast the right and privilege to do as Thou pleasest. Not our opinion, our will, but Thy will, Thy counsel, be done! Who are we to be disobedient to Thy will, so clearly expressed by the storm, by Jonah's confession, Thy prophet's demand? So they took up the prophet and hurled him into the raging waters (v. 15). While their hurling the cargo into the sea had not the slightest effect on the storm, this hurling at the command of God's prophet, in keeping with God's will, immediately accomplished its purpose. The sea ceased from its raging.

227

D. The Effect of the Miracle upon the Sailors, v. 16

16 Then the men were filled with profound fear of the LORD and offered sacrifice to the LORD and vowed vows.

"Feared exceedingly," literally, feared a great fear. They were overcome with awe and amazement. Vividly they felt their own puniness and helplessness over against the majesty of Him who in a moment had stopped the howling tempest and quieted the raging sea. At the same time they had experienced in so marvelous a manner the grace and mercy of the Helper of the helpless. In adoration of His power and loving-kindness they offered what sacrifices were available on the ship and made solemn vows of allegiance and further service and sacrifices to their newly found God. Jonah's sacrifice of his own life had not only saved the sailors' lives, but was also the means — again unintentional on his part — of strengthening their faith in the Lord of salvation. How marvelous are the ways of our God!

PART II

The Lord Delivers His Repentant Prophet

Chapter 2:1-11 (A. V., 1:17—2:10)

CHAPTER 2

A. Jonah Swallowed by a Fish, M. T., 2:1 (A. V., 1:17)

2:1 (A. V., 1:17) Now the LORD assigned a large fish to swallow Jonah; and Jonah was in the belly of the fish three days and three nights.

Grammatical Notes

V. 1 (A. V., 1:17). "Prepared." קָנָה, Qal, to count, ten times (cp. Gen. 13:16; Ps. 90:12). To apportion, appoint (cp. Is. 65:12; Ps. 147:4). Pi., to assign, appoint (Job 7:3; Ps. 61:8; Dan. 1:5, 10, 11; Jonah 2:1; 4:6, 7, 8). Pu., passive (once, 1 Chron. 9:29). The term never occurs in the sense of prepare, or create. — "Fish," dag, דָּג; the masculine form is used here and v. 11, while v. 2 the feminine, דָּגָה, is used. Gen. 1:26 f. and Ex. 7:18, 21 the feminine is used in designation of all the forms of aquatic animals created by the Lord (Gen. 1:22). — "Three days and three nights." Not necessarily seventy-two hours. (Cp. Esther 4:16 and 5:1; Matt. 12:40 and 16:21; 1 Cor. 15:4.)

This story of Jonah's survival in the belly of the fish for three days and three nights (Gr. N.) has been the butt of ridicule by unbelievers throughout the centuries. People who know little more about the Bible than this story consider it as sufficient to regard the

Bible as a book of fables, unfit to be taken seriously by men of intelligence. Luther writes: "This narrative seems almost unbelievable, yea, sounds like a greater falsehood and folly than any fable of the poets. If it were not recorded in Scripture, I would regard it as a ridiculous lie." And he repeats: "I myself would not believe it, were it not written in Holy Scripture." That latter fact, indeed, changes the whole matter. It is written in Scripture! We believe that Scripture is given by inspiration of God (2 Tim. 3:16). We believe our Lord Jesus who says, "Scripture cannot be broken" (John 10:35); and again, "Thy Word is truth" (John 17:17). Christ believed the story narrated here, and with Christ and with Luther we believe it.

"Now the Lord had prepared a great fish." This great fish (Gr. N.) may have been a huge whale, or one of the many species of the shark family, or any other sea monster. It is not a miracle that a man is swallowed by a huge fish, nor is it unheard of that a man so swallowed has been rescued within a short time. Yet none of these stories, even if true, explain in any manner the miracle here recorded. Nor was this a special fish created by the Lord for this special purpose. The word translated "prepared" never is used in the sense of "create" in Scripture. It always denotes to count, or to assign, commission (see Gr. N.). God is the Ruler of earth and sky and sea, and the inhabitants of the latter obey His direction and do His will. At God's direction this fish swallowed Jonah alive, and by God's almighty power the prophet was kept alive and conscious, or, if he temporarily lost his consciousness, was restored to it so that he could pray to the Lord, as we are told in the next verse. To be sure, this is a miracle past understanding. Of course, natural reason finds it impossible to believe this story. Yet by the grace of God we cast down imaginations and every high thing that exalteth itself against the knowledge of God and bring into captivity every thought to the obedience of Christ (2 Cor. 10:5). While our reason may advance many an argument against its possibility, we accept the story in its entirety at par value, because it bears the imprint of the omnipotent Lord and Creator and carries the attesting signature of our Lord and Savior (Matt. 12:40).

B. Jonah's Prayer, Vv. 2-10 (A. V., 2:1-9)

2 (A. V., 1) Then Jonah prayed to the LORD, his God, from the belly
3 (2) of the fish, saying: I called out of my distress to the LORD, and He answered me! From the womb of hell I pleaded. Thou hast
4 (3) heard my voice! For Thou didst cast me into the deep, into the heart of the seas, and the flood surrounded me; all Thy breakers and Thy rollers passed over me.
5 (4) Then I said, I am cast out of

Thy sight! Surely, I will look again upon Thy holy Temple!
6 (5) Waters encircled me (coming) to my soul. The deep encompassed me. Seaweed was wound around
7 (6) my head. To the ends of the mountains I went down. The earth — her bars were behind me forever! Yet Thou hast brought up my life from the pit, O LORD, my

8 (7) God! When my soul fainted within me, I thought of the LORD; and my prayer came in unto Thee,
9 (8) into Thy holy Temple. They that regard deceitful vanities for-
10 (9) sake their Mercy! But I with the voice of thanksgiving will sacrifice to Thee! What I have vowed, I will pay! Salvation is of the LORD.

Grammatical Notes

V. 4 (3). "Billows," "waves." The Hebrew word for billow denotes the breakers, short, rough, choppy waves, while "waves" are rollers, long, swelling waves.

V. 5 (4). "Yet," אַךְ = surely, certainly (Gen. 9:5; 26:9; 1 Kings 22:32); here it denotes assured confidence in spite of

all circumstances pointing to the contrary.

V. 7 (6). "Corruption," שַׁחַת = pit (see Ps. 9:16; 94:13; Prov. 26:27), the grave (Ps. 30:10; Job 33:22, 24, 28).

V. 9 (8). "Observe," שָׁמַר, here = attend, to worship, serve (Hos. 4:10; Ps. 31:7; Prov. 27:18).

V. 2 (A. V., 1). St. Paul exhorts, "I will that men pray everywhere" (1 Tim. 2:8). A Christian cannot come into a place so abnormal that he could not pray to God there. — We cannot imagine a place more fantastic, more horrible, more filthy, than the one where Jonah was, in the belly of a horrible monster, in the dreadful sea, all alone, cast away from mankind." (Pardieck, *Lehre u. Wehre*, 61 [1915], 244.) Yet Jonah prayed there a model prayer as St. Paul describes it: request, prayer, supplication, thanksgiving (Phil. 4:6). The belly of this sea monster was the prayer chapel from which ascended a prayer pleasing to God, accepted and answered by Him in a truly marvelous manner. We may divide this prayer into four paragraphs, vv. 3; 4, 5; 6-8; 9, 10 (A. V., 2; 3, 4; 5-7; 8, 9). The first three describe first the agony and anguish threatening to overwhelm Jonah, only to be supplanted by the firm assurance of God's deliverance, while in the last paragraph Jonah rises to a confidence so certain that he regards his deliverance as already accomplished. (Cp. Ps. 55:17 f., A. V., 16 f.; 57:2-12, A. V., 1-11; Is. 65:24.)

V. 3 (2). "I cried by reason of," literally, from out of, mine affliction, my straits, my anguish. — "Out of the belly," the inner part of "hell," sheol, the realm of death. When Jonah saw the men approaching him to do what he had told them, when they lifted him off his feet and carried him to the side of the ship, when they hurled him through the air into the raging sea, then, indeed, he was in

230

affliction, then dread, fear, the anguish of death and hell held him in its grip. Yet God had heard him in his distress; even in his deepest anguish the Lord of the Covenant heard the voice of His agonized servant.

Vv. 4, 5 (3, 4). "For," rather, "and," connecting this verse with the preceding thought and adding another instance of his agony turning into confident thanksgiving. As he felt the waters surrounding him, his conscience upbraided him. It was God who had cast him into the deep. The sailors were merely the instruments of His wrath. And as he sank deeper, as the mighty floods and currents engulfed him, as God's "billows and waves" (Gr. N.), His breakers and rollers, passed over him, he felt that he had been cast out of God's presence forever, as if he had been altogether forsaken of the Lord. Yet suddenly he realized that he was no longer in the water, that he had not drowned, that he was in darkness, in the gruesome maw of a fish — yet alive! God had not forsaken him. Though he had been unfaithful to his God, the Lord of the Covenant had remained faithful. He had not slain the wayward prophet, not cast him into eternal damnation. A sudden ray of hope illumes the darkness of gloom. "Yet" (Gr. N.), surely, certainly I will look again toward Thy holy Temple. What strange power of faith! (Cp. Heb. 11: 1.) Faith looks forward confidently to continued grace and final delivery on the basis of past deliverance from physical or spiritual anguish. Momentarily his affliction was forgotten and joyous confidence filled his heart. Yet only momentarily!

Vv. 6-8 (5-7). (Cp. Ps. 18: 5-7, A. V., 4-6; 69: 2, 3, A. V., 1, 2; 88: 4, 5, A. V., 3, 4.) Once more the horror of drowning is vividly described. He had despaired of his life when the waters surrounded his soul, the seat of life, and the deep had enclosed him, and the seaweeds had wound round his head, as if to hold him in their grasp forever. He had gone down to the lowest depths of the sea, where it rested upon the foundations of the mountains as on its bed. No escape there! And as far as the earth was concerned, that had closed and barred its doors against him forever! The sea, the mountains, the earth, had joined in conspiring against his life. But there was One mightier than earth and mountains and sea — the Lord, Jehovah, his God. He had in His everlasting mercy and grace brought up his life from corruption (Gr. N.), from the pit. (Cp. Ps. 30: 4, 10, A. V., 3, 9.) "When my soul fainted," was utterly exhausted, at death's door, I thought of Thee, the God of the Covenant, I, the miserable, unfaithful, runaway servant, remembered Thee. And what I could find nowhere else, I found with Thee! My prayer, uttered in the lowest sea, in deepest anguish, came

231

in unto Thee, into Thy holy Temple, and was not refused entrance! The prayer of a sinful, dying man, manifestly lost, was heard by the holy Lord!

Vv. 9, 10 (8, 9). "They that observe," hold fast, serve (Gr. N.), lying vanities," deceitful nothings, forsake their own Mercy. Mercy is here, like in Ps. 144:2 (Goodness used as a proper noun), a name of God, who is Love. Jonah had become guilty of that folly. He had followed the dictates of his own wicked and deceitful heart (Jer. 17:9) rather than Him who is Mercy. Never again will he do that! The Lord shall be his God, whom he will serve, to whom he will sacrifice with the voice of thanksgiving, to whom he will pay his vows, for He alone is the Lord of his salvation. On this note of joyous assurance of deliverance and sincere promise of grateful service ends this remarkable psalm.

Did Jonah actually pray this psalm while he was in the belly of the fish? He tells us that he did. That is not impossible. The prayer is saturated with quotations from, or reminiscences of, psalms written by David or in his age and therefore well known to pious Israelites. Compare (in A. V.) Jonah 2:2 with Ps. 18:4-6; 30:3; 120:1 — v. 3 with Ps. 42:7 — v. 4 with Ps. 31:22; 5:7 — v. 5 with Ps. 18:7; 69:1f. — v. 6 with Ps. 18:16; 30:3; 103:4 — v. 7 with Ps. 142:3; 43:4; 18:6; 5:7; 88:2 — v. 8 with Ps. 31:6 — v. 9 with Ps. 42:4; 50:14, 23; 116:17. How many Christians have voiced their prayers in hours of extreme anguish by repeating familiar passages from Scripture or from their hymnbook! So even Christ in His agony on the cross (Matt. 27:46; Luke 23:46; cp. Ps. 22:1; 31:5a). The thoughts and emotions recorded in Jonah's prayer were those that actually passed through his mind during his imprisonment, and he may have given expression to some of them in the very words recorded. The final form of great poetical perfection and logical sequence found in ch. 2 was composed by him after his deliverance.

C. Jonah's Deliverance, V. 11 (A. V., 10)

11　(10)　And the LORD spoke unto the fish, and it vomited out Jonah upon the dry land

---

Now the Lord releases His repentant prophet from his prison. At His command the fish spews Jonah out, not into the waters of the sea, but upon the dry land. "It is also related that . . . he was vomited out upon the Euxine Sea," the Black Sea. (Josephus, *Antiquities* IX, X, 2.) That is a legend, for which there is no authority in Scripture.

PART III

Jonah's Preaching and Nineveh's Repentance

CHAPTER 3

1 Then the word of the LORD came to Jonah a second time, saying,
2 Arise, and go to Nineveh, that great city, and proclaim unto it the proclamation which I shall tell you.
3 So Jonah arose and went to Nineveh, as the LORD had told him. Nineveh was a great city before God, a journey of three days. So
4 Jonah began to go into the city one day's journey, while he was proclaiming and saying, Forty days more, and Nineveh shall be overturned!
5 Then the people of Nineveh came to believe in God, and they proclaimed a fast and put on sackcloth from the greatest to the least.
6 When the matter reached the king of Nineveh, he arose from his throne and took off his robe and put on sackcloth and sat in the dust.
7 And sent criers to say in Nineveh, By decree of the king and his nobles: Let neither man nor beast, neither cattle nor sheep, taste anything, let them neither feed nor
8 drink water. And let them put on sackcloth, both man and beast, and call to God fervently, and let them turn, each one, from his wicked way and from the violence they are
9 committing. Who knows? God may turn and relent; and He may turn from the furor of His anger, so that
10 we shall not perish. So, when God saw their actions, that they turned from their wicked way, God relented of the evil which He had said He would do to them, and did not do it.

Grammatical Notes

V. 2. "The preaching." קְרִיאָה occurs only here in Biblical Hebrew. — "Bid," דָּבֵר, to speak, here with אֶל = command. (Cp. Gen. 16:13; Ex. 6:29.)

V. 3. "Nineveh was." The perfect often denotes a past action or state which still continues at the speaker's time. (Cp. Ex. 2:22; Gen. 18:13; 27:4; 49:18; Num. 11:5, etc. G.-K. 106 g.) — "Journey." מַהֲלָךְ occurs only five times, denotes a walk, on which one walks, a path (Ezek. 42:4; Zech. 3:7), or a journey (Neh. 2:6; Jonah 3:3, 4). The term says nothing about the direction of the journey, whether straight ahead, or zigzagging. The context alone can give this information.

V. 4. "Began" is construed with the infinitive and לְ (e. g., Gen. 6:1; 10:8; 11:6, etc.; so here), "to enter"; also with strong waw and imperf. (Gen. 9:20; Ezra 3:8). Here the two constructions are found side by side: He began to walk and to preach.

V. 5. "Believed," from אָמַן, to be firm, sure, true; the English "amen" is the same word. Hiph. = to regard or make firm, by saying yea and amen; to believe, confide, trust in a person or object.

V. 7. "Decree," טַעַם. The Hebrew word occurs in the sense of taste (Ex. 16:31; Num. 11:8); also, sensation, understanding, reason (1 Sam. 25:33; Prov. 11:22; 26:16). Here Jonah uses the Assyrian-Babylonian term "temu" = decree, royal edict.

V. 9. "God." The king uses the article before Elohim, in order to denote the one, the true God.

Vv. 1, 2. God did not dismiss His disobedient servant. Nor did He wait until Jonah had of his own accord set out for Nineveh. In order to assure Jonah that his willful disobedience had not made him ineligible for the Lord's service, He once more commissions him to go to Nineveh (v. 2) and to preach the preaching (Gr. N.) which the Lord would "bid" (Gr. N.), or keep on telling him. But He does not inform Jonah of His purpose. The prophet's and preacher's duty is to preach not his own mind, but only whatever the Lord tells him (Jer. 1:7, 9) and to leave the success or non-success of his preaching to the Lord.

V. 3. In obedience to the Lord's command, Jonah arose, made the necessary preparations for the long journey, and set out on his way to Nineveh, "according to the word of the LORD." There may have occurred moments of hesitation, of unwillingness, of the need to bring his flesh into subjection to the spirit (cp. 1 Cor. 9:27); but God's will and word helped him to gain the victory. He kept on until he came to Nineveh, the capital city of the Gentile world empire. "Nineveh was a great city" does not warrant the assumption of many critics that Nineveh must have been destroyed for a long time before the author wrote this story. Jonah simply states that when he arrived at Nineveh it had been, and still was (Gr. N.), a large city. Moreover, he states that it was an "exceeding" great city, literally, a large city "for God," great in God's eyes, an object of living concern for Him (cp. ch. 4:11). Even though Jonah saw only its wickedness when he came there, it was for God a great city, a city whose eternal welfare He sought. It is a chastened and repentant Jonah that speaks here in retrospect, not the dissatisfied prophet of Jonah 4:1-9. "Three days' journey" (Gr. N.) refers according to the context not to the circumference or to the diameter of the city, but to the length of time he required to preach to all the people.

V. 4. "Began" (Gr. N.) refers to "to enter" and to "he cried." Jonah does not mean to say that he had walked a day's journey on Main Street before he began to preach. He knew that he was not to make this a sight-seeing tour. He was sent to preach, and to preach not to one individual, as, e. g., Moses (Ex. 6:11, 29), Nathan (2 Sam. 12:1), Elijah (1 Kings 18:1). He was sent to preach to Nineveh, that great city (ch. 3:2). This meant that he was to preach not merely to the walls and houses, but to the people of Nineveh. These people were not assembled at one place, nor were they lined up on Main Street to watch a parade. At the first opportunity after coming to Nineveh, perhaps to the very first group he saw, or even to the first individual he met, perhaps already in the suburbs, at the very beginning of his

234

entering the city, he began to proclaim his message: "Yet forty days, and Nineveh shall be overthrown!" He predicts the fate of Sodom and Gomorrah, total destruction (Gen. 19:21, 25, 29) to proud, invincible Nineveh. For three days he continued with his proclamation.

Vv. 5-9. Nineveh's repentance. — News of the strange prophet and his strange message spread like wildfire throughout the city, and soon he may have preached to huge crowds coming from every quarter of the city to hear him. Idle curiosity changed suddenly to fear and consternation, their own conscience condemning them. Is there any possibility of escaping the wrath of Jehovah? Perhaps if we turn to Him in prayer, He will relent! And behold, what Jonah had never hoped, what was directly contrary to his own wishes, what he had actually feared (ch. 4:1 f.) now happened! The people of Nineveh, these wicked Gentiles, "believed" God (Gr. N.). The prophet uses the same word that Moses used to describe Abraham's saving faith (Gen. 15:6; cp. Ex. 14:31; 2 Chron. 20:20), a term that denotes saying yea and amen to God's Word as it was revealed to them by the prophet. In proof of the sincerity of their sorrow for their wickedness and of their turning to God, they proclaimed a fast and wore sackcloth. Even the king of Nineveh (v. 6) descended from his throne in humble submission to Jehovah, exchanged his royal robes for coarse, ugly sackcloth, and sat in ashes. (Cp. Esther 4:16; Job 2:8; 42:6; Dan. 9:3.) By royal decree (Gr. N.) both man and beast were to refrain from food and drink, and all be shrouded in sackcloth (vv. 7, 8). Such mourning extending even to the animal world is not unexampled. Herodotus relates that after the death of Masistios, the leader of the Persian cavalry, who was slain by the Greeks in the battle of Kithairon, 479 B. C., Mardonios, the Persian general, together with the whole army, mourned his death by cutting off their hair and the hair of their horses according to their custom (Herodotus IX, 24); cp. Judith 4:10, 12 (the Jews placed sackcloth on their cattle and about the altar on a day of prayer and repentance). The king was not satisfied with a mere outward expression of sorrow; he demanded a change of life, a turning away from their evil way and from violence, oppression, their besetting sin (Nah. 3:1, 19). And he expressed his hope that God (Gr. N.), the one true God revealed to them by Jonah, might turn from the fierceness of His anger, so that they would not perish (v. 9).

Critics tell us that such a mass conversion is impossible from the historical as well as the psychological point of view. There is no historical record of such a change of religion in the Assyrian inscriptions.

Granted! But this fact does not make the statement unreliable or untrustworthy. For centuries Is. 20:1 was the only known reference to Sargon, so completely had his memory been wiped out. Yet he is now known to have been one of the most powerful rulers of Assyria and the builder of a magnificent palace at Nineveh. Was Isaiah's reference to Sargon less true or reliable because it was the only one? Must every historical statement of the Bible be confirmed by other witnesses before it can be accepted? Has any historical statement of the Bible ever been disproved? Have they not times without number been corroborated in a marvelous manner? "The Scripture cannot be broken," says Christ, who is the Truth (John 10:35; 14:6).

But the conversion of an entire city in so short a time is psychologically impossible, we are told. Really? Does not psychology know of mass psychoses? Did not Orson Welles's purely fictional broadcast of a Martian invasion of America (October 30, 1938) terrify millions of Americans and "spread wild disorder and terror from coast to coast," so that "police headquarters, newspapers, and radio stations were swamped with anguished calls," "whole neighborhoods were evacuated as inhabitants rushed into the streets with wet handkerchiefs pressed to their noses to defend themselves against poison gas," "families huddled in desperate prayer"? (*Reader's Digest*, February, 1951, p. 17.) At Nineveh the speaker was not a sensationalistic broadcaster. He was a prophet of Jehovah! If Peter's sermon converted 3,000 Jews, many of whom had only fifty days before cried "Crucify Him!" why should we limit the omnipotent grace of the Lord to a number of people suitable to the psychology of modern unbelief? Here is the psychology not of mortal man, but of the Lord of Lords, with whom nothing is impossible (Luke 1:37; Matt. 19:26), the conversion of an entire city as little as the conversion (impossible to human strength) of a single human being dead in trespasses and sins (Eph. 2:1-7, 19, 20).

Was the repentance of the Ninevites sincere? Keil says that Jonah's preaching did not effect a thorough conversion, rather only a powerful incitement to conversion, which did not last long. Others have pointed to the example of Ahab, whose penalty was postponed because he at least outwardly humbled himself before God at Elijah's reproof (1 Kings 21:27-29). Yet the Biblical record tells us that the people of Nineveh believed God. The Searcher of hearts (Jer. 17:9) sees faith and its effect, a change of life. Moreover, Christ, who knows what is in man (John 2:24f.), assures us that the Ninevites repented (Matt. 12:41). There ought to be no doubt therefore that the faith and contrition of these people were sincere and serious. Whether all of them continued in faith is a different question. Some may have remained faithful, others may have permitted their faith to be choked by the cares of this world or to die in times of persecution and tribulation (Matt. 13:20 ff.).

V. 10. God's repentance. The unchanging I AM THAT I AM (Ex. 3:14) repents! How is that possible? Just because He is the God of unchanging grace, forgiving iniquity and remitting the punishment to all that believe, while hating and punishing all that hate Him and refuse to believe and obey His Word, which calls them to repentance. That is His norm of action with all nations, Jews and Gentiles, as He Himself has revealed it (Jer. 18:7 ff.).

PART IV

Jonah's Complaint and God's Rebuke

CHAPTER 4

1 And Jonah's feelings were bitterly hurt, and he burnt with anger.
2 So he prayed to the LORD and said, Ah, LORD! Wast not this what I said when I was still in my own land? Therefore I fled so hurriedly to Tarshish! For I knew that You are a God gracious and merciful, slow to anger and of great loving-kindness and relenting
3 of evil. And now, O LORD, take my life, I pray thee, from me! For I would rather be dead than alive!
4 Then the LORD said, Is it right for
5 you to be angry? Then Jonah left the city and sat down on the east side of the city, and he made a booth for himself and sat under it in the shade, until he should see what would happen in the city.
6 And the LORD God ordered a gourd, and it grew up over his head to deliver him from his irritation; and Jonah was overjoyed because of the gourd, in happy de-
7 light. Then God ordered a worm, when the dawn came up the next day, to strike the gourd so that it
8 dried up. When the sun rose, God ordered a hot east wind, and the sun struck Jonah's head so that he became faint and asked that he might die, and said, I would rather
9 die than live! Then God said to Jonah, Is it right for you to be angry over the gourd? And Jonah said, I have a right to be angry
10 unto death! The LORD said, You are sorry for the gourd, for which you did not go to any trouble, and did not make it grow up, which came into being overnight, and per-
11 ished overnight, and I — should I not be sorry for Nineveh, that great city, in which there are more than one hundred and twenty thousand persons that know not to distinguish between the right hand and the left hand, and many cattle?

Grammatical and Textual Notes

V. 1. "It displeased." רָעַע, to be bad, evil, to regard as evil, dislike. The added "a great evil" emphasizes the bitterness of his dissatisfaction.

V. 2. "Before," קָדַם, Pi., to go before, to hurry in order to arrive early or to forestall.

V. 4. "Doest thou well"; the Hi. of יָטַב,

237

to do a thing well, in a thorough manner. (Cp. Deut. 9:21; 18:17.) Hence some translate, Are you very, thoroughly, angry? In a number of passages the term is used of doing well morally (Gen. 4:7; Is. 1:17; Jer. 4:22; 13:23; cp. Lev. 5:4; Zeph. 1:12; etc.). G.-B. translates: "Is it right?" So also Sellin and others. This translation suits the situation better.

V. 6. "Gourd," Hebrew: *kikayon;* only here, vv. 6-10; LXX, Syriac, Arabic versions = colocynth, gourd, pumpkin. The Talmudists connected it with the Egyptian kiki, ricinus, the castor oil plant; also called Palma Christi, palmcrist, because the large leaves resemble the palm of a hand. Others, e. g., W. J. Deane, *Pulpit Comm.,* J. M. Powis Smith in *The Complete Bible,* retain the rendering of the Septuagint, Luther, A. V., which is at least as well founded as that of the Talmud.

V. 7. "Worm," destroying plants (Deut. 28:39), cutworm, caterpillar, borer, etc.; maggot (Ex. 16:20; Is. 14:11; 66:24).

V. 8. "Vehement," חֲרִישִׁית, of unknown etymology; LXX, burning hot; others, sultry.

V. 10. "Labor," עָמָל, toil. (Cp. Ps. 127:1; Prov. 16:26; Eccl. 2:11, 21; 5:15; 8:17.) — "Came up in a night," literally, came into existence as "a son of a night," as if the night had given birth to it; and it perished in a night, "as the son of a night," not having seen the light of another day. G.-K. 128, 2, s-v, speaks of "very numerous combinations of the masculine, feminine, and plural constructs of *ish, baal, ben,* man, master, son, with common nouns in order to denote a person (in poetry even an inanimate object) as possessing or standing in some relation to a person or attribute or state"; e. g., "a man of words," an eloquent man (Ex. 4:10); a son of hundred years, a centenarian (Gen. 21:5; cp. 2 Sam. 16:7; Prov. 22:24; 27:15, etc.). As examples of inanimate objects G.-K. lists Is. 5:1, "a very fruitful hill," literally, a horn or hill of a son of oil; Job 5:7, "sparks," literally, sons of the flames; ch. 41:20 (A. V., 28), "arrow," literally, son of the bow; Lam. 3:13, "arrows," sons of the quiver; Eccl. 12:4, "daughters of music," or song, the individual sounds or notes.

V. 11. "Spare," same word as "had pity," v. 10. — "Thousand," רִבּוֹ, ten thousand, occurs already Ps. 68:18 (A. V., 17), a Psalm of David, v. 1; also Hos. 8:12 K'tib, where the Q'ri reads רִבֵּי, multitudes, a plural which does not occur elsewhere. "Twelve ten thousand" = 120,000. This term certainly cannot be used to prove post-Exilic authorship of our book.

Israel and the Gentile Nations

The distinction between Israel and Gentiles traces its origin back to the Lord's call to Abraham (Gen. 12:1 ff.). Abraham was commanded to separate himself from his home and his kindred and his father's house. He was told to go to a country that the Lord would show him. There God would make him a great nation and a blessing to all other nations through his Seed, the promised Deliverer. This separation was emphasized when God established the rite of circumcision as the token of His covenant and the unalterable condition of membership in the covenant nation (Gen. 17:7-21; cp. Ex. 4:24-26; 12:43-49; Joshua 5:2-10). To this nation the Lord promised a special country, the land of Canaan, as its lasting possession (Gen. 12:7; 15:18 ff.; 26:3, 4; 28:13; Ex. 3:8). The distinction between Israel and the Gentiles came into special prominence when Israel as a nation was received into a special relationship with the Lord, revealing to all people not only His Moral Law in its perfection, but commanding to them many rites and customs to be observed in their daily religious, social, and civic life. (Ex. 17 ff., Lev., Num., Deut.) To them He gave the sacrificial ordinances, foreshadowing the great High Priest and His vicarious offering of Himself, as the firm assurance of divine forgiveness and everlasting salvation. Moses could truthfully say: Deut. 4:7, 8; and David: 2 Sam. 7:23-29; and the psalmist: Ps. 147:19 f. (Cp. Rom. 3:1, 2; 9:4, 5.) By these ordinances the Lord separated, severed Israel from other people that they should be His (Lev. 20:24, 26; 1 Kings 8:53). Particularly the many ceremonial rites were to serve, as St. Paul writes, as a wall of partition between Israel and the Gentiles, to be removed only by Christ's death (Eph. 2:11-22; cp. Col. 2:11-23).

The fact that God had chosen Israel alone as His covenant nation (Ex. 19:5-6; Amos 3:2) does not mean that He had at any time intended to restrict His saving grace to this one nation. The first promise of a Savior (Gen. 3:15) was as universal as mankind. Noah foretold that both Ham and Japheth, the Gentile nations, were to participate in the salvation originating from the tents of Shem (Gen. 9:25 ff.). The blessing given to Abraham, Isaac, and Jacob included all the families of the earth (Gen. 12:3; 18:18; 22:18; 26:4; 28:14). Israel was to be a leaven among the nations, a wellspring of living water, a constant invitation for the Gentile nations to learn saving and sanctifying wisdom. Compare Deut. 4:6; the examples of Rahab (Joshua 2:1 ff.; 6:22 ff.; Heb. 11:31), Ruth (ch. 1:16 f.), Naaman (2 Kings 5:17). David speaks of the world-wide rule of Messiah (Pss. 2; 22:28 ff.; 110), Solomon (1 Kings 8:41 ff.; Ps. 72). (See Pss. 45, 47, 67, 87, 89, 95—100, 117, etc.)

Yet the Jews were always in danger of forgetting that it was part of their mission to be a light unto the Gentiles. Too readily they were satisfied with possessing the Gospel for themselves; finally they became bigoted nationalists, opinionated separatists, repelling the surrounding nations rather than attracting them and winning them for Jehovah.

In this respect Jonah was thoroughly a Jew. The very idea that the Gentile nations, particularly wicked Nineveh, were to participate in the saving grace of God was repugnant to him (ch. 4:2, 3). "He whose all-seeing eye penetrates the secret recesses of the human heart (Heb. 4:12 f.) pictures to us the character of Jonah in order to teach us that man usually is more eager for his own glory than for the glory of God, so that even the grace of God which he has experienced will fail to make him willing unselfishly and without the least envy to help in bringing the same grace to others and to rejoice wholeheartedly in their possession of it" (Delitzsch).

Jonah was merely the representative of Jewish particularism. The Jews would have failed to fulfill their mission unless this fatal lack of mission-mindedness would be changed into fervent zeal to bring Jehovah and His salvation to the nations. Therefore at this important crisis in the national life of Israel, when the nation was coming in contact with the world powers of the East, Assyria and Babylonia, God Himself acted directly and miraculously. By His supernatural direction of Jonah's mission He intended to teach Israel that only through repentance, loyal service to God, and solicitous efforts to bring salvation to the Gentiles could they hope to retain their own spiritual blessings together with their national existence. Had Israel in fervent missionary zeal sought to gain Assyria for the kingdom of the Lord at the time of Assyria's national weakness (see p. 295), who can tell whether the history of Israel as well as of Assyria might not have been changed completely! A church no longer mission-minded has lost its right of existence. Only a mission-minded church will continue to grow and flourish.

The lesson Jonah had to learn had to be learned by the apostles and the early Christian Church. God had to perform many miracles before they learned and heeded this lesson. (See Acts 10:3 f., 11, 19, 28, 44-48; 11:1-26; 13:1-4; 15:1-35.) We have no right to sit in judgment on Jonah.

V. 1. "But it displeased" (Gr. N.). Jonah's proclamation had been blessed by the Lord with a success unique in the history of preaching. Surely, Jonah should have been grateful, happy. Yet he confesses that his success displeased him greatly. The Hebrew expression is still more forceful. It was evil to Jonah, a great evil. He was "very angry," fierce wrath burned in him.

Vv. 2, 3. This time he does not run away from God. He turns to the Lord in prayer; not a prayer of praise and adoration, but a prayer unbecoming to a prophet, a prayer of bitter resentment, not of God's judgment, but of His grace. He knows well the definition which God Himself had given of His name Jehovah (Ex. 34:6f.). He repeats this definition in almost the identical words. Yet though he calls his God Jehovah, He resents the very idea which this name is to convey to the Israelite. God's grace and loving-kindness, better than life (Ps. 30:5; 63:3), is displeasing to him, provoking him to burn with fierce anger. And this is not spoken in a momentary fit of anger. It was his "saying," his word, his inmost thought already in his homeland when the Lord had told him to preach to Nineveh. For this reason he had fled "before" (Gr. N.), literally, hurriedly, hastening to forestall and frustrate God's gracious will. And now the marvelous manifestation of God's grace so completely upsets him, so enrages him, that he not only reprimands God because of His loving-kindness, but actually asks God to take his life, "for my dying is better than my living" (v. 3). Elijah had expressed a similar desire, but from an entirely different motive. Elijah was disappointed because of his seeming failure (1 Kings 19:4, 10-14); Jonah is vexed because of the repentance of Nineveh, the success of God's mercy and grace.

V. 4. God does not take the prophet at his word. He does not slay His grumbling child. Quietly He asks him a single question: "Doest thou well" (Gr. N.), is it right, proper, good, for you, "to be angry?" The original has only three brief words, the first of three syllables: *Haheteb,* Is it good; the second, two: *charah,* to be angry; the third, one: *lak,* for you? You who have just experienced My grace, when in disregard of your disobedience I delivered you in so miraculous a manner from well-deserved death, are you angry because this same grace is ready to help and save not only you, not the Jews alone, but likewise the Gentile nations? Is it proper, right, good for you so to do? No answer is recorded, very likely because Jonah knew no answer. He is not quite ready to say what he said later, "I do well to be angry" (v. 8). Yet he certainly is not ready or willing humbly to confess, "No, I am not doing right. Lord, forgive my wicked grumbling!"

V. 5. Displeased and angry because Nineveh had repented, peeved

at the Lord's reproof, Jonah left the city. On its east side "he made
him a booth" (cp. Hos. 12:10 on "tabernacle," p. 94), a temporary
shelter made perhaps by intertwining a few branches. There he sat,
not praying for the salvation of Nineveh, nor to gather strength for
another preaching tour, but that he might see what would become of
the city. He cannot reconcile himself to the thought that Nineveh is
to be spared. He still looks forward to the day that the mistress of the
world shall be humbled into dust. Surely, says Luther, a strange,
peculiar kind of saint, to be angry because God is gracious to a Gentile
city, grudgingly to deny her any share in God's love, to wish her
only evil.

V. 6. Now, as Luther puts it, God begins to play with Jonah, as
a mother will play with her distressed child in order to cheer him.
He "prepares" (see Gr. N. on ch. 2:1, A. V., 1:17, p. 228). Three times
this term occurs here (vv. 6, 7, 8). It is God's providence that sends
both weal and woe to His children, as He in His loving wisdom sees fit.
Every sorrow as well as every pleasure is sent by a loving Father
who governs all the world for the welfare of His chosen children
(Rom. 8:28). His providence, His government, extends not only over
mankind, but even over the whole realm of nature, over sea and wind
and storm (1:4, 12-15), over the monsters of the sea (1:17; 2:10),
over the plant life (4:6), over creeping things and worms (4:7), over
heat and cold (4:8). All are governed by His will (Acts 14:17;
17:24-28). All His creatures are His servants whom He uses for the
guidance and shaping of the life of His children, for their training,
disciplining, teaching, to comfort, to gladden, or to chasten them;
always having in mind their temporal and eternal welfare. In Jonah's
case the Lord appointed a "gourd" (Gr. N.), either a ricinus plant,
the castor bean, or preferably one of the various creepers of the gourd
family. In order to comfort His prophet, the Lord causes this plant
to grow miraculously fast, so as to cover his rude hut overnight (v. 10).
Awakening from his sleep, he sees to his amazement and joy a green
plant covering his hut with its dense foliage, promising protection from
the rays of the fierce desert sun. For once he is happy! He confesses
that he was exceedingly glad of the gourd. — How often will a comparatively small matter help us to forget our sorrow at least for
a while! Yet Jonah's joy was centered only on the gourd. God's purpose had been to remove his "grief," his evil (same word as "displeased exceedingly," v. 1), his displeasure at Nineveh's preservation
and God's grace. But it remains rankling in his breast.

241

Vv. 7, 8. Since Jonah refused to change his mind in spite of all the favors shown him, God resorts to sterner measures. Jonah must learn his lesson the hard way. All day long he had watched the growth of the plant and enjoyed its refreshing shade. Joyfully he had fallen asleep. In the early dawn of the next morning a "worm" (Gr. N.) smote the gourd, and quickly the plant withered. Now the sun arose, foreboding another hot day (v. 8). In addition the Lord prepared, provided, a "vehement" (Gr. N.) east wind. The sultry atmosphere made the heat unbearable. Jonah lost completely what little patience with God's way he had possessed. Once more the prophet was gripped by bitter disappointment to the point of despondency. He wished "in himself" (Gr. N.), for his soul, to die. (Cp. 1 Kings 19: 4.)

Very definitely all these natural phenomena (vv. 6-8) are designated as having been appointed by the Lord, who is called "Jehovah God," v. 6, the gracious Covenant God and almighty Creator about to comfort His harassed prophet, "the God," v. 7 (the Hebrew adds the article = the one and only God), chastening His rebellious messenger, "God," v. 8, the almighty Creator and Ruler of life and death, causing the plant to die, v. 8.

Vv. 9-11. Once more God kindly, leniently, rebukes His dissatisfied prophet; cp. v. 4. Will grumbling help you? But this question seems to add insult to injury, like pouring oil into the fire of Jonah's anger. Of course I have a right to be angry! Of what use is life to me any longer? I wish I were dead! Does God surrender him to despair, death, damnation? Oh, no! He is not willing that even wicked Jonah should perish (cp. Ezek. 33: 11). How kindly, how lovingly does He deal with Jonah! Graciously He overlooks the fact that Jonah's pity for the gourd was largely self-pity, pity for his own personal loss and the resulting inconvenience for himself. Still He calls it pity on the gourd and tells Jonah: See here! You are sorry for the gourd, filled with pity for a mere plant; a plant for which you did not labor, which you did not cause to grow up (v. 10). I did that, not you! It grew while you were sleeping. This gourd, moreover, came up in a night (Gr. N.), was a child of the night, and like a child of the night it perished. It had no living soul, to be filled with the light of everlasting life. Yet you are sorry that it died! Should not I "spare" (v. 11) (Gr. N.), feel sorry for, have pity on, Nineveh, that great city, wherein dwell more than 120,000 persons who cannot yet distinguish between their right hand and left, little children too young to have reached the age of discretion? And besides them the many thousands and tens of thousands of grown people. They all are "persons" (Gr. N.), human beings, having not only a body, but also an immortal soul; persons, to all of whom My blessing through the Woman's Seed, the Seed of Abraham, Isaac, and Jacob is promised (Gen. 22:18; 26:4; 28:14). "And also much cattle." The Lord's pity extends also to the animal world (Ps. 36:6; 136:25; 147:9; Matt. 6:26; 10:29; Luke 12:6). How many animals would have perished if Nineveh had been overthrown!

With this question the book of Jonah closes. The prophet rather abruptly drops the curtain, draws a veil over his further life's history. Naturally we ask, Did Jonah repent of his stubborn opposition to the universality of God's grace? Jonah does not answer this question directly. But his very silence on this point and the entire tenor of his book speak louder than words. Jonah would not have written so frank and self-humiliating a confession of his sin if he had not been sincerely repentant and had not hoped to preserve and save others from similar bigotry and grumbling. "By the very act of penning it [his confession], Jonah at once merges out of his former character and appears in our view not merely as a prophet, but as a remarkably humble and noble-spirited saint" (Huxtable in *The Bible Commentary,* VI, 582). Particularly the conclusion of his book corroborates this view. At last he no longer finds fault with God's ways. No longer does he voice his anger and displeasure with the universality of God's grace. God's revelation of His fathomless pity embracing all His creatures, cattle as well as men, young as well as old, Gentiles as well as Jews, this revelation has melted Jonah's icy heart. In silent adoration (cp. Hab. 2:20; Zech. 2:13) he sinks down before this God of grace. Thy will, Thy good and gracious will, be done in earth as it is in heaven! Says Delitzsch: "The book begins with the statement that God spoke and closes with a word spoken by God, and the prophet, like Job (Job 40:3, 4), is silenced. In this concluding speech of God all the dissonances are resolved in an effectual harmonious finale. The silence of the prophet exhorts every reader in silence to contemplate and deeply to meditate on the mercy of God. The *kikayon* [gourd] of Jonah is a beautiful symbol, testifying to all souls longing for salvation the sincere and gracious good will of God intent on their salvation. The prophet dwelling complacently under the shady foliage of the gourd, but giving way to angry complaints because of its sudden wilting, is a warning proclamation of judgment directed against every form of Pharisaism, coarse or subtile. To me the book appears as the confession which the prophet after his restoration wrote by inspiration of the Holy Spirit in a feeling of deep shame and in divine self-denial. It was incorporated in the prophetic books because Jonah, who had prophesied even when he had no such intention, was a type of the coming Christ, in whom alone and through whom alone the believers also of the Old Testament eon (Jonah 3:5) were the recipients of grace. Hence the Book of Jonah is a historical painting of equally deep psychological, dogmatical, and typical meaning. From its dawn-like background, Christ Jesus, the Savior not only of the Jews, but also of all nations, shines forth brightly. We find here also a confirmation of the ancient teaching of the Synagog: The goal of all prophecies are the days of the Messiah." (Fr. Delitzsch, *Zeitschrift fuer lutherische Theologie und Kirche* [1840], p. 121 f.)

M I C A H

Superscription, V. 1

1 The word of the LORD which came to Micah the Morashtite in the days of Jotham, Ahaz, and Heze-kiah, the kings of Judah; which he saw concerning Samaria and Jerusalem.

V. 1. Little more is known of the life of Micah than we learn from these few words. It is not so much the circumstances of his life as his wondrous message that makes this minor prophet truly great. He is called Micah the Morashtite. Compare Jer. 26:18ff., where this cognomen distinguishes him from Micah, or Micaiah, the son of Imlah (1 Kings 22:8ff.), living in the time of Jehoshaphat and Ahab (ca. 900 B. C.). The name Micah is the shorter form of Micaiah = Who is like Jehovah? (Cp. ch. 7:18.) Micah's native town is called Moresheth-Gath (ch. 1:14). Excavators have identified it with the ruins of Tell-el-Judeideh, six to seven miles northeast of Gath, one of the chief cities of ancient Philistia (1 Sam. 5:8; 7:14; 17:4; 21:10; 27:2 ff., etc.). It lay about three miles off Tell-Sandahannah, identified with Mareshah (ch. 1:14), and six miles north and slightly east of Tell-el-Duweir (Lachish, v. 13). Micah hailed from a small, insignificant village whose site was defined by its proximity to well-known Gath. He was the subject of a relatively small country, consisting chiefly of desert lands and hills. Yet this man had a message not only for Jerusalem, the capital city of "the kings of Judah," not only for Judah's northern neighbor, Samaria, far larger and more fertile than little Judah. He is a prophet of Jehovah, who is not merely the local God of Moresheth, the tribal God of Judah, the national God of Israel. He is the everlasting, omnipotent Ruler of all the earth, and Micah, no matter how insignificant his birthplace and ancestry, is the spokesman of the Lord, whose word came to him (cp. Hos. 1:1). Micah proclaims not only his personal views, his own philosophy of life, his own social and civic program. He announces the Lord's revelation, proclaims Jehovah's program in words which the Lord Himself puts into his mouth. On the contemporary history see pp. 10 ff.

PART I

Chapter 1:2—2:13

God's Threat of Destruction and Promise of Deliverance Addressed to Israel and Judah

A. The Severity of the Judgment, Vv. 2-9

2 Hear, O nations, all of you! Attention, O earth and its fullness, and let the Lord God be a witness against you, the Lord from His holy
3 temple! For behold, the LORD is coming forth from His place, and He descends and treads on the
4 heights of the earth. The mountains shall melt under Him, and the valleys shall split apart, like wax before the fire, like waters poured
5 down a cliff. For the rebellion of Jacob all this is coming on, and for the sins of the house of Israel. Who is the rebellion of Jacob? Is it not Samaria? And who are the high places of Judah? Are they not
6 Jerusalem? But I will turn Samaria into a heap of ruins in the field, as the plantings of a vineyard; and I will pour out her stones into the valley, and her foundations
7 I will lay bare. And all her carved images shall be broken to pieces, and all her temple gifts shall be burned with fire, and all her statues will I lay waste. For of harlot's hire did she gather them, and to harlot's hire they shall return.
8 For this, oh, let me mourn and wail, oh, let me walk stripped and naked. I am making a mourning like jackals and a wailing like that
9 of ostriches. For her wounds are incurable; for it has come to Judah! It is striking at the gates of my people, even Jerusalem!

Grammatical Notes

V. 5. "Transgression," פֶּשַׁע, see Gr. N. on Amos 1:3. The verb פָּשַׁע is translated "rebelled" 1 Kings 12:19. The Northern Kingdom was born in rebellion against the divinely instituted kingdom and worship (1 Kings 12:26 ff.; 14:9). — "Sins," חַטָּאות. The etymological meaning of חָטָא = to miss the mark, fail to find (Job 5:24; Prov. 8:36 in contrast to v. 35, "find"; 19:2; Hiph., Judg. 20:16, "miss"). The dreadful consequence of missing the mark is stated Prov. 8:36. — "What," מִי in both questions. מִי is sometimes used instead of מָה, when the underlying idea is that of persons rather than things. (Cp. Gen. 33:8; Judg. 9:28, "Who is Shechem" = the Shechemites? Ch. 13:17, "What is Thy name?" = Who are You? 1 Sam. 18:18, "Who" — "what"? 2 Sam. 7:18, "Who" — "what"? G.-K. 137 a.)

V. 7. "Beaten to pieces," יֻכַּתּוּ, Hoph. impf. of כָּתַת. (Cp. Is. 24:12; Jer. 46:5; Job 4:20. G.-K. 67 y.)

V. 8. "Wail." The K'tib has endeavored to imitate the long-drawn-out notes of the wail by the full vowels אֵילִילָה, אֵילְכָה, and even שֵׁילָל instead of the usual שׁוֹלָל; see Q'ri. — "Stripped." שׁוֹלָל = deprived of upper clothing; not "barefoot" as some translate. Barefoot = יָחֵף (2 Sam. 15:30; Is. 20:2-4; Jer. 2:25, "unshod." — "Dragons," תַּנִּים = jackals (Job 30:29; Is. 13:22; 34:13, etc.). — "Owls," בְּנוֹת יַעֲנָה, daughters of the desert. יַעֲנָה occurs only in this phrase, the ostrich (Job 30:29; Lev. 11:16; Is. 13:21, etc.).

V. 9. "Unto." Note the threefold עַד, which implies arrival at one's goal.

V. 2. This proclamation is addressed to all nations. To hear Jehovah's words is the primary duty of all that have ears to hear. All the earth, all that dwell in it, are called to attend to this divine proclamation and to let the Lord, *Adon,* the authoritative Ruler, even Jehovah, the I AM THAT I AM, "be a Witness against you"; the Lord from His holy temple in the heavens above, of which temple His sanctuary at Jerusalem is but a feeble mundane image and symbol.

The Lord's revelation concerning Samaria and Jerusalem. The two kingdoms are to serve as God's witnesses against all the nations steeped in idolatry and wickedness. His unchanging holiness, His unfailing insistence on fulfillment of His Law, as written in the hearts of all men and published in unmistakable language from Mount Sinai, the destructive character of His judgments against all transgressors, the absolute impartiality of Him who knows no respect of persons, and at the same time His unfathomable grace and mercy and lovingkindness shall become apparent to the whole world from His ways and judgments with regard to His own chosen people. His just punishments are brought out first to reveal to the nations His holiness and righteousness (ch. 1: 4—2: 12, and in every succeeding chapter throughout the book). His grace is revealed in His first promise of a Deliverer, the Breaker (ch. 2: 13), and in the other promises (ch. 4: 1-8, 12, 13; 5: 1ff.; 7: 7-20). This is the twofold witness repeated again and again to all the earth, in order to show to all nations the futility of idolatry and sin service and to win them over to His kingdom of grace and peace and righteousness and everlasting salvation.

V. 3. The Lord's "place"; see 1 Kings 8: 27; Is. 66: 1; Eph. 1: 20-23.— "Tread upon the high places of the earth." To do that, the Lord, humanly speaking, must descend from His throne, infinitely higher than the highest mountains. The expression is used to denote the victorious march of a conqueror (Deut. 32: 13; 33: 29; Is. 58: 14), of God (Amos 4: 13). Possession of the high places guaranteed conquest of the land.

V. 4. Once the Lord came down to destroy the idolatrous nations of Canaan and to give their land to Israel (Gen. 15: 16 ff.; Ex. 3: 17; Amos 2: 9, 10), now He comes down to destroy His people and their land, as earthquake and storm leave destruction and ruin in their path. — "Wax" and "waters" refer to both "mountains" and "valleys." Heat causes wax to spread in all directions. So shall mountains and valleys lose their characteristics. Waters rushing down a steep hill are symbolic of disaster and devastation. Mountains shall be changed to stony plains, fertile valleys to arid wastes. Surely a catastrophic change!

V. 5 states the reason: "transgression," literally, rebellion (Gr. N.), "sins," missings of the mark (Gr. N.). — "Jacob," the man received into grace; "Israel," the conqueror of God (Gen. 32:10, 24-28), both terms here designate the entire nation, which shamefully missed the mark, ungratefully abused its high calling, revolted against God to whom it owed all it was and all it had. — "What," both times "who" (Gr. N.) — "Transgression" = rebellion, and "high places" = idolatry, are personified. Jacob again denotes the entire nation; Judah, the Southern Kingdom. From Samaria, the capital city, Baalism, introduced by Ahab (1 Kings 16:31-33), permeated not only the Northern Kingdom (1 Kings 18:18-22; 19:13-18, only 7,000!); it also invaded Judah through the son-in-law of Ahab, Ahaziah (2 Kings 8:26 ff.; 11:1, 2, 17-20). And the former kings of Judah had introduced and tolerated the "high places" with their shameful rites (1 Kings 11:1-8; 14:21 ff.; 15:14; 22:43; 2 Kings 12:3, etc.). The kings, who were to safeguard the true worship of the Lord (Deut. 17:18 ff.), failed to do their duty and introduced, or fostered, or tolerated, idolatry instead of suppressing it, as Hezekiah, and later, Josiah did. The leaders in God's Church are held responsible for the maintenance of truth against all errors. How often has error seeped from the pulpit into the pew!

V. 6. Proud Samaria, the unconquerable fortress, shall become as a stone heap in the field; its steep ascents shall be used for the peaceful occupation of the vineyardist, its mighty walls destroyed and rolled down into the surrounding valley, 300 feet deep, its palaces and bastions destroyed to their very foundations. Sellin denies any reference to the destruction of Samaria by the Assyrians, since only an earthquake could have caused so complete a destruction. But see 2 Sam. 17:13; 2 Kings 25:10; Neh. 2:13 ff.; Luke 19:44; 21:6; etc.

V. 7. "Graven images" denotes images carved out of wood (Is. 40:20; 44:15, etc), or molten (Is. 40:19; 44:10; cp. Jer. 10:14). "Hires," the harlot's wage (cp. Hos. 2:14, A. V., 12; 9:1). Idolatry is adultery (Hos. 1:2; 2:2), and all the money spent for an idolatrous worship and its upkeep, its votive gifts, sacrifices, ornaments, etc., are regarded by the Lord as wages paid to a harlot. All images and "hires" shall be smashed (2 Kings 25:14 f.; Jer. 52:17-23). As Israel had gathered all these things for the adulterous worship of idols, used them as harlot's wages, so they shall in turn be devoted to the hire of an harlot, be placed into the temple of heathen idols, and used for their riotous festivities in honor of their gods (Ezra 1:7 ff.; Dan. 5:1 ff.). Compare the edict of Cyrus, speaking of the gods placed in Babylon's temples by former kings as having been returned by him to their former shrines. (Barton, *Archaeology*, 1933, p. 484.)

V. 8. "Go stripped" (Gr. N.), deprived of all fineries (cp. Job 12:17, 19, "spoiled"); "naked," not nude, but poorly dressed (Is. 58:7; Job 24:7, 10), without the upper garment (1 Sam. 19:24; Is. 20:2-4), a symbol of deep sorrow. — "Dragons" = jackals; "owls" = ostriches, whose roar is similar to that of the lion.

V. 9. Micah sees no help for Israel, whose wound, inflicted by the Lord in penalty of her sin, is incurable. Destruction is rapping at the very gates of Jerusalem (cp. 2 Kings 19:1-5; Is. 37:1-4). The marvelous delivery of Jerusalem by the Angel of the Lord had not been revealed to Micah when he composed this dirge, nor even to Isaiah until shortly before it occurred. Micah saw prophetically only the enemy approaching to the very gates of Jerusalem, and he knew that the wicked city deserved the destruction threatened already by Moses to apostate Israel (Deut. 28:15 ff.).

B. The Extent of the Judgment, Vv. 10-16

10 Publish it not at Gath! Do not weep bitterly. In Beth-L'aphrah
11 roll yourself in the dust. Pass away, O inhabitant of Shaphir, in shameful nakedness! The inhabitants of Zaanan have not gone forth! The mourning of Beth-ezel has taken away from you its refuge
12 place. The inhabitants of Maroth waited painfully for good, for evil has come down from the LORD to
13 the very gate of Jerusalem. Hitch the chariot to the horses, O inhabitant of Lachish. She is the beginning of sin for the daughter of Zion, for in you are found the re-
14 bellions of Israel. Therefore you will give letters of dismissal to Moresheth-Gath. The houses of Achzib shall be a deceptive lie to
15 the kings of Israel. I will yet bring to you the dispossessor, O inhabitant of Mareshah. To Adullam shall the glory of Israel ascend.
16 Make yourself bald, and shear yourself for your darling children! Make your baldness large like that of a vulture! For they are deported from you!

Grammatical Notes

V. 10. "Weep," בְּכוֹ is not to be changed to בְּעַכּוֹ, "in Acco," LXX, ἐν ᾿Ακείμ; it is abs. inf. of בָּכָה, emphasizing the idea of the jussive: Weep not bitterly! — "Roll thyself," הִתְפַּלָּשְׁתִּי; occurring only in Hithp., and only here, Jer. 6:26; 25:34; and Ezek. 27:30. The K'tib reads first pers. perf., "I will wallow," the prophet speaking in the name of the people; the Q'ri demands the imperative, Roll yourself!

V. 11. "Pass ye away," עִבְרִי, imperative fem. of עָבַר in sense of go away! On your way! (Cp. Cant. 5:6; 2 Sam. 16:1; Judg. 19:18, etc.) — "Ye," לָכֶם, dative commodi, for your own welfare.

The imperative = sing., collective; לָכֶם, yourselves, distributive, every one of them. — "Shame naked." עֶרְיָה־בֹשֶׁת = nakedness, shame; modal accusative: in shameful nakedness. — Zaanan, the prophet connects it with יָצָא, go forth, march; others prefer connection with צֹא, flock. — Beth-ezel, אֵצֶל = at the side of, close to, neighbor. (Cp. Prov. 8:30; 1 Kings 4:12, "by"; Jer. 41:17, "by.") — "In the mourning," מִסְפַּד, begins a new sentence. — "He shall receive of you," יִקַּח, shall take away from you. — "His standing," עֶמְדָתוֹ. The verb is often used = to stand still, tarry, remain at a place for conversation, rest,

refreshment, refuge (Gen. 18:22; 19:17; Ex. 9:28; Jer. 4:6, etc.). The noun occurring only here = place of rest or refuge.

V. 14. "Presents," שִׁלּוּחִים, dismissal, sending away (cp. 1 Kings 9:16, "present"), "to," עַל = concerning, with reference to. — "Achzib," the deceptive, lying brook. Cp. אַכְזָב, a brook that fails (Jer. 15:18).

V. 15. "Bring," אָבִי, Hi. 1st pers. of בּוֹא. — "An heir," יֹרֵשׁ, a play on the name of the city: "Inheritance City." The verb = to obtain possession by inheritance (Lev. 25:46; 2 Sam. 14:7, etc.) or conquest (Deut. 1:8, 21; 2:24, 31, etc.).

Note on Ch. 1:10-16

In this dirge the play on words is used to a greater extent than in any other passage of Holy Writ. Paronomasia is a much-abused figure of speech, but, if properly used, very effective. The prophet employs it here as an efficacious means of driving home the lesson in the briefest possible manner.

"The text," says Sellin, "is mutilated to such an extent that at times we may arrive at an acceptable understanding only by means of daring conjectures. Already Duhm and Budde have made quite successful attempts in this direction, so that a rather high degree of probability has now been achieved." (*Zwoelfprophetenbuch*, p. 313 f.) Sellin has made no fewer than twenty alterations, some rather radical, in these seven verses, partly based on LXX, partly on suggestions by other scholars, partly on his own studies. We feel that as long as the M. T. permits an intelligible translation, without violating any grammatical rules, it is to be accepted, unless it is ruled out by the context or contradicts clear teachings of Scripture. The duty of the interpreter is to set forth the meaning of the text to be interpreted, not to change it so that it expresses what it ought to say according to the interpreter's conception. The text may present difficulties of various kinds. If these difficulties are insuperable, they should be acknowledged as such, but not be supplanted by guesswork. Many of the difficulties may stem from the impossibility to fully understand in our time certain references which may have been perfectly clear to the hearer or reader at the time they were spoken.

V. 10. In an agonized dirge (vv. 10-16) Micah bewails the enormity and the extent of the destruction. "Declare it not at Gath," the well-known city of Philistia (see p. 169). This is a quotation from 2 Sam. 1:20, "a plaintive entreaty," which "touchingly indicates the fatal nature of the calamity." (*Pulpit Commentary* on 2 Sam. 1:20.) Like David, Micah would have preferred that the news of the calamity about to come upon Judah be kept from the enemies, that no public proclamation be made, no bitter weeping betray the totality of Judah's destruction. Yet he knows that this judgment is unalterably decreed by the Lord and that his people must be made aware of its imminent approach, in order that by sincere repentance the Lord might be moved to restrain the fury of His wrath, even though the calamity could not be entirely averted (cp. Jer. 18:6-11). Just as David in spite of his plea (2 Sam. 1:20) describes the grievous loss sustained and calls on the women to weep (op. cit., vv. 21-27), so Micah now goes on to describe in gruesome detail the catastrophe so soon to overwhelm them. "In the house of Aphrah," or Beth-L'aphrah. "House," Beth, in the names of localities is our "town," "city," here: In Dust-town roll thyself (Gr. N.) in the dust, a symbol of sorrow, poverty, shame, repentant humiliation (Job 16:15; 42:6; Is. 2:10; 25:12; 26:5).

V. 11. "Pass ye away" (Gr. N.). On your way to captivity! "Inhabitant, dweller," the singular is collective, the entire population. "Saphir," Hebrew: *Shaphir* = Beauty, identified by Sellin with Sawafir, west of Ascalon, but doubtful. She will be stripped of every vestige of her beauty and stand before the world in shameful nakedness (cp. Hos. 2:3). We have here, perhaps, an allusion to the shameful treatment accorded by Assyrian and Babylonian armies to their captives, men and women (Jer. 13:22, 26; Nah. 3:5). — "Zaanan" (Gr. N. Cf. Joshua 15:37). "Going forth," will not be able to come forth. Enclosed like a bird in the cage, it will perish by famine and pestilence. "The mourning," the death wail "of Beth-ezel" = Neighbortown" (site unknown); "receive" (Gr. N.), rather, will take away, remove from you its "standing." It will no longer serve as a "near-by" town where one could find rest, refreshment, refuge (cp. modern motels). Who would seek that in a locality wailing in its death throes?

V. 12. "Maroth = Bitternesses (site unknown), waits anxiously, yet in vain, for good. Bitterness-town tastes only bitterness that cannot be removed, because it comes from the Lord. He sends evil even to the gates of Jerusalem, the city of peace (Heb. 7:2; Ps. 122:6 ff.). If the Lord's city of peace is not spared, how can Bitternesses expect relief? Note that Micah does not speak of Jerusalem's destruction, but sees the enemy at the very gates. (Cp. 2 Kings 18:17, 26 f.)

V. 13. "Lachish," large fortress about twenty-five miles southwest of Jerusalem, the modern Tell ed-Duweir. (Cp Joshua 10:3-35; 2 Kings 18:14, 17; 19:8; Jer. 34:7.) Its strategic position made it a very important military and trading post. — "Swift beast" = horses (1 Kings 5:8, A. V., 4:28, "dromedaries"; Esther 8:10, 14), evidently a special breed noted probably for its beauty and speed. The mention of horses and chariots suggests the possibility of Lachish being one of the cities from which Solomon carried on his flourishing horse trading business (1 Kings 10:28, 29). Micah sees not the glory, but only the sinful manner in which this glory was gained by transgression of God's commandment (Deut. 17:16, 17) and impoverishing and estranging the people by heavy taxes (1 Kings 12:4 ff.), thus laying the foundation for the division of the kingdom. Lachish was the beginning of Jerusalem's "sin," missing of its high mark (cp. Gr. N. on v. 5); and there was found the "transgression" (see same note), the revolt of Israel. Trade with surrounding heathen countries led to unholy alliances and unholy marriages. Solomon's idolatry is brought into close connection with his horse-trading business and multiplying of chariots (1 Kings 10:26—11:9).

V. 14. Pharaoh had given Gezer to his daughter as a wedding present on her marriage to Solomon (1 Kings 9:16), and both Pharaoh's daughter, for whom he built a special palace (9:24), and the fortification of Gezer (9:16) contributed to increase the levy Solomon was obliged to impose on the nation (9:15). Because of the sinful policies pursued by the kings and the people of Israel, the nation would have to "give presents to" (Gr. N.), rather, letters of dismissal concerning Moresheth-Gath. In other words, this city would be lost to Israel and returned to the enemies. Moresheth was, indeed, only a small town, yet so dear to the prophet, the home of his ancestors, his birthplace, now in foreign, heathen possession! — Achzib (Gr. N.), False-town, shall prove true to its name. Its houses, i. e., their inhabitants, will prove to be as a failing brook that dries up when water is most needed, to the kings of Israel, the royal house.

V. 15. "An heir" (Gr. N.) = the possessor, or conqueror, whom the Lord will bring upon Mareshah, the modern Sandahannah (see notes on v. 1, p. 245). The first "heir" was Israel; the second, "again," the Assyrian. The glory of Israel, the aristocracy (Is. 5:13), their riches (Is. 10:3), all they were proud of, shall go up, ascend to — Adullam! the well-known place where David sought refuge in one of the caves (1 Sam. 22:1, 4; 2 Sam. 23:13), an "ascent" into poverty and humiliation!

V. 16. "Make bald," "poll," shave, cut off your hair, a sign of mourning (Lev. 21:5; Amos 8:10; Jer. 7:29; 16:6; Job 1:20). — "Delicate," literally, children of your delight, your darling children. "As the eagle," the vulture, whose head and neck is almost completely bare. The reason for such deep sorrow: Exile! Capitvity! For Israel, 722 B. C., for Judah, 586 B. C. Undoubtedly a number of Jews were also deported during the Assyrian campaigns against Hezekiah. (Cp. 2 Kings 18:13, 30 ff.)

CHAPTER 2

C. Sin and Salvation!

1. The brutalities of the upper classes and their punishment, vv. 1-5

1 Woe to them that devise iniquity and work out wickedness on their beds! In the light of the morning they carry it out, for it is in the 2 power of their hands. They covet fields and seize them, houses, and take them away. They crush a man and his house, a man and his her- 3 itage. Therefore thus says the LORD: Behold, I am planning against this tribe an evil from which you shall not extricate your necks. You shall not keep on walk- ing in haughtiness, for this shall be 4 an evil time. In that day they shall chant a taunting song, and a bitter lamentation shall be wailed: We are utterly ruined! He has changed the allotted possession of my peo- ple! How completely has it gone! To the apostates He has allotted our 5 fields! Therefore you shall have no one to stretch the measuring line by allotment within the congrega- tion of the LORD.

Grammatical Notes

V. 1. "Power," אֵל, used here in its orig- inal sense, strength, power, might.

V. 2. "Man" . . . "man." גֶּבֶר = the strong, influential man; אִישׁ here used in general sense. When אִישׁ is used in connection with אָדָם, the latter denotes the humble origin of man, earth, dust (Gen. 2:7).

V. 4. "One," the third person sing. or plural is often used to denote an in- definite personal subject. (Gen. 11:9; 16:14; 19:22, etc. G.-K. 144 d.) — "Par- able." מָשָׁל, originally, short, pithy proverbs (e. g., 1 Sam. 10:12; 1 Kings 20:11), various forms of wisdom, litera- ture, riddles (Prov. 6:16-19; 30:15-31; cp. Judg. 14:12-18), parables (Judg. 9:8 ff.; Prov. 9:1 ff.), taunting songs (Jer. 38:22; Hab. 2:6-8).

Vv. 1, 2. Devise iniquity, work evil. (Cp. Ps. 36:1-4.) The wicked deeds which they have planned on their beds are carried out at earliest opportunity, as soon as the day dawns. What is schemed secretly is done publicly, for they have the power (Gr. N.) to do it. No one can resist their reign of terrorism. Gangsterism is as old as human greed. Either under cover of laws made for that purpose or by open violence they obtain whatever they covet, fields (cp. Ahab's theft, 1 Kings 21) and homes (v. 2). They are not respecters of men. Whether it is the home of a man of influence (Gr. N.) or the heritage of one of the common people makes no difference (see ch. 3:2, 3; 6:10 ff.).

V. 3. While their wicked schemes may prosper for a while (Ps. 37:35; 73:3 ff.), there is Another who also plans evil, the well-deserved penalty for these heartless oppressors, an evil from which they cannot escape. Money, influence, threats, henchmen had helped them to extri- cate themselves out of many a noose about to tighten around their

253

necks. Yet there is coming for them an evil time, the day of the Lord's vengeance (Ps. 79:12; 94:20 ff.; Jer. 51:6). The Lord of irresistible power and of implacable justice for all who have rejected His grace, will be their Judge. No longer will they hold their heads "haughtily," high, in vain pride and haughty defiance of all the laws of God and man.

V. 4. "One," "parable" (Gr. N.). All who were oppressed by them shall shout a taunting song against them, mockingly aping the doleful lamentations of their former oppressors. "Utterly, completely ruined are we!" so they sing in chorus. Then the individual's lament: "He hath changed the portion of my people!" "The land allotted to my people has changed ownership" (in just penalty of their stealing the property of others, v. 2). "How hath He removed it from me!" Instead of bewailing their sins they weep only for their losses! Impenitent to the last! And once more the chorus: "Turning away" (Gr. N.) "He hath divided our fields." "To the apostate He has allotted our fields." Forgetting their own apostasy, they cannot understand the reason why God should punish His people so severely.

V. 5. The Lord adds His yea and amen to the taunting song. No member of this nation shall have any property allotted to him within the Lord's congregation. (On measuring one's allotted portion, cp. Joshua 14:1-16; 18:1-10; Ps. 16:5, 6.) In other words, they are excluded from the congregation of saints (Acts 8:21).

---

2. Micah's controversy with the false prophets, vv. 6-11

6 "Do not drip," they keep on dripping. "If they will not drip to such as these, there will be unceasing
7 shames for them!" Are you called the house of Jacob? Is the Spirit of the LORD cut short? Or are such His doings? Do not My words do good to him that walks up-
8 rightly? For a long time My people have risen against Me like an enemy. You have torn the mantle off the clothes of those passing by unsuspectingly, unaware of war.

9 The women of My people you evict from the houses they love. From their children you take My glory away forever. Arise! On your way!
10 For this is not the resting place because of the defilement which brings destruction, incurable de-
11 struction! If a man walking in wind and deceit would lie, "I will drip for you about wine and liquor," that would be a dripper for this people!

Grammatical Notes

V. 6. "Prophesy," נָטַף = to let drop, drip (cp. Judg. 5:4), figuratively, of words "dripping" from the lips (Prov. 5:3; Cant. 4:11; 5:13; Amos 7:16). The same idea is expressed Deut. 32:2 by the two expressions "drop as the rain" and "distil as the dew."

V. 7. "O Thou," הָאָמוּר. הַ is the interrogative. Here it has the force of an exclamation.

V. 8. "Yesterday," like 1 Sam. 10:11 ("beforetime"), Is. 30:33 ("of old"), here denotes indefinite past time, long ago. — "Risen up," קוֹמֵם. The Pi not causative, but in its primary force, intensive. The perfect views all the past uprisings as one complete act. — "Averse from war," שׁוּבֵי, part. pass., that are turned away from war, have no inclination for strife, litotes = are peaceful.

V. 9. "Glory," הָדָר, beauty, ornament, glory. Here the glory that God gives, His blessing.

V. 11. "Spirit," רוּחַ, a play on its original meaning, "wind." Professing to be a man of the Spirit, he walks in wind, or as wind, a walking windbag. (Cp. on this use of "walk" Prov. 2:7; 6:12; Is. 33:15.) — "Falsehood," deception, "do lie." Note the chiastic construction, the two verbal forms enclosing the two nouns.

V. 6. "Prophesy not" (Gr. N.). Do not constantly let accusations and threats and lamentations drip from your lips like an all-day rain! So they, the opponents, tell the prophet, unaware that they are doing the identical thing for which they fault the prophet. They charge the prophet with endless repetitions, harping on one string, while they as endlessly tell him to stop. The prophet speaks because God tells him. The people speak, because God's word is disagreeable to them. God answers their charge, defends His prophet, and once more warns the stubborn people. If the prophets were not constantly "dripping," repeating God's warnings, the judgment would be inevitable. The believing remnant — faithful prophets proclaiming God's Word, and faithful hearers, directing their lives according to this word — are the only ones to retard God's judgments upon a wicked nation (Gen. 18:23-32; Jer. 5:1).

V. 7. Israel has become utterly unlike his father Jacob, "O thou," etc. (Gr. N.), literally, Are you called the house of Jacob? The question practically has the force of an exclamation. God asks them as if in astonishment at their ignorance of what their name implies. As the house of Jacob, they were the descendants of a man to whom God appeared in the darkest hours of his life and assured him of divine guidance and blessing, of the coming of the Messiah (Gen. 28:11 ff.; 32:24 ff.; 35:1-15; 46:1 ff.). Did not the Lord keep His promise to Jacob and his house? Or is the spirit of the Lord straitened? The spirit of the Lord of life is the Lord's willingness and power to sustain the life and activity of the universe (Ps. 104:30; Is. 34:16). The Lord is willing to make man truly wise (Job 32:8), to lead him on the paths of righteousness (Ps. 51:13; 143:10; Hag. 2:5). Has this spirit lost its power? Surely, your father Jacob did not think so! (Cp. Gen. 48 and 49, Jacob on his deathbed.) Are these judgments His doings, characterizing Him as a vengeful, bloodthirsty tyrant? Why, no! Do not My words which promise good things, rich blessings to those who walk in My ways uprightly, carry their fulfillment within themselves? Have they ever failed? (Cp. 1 Kings 8: 56 ff.) By the same token, are not My judgments the indisputable evidence that you are no longer walking according to My will?

V. 8. "Yesterday," "risen up" (Gr. N.). Throughout the ages My people were engaged in violent uprising as an enemy of their God and their fellow men. A number of these social injustices violating at the same time God's Law are named. The robe, the outer garment, usually well made and highly prized by the owner, was ruthlessly torn away, so that only the nether garments remained to cover them. This may have been done by actual theft or by forcing them to pawn their best clothes to meet the payments due on interest or capital. And they did that without provocation, merely to satisfy their hunger for money. They committed these outrages on people "passing by securely," pursuing their way unsuspectingly, entrusting themselves to these Shylocks without knowing their true character, "averse from war" (Gr. N.), peace-loving people, not realizing that not all other people were, like them, trustworthy, peaceable people, ready to help the needy.

V. 9. Women of God's people, the mothers and sisters of their fellow men, were evicted cold-bloodedly from the homes they loved; and their children were deprived of God's glory (Gr. N.), His blessings. God's material gifts, their few possessions, their very clothing to cover their nakedness, were taken by these avaricious money sharks in brazen disregard of God's Law (Ex. 22:21-27; Lev. 25:35-41; Deut. 24:10-15). "Forever," eternally, they inflict irreparable loss.

V. 10. The people are told to leave the Promised Land. It is no longer "the rest" (Deut. 12:9; 1 Kings 8:56), where they enjoyed God's protection (1 Kings 4:24, 25), peace, and prosperity. They had defiled the land of the Lord, and the land would now destroy them in a destructive calamity (cp. Lev. 18:24-30; 20:22-26).

V. 11. In bitter irony the prophet voices his resentment of his people's attitude. If he were one of those walking "windbags" (Gr. N.) who delighted in speaking the lying deceits proceeding from his own wicked heart, if his lips overflowed with promises of all the wine and liquor they longed for, then, indeed, would he be a prophet, a dripper, for this kind of people. Then they would be running after him with the request, Drip some more, instead of telling him, Do not drip! (V. 6.)

3. Deliverance by the Breaker! Vv. 12, 13

12 I will surely assemble all of you, Jacob! I will surely gather the remnant of Israel. Together I will place them as a flock of Bozrah, as a flock in the midst of its pasture.
13 They shall hum with men. The Breaker has come up before them. They have broken through and are passing through the gate and going forth from it, while their King is going on before them, and the LORD at their head.

Grammatical Notes

V. 12. "Put together," יַחַד, I will place them as one, a union, the division of Judah and Israel into two kingdoms will cease (Jer. 3:18; Hos. 2:2; A. V., 1:11; John 10:16).

V. 13. "Come up," "broken through," perfects denoting the act in its completion. — "Have passed through," "are gone out," "shall pass," three progressive imperfects connected with the two perfects by strong waw. As a result of the completed acts a continuous stream of liberated people pass through, etc.

Vv. 12, 13. Unexpected, undeserved salvation! Jacob, Israel, each name denotes the entire nation (cp. ch. 1:5; 3:9, 10), the twelve tribes as God's covenant people; particularly, the true Israel, defined here as the remnant, the whole number of those who were faithful to the Covenant (see 2 Kings 19:30, 31; Is. 10:20-22; 11:11, 16; Micah 5:6; Rom. 9:27 ff.). Though at present they were oppressed by the wicked leaders, though they also were to share the exile together with the wicked (v. 10), yet the Lord has not forgotten nor forsaken His own (Is. 49:14 ff.). He will provide a deliverance from all that oppress them. He will assemble, gather, all His own, so that not one of His chosen children shall be missing. "Together" (Gr. N.), united into one flock, though separated by nationality, race, sex, language (cp. Gal. 3:26-28), yet one by common faith in their One Shepherd (John 10:14-16; Eph. 4:4-6). "Sheep of Bozrah," a city in Edom noted for its large flocks of sheep (Is. 34:6). They will be as the flock in the midst of their fold, well fed and provided for (Ps. 23). "Make great noise," denotes the sound of a great multitude (1 Kings 1:41; Is. 17:12), raising their voices to their God in prayers of supplication, of praise and thanksgiving; of a busy city (Is. 22:2), of the Church's activity in spreading the Gospel, building the Church at home and abroad, "men," sons of Adam (see Gr. N. on v. 2), dust of dust, yet by the grace of God active in the service of the Most High. What an assembly! (Cp. Rev. 7:9.) One holy, Christian Church, the communion of saints! This gathering will be made possible by the coming of a Deliverer (v. 13), who shall free them from their oppressors, the Redeemer promised Gen. 3:15, whose coming was being foretold with special clarity and with the addition of many new details in Micah's age (Amos 9:11 ff.; Hos. 13:14; 14:6-9, A. V., 5-8; Is. 7:14; 9:1-7; ch. 53, etc.; Micah 5:1 ff.). This Redeemer is pictured as the Breaker, who will break down the gates of the prison in which they were held captives, Satan's stronghold of sin and death and damnation. This Breaker has come up. Looking into the distant future, Micah sees His breaching the gates of hell as an accomplished fact (Gr. N.). Redemption, deliverance, has been accomplished! The captives have broken through the gates opened by the Breaker, and now the prophet sees them in a never-ending stream passing through the gates and going out into freedom, into full use of that liberty wherewith the Breaker has made them free (Gal. 5:1). Nor does the Breaker leave them. As their King He keeps on passing before them, coming to each individual by means of Word and Sacrament. This one is not a human king, He is Jehovah at their head! Cp. Gen. 4:1; Ex. 23:20; Jer. 23:5, 6; also Is. 40:10, 11; Ezek. 34:1-31; John 10:11-16.) Under the leadership of Him who is Jehovah Our Righteousness (Jer. 23:5, 6), God's people, delivered out of Satan's power, walk on the highway of holiness leading onward, upward, to everlasting joy (Is. 35:8-10).

PART II

Israel's Deepest Degradation and Greatest Glorification

Chapters 3—5

CHAPTER 3

A. The Leaders of Israel Have Led the People into Sin and Destruction

1 And I said, Pray, hear, O heads of Jacob and magistrates of the house of Israel! Is it not for you to know
2 judgment? Haters of good and lovers of evil! Who tear their skin off them and their flesh from their
3 bones, and who eat the flesh of My people and flay their skin off them and break their bones. They spread them out as in a caldron and as
4 meat in a pot. Then shall they call to the LORD, and He will not answer them, but hide His face from them at this time, according as they
5 have done only evil deeds. Thus speaks the LORD against the prophets who are leading My people astray, who are biting with their teeth and cry, Peace! And whoever will not put into their mouths, against him they prepare
6 war. Therefore it shall be night for you without vision, and darkness without divination; and the sun shall go down upon the prophets, and the day shall be dark upon
7 them. Then shall the seers be put to shame and the diviners incur disgrace, and they shall all cover their upper lip; for there shall be
8 no answer from God. But I, on the contrary, I am full of power, of the

Spirit of the LORD, of judgment and courageous strength to proclaim to Jacob his trangression and 9 to Israel his sin. Oh, hear this, you chiefs of the house of Jacob and you magistrates of the house of Israel, who detest judgment and twist everything that is straight, 10 who would build Zion with blood 11 and Jerusalem with iniquity. Her chiefs pronounce judgment for a bribe, and her priests teach for hire, and her prophets divine for silver. Yet they lean on the LORD, saying, Is not the LORD within our midst? No evil shall come 12 to us! Therefore, for your sakes Zion shall be plowed as a field, Jerusalem shall become heaps, and the mountain of the house as hills in the forest.

Grammatical Notes

V. 1. "And I said," וָאֹמַר, the imperfect of progress. The strong waw connects this section with the foregoing. We might translate, I continued to speak.

V. 5. "Make err," "bite." The participles denote the constant performance of the verbal idea; the characteristic trait.

V. 7. "Cover their lips," שָׂפָם = beard, mustache (cp. Lev. 13:45; 2 Sam. 19:24; Ezek. 24:17, 22). Others regard it as an irregular form for שְׂפָתָם, "their" lip.

V. 1. "And I said" (Gr. N.) connects the second part with the first. Chs. 1 and 2 were addressed to all nations (ch. 1:2); here is a compilation of prophecies addressed particularly to the "heads," the general term for officials in church and state, and the "princes," judges and other magistrates (cp. Joshua 10:24; Is. 1:10; 3:6, 7) of Jacob and Israel (see ch. 1:5). It is their special business and duty to know the constitutional Law (see Ex. 18:13-27; Num. 11:16-30; Deut. 17:1-20; 33:8-10, etc.).

Vv. 2, 3. Instead of making God's Law the norm of their judgment (Matt. 22:36-40), they hated what was good, pleasing to God, and beneficial to the community, and loved what was evil, wicked. Their sole aim was to satisfy the desires of their own sinful, depraved flesh, to obtain and enjoy riches, luxury, power. Their tyrannical rule was directed particularly against "My people," the God-fearing Israelites, whom they hated for their very uprightness. In scathing language Micah describes their heartless cruelty in terms of cannibalism. They treated their own flesh and blood like beasts brought to slaughter. Having stripped them, they flayed them, broke their bones, and were ready to feast on the very flesh of their brethren.

V. 4. As they knew no mercy and refused to listen to the pleas of their downtrodden brethren, so the Lord will turn away from their agonized cries (Ex. 21:23 f.; James 2:13 a; 5:1-6). His face, beaming with love and mercy for His own, will be hid from these wicked oppressors. Nothing but wrath for them!

259

Vv. 5-7 are directed against the false prophets purporting to be the Lord's spokesmen, while they make God's people err (Gr. N.). Instead of leading God's people to God, aiding them to remain faithful to the Covenant Lord, they deceive and seduce them by word and example to become covenant breakers. Their chief concern in life is to "bite with their teeth" (Gr. N.), to feast and dine and wine (1 Cor. 15:32 b, 33). In order to gain the favor and support of the people, they preach to them according to their itching ears, what these people wish to hear, Peace! Peace! There is no danger! You are God's people! How can the Lord forsake His own? He is not a cruel God, as Micah tries to tell you. Vain promises, empty, hollow words, yet exactly what the people demanded and were willing to pay for. These apostles of peace, of a god of love and kindness who will harm no one, these self-same prophets oozing love and liberality are the bitter enemies of God's prophets and God's people. Whoever will not fill up their mouths, give them something to eat, do them favors, will be mercilessly persecuted. And this hatred will not merely be voiced in empty words! No, they prepare warfare, literally, sanctify war; make it the solemn duty of the people to do away with prophets daring to speak of God's wrath against His chosen people. Away with such unpatriotic troublemakers, isolationists, calamity howlers! Peace! Peace!

Four times the darkness is described which will envelop these self-styled prophets of the Lord (v. 6). No more visions of peace shall they have in this utter darkness. Even their divination, seeking an oracle by means of arrows or other superstitious means, will yield no result. When they face the sunset of the nation, the darkness of the night of total destruction suddenly coming upon them, they no longer speak, nor dare to speak, of peace. The seers, who had seen visions, dreamt dreams, the diviners who had used superstitious means, all alike shall be abashed (v. 7), put to shame, cover their lips (Gr. N.) in sorrow and consternation. For there is no answer from God, no yea and amen to their former prophecies of peace, but the stark reality that God's true prophets revealed: Destruction! Ruin! Night!

V. 8. Micah contrasts himself with these miserable caricatures of the Lord's prophets. Yet in doing so he gives all the glory to the Lord and His life-giving Spirit. (Cp. 2 Cor. 11 and 12.) This Spirit has filled him with power, the inner strength of conviction; with "judgment," the ability to realize what is right and just, what God demands to be done under prevailing circumstances. "Might," that manly courage which boldly confesses and defends what one knows to be true and what is necessary to be preached to the people at this particular time. Therefore he proclaims to all of Israel their rebellious iniquities and sins (cp. 1:5).

Vv. 9-11. He proves his courage by again addressing the rulers and leaders, princes (v. 9), priests, and prophets (vv. 10, 11). The princes, the judges and magistrates (v. 1), prove by their judicial decisions that justice and judgment is an abomination to them. Regardless of the justice of a case, they know how to twist it so that the innocent is condemned. "They build up Zion" (v. 10), put it on the map, make it renowned by blood, bloody crimes (Is. 1:15-18, 21; Ezek. 22:2-12), gangsterism, judicial murders, a "wide-open town." Judges, priests, and prophets alike are money-mad. Reward, hire, money, is the beginning and end of their ambition. And still they "lean," rely on the Lord, look to Him for support and help. No evil can come to us! We are the Lord's people! (Cp. Is. 1:10 ff.; Jer. 7:8-11.)

V. 12. Such shameful hypocrisy is an abomination to the Lord, worse than open rebellion and paganism. "For your sakes" the "builders" of Zion (v. 10) are its destroyers. Zion, Jerusalem, the mountain of the house, the most sacred places, the very proofs of God's presence, regarded as absolute guarantees of safety, whose destruction was impossible, will be plowed up by the machines of war, changed to a field of ruins and heaps of stones, to "high places of the forest," become hills of a jungle, overgrown with thorns and brambles. (Cp. 2 Kings 25:8 ff.; Lam. 1:1; 2:1 ff.; 4:1; 5:18.)

CHAPTER 4

B. The Glorification of the Church

1 It shall come to pass in the end of the days that the mountain of the house of the LORD shall be established on the top of the mountains, and it shall be elevated above the hills, and nations shall stream to it.

2 And many nations shall go and say, Come, and let us go up to the mountain of the LORD and to the house of the God of Jacob, that He may instruct us in His ways and that we may walk in His paths. For from Zion goes forth instruction and the Word of the LORD

3 from Jerusalem. And He shall judge between great peoples and render decisions for strong nations afar off. Then they shall beat their swords into plowshares and their spears into pruning hooks. Nation shall no longer lift its sword against nation, nor shall they learn

4 war any more. But they shall sit each under his vine and under his fig tree, and no one shall frighten them; for the mouth of the LORD

5 of Hosts has spoken! For all the peoples walk each in the name of its god, but we, we walk in the name of the LORD, our God, for-

6 ever and ever. On that day, is the oracle of the LORD, I will gather her that is limping, and her that is cast out will I assemble, and her

7 whom I have afflicted. Then I will make her that is limping a remnant and her that is far removed a strong nation. And the LORD shall

reign over them on the Mount of Zion from now on and forever.

8 And you, O Migdal Eder! Ophel, the daughter of Zion, shall come to you! And the former dominion, a kingdom, shall come to the daugh-

9 ter of Jerusalem. Now, why do you cry so bitterly? Is there no king within you? Or has your counselor perished? For anguish has gripped

10 you like a woman in travail. Be in anguish and bring forth, O daughter of Zion, like a woman in travail. For now you will go forth from the city and live in the field, and will come to Babel. There shall you be rescued. There the LORD shall re-

deem you from the hand of your
11 enemies. But now there shall be gathered against you many nations who shall be saying, She is polluted! Let our eyes feast on Zion!
12 But they do not know the plans of the LORD, nor do they understand His counsel; for He shall gather them as sheaves to the threshing
13 floor. Arise and thresh, O daughter of Zion! For I will make your horn iron, and I will make your hoofs brass, so that you shall crush many peoples and shall devote their riches to the LORD and their wealth to the Lord of all the earth.

Grammatical Notes

V. 5. "Forever and ever," עוֹלָם וָעֶד. On *olam* see p. 270. עַד occurs only with וְ otherwise עַד, from עָדָה, to go on, denoting unlimited or unknowable progress; of past time only (Job 20:4), of unknown duration in time (Ps. 104:5), of God = absolute eternity (Ex. 15:18; Ps. 10:16; 45:7), of everlasting damnation (Ps. 9:6), of eternal life after resurrection (Dan. 12:3). The eternal God is our God in time and eternity. (Cp. Ps. 48:14; 45:17; 52:8; 145:1, 2, 21.)

V. 7. "Cast off," הַנַּהֲלָאָה, occurs only here; a denominative of הָלְאָה, "away, afar off" (Num. 17:2, A. V., 16:37, "yonder"; 1 Sam. 10:3, "forward"); hence, "to be removed far away, cast off."

V. 8 presents difficulties. LXX regards it as a threat and translates, "O defiled tower of the flock, daughter of Zion, against you shall come and approach you, the first power, a kingdom from Babylon, to the daughter of Jerusalem." Similarly Vulgate. Both take עֹפֶל in the sense of dirty, defiled, which cannot be established. (See excursus on Ophel

below, p. 263. Luther: "Your golden rose shall come" = the Messiah; he read עֶדְיֵךְ, "your ornament," instead of עָדֶיךָ, "to you." Sellin: "And you, O tower of the flock, watchtower of the daughter of Zion, to you shall come ['and come' = a gloss] the former dominion, the royal rule of the house [instead of 'the daughter'] of Jerusalem." R. S. V.: "And you, O tower of the flock, hill of the daughter of Zion, to you shall it come, the former dominion shall come, the kingdom of the daughter of Jerusalem." None of these translations does justice to the M. T. Ophel does not mean "watchtower." It is the hill Ophel (see below, p. 263). There is no need to regard "and come" as a gloss. It is a perfect with strong וְ as the accent on the ultimate proves (see G.-B. sub בּוֹא). We, therefore, in keeping with the pointing of the M. T. translate as above. — תֶּאֱתֶה, from אָתָה, which occurs only in poetic language. (Cp. Is. 21:12; 41:5, 23; 44:7; Job 16:22; 30:14, etc.)

Jerusalem — Zion — Ophel

Jerusalem, called Salem (Gen. 14:18; cp. Ps. 76:2), Jebusi (Joshua 18:28), Jebus (Judg. 19:10 f.), city of Jebusites (Judg. 19:11), "side" (= slope) of Jebusites (Joshua 15:8; 18:16), shares with Damascus (Gen. 14:15; 15:2) the honor of being the oldest city still existent. It is situated on the central ridge of Palestine extending from Beersheba to Lebanon. Its highest point is 2,593 feet above sea level and ca. 3,850 feet above the Salt Sea. At the time of Micah it occupied that part of the ridge bounded by the deep valley of Kidron on the east, from 60 to 150 feet deep today and from 20 to 50 feet deeper in ancient times (Barton, *Archaeology and the Bible*, p. 168), the Valley of Hinnom on the south and west. The north side alone was unprotected by natural defenses. The plateau between Kidron and Hinnom was divided by a shallower valley running north and south into two unequal parts, the wider and higher part toward the west, a narrower spur on the east. The name of this valley is not preserved in the Bible. Josephus calls it the Tyropoeon (cheesemakers') Valley. This eastern spur is composed of two hills, the southern, Hill of Zion, the site of Jebusite Jerusalem, and a northern hill, Mount Moriah, the later site of Solomon's Temple (2 Chron. 3:1; cp. 2 Sam. 24:12-25; 1 Chron. 21:9 ff.). Between these two hills forming the eastern ridge excavators in 1923—24 found a shallow valley running eastward from the Tyropoeon Valley and forming a natural defense about halfway to the Kidron Valley, extended to the latter by an artificial ditch ten feet wide and eight feet deep. Already in early times (ca. 1600 B. C.) this ditch was filled up and later the entire valley was gradually filled up. (*A Century of Excavation in Palestine*, R. A. C. MacAlister, p. 99 f.) The only water supply came from two springs in the Kidron Valley, one just south of the valley joining Zion and Moriah, the other south of the juncture of the Kidron and Hinnom valleys. The former, Gihon, was connected by a subterranean aqueduct with the Pool of Siloam by King Hezekiah (2 Kings 20:20; cp. Siloam inscription, Barton, *Archaeology*, p. 475).

For many centuries the western hill of Jerusalem, the modern Zion, the Jewish section of the city, was regarded as the site of Jebus, the city of David (2 Sam. 5:9; the exact nature and site of "Millo" are still unknown). Yet excavations have made the identification of Zion and the southern half of the eastern ridge practically indisputable.

Ophel (Micah 4:8, "stronghold") has been variously identified. It denotes a "bulge" or "hump," occurs 2 Kings 5:24, "tower" (a hill in Samaria); 2 Chron. 27:3; 33:14; Neh. 3:26 f.; 11:21; Is. 32:14; Micah 4:8, in connection with Jerusalem. Ges.-Buhl: the southeastern part of the Temple hill. The *Westminster Atlas* (p. 101) places the name Ophel between Zion and Moriah and says that the hill of Zion "in ancient times was called, in its northern part at least, Ophel" (p. 97 A). Marston (*New Bible Evidence*, pp. 26, 120, 231) and Garstang (*Joshua and Judges*, p. 388 f.; Plate XXXVIII opp. p. 170) identify it with ancient Zion, now outside the city walls and used as vegetable gardens, and Garstang places the "wall of Ophel" between Mount Zion and Mount Moriah.

The total area of the City of David may have been eleven to thirteen acres. In later times the name Zion, or Mount Zion, included the Temple hill (Is. 10:12; 24:23; Joel 3:5; Zech. 1:14, etc.); and the entire city (Jer. 3:14; Amos 6:1; Micah 3:10, 12, etc.).

---

1. The Church's glory, vv. 1, 2

V. 1. "In the last days," the New Testament era (see Hos. 3:5). "The mountain of the house of the Lord," see excursus on "Jerusalem, Zion, Ophel" above. "In the top." This cannot mean that at some future time Mount Zion will grow higher than the mountains. The article is generic, comprising all mountains. A number of interpreters insist on the physical growth of Zion until it becomes the highest mountain. Aside from the physical impossibility of the nations, men and women, young and old, ascending a mountain overtopping Mount Everest, an undertaking correctly called by E. Koenig "eine halsbrecherische Bergfahrt," a breakneck ascent, other valid reasons oblige us to reject this interpretation, although it is held by Guthe (Kautzsch, *Komm.*), Procksch, Margolis, and others. "In the top" does not necessarily denote greater physical height. The context demands the sense of leadership, higher rank here. Nor is the ascent a physical one. According to v. 2 the nations go up to Zion because from Zion the Word of the Lord goes forth. The kingdom of God, the Church of Christ, comes to the nations in the preaching of the Gospel, and by faith in this Gospel the nations enter Zion, go up to Jerusalem (cp. Heb. 12:22 ff.).

Hofmann, Delitzsch, and others limit the growth of Mount Zion to one surpassing the neighboring mountains. This does not do justice to the generic article and is equally opposed by the context and Dan. 2:37-45.

In the Messianic era the Church of God, Mount Zion, God's Kingdom of Grace, will in every respect be "at the head," the chief of all kingdoms. In point of importance it was that already in Moses' time (cp. Num. 23 and 24, Balaam's prophecies; Deut. 4:6-8; 33:26 ff.; Rom. 9:1 ff.). The New Testament Church will excel this glory of the Old Covenant (Jer. 31:31 ff.; Col. 2:10-17; Heb. 8—10) and will lead all kingdoms in point of extent also. People, nations shall "flow," stream in mighty numbers to this kingdom reaching to the uttermost parts of the earth (Ps. 72:8-11; Luke 24:47; Acts 1:8; Rom. 10:18; Rev. 14:6). And while the most powerful kingdoms shall vanish (Dan. 2:31-44; Hag. 2:21, 22), God's Kingdom of Grace, Mount Zion, shall be established forever, firm, immovable, leading all kingdoms in this respect also (Ps. 45:5-7; Dan. 2:44 f.; 7:13, 14, 27; Matt. 16:18; Heb. 12:28).

V. 2. The nations will urge one another to join God's kingdom, will be engaged in world-wide mission work, new territories being conquered, and these in turn spreading the Gospel to people unacquainted with it, or seeking to regain territories once under the rule of Christ the King, but later apostatized. They will proclaim the glory of Jehovah (Ex. 3:14; 34:6, 7; Is. 40; Micah 7:18 ff.), of the God of Jacob, who came to sinful Jacob and graciously encouraged, comforted, strengthened him in every crisis of his life (Gen. 28:10-22; 32:24 ff.; 35:1-15; 46:1-4) and on his deathbed (Gen. 48 and 49). A twofold purpose and blessing for joining this kingdom: (1) God teaches man "of" His ways, not all of them (Is. 40:13-28; 55:8, 9; Rom. 11:33 ff.), but enough for salvation (Is. 55:1-4). (2) We will walk in His paths. His teaching, spirit and life (John 6:63) give us strength to lead a God-pleasing life. "For" motivates the invitation. "The Law" here in the sense of instruction, as the parallel "Word of Jehovah" indicates. The Church, Zion, Jerusalem, not only knows the Word of God, His Law and His saving Gospel. From the Church this instruction, justifying, sanctifying, also goes into the world (Is. 40:1-9; Matt. 28:19 f.; Luke 24:45 ff.).

2. The Church's peace, granted to her by her Lord. vv. 3-5

V. 3. "Judge." The judges during the early history were the deliverers of their people, their protectors, instructors (cp. Judg. 2:11-18; chs. 4 and 5; 1 Sam. 3 ff.). "Rebuke," literally, to decide, make decisions; to defend and protect the right; to teach and train by admonition, chastisement, punishment. The Lord will judge and rebuke among many nations. His Word will be the norm of life not only in little Judah, but also throughout the wide world. In Asia, in Africa, in Europe, and in America the Church has no other norm than God's Word. Though the civic laws of the various nations differ, sometimes greatly, the Church everywhere acknowledges the Triune God and His Word as her highest norm. The Lord will also "rebuke," protect, and defend the rights of His Church against all opponents. Neither the wisdom of Greece nor the power and hatred of pagan and papal Rome could destroy the Church, nor will any other force succeed in its efforts against God's Kingdom of Grace (Matt. 16:18).

The purpose and result of such judging and rebuking is the establishment and maintenance of a kingdom of peace on this earth; nations shall beat their swords into plowshares, etc. Does this mean that "when the eternal Lord by His guidance of the history of the world — we think, e. g., of the catastrophe annihilating Sennacherib's army (Is. 31:8; 37:36), or of the hard winter of 1812 — shall arise as the Arbiter among the peoples of the world, then the nations, overwhelmed by these soul-stirring divine actions, will no longer be inclined to settle their quarrels by force of arms"? (Koenig, *Das Buch Jesaia*, pp. 56, 57.) The Lord of this kingdom knows of no such universal peace. He knew only of wars and other calamities as the beginning of sorrows to continue until His appearance on the Last Day (Matt. 24:7 ff.). The divinely appointed herald of Christ (Luke 7:27) did not demand that the soldiers beat their swords into plowshares before they could become disciples of the Prince of Peace (Luke 3:14). Nor did Peter, the first messenger of Christ to the Gentiles (Acts 15:7), having accepted the invitation of a Roman centurion transmitted by a soldier, and preaching in a soldier's home before military men, demand that they must beat their spears into pruning hooks before they could join the

265

Church of the Gospel preaching peace by Jesus Christ (Acts 10:7, 33 ff.). And Micah himself speaks not of an era of political peace among the nations of the world. He speaks here very definitely of God's Kingdom of Grace established by the Word of God proceeding from Zion and Jerusalem and gathering God's people throughout the world into one holy Christian Church (Luke 24:47; Acts 1:8). The Christian from Alabama and the Christian from Ohio, one wearing the Southern gray, the other the Northern blue, were fighting against each other in bloody battles, yet both were brethren in Christ, both members in His kingdom of peace, both one in faith of their common Savior, both enjoying the peace procured for them by the Prince of Peace and praying for the spiritual welfare of each other. (Ch. 4:1-3 and Is. 2:2-4 are almost identical prophecies.)

V. 4. Sitting under one's vine and fig tree is an emblem of peace, security, happiness. Again, Micah speaks here of spiritual gifts enjoyed by the members of God's Church. The peace of God procured by the Prince of Peace and implanted into the heart of the believer by the Gospel keeps him free from cares and worries (cp. Ps. 23:4; 27:1, 3; 56:11; Is. 41:10, etc.). This is indeed a peace passing understanding, mingled with fightings and fears within and without as long as we live in this world of imperfection. Its fullness will be enjoyed only in the realms of eternal peace above. Yet to assure us of God's peace and to keep us in this peace, the prophet solemnly declares that the promise of such peace is not that of a mere man. It is the mouth of the Lord of Hosts, the Ruler of the universe, that has spoken!

V. 5. All peoples, and every individual member of these peoples outside the Church, walk in the name of their god. The name is the revelation of one's nature, what one knows about another. What the nations know about their gods, the creation of their own minds, is what their own reason, or their prophets, or their traditions, handed down from generation to generation, tell them. Their gods are at best glorified men reflecting in their character the character, the foibles, the sins and vices of sinful, wicked men, whose creation they are. And in turn these gods, jealous, cruel, lecherous, covetous as they are, serve as patterns for the lives of their worshipers. The character of a nation corresponds to the character of its god. The Church walks in the name of Jehovah, her God, firmly trusting in His grace and forgiveness and salvation as revealed in His Gospel and willingly obeying His commandments revealed in His Law. — "Forever and ever" (Gr. N.). While nations perish and individuals die and are lost forever because their man-made gods cannot help them (Jer. 10:2-16), the Church and her individual members have the promise of everlasting life through the revelation of the Lord of Life (Gen. 5:29; 48:15, 16; 49:18; Job 19:25 ff.; Ps. 17:15; 90:1 f., etc.). Even death cannot deprive them of their peace.

3. The Church's strength, vv. 6, 7

Vv. 6, 7. "In that day," the Messianic era (cp. v. 1), the Lord will keep on gathering her that "halteth," limps, is lame. The word occurs only here, Gen. 32:31, and Zeph. 3:19; an allusion to Jacob's lameness after battling with God, as a constant reminder of his own weakness. So the children of Jacob, believing and blessed children of God, still "halt" and because of their sins must be disciplined. Israel was "driven out" (same word as Deut. 30:4), exiled; the Lord "afflicted" her. Though the enemies exiled and afflicted Israel, they were only God's instruments. He scattered Israel (cp. Deut. 30:3). Yet the halt, the limping Church shall by the Lord's almighty grace be made a remnant (v. 7; cp. Micah 2:12; 5:6 f.), the chosen children of God (John 10:27 ff.; Rom. 8:29-39). The "cast off" (Gr. N.) shall become a strong nation, just as limping Jacob came forth from his battle a strong man, an Israel, a conqueror; indeed, more than conquerors, through Him that loved them.

4. The Church's kingdom, v. 8

V. 8. "Tower of the flock" (Gr. N.). Migdal Eder (Gen. 35:21; cp. vv. 16-20). According to Jerome (*Ad Eust.*, ep. 108, cp. *Peregrinatio S. Paulae*, ch. 9), it was located about one Roman mile (ca. 4,900 feet) from Bethlehem. No other Migdal Eder is mentioned in Biblical or ancient non-Biblical literature. On the fields of Bethlehem shepherds watched their flocks by night. There came the first public announcement of the birth of the Christ Child; there the angels praised God for the birth of the Prince of Peace, who brought God's good will to men. There the Eastern Magi found the newborn King of the Jews. From the fields of Bethlehem, marked by the "tower of the flock," the "former" kingdom, promised to Judah (Gen. 49:10 ff.) and to David (2 Sam. 7:12-16; cp. Ps. 2:6 ff.; 45:6; Dan. 7:13 ff.), came to Jerusalem. This was not a political, but a spiritual kingdom (Hos. 1:7; Zech. 4:6 b; Micah 7:18-20). When Israel rejected its King and His Kingdom of Grace, it lost the privilege of being as a nation "a kingdom of priests" (Ex. 19:6; Matt. 8:10-12; 21:43; Acts 13:46 ff.; 1 Thess. 2:14-16). When Christ established His Church of the New Testament, the former dominion, a priestly kingdom in the noblest sense of the term (1 Peter

2:9; Rev. 1:6; 3:21; 5:10), came to the New Testament Jerusalem, the spiritual Zion (Gal. 4:26; Heb. 12:22 f.), composed of believing Jews and Gentiles (Is. 49:6; Rom. 9:23—10:17), as the bridal gift of the King of Kings.

5. The Church's victory after seemingly hopeless defeat, vv. 9-13

Vv. 9-13. The prophet sees his nation weeping aloud and writhing in agony. He asks for the reason: "Are kings and counselors perished?" He knows the bitter truth, and the full truth is yet hidden to them. Judah shall be deprived of her rulers! But that loss is only a fraction of her oncoming disasters. He calls upon her to "be in pain" (v. 10), to writhe, and "labor to bring forth," go to full length of anguish. (Cp. Luke 23:28 ff.) For she shall be forced to leave her city, her homeland, and dwell in the field, shelterless, exposed to danger. Far away, to distant Babylon! Exile! (Cp. Is. 39:3-6.) Lest despair overtake her, a glorious promise of deliverance is added. Judah will be delivered, literally, "drawn out," "plucked out" (Zech. 3:2), saved, not by her own efforts, but by her Redeemer, who has bound Himself to the duty of a redeemer, by becoming her kinsman (Lev. 25:25 ff.); her brother (Heb. 2:11-15). Lest she give up hope when the Holy City will be cruelly defiled by heathen hosts and she herself be made the gazingstock of her enemies (v. 11), the Lord assures her of His secret thoughts and counsels (vv. 12, 13; cp. Jer. 29:11). The Lord will gather her oppressors like sheaves upon the threshing floor. There Judah shall thresh them with the strength of iron and hoofs of brass (cp. ch. 5:5b-9). Converted Judah will proclaim the holy Law and the saving Gospel, the power of which (cp. Jer. 23:29; Is. 61:1f.) she has experienced herself. The chaff, the unbelievers, shall be swept away; the wheat, the elect, be gathered into God's granaries. The Lord Himself will consecrate their gain, literally, their "cut," dividends, profit, and their "substance," strength, wealth, power, by putting it into His service. Very appropriately He is called the God of the whole earth, who has first claim on all the fruits of the progress made by man in subduing the treasures and forces of the universe. The Church will gladly put them into the service of the Gospel.

CHAPTER 5

C. The Church's Glorious King, Ch. 4:14—5:14 (A. V., 5:1-15)

14 (A. V., 5:1) Now gather in troops, O daughter of troops! He has besieged us! With a rod they strike upon the cheek the judge of Israel.

1 (A. V., 2) And you, Bethlehem Ephratah, too little to be among the thousands of Judah, from you shall come forth unto Me He that

is to be Ruler over Israel, whose forthcomings are from of old, from 2 (3) the days of eternity. Therefore He will give them up until the time when she who is with child shall have given birth. And the remnant of His brethren shall return together with the children of 3 (4) Israel. And He shall stand and do the work of a shepherd in the strength of the LORD in the majesty of the name of the LORD, His God. And they shall dwell in safety; for now will He be great unto the ends of the earth. 4 (5) And this One shall be Peace! When Assyria shall come into our land, and when he treads upon our palaces, then shall we raise up against him seven shepherds and 5 (6) eight princes of men; and they shall shepherd the land of Assyria with the sword and the land of Nimrod in her gates. And He shall effect a rescue from Assyria when it comes into our land and when it treads on our territory. 6 (7) And the remnant of Jacob shall be in the midst of many peoples like dew from the LORD, as showers on the vegetation, which

do not wait for man nor tarry for 7 (8) the children of men. And the remnant of Jacob shall be among the nations, in the midst of many peoples, like a lion among the beasts of the forest, like a young lion among flocks of sheep, who, when he passes through, tramples and tears with none to deliver. 8 (9) Your hand shall be exalted above your oppressors, and all your 9 (10) enemies shall be cut off. And it shall come to pass on that day, is the oracle of the LORD, that I will cut off your horses from the midst of you, and destroy your 10 (11) chariots. And I will cut off the cities of your land and raze all 11 (12) your fortresses. And I will cut off witchcraft from your hand, and you will have no more sooth- 12 (13) sayers. And I will cut off the carved images and the pillars from the midst of you, so that you shall no longer worship the work of your 13 (14) hands. And I will uproot your Asherahs from the midst of you and destroy your cities. 14 (15) And will wreak vengeance in anger and fury upon the nations that have not obeyed.

Grammatical Notes

Ch. 4:14 (A. V., 5:1). "Gather thyself in troops." תִּתְגֹּדְדִי, from גָּדַד; the Hithp. is used in a twofold sense, "to make incisions," cut, mutilate oneself, in sorrow or fanaticism (Deut. 14:1; 1 Kings 18:28; Jer. 16:6; 41:5; 47:5). So Sellin and others translate here. We prefer with A. V. to connect it with גְּדוּד, troop, band, company (cp. Gen. 49:19; 1 Sam. 30:8, 15, 23; 2 Sam. 4:2; 1 Kings 11:24, etc.). — "He hath laid siege." The indefinite עָל, "one," in the sense of passive: We are besieged. (G.-K. 144 d.)

5:1 (2). "Bethlehem." בַּיִת is always masculine; Bethlehem always feminine, but here followed by a masculine adjective, perhaps to call attention to the symbolism of the name. — "In Israel."

מָשַׁל בְּ always means rule over (Gen. 3:16; 4:7; Prov. 22:7, etc.). — "Thousands," here a family or commonwealth of about a thousand more or less; then, any tribe or family (Judg. 6:15; 1 Sam. 10:19, etc.) smaller than a tribe. Num. 1:16; 10:4; Joshua 22:21 it is synonymous with tribe. — "Goings forth." מוֹצָאוֹת is derived from יָצָא, to go forth. The feminine plural occurs only here and in the Masoretic correction of the vulgar Hebrew word for "privy," A. V., "draught house" (2 Kings 10:27), מֹחֲרָאוֹת, substituting for it "outgoings" = excrements. The masculine form occurs quite frequently and may mean (1) the place of going forth (e. g., Ezek. 42:11; 43:11, "goings out" = gates; 2 Kings

269

2:21, water springs); (2) that which proceeds from (Num. 30:13; Deut. 8:3; Jer. 17:16); (3) the act of going forth (2 Sam. 3:25; Ps. 19:7, A. V., 6; Hos. 6:3; Ezek. 12:4; Dan. 9:25). In our passage it can mean only the act of going forth, since eternity is no place. The plural may refer to a number of "goings forth," or it may be the plural of amplification, referring to a single act, but viewing this act in its various stages or steps. Compare Jer. 2:2, where both "thy youth" and "thy espousals" are plural in the Hebrew text, although the reference very clearly is to only one youth and one espousal. So *shilluchim,* plural, literally, "sendings away," is "divorce," singular, Ex. 18:2; *kippurim,* Ex. 29:36; 30:10, etc., not atonements, but atonement; *binot,* feminine plural, Is. 27:11, insight. (G.-K. 124 e, f.) We might compare the English "news," "tidings." — Again the context must decide whether the plural refers to one outgoing or a number of them. — "Of old," מִקֶּדֶם. קֶדֶם properly is that which lies before; transferred to time, that which lies before us in the more or less distant past. That may be a century, or a millennium, several millenniums, or that timeless, ageless eternity, which no man's mind can comprehend, where nothing existed save He who calls Himself I AM THAT I AM. The context must decide whether *kedem* denotes "old, ancient," in the sense of time or of ageless eternity. It is used in the former sense, e. g., Deut. 33:15 ("mountains of old"); Is. 19:11 ("kings"); Ps. 143:5, etc.; in the latter sense, e. g., Ps.

55:19; Hab. 1:12; the plural, Prov. 8:23. — "From everlasting," מֵעוֹלָם. עוֹלָם, derived from a root = "to be hidden," is used to denote time "hidden," time of which the beginning, or the end, or both, are unknown, unknowable, or nonexistent. Koenig: verhuellte Zeit: veiled, shrouded time. That *olam* is a term for eternity when ascribed to God, is evident from such passages as Ps. 90:2; Prov. 8:23; Is. 63:16, etc.; that it refers to His acts in time, from Is. 42:14; 44:7; 63:9; Jer. 2:20. Again the context must decide whether it refers to time or to eternity.

V. 2 (3). "Travaileth, hath brought forth," יוֹלֵדָה יָלָדָה. (Cp. יוֹלֵדָת, Is. 7:14.) A very definite reference to Isaiah's prophecy. — "Remnant." יֶתֶר frequently denotes something beside what is mentioned in the context, sometimes translated "rest" (Judg. 7:6; 1 Sam. 13:2; 2 Sam. 10:10), sometimes "residue" (Is. 44:19; Jer. 27:19, etc.). Compare the frequent phrase "the rest of the acts of. . . ." (1 Kings 11:41, etc.) "Unto." עַל, either "to" or "together with" (Gen. 32:12, A. V., 11; Hos. 10:14).

V. 3 (4). "Abide." יֵשְׁבוּ = dwell safely, quietly. (Cp. Lev. 26:5, 6; 2 Sam. 7:10; Micah 4:4.)

V. 4 (5). "Principal men," נְסִיכֵי אָדָם, literally, princes of, or among, men. (Cp. Is. 29:19, "poor among men"; Prov. 15:20; 21:20, "a foolish man," fool among men; our "prince of a fellow." G.-K. 128 l.)

---

1. The coming of the King preceded by a time of deepest degradation, ch. 4:14 (A. V., 5:1)

The prophet had ended his prophecy with a note of joyous hope. Yet the day of victory was still in the distant future. A time of deep degradation would precede the Messianic kingdom. Judah is told to gather herself in troops, huddle close together in fear and distress.

The imperative indicates the certainty of such times. Enclosed, restrained, harassed, deprived of her liberty by powerful cruel enemies. Even her judges, her rulers, would be smitten on the cheek, insulted, maltreated. We think of Hoshea (2 Kings 17:4); Manasseh (2 Chron. 33:11 f.); the last kings of Judah (Jer. 22:18-30; 52:8-11, 24-27); the bloody persecutions under Antiochus Epiphanes and Herod, etc. At this time when the scepter had departed from Judah, when an Idumaean, ruling by the grace of Rome, pompously calling himself Herod the Great, was king of the Jews, at this time of deepest humiliation and degradation, the Messiah came!

2. The twofold miraculous birth of the Ruler, ch. 5:1, 2 (A. V., v. 2, 3)

5:1 (A. V., 2). "Bethlehem" = House of Bread (Gr. N.); Ephratah = Fruitful. Micah adds the ancient name (Gen. 35:16, 19) in order to distinguish it from Bethlehem in Zebulon (Joshua 19:15). Here He was to be born who was indeed the Bread of Life (John 6:48), the fruitful Progenitor of innumerable children of God (Ps. 22:31, 32, A. V., 30, 31; Is. 53:10 ff.; Hos. 2:1, A. V., 1:10). Near Bethlehem, Benjamin was born and Rachel buried (Gen. 35:16 ff.); here Ruth gleaned (Ruth 2:1 ff.); here David was born (1 Sam. 16:1; 17:12). Later it was fortified by the Philistines (2 Sam. 23:14) and by Rehoboam (2 Chron. 11:6). Yet it always remained a small town. It is not named among the more than hundred cities allotted to Judah (Joshua 15:21-63). After the Exile it is named in Ezra 2:21 and Neh. 7:26. Too little indeed to be numbered among the thousands (Gr. N.), towns of more than a thousand inhabitants (cp. John 7:42, town = village). Yet the Lord, who usually chooses the small and insignificant to work His miracles, had selected this little town of Bethlehem as the birthplace of the incarnate Son of God.

"Come forth" does not per se denote birth (cp. Micah 4:10). It derives this meaning only from the context (Gen. 25:25 f.; 2 Kings 20:18). The word tells us that the Ruler would issue from Bethlehem, not from the royal city, Jerusalem. The context, however, very clearly defines this going forth as the bringing forth by her "which travaileth" (v. 3), as the birth of a human child by a human mother. So the chief priests and scribes correctly understood this prophecy (Matt. 2:1 ff.), and the people as well (John 7:42). This human child was to be "Ruler in Israel" (Gr. N.), rather, "over Israel," of all to whom this name applies. Such a ruler had long ago and time and again been prophesied (Gen. 49:10f.; 1 Sam. 2:10; 2 Sam. 7:12ff.; Pss. 2; 22:23ff.; 45; 47; 72;

110; Is. 9:6 f., etc.). Now Micah is the first one to name the birthplace of this Ruler: Bethlehem.

"Goings forth"; "from of old"; "from everlasting" (Gr. N.). The Jewish rabbis in the Christian era refer these words either to the naming of the Messiah's name in eternity or to the idea of the Messiah existing in God's mind before the creation of the world. Rationalistic interpreters of the early nineteenth century generally adopted these interpretations. Modern Jewish and Protestant interpreters generally refer "from of old," "from everlasting," to the time of the rise of the Davidic dynasty. (Margolis, *Micah*, p. 52; Guthe in Kautzsch, *Die Hlg. Schr.*, etc.) Yet a lineage dating back to ancient times could not possibly have served as a special characteristic of the future Ruler. Every descendant of David and even of Abraham and Adam could trace his lineage back to creation (cp. 1 Chron. 1:1-28; 2:1-15). Nor can the words denote "the many preparations made by God from the earliest times in prophecy and history for the founding of the Messianic kingdom" (Orelli). For the words speak not of the founding of a kingdom, nor of the preparations for such a kingdom, nor of the prophecies of the going forth of the Ruler. The prophet here speaks of the goings forth and of the birth of a future Ruler. A quite different matter. Keil regards the plural "goings forth" as referring both to the origin of the Messiah before all worlds and to His appearances in the olden time. Sellin (*Zwoelfprophetenbuch*, 1929, p. 336 f.) sees in this ruler one who has once before appeared, existed, in ancient times. He identifies him later with David, who according to popular conception would personally return to rule Israel. He quotes Ezek. 34:23; 37:25; Hos. 3:5; Is. 9:6; 11:1.

Scripture speaks of another birth of this Child, born at Bethlehem of a human mother. God Himself, speaking of His Anointed, the Messiah, tells Him Ps. 2:7. Wisdom, the Son of God, speaks of His birth before all times (Prov. 8:22-31). Because of this birth the future Messiah is Immanuel, God with us (Is. 7:14), the Mighty God, the Everlasting Father (Is. 9:6; cp. also John 1:1-3, 14; 9:35-38; Col. 1:15-17; Heb. 1:1-12). It is to this birth in the timeless eons of eternity that Micah refers here. This generation from eternity distinguishes the Child of Bethlehem from all other descendants of David, and this generation alone qualifies Him for His work as Ruler of Israel, His Church.

V. 2 (A. V., 3). "He" = Jehovah; "them" = Israel. Micah had foretold the destruction of Israel because of its apostasy (ch. 3:1ff.; 4:9—5:1). This humiliation will continue "until the time that she which travaileth hath brought forth." Here is a clear, unmistakable reference to Is. 7:14 (see Gr. N.). The one bringing forth has brought forth. While Israel's oppression would last until the birth of this Child, this Babe is the Ruler, the Shiloh, in whom the scepter would be returned to Judah (cp. ch. 4:8). As Jerusalem of the Old Testament owed its royal glory to the man David born at Bethlehem, so the New Testament Jerusalem, the Israel of God (Gal. 4:26; 6:16; Heb. 12:22 f.), owes all its glory to the virgin-born Child of Bethlehem, whose goings forth are from of old, from everlasting. — "Remnant of His brethren" (Gr. N.). Besides the Israelites here mentioned, who are brethren of the Messiah according to the flesh, there are other brethren, not by common descent from Abraham, but by spiritual relationship, by faith in the promised Redeemer (Micah 4:2-5; Is. 11: 10-12; Eph. 2:11-22; Rom. 9:24-26). These the Ruler of Israel is not ashamed to call His brethren (Heb. 2:11; Matt. 12:50; John 11:51 ff.). What an honor to be acknowledged as a brother by Him who is the Everlasting!

3. His rule of peace, vv. 3, 4a (A. V., 4, 5a)

V. 3 (A. V., 4). "He shall stand." The Shepherd-King is pictured not as sitting, but as standing and feeding, doing His Messianic work. His strength is that of the Lord (Is. 9:7), an irresistible, omnipotent strength, tested to the utmost on the cross, where in the midst of hell He stood unconquered, invincible. — "In the majesty of the name of the Lord, His God." As one born of a human mother, the Lord is His God ("My God!" Matt. 27:46). Born of the Father from eternity, the Lord's name is in Him (Ex. 23:21), His is the majesty of the Lord's name, the very Being and Essence of Jehovah (John 1:14; 10:30; 14:9; Eph. 1:20 ff.; Phil. 2:9 ff.; Rev. 5:6-14). This power and majesty the Messiah employs in feeding, shepherding His people as their Shepherd-King. In Him are combined the majestic power of Deity and the tender love of the Shepherd who loved us and gave Himself for us. What marvelous honor bestowed on human, frail, sinful mortals! — "They shall abide" (Gr. N.), dwell quietly in safety; a security far more reliable than any scheme of health insurance, old-age pension, or social security can possibly guarantee! For this Shepherd, exalted far above all heavens, "shall be great unto the ends of the earth." The iron fist of Assyria and Babylon held all the world in fearsome subjection. The power of Rome was respected throughout the world. (Cp. Acts 16:37-40; 22:25-29; 23:26-35.) Here is the King clad in the royal robes of Jehovah's power, and He is our Shepherd, watching with eyes of love every sheep and lamb of His flock, and no one shall

273

pluck them out of His hands! A superhuman job, yet a work of love
with Him! Such is our King!

V. 4 a (A. V., 5 a). "And this Man shall be the Peace" (Gr. N.),
literally, Peace. The Babe of Bethlehem is not only the Prince of
Peace (Is. 9: 6), He *is* Peace (Eph. 2: 14). Having Him, we have peace
in the fullest sense of the term. This peace gives us the assurance
that our sins have been atoned for (Is. 53: 6; 2 Cor. 5: 18 ff.), forgiven
(Micah 7: 18, 19), propitiated (1 John 2: 2), blotted out of God's
memory (Jer. 31: 34; 50: 20); that our sentence of eternal damnation
has been quashed by the death of the Prince of Life (Rom. 8: 34); that
all accusing voices shout in vain (Is. 54: 17; Rom. 8: 33); that our punishments have been changed to wholesome discipline (Heb. 12: 9-11);
that our conscience is cleansed (Heb. 9: 14; 10: 22); that God has become our reconciled Father of mercies (2 Cor. 1: 3; 5: 19); that we have
been released from the bondage of the Law (Gal. 4: 4, 5), made members of God's household (Eph. 2: 19), God's children and heirs (Rom.
8: 14-17; Gal. 4: 7). It is a peace enabling the believer to glory even
in tribulation (Rom. 5: 1 ff.), which removes death's sting and opens
the portals of eternal rest and peace (Is. 57: 1b, 2; Luke 2: 27ff.; Rom.
14: 8, 9). Jesus is Peace! Three short words, also in the original
Hebrew. Yet an eternity of study cannot fathom its depths, millions
of words cannot exhaust its meaning. That is the peace foretold in
the Old Testament, proclaimed by the angels on the fields of Bethlehem, invoked by Paul upon his readers in every one of his letters,
forming the burden of the everlasting hymns of the redeemed in
heaven, in which the innumerable host of angels will join in praise
and adoration: This Man is Peace!

4. The Messiah's loyal army, vv. 4b-8 (A. V., 5b-9)

V. 4b (A. V., 5b). "The Assyrian!" Emphatically the name of
this archenemy of Israel stands at the head of this paragraph. (Cp.
2 Kings 15: 19-29; 16: 7-12; 17: 3-6, 23-27; 18: 7—19: 37.) Assyria is a
type of all external enemies of the Church of Christ: Rome, imperial
and papal; rationalism; Modernism; atheism; Communism; Gog and
Magog of Rev. 20: 8, 9. Assyria, the very name struck terror into the
heart of every Israelite, just as the thought of the vast host of enemies
fighting against the Christian Church fills the heart of the believer
with anxious forebodings. Yet the Church is not panic-stricken.
It shall raise "seven shepherds and eight men." As three and four
(Amos 1: 3-11), four and five (Is. 17: 6), six and seven (Job 5: 19;
Prov. 6: 16), so seven and eight here (also Eccl. 11:2) are not to be

regarded mathematically, but as rhetorical figures, used to express an indefinite number, with or without the connotation of intensification. While sometimes the figure denotes a scanty measure, two, at the most three, e. g., Is. 17:6, here, as in Amos 1:3-11, it is used in the sense of *satis superque,* enough and more. Shepherds are the spiritual leaders of the people, clerical and laic; leaders, not like the false shepherds so bitterly denounced by Micah (ch. 3:1-11) and later by Jeremiah (ch. 23:1, 2, 9-32), but leaders who are at the same time "principal men" (Gr. N.), princes of, or among, men. These leaders shall oppose the enemies of the Church ruled by Christ. We think of the great leaders and reformers raised by the Lord throughout the centuries, men like Paul and the other apostles, Athanasius, Augustine, Wyclif, Luther, Tyndale, the missionaries to heathen lands, faithful pastors and teachers in parochial and Sunday schools, consecrated laymen, Christian fathers and mothers, etc.

Vv. 5-8 (A. V., 6-9). Nimrod (v. 5, A. V., 6) was one of the earliest empire builders (Gen. 10:8-12); Shinar = Sumeria, northwest of the Persian Gulf, along the lower course of the Euphrates. He was the founder of Babylon and Assyria, later the archenemies of Israel (cp. v. 5). Refrainlike, the prophet repeats v. 5 b, testifying to the terror caused by Assyrian invasions. The believing child of God still shudders at the memory of fierce battles against Satan's temptations, which almost robbed him of his faith and salvation. Yet the Church's battle is not hopeless. Not only will the Church repulse the attacks of the enemies, it will also attack the enemy, attack his territory, lay it waste "in the entrances thereof," the gates, and through them enter into the conquered city. Their weapons, of course, are not carnal, but spiritual (2 Cor. 10:1-6; Eph. 6:11-20). "Thus shall He deliver us." The Church carries the banner of her divine Ruler to all nations. Yet the Church knows that it is not her own efforts, wisdom, experience, psychological insight, progressiveness, or any other human skill or aptitude that gives her success (1 Cor. 3:5-7; 15:10; Phil. 4:12, 13).

In contrast to the twofold mention of the Assyrian army (vv. 4, 5) there follows a twofold presentation of the Church's victory over the enemy (vv. 6, 7, A. V., 7, 8). "The remnant" (cp. ch. 2:12; 4:7; Is. 10:20-22). Jacob's children they are, utterly unworthy (Gen. 27:1-36), yet by the grace of God His chosen people (Gen. 32:10; Rom. 9:6b-12). They are like dew (cp. Hos. 14:5), fructifying the barren earth, bringing life to nations dead in sins and unbelief. They know the Babe of Bethlehem, their Peace, their Life. Of Him they testify by words

(2 Kings 5:1-3; Acts 8:4-12, 27ff.; 11:19ff.) and by their lives (Matt. 5:14-16; Phil. 2:15; 1 Peter 2:12; 3:1, 2). This testimony comes down like dew from heaven upon the barren hearts of their fellow men, and like showers from on high mellows their hard hearts and changes them from thickets of thorns to beautiful gardens of the Lord. This dew is the dew of the Lord. As the dew and the showers wait not for man, but are independent of man's wishes to come or go, so it is indeed Paul that labors and Apollos that waters, but God who giveth the increase (1 Cor. 3:6). The scattering of God's chosen nation among the Gentiles seemed to be the tragic end of the glory that was Israel, yet it shall serve to make them the means of spreading the Gospel of the Kingdom already in the Old Testament era. — Daniel and Ezekiel proclaimed it in Babylonia; other pious Israelites spread it elsewhere throughout the then known world (Acts 2:8-11). Jewish synagogs throughout the Roman Empire were usually the starting point of Paul's mission work. And so the Christians of all times and countries are to be and will be like dew and showers to a barren earth. — "As a lion, a young lion." Feeble Jacob, the playball of the nations, God's Church, afflicted, tossed with tempest (Is. 54:6, 11), shall become a powerful lion, breaking into the folds of Nimrod, Satan, depriving him of his sheep, treading down his strongholds of unbelief, sin, and superstition, delivering those who had been held captive by the prince of darkness, making constantly new inroads on his vast empire, gaining constantly more territory; a victorious Church (v. 8, A. V., 9) whose individual members are more than conquerors (Rom. 8:33-39; 1 Cor. 15:55-57). And while the Gospel of the virgin-born Shepherd-King for many will be as life-giving dew and vivifying showers, a savor of life unto life, to others, who steadfastly refuse to give up their opposition, it will become a savor of death unto death (2 Cor. 2:15, 16). He that believeth not is damned (Mark 16:16), is trodden down, hopelessly lost, one whom "none can deliver" (v. 7, A. V., 8; cp. John 3:36).

5. The cleansing of the Church and execution of vengeance upon her enemies, vv. 9-14 (A. V., 10-15)

Vv. 9-14 (A. V., 10-15). The Lord will sanctify His Church by removing all forms of idolatry and superstition and finally will execute His vengeance upon all that refuse to accept His Word. — "In that day" refers to the rule of the Messiah. His kingdom is not of this world and will not be established or propagated by force of arms. (Cp. Zech. 4:6; John 18:36; 2 Cor. 10:3 ff.; Eph. 6:10-13.) Therefore God will purge His Church of misplaced trust in any means or devices of her own beside the power of God's Spirit. In order to maintain the independence of his kingdom, Jeroboam had introduced the calf-worship. This worship, though nominally a worship of Jehovah, was in itself apostasy from the Lord (1 Kings 12—14). Having lost their trust in Jehovah, who had from the earliest period in the history of Israel as His covenant people proved Himself a "man of war" indeed (Ex. 15: 3; cp. Ex. 3—14), a very present Help in every trouble (Ps. 46:2, A. V., 1), they sought other means of aid, horses and chariots (v. 9, A. V., 10), fortified cities and impregnable strongholds (vv. 10, 13 b, A. V., 11, 14 b). They sought counsel not from the living God, but resorted to witchcraft and soothsaying (v. 11, A. V., 12), superstition of the worst sort (cp. Is. 2: 6; 8: 19). Besides the golden calves, images of Jehovah, they worshiped "graven," carved images, and "standing images," pillars of stone or metal (v. 12, A. V., 13); "groves," the *asherim,* emblems of the female deity Asherah, the star Venus, the queen of heaven (v. 13, A. V., 14). Idols all of them, more helpless and unreliable than they whose handiwork they were (Is. 44: 9 ff.; Jer. 10: 2 ff.). All these objects of their trust will be cut off, plucked up, destroyed by the Lord in that day, the New Testament era, when God's Church will be the invisible communion of saints, the Church of the elect in Christ Jesus (1 Cor. 1:2; 1 Peter 1:2). They need no other means to build the Church than the Gospel of Christ, the Word of God, which liveth and abideth forever (1 Peter 1: 23 ff.; cp. John 6: 63). And they need not the force of arms or any other means to defend the Church of God against her enemies, for God Himself will execute vengeance upon all the opponents of the Church. He will protect His Church (Matt. 16: 18; Rev. 20: 7-10).

PART III

God Goes to Law with His People

Chapters 6 and 7

CHAPTER 6

A. The Lord Presents His Charge

1. Israel has repaid God's kindness with apostasy, vv. 1-5

1 Oh, hear what the LORD is saying! Arise, contend with the mountains, and let the hills hear your voice!
2 Hear, O mountains, the controversy of the LORD, and you enduring ones, you foundations of the earth! For the LORD has a controversy with His people, and He will argue
3 with Israel. O My people, what have I done unto you, and wherewith have I wearied you? Answer
4 Me! For I brought you up from the land of Egypt, and I redeemed you from the house of bondage. I also

sent before you Moses, Aaron, and
5 Miriam. O My people, remember
what Balak, king of Moab, devised,
and what Balaam, the son of Beor,

answered him from Shittim to Gilgal, that you may know the righteous deeds of the LORD.

Grammatical Notes

V. 1. "Before the mountains." אֵת with רִיב is invariably used in the sense of contend with, raise charges against (cp. Judg. 8:1; Is. 49:25; 50:8, etc.), not, contend "before."

V. 2. "The strong foundations." The M. T. regards "foundations," etc., as an apposition to "strong," firm, lasting.

Vv. 1, 2. Isaiah was told to call the mountains to rejoice at Israel's redemption (Is. 44:23; 49:13; Is. 55:12). Micah is commanded to summon the mountains and the "strong foundations" of the earth (Gr. N.) into court, to contend "before," rather with them (Gr. N.), to pronounce God's punishment upon them. For the sake of man's sin the whole earth was cursed by the Lord (Gen. 3:17 b) and must suffer the consequences of man's sin (Rom. 8:20-22). The mountains especially were defiled by idolatrous altars and riotous festivities (1 Kings 14:23; Jer. 3:6) and are now to hear their Creator pass His sentence upon them (cp. Is. 42:15; Jer. 44:2; Ezek. 33:28). This sentence, however, does not affect only, or even primarily, the mountains. The Lord has a controversy with His people, Israel, the highly favored nation, as its very name indicates (Gen. 32:27, 28).

Vv. 3-5. The Lord enumerates His favors toward Israel. He appeals to His people to tell Him wherewith He had wearied them, as if He might be at fault. What has He done to merit their ingratitude and shameful rejection? Tell Me! "Testify against Me!" You cannot show any one instance of unfairness on My part. He it was that brought them up out of the foreign land by redeeming them from slavery to His service (Ex. 3—15). It was He that gave to them that noble triad of leaders, whose names are revered to this day. When Balak asked Balaam to curse Israel, the Lord commanded Balaam to pronounce blessings instead (Num. 22—24). And when Balaam's vicious advice to Balak to seduce Israel to idolatry and immorality (Num. 31:16) proved successful (Num. 25:1-18), the Lord punished them severely (Num. 25:4-9), but did not reject them. From Shittim, the place of their shame and God's forgiving grace, He led them through Jordan (Joshua 3:1-17) to Gilgal, where even during the days of physical weakness of their fighting men (Joshua 5:2-8) the Lord protected them by striking their enemies with paniclike fear

278

(Joshua 2:9-11, 24; 5:2). He did that in order to prove to Israel the righteousness of His Law in punishing their sin; the righteousness of His Gospel in forgiving their sins and bringing them to the Promised Land. Remember that, O My people! The people harden themselves against His appeal. They refuse to accept His grace freely offered in His Gospel. They insist on walking according to their own will.

---

2. The people reply to God's charge, vv. 6, 7

6 With what shall I come before the LORD, bow myself before the God on high? Shall I come before Him with burnt offerings with calves 7 a year old? Will the LORD be pleased with thousands of rams and ten thousand streams of oil? Shall I give my first-born for my transgression, the fruit of my body for the sin of my soul?

Vv. 6, 7. The people's reply betrays their appalling spiritual ignorance. Though they constantly used His name, Jehovah, they had no understanding of the real meaning of this name, so clearly revealed to them in such passages as Ex. 3:14 ff.; 34:6, 7. There is not the slightest realization of the unalterable holiness of God, which is satisfied with nothing less than perfect holiness in man (Ex. 19:6; Lev. 11:44; 19:2), perfect love toward God and man (Deut. 6:5; Lev. 19:18; cp. Matt. 22:36-39); no recognition of the wickedness and damnableness of every sin (Deut. 27:26; 28:15 ff.; 32:22). Nor is there the least desire for mercy, the faintest plea for grace and forgiveness. As His holiness is an offense, so His mercy is a stumbling block to them. They will not be poor beggars before God's throne. They are convinced that they can merit God's good will by their own efforts. They are willing to bargain with God, as if He were a bargainer like themselves. They are ready to buy His favor, as if He were a venal judge who would overlook their failings, if only they paid His price. They are ready to bid high. If the Lord is not satisfied with the choicest calves, they are ready to slay thousands of rams and pour out myriads of rivers of finest olive oil (v. 7). If all this will not satisfy Him, they are ready to sacrifice their sons and daughters. Self-righteous, proud of their ability to pay for any favors God gives them! We have there the same self-satisfaction of an impenitent people that characterizes the prayer of the Pharisee (Luke 18:11, 12). At the same time an undercurrent of impatience and dissatisfaction runs through their bargaining, as if God were a greedy, bloodthirsty tyrant, hard to satisfy, punishing people who are willing to make great sacrifices, as if they were unworthy criminals.

3. The prophet's reply to the people's questions, v. 8

8 It has been declared unto you, O man, what is good and what the LORD requires of you: No more than to establish judgment and to love kindness and to walk humbly with your God!

Grammatical Notes

"He hath showed." The Hebrew has the indefinite third person, one hath told (you, or passive, It has been declared (Cp. G.-K. 144 d.) — "O man!" אָדָם, see Gen. 3:19. — "Do justly" denotes not merely the "doing" of justice, but the establishment of justice, of proper norms of judgment. (Cp. Ps. 99:4, where the phrase occurs in parallelism with כּוּן, to establish. See also Ps. 103:6; 146:7; Jer. 9:24; 22:3,15; Koenig, *Die Psalmen*, on Ps. 146:7; Volz, *Jeremias*, on Jer. 23:5; 33:15.)

V. 8. The prophet's answer. Why do you ask what God demands? You have been shown very clearly what is good and pleasing to Him, O man! (Gr. N.) The great Lord of the universe has condescended to reveal His will to man who is dust and ashes (Gen. 2:7), who by his own fault lost his original righteousness and holiness (Gen. 1:26 f.). We must not overlook the one basic fact, without recognition of which we cannot properly understand this verse: It is Jehovah who speaks here. Jehovah is not only the God of unalterable holiness, righteousness, and justice (Ex. 34:7; Nah. 1:2), who will not like a venal judge clear anyone who has not a perfect righteousness. Yet the same Jehovah is also the God of unalterable grace and mercy (Ex. 34:6), who has promised a Redeemer (Gen. 3:15), a Comforter against the curse (Gen. 5:29), faith in whom is counted for righteousness by the Lord (Gen. 15:6); a Savior, vicariously suffering our penalties, bearing our sins, and offering His righteousness to all (Is. 53:4-6, 11). This Lord has clearly told man what He asks of him. Three items are mentioned. "Do justly" (Gr. N.), literally, establish the norm of justice and judgment, not a human norm, but the unalterable norm of the Lord. His norm of the Law, which demands perfect righteousness, and His norm of the Gospel, which gives to man the perfect righteousness procured by Christ and made man's own through faith in Christ. This latter norm does not annul the former, but establishes it (Rom. 3:31), by engendering and nourishing in man that love toward God and man demanded by the Law. The establishment of God's Gospel is the chief duty of the Church. Where this duty is conscientiously carried out, the second and third duties will naturally be performed. "Love mercy," again not what man calls mercy, but the mercy demanded by the Lord of mercy, patterned after His mercy (Micah 7:18), and defined by Him in His Word as unselfish love toward God (Jer. 2:2; Is. 57:1;

Hos. 6:4, "goodness"; v. 6, "mercy"; cp. Deut. 6:5), and warmhearted, compassionate love towards one's fellow man (Gen. 21:23; 1 Sam. 20: 14-17; 2 Sam. 1:26; 9:1, 3, 7). "Walk humbly with thy God," not puffed up by conceit, but always aware that we are dust and ashes (Gen. 18:27, 31, 32); always remembering that if there is any good in us, we owe it all to the Lord God (1 Cor. 4:7); and we therefore humbly accept whatever He sends us, good or evil (1 Peter 5:6, 7). We must not overlook the small word "thy." God has given Himself, all His grace, all His power, all His wisdom to His believing followers. What an honor, and what an incentive gladly, willingly to do what this Lord has shown us to be good, pleasing to Himself, profitable for us (Rom. 14:18; 1 Tim. 2:3; 6:6).

---

4. Rejection of God's Word brings ruin and destruction, vv. 9-16

9 The voice of the LORD is calling to the city, and it is true wisdom to keep in sight His name. Obey the rod and Him who has ap-
10 pointed it! Are there yet in the house of the wicked, treasures gotten by wickedness and the accursed
11 ephah of leanness? Can I be pure with wicked scales and with a bag
12 of false weights? Because their rich men are full of violence and her inhabitants speak lies and their tongue is deceit in their mouths.
13 And I also have made you sick by smiting you to lay you in ruins for
14 your sins. You shall eat and not be satisfied; and there will be shrinkage in your midst. You shall put away and not save, and what you
15 save I will give to the sword. You shall sow, but not reap; you shall tread the olives, but not anoint yourselves with oil; and there will be new wine, but you shall not
16 drink wine. They zealously observe the statutes of Omri and all the deeds of the house of Ahab, and so you walk in their counsels in order that I will surrender you to desolation and your inhabitants to mockery, and you shall bear the shame threatened to My people.

Grammatical Notes

V. 9. "The man of *wisdom*," תוּשִׁיָּה, the ability to help oneself, to bring a matter to successful conclusion, cunning, shrewdness, wisdom. "See" = understand, grasp (cp. 1 Sam. 12:17; 1 Kings 10:4; Is. 40:5). The imperfect progressive, keep in sight; understand ever better.

V. 10. "Are there." אִשׁ = יֵשׁ, the existence of something (cp. 2 Sam. 14:19), used adverbially here: Are there?

V. 11. "Count them pure." אֶזְכָּה, first person perf. Qal of זָכָה, to be pure, clean, innocent. "Am I pure?"

V. 14. "Thy casting down." יֶשְׁחֲךָ, meaning uncertain; LXX, darkness; Syr., dysentery; Vulg., Kimchi, humiliation; Aquila, I will plant; Ewald, hunger; Harkavy, shrinking (from hunger).

V. 9. The Lord's voice as it sounds forth in the oral and written message of the prophets cries loudly to the city. Turning to this Lord, the prophet exclaims, "Wisdom" (Gr. N.), profitable wisdom, such as the Lord alone can give and will give to the righteous (Prov. 2:7). "Will see" (Gr. N.) "Thy name," God's revelation of Himself, His inmost essence and being as far as He has seen fit to reveal it (Ex. 23:22; John 1:15); and true wisdom will make ever greater progress in grasping, understanding God's Word. Turning now to his people, the prophet urges them to "hear the rod," to listen to the message the Lord intends to convey by His chastising rod and to obey this rod and Him who has appointed it. It is Jehovah, the Covenant God, that speaks by word and deed, who even by stern rebuke and severe punishment seeks their temporal and eternal welfare, endeavors to win them back to Himself by showing them the wickedness and folly of serving other gods. Alas, there is no sign of a return, of repentance.

V. 10-12. "Are there?" (Gr. N.), etc. A rhetorical question, the answer an emphatic Yes! There is no need for an investigation committee. The evidence is manifest. All their treasures are procured by wickedness, by the sweat and blood of the oppressed. On all markets and in all business establishments the "scant measure," fraud and deception so abominable to God, is being practiced. "Shall I count them pure" (Gr. N.) (v. 11), literally, Shall I be accounted innocent, honest, if I were to use "wicked balances," false scales used by wicked people, and come to you as a buyer or seller with a double set of "deceitful weights," stones used as weights, one set, too small, used for selling, the other, too large, used for buying? Were I to use such tactics, you would be the first to condemn me. Yet not only the rich (v. 12), but also the entire nation is a band of oppressors and deceivers! How can you hope to escape God's judgment?

Vv. 13-16. Already the Lord is withholding His blessing, "making them sick," depriving them of their civic health and well-being. He is fulfilling His threats spoken centuries before (Deut. 22:38 ff.; cp. Joel 1:5-12, 16 ff.; Hag. 1:6; 2:16 f.). "Casting down" (Gr. N.), shrinkage. "Take hold" in a vain effort to save from marauding enemies. — "The statutes of Omri and Ahab" (v. 16), the two kings described as worse than all before them, introducing Baalism as the official religion of the Northern Kingdom. Their example was followed by Judah's kings Jehoram (2 Kings 8:18), Ahaziah (v. 26 f.), and Ahaz (ch. 16:3-18). This wickedness served only one purpose: to invoke the curse of God, which they had deliberately chosen instead of the promised blessings (Deut. 30:16-20; Hos. 8:4).

CHAPTER 7

B. Israel's Repentance and Grateful Adoration of the Lord's Mercy and Faithfulness

1. Confession of sin, vv. 1-6

1 Woe is me! For I am become like the gathering of summer fruit, like the gleaning of the vintage, when there is not a grape cluster to eat, nor any early fig such as my soul 2 desires. Perished is the pious from the earth, and there is none upright among men. All lie in wait for bloodshed; each hunts his 3 brother with the net. Their hands are intent on doing wickedness successfully. The prince makes demands, and the judge asks for bribes, and the great man, he voices the desire of his soul, and so they 4 weave their plans. The best of them is like a briar, the most upright worse than a hedge of thorns. Coming is the day of your watchmen, your punishment! Now shall 5 come their consternation! Do not trust a friend! Do not rely on an intimate! From her that lies in your bosom guard the doors of your 6 mouth! For the son has no respect for his father; the daughter rises up against her mother, the daughter-in-law against her mother-in-law. A man's enemies are the members of his own household.

Grammatical Notes

V. 2. "Good," חָסִיד, one who practices חֶסֶד, unselfish love of God and his fellow men, hence "pious" in the best sense of the term. — "Upright," יָשָׁר, straight, right, righteous, honest; opposed to crooked, deceptive.

V. 3. "Mischievous desire," הַוַּת נַפְשׁוֹ, from הָוָה, breathe; hence eagerness, desire, used only in an evil sense, lust; cp. Prov. 10:3 ("substance"), 11:6 ("naughtiness"). Others derive it from הָוָה in sense of fall, destruction (Prov. 19:3); what causes destruction, mischief (Prov. 17:4).

Vv. 1-6. The Church laments her sad condition. Her fruit, her prosperity, her growth in good works have ceased. Like fields and orchards after harvest and gleanings (Lev. 19:10; Deut. 24:19ff.), the Church stands bare and fruitless. In vain does she long for a cluster to eat, for the first ripe fruit; the barrenness continues from one season to another. Wretched, miserable, poor, naked she stands (Rev. 3:17). The "good men" (Gr. N.), the unselfishly kindhearted and merciful, are perished (v. 2). The "upright" (Gr. N.), walking without deviation in the way of God's Law, is no more to be found. Bloodshed, manhunting, persecution everywhere. Their hands are eager to do only evil and do it thoroughly (v. 3). Money-madness, the accursed hunger for gold, rules the rulers. The prince, who always needs money, is constantly asking, demanding, and the judge is after a reward, and the great man, the man of influence of power, speaks the desire (Gr. N.) of his soul — money! And so the three combine to "wrap it up," literally, twist it, pervert the right to gain their end, spin their net about their victims. So completely has piety and uprightness vanished that even the most upright is like a briar and sharp thorn (v. 4). This universal wickedness portends the closeness of God's judgment, the day of their watchmen, prophesied so often by God's prophet's and sneered at by the people. Their visitation is coming, when God will requite them for all their evil deeds and schemes. Then "shall be their perplexity." Their cocksureness, their shrewdness, their boldness will be changed to consternation and panic. So widespread has deceit and perfidy become that one can no longer trust one's friend, nor one's "guide," one's intimate, confidential companion; no, not even the wife of one's bosom (v. 5). Gone is the God-fearing home, where children were brought up in keeping with God's command (Deut. 6:6 ff.), where husband and wife and the entire household lived in peace and harmony and mutual love and trust (v. 6; cp. Pss. 127 and 128; Prov. 31:10 ff.). Quarrel, strife, hatred, distrust have disrupted the family. The closer the ties of kinship, the greater now the hatred and perfidious betrayal of trust.

---

2. Confession of faith, vv. 7-10

7 But I will watch for the LORD. I will wait for the God of my salvation. 8 My God will hear me! Rejoice not over me, O my enemy! Though I have fallen, I shall rise! Though I sit in darkness, the LORD 9 is my Light! I must bear the wrath of the LORD, for I have sinned against Him, until He will plead my cause and establish my right. He will lead me out into the light, 10 I shall behold His salvation. My enemy shall behold, and shame shall cover her who said to me, Where is He, the LORD, thy God? My eyes shall behold her with satisfaction. Now she shall be trampled on like the mud of the streets.

Grammatical Notes

V. 7. "Look unto." צָפָה = watch, be on the lookout. Pi. intensifies the idea, eagerly watching for.

V. 8. "Enemy," here and v. 10 the feminine participle, frequently used as a collective (cp. Micah 1:11 f.; 4:6 f.; Is. 12:6, etc.; G.-K. 122 s).

Vv. 7-10. Even under such discouraging, lamentable circumstances the Church does not lose her faith and trust in her God. "Therefore," for the very reason that unbelief, unfaithfulness, treachery surround her on every side, she turns unto the faithful Lord and "looks unto Him" (Gr. N.), continues the attentive, untiring alertness of a faithful watchman. The Church is sure that the God of her salvation will not fail her. In Him she has a friend that sticketh closer than a brother

(Prov. 18:24). He will hear her prayer (Is. 43:1 ff.; 54:4-17). Confidently, therefore, she faces her enemies (Gr. N.), bidding them not to rejoice over her sad plight (v. 8). When I fall, I shall arise! The latter fact is as sure as the first. She does not, and cannot, deny that she has fallen, but that does not shake her trust in her God. That is not the language of self-reliance, of vaunting pride, but the language of humble, yet unwavering trust in the God of grace forgiving iniquity (Ex 34:6, 7), as the very next words prove. When I shall continue to dwell in darkness, even when sorrow, persecution, and shame shall remain my lot, yea, though He slay me, yet I will trust in Him (Job 13:15), for the Lord and His word of grace "shall be a light unto me." He changes the night of sin and sorrow and suffering into bright sunshine (Rom. 5:1-3; James 1:2 ff.). Humbly submitting to God's chastening hand, the Church will bear the "indignation," the wrath of God (v. 9). She knows that her failings and sins have deserved God's punishment. Therefore she will not rebel, but bear it without grumbling, until He in His own time will plead her cause as her Advocate and establish her "judgment," her right to call herself His own, His elect, His bride. "He will bring me forth to the light, and I shall behold His righteousness" in unfailingly keeping His glorious promises (see v. 11 ff.). Then the enemy who sneeringly asked, "Where is the LORD, your God?" (2 Kings 18:30-35; Ps. 42:3; Joel 2:17) shall see that the Church's trust in the Lord was not in vain (v. 10). Now the enemies will be covered with shame (cp. 2 Chron. 32:21, "returned with shame"; Ps. 37:35 ff.; 73:18 ff.; Nah. 1—3), trodden under foot (Is. 5:5; 10:6, etc.), in utter contempt (Is. 66:24; Mark 9:46 ff.; Rev. 20:10; 21:8).

---

3. God's promise in answer to the Church's confession, vv. 11-13

11 The day to build your walls, this is the day on which the decree shall
12 be removed. This is the day on which they shall come to you from Assyria and the cities of Egypt and from Egypt to the Euphrates, and from sea to sea and mountain to
13 mountain. Yet the land shall be desolate because of its inhabitants on account of the fruit of their deeds.

Grammatical Notes

V. 12. "Fortified cities," "fortress." מָצוֹר, here as 2 Kings 19:24; Is. 19:6; 37:25, nom. propr. = Egypt. For the second *Mazor* LXX reads צוֹר, Tyre. — "From sea to sea," rather to sea (locative) from sea.

V. 13. "Notwithstanding" = adversative ﬥ, yet, but. — "The land" = Palestine, as, e.g., Jer. 1:14; Hos. 4:3; Joel 1:2.

Vv. 11, 12. The day of the building of Zion's walls is identified with "that" day on which people from all nations come to Jerusalem. "From Assyria" (v. 12) and from the fortified cities (Gr. N.) and from the fortress (Gr. N.), Egypt, to the river. Assyria and Egypt (the fortified cities) were the two ancient enemies of Israel, one to the east, representing the vast areas of Asia, the other to the south, representing dark Africa. The "river" = Euphrates. From Assyria to Egypt, from Africa to Asia, the nations come to Zion. And from sea to sea, from mountain to mountain, from all islands and continents bounded by sea or ocean, from all countries shut in by mountains ever so high, they come to join the Church. This definitely places the situation of vv. 11 and 12 into the New Testament era, when people from many parts of the world become members of the Christian Church. And so the Church will "build her walls," will spread beyond all political and natural boundaries, become a world empire of unlimited extension. V. 12 makes it impossible to refer the "day" of v. 11 to the era of Nehemiah, who rebuilt the broken-down walls of physical Jerusalem. And v. 12 also sheds light on the nature of the "decree" to be far removed on that day. The fact that not only Jews, but also Gentiles from all nations will come to the Church of God makes it necessary to refer the decree to be removed completely to the decree making Israel God's special people (Ex. 19: 5, 6; Amos 3: 2; cp. Ps. 147: 19, 20) by separating them from other nations by definite rites and ceremonies and laws (Gen. 17: 9-14; Ex. 12: 14 ff.; Lev. 1—27) and by allotting to them a special land (Num. 23: 9; Deut. 33: 28; cp. Micah 7: 14). This decree of separation was to be abolished in the New Testament era (Jer. 3: 16, 17; 31: 31-34; Acts 10 and 11; Eph. 2: 11-22; Col. 1: 18-29; 2: 16-23).

V. 13. Again the prophet adds a warning not to expect the coming of this day in the immediate future. First comes devastation! (Cp. 4: 6-8, promise; v. 9f., threat; 5: 2, 3 a.)

---

4. The Church's prayer for God's guidance and the Lord's answer, vv. 14-17

14 Shepherd Thy people with Thy staff, the flock of Thy heritage, which dwells alone in the forest in the midst of Carmel. Let them feed in Bashan and Gilead as in the 15 days of old. As in the days when you went forth from the land of Egypt, I will show him wondrous 16 things. The nations shall see and be ashamed of all their own strength. They shall put their hands to their mouth. Their ears 17 shall be deaf. They shall lick the dust like a serpent; like creeping things of the earth they shall come trembling from their strongholds toward the LORD, our God; they shall tremble and fear before Him.

V. 14. Feed = shepherd Thy flock (Ps. 23:1; 78:52; Is. 40:11; Jer. 31:10; Ezek. 34:11-23), as only Thou canst shepherd it. "With Thy rod." The shepherd used his rod to lead the sheep out of the fold to the nourishing pastures and the refreshing brooks of water, to prod on the lagging sheep, to bring back the straying members of the flock, to ward off wild animals, to lead his flock back at eventide to the safety of the fold to rest and sleep after the wanderings of the day. Micah asks the Lord of everlasting grace to guard His flock against all danger, shelter them, keep them as His own, who are His heritage, His chosen possession in time and eternity (Deut. 4:20; 9:26, 29; Ps. 100:3; John 10:27 f.). "Dwell solitarily," see remarks on "decree," v. 11, p. 286, and cp. 2 Cor. 6:14-18. Not separatism, but separation from sinful doctrine and sinful life is a characteristic of the true Church of God. — "In the wood, in the midst of Carmel." Carmel, a mountain range reaching a height of 1,800 feet, extending about twelve miles from the sea in a southeasterly direction, was known for its beauty (Cant. 7:5; Is. 35:2); and to this day, though the ravages of centuries of war and maladministration have robbed it of much of its glory, it is still an outstanding beauty spot of Palestine. Along the northern slope of Carmel ran the Kishon River through the valley of Accho bordering the seashore, as a part of the fertile plain of Esdraelon, extending from the Mediterranean Sea to the Jordan. The mountain range of Carmel with its wooded slopes and the lush fields and vineyards and olive groves of Esdraelon formed the most beautiful region in the Promised Land.

"Let them feed in Bashan and Gilead." These two provinces formed the eastern part of Israel's possession. Bashan in the north, just east of the Sea of Galilee; Gilead extending southward along the Jordan to the northern edge of the Dead Sea. Bashan was noted for its cattle (Ezek. 39:18; Amos 4:1; Ps. 22:12) and together with Gilead offered such splendid pastures that Reuben, Gad, and one half of the tribe of Manasseh asked Moses to allot this Eastjordanland to them (Num. 32:1-5, 16, 24, 33, 40; cp. Song 6:5). The congregation asks God to feed Israel in fertile, blessed areas, where both body and soul enjoy the loving leadership of the Shepherd.

"As in the days of old," the former days, the past (cp. ch. 5:1, A. V., 2, "everlasting"). This may refer to the times of Moses and Joshua, when God Himself led His people as a flock of sheep (cp. Ps. 77:20; Ex. 3:17; 23:20-31; 34:10, 11), fed and clothed them (Deut. 8:3, 4), when the tribes first occupied Gilead and Bashan (Num. 32).

Or it may refer to the early days of the kingdom of David and Solomon, when the boundaries of Israel extended from the Euphrates River to the boundary of Egypt, each man dwelling under his own vine and fig tree, enjoying peace and prosperity (1 Kings 4:20-25). Micah refers to this era (ch. 4:4), which was at the same time an age of spiritual blessings (David's Psalms, his labors for the proper Temple services, 1 Chron. 23—27; the building of the Temple of Solomon). In our text Micah may have thought of both eras.

Vv. 15-17. God's answer to the Church's prayer. In the days of the Messiah (cp. vv. 11, 12) the Lord will perform miracles even greater than those characterizing the days of Israel's deliverance out of Egypt. Throughout the history of Israel the deliverance out of Pharaoh's bondage was used as a symbol of the redemption by the Woman's Seed, the Messianic deliverance. The deliverance out of Egypt, which made the establishment of Israel as God's covenant people in the Promised Land possible, was accompanied by miracles so great and so numerous as to make the Mosaic era unique in the history of Israel (Deut. 34:10-12; cp. Ex. 15:1-19; Joshua 24:2-18; Pss. 105 and 106, etc.). Marvelous as these miracles of God's power and grace were, they are far excelled by the miracles ushering in the coming and the work of the Messiah and the foundation of the New Testament Church, the miracles of the Incarnation, of Gethsemane and Calvary, the crucifixion of the Lord of Glory, the death of the Prince of Life, His resurrection, His ascension, the outpouring of the Holy Ghost. Marvelous things indeed!

V. 16. "The nations shall see and be confounded at all their might," be ashamed of their own strength in which they trusted. Not only God's people will see His marvelous deeds (v. 15). Already in vv. 11 and 12 the Lord had foretold the coming of the heathen to God's Church; they also shall see God's glorious redemption (cp. Is. 52:10). The nations place their confidence in their own power, their riches, their commerce, their statesmanship, their powerful armies and war machinery, their wisdom and philosophy. And where has it gotten them? They see disorder, chaos, dissolution everywhere! They are bankrupt, whether they acknowledge it or vainly endeavor to cover it up by boastful oratory. While most of them remain obstinate, there are many whose eyes are opened to see what mighty and marvelous things the Lord God of Israel has done for their redemption. And now they are deeply ashamed of "all their might," of what they regarded as their strength. "They shall lay their hand upon their mouth," a gesture of reverential silence from astonishment and admiration (cp. Job 21:5; 29:9; 40:4, 5). They cease to extol their own accomplishments, will cease their ridicule and mockery and blasphemies of the Lord and His Church. "Their ears shall be deaf" to such effusions as well as to the alluring voice of sin, self-righteousness, and self-indulgence. Overawed by the majesty of the infinite power and justice and grace displayed in God's redeeming work, they lack words to express their thoughts.

V. 17. "Lick the dust" denotes the attitude of defeated enemies unconditionally surrendering to the victor (Ps. 72:9; Is. 49:23; Lam. 3:29). "As the serpent." "The serpent, moving as it does with its mouth upon the ground, may readily be supposed to swallow more dust than other animals" (Margolis, *Micah*, p. 78). "Worms of the earth." The word occurring only here and Deut. 32:24 denotes the creeping, crawling creatures. The mighty men of this world, like creeping, crawling things before the Lord! "They shall be afraid of the Lord, our God, and shall fear." But that is not the slavish fear of a criminal caught in the act and fearing nothing but the punishment. They do not in fear crawl back into their hiding places as did Adam and Eve. No, "they shall move out of their holes," literally, they shall tremble out of their hiding places; to the LORD, our God, they shall come in trembling awe, "and they shall fear Him." While lying in the dust before the Lord, ashamed to lift up so much as their eyes unto heaven, while smiting upon their breast, yet they exclaim with the repentant publican: "God, be merciful to me, a sinner!" While the majesty of the mighty works of God shattered their trust in their own strength, showed them their sinfulness and unworthiness, yet these marvelous works brought to their attention a salvation so glorious, a love so transcending, a wisdom so profound, a mercy so unequaled, that they were attracted to this God by a mysterious power, were drawn, in fact, by Him with loving-kindness to Himself, their God of mercy and love. To Him they come, trembling under the burden of their guilt, shivering with shame at the atrocity of their sin, yet trembling with a holy joy never before experienced at the knowledge of sin forgiven, of a conscience purged of dead works, of the peace of God surpassing all understanding. And the deeper a believer delves into the mysterious miracle of God's redemption, the greater will become his awe at the stupendous power, the infinite justice, the incomprehensible mercy revealed in the marvelous things accomplished by our Lord in the redemption, justification, conversion, and sanctification of sinful man.

That is the history of God's Church: a record of marvelous miracles performed by God. Savage nations as well as highly cultured peoples have become docile followers of the Redeemer. Mighty emperors and kings in the realms of art and science have cast their scepters and crowns before the throne of Jehovah, have brought into captivity every thought to the obedience of Christ (2 Cor. 10:5). And so these miracles go on unto the end of days, till the whole number of elect has come into the Kingdom of Grace, and then the Day of the Kingdom of Glory, which knows no night, shall dawn.

---

5. The Church's grateful adoration of God's mercy and faithfulness, vv. 18-20

18 Who is a God like unto Thee? Who lifts away iniquity, who passes by the transgression of the remnant of His heritage, who does not eternally retain His wrath, for He delights in 19 mercy! He will turn again, He will have compassion; He will trample underfoot our guilts. Thou wilt cast all our sins into the depths of the 20 sea. Thou wilt show faithfulness to Jacob, mercy to Abraham, as Thou hast sworn to our fathers from the days of old.

V. 18. Overwhelmed by the wonderful outlook, Micah bursts forth in one of the sublimest hymns of praise in honor of the Lord's grace and mercy. "Who is a God like unto Thee?" (Cp. Ex. 15:11; Ps. 18:31; 89:6; 113:5; Is. 40:18, 25.) — "Pardoneth iniquity." The Hebrew term for "iniquity" is one of the strongest terms for sin, denoting perverseness, crookedness which makes man guilty, a debtor before God, with no possibility of ever ridding himself of that guilt. God does the marvelous thing no man can do. He "pardons" iniquity, literally, lifts that burden off the guilty conscience and places it on the Man who shall be Peace (ch. 5:5; cp. Is. 53:4-12). For this reason the God of Justice can now pardon our iniquity and pass by the transgression, the rebellion, the revolt of "the remnant of His heritage" (see ch. 2:12; 5:7; 7:14; Is. 10:22 ff.). Regardless of the wickedness of their guilt and rebellion, the Lord pardons, passes by them. Micah uses the participial form of the two verbs "describing a person in continuous, uninterrupted performance of an activity" (G.-K. 116 a). In His Christian Church the Lord "daily and richly forgives all sins to me and all believers." — "He retaineth not His anger forever." If the Lord continued to cling to His anger, what would become of us? But He "delights in mercy," in loving-kindness, in good will; and this delight moves Him to turn from His anger to compassion, pity, sympathy, even as a mother has compassion upon the child of her womb (Is. 49:15; cp. Lam. 3:31, 32). The imperfects picture the turning and pitying

290

as constantly recurring, always being new (Lam. 3:22, 23), ceaselessly being in action as the waves of the sea ceaselessly, day and night, year in, year out, wash the sandy shore.

V. 19. "Subdue," tread down, trample down. Our debts, our manifold guilt, which we daily amass by sins of commission and omission, which disturb the believer's peace, our conscience, all these sins He tramples underfoot. They have no right to disturb the peace of those He calls His own. Their attacks upon His children the Lord regards as an insult to Himself, as charging Him with not having finished His work of redemption, as having failed in His work of atonement. And, therefore, as often as sin raises its accusing voice against a child of God, so often does the Lord take that sin, hurl it to the ground, and trample it underfoot. And if, in spite of being ground into the dust, our sin still continues to shriek out its accusations against us and its protests against God's forgiveness, the Lord takes that sin and casts it into the depths of the sea. The God who has determined to forgive the sins of His children, who has forgotten them so thoroughly as to wipe them out of His memory, does not want His children to be disturbed by any accusation, any memory of sins forgiven. (Cp. Ps. 103:3-13; Is. 26:3, 4; 32:17, 18; 54:10, 13; Jer. 31:34; 50:20.) Who is a God like unto our God?

V. 20. While the English translation "perform the truth," or "show faithfulness" (Smith and Goodspeed, *The Complete Bible*), stresses the faithfulness of God, the Hebrew "give, grant, faithfulness" emphasizes in equal measure the utter lack of merit on the part of the recipient. God's keeping of faith with man is altogether independent of any worthiness in man. It is a free gift of grace, granted by the God who delights in mercy. This becomes evident also from the word "mercy" used in parallelism with "truth." The Lord, our God, who Himself determines all His actions by His own free will, had sworn to Abraham and Jacob that their seed would be like sand on the shore of the sea and that in them and their Seed all nations were to be blessed (Gen. 12:2, 3; 15:5; 18:18; 22:16-18; 28:14). Having determined on this action, having made this promise, and having confirmed it with a solemn oath (cp. Heb. 6:13-18), the unchanging God, with whom is no variableness neither shadow of turning, will do what He has promised and affirmed with His oath. Who is a God like unto the Lord Jehovah?

At the close of his exposition of Micah, Luther quotes Jerome's prayer with which the latter ends his commentary on this prophet:

"O God, who is a God like unto Thee? Who pardonest iniquity, passest by the transgression of the remnant of Thy people; who retainest not Thine anger forever because Thou delightest in mercy! Thou hast turned to us again and hast had compassion upon us. Thou hast subdued our iniquities and hast cast all our sins into the depths of the sea. Oh, preserve unto us this Thy mercy forever and ever, so that we may walk in the light of Thy Word and escape all dangers threatening us from Satan and the world, through Jesus Christ, Thy Son and our Redeemer. Amen. Amen. Amen." (Luther's *Saemmtl. Schriften,* St. Louis, XIV, 1169.)

N A H U M

Nineveh's Destruction a Manifestation of the Lord's Zeal for His Honor and the Salvation of His People

PART I

Chapter 1:1—2:1 (A. V., 1:1-15)

A. The Lord Is Ready to Destroy Nineveh, Ch. 1:1-14

1 A prophecy concerning Nineveh. The book of the vision of Nahum
2 the Elkoshite. A zealous and avenging God is the LORD! An avenger is the LORD and a Lord of wrath. An avenger is the LORD to His adversaries, and He reserves wrath
3 for His enemies. The LORD is slow to anger and great in power. The LORD will not leave the guilty unpunished. In storm and in whirlwind is His way, and the clouds are
4 the dust of His feet. He rebukes the sea and dries it up. All the streams He drains. Withered is Bashan and Carmel, and the vege-
5 tation of Lebanon, withered! Mountains quake before Him, and the hills tremble; the earth heaves before Him, the world and all that
6 live on it. Before His fury who can stand? And who can abide in the heat of His anger? His wrath is poured out like fire, and the rocks
7 are smashed before Him. Good is the LORD as a refuge place on the day of trouble, and He knows those
8 who trust in Him; but with an overwhelming flood He will make an end of her place and will pursue
9 His enemies into darkness. What do you think of the LORD? He is about to make total destruction. Affliction shall not arise a second
10 time! For though they are woven together like thornbushes and intoxicated as by their wine, they shall be completely consumed like
11 dry stubbles. From you proceeded one who plotted evil against the LORD, a counselor of wickedness.
12 Thus says the LORD: Though in full possession of power and likewise great, likewise they shall be shorn and shall pass away. And I have afflicted you, and will afflict
13 you no more. And now I will break his rod from upon you, and your
14 bonds I will burst asunder. And the LORD has issued a decree against you. No longer shall any of your name be sown. From the house of your gods I will cut off carved and molten images. I will appoint your grave, for you are despised.

Grammatical Notes

V. 1. "Burden," מַשָּׂא. Following the Vulgate "onus," Luther has translated "Last," A. V., "burden." The Hebrew term occurs some 20 times in this sense, literally, that which is lifted up, a load, a burden. (See Ex. 23:5; Num. 11:11, 17; Is. 46:1, etc.) Yet we can see no reason why this sense should be forced upon every passage where it occurs in connection with prophecy.

293

The verbal stem denotes to lift up, and in connection with קֹל, voice, to lift up one's voice; cp. Gen. 27:38, in weeping; Judg. 9:7, shouting; Is. 24:14; 52:8, rejoicing, singing. The verb, however, occurs frequently in these senses without the addition of קֹל, voice; see Ex. 20:7; Deut. 5:11, "take," lift up = utter, speak; Ex. 23:1, "raise" = utter; Num. 14:1, "lifted up their voice," Hebrew only "lifted up" = in crying, weeping; Num. 23:7, "took up" = spoke, so also v. 18; ch. 23:3, 15, 20, 21, 23; Ps. 15:3, "taketh up" = speaks; Is. 3:7, "swear," literally, lift up = say, assert; ch. 42: 2, 11, "lift up" = shout; Amos 5:1, "take up" = proclaim. From this sense of the verb the noun massa, that which is lifted up, uttered, spoken, received its meaning of utterance, proclamation.

The argument that the term massa, translated "burden" (A.V.), "Last" (Luther), invariably is used to introduce a minatory, or judgment, prophecy, loses sight of the actual facts. While it is used to introduce also this kind of divine proclamations, yet many of these "burden" utterances end in marvelous promises (e. g., Is. 19:1, "burden," but see vv. 19 ff.; Is. 22:1, also vv. 20 ff.; 23:1, also vv. 16 ff.). Zech. 12:1 the glorious promise of the Church's victory through faith in the pierced Redeemer and by the Spirit of grace and supplication (v. 10) is called a massa, "burden." The Book of Malachi is called a massa (ch. 1:1), yet it contains truly marvelous promises (ch. 1:2, 11; chs. 3 and 4). Finally, Jeremiah calls the utterances of the false prophets massa (Lam. 2:14), "false burdens." Yet these massas did not prophesy judgments, burdens, but

peace, peace (cp. Jer. 6:14; 8:11; 5:12). The term massa therefore cannot denote only judgment prophecies. It is a synonym of prophecy, proclamation, prophetic utterance.

V. 2. "Jealous," קַנּוֹא, the fuller form, occurring only here and in Joshua 24:19, is used for emphasis. The adjective used of God denotes the rightful and righteous, jealous anger of Him who is man's Creator and Preserver and Israel's Husband (Jer. 3:14; Hos. 1:2; 2:4, 21, 22, A. V., 2, 19, 20. Cp Ex. 20:5; 34:14; Deut. 4:24; 5:9, etc.).

V. 3. "Not at all acquit." The absolute infinitive before the predicate emphasizes the certainty or intensity of the finite verb. (G.-K. 113 n.) The Pi. of נָקָה = to declare innocent (Job 9:28; 10:14; Ps. 19:18); to declare free from punishment (Ex. 20:7; 34:7; Num. 14:18).

V. 5. "Is burnt." נִשְּׂאָ here is used intransitively or reflexively, rises, lifts itself. (Cp. Ps. 24:9; 89:10; Hos. 13:1; Hab. 1:3).

V. 8. "Pursue." The subject is still the Lord; the Pi. is intensive; "darkness," the accusative of direction (G.-K. 118 d). Others prefer the rendering of A. V.

V. 9. "Imagine against," אֶל, like עַל in Jer. 29:11, may be "concerning." Both Judah and Assyria are addressed, and both have a wrong conception concerning God. — "The second time," פַּעֲמַיִם, two times (Gen. 27:36; 41:32; Num. 20:11).

V. 11. "Come." The Hebrew perfect here, like the Greek aorist, denotes truth proved by experience (Is. 40:7; 8, 23; Ps. 10:3, 6; 14:1-5).

Note on Nineveh's Fall

The exact date of Nineveh's fall was not known until 1923, when C. J. Gadd in *The Fall of Nineveh*, London, published the Babylonian text found among the tablets in the British Museum (No. 21901), which chronicles the events of the tenth to the seventeenth year of Nabopolassar, king of Babylon (625—605). Unfortunately the sections referring to the fall of Nineveh are damaged, so that it is quite impossible to get a clear picture of Nineveh's fall. Yet we learn many details, unkown before, concerning the events leading up to the destruction of Nineveh. We learn that as early as in his tenth regnal year (616/5) Nabopolassar attacked Assyria with varying success after having gained his independence from Assyrian rule 625. In December, 615, "the Mede came down unto Arapkhu [ca. 100 miles southeast of Nineveh] and fought against the city." In July/August, 614/3, "the Mede went against the city of Nineveh as . . . and hastened, and captured Tabriz, a city of the district of Nineveh [200 miles northeast of Nineveh and 200 miles northeast of Arapkhu, the modern Tabriz in Iran, of some 220,000 inhabitants]. . . . He marched down the shore of the Tigris against the city of Asshur and fought against Asshur. . . . The city he destroyed and accomplished cruelly the destruction of the principal people; he seized their plunder and took their booty. The king of Akkad (Babylon) and his army, who had gone to the help of the Mede, did not arrive for the battle. The city. . . . The king of Akkad and Cyaxares [the Median king] met one another near the city and made a covenant of friendship and amity. . . . Cyaxares and his army returned to their country; the king of Akkad and his army returned to their country." During the next year the Babylonian king suffered a severe defeat by the Assyrians. Then the chronicle continues: "The king of Akkad . . . and Cyaxares . . . he caused to cross, and along the bank of the Tigris they marched and . . . against Nineveh . . . they from the month Simanŭ [May/June] to the month Ab [July/August] three battles. . . . In the month of Ab on the . . . day. . . . He accomplished the destruction of the principal people on that day." "They took the spoil of the city, a quantity beyond computation [cp. Nah. 2:9], and turned it into a mound and ruin." (Barton, *Archaeology*, p. 538 ff.) An Assyrian nobleman, Ashuruballit, escaped to Haran cp. Gen. 11:31 f.; 12:4 f.), proclaimed himself king, and sought to re-establish the old empire. Nabopolassar drove him out of Haran and plundered the city. Ashuruballit sought the aid of the Egyptian king, who willingly came in the hope to enable Assyria to remain a thorn in the flesh of powerful Babylonia. On Pharaoh Necho's march through Palestine Josiah opposed him (2 Kings 23:29) and was slain. The combined armies of Egypt and Assyria failed to reconquer Haran, and Ashuruballit passes out of history. In 605 the Egyptian army was routed at Carchemish by Nabopolassar (Jer. 46:1-26), and world sovereignty definitely passed over to Babylonia until 536.

V. 1. The "burden" (see Gr. N.). The little book records a proclamation directed against the great city of Nineveh. On "vision" see Obad. 1, p. 193. This vision was revealed to a man of whom we know nothing but his name, Nahum, "comforter," and the name of his native city. Not the man, but the message he proclaims is the important factor. Elkosh has been identified with the modern village of Al Qosh in Iraq, ca. 25 miles north of Mosul. Here is shown the site of Nahum's tomb, at which Christians, Jews, and Mohammedans have worshiped since the sixteenth century. Yet Al Qosh has never before that time been mentioned as Nahum's city. Jerome's statement in his Preface to Nahum is far more trustworthy: "Elcesi is even to this day a little village in Galilee, small indeed, and scarcely indicating by its ruins the traces of ancient buildings, yet known to the Jews, and pointed out to me too by my guide." (Quoted by Pusey, *The Minor Prophets*, p. 357.)

As Obadiah was called to be God's prophet against Edom, and as Jeremiah later was ordained a prophet unto the nations (Jer. 1:5), the spokesman of the Lord to Jews and Gentiles (ch. 1:9, 15), so the

Lord, the Ruler of the nations (Ps. 33:13, 14), honored Nahum to be His spokesman to Nineveh the Great. On Assyria and Nineveh see Hos. 7:11; 8:9; 9:3; 10:6; 11:11; Jonah 1:2; 3:3, p. 234; Micah 5:6; 7:12, p. 13; Zeph. 2:13, pp. 372 f.

In the first chapter Nahum pictures the Lord Jehovah sitting upon His eternal throne, while Judah and Nineveh are gathered before it. Through His spokesman the Lord addresses the assembly, revealing first in majestic terms the nature of the Ruler of the world (vv. 1-5), applying these truths to the whole assembly (vv. 6-8), and then in turn addressing Nineveh (vv. 9-11), Judah (vv. 12, 13), Nineveh (v. 14), Judah (v. 15). Yet the words addressed in particular to one of the two nations are spoken in the hearing of both. It is the Lord's message spoken before a mixed multitude, with important lessons for each and every individual in that vast gathering, lessons profitable for doctrine, for reproof, for correction, for instruction in righteousness, for eternal salvation; lessons for our learning, who are living 2,600 years after they were first spoken.

V. 2. In a remarkable oracle, approaching in grandeur God's self-revelation to Moses (Ex. 34:6, 7), the prophet depicts the majestic and incomprehensible nature of Jehovah, the Covenant God of Israel, to whom nothing can be likened (Is. 40:18, 25; Rom. 11:33). Rarely is the absolute, essential unity of divine attributes, which to the human mind seem contradictory opposites, brought out as forcefully as in this passage. On the one hand the furious wrath of God is presented in language that seems to make impossible any thought that this selfsame God is a God of grace and mercy and loving-kindness. And then these latter attributes are set forth in such brilliance as to seemingly shut out every possibility of anger, wrath, fury. And yet it is the same God, the unchangeable Jehovah, I AM THAT I AM (Ex. 3:14), whose wrath is as boundless as His grace, whose mercy as limitless as His anger. Let all the earth keep silence before Him! (Hab. 2:20.)

God is jealous (Gr. N.). The adjective invariably denotes God's zealous, eager jealousy, which cannot tolerate any rival to the perfect love and fear and trust He demands from all mankind, and which will wreak the fullness of His everlasting, burning wrath upon every human being failing to grant first place to God in his affection, his fear, and his confidence. "The Lord revengeth"; the Hebrew participle denotes the characteristic attribute. The unchanging God is an avenging Lord. This term is repeated and another synonym added, "furious." The Hebrew is stronger: a "lord," a master of heat, fury, one who owns fury. The Lord is the perfect Lord, and His fury is perfect fury, than which no fury is greater (cp. Deut. 32:22). A third time the term "take vengeance," revengeth, is used and the vengeance described as directed against His enemies and His adversaries, against whom He "reserves" wrath, lays it up, retains it. His wrath is as eternal as He Himself (Is. 66:24; Mark 9:43-48).

Vv. 3-5. Lest anyone receive an altogether wrong conception of divine wrath, it is further defined. It is not the whim of a cruel tyrant, the unreasonable flaring up of the temper of one who has not learned to control his passion, not the fury of a hothead who strikes out without rhyme or reason, letting his blows fall where they may. The Lord is slow to anger (Gr. N.). His anger is a well-considered wrath; His fury a justified vengeance, coming only after He has carefully weighed the whole matter. Yet it is not the wrath of one who cannot carry out his revenge or satisfy his wrath. His fury is the fury of Him who is "great in power," the omnipotent Ruler, with whom nothing is impossible (Gen. 18:14; Jer. 32:17, 27). For that very reason He will not at all acquit the wicked (Gr. N.), literally, as to declaring innocent, I will not declare innocent. When a judge declares an accused person innocent, he declares him free from the wrong or guilt with which the accused was charged, and free from the penalty demanded by the law. Jehovah is the Judge of the world, a Judge of unchanging justice. He cannot be persuaded either by flattery or force to declare any transgressor of His Law free of guilt. Nor will He remit the penalty of anyone deserving punishment. His demand of perfection is irrevocable; His judgment of death and damnation for every sinner stands eternally unchanged. He also has unlimited power to execute such judgment. He is the Ruler of the universe. The paths of whirlwind and storm, uncontrollable to man's power and wisdom, are His "way," on which He walks through the earth to carry out His plans of destruction. The clouds racing across the continents are to Him but the fine dust that arises when a man walks on the street. He speaks to the sea (v. 4), and it turns into dry land (cp. Ex. 14:16 ff.). At His word the rivers run dry (Joshua 3:13 ff.; 1 Kings 17:1, 7; 18:5, 6). Dry are beautiful Bashan and parklike Carmel, symbols of fertility (Is. 33:9; 35:2; Micah 7:14). Even Lebanon, whose "flower," sprouting vegetation, from the least blade of grass to the towering cedar, is fed by the waters of perennnial snow, stands dry and sere. Before His presence the mountains quake (v. 5), the hills melt, pouring their lava over the surrounding country; the earth "is burned" (Gr. N.), lifts up,

297

quakes, as does the "world," the cultivated, inhabitable earth, and all that dwell therein, man and beast, all quake in fear. (Ex. 19:16 ff.; 20:18 ff.; Heb. 12:18 ff.; Luke 21:25 ff.)

V. 6. His "indignation," His punitive wrath, His fierce anger, His fury poured out like fire, tearing down masses of rock — what is man against Him? Can puny man hope to stand before Him? Can sinful mortals ever hope to rise up successfully against Him? What folly, what wickedness for man to rebel against the LORD!

V. 7. Abruptly, without connective, the tone changes: Good is the Lord! God's "goodness" is His good will, His loving-kindness, as manifested in various ways. Ps. 25:7, 8 it stands in intimate connection with forgiveness (v. 7) and with teaching of God's ways (v. 8), justification and sanctification, embracing the entire life of the believer (Ps. 73:1, 23, 28; Ps. 106:1; 107:1; the two psalms are a commentary on God's goodness). In our passage (as in Ps. 34:8; 54:6) God's divine protection is placed in close connection with His goodness. Lam. 3:25 teaches us that even in deepest anguish His goodness upholds and comforts us. The very fact that He is slow to anger (Nah. 1:3) proves His unchanging good will. What a blessing to be sure of the Lord's protection in the day of trouble, in physical and spiritual need, in life, in death! (Ps. 27:1; 28:8; Prov. 18:10.) — "He knoweth them," encompasses them in His loving, affectionate, and effective knowledge (Amos 3:2, p. 149; Is. 46:16; John 10:27 ff.). This knowing is, as the Hebrew participle indicates, a characteristic trait of God, directed toward those that "trust" in Him, that make it their life's principle to seek refuge, not in their own power or wisdom, but in the Lord (cp. Ps. 2:12; 5:12; 18:31). Like the proclamation of God's wrath (vv. 2-6), this announcement of His goodness is spoken in the presence of the entire assembly. It applies to Assyria as well as to Israel; a gracious invitation to the former to turn from its dead idols to the living God of goodness and grace; and to the latter, an exhortation to remain, or again become, faithful to its Covenant God.

V. 8. "But," literally, and, connects v. 8 closely with v. 7. God's goodness does not change in the least the fact that He is and ever remains a God of vengeance against all His enemies. With an overwhelming flood He will annihilate her (Nineveh's) place. (Cp. ch. 2:6, M. T., 7.) The Ruler of the universe will use a flood to destroy proud Nineveh. While no reference to such a flood has been found in the extant inscriptions, the Greek historian Diodorus Siculus, living about the time of Christ, has an interesting passage in his *Library of History:*

"In the third year [of Nineveh's siege by the Medians and Babylonians] a series of heavy rains swelled the Euphrates [an error for "Tigris"], flooded part of the city, and overthrew the wall to a length of twenty stadia" [more than two miles], op. cit. II, 27. This breach in the city walls gave the hostile armies access to the city, enabling them to destroy it. "Darkness shall pursue" (Gr. N.) "His enemies," rather, He will zealously, unremittingly pursue Nineveh into darkness, oblivion. He covered the ruins of the city with huge sand dunes, beneath which she lay buried for 2,400 years, and which ruins to this day have not been fully explored or removed. This darkness is merely a symbol of that utter darkness, of being forever rejected from the light (Amos 5:18-20; Zeph. 1:15; Jude 13 b).

V. 9 is again directed to the entire assembly. What do you imagine "against" (Gr. N.), rather, concerning the Lord? Do you Assyrians imagine that you will be able to resist successfully this Lord or destroy His people? Judah, do you think that this Lord will not be able to protect you even against powerful Assyria? Why do you seek alliances with other nations instead of relying on the Lord? Listen, both of you! Assyria, the Lord will make an utter end of you! Judah, affliction, straits shall not arise against you "a second time" (Gr. N.)! Never again shall Nineveh oppress you!

V. 10 explains the last statement. "Folden together as thorns." A dense hedge of thorns and brambles closely interwoven may offer protection against attacks by man or beast. Against the Lord even the monstrous fortifications of Nineveh cannot avail. Nineveh may feel secure and absolutely safe, so safe that even while besieged her people will continue in their riotous revelries. Suddenly the fiery anger of the Lord will destroy them, as stubbles dried and sere are consumed by fire.

V. 11. A grave charge! "There is one come" (Gr. N.). "A wicked counselor," one who counsels Belial (Deut. 13:13; Judg. 19:22; 1 Sam. 1:16; 2:12), something unprofitable, worthless, wicked, that will end in his own and other people's destruction. The whole history of the Assyrians is a record of willful suppression of the natural knowledge of God written in their heart (Rom. 1:18 ff.), of opposition to the Lord Jehovah, of ruthless trampling underfoot every consideration of their fellow men, a brazen service of self. Yet the Lord, slow to anger (v. 3), is now ready to open the floodgates of His wrath.

V. 12. "Though they be quiet," unharmed, in full possession of their strength, seemingly invincible, their hosts innumerable, yet "thus," in full enjoyment of their power, "shall they be cut down, when he shall," etc., rather, "and it," Nineveh, shall pass away. — Once more the Lord turns to Judah, "I have afflicted thee," etc. This must be read in the light of v. 7 b, if Judah will trust in Him (cp. Jer. 18:9 ff.).

V. 13. The Assyrian yoke will be broken, while Judah will be freed from her bondage.

V. 14. Again Nineveh is addressed. God has decreed that no more of Nineveh's name shall be sown, she will have no more progeny, her national life shall cease completely. Their temples will be robbed of their carved and molten images. God Himself, the Fountain of life, will dig Nineveh's grave, "for thou art vile," light, despicable, "weighed and found wanting" (Dan. 5:27; 1 Sam. 2:30).

B. Nineveh's Destruction Insures Judah's Salvation
Ch. 2:1 (A. V., 1:15)

1 (A. V., 1:15) Behold, upon the mountains the feet of one bringing good tidings, announcing peace. Celebrate your feasts, O Judah! Pay your vows! For no longer shall the wicked continue to pass over you! He is cut off completely!

V. 1 (A. V., 1:15). The prophet quotes Is. 52:7 with slight changes. Over the mountains surrounding Jerusalem hurry the feet of a messenger bringing good tidings of great joy to the sorrowing people of God, the message of peace! Nineveh, the archenemy of Judah, is no more! The wicked destroyer shall no more pass through you (cp. ch. 1:9). So shall perish all your foes! So shall be foiled all the plans of Satan and his hosts to destroy you! O Judah, O Church of God, keep your solemn feasts! Your joyous hope of a Redeemer, commemorated on these feasts, shall not be disappointed! Perform, pay your vows! Your salvation is assured! It will not and cannot fail. As Nineveh, so shall all the enemies of your salvation be overcome! Both Isaiah (ch. 10:5-27) and Micah (ch. 5:4, 5) had foretold the destruction of Assyria prior to the coming of the Messiah as a guarantee of the ultimate destruction of all the enemies of the Church and of the salvation of God's people. Nahum's prophecy of Nineveh's fall is therefore a further guarantee that all Messianic prophecies shall be fulfilled in due time. While Nahum, therefore, does not name the Messiah, his prophecy implies and includes the assurance of Messiah's future salvation in the good news to be brought to Zion. See also remarks on Hab. 1:12: We shall not die! p. 324.

300

PART II

Nineveh's Destruction Will Be Complete Annihilation

CHAPTER 2:2-14 (A. V., 2:1-13)

2 (A. V., 2:1) A Scatterer shall come up against you! Guard the ramparts! Watch the way! Strengthen your loins! Bring your forces to
3 (2) fullest strength! For the Lord will restore the glory of Jacob as the glory of Israel; for plunderers have plundered them and have
4 (3) destroyed their vines. The shields of his warriors are tinted red; the valiant men are clothed in scarlet; the chariots sparkle like fire on the day of his preparation. Their spears of cypress wood are
5 (4) brandished. On the streets the chariots race like mad: they rush onward through the open places, in appearance like torches, like light-
6 (5) ning they run. He urges on his heroes. They stagger in the ways; they hurry to the wall; the
7 (6) battering ram is set up. The gates of the great river are thrown open and the palaces swept away.
8 (7) And Huzzab is stripped; she is deported, and her maidens are leading the way as with the mourning voice of doves, while they
9 (8) strike their breasts. Nineveh had been like a pool of waters since the day she came into existence. Yet they are fleeing! "Halt! Halt!"
10 (9) But no one turns back! Plunder silver! Plunder gold! For there is no end to the treasures! Riches of every kind of precious wares! —
11 (10) Void and devoid and desolate is she! And hearts are despairing, and there is shaking of knees and anguish in all loins, and the faces of all of them grow livid
12 (11) with fear. Where is the den of lions, that feeding place of young lions, where the lion walked, the lioness, the lion's whelp, while no
13 (12) one disturbed them? The lion kept on tearing to pieces sufficient food for his whelps and slaying for his lioness; and he filled his caves with ravin and his dens
14 (13) with rapine. Behold, I am against you! is the oracle of the LORD of Hosts. And I will burn her chariots in smoke, and the sword shall consume your young lions. And I will cut off from the earth your prey, and the voice of your messengers shall no longer be heard!

Grammatical and Textual Notes

V. 2 (A. V., 1). "Dasheth in pieces," Hi. of פוּץ, to spread, Hi., causative = scatter; seed, Is. 28:25; a nation, Is. 24:1; defeated armies, Hab. 3:14. Shattered Nineveh shall be scattered.

V. 3 (2). "Hath turned away." שָׁב here in sense of turn, restore (cp. Job 39:12; Ps. 85:5, A. V., 4). Cp. *shub shebut* = turn a turning, restore the former state.

V. 4 (3). "Flaming torches." פְּלָדוֹת occurs only here, probably a Persian word adopted by the Babylonians and Israelites, usually rendered iron, steel; the iron ornaments on chariots. Flam-

ing, אֵשׁ = fire, fiery gleam (cp. Ezek. 28:14, 16, "stones of fire" = glittering stones or gems). Hence here "glittering iron." — "Preparation," here lining up in battle formation, fully prepared to attack the enemy.

V. 5 (4). "Rage," literally, to be foolish, insane; Hithpolel = to become crazy, frenzied (Jer. 25:16; 46:9; 51:7).

V. 6 (5). "Recount," literally, remind. Cp. Is. 43:26, "put Me in remembrance"; 62:6, "make mention of" = remind Him. As the remembrancers of the Lord should not rest, and give Him no rest, so the leader of troops reminds them of their duty, urges them on, encourages them to ever greater efforts. — "Defense," from a stem denoting to cover protectingly. The Assyrians used smaller, hutlike shelters which could be readily carried by a few men, or larger, towerlike structures rolled on wheels to the top of the embankments built round about the besieged city. The sheds offered protection to the soldiers while building these embankments, and later while seeking to undermine the foundations of the walls to hasten their collapse. The towers were provided with machines hurling stones and firebrands against the walls and into the city, in order to smash the fortifications and start conflagrations. Moved close to the walls, they also offered vantage points for attack by the soldiers.

V. 7 (6). "Rivers." The plural here is intensive: the great, or mighty, river. Cp. Job 41:4 (A. V., 12), "power," Hebr., plural = great strength; Is. 40:14, "understanding," plural = thorough understanding; v. 26, "power," plural = omnipotence. (G.-K. 124 d.) — "The palace" may be generic, denoting the entire class.

V. 8 (7). "Huzzab," the Hophal of נָצַב; Qal does not occur. Niph. = to be set up, stand, be firm (Ex. 15:8; Ps. 119:89; quite common); Hiph., causative = to set up, place, establish (Gen. 33:20; Deut. 32:8; Jer. 31:21); Hoph., passive, occurs only Gen. 28:12 (a ladder "set up") and here. S. Schmidt, Keil, and others translate "It is decreed, She shall be led away," etc. We prefer to regard the term as an appellation for Nineveh: He

is established, made firm. The masculine form is used because Nineveh is compared to a giant, a Goliath, made invincible by her powerful rulers. The feminine predicates are chosen to indicate that not the king, but the city is so designated. Cities and countries take the feminine when they are regarded as the mothers of their inhabitants (see 2 Sam. 20:19, "mother"; Ps. 149:2; Joel 2:23; Zeph. 2:9, "children"). When the name of a city or country stands for the inhabitants, the predicate is either masculine (Num. 20:20; Is. 3:8) or feminine (Gen. 41:8; Ex. 10:7; 2 Sam. 8:2; Is. 7:2, etc. G.-K. 122 h, i). — "Led." נָהַג in Biblical usage always = to lead, drive, as a shepherd leads his flock (Gen. 31:18; Deut. 4:27; Is. 49:10), or lead away (Gen. 31:26), never in the sense of groan. Nor does the context demand the latter sense.

V. 9 (8). "Of old," מִימֵי הִיא, from the days of her = since she existed (G.-K. 130 d. Note 1).

V. 13 (12). "With prey," "ravin," tereph, teraphah, tearing, and torn things. The Bible Commentary renders well: "ravin," "rapine."

V. 14 (13). "In the smoke," בְּ of the accompanying circumstance, a fire accompanied by smoke, a huge fire. (See Gen. 3:16, "in sorrow"; Ps. 73:8, "wickedly" = in a wicked manner.) — "Thy messengers." מַלְאָכֵכָה, an abnormal form of the suffix; probably purposely chosen as a fuller form at the end of a section. (Cp. אֹתָכָה, Gen. 25:39; G.-K. 91 l.)

V. 2 (A. V., 1). "Dasheth in pieces" (Gr. N.), literally, the Scatterer. "To thy face" = into your presence, to your very gates. Rarely, if ever, had Nineveh been besieged during the past centuries. Now the haughty mistress of the world will have to do what her victorious armies so often had forced other cities to do. "Keep the munitions," guard your bulwarks and fortifications! — "Watch," keep a sharp look-out on all the highways leading to your city, to guard against any sur-prise attack! — "Make your loins strong," muster up all the courage you can. You will have need of it! (Cp. v. 10, weakened knees and paining loins.) "Fortify thy power mightily," make use of every pos-sible means to present a solid, strong front. The Lord knows that all their efforts will not save the nation from disintegration. The Scatterer will come and do His job thoroughly. The danger of disintegration of so vast an empire had been foreseen by that shrewd statesman Tiglath-Pileser (745—727 B. C.). For this reason he had introduced the system of deporting either entire cities and nations, or at least the influential citizens, and settling them in sections of his empire far remote from their homeland. The cities or countries left vacant were repeopled by colonists from other parts of his empire. (See 2 Kings 15: 29; 16: 9; 17: 6, 23, 24.) These deported people would gradually forget their native soil, would adopt Assyrian language and customs and religion. Assyria became their homeland. Man proposes, God disposes. The Scatterer, the Lord Himself, whose instruments the enemies of Nineveh were, would inflict on Assyria the same penalty it had inflicted on so many cities and nations. It would pass out of history as a nation; its role of world domination would be taken over by its hated rival Babylon and by the despised "barbarians," the Medes and Persians.

V. 3 (2). The Lord Jehovah, whom Nineveh had despised and blasphemed (2 Kings 18: 32 ff.), whose people Nineveh had deported, in whose temple an altar dedicated to the god of Assyria had taken the place of Jehovah's altar (2 Kings 16: 10-18), this Lord was, after all, the world Ruler and would come to the aid of His people. "Hath turned away" (Gr. N.), has returned the "excellency," the glory of Jacob, the sinful, homeless fugitive. On the glory of Jacob cp. Ex. 19:5, 6; 24: 1-18; Deut. 4: 5ff.; Rom. 9: 4ff. "As the excellency of Israel." Israel was the honorable name of Jacob (Gen. 32: 24-29). The children of Israel, the man blessed by the Lord, had become children of Jacob, the sinful fugitive. (Cp. Ezek. 36: 17-21.) Yet the faithful Lord of the Covenant, who had not yet rejected His people, would restore, return to them the full excellency promised to Israel. He had sent the Assyrians in chastisement of His people. Yet they refused to realize that they were only the Lord's instruments. They had perverted their divine mission (Is. 10: 5-19; Zech. 1: 15), had plundered Israel like cruel robbers, and had "marred," laid waste, the branches of the Lord's vineyard (Ps. 80:8-16; 89:40 f.; Is. 5:1-7). Now the Lord arises for the deliverance of His people and the destruction of their haughty enemy.

V. 4 (3). According to Ezek. 23:14, corroborated by ancient sculptures, Assyrian and Babylonian soldiers had their shields painted red, their cloaks colored scarlet; so also the Medes, as Xenophon informs us, *Cyropaedia*. "With flaming torches" (Gr. N.), in the fiery gleam of iron, refers to the brightly burnished iron ornaments on their war chariots and the trappings of their horses. "In the day of his preparation" (Gr. N.), when they lined up in battle formation, "terribly shaking," brandishing their "fir trees," or cypresses, here the spears, lances, javelins, etc., of cypress wood, they presented indeed a terrifying spectacle.

V. 5 (4). On every street and highway leading to the city, once crowded with caravans of merchants, now "rage" (Gr. N.), run like mad, the war chariots. The "broadways," *rechoboth* (see Gr. N. on Amos 5:16, p. 160), were the open, parklike spaces surrounding the city and its suburbs (cp. *Rechoboth Ir*, Gen. 10:11; Park City). These parks, where young and old had met for joyous play or serious discussions, now are filled with chariots jostling, crowding, bumping one against the other; like flaming torches, their ornaments shining, they race on like streaks of lightning, swiftly, fear-inspiring.

V. 6 (5). He, the Scatterer (v. 1), the chief Commander, "recounts" (Gr. N.) His "worthies" (same word as "nobles," ch. 3:18, denoting here His "heroes"), His heroic troops, whom He reminds of their past victories, encourages and urges them on to forget their weariness, to labor and fight on in unflagging courage. They "stumble," they stagger under the heavy loads of rubbish and earth they must carry on their shoulders in order to build the embankments ever higher. (See Hab. 1:10; Ezek. 29:18.) They flounder through the masses of debris, of wreckage, of dead bodies, seesawing in their efforts to dodge the missiles hurled at them from the city walls. Yet they do not rest. Overcoming their weariness, they hurry as fast as they can; and soon the "defense" (Gr. N.) is erected; the first stones thunder against the walls.

V. 7 (6). Nahum does not state the manner in which the gates of the river shall be opened. Undoubtedly he refers to the overwhelming flood of ch. 1:8, which also Diodorus mentions; see p. 298 f. On "rivers" and "palace" see Gr. N.

V. 8 (7). "Huzzab" (Gr. N.). We regard this term as an appellation of Nineveh: It is established! Firmly founded! The seemingly unconquerable city shall be laid low. Nineveh had cruelly deported the nations she had conquered. And now she is to suffer like shame, to be stripped (cp. 3:5). She shall be brought up (Gr. N.), led away into captivity. Her maidens, who had so often led the rejoicing population out of the city to meet the returning victorious army, now again will lead (Gr. N.) the people out of Nineveh. No longer will they joyously sing, but "with the voice of doves," wailing incessantly like mourning doves, "tabering," beating, not their tambourines, but their hearts in bitterest sorrow. The heart is named to indicate the depth of their sorrow, affecting the inmost seat and center of their lives.

V. 9 (8). "Pool," an artificial reservoir fed by springs. (Cp. Eccl. 2:6; 2 Kings 20:20, etc.) "Of old" (Gr. N.), since her earliest days (cp. Gen. 10:11, "great city"), Nineveh had been like a pool of water, overflowing with people, spreading ever farther (cp. Rev. 17:15, Babylon), until she had become a huge metropolis (Jonah 1:2; 3:3). Now Nahum sees these "waters," her people, flee away. He hears the frenzied cries, Stand! Halt! Stop! Yet no one listens, no one turns back.

V. 10 (9). Suddenly the scene shifts from the fleeing populace to the conquerors invading the city. The prophet hears the triumphant shouts of the enemies rushing through the streets, Plunder silver! Plunder gold! Help yourselves to the riches! He hears the astonished cry of the plunderers, What endless mass of materials! What "glory," what beauty! What unlimited quantities of every sort of precious objects!

V. 11 (10). The plunderers do a thorough job. Empty, void, waste is rich Nineveh! The original is even more forceful: *Bukah, umebukah, umebullakah!* each term picturing the horrible void more vividly. The heart of the people, their spirit, once so fearless, so proud, so indomitable, now is melted like wax. Alarm, fear, terror, consternation, black despair grip them. No longer can they form any plan of resistance; their knees tremble; sickening anguish, nauseating horror grips their loins. Their faces "gather blackness," assume the livid, ashen color of people frightened to death.

Vv. 12-14 (11-13). Nineveh had long been like a lion's den, into which the ravaging, invincible killer lion had brought ever-increasing masses of spoils for his lioness and their cubs. There they enjoyed their wealth to their heart's content, while no one had dared to disturb them. Where is their lion's den? Gone forever! Jehovah, the Lord of Hosts, has turned against them (v. 14, A. V., 13). He whom no one can resist will kindle a huge fire and will burn her chariots in the smoke (Gr. N.), reduce them to smoke. Their young lions, the youth of the land, He will slay with the sword. Their stolen treasures He will cut off the earth, bury them in the sands. The voice of their ambassadors, enticing with seductive flatteries and deceptive promises, or terrifying by dreadful threats, will no longer be heard! That is the dire doom of Nineveh proclaimed in advance by the spokesman of Him who knows all His works from the beginning of the world (Is. 45:5 ff.; 46:9 ff.; Acts 15:18), the almighty Ruler of the world.

PART III

The Iniquity of Nineveh Makes Its Destruction Inevitable

CHAPTER 3

1 Woe to the bloody city! Lies throughout, filled with booty, un-
2 ceasingly she plunders! Crack of whip, and rumbling wheels; galloping horses, and rattling chariots;
3 plunging steeds, and flashing swords, and glittering spears, and numbers of slain, and masses of carcasses, and no end to the corpses! They stumble over the
4 corpses. Because of the many harlotries of the harlot, the lovely beauty, the bewitching mistress who sells nations by her harlotry
5 and tribes by her spells, behold, I am against you, is the oracle of the LORD of Hosts, and I will lift up your skirts over your face, and I will show to the nations your nakedness, and to the kingdoms
6 your shame. And I will throw vile filth on you, and treat you contemptuously, and make you a gaz-
7 ing stock, so that everyone seeing you shall flee from you, and say, Nineveh is destroyed! Who shall pity her? Where shall I seek com-
8 forters for you? Are you better than Thebes that sat on the great river? Waters surrounded her, whose defense was the sea, her
9 wall of sea? Ethiopia was strength and Egypt unceasingly, Put and

10 Lubim came to your aid! Yet even she became an exile, she went into captivity. Her children were dashed in pieces at the head of every street; and upon all her honored men they cast lots, and all her great
11 men were bound with chains. You also shall become drunk, become hidden; you also shall be seeking
12 refuge from the enemy. All your fortresses shall be as fig trees with early figs which, when they are shaken, fall into the mouth of the
13 eater. Behold, your people shall be women in the midst of you. To the enemies the gates of your land will be opened wide. Fire will consume
14 your barriers. Draw for yourself water for the siege! Strengthen your fortresses! Go into the clay and tramp in the potter's clay!
15 Take hold of the brick mold! There fire shall consume you; the sword will cut you off; it will devour you like the locust does. Increase like the licker! Increase like the locust!
16 Though you have made your merchants more numerous than the stars of heaven — the licker has
17 plundered and flies away. Your watchmen are as locusts, your scribes as swarms of grasshoppers, which settle in the hedges in the

306

cool of the day. When the sun rises, they flee; and unknown is the
18 place where they are. Asleep are your shepherds, O king of Assyria; lying quiet your noble men; scattered on the mountains your people; and no one gathers them!

19 There is no remedy for your ruin; incurable your wound! All that hear the report about you will clap their hands over you. For over whom has not your wickedness passed continually?

Grammatical and Textual Notes

V. 8. "Populous No." No is Thebes in southern Egypt. "Populous," rather, Amon, the deity of Thebes and the supreme deity of Egypt (Jer. 46:25; Ezek. 30:14-16).

V. 9. "Her strength," עֻצְמָה, a feminine variant of עֹצֶם (cp. Is. 40:29; 47:9); hence "her" is to be omitted. — "Thy helpers," בְּ *essentiae* denotes the character, manner, etc., of the person or object.

V. 11. "Hid." וְנַעֲלָמָה always = hidden, never = fainted (Nowack, Sellin, and others; cp. Lev. 5:2-4; Num. 5:13).

V. 12. "With" denotes any connection of one object with another; here "with" figs = bearing figs.

V. 15. "Make thyself many," *hitkabbed, hitkabbedi.* The first may be abs. inf., which may take the place of any verbal form (G.-K. 113 y, bb); or it may be the masc. imperative (since the masculine form is often placed at the beginning of a sentence even if the following subject is feminine. (G.-K. 145 o.) The two imperatives state conditions to which a third condition is added in v. 16.

V. 16. "Thou hast multiplied." Here the simple perfect introduces the condition. (G.-K. 159 h; cp. Ex. 20:25; Prov. 18:22,

etc.) The final clause is stated v. 16 b, "the cankerworm," etc. "Spoileth," פָּשַׁט, plunder, rob, raid, forage (Hos. 7:1; Judg. 9:33, "set upon"; 1 Sam. 27:8, "invaded"; v. 10, "road" = inroad, raid; 30:1, etc.). The verb is also used in the sense of disrobe, shed one's clothes, and therefore some commentators render it "molts," but the word never occurs in that sense and would not suit the context. The enemies did not molt and fly away, nor did the Ninevites willingly disrobe or fly away to continue their depradations as the locusts do after molting.

V. 17. "Crowned." The Hebrew stem is נָזַר, set apart; a crown or diadem (*nezer*) is the symbol of one set apart, or appointed. The word denotes some official, but the exact duties are not known. — "Captains." The Assyrian *Taphsarim* (Jer. 51:27) are scribes, perhaps enlisting officers. — "Great grasshoppers," גּוֹב גֹּבָי, only here; the former also Amos 7:1; another term for locust. The repetition of two nouns of the same or a related stem denotes the superlative: *shabbat shabbaton* = the supreme day of rest; *shalom shalom* (Is. 26:3), perfect peace, nothing but peace; here, *gob gobai*, innumerable grasshoppers. (Cp. G.-K. 133 i.)

V. 1. The bloodthirsty city filled with the blood of her own people. "Bloody city," the city of bloods, bloodshed. Cp. remarks on Nineveh's wickedness, Jonah 1:2, p. 221. One of the reliefs discovered in Ashurbanipal's palace pictures him with his queen, celebrating his victory over the Elamites. In the banquet hall is shown near the table a fruit tree from one of whose branches dangles the head of the defeated king. Bloody Nineveh, indeed! "Lies," fraud, deception in business and politics, see v. 4. "Robbery," that which is violently torn off. (Cp. Gen. 49:9; Amos 3:4; Ezek. 19:3, 6.) "Prey." The verb denotes tearing to pieces like wild animals (Nah. 2:13, A. V., 12; Hos. 5:14; Micah 5:7); the noun here, the act of cruelly tearing to pieces. "Departeth not," never stops, goes on unceasingly.

Vv. 2, 3. While above in the Bible text, we have offered this marvelous piece of poetry in the translation of J. M. Powis Smith, in *The Complete Bible,* we now offer the translation by Geo. Adam Smith in *The Expositor's Bible.*

> Hark the whip,
> And the rumbling of the wheel,
> And horses galloping,
> And the rattling dance of the chariot!
> Cavalry at the charge, and flash of sabres.
> And lightning of lances,
> Mass of slain and weight of corpses,
> Endless dead bodies —
> They stumble over their dead!

"It is a fearful thing to fall into the hands of the living God!" (Heb. 10:31.) Yet this horrible punishment is the well-deserved judgment executed by the just and holy God.

V. 4. The bewitching harlot will meet the harlot's fate. Nineveh is called a harlot committing a multitude of whoredoms, a scarlet woman. Yet she is not an ugly, worn-out, repulsive hag. She is "well favored," of perfect beauty, of fascinating loveliness. Her power, her world-wide commerce, her invincible military machinery, her riches, her architecture, her learning had bewitched "nations," great powers as well as "families," smaller tribes and clans. All wooed this beautiful mistress of the world, sought her favor, basked in her sunshine. "The mistress of witchcrafts" knew how to use her captivating beauty, how to weave the net of intrigue and trickery, of flattery and high-sounding promises (2 Kings 18:31ff.), or of sharp threats, if that suited her better, until the helpless victims were enmeshed, until she possessed them body and soul, heart and mind. As long as they were her obedient slaves, she protected them, but was ready to cast them off, crush them underfoot, sell them down the river, as soon as they refused to obey her slightest wish or whim. In spite of her loveliness she was a vile, cruel prostitute, whose every thought and act had but one aim: to satisfy her passion for power, her lust of plunder, her desire for world supremacy. Witness the history of Ahaz and Judah. Having lost confidence in the Covenant God (Is. 7:1-13), Ahaz wooed the well-favored harlot (2 Kings 16:7), gladly paid her the harlot's fee (v. 8). While freed from one enemy (v. 9), he had fallen victim to a pitiless tyrant. Nineveh had come not to strengthen or help him, but to distress, oppress Judah (2 Chron. 28:20 ff.), to ruin king and people politically by depriving them of their independence; financially, by exacting heavy tributes ("took away a portion," v. 21 = plunder); socially, by their aping Assyrian customs (Zeph. 1:8 b); spiritually, by Ahaz's introducing Assyrian idolatry into the Lord's Temple (2 Kings 16:10-18; 2 Chron. 28:24; 29:3-7). See also Manasseh's experience (2 Chron. 33:1-11) and the bitter end (ch. 36:5-21). Nineveh, in spite of her grandeur, was a vile, cruel, selfish, dangerous harlot!

Vv. 5-7. Yet this harlot had reckoned without the Lord Jehovah, whom she had despised and blasphemed (2 Kings 18:32 b-35). He says, Behold, I am against thee! (Cp. ch. 2:13.) He will reveal her true character, her shame to all the world. The beautiful harlot will receive the harlot's punishment (Hos. 2:3; Is. 47:3). Nineveh will be put to public shame, vilified, pilloried, made a horrible example to all the world. Everyone seeing her, stripped of her beauty, runs away in horror. Her former lovers and friends stand aloof from her sore, her kinsmen stand afar off (cp. Ps. 38:11). After all, she never had succeeded in gaining the affectionate and faithful love of her wooers. They were good-weather friends. Now there is none to bemoan, to pity her. Even the most diligent search will fail to find a single comforter for her. Forsaken of men! Forsaken of God!

Vv. 8, 9. The self-confident empress will be laid low. — Nineveh regarded herself as invincible. She is doomed to bitter disappointment. Pointedly the Lord asks her, Are you better than "populous No" (Gr. N.)? No Amon, the ancient Egyptian name of Thebes, situated on both banks of the mighty Nile, is here called a "sea." (Cp. Is. 19:5; Ezek. 32:2, Nile; Jer. 51:36, Euphrates.) The ruins of Thebes at Luxor on the eastern bank and Karnak on the western still rouse the amazement of all visitors. "Rampart" = a glacis, a defensive slope or wall placed before the main fortifications in order to increase the difficulties of attack. In addition to the long march through Egypt, some 500 miles, the mighty river and its many canals surrounding the twin city, made a successful attack from the north, a protracted siege, a final conquest almost impossible. From 711 to 663 Thebes was the capital city of Egypt. Ethiopian kings had subdued the empire, which now extended from the shores of the Mediterranean Sea, including Libya west of Egypt, down through Ethiopia and Put, the latter either part of Libya or, most probably, the modern Somaliland in eastern Africa, extending along the Gulf of Aden and southward along the Indian Ocean to the equator. "Her strength" (Gr. N.). "Infinite," literally, there was no end. Thebes's territory was practically limitless (cp. remarks on Zeph. 2:12, p. 371). "Thy helpers" (Gr. N.); the Lord addresses Thebes. Such sudden changes from third to second person and vice versa are rather frequent (cp. Hos. 2:5-23).

V. 10. Yet mighty Thebes was destroyed, her inhabitants deported, her babes cruelly killed, her honorable men sold into slavery by lot, her great men dragged away, ignominiously bound in chains. "Top of the streets," literally, the head of the streets, the street corners. Assyria had conquered her mighty rival for world supremacy, but only after bloody campaigns. Esarhaddon reached Memphis, about 300 miles north of Thebes, 673 B. C., but was defeated. Two years later Esarhaddon conquered the land as far south as Thebes, but the Nubian or Ethiopian king Tirhaka reoccupied the entire land by 669. On his next campaign, 668, Esarhaddon died. His son Ashurbanipal finally conquered Thebes and sacked it 663. The Lord draws a lesson for Nineveh from the fall of Thebes. If that happened to your powerful rival, are you immune from similar destruction?

V. 11. You are not! "You shall be drunken," reel, totter, like an intoxicated person who has lost control over himself and finally lands in the gutter. "Hid" (Gr. N.), secreted beneath huge masses of sand, gone from sight. "Seek strength," rather, refuge. You, at whose word nations trembled, will flee for protection from your enemy (cp. ch. 2:8).

V. 12. "With" (Gr. N.). Early, first ripe figs were regarded as a delicacy (Is. 28:4; Jer. 24:2; Hos. 9:10; Micah 7:1). They were readily shaken from the branches. So all the fortresses round about Nineveh will easily fall (cp. Notes on Fall of Nineveh, pp. 294 f.) like delicious figs, welcome sweets, into the mouths of the conquerors, to be devoured by them.

V. 13. Nineveh's people, seized by panic, will be like defenseless women. In order to escape certain death and destruction, they will open "the gates of her land," surrender the outposts which were to protect the city. "Bars," the heavy timbers used as crossbars to close the city gates, here represent all defensive means.

Vv. 14, 15. A warning to prepare for a protracted siege. The river water was not fit to drink unless it was purified by being stored in public reservoirs or private cisterns. All their fortifications were to be replaced and strengthened. The entire population must go into the mud, tread the clay, "make strong" = take hold of, the "brick kiln," the mold in which the clay was formed into bricks and then hardened by fire. And "there," wherever they are busily preparing for the siege, fire shall cut them off, the sword consume them (v. 15). The ruins still show the effects of the fierce conflagrations raging through the magnificent palaces. The "cankerworm," literally, the licker, one of the stages in the development of the locust, jumping rather than flying (cp. Joel 1:4, pp. 114 f.), leaving not a vestige of green on the field and in the garden. "Make thyself many" (Gr. N.) is a conditional clause describing the impossibility of escape. Even if you multiply like hoppers and locusts, you shall be completely destroyed.

V. 16. Most of the main trade routes led to Nineveh and radiated from that city into all parts of the world. It was the commercial center of the ancient world, where numberless merchants and representatives of distant commercial and manufacturing establishments did a flourishing business. Suddenly this will stop! The cankerworm "spoileth," despoils, plunders, and flieth away, disappears. John D. Whiting, describing Jerusalem's locust plague of 1915, writes: "In passing the Jordan Valley these fliers of recent date came in clouds sufficiently dense to darken the sun and cleared this Jericho oasis of its vegetable gardens and the leaves from the fruit trees, rendering it for a while as barren as the parched wilderness encircling it. — The entire devastation was wrought by two visits lasting but a day or so each, after which diligent search could not produce a single locust." (*National Geographic Magazine,* December, 1915, p. 544, col. B.) The sudden and complete disappearance of the plunderer is the point of comparison here. The merchants, feeding themselves on the fat of the land, filling the city with fraud and their pockets with robbery (ch. 3:1), these plunderers shall suddenly disappear. For centuries the most diligent search would not find a single merchant in Nineveh.

Vv. 17, 18. Not only the merchants will disappear. Her "crowned" (Gr. N.), most likely princes; her "captains," an Assyrian term for some high official, scribe, perhaps enlisting officer (cp. Jer. 51:27), are like locusts and grasshoppers (Gr. N.) which camp in the hedges, the rubble walls enclosing the gardens and fields, where in the evening innumerable locusts gather like an enemy in its camp, lie quietly

311

during the night and the cold morning, until the sun rises and the whole swarm "flies away," disappears, no one knows whereto. Again the sudden and complete disappearance to places unknown is the point of comparison. "Shepherds" (v. 18), the secondary rulers appointed by the Assyrian king, "slumber," sleep the sleep of death. "Nobles," called "worthies" (ch. 2:5), here perhaps the heroic warriors of Nineveh "dwell in the dust," literally, dwell quietly — in the grave. The people of Nineveh are scattered upon the hills (1 Kings 22:17; Zech. 13:7; cp. also Num. 27:17). They fled to the hills in the vain hope of escape. Having no shepherds to "gather" them, to guide and feed and protect them, they fall victims to the hardships of the flight, to the sword of the pursuing enemy.

V. 19. "No healing," literally, quenching, soothing of their "bruise," their shattering destruction; so grievous, so mortal is their wound. All that hear the "bruit," the report, of Nineveh's fall, clap their hands in joy and mockery. There is none to pity or comfort (see v. 7), for there is no nation that was not constantly harassed and oppressed by wicked Nineveh. Overwhelming wickedness, tyranny, cruelty forever, that is Nineveh's sin. That caused Nineveh's fall. That shall be the judgment overtaking every individual, every nation, no matter how powerful, that dares to oppose the Lord Jehovah and seeks to destroy His Church.

H A B A K K U K

Introductory Remarks

1. Habakkuk's Personality

We know no more about the personality of Habakkuk than what ch. 1:1 and 3:19 reveal. Luther connects his name with a verb denoting "to embrace," the embracer. Sellin, G.-B., connect it with Assyrian *hambakuku,* the name of a garden plant, also used as a personal name. He calls himself "the prophet," 1:1, the *nabi.* This does not justify the charge raised by Sellin and others that he was an ecstatic, "one of that class of prophets," *nebiim,* so severely condemned by Jeremiah 6:13 f.; 23:9ff. Jeremiah does not hesitate to call himself a *nabi* (Jer. 1:5; 20:2; 25:2; 28:5f., 11-15, etc.). Nor is it true that Habakkuk "lacked entirely the deeper understanding of the increasing sinfulness of Judah" or that "his conception of an ideal life, consisting in diligent labor, quiet enjoyment, and of industry based on justice and equity, stamps him a somewhat narrow-minded plebeian (etwas beschränkten Spiessbuerger)," Sellin, p. 383. Strange to say, on the same page the same author calls Habakkuk a true messenger of the living God, "rising towerlike above the exclusiveness of many of his contemporaries, and whose subjective veracity is not to be denied." We shall learn that Habakkuk had a keen insight into the wickedness of his people and a thorough conviction of the only possible cure: faith in the promised Redeemer, the Justifier and Sanctifier of His people (ch. 2:4; 3:13, 18f.).

Another bit of information concerning Habakkuk's personality may be gathered from the subscription, ch. 3:19 b. We can see no valid reason for eliminating or changing this subscription. (See Gr. N., p. 351.) The prophet evidently was a member of the Temple choir, hence a Levite. (Cp. 1 Chron. 23:3-6.) Since he speaks of "my instruments" (plural), he may have been one of the musical leaders or directors.

2. The Date of Habakkuk's Activity

Modern scholars as a rule place Habakkuk's activity in the age of Jehoiakim (609—598 B. C.), since only at that time the Chaldeans began to oppress Judah (Dan. 1:1ff.). Bewer, 605—590; Sellin, in second edition of his commentary, 600—587; Budde, 615; Oesterley-Robinson regard the book as a compilation of various oracles completed no earlier than the beginning of the fifth century B. C. Duhm regarded the Hebrew *Chasdim,* Chaldeans (ch. 1:6), as a scribal error or a gloss for *Kittim* = Cyprians, Greeks, and placed the book in the age of Alexander the Great. He was followed by Procksch, Torrey, Nowack, Sellin in first edition of his commentary. Pfeiffer: If "Chaldean" is correct, 615—600; if *Kittim,* then the era of Alexander. O. Happel, 1900, the time of Antiochus Epiphanes, about 170 B. C. Eissfeldt is one of the few who date it as early as 625—612. A careful study of the book and contemporaneous history will positively establish the date of Habakkuk's activity as either the last years of Manasseh's long reign (698—643) or preferably the early years of Josiah (641—609).

Two divine statements in ch. 1:5 will be helpful in determining the approximate time of Habakkuk's activity. The coming of the Chaldean (v. 6) is described in v. 5 as a marvelous work of the Lord, so wholly unexpected as to seem impossible, unbelievable, to the people of Habakkuk's time. This fact very effectually disposes of the possibility of dating Habakkuk's activity as beginning in Jeroboam's rule, when the Chaldeans already had gained the world supremacy by destroying Nineveh, in 612, and in whose third year the first Jews were deported to Babylon by Nebuchadnezzar (Dan. 1:1ff.). Yet these unbelievable prophecies would be fulfilled "in your days," within the lifetime of the generation then living. The raising of the Chaldean cannot imply that the Chaldeans were a nation entirely unknown to the Jews of that era, just as Judg. 3:9; 1 Kings 11:14, 23; Amos 6:14 do not mean to describe the persons "raised up" as hitherto unknown. The article before "bitter and hasty nation" points to a well-known characteristic of the Chaldeans, who had infiltrated into Babylon many centuries before and were continually stirring up dissatisfaction and rebellion against the Babylonian rulers. Merodach Baladan (2 Kings 20:12ff.; Is. 39:1ff.), an ancestor of Nabopolassar, the father of Nebuchadnezzar, was a Chaldean.

The Chaldeans were not unknown to the Jews of Habakkuk's time. Yet the unbelievable miracle, which the World Ruler alone could perform, was the fact announced by Him that not the Assyrians, nor the Babylonians, but the Chaldeans, who after all had so far played only a minor role in the history of the world, were to be the power destroying the Jewish nation.

For centuries the Assyrians and the Babylonians vied with each other for world supremacy, and while Assyria had at times been forced to yield its superiority to its rival, it had shown a remarkable ability for rejuvenation. After one of these temporary declines (783—745), Tiglath-Pileser (745—727) (cp. 2 Kings 15:29; 16:7 ff.) had re-established the supremacy of Assyria. He was followed by powerful rulers, Shalmaneser (727—722), Sargon (722—705), Sennacherib (705—681, who put the torch to rebellious Babylon), Esarhaddon (681—668), and Ashurbanipal (668—626). During the entire century Assyria had been the chief oppressor of Israel and Judah (cp. 2 Kings 15:19f., 29; 16:7-19; 17:1-6, 23, 24; 18:13—19:37; 2 Chron. 33:11). Under Ashurbanipal the empire extended eastward to a line running from the southeastern shore of Lake Urmiah southward to the northeastern coast of the Persian Gulf, along its northern coast, then southward along its western coast into the Arabian Desert, across it westward to Egypt, northward to Cappadocia and along the boundary of Armenia back to Lake Urmiah. Only twenty years before the enthronement of Josiah (641), Ashurbanipal, after a number of disastrous campaigns by his father and himself, had conquered Egypt and sacked Thebes, its southern capital city, 400 miles south of the Mediterranean Sea (663). Proud and cruel Assyria seemed to be the invincible mistress of the world. True, the strenuous campaigns against Egypt had severely strained the resources of Assyria, so that it could not prevent Egypt from regaining its independence, about 660. But when Shamash-shum-ukin, king of Babylon, rebelled against his brother Ashurbanipal, he was defeated by the latter and committed suicide, 648. Now Ashurbanipal assumed the throne of Babylon, and Assyria's world supremacy again seemed to be securely established. Ashurbanipal directed his attention to the internal affairs of his vast empire and to the maintenance of peace and prosperity in his vast domain. Under his guidance, Assyrian art, architecture, literature, and culture reached a point surpassing that of any other Oriental nation. He established a huge library at Nineveh, collecting over 22,000 tablets copied from ancient archives of Babylon and Assyria, returning the originals to their place. This era of the Assyrian Empire has been compared not improperly to the Augustan period of the Roman Empire. Yet only fifteen years after Josiah's enthronement and only two years after the beginning of his reform (628) Ashurbanipal died. Now Babylon, under the rule of a Chaldean, Nabopolassar, a descendant of Merodach Baladan, gained its independence from Assyria, 625. Thirteen years later the Chaldeans, aided by the Medes, had destroyed Nineveh, 612, literally wiped it off the face of the earth (see pp. 4, 5). When

Pharaoh Necho of Egypt made his ill-fated campaign against the new aspirant for world power, Necho was disastrously defeated at Carchemish, 605. (Cp. Jer. 46: 2-26; 2 Kings 24: 7.) What had seemed unbelievable had become an incontrovertible fact. A Chaldean was the world ruler, and his son, the Chaldean Nebuchadnezzar, became God's instrument to punish wicked Judah and Jerusalem (Dan. 1: 1 ff.; 2 Kings 24—25; Jer. 27—29; 36—44; 52). God's word never fails. (Cp. Hab. 2: 3.)

The subscription, ch. 3: 19 b, points to a time when the Levitical Temple service as instituted by the Lord and regulated by David (1 Chron. 23:2 ff.) was being observed. This time might be, as a number of scholars have held, the period after Manasseh's repentance and restoration of the divine worship (2 Chron. 33: 10-17) or preferably the early years of Josiah's rule and reformation. We do not know at which time during the 55 years of Manasseh's rule he was imprisoned nor when he was released. Even if his release had taken place only ten years before his death (643), a period of almost 50 years would have elapsed before the Chaldean began to harass Judah (Hab. 1: 6 a; Dan. 1: 1 ff.). This would hardly suit the expression "in your days" (Hab. 1: 5), since in 606/5 only a comparatively small number of people living in 653 would have remained. Moreover, we know very little about the period of Manasseh's reform, 653—643, and the prevailing social and religious conditions, except the brief notice in 2 Chron. 33: 17. It would then be far more suitable to date Habakkuk's activity in the early years of Josiah's rule and reform 641—628. Jeremiah was called into office one year after Josiah's reform began (cp. Jer. 1: 2; 2 Chron. 34: 3 b). In his early prophecies (chs. 1—6) he denounces in the most scathing terms the violent reaction to Josiah's reform. Habakkuk was face to face with the same situation, denounces the same evidences of national depravity, and predicts the same divine judgments in terms just as severe, and in language often almost identical with that of Jeremiah. (Compare Hab. 1: 2 f. and Jer. 6: 7 f.; 5: 26-31; Hab. 1: 6 and Jer. 5: 15, "I will raise up" — "bring"; Hab. 1: 6, "bitter, hasty," and Jer. 6: 23, "cruel, no mercy"; Hab. 1: 8 and Jer. 4: 13; 5: 6.) Both prophets were so deeply disturbed by the Lord's seeming apathy that they were harassed by grave doubts concerning His justice and righteousness in His government of the world. (Cp. Hab. 1: 2, 12; 2: 1, 18, 19 and Jer. 12: 1 ff.; 15: 10-21; 20: 7-18.) The social and religious conditions as described by Habakkuk demand the dating of his activity in the early years of Josiah.

HABAKKUK

3. Language and Style

"His language," says Delitzsch, "is classical throughout, replete with rare words and idiomatic phrases peculiar to him. His manner of presentation bears the impress of independent power and consummate beauty. That his thoughts rush swiftly onward and soar to the greatest heights, does not, however, interfere with the clarity of organization and the artistic form of the entire book. Like Isaiah, Habakkuk is comparatively much more independent of the former prophets. His book reflects the era of greatest prophetic glory. While the religious life of the Church had hitherto expressed itself in sacred song and lyrics, there now arose in its place by an even mightier divine interposition, poetic prophecy. Its mighty voice served to reawaken in the Church, at the point of spiritual death, the consciousness of God, which had almost completely disappeared." (Delitzsch, *Der Prophet Habakkuk ausgelegt,* 1843.)

Another authority says: "Chapter 3 consists of a lyrical ode, which, for sublimity of poetic conception and splendor of diction ranks with the finest (Ex. 15; Judg. 5) which Hebrew poetry has produced" (Driver, *Introduction,* 1912, p. 339).

4. Literary Form

The literary form of the book is unique. It is not merely the record of a divine message, but that of a dialog between the prophet and his God, who finally appears in a marvelous theophany, ch. 3, described by the prophet in the form of a prayer in which he pleads for speedy fulfillment of the divinely promised deliverance (vv. 3-15) and expresses his joy in the God of his salvation (vv. 16-19). This is not merely a dramatic construction, the artistically executed plan of a skillful writer, but the natural result of the manner in which God dealt with His prophet. The book was intended as an urgent call to repentance for the wicked, as a message of consolation for the little flock of believers, and as an admonition for the latter to continue steadfast in their trust and confidence in the promised salvation and Savior.

The Unsearchable Ways and Judgments of God in Carrying Out His Plan of Salvation

PART I

Habakkuk's First Complaint and God's Answer

CHAPTER 1:1-11

A. Habakkuk's Complaint, Vv. 1-4

1 The oracle which Habakkuk the
2 prophet saw. How long, O LORD, must I cry for help, and Thou wilt not hear? I cry unto Thee, Vio-
3 lence! yet Thou wilt not save! Why dost Thou make me look upon iniquity, while Thou calmly viewest oppression? And affliction and tyranny confronts me! There is strife,
4 and discord arises! Therefore the Law is crippled, and judgment never goes forth; for the wicked hem in the righteous; therefore judgment goes forth perverted.

Grammatical Notes

V. 3. "Why dost Thou show me?" הַבִּיט is never used in a causative sense, "to show." It always means "to behold," to look attentively (Is. 18:4; 63:5; 64:8), with satisfaction, complacency, joy (Ps. 92:12, A. V., 11; Amos 5:22; Lam. 4:16).

V. 1. On "burden" see Gr. N. on Nah. 1:1, pp. 293 f. On Habakkuk, his personality, time, style, etc., see pp. 313—317.

Vv. 2-4. Habakkuk lived at a time when "violence," oppression, and "iniquity" (a term comprehending falsehood, vanity, idolatry, injustice) prevailed, and "grievance," mischief, oppression, and "spoiling," theft, robbery, and "strife," every form of quarreling, with the members of the family or with the neighbors, legal and illegal lawsuits, and "contention," disputes, wrangling, were rampant throughout Judah. Under such conditions it was natural that the Law was "slacked" (v. 4), paralyzed, a dead letter. God's own Law, the constitution of the nation, the heart and soul of Judah's political, religious, and social life; God's Law, the neglect of which would inevitably bring on the ruination of God's land and people (Deut. 28:15 ff.), this Law was crippled so that "judgment doth never go forth," literally: there is forever a nonissuance of judgment, a failure to carry out justice and equity. The few righteous people remaining in the land were surrounded, hedged in, restrained by the wicked so completely as to nullify all their efforts to re-establish the authority of God's Law. Therefore "judgment," judicial decisions, went forth perverted, in

318

utter disregard of the justice or injustice of the cause, the judges invariably favoring the "right people," their own cliques (v. 4).

For a long time (v. 2) Habakkuk had cried to God, "Violence! Oppression!" Yet the Lord, who had chosen Canaan as His land and Judah as His people, had not "saved," had sent no relief to His oppressed children. He had continued to "show," to make the prophet see, iniquity without seemingly moving as much as a finger to punish the evildoers and deliver His oppressed people. On the contrary, the Lord had "caused him to behold" (Gr. N.), literally, had looked complacently, with seeming satisfaction, on the "grievance," mischief, and upon the people perpetrating such atrocious crimes (v. 3). Had God forgotten that in His land His glory was to dwell, mercy and truth were to meet together (Ps. 85:9-13)? Had He lost His power to establish law and order in His land? Why had He not done anything to make it once more a holy land, and Judah a holy people? Why did He not answer the prophet's prolonged cries? Why must the righteous suffer, while the wicked flourish? (Cp. Ps. 73; Jer. 12:1-4; 15:15-18.) Why?

B. God's Answer: The Chaldeans! Vv. 5-11

5 Look round among the nations, and observe, and be astonished, yea, astonished! For one is doing a deed in your days that you would not
6 believe if it were told! For behold, I am going to raise up the Chaldeans, that cruel and impetuous nation, that proceeds through the breadth of the earth to take possession of dwelling places not his
7 own. Terrible and dreadful is he! From himself proceeds his judg-
8 ment and authority. Swifter than leopards are his horses, and shrewder than the wolves of the evening. His horsemen prance proudly, and his horsemen come from afar. They fly like the vulture
9 that hastens to devour. Everyone comes for oppression. Eagerly their faces are turned forward; and he
10 gathers captives like sand. He scoffs at kings, and princes are a mockery to him; he laughs at every fortress and heaps up dust and cap-
11 tures it. Then he rushes onward — the windstorm! — and passes on, and becomes guilty; this his strength is his god.

Grammatical Notes

V. 5. "I will work a work," פֹּעַל פֹּעֵל, literally, one is working a work. (G.-K. 144 f.) The term פֹּעַל is not restricted to human "works," but is used just as frequently of God's miraculous deeds. (Cp. Deut. 32:4; Ps. 64:10, A. V., 9; 77:13; 90:16; 111:3; Is. 5:12, etc.) Purposely the speaker does not at once reveal the author of the work, but keeps the hearers momentarily in suspense. V. 6 reveals the author as well as the exact nature of the work.

V. 9. "Sup up." The Hebrew term is of doubtful meaning. Symmachus renders it "appearance," so also the Syriac translation; LXX, ἀνθεστηκότας, opponents. The ancient rabbis connected it with a root = "to swallow, sip, gulp"; cp. Gen. 24:17, "Let me drink," denoting Eliezer's eagerness to quench his thirst. In Job 39:24 the verb is used of the horse "that swalloweth the ground with fierceness and rage," eagerly rushing forward to meet the enemy, "swallowing up" the distance separating it from the hostile forces. This sense suits the context also. See p. 322.

V. 5. The Lord had not answered the former complaints of the prophet. When He does speak to Habakkuk, He does not answer the prophet's "Why?" Nor does He tell him the reason for delaying His answer so long. The Lord is the sovereign I AM THAT I AM. He owes no apology and no explanation of the whys and wherefores of His ways and actions to anyone. He always remains the Lord of unwavering justice and unchanging grace, even though we cannot understand His dealings with mankind. The Lord addresses His answer to Habakkuk, who as God's spokesman is to transmit it to God's people. Hence He uses the plural predicates. They are to behold and "regard," observe closely, the events occurring among the nations of the world, for He is about to "work a work" (Gr. N.) manifesting His glory in governing the lives of nations. They are to "wonder marvelously," literally, be shocked, shudder, for the work to be done would be so horrifying that the very telling of it would seem incredible. "I will work" (Gr. N.), literally, one will work, the person performing the work being unnamed. This work will be wrought "in your days," in the lifetime of the present generation, any time between the first and thirtieth year following. The Lord does not state a definite date, although He knows the exact time. His purpose is to rouse them to immediate repentance, so that they might be saved, as Jerusalem had been delivered in the time of Hezekiah in answer to his humble, penitent, trusting prayer of faith (2 Kings 18 and 19).

Vv. 6, 7. The terrifying, almost incredible work is now described in detail. The Lord is about to raise up the Chaldeans, whose capital city, Babylon, was already mentioned by Isaiah as the city of Judah's captivity (Is. 39:6 ff.). The Chaldeans, "an ancient nation" (Jer. 5:15), were a Semitic people appearing in history about 1000 B. C., when they invaded the marshlands of southern Babylon, subduing the Babylonians. Under the leadership of the Chaldean Merodach Baladan (cp. Is. 39:6 ff.) the two united nations temporarily regained their independence from Assyrian rule, ca. 721—710 B. C. A century later, Nabopolassar, a descendant of Merodach Baladan, established himself as king of Babylon and founded the Chaldean or Neo-Babylonian Empire (626—539).

As in the year of Jeremiah's call (628) the Lord told the young prophet: Behold, I am about to call all kingdoms of the north against Jerusalem (Jer. 1:15), so here the Lord informs Habakkuk that He is at that very moment raising up, placing into power, the Chaldeans as His instrument in carrying out that incredible work announced in v. 5. His characterization of this nation was horrifying enough to strike fear and terror into the heart of the prophet and the Jews, to make their very blood run cold.

"Bitter," fierce, pitilessly cruel, bitter as poison; "hasty," literally, hurrying themselves onward, impetuously rushing on, never resting until their goal was reached. The rapidity with which the Chaldean or Neo-Babylonian Empire became the ruling world power is almost ınbelievable. Nabopolassar's revolt against Assyria (626) was crowned with success. Only thirteen years later (612) proud Nineveh lay at his feet a heap of ruins (see Nahum). Seven years later, Egypt, the only remaining rival for world supremacy, was disastrously defeated by Nebuchadnezzar, the crown prince, who pursued Necho and his army as far as Egypt (605). (See Jer. 46: 2-26.) Jerusalem was destroyed in 586, Egypt overrun and humbled in 568. Proud Nebuchadnezzar could boastfully yet truthfully write in one of his inscriptions: "In exalted trust in him [Marduk] distant countries, remote mountains from the upper sea [Mediterranean] to the lower sea [Persian Gulf], steep paths, blockaded roads, where the step is impeded, [where] was no footing, difficult roads, desert paths, I traversed, and the disobedient I destroyed. I captured the enemies, established justice in the lands [cp. Hab. 1:7]; the people I exalted; the bad and evil I separated from the people." (See Barton, *Archaeology*, p. 477.) In their insatiable hunger for world power, the Chaldeans were not satisfied with acquiring unoccupied areas; they marched through the length and breadth of the land, lusting particularly for the conquest of countries inhabited by other nations. Why? They are "terrible" (v. 7), their very nature impels them to strike fear and terror into the hearts of others; "dreadful," literally, to be feared, demanding reverence and humble abject subjection. "Their judgment," etc. Their greatest ambition is to impose upon others their own "judgment," their presumptuous claim to demand obedience to their laws and to call to account all that dared to deny this right. His "dignity" = his self-assumed superiority. Both their judgment and their dignity "proceeded of themselves," originated only in their own arrogance. As if to the manner born, they claimed and exacted acknowledgment of their high estate, slavish obedience from all other nations. There were once more "giants in the earth," as in the days before the Deluge (Gen. 6:4). "This brings to our mind Nietzsche's *Uebermensch,* G. B. Shaw's *Superman,* Goethe's *Prometheus,* W. W. Henley's *Invictus,* and other examples." (L. Fuerbringer, *The Eternal Why,* p. 20.)

V. 8 pictures the Chaldean cavalry swiftly overrunning a country, looting, raping, killing, spreading fear, horror, panic throughout the nation, foreboding worse things to come when the main army would roll like a death-dealing machine over the luckless people. "Swifter than leopards," exceeding in agility, mobility, cruelty, the ferocious leopard. "More fierce," literally, sharper, more cunning, keener, "than the evening wolves" (cp. Zeph. 3:3), who, after spending the day in their dens gather at evening for their murderous raids, by their cunning elude the traps and pitfalls set for them. "Horsemen shall spread themselves," literally, jump up (Jer. 50:11). "From afar" they come, from the distant steppes of Asia, pressed into service by the lordly Chaldean. Distance is no obstacle to them. Like the "eagle," or vulture, that sees the carrion from incredible distances, so they hasten with unbelievable speed "to eat," to satisfy their lust for slaughter and fill their pockets with gold and plunder. (Cp. Deut. 28:49 ff.; Jer. 4:13, 20-31.)

Vv. 9, 10. Every one of that vast army comes for "violence," for oppression. That is the just punishment of the holy God for the wicked Jews, whose delight it was to oppress their brethren. (Cp. vv. 2 ff. and Ex. 21:24 f.; Lev. 24:19 f.; Deut. 19:21.) "Sup up" (Gr. N.), the faces of the Chaldean forces are eagerly set on what is before them, burning with eager desire to rush onward to ever new conquests, gathering captives like sand, innumerable. (Cp. Gen. 22:17; 41:49.) Kings, however mighty, are scoffed at (v. 10); princes, no matter how many, are objects of ridicule. Do strongholds bar their way? They heap up dust, earth, rubbish into embankments (cp. Ezek. 26:7-14) from which cities are attacked and swiftly taken.

V. 11. "Then shall his mind change," rather, then, after having captured the stronghold, he rushes on—a windstorm—and passes on. Puffed up by his success, he "offends," becomes guilty of self-deification. His strength (the Hebrew term denotes inherent strength, physical and mental ability, power) is his god.

This characterization of the Chaldeans (vv. 6-11) does not prove that Judah must have been harassed by the Chaldeans for some time and have known its cruel oppressors by personal experience, since the prophet could not have included in his characterization certain traits which came into evidence only after they had attained world sovereignty. Nor does it prove that Habakkuk wrote only after the fall of Nineveh, perhaps under Jehoiakim's rule. No, here is the prophetic characterization by the eternal and omniscient Jehovah (Acts 15:18; cp. Deut. 28:49 ff.; Is. 39:6 f.; 44:24—45:7; Jer. 1:11-17, etc.). What Habakkuk knew of the Chaldeans by divine revelation (ch. 1:5-11), together with his knowledge of their constant revolts against Assyria and their endeavor to draw Judah into an alliance in Hezekiah's day (Is. 39:1-6), fully justified his fears and doubts expressed in vv. 12-17. There is no need, therefore, of rearranging this chapter, as, e. g., Geo. A. Smith does in *The Expositor's Bible,* 1:1-4; 1:12—2:4; 1:5-11; 2:5-20. Nor is there any justification for Sellin's charge that Habakkuk had no deep insight into Judah's sinfulness (see pp. 318 f.).

PART II

Habakkuk's Second Complaint and God's Answer

CHAPTER 1:12—2:20

A. The Prophet's Complaint, Ch. 1:12-17

12 Art Thou not from everlasting, O LORD, my God, my Holy One? We shall not die?! O LORD, for judgment hast Thou appointed him? And, O God, for correction 13 hast Thou established him? Thou art purer of eyes than to look with pleasure upon wickedness, and Thou canst not look with favor upon affliction! Why dost Thou look with favor upon treacherous men, art silent while the wicked swallows him that is more righteous 14 than he? Thou makest men like fish of the sea, like creeping things that have no ruler over them. 15 He lifts them all with the hook and drags them away in his net and gathers them in his seine. Therefore he rejoices and shouts for joy. 16 Therefore he sacrifices to his net and gives offerings to his seine, because by them his portion is fat and his food luscious. Shall he 17 therefore empty his net and forever murder nations unsparingly?

Grammatical Notes

V. 12. "We shall not die." Luther: "We may regard this sentence as a question. Is it not true, Lord, that Thou art my God of old, my Holy One, so that we shall not die, but that Thou wilt use him to punish and correct us? He speaks to God in the form of questions." (St. L. XIV, 1446, par. 60.) Sellin also translates v. 12 in the form of two questions. The context presents the prophet as being harassed by grave doubts, as violently disturbed, stricken to the very

323

core by the unexpected turn of events (see notes on vv. 12-17). And from a heart torn by dreadful fears comes the anguished cry, We shall not die!?

V. 13. "Behold," רָאָה here = to view with pleasure, approbation. (Cp. 1 Sam. 6:19; Obad. 12; Prov. 23:31; Is. 53:2.)

V. 12. God's revelation of His judgment impending upon Judah came as a heart-rending blow to the prophet. The announcement that this fierce, beastly cruel nation was to be God's instrument in punishing wicked Judah seemed to sound the death knell for the nation and therefore the renunciation of His covenant relation not only with Judah but also with mankind. God's covenant with Israel was based on His covenant with the patriarchs (Ex. 3:6-17; 6:3; Deut. 9:5), which culminated in the promise that in Abraham's Seed all the nations of the world should be blessed (Gen. 12:3; 18:18; 26:4; 28:14). This latter covenant, in turn, was based on God's promise of the Bruiser of Satan's head (Gen. 3:15). The fulfillment of this promise of a universal Redeemer was later inseparably linked with the tribe of Judah (Gen. 49:10 ff.) and with the house and lineage of David (2 Sam. 7:2 ff.; Matt. 21:9; 22:42; Luke 2:4; John 1:46; 7:41 f.). If Judah or the house of David would become extinct before the fulfillment of this promise, the coming of the Redeemer would be rendered, humanly speaking, impossible. The deportation of the ten tribes (722 B. C.) had been an appalling calamity; but far more catastrophic would be the annihilation of Judah. Yet what God had just announced appeared to the prophet as the Supreme Judge's death sentence upon Judah. In horrified shock he cries out, We shall not die! (Gr. N.) That cannot be, O God! That would contradict Thine own self-revelation, Thy very nature. And at once he begins to "complain" (see ch. 2:1), to argue, remonstrate with the Lord. "Art Thou not from everlasting," the eternal I AM THAT I AM (Ex. 3:14)? Hast Thou, the Unchangeable, changed? O Lord, Jehovah, the Covenant God, shall Thy promise of a Redeemer remain unfulfilled, Thy covenant be broken by Thyself? My God, my strong, omnipotent God, has Thy power to do what Thou hast promised suddenly failed? My Holy One, has Thy hatred of sin and Satan ended? Wilt Thou, canst Thou permit Thine enemies to foil Thine eternal plan of salvation? Wilt Thou, canst Thou, permit Thy people to perish and with them all hope of life and salvation to be annihilated? Shall we as a nation die? Shall with us all mankind hopelessly die eternal death, suffer hopelessly, endlessly, eternal damnation? Surely, "Thou hast ordained them for judgment," placed

324

them, the Chaldeans, as a punishment! We acknowledge that we have deserved that. I even asked Thee to punish the wicked nation (vv. 2-4). "O mighty God," literally, O Rock! (Deut. 32: 4, 15, 18, 30 f.; Ps. 18: 31; Is. 26: 4; 30: 29.) Tossed about by agonizing doubts, the prophet clings with the hands of faith to the firm, immovable Rock of Ages. Face to face with the possibility of the death of his nation, he hopes that the Covenant God in wrath will remember mercy, that His judgment will take on the nature of correction, paternal chastisement for the betterment of His wayward people (Prov. 3: 11 f.; Heb. 12: 5-11). Luther says: "The prophet here describes the state of faith in times of trial and temptation. Then faith seems so weak as if it no longer believed, but were about to sink and doubt because of the great weight oppressing it. For although faith remains firm, it cracks under the severe strain of affliction and temptation and, while in the midst of battle, uses language far different from that employed after it has gained the victory." (St. L., XIV, 1446.)

V. 13. Habakkuk fully realized that a nation fast approaching the wickedness of Sodom and Gomorrah (Is. 1: 9 f.; Hab. 1: 2-4) deserved God's punishment and was sorely in need of His correction. Yet the means employed by the Lord for such punishment presents another problem which he cannot solve. On the one side, there is God, the Holy, Immaculate One. His eyes are too pure complacently to behold (Gr. N.) evil, wickedness. Nor can He regard with satisfaction "iniquity," literally, trouble or burdens inflicted on others. On the other side, there is the Chaldean, "dealing treacherously," characteristically perfidious, unfaithful to God and man. His greatest delight is to oppress people, inflict hardships upon them, make life a burden to them. How can God regard this treacherous people with such satisfaction as to employ it as the instrument of His holy wrath? How can He look on silently, approvingly, while a wicked nation unmercifully devours, swallows such as are more righteous than itself? The prophet, of course, does not think here merely of civic righteousness. He uses the term in the same sense as does the Lord God in ch. 2: 4. He thinks here of the small remnant of such as are righteous by faith in the promised Redeemer. Yet they must suffer together with the mass of unbelieving Jews, and in like manner, the inhuman cruelties of the Chaldeans. Why does God permit, and even decree, such a judgment? How does this agree with His holiness and justice?

V. 14. Still another problem worries the prophet. Why does God make men (Gr. N.), mankind in general, Gentiles as well as Jews, as the fishes of the sea and the "creeping things," the many forms of animal life with which the sea teems (cp. Gen. 1:21; Ps. 104:25)? "No ruler." "These creatures," says Luther, "have no government or direction to defend themselves against anyone. Whosoever will, catches and takes them. Man catches and devours them, large fish and otters devour them, eagles devour them, beavers and other animals devour them. They are only food for others, for man and birds and beasts need fishes. In like manner Thou hast given all countries and peoples to the Chaldeans, that they may catch, devour, glut, and gorge. Is it not vexatious that for such wicked, ungodly people all good people are only like fish for their kitchens, whom they may catch and kill and devour as they please?" (St. L., XIV, 1451.) Is that right, O God? Why hast Thou made all the nations leaderless, defenseless, helpless, against so wicked an enemy? Why?

Vv. 15, 16. "Angle," "net," the smaller net, cast by hand; "drag," the larger net, seine, weighted to sink to the bottom and dragged to the boat or the shore. Here the three are symbols of the Chaldeans' war machinery, including every means or device for defeating, capturing, deporting, killing, destroying the people. "All the major Babylonian deities, Ningirsu, Shamash, Enlil, Marduk, etc., are pictured holding or dragging a net in which the captured enemies squirm, the ancient symbol of the world sovereign." Cp. Prinz, *Altorientalische Symbolik,* p. 135, and Sellin on Hab. 1:16. The greater the destruction of men and women and children and property, the greater was their joy, the louder sounded their triumphant paeans. Instead of turning to the true God in gratitude for the victories He alone could grant, they "sacrificed unto their net" (v. 16), they attribute their success to their war machinery, their military prowess, their leadership, their bravery. They continue their depredations, because by them their portion becomes fat, prosperity increases, and everyone has enough to eat. The full dinner pail was and remains one of the chief purposes of warfare.

V. 17. Shall they "therefore" — because they are idolatrous, treacherous, cruel wolves and leopards — shall they keep on emptying their net after having made another rich catch, keep on amassing riches, works of art, silver and gold, power, glory? Shall they never spare, but go on unmercifully and continually to slay entire nations? Shall they succeed in slaying Judah? Shall we also die, die at the hands of such wicked people, die before Thou hast fulfilled Thy promise? Hast Thou hopelessly condemned Thy people to everlasting death, and must with them all the nations perish in their sins? Else, wherefore hast Thou surrendered us to so wicked, bloodthirsty, murderous a nation? Why?

CHAPTER 2

B. The Prophet Waiting for God's Answer Is Granted a Marvelous Vision

1. The prophet's anxious watch, v. 1

1 Upon my watch will I stand, and I will station myself on a stronghold, so that I may be on the lookout to see what He will say to me and what I shall respond to my complaint.

Grammatical Notes

V. 1. "I will stand," "will set me," will place myself. The cohortatives "graphically depict the eagerness of the watchman preparing for his post" (Driver, *Hebrew Tenses*, par. 54). — "Watchtower." מִשְׁמֶרֶת never is used in this sense. It denotes (a) the act of watching or observing, guarding, keeping (Ex. 12:6; 16:32 ff.; 1 Sam. 22:23; Num. 1:53; 3:28), observing God's Word (Joshua 22:3); (b) that which is to be observed, watched, kept (Lev. 8:35; Deut. 11:1; Zech. 3:7; Mal. 3:14), a charge; (c) the person watching, a watchman (Neh. 7:3; 1 Chron. 9:23). In every instance the word stresses the idea of watching, irrespective of the place which may, or may not, be stated in the context. — "The tower," מָצוֹר, from צוּר, to enfold, bind up, for the purpose of safekeeping (Deut. 14:25; 2 Kings 5:23; 12:11); in hostile sense, to hem in, besiege (Deut. 20:12; 1 Kings 15:27; 16:17; 20:1). The noun is used in both senses; hostile, e. g., Deut. 20:19 f.; 28:53, 55, 57; protective, a wall "enfolding" a city; a fortification, a stronghold. So 2 Chron. 8:5, where "fenced" cities are defined; 2 Chron. 11:5; Ps. 31:22 (21). Hence neither "watch" nor "tower" warrants the assumption that Habakkuk was a "visionary" who had to go to some solitary height in order to induce visions. — "When I am reproved." תוֹכַחְתִּי is a noun with suffix = my reproof; how I shall answer my reproof, my charge against God.

V. 1. Far from solving Habakkuk's problem, the Lord's revelation of His impending judgment upon Judah had raised only new questions, new doubts, new fears. Yet he did not permit his perplexity to turn him away in unbelief from the Lord, even though His ways and judgments were incomprehensible to him and seemed to be in conflict with God's revelation of Himself. The very fact that the High and Lofty One (Is. 57:15) had graciously condescended to speak to him, a sinner, encouraged him to approach this Lord for the third time in the hope that he will finally receive a satisfying answer. He does not insist on an immediate answer. Patiently he will stand (Gr. N.) upon his watch (Gr. N.), waiting till God's time to answer him has arrived. Nor does he prescribe the manner of God's response. He will set himself "upon the tower" (Gr. N.), literally, something strong, firm, reliable. Solomon had compared the name of the Lord, His revelation of Himself, particularly in Holy Scripture, to a strong tower, running into which the righteous man is safe (Prov. 18:10; cp. also Ps. 73:16f.). Habakkuk himself cannot answer the questions his reason raises. He has tried until he is at his wit's end. Now he will quietly wait to see what God will say unto him either by direct revelation or through His holy Word, God's ordinary way to reveal Himself to man. That the prophets searched the Scriptures to find an answer to their problems is proved by the many quotations from, and allusions to, the earlier writings by the later prophets. (Cp. also Dan. 9:2, 11, 13; 1 Peter 1:10-12.)

The prophet's desire for further information sprang not from idle curiosity nor from a vain endeavor to pry into the secret counsels of God. He rather hoped to receive some instruction or revelation from the Lord, telling him "what I shall answer when I am reproved" (Gr. N.), rather, what I shall say in response to my reproof. He used a rather strong term for his complaint. Like Abraham (Gen. 18:23-32), Moses (Ex. 32:11—33:17; Num. 14:11-19), and, later, Jeremiah (Jer. 12:1 ff.; 14:11-22; 15:10-21; 20:7-18), Habakkuk had dared to contend, to argue, to remonstrate with God. God's answer had not silenced his doubts, had not answered his "Why?" How could he boldly and confidently preach to his people if he himself was doubtful, unsettled, perplexed? If he could find no answer to his own complaint, how could he hope to answer the same or similar charges raised by the people? Before the preacher can properly teach, he must be sure of his ground (Titus 1:9-13; 1 Peter 3:15 b).

---

2. God's answer, vv. 2-20

a. Divine prophecy will be fulfilled in its divinely appointed time, vv. 2, 3

2 Then the LORD answered me and said: Write a vision, and inscribe it clearly upon tablets, so that anyone reading it may be on the run.
3 Surely, vision is still for the appointed time. And it gasps for the end and will not lie. If it tarries, wait for it. For it will surely come; it will not delay.

Grammatical Notes

V. 2. "Write the vision." The article is not placed in the Hebrew text, though in this context it is used a number of times where it could have been omitted: the tablets; the appointed time (v. 2), the end (v. 3), the wine (v. 5). Evidently the article is omitted intentionally, to stress the qualitative force of the term, vision as vision, vision in general. — "Make it plain." בָּאֵר occurs only here and Deut. 1:5; 27:8. It means to make clear, either by explaining the full content of a message (so Deut. 1:5) or by writing the message in large, clear letters, readily legible (so here and Deut. 27:8; cp. Joshua 8:31 ff.). The underlying idea is not that of permanence, but of clarity. It is not a synonym of engrave, although the letters may be engraved. — "Tables." Here M. T. has the article, called by Koenig (on Deut. 1:5) the article of necessary, obligatory appurtenance. It does not necessarily point to tablets already erected for public announcements. — "He may run." יָרוּץ is the predicate, the imperfect describing the action in movement, in progress. "That readeth it," participle, one reading it, its reader, may be in process of running, may be "on the run" (as J. M. Powis Smith translates in *The Complete Bible*), while he reads.

V. 3. "For the vision." Again the article is omitted, hence, vision in general, prophecy (see Gr. N. on v. 2, "Write the vision"). This statement is quite generally regarded as a causal sentence stating the reason why the vision was to be written: it was to be preserved until the day of its fulfillment and by its fulfillment strengthen the faith of the people. Yet it is extremely improbable that the tablets were still standing at the time of Christ's coming. Nor did its preservation demand its writing in clear, large letters. Innumerable cuneiform tablets are still extant and can be read, though written in very small characters. Moreover, if "vision" was to refer to the special vision spoken to Habakkuk at this time, then the article or a demonstrative pronoun would have had to be added in v. 3. Compare Dan. 8:1, where A. V. correctly translates "a vision," while v. 2, "a vision," A. V., has the article in the original; so vv. 13, 15, 16, 17, 26 (twice), 27, all referring to the vision first mentioned in v. 1. Hence, Hab. 2:3 the anarthrous חָזוֹן is to be taken in the general sense, vision as vision, prophecy. This also is in keeping with the subsequent context. — "For." כִּי frequently is not the causative conjunction, but an affirmative interjection. (Cp. Gen. 31:42; 43:10; Lam. 5:22 with אִמְנָם, Ruth 3:12; Job 12:2; 36:4. See also G.-K. 148 d.) — "It shall speak," יָפֵחַ, Hiphil of פּוּחַ, the Qal occurring only Cant. 2:17; 4:6, the shadows flee away, literally, the day blows, of the evening wind; Hiphil, to cause to blow; it is used of blowing or spreading scandals (Prov. 6:19; 12:17, etc.); of kindling revolt (Prov. 29:8). Ps. 10:5, "he puffeth at them"; Ps. 12:6 (5), "puffeth at him." The latter passage is translated by Koenig: "I shall grant salvation to him who pants for it," *keuchend strebt* (cp. Ezek. 21:36, A. V., 31, "I will blow against thee in the fire of My wrath"). To blow hard, pant, suits our passage best. . . . "Tarry." The first "tarry," from מָהַהּ, to hold back, occurs only in Hithpael, to cause oneself to hold back, to tarry, delay; the second "tarry," אָחַר, to be late; often the consequence of tarrying, loitering.

V. 2. In answer to Habakkuk's prayer the Lord speaks to him. Habakkuk had voiced his "complaint," his own views. Now he is told to write something not originating in himself, but coming from without; not from any human source, but from the Lord Himself in the form of a divine vision. On "vision" see Obad. 1:1, pp. 193 f. It denotes

329

a divine communication by means of the eye, or ear, or both (Is. 1:1; 6:1 ff.; Dan. 8; Zech. 1—7). The vision was granted not only for the prophet's own information and comfort. He also was to write it that others might read it. And he was to "make it plain" (Gr. N.), write it in large, clear letters, so that even "he that runs" (Gr. N.) could read it. It was to be written, or engraved, in "the tablets" (Gr. N.), either large stone slabs or tiles (cp. Job 19:24; Jer. 17:1). These tablets were to be erected in public places, on highways, perhaps in the Temple courts; wherever they would attract the attention of the people hurrying, rushing, on their way to work, or business, or worship, or play, or sin. Many a person might read what was so conspicuously displayed, and remember and ponder the message and derive everlasting benefit. On the erection of such tablets see Is. 8:1; Jer. 17:1; 1 Macc. 14:25-49 (a lengthy inscription, vv. 27-49, inscribed on brass tablets erected on Mount Zion). Just how long the inscription to be written by Habakkuk was is hard to tell. Since it could be read by people hurrying past, it may have included only vv. 3-5.

V. 3. "For the vision." (Gr. N.) Habakkuk lived in the Old Testament, which was the era of vision, prophecy, to be fulfilled in the New Testament. (Cp. Mark 1:15; Gal. 4:4; Col. 2:17; Heb. 8:5; 9:9, 23; 10:1.) This era of visions had its "appointed," divinely determined, time. God could have fulfilled immediately His Eden promise of sending the Redeemer. Eve and Lamech had hoped He would (Gen. 4:1; 5:29). Yet it had pleased the I AM THAT I AM to choose together with the person of the Redeemer also the time of His appearance. The long interval between the first promise and its final fulfillment was to serve the purpose of keeping His people watchful, hopeful, ever alert for the advent of the Woman's Seed. At Habakkuk's time the believers had waited, hoped, prayed for more than thirty-three centuries, and God tells the prophet, "Vision is yet for an appointed time." Not because God had forgotten His promise or was no longer willing or able to fulfill it. He was still Jehovah, the eternal, almighty God. Only His appointed time had not yet arrived. "But at the end it shall speak!" The Hebrew is still more forceful and impressive: "It gasps toward the end" (Gr. N.). Not only the prophet and God's people were anxiously waiting for the "end," for the fulfillment of prophecy. In a bold but very effective personification, the prophet, or rather God speaking to His prophet, has also vision joining the believers in their eagerness to hasten the fulfillment. It gasps, pants. As the runner, seeing the goal coming nearer, strains every muscle, runs the faster, until his breath comes in loud gasps, so vision sees fulfillment coming ever closer; and as the distance decreases, so its eagerness to arrive at the goal increases. It will not lie, will not deceive the eager expectation of God's children. To the waiting believers vision seems to "tarry" (Gr. N.). How long have they waited! Will fulfillment never come (Ps. 14:7)? Fear not! says God. Though you are worried by anxious thoughts, by doubts and fears, wait for it! Hope on! Only believe! It will surely come, literally, it is coming, a-coming! It will not tarry (Gr. N.). It will not be too late, not a year, not a minute later than the appointed time. The Chaldean may conquer and deport you, but he cannot stop, not even delay, the coming of the Redeemer and your salvation. This is God's answer to the prophet's anguished cry, We shall not die?! (Ch. 1:12.) The answer is a divine, emphatic No! The death of Judah as a nation would involve the nonfulfillment of vision, of God's promise concerning the Redeemer coming out of Judah and the house of David. This vision cannot fail! It will surely come at its appointed time, and the nation will not and cannot die before the advent of Him of whom the vision spoke and who is the sole Author of man's salvation and the only Foundation of the believer's faith (Luke 24:26 f., 44 ff.; Acts 4:10 ff.; 10:43).

---

b. *The proud and wicked Chaldean will perish, while the just shall live by his faith, vv. 4, 5*

4 Behold, puffed up, not upright, is his soul in him; but the righteous,
5 by his faith shall he live. Moreover, wine is a deceiver. An arrogant man is he. He never dwells quietly, he who enlarges his desire as the grave and who, like death, is never satisfied, but gathers to himself all nations and assembles to himself all peoples.

Grammatical Notes

V. 4. "Lifted up," third person fem. Pual of a stem denoting to bulge, puff up, as a boil (cp. Deut. 28:27, "emerods," hemorrhoids, piles; 1 Sam. 5:6, 9, 12, a hill; Is. 32:14; Micah 4:8, Ophel); here, to be puffed up, bloated, with pride and arrogance.

V. 5. "Yea, also," יִ אַף. This phrase is most frequently used to introduce a climax, advancing from the lesser to the greater, "how much more," or an anti-climax, "how much less." Yet in all these instances both the principal and the final clause have verbal predicates, or the verb is easily supplied in the final from the principal cause. That is not the case here. Therefore Sellin finds it necessary to change the text to read, "Behold, 'the puffed up'! His soul shall not 'dwell' in him, while the righteous man through his faithfulness remains alive. How much more shall the deceiving 'evildoer,' the arrogant man, not 'be built' (succeed)." J. M. Powis Smith in *The Complete Bible*: "How much less shall the faithless man live?" — There is no need to change the text. אַף כִּי, literally translated = also—

that, indeed — that, so in the question: Is it indeed that God has said? Has God really said? (Gen. 3:1.) It is used in the sense of moreover, in addition. (1 Sam. 14:30; 2 Kings 8:27; Neh. 9:18; Ezek. 23:40.) The Lord adds other traits to the characterization of the wicked

Chaldean — "Man," גֶּבֶר. The root idea is that of strength, a he-man. — "Keepeth at home," יִנְוֶה. The verb occurs only here, evidently from the same root as נָוֶה, habitation, used of the fold of the sheep, where they were safe and satisfied.

V. 4. Another question agitating the prophet concerned God's government of the Church and of the world at large (ch. 1:13-17). The Lord answers this question also, but again in His own manner without stating His reason (ch. 1:5). He comforts (cp. 2 Cor. 1:3 f.) His prophet by calling to his attention certain truths well known to the prophet and asking him to draw his own conclusions. He places the Chaldean side by side with the just. On the one side is the Chaldean. Consider him! His "soul," the seat of his life, particularly of his emotions, is "lifted up" (Gr. N.), puffed up, swollen with pride and self-glorification. See ch. 1:7 b, 10, 11; "not upright," not straight, but crooked, perverted. The Chaldean is spiritually dead, bearing within himself the germs of temporal and eternal death, individually as well as nationally. (Prov. 4:16 f.; 11:2; 12:8; 16:5, 18; 17:20; 29:22 f.) On the other side are the just; not, of course, Judah as a nation, but the righteous by faith, believing God's vision, God's promise, trusting in the coming Redeemer. They shall live, and live by their faith! The purpose of My punishment is not to slay them, but to correct them, to keep them from becoming proud and perverted. Even if they smart under the scourge, keenly feel the cruelty of the heartless enemy, yet they shall live by virtue of the promised Redeemer, whom they have embraced by faith. Like Lamech, they know Gen. 5:29; like David, Ps. 25; like the sons of Korah, Pss. 42 and 43; like Asaph, Pss. 73 and 77. Even death cannot deprive them of their life and salvation. (Gen. 48:15 f., 21; 49:18; Job 19:25 ff.; Ps. 17:15; 31:5.) Do not ask why I am using the wicked Chaldean to punish My people, righteous through faith. Leave that to Me, the all-wise God, who rules every detail of your entire life for your temporal and eternal welfare. Remain faithful, trust Me, and you shall live!

V. 5. "Yea, also" (Gr. N.), moreover. V. 5 adds more details to the characterization of the Chaldean. "Because he transgressed by wine," literally: Wine is a deceiver. (Cp. Prov. 20:1; 23:30-35; Hos. 4:11; Is. 28:7 f.) It robs man of the proper use of his physical and mental faculties. Alexander, the world conqueror, was conquered by wine, cut off in the prime of his life. Excessive love of wine was one of the besetting sins of the Chaldeans and helped to destroy the proud and perverted Chaldean empire (Dan. 5:1-31). — There is another wine, equally destructive, the heady wine of pride, vanity, self-adoration (cp. vv. 4, 15 f., where the Lord compares pride with wine). Wine deceives men; wine makes man boastful; wine makes man restless, dissatisfied with his home; wine enlarges the desire. The winebibber is never satisfied, always thirsty, always calling for more wine till he lies on the floor like a dead man, an object of ridicule and disgust. All this is true of the wine of pride and arrogance. The Lord calls the Chaldean a "proud man." Man here = the strong, powerful man (Gr. N.), as in fact the Chaldean proved himself to be. Yet he did not use his strength properly, as the "proud" indicates. This Hebrew term occurs only once more, Prov. 21:24, where it describes the self-conceited, haughty mocker of God and His Word. It denotes one who acts without mature deliberation, is as precipitate in his actions as he is rash in his judgment, inconsiderate of the feelings of others, irreverent toward all that is sacred to God or man, contemptuous of anything that does not agree with his own will or whim. "Neither keepeth at home" (Gr. N.). He is not satisfied to remain in his homeland, to sit quietly and contentedly under his vine and fig tree. The Chaldeans left their native land, infiltrated into Babylon, finally conquering it; fought for world supremacy with Assyria, destroyed Nineveh in 612 B. C. Their successes served only to increase their thirst for power. "He enlargeth his desire," literally, his soul, "as hell"; his ambition grew wide as hell, Sheol, the grave. "As death, and cannot be satisfied," ever yearning for more possessions, more conquests, more riches and power. "But gathereth unto him all nations," such as are descended from a common ancestor, "and heapeth unto him all people," a commonwealth united by common political principles. Such bloated pride, such almost demonic lust for power will work the Chaldean's ruin. This is brought out in the five woes pronounced by the Lord and put by Him into the mouths of the suppressed nations. As the Chaldean's success was phenomenal almost beyond belief, so his downfall will be almost unparalleled.

---

c. Five woes upon the wicked slayer of nations, vv. 6-19

(1) The first woe: The plundering Chaldean will be plundered, vv. 6-8

6 Shall not all these take up a taunting song against him, and a vexing proverb, riddles, referring to him? And they will say, Woe to him that increases what is not his own! How long? And who loads upon himself 7 a burden of pledges! Will not your creditors rise up suddenly and your

agitators wake up to plunder you?
8 Because you have plundered many
nations, all the remnant of the people shall plunder you, because of
the blood of men shed by you and
the violence committed against the
land, the city, and all that dwelt
therein.

Grammatical Notes

V. 6. "Parable," the Hebrew *mashal*,
literally, a comparison for the purpose
of teaching a lesson, either in a short,
terse form, or in a more or less lengthy
discourse. — "Taunting proverb," a
taunting song in the form of riddles, the
real meaning being skillfully hidden or
at least obscured by using words which
have a twofold sense, the intended
meaning being brought out by emphasizing certain words, or accompanying
the words with a significant look or
gesture, or becoming apparent only
after careful study.

V. 6. "Parable," "taunting proverb" (Gr. N.).

Each woe describes one of the characteristics of the Chaldeans.
These sins are not occasional slips, isolated failings. The prophet uses
the participial form, denoting customs, habits, characteristic traits:
"increasing" (v. 6), "coveting" (v. 9), etc. The Lord presents the
Chaldean as He sees him stripped of his power and glory before men.
(Cp. 1 Sam. 16:7; Is. 59:18.) By foretelling through His prophet the
future history of the Chaldean and revealing his motives, the Lord
proves that He is the Searcher of the hearts (Jer. 17:10; Ps. 139:1 ff.),
the Ruler and Judge of the world (Eccl. 12:14; Is. 59:18). At the same
time this prophecy served to strengthen the faith of the believers.
As they lived to see the fulfillment of this prophecy, so the final
destruction of all enemies of the Church and the promise of Messiah's
eternal salvation shall surely be fulfilled in God's appointed time.
Wait! Hope! Believe!

The first woe refers to the rapacity of the Chaldean, his eagerness
to enrich himself at the expense of others (see 1:6, 9f., 16; 2:5b) by
conquest of their home countries, making vassals of the nations, ex-
torting from them huge contributions of materials, money, and men,
bleeding them white. "Woe to him," so runs the taunting song, "that
increaseth that which is not his!" The last phrase consists of two words
of like sound but different spelling: *lo, lo*, which if spoken may mean
"his, his!" or "not, not!" or "not his." Tauntingly the nations ask,
"How long?" i. e., will he enjoy it? And he is constantly lading himself
with "thick clay," a word composed of two syllables, *ab-teet*, the first
denoting density, a dense mass, a cloud; the second, mud, mire (cp.
Nah. 3:14; Zech. 9:3). The two syllables combined into one word
denote a pledge, or pawn. The heavy pawns, the humiliating pledges
exacted by the Chaldean from his conquered enemies, will change into
a thick, dense mass of mud, of gumbo, from which he cannot extricate

himself. Instead of gaining their lasting love and loyalty by judicious and kind treatment, he by his harsh cruelty, particularly his continuation of the Assyrian custom of deportation, of shifting whole nations like pawns on a chessboard, alienated them and made them willing to join the ranks of any enemy or revolting nation.

Vv. 7, 8. "Shall bite thee," the participle form of a verb used in Deut. 23:21 f. in the sense of lend to, hence, your creditors, while Gen. 49:17 and Prov. 23:32 it means to bite. The nations who were forced to lend him their money, their men, now became hardhearted creditors, biters, exacting their money with interest. "They shall awake that vex thee," rouse themselves from the sleep of fear that held them spellbound, and vex, harass, torment, bite their former oppressors. The Chaldean wealth shall become "booties," spoils of war, for the nations. Because the Chaldean had "spoiled" (v. 8), plundered, many nations, all the "remnant," the surviving members of these people, shall spoil, plunder the riches of the Babylonian enemy. "Suddenly," unexpectedly, the end came less than 25 years after great Nebuchadnezzar's death (562 B. C.), when Cyrus, the Persian ruler, took Babylon and made it a province of his vast kingdom (539 B. C.). Such was God's judgment upon the wicked, treacherous Chaldean for his bloody violence against countries and cities and all their inhabitants. Be not deceived; God is not mocked.

---

(2) The second woe: Ambitious schemes recompensed by shame, vv. 9-11

9 Woe to him who gains unjust profits for his house in order to set his nest on high, to save himself 10 from the grasp of disaster! You have planned disgrace for your house! Cutting off many nations, you have forfeited your own life. 11 For the stone will cry from the wall, and the beam from the woodwork will answer him.

Vv. 9-11. "Coveteth an evil covetousness," literally, "cuts an evil cut"; compare "my 'cut' of the loot." The Yiddish term *schnitt*, "cut," for gain, profit, is an exact rendering of this word. The phrase denotes the love of illegal gain, greedy profiteering (cp. Prov. 1:19; Jer. 6:13; 8:10), which idea is emphasized here by "evil," wicked. The Chaldean's covetousness is directed "to his house," here, as in v. 10 to his family, his dynasty. On this sense cp. 2 Sam. 7:11, 16. His ambition was "to set his nest on high," to make the sovereignty of his house so secure that it would be immune against the "power," literally, the hand, the grip, "of evil," disaster, overthrow. His life's goal was the establishment of an illustrious, lasting dynasty. In one of his building inscriptions Nebuchadnezzar states that one of his chief purposes in strengthening the walls of Babylon and beautifying the city was to make "an everlasting name for his reign." And he prays: "O Marduk, lord of the gods, my divine creator, before thee may my deeds be pious, may they endure forever! Life for many generations, an abundant posterity, a secure throne, and a long reign, grant as thy gift. Truly, thou art my deliverer and help, O Marduk! By thy faithful word that changes not, may my weapons advance, be dreadful and crush the arms of the foe!" (Rogers, *Cuneif. Parallels*, p. 369. Cp. also Dan. 4:10 ff., 20 ff., 29 f.) His high-flying plans were to be rudely shattered. In fact, his ruthless "cutting off many people" (v. 10), his adoption of the Assyrian melting-pot system by deportation of entire nations and settling foreigners in the vacated countries was not wise statesmanship. It was, as the Lord says, "consulting," devising, planning the shame of his house, sinning against his own soul, the seat of life — forfeiting his very life and being. The conquered nations rebelled at every opportunity or joined the enemies of Babylon. The brief glory of Babylon ended in disgrace and shame. Nebuchadnezzar's son, Amel Marduk (Evil-Merodach, 2 Kings 25:27), was assassinated after ruling only two years (562—560), by his brother-in-law Nergal-Shar-Ussur, who ruled four years. His son succeeded him but was murdered nine months later. One of the conspirators was Nabonidus, a son-in-law of Nebuchadnezzar, who appointed his son Belshazzar coregent of Babylon (cp. Dan. 5). The magnificent structure of the Neo-Babylonian Empire, which the Chaldean had built for the house of his kingdom, by the might of his power, for the honor of his majesty (Dan. 4:30), is compared by the Lord to a house struck by a sudden whirlwind and gutted by fire. In the creaking of the beams connecting the "timber," the woodwork of the roof, and in the grating of the cracking stone walls (v. 11), one can hear an awesome dirge, the stones intoning the chant, the beams responding in antiphonal death song, until they also crash down into a heap of ruins and ashes. Babylon, at whose name the world trembled, is marked on the map and the index of the *Encyclopaedia Britannica World Atlas* with the notation, "Babylon, Ruins of." Map 48; Index, p. 210. On the Bagdad Railroad it is a whistle stop for archaeologists. *Sic transit gloria mundi.*

---

(3) The third woe: Sinful building repaid by destruction, vv. 12-14

12 Woe to him that builds a city by bloodshed and establishes a town 13 by perversity! Behold, is this not from the LORD of Hosts that nations tire themselves for fire, and 14 people wear themselves out for naught? For the earth shall be filled with the knowledge of the glory of the LORD as waters cover the sea.

Vv. 12-14. The third woe is directed against the bloodthirsty cruelty of the Chaldean king. His vast building program was carried out at the price of the sweat and blood of the conquered nations. "Buildeth," "stablisheth"; the Hebrew participles here denote the habitual custom to build and stablish, strengthen walls, fortifications, palaces. While Assyrian kings boast chiefly of their military successes, it is remarkable that, although "many inscriptions of Nebuchadnezzar are known, most of them relate to buildings." (Barton, *Archaeology,* p. 477.) In one he boasts of having done what no king before him had done, "in that on the outside of Babylon a great wall to the eastward of Babylon I placed about the city . . . which like a mountain cannot be moved. . . . Its head I raised mountain-high." (Rogers, *Cuneiform Parallels,* p. 368 f.) R. Koldewey, who led the excavation of ancient Babylon under the auspices of the Deutsche Orient-Gesellschaft from 1899 to 1917, states that the walls of Babylon measured 17 to 22 meters, 55 to 71 feet, in width, the usual city walls measuring three to seven meters, 10 to 22 feet. The city was covered by rubbish varying often from 50 to 80 feet. (*Das wiedererstehende Babylon,* p. 111.)

Babylon's magnificent palaces, its costly temples, its grand processional street, aroused the awe and wonder of all visitors, and its mountain-high walls forced upon them the impossibility of conquering this city. Yet the Lord Jehovah was unimpressed by Babylon's strength and grandeur. He saw only the blood of untold numbers of people who were slaughtered in ruthless warfare in order to obtain the means which made these buildings possible. He saw only the iniquity, the perversity, the crookedness of the builders, and while stone was added to stone, and ornament to ornament, He pronounced His sentence of doom (v. 13). All the labor spent in building the city shall have no purpose other than to be "in the very fire," literally, "sufficiency," food, for the fire. And all the ceaseless, wearying work shall be for the sufficiency of "vanity," emptiness, nothingness! Ruins, rubbish, ashes! For the whole earth shall be filled with the knowledge of the glory of the Lord! (V. 14.) Not only shall the destruction of Babylon manifest the glory of Jehovah, who was powerful enough to overthrow this city. No, there shall come a time when all the earth shall be filled with the glory of God revealed in the coming of the promised Redeemer and in the preaching of His Gospel to the uttermost parts of the earth (Luke 24:47; Acts 1:8). "As the waters cover the sea" = in overflowing abundance. And all the enemies of the Church can see in the ruins of Babylon their own ruin, the hopelessness of dethroning Jehovah. (Ps. 2; Rev. 20:7-15.)

(4) The fourth woe: The debaucher of nations will be debauched, vv. 15-17

15 Woe to him that gives drink to his neighbor, mingling with it thy poison, and also makes him drunk so that he may gloat on his nakedness.

16 Thou hast sated thyself with shame rather than glory. Drink thou also! And show thy foreskin! The cup of the LORD's right hand shall turn to thee, and shameful spewing shall

17 be on thy glory. For the violence done to Lebanon shall cover thee, and the destruction of the beasts which terrified them; for the blood of men shed by you and the violence committed against land and city and all that dwell therein.

Grammatical Notes

V. 15. "Puttest thy bottle." "Puttest," מְסַפֵּחַ, participle Pihel, add, join, mingle (1 Sam. 2:36; Is. 14:1; Job 30:7); others combine it with שָׁפַח, pour out. "Bottle," חֵמָה, heat, anger, fury (Gen. 27:44; Is. 51:13), poison (Deut. 32:24, 33; Ps. 58:5, A. V., 4; 140:4, A. V., 3; Job 6:4).

V. 16. "Art filled." The change from imperfect to perfect makes it preferable to regard this as a description of past iniquities He had regarded the satisfaction of his hunger for conquests as his glory; but it will turn out to be his shame. — "Show thy foreskin," the verb is related to the noun. The foreskin or uncircumcision was regarded as an evidence of unbelief and enmity against God and His Church. (Cp. 1 Sam. 17:26, 36; 1 Chron. 10:4; Ezek. 28:10; 32:19-32.) — "Shameful spewing." קִיקָלוֹן, a composite noun of קִיא, to spew, vomit (Lev. 18:28; 20:22; Jer. 25:27; the noun, Is. 19:14; 28:8; Jer. 48:26) and קָלוֹן, shame, disgrace (Prov. 11:2; 12:16, etc.), used to denote the shame of nakedness (Jer. 13:26; Nah. 3:5). In our passage the two words may have been combined to describe the Chaldean lying naked in his own vomit.

Vv. 15, 16. "That puttest thy bottle to him" (Gr. N.), that deliberately adds deadly poison to the drink he gives to his neighbor, whom he ought to love and respect as he respects and loves himself. He gives his neighbors wine to drink, invites them to his banquet, asks them to become his friends and allies, offers them honor, power, riches, his protection, yet at the same time he mingles deadly poison into the heady wine. His purpose is to make them drunk, intoxicate them with the honor of being his chosen friends, while his real aim is to "look on their nakedness." He is worse than Ham (Gen. 9:22 ff.), who did not make his father drunk. The Chaldean offers poisoned wine to his neighbors for the very purpose of gloating on their nakedness. In their intoxication they strip themselves of their liberty, denude themselves of independence, cast aside their greatest glory to become shameful puppets, disreputable slaves, living only by the whim of their master, who unmercifully punishes every attempt at regaining their liberty and indepedence. Woe on this deceitful enslaver! "Thou art filled" (v. 16, Gr. N.). The Chaldean had shamefully abused his honorable

338

position which the Lord had given to him. His conquests, his cruel oppression, his palaces, his temples, in which he gloried, were in God's eyes disgraceful shame, abominable wickedness. Now the same poison cup which he had forced upon his neighbors will be put to his own lips, and he will have to drain it to the very dregs (cp. Jer. 25: 9-26). "Thy foreskin" (Gr. N.). "Shameful spewing" (Gr. N.). Dead drunk, the proud Chaldean shall lie naked on the floor in his own vomit, an object of horror and ridicule for all the world.

V. 17. Again the cause of the Chaldean's downfall is named: his violent and shameful abuse of God's creation for selfish purposes. Lebanon denuded of its cedars to furnish material for his military operations and his building program (cp. Is. 14: 4 ff.); beasts cruelly maltreated, driven to death; whole countries and cities depopulated and destroyed for Babylon's glorification! Animate and inanimate creation, rational and irrational products of God's wisdom and power, all alike were treated with contemptuous disdain; all alike groaned under the heavy yoke of the oppressor; all alike shall be avenged!

---

(5) The fifth woe: The idolater will be forsaken by his idol, vv. 18, 19

18 What will a carved idol profit, so that its molder should carve it, a molten image, and a teacher of lies? that a molder molding it should place his trust upon it, so as to
19 make speechless idols? Woe to him who says to wood, Awake! Arise! to silent stone. That, a teacher? Behold, it is encased with gold and silver, and there is not the least breath within it!

Grammatical Notes

V. 19. "It shall teach." The arrangement of v. 19 and the Hebrew accents demand that this clause be connected not with "Arise," but regarded as a question. — "No breath at all." The Hebrew is very emphatic, "a nonexistence within it of any breath."

Vv. 18, 19 is not a later gloss. It connects the fifth woe with the preceding ones by pointing out the fountainhead of their wickedness and the real cause of their destruction, idolatry, which had been named as one of their characteristic sins (ch. 1: 16). They refused to accept Jehovah as the Supreme Lord, rejected His Gospel as well as His Law, because both clashed with their self-made "judgment and dignity" (ch. 1: 7). Professing themselves wise, they became fools! What folly for man, gifted with reason, to put his trust in stone and wood, in man-made idols, existing as gods only in his own fancy, more readily destroyed than they were made! What folly to worship the work of one's own hand! Pray to it, and it will not respond; plead with it, and it will not answer; cry out with a loud voice and torment yourselves (1 Kings 18:26-28), it will remain what it is, a deaf and dumb idol, beautifully decorated, but absolutely void of any breath within itself (Gr. N.), a dead, helpless block of wood and metal. In bitter irony the prophet cries out, That — pointing to the idol — that, your teacher? (Gr. N.) What can it possibly teach you? What does it know about God and His will? It is a creature of your imagination, no better morally than your own corrupt heart. When God made man in His own likeness, He made man like unto Himself, righteous, sinless, holy. When sinful man makes his own god, he cannot but make him in the image of his own depraved, sinful, corrupt nature. The heathen gods are morally as corrupt as their makers. What wickedness to worship them instead of the true God, whose nature and will they had ample opportunity to learn from His prophets and from their contact with His people and His Scriptures. (Cp. Dan. 1—6; Jer. 40: 2 f.; Ezek. 1:1 ff.) As all sins have the germ of death within themselves (Gen. 2:17; James 1:14 f.), so idolatry leads to destruction, eternal death. Woe unto him! says the Lord to all idolaters.

C. Conclusion, V. 20

20 But the LORD is in His holy temple. Let all the earth keep silence before Him!

V. 20. The Lord, the high and lofty One that inhabiteth eternity, whose name is Holy (Is. 57:15), is in His holy temple. There He, whom the heaven and heaven of heavens cannot contain (1 Kings 8:27; Is. 66:1), sits in transcendent majesty (Is. 6:1 ff.; Rev. 4:2-11), the God of absolute holiness and sinlessness, who, however, has found a way to dwell with him who is of a humble and contrite spirit, to revive his heart (Is. 57:15); the God of Zion, of His Church and every member of it unto all generations (Ps. 146:10). Before Him, silence! Hush, all the earth! Opposition to Jehovah, raving and raging against Him, is folly, is futile, is self-destruction (Ps. 2). Ye nations, hear His voice! Wherefore will ye die? Come unto Him, hear, and your soul shall live! (Is. 55:3.) Silence before Him also you children of the Lord! This does not mean that no one shall dare ever to speak to Him. He has commanded us to pray and has promised to hear us (Deut. 4:7; Ps. 37:5; 50:15). But it does mean that we are not to dictate to Him, to present to Him our own program or plan, expect Him to carry it out in every detail, and charge Him with a lack of love or worse if He deviates from our wishes. It does mean quiet submission to God's will, humbly letting Him lead us on the paths He has chosen (Ps. 73:23-26), in firm confidence that His ways are best, even if we cannot understand them.

Habakkuk's prayer in chapter 3 is a truly wonderful example of such prayer and keeping silence before the Lord.

On v. 20 see Ps. 11:4; Zeph. 1:7; Zech. 2:13.

PART III

Habakkuk's Prayer in Grateful Adoration of the Lord for the Vision Granted to Him

CHAPTER 3

A. The Superscription: A Prayer of Habakkuk the Prophet According to Shigyonoth

Grammatical Notes

V.1. *Shigyonoth,* occurring only here, is the plural form of *Shiggayon* (only Ps. 7:1), derived from שָׁגָה, to go astray (Ezek. 34:6); to err, sin (Lev. 4:13, etc.); to stagger, reel, like a drunkard (Prov. 20:1; Is. 28:7); to be intoxicated with love, be ravished (Prov. 5:19 f.); to reel with emotion, passion; the noun = an emotional, passionate hymn, a dithyramb. — "Upon," עַל, here = according to, in the manner of (cp. Ex. 6:26; 12:51; Ps. 110:4). In the superscription of Psalms it indicates, as here, the literary style; in other instances, the melody according to which the Psalm is to be sung (Ps. 9:1; 22:1; 56:1, etc.).

V.1. Chapter 3 is a prayer in the form of a psalm to be sung by the Levites in the Temple service (1 Chron. 25:1-8). Cp. the superscription, the Selahs, vv. 3, 9, 13, and the subscription. David's Psalms are frequently called prayers, the outpourings of a believing heart, giving expression to his hopes and fears, his desires and doubts. See Ps. 4:2 (A. V., 1); 6:10 (9); 55:2; 61:2 (1); 72:20. Quite naturally the reflections of the believer on his own life's experiences, on conditions of the world at large, on the ways and judgments of God, will pass over into prayer. Intercessory prayer was also one of the duties and privileges of God's prophets. (Gen. 20:7; Ex. 32:11 ff., 31 f.; Ezra 9:5-15; Jer. 14:7 ff., 19 ff.; Is. 63:15—64:12; Dan. 9:3-19.) Very appropriately Habakkuk places his prayer immediately after his reference to the folly of idolatry (ch. 2:19) and the admonition to stand in silence before the Lord. Habakkuk particularly calls attention to the fact that he is a prophet. He speaks here not only as a believing child of God, but also as the Lord's spokesman, telling his readers what the

Lord had revealed to him by word of mouth (chs. 1 and 2) and in a vision (ch. 3: 3 ff.).

This prophetic psalm is cast in the form of *Shigyonoth* (Gr. N.). It depicts the battle of conflicting emotions going on within himself while contending (ch. 2: 1) with God. Indignation at the wickedness of Judah (1: 2-4), horror at God's threatened punishment (1: 5-12), doubts as to God's justice and wisdom (1: 13-17), patient waiting (2: 1), joy at salvation promised (2: 2-20), fear at God's majesty (3: 2 a, 16), adoration of God's glory (3: 3 f.), joy over salvation (3: 8, 13, 18), deep disappointment at the delay of God's help (3: 16 c), jubilant confidence in the Lord, his Strength, and in God's final victory (3: 19) — such were the deep and violent emotions rolling over the prophet like surging waves and billows, tossing him to and fro, until he finally found peace, contentment, joy in Jehovah. This psalm is truly a *Shigyonoth*, a dithyramb!

Since, therefore, the chapter is a unit, the vision which roused such feelings must have been experienced by him prior to his composition of this chapter. We might, therefore, translate the verbs vv. 3-15 as past tenses, as did A. V. and Luther. The LXX uses futures in vv. 3 a, 4 a, 5, 7 b, 9, 10 a, etc., and aorists in vv. 3 b, 4 b, 6, 7 a, 8, 10 b, etc.; the Vulgate, perfects and futures. Since the prophet describes the vision so vividly as if he were seeing it at that moment, we prefer to use the present tense. The scenes as well as the language are reminiscent of past theophanies narrated by Scripture. On the scenes cp. Israel's deliverance out of Egypt, particularly the crossing of the Red Sea and Jordan, the Lawgiving at Mount Sinai, the deliverance of Israel in the time of the Judges, etc.; on the language, cp. v. 3 and Deut. 33: 2; Judg. 5: 4 f.; v. 5 and Ps. 18: 8; 68: 25 (24); v. 8 and Ps. 18: 10; 68: 5 (4), 34 (33); vv. 10-15 and Ps. 77: 17-21 (16-20); v. 19 and Deut. 32: 13; 33: 29; 2 Sam. 22: 34; Ps. 18: 34 (33). The psalm, however, is not to be interpreted merely as a narrative of God's guidance of Israel from the time of the Egyptian plagues to the days of Joshua and Gideon, in order to assure Judah that He who delivered Israel in their youth will not forsake them in the midway of their career ("in the midst of the years," v. 2). So Calvin, as quoted approvingly in *The Expositor's Bible,* and followed by many interpreters. Habakkuk is speaking here as a prophet, revealing to his people what God had revealed to him, God's plan for the future history of the Church until the end of time. See also notes on v. 3, pp. 344 f. The prophet does not state the exact time when the vision was granted him.

B. The Prophet's Prayer, V. 2

2 O LORD, I have heard Thy report. I am overawed! O LORD, in the midst of the years call to life Thy work! In the midst of the years manifest it! In wrath remember mercy!

Grammatical Notes

"Revive it." חַיֵּיהוּ denotes not only bringing back to life, renewing it; it also denotes the creation of life. (Cp. Gen. 7:3; 19:32, 34; Deut. 32:39.) — "In the midst of the years." Sellin regards this as the only possible translation of the text. "Such a prayer, however, would be extremely strange, both linguistically and materially"; therefore he changes the text to read בְּקֶרֶב, "in the nearest of the years." We shall see that there is no need of such a change. — "Wrath." רֹגֶז is derived from a stem = "to be disquieted," excited; by fear (Ex. 15:14), anger (Gen. 45:24; Job 12:6, provoke to anger; Prov. 29:9; Is. 28:21). The noun occurs in the sense of anger in Job 3:17 (hateful rage), 37:2 (angry roar of thunder), and Hab. 3:2.

V. 2. Jehovah! is the first word of this truly remarkable prayer. In the face of the prophet's misgivings, the wickedness of Judah, the fierce hatred of the powerful Chaldean, Jehovah still is what His name implies, the unchanged and unchangeable I AM THAT I AM (Ex. 3:14), Judah's Covenant God. Jehovah has spoken, has appeared to His prophet. While His revelation in word and vision had caused Habakkuk to fear (cp. Ex. 3:6; 14:31; 19:16; 20:18-21; Dan. 10:7-11), yet his fear did not drive him away from God. In humble adoration, in childlike trust he pleads with the Lord, as a loving child pleads with his loving father, to hurry His deliverance, the Grand Day of Salvation. No longer does he doubt the wisdom or justice or grace of God's actions, His "work" (cp. Gr. N. on ch. 1:5). He knows that Jehovah's work is right, perfect (Deut. 32:4), even if it passes man's understanding. "Revive" (Gr. N.), bring into life and reality the salvation Thou hast promised in word and vision. Do it "in the midst of the years" (Gr. N.). Do not delay Thy coming (cp. 2:3, "tarry"). Cut in half that long period of waiting Thou hast appointed. "Make known," make publicly manifest (on this sense see Ps. 77:15, A. V., 14; 98:2 a; 103:7; Ezek. 39:7) Thy deliverance! Truly, a bold prayer of longing faith and hope. Cp. Rev. 22:20 and Ringwaldt's prayer: "O Jesus Christ, do not delay, But hasten our salvation" (*The Lutheran Hymnal,* Hymn 611, st. 7; also 606, st. 2).

In wrath remember mercy! Let not Thy wrath (Gr. N.) blot out Thy mercy! This is a confident prayer based on Ex. 34:6 f., where wrath and mercy are placed side by side as essential attributes of God in the Lord's own definition of His name. This prayer is a prophetic

343

prayer, the fulfillment of which must come as surely as the Lord is the unchanging God of unalterable holy wrath and never-ceasing mercy. I see no reason why the mercy to be remembered by God in the midst of His wrath should be restricted to God's people, His believing children. While sending His judgments upon wicked Judah through the Chaldeans, the Lord is asked to remember His people in mercy and grant them His grace unto sincere repentance (cp. Deut. 30:1-6). And may the Lord likewise be gracious to the wicked Chaldeans and pluck them like brands out of the fire! Was the preaching of Ezekiel and Daniel, whom the Chaldeans had taken captive, altogether without success as far as the conversion of heathen is concerned?

In order to encourage his fellow men to like humble, yet confident prayer, the prophet now pictures the vision which had moved him to pray as he did.

C. The Advent of the Lord, Vv. 3-15

1. Its majestic, awe-inspiring glory, vv. 3-7

3 God is coming from Teman, and the Holy One from Mount Paran, Selah. His glory covers the heavens; His praise fills the earth.
4 Brightness appears like light! Rays of light are at His side; there is the
5 cover of His power. Before Him walks pestilence, and plague goes
6 forth from His feet. He stands, and rocks the earth. He looks, and makes nations tremble, and the everlasting mountains smash to bits, the ancient hills sink down.
7 His are the ways of old! Under affliction I see the tents of Cushan; the tent curtains of the land of Midian are flapping.

Grammatical Notes

V. 3. "Selah." G.-B.: Meaning and etymology of the term is entirely obscure. Koenig (*Psalmen*, p. 30 f.) explains the term as a locative of a substantive סַל, from סָלַל, to heap up, make high; cp. מְסִלָּה, highway, Is. 62:10; 57:14; Prov. 15:19; Jer. 18:15; hence, elevation, with ה loci, "on high"; a call directed to the musicians to play louder, forte! fortissimo! But there is no dagesh in the ל! Occurring about 74 times, the term is found almost invariably at the end of a paragraph or of exalted, strongly emotional statements. LXX translates διάψαλμα, interlude, the musicians playing louder than while accompanying the singing Levites.

V. 4. "Was." תִּהְיֶה here = to appear, come into existence. (Cp. Gen. 1:5; 9:16; 26:1; Ex. 19:16; Jonah 1:4, etc.). — "As the light." The absence of the article emphasizes the qualitative force of the term, light as light, in its purest form. — "Horns." קֶרֶן denotes also rays of light, because of their similarity to horns. (Cp. Ex. 34:29 f., 35; 2 Cor. 3:7, 13-16). — "Hand" frequently denotes side (1 Sam. 4:18; 19:3; 2 Sam. 18:4; Zech. 14:13, etc.).

V. 6. "Measured," יְמֹדֵד, here a variant of מוֹט, to set in motion, shake, rock, cause to quake. — "Drove asunder," נתר = to jump (with fear), Job 37:1; Hiphil = to cause to jump, or quake. — "Were scattered," פוץ = to spread, Hithpolel, causative reflexive, they caused themselves to spread, to disintegrate.

In this remarkable vision the prophet sees the New Testament realities in the mold of Old Testament types and figures. The New Testament Church is Israel, Judah; its enemies the Chaldeans and their allies, the Edomites, Midianites, etc. Moreover, God grants His prophet the gift of seeing history in a manner similar to that of the eternal God, who is not bound by any restrictions of time and space (Ps. 90:4; 2 Peter 3:8; Ps. 139:3-12; Jer. 23:23 f.). The prophet sees in one brief moment, as if they were closely connected, events which lie centuries and millenniums apart. All divine deliverances through time and eternity, from every form of evil of body and soul, property and honor — all these he sees as one deliverance, the result of that great battle of God's Anointed on Calvary, at the end of which he cried, It is finished! (Ps. 22, particularly v. 31, "He hath done!") In fact, all deliverances of God's people prior to Calvary are not only foreshadowings and prophecies of this great redemption; and all deliverances following it in time and eternity are not only reminders of it. They owe their very reality to the victory of God's Anointed on Golgotha.

Vv. 3, 4. "Teman" (see Obad. 1, p. 194). Paran, the modern Faran, is a mountain range west and south of Edom, north and slightly east of Mount Sinai. On Sinai the Lord had established His covenant with Israel. He has lost none of His power. He is still "God," Eloah, an ancient designation of the Deity, found only here, some 40 times in the Book of Job, and Deut. 32:15, 17; Ps. 50:22; 139:19; Prov. 30:5. He comes as the Holy One (Is. 6:3), in absolute sovereignty and exaltation over all created beings, as the sinless, immaculately pure God, who hates and detests sin and wickedness, and who will destroy all who oppose and oppress His Church, which He has sanctified unto Himself (Lev. 20:8; 21:8, 15, 23). Selah (Gr. N.): the musical instruments announce His advent, as He moves onward on a front reaching across the southern horizon from east to west. The heavens are covered with His majestic glory, far surpassing that of the noonday sun. The whole earth is full of the praises of Him who is its Creator and Ruler (Is. 6:3). As Habakkuk looks, he sees a brilliance like light (v. 4) (Gr. N.), purest light, emanating from Him; "horns" (Gr. N.), beams of light streaming forth from His "hand" (Gr. N.), His side. "There," in this supermundane brightness surrounding Him and flowing from Him in undiminishing clarity and dazzling splendor, "was the hiding of His power." This brilliance served as a garment, a veil, for the hiding of His essential glory (Ex. 33:18), His "face" (Ex. 33:20), which no mortal man can see and live (Ex. 33:20-33; Ezek. 1:27; 1 Tim. 6:16; Heb. 1:1-3). Oh, the brilliance of that unexplored and unexplorable Light, which hides its glory behind brightness outshining the very sun! Oh, the glory, to behold Him face to face! (1 Cor. 13:13.) His "power," not merely His omnipotence, but the sum total of all His attributes, the fullness of His glory (Ex. 15:13, "strength"; Ps. 89:11; parallel to glory of the Ark of Covenant, Ps. 132:8; 150:1; Micah 5:3).

Vv. 5-7. Before this gloriously holy God goes "pestilence," slaying all who dare to oppose Him; and "at His feet" go forth burning coals, vivid, horrible emblems of the everlasting fire of His wrath burning to lowest hell (Deut. 32:22) against all that dare to array themselves against Him and His people. "He stood" (v. 6), has taken His firm and resolute stand. It is the pause before the battle, the lull before the storm. "Measured" (Gr. N.), He causes the earth to tremble as if shaken by fierce earthquakes. "Drove asunder" (Gr. N.), rather, causes to quaver, disintegrate. The nations, however powerful they may be, shudder in mortal fear. Even the everlasting mountains, emblems of eternity, are scattered (Gr. N.), lose their stability, are smashed to bits, while the perpetual hills bow down, sink down into the valley surrounding them. All nature is out of joint. "His ways are everlasting," rather, "of old." The ancient God of salvation once more comes to the rescue of the people, as He did in their early history (Ex. 3—15). And again the nations fear (cp. Ex. 15:14-16). The "tents," the "curtains" (v. 7), here for the people dwelling in the tents. "Cushan," either a different form of Cush = Ethiopia, or some unknown nomadic tribe. The word occurs only here. Others suggest to read Jokshan, descendants of Abraham and Keturah; a brother nation of Midian (Gen. 25:2 f., 1 Chron. 1:32). Midian was an ancient enemy of Israel (Num. 22:4 ff.; 25:6-18; 31:2; Judg. 6 and 7), representing all the enemies of God's people.

---

2. Its twofold purpose, destruction of the enemies, salvation for Israel, vv. 8-15

8 Does the LORD rage against streams? Is Thy wrath directed against the streams, or Thy fury against the sea, that Thou ridest on Thy horses, Thy chariots of salva- 9 tion? Thou art wholly unsheathing Thy bow. Missiles have been sworn into service by a word. Selah. Streams are splitting the earth. 10 Mountains see Thee and quake; a cloudburst passes by; the deep utters its voice and lifts its hands

11 on high. Sun and moon stand still
in their habitation; they have gone
away at the gleam of Thy arrows,
at the glittering flash of Thy spear.
12 In fury dost Thou stalk through the
earth, in anger dost Thou thresh
13 the heathen. Thou art proceeding
for the salvation of Thy people, for
the salvation of Thine Anointed.
Thou dost smash the head from off

the house of the wicked, pouring
out its foundation up to the neck.
14 Selah. With his own spear Thou
dost pierce the head of the villagers
who are rushing onward to scatter
me like those determined to devour
15 the poor in secret. Thou dost tread
on the sea with Thy horses, on the
turbulent billows of great waters.

Grammatical Notes

V. 8. On the change of the third to the
second person in speaking to the Lord,
see Hos. 2:6–9, 17–21 (A. V., 4–7, 15–19).
"Thy chariots of salvation." Salvation
is in apposition to "Thy chariots," qual-
ifying the latter, Thy chariots which are
salvation, or, Thy chariots, salvation.

V. 9. "Quite naked." עֶרְיָה תֵעוֹר, literally, as nakedness didst Thou lay bare,
lay bare completely, Thy bow by keeping it unsheathed until it had finished
its work. — "According to the oaths,"
etc. Delitzsch has counted more than
a hundred different interpretations of
this sentence. "Oaths"; שְׁבֻעוֹת may be
rendered seven, sevens, sevenths, weeks,
sevenfold, sworn, put under oaths;
"rods" = branches, or staffs (for protection, Ex. 4:2; or for punishment, Is.
9:4, "staff"); or tribes (Ex. 31:2). —
"Word." אֹמֶר occurs once in the sense
of thing, matter (Job 22:28); twice of
heaven's "speech" (Ps. 19:3 f., A. V.,
2 f.); twice of God's word of promise
(Ps. 68:12, A. V., 11; 77:9, A. V., 8).
Habakkuk evidently refers here to the
oracle recorded Deut. 32:40–42. See exposition, p. 348. This is proved also by
comparing Hab. 3:11 with Deut. 32:41,
the only Biblical passages in which the
Hebrew word for "glittering" is applied
to God's weapons. Cp. also Hab. 3:13 f.,

"head out of the house," "head of his
villages," with Deut. 32:42, "from the
beginning of revenges," literally, "from
the head of the leaders" (Koenig, Deu-
teronomium, on Deut. 32:42), or "from
the hairy head," "the bare head" (Luther).

V. 13. "Thou woundedst." מָחַץ = to
smash (Num. 24:17; Judg. 5:26); inflict
a mortal wound. — "By discovering,"
עָרוֹת, to lay bare (Ps. 137:7), to pour
out, empty (Gen. 24:20; 2 Chron. 24:11;
Ps. 141:8, "leave destitute"; cp. Hiphil,
Is. 53:12, "poured out his soul").

V. 14. "Villages." פָּרָז, a "villager" =
one living in open country, or unwalled
cities (Deut. 3:5; 1 Sam. 6:18; Esther
9:19; cp. also פְּרָזוֹת, Esther 9:19; Ezek.
38:11; Zech. 2:8). The defective writing
of the third person singular in plural
nouns is quite common (G.-K. 91 k, last
sentence). Sellin substitutes "horsemen." — "As to devour," etc., is an abbreviated comparison: their rejoicing is
as the rejoicing of such as, etc.

V. 15. "With thine horses." סוּסֶיךָ is the
adverbial accusative, here instrumental. — "Heap." חֹמֶר is derived from a
verb = "to ferment," be violently moved
(Lam. 1:20; 2:11; Ps. 46:4); the noun,
the surging billows, only here.

Vv. 8, 9. When the Lord parted the waters of the Red Sea (Ex.
14:15 ff.), and forty years later, the waters of Jordan (Joshua 3:14 ff.),
He did not do this in anger against the waters of the sea or the river.

So the Lord coming from Teman comes not in furious displeasure
(Gr. N.) with the rivers and streams of the earth, or in overflowing
wrath against the sea, the vast mass of water lying to the west of
Canaan, connecting with the mighty oceans. No! The Lord comes
riding on His horses hitched to chariots of salvation (Gr. N.), literally,
chariots, salvation. His advent has primarily the purpose of redeeming, delivering, saving His people from the hands of their enemies.
(Cp. 1 Sam. 2:1-10; Luke 1:51 ff., 68 ff.) "Salvation," the Hebrew
term *Jeshuah* is derived from the same root as the name given to
Mary's Son, Jesus, and defined by the angel as salvation, saving from
sin (Matt. 1:21). This salvation necessitates a fierce battle. Yet the
Lord is well prepared. "Thy bow was made quite naked" (v. 9)
(Gr. N.), laid bare, removed from its sheath, to be used without
remission until there is no other enemy to conquer (Ps. 110:1; 1 Cor.
15:24-27). "According to the oaths of the tribes, even Thy word"
(Gr. N.). Of all the various translations and emendations of this
passage, we prefer Keil's rendering: Rods are put under oath, i. e.,
sworn into service, by Thy word. Long ago, in the time of Moses, the
Lord had by a solemn oath sworn rods, staffs, missiles, arrows, and
spears, weapons of war, into His service. (See Deut. 32:40-42.) As the
Lord had already in eternity appointed the Person who was to save
His people and defeat His enemies (Ps. 110, etc.; Acts 2:23; 4:28) and
had announced His coming from the days of Paradise (Luke 1:70;
1 Peter 1:20), so He had also sworn into His service His rods, all the
instruments of war needed for this battle long before it was actually
fought. "Selah" again calls upon the musicians for an interlude, emphasizing the peculiar solemnity of this verse, its message of hope for
the anxiously waiting Church, of consternation for the enemies.
"Thou didst cleave," etc., denotes either a splitting of the ground into
crevices, dales, valleys, in which rivers began to flow, or the formation
of water bodies by the overflowing sea. G.-B. translates "opening up
waters" and compares the use of the same word in Job 28:10, miners
on their search for gold, splitting the rock and "cutting out," opening,
springs of water; also Ezek. 13:11, the wind "rending," splitting a wall.

V. 10. "The mountains," cp. v. 6. "The overflowing of water" denotes a cloudburst. The windows of heaven were opened as at the
time of the Deluge; "the deep," the vast reservoirs of underground
waters roared as they were released from their confinement (cp. Gen.
6:11). "Lifted up their hands on high," terrified at the presence of
Jehovah, as if groaning in anguish and travail (Rom. 8:19 f.).

V. 11. Sun and moon stand still in their habitation. Cp. Ps. 19:4-6, their "tabernacle," or dwelling place, the firmament of heaven (Gen. 1:16 f.). Now they stand still, as in the days of Joshua (Joshua 10:12), this time in terror at the brightness of the Lord's spears and arrows; then they go away in order to hide themselves (cp. Matt. 24:29; 27:45).

Vv. 12, 13. The reason for such uproar of the entire creation is God's indignation. The Hebrew word denotes particularly God's avenging wrath (Is. 10:5, 25; 26:20; Dan. 8:18, etc.). Majestically the Lord strides through the earth on a punitive expedition, to thresh, flail, destroy the heathen, the *goyim*, the nations opposing His Church. At the same time this is a rescue mission (v. 13) for the deliverance of His people and of His Anointed, the Messiah, a name familiar to the Israelites as designating the promised Redeemer. (Cp. 1 Sam. 2:10; Ps. 2:2; 45:6 f.; Is. 61:1.) God's Anointed was to be the Captain of our salvation, girding His sword upon His thigh to fight the Lord's battle (Gen. 3:15; Num. 24:17-19; Ps. 45:3-5; 110:1-7). In this fierce battle He was to cry to the Lord for help (Ps. 22:1, 11, 19-21; 40:12, 14; cp. Matt. 26:39-44; 27:46; Heb. 5:7), a prayer that was heard (Ps. 110:1; Heb. 5:7-9; Phil. 2:7-11; Eph. 1:20-23). "Thou woundedst" (Gr. N.). The Lord smashes "the head out of the house of the wicked." "House," here in the sense of realm, kingdom (2 Sam. 7:1-13; 1 Kings 12:16, 19; 14:10). "The house of the wicked" is the kingdom of ungodly, wicked people, with Satan at their head, carrying on an unceasing battle against the kingdom of God and His Anointed (Gen. 3:15 and Ps. 2). The Lord speaks of a "house," of its "foundation," its "head," or roof, its "neck," the upper part of the walls on which the roof rests. When the head, the roof of a house, is smashed off, when it is unroofed, it no longer can protect its inhabitants against wind and weather, storm and sleet. The foundation is "discovered" (Gr. N.), literally, poured out, deprived of its contents, its stones. "Unto the neck." Like the roof and the foundation, its walls are demolished, as a house struck by lightning in a fierce windstorm is gutted by fire, unroofed, demolished. The warfare between God's Anointed and Satan's kingdom of sin and wickedness culminated in the great battle on Golgotha, which ended in Satan's complete and everlasting defeat, in full and eternal salvation of God's Church. There the head of the house of the wicked received his mortal wound; the foundation of this house was revealed as falsehood, sinking sand; its walls, as fraud and deception; its interior, as chambers of iniquity, inhabited by the dead, the guests of deepest hell (Prov. 9:18). Selah! See vv. 3, 9.

V. 14. Satan's head was indeed bruised! And Satan was "stricken through," pierced, mortally wounded with his own "staves," the same word translated "rods" in v. 9 (A. V., "tribes"). The staves, the weapons, whereby Satan deceived and held captive mankind were sin, death, damnation. And the Anointed, by being made sin for mankind (2 Cor. 5:21), by permitting Himself to be numbered with the transgressors, by bearing man's sins (Is. 53:6, 11 f.), procured for man an everlasting, perfect righteousness (2 Cor. 5:21; 1 John 2:2). By pouring out His soul unto death (Is. 53:12), the Messiah through death, through Satan's weapon, destroyed Satan and delivered his captives (Heb. 2:14-18). By being forsaken of God (Ps. 22:1; Matt. 27:46), by being made a curse for mankind, Christ redeemed man from the curse of the Law (Gal. 3:13). With Satan's own weapons the Lord's Anointed mortally wounded, crushed the head of the wicked Serpent. Satan is here called the head of "his villages" (A. V., see Gr. N.), literally, villagers, the inhabitants of unfenced cities or the open country. The Chaldean ruled not only over strongly fortified cities like Babylon. His realm extended over innumerable unwalled cities and immense stretches of steppes, prairies, semidesert regions, populated by nomadic peoples. All of them were subject to Chaldea's power and had to furnish their quotas of men and material for Chaldea's campaigns of conquest. Satan's kingdom includes not only the large cities, usually the hotbeds of sin and vice and crime. It extends also throughout the world, wherever sinful Adam's children are to be found (Ps. 14:2 f.). They all are part of Satan's vast army and show their enmity against God by coming out "as a whirlwind to scatter me." Habakkuk speaks in the name of the Church. The enemies' rejoicing is "as to devour" (Gr. N.), a rejoicing like that of those whose object it is "to devour the poor secretly." Here the prophet names another class of Satan's hordes, already referred to in ch. 1:2-5, the ungodly, wicked people within God's kingdom, the visible Church. Nominally members of God's kingdom, they are actually allies and slaves of Satan and will meet the fate of their head and his kingdom of wickedness, death, eternal destruction.

V. 15. As the Lord rode through the Red Sea for the deliverance of His people (Ex. 14:19-22, 29; 15:13, 19) and the destruction of His enemies (Ex. 14:24-28; 15:3-12, 19), so He shall throughout the life of His Church on earth ride in His chariots with His horses (Gr. N.) through the heap of great waters, through the wildest and stormiest waves of persecution and bloodshed threatening to overwhelm and swallow forever the Church of God. He shall ride to the salvation of His faithful flock (Is. 54:5-17; Pss. 46, 93).

3. The prophet's horror turns to confident joy, vv. 16-19

16 When I heard it, my heart trembled; my lips quivered at the sound. Rottenness entered my bones, and my feet tottered under me, because I must quietly wait for the day of trouble to come on the people that

17 oppress us. Though the fig tree does not blossom and there be no fruit on the vine; though the product of the olive fail and the fields produce no food; though the flock be cut off from the fold and there

18 be no cattle in the stalls, yet I will rejoice in the LORD, I will exult in

19 the God of my salvation. The LORD Lord is my Strength, and He makes my feet like hinds' feet, and He makes me walk on my heights. To the choir leader, on my stringed instruments.

Grammatical Notes

V. 16. "Belly," בֶּטֶן, "the inner parts of man when he receives mental and spiritual impressions" (G.-B.). (Prov. 18:8; 20:27; 22:18; Job 15:2, etc.) — "In myself," תַּחְתַּי, under myself. — "That I might rest," אֲשֶׁר here = because. (Cp. Deut. 3:24; Job 34:27; Dan. 1:10.)

V. 19. "Chief singer"; the participle Piel of נצח = to be prominent, leading (1 Chron. 23:4; 2 Chron. 2:1; Ezra 3:8f.). Here the musical director, the choirmaster (Ps. 4:1; 5:1; 6:1; 39:1, etc.). — "On my stringed instruments." נְגִינָה denotes a stringed instrument, most probably a zither, one of the various instruments used by the Levites in accompanying the hymns sung by the Temple choir. The term occurs in the superscription of a number of Psalms, in the singular only in Ps. 61; in the plural in Pss. 4, 6, 54, 55, 67, 76. These superscriptions are directions to the chief musical leader to compose a suitable melody for the public rendering of the Psalm by the singers and musicians in the Temple service; or to use the melody of the hymn named in the superscription. (Cp. Ps. 9:1, muth labben = "die for the son," Ps. 22:1; Pss. 53, 56, 57, 58, 59, 71, etc.) — "On my stringed instruments," בִּנְגִינוֹתָי. A number of scholars regard the final syllable not as the suffix, but as an Aramaism "ai" for "i." G.-K. lists as "indubitable" examples of such endings proper nouns, like Barzillai, 2 Sam. 17:27; as "prob-able," e. g., kilai, Is. 32:5; chorai, Is. 19:9; "perhaps" also gobai, grasshoppers, Amos 7:1; Nah. 3:17; "hardly" (schwerlich) neginotai, Is. 38:20; Hab. 3:19. Is. 38:20 certainly may be translated "my stringed instruments." Hezekiah had in obedience to God's command ordered the priests and Levites to sanctify themselves and cleanse the Temple from every trace of idolatry (2 Chron. 29:1-24). He had also restored the sacred music, instrumental and vocal, in the Temple service (2 Chron. 29:25 f.). As the musical instruments introduced by David are called David's instruments (2 Chron. 29:26 f.), so Hezekiah could very properly call the musical instruments whose use had been restored by him, "my stringed instruments" (Is. 38:20). There is consequently no valid grammatical reason to change the translation of Luther, A. V., Jewish Publ. Society, 1941; Keil, Orelli, F. C. Cook in Bible Commentary, J. M. Powis Smith in The Complete Bible. The LXX, "He makes me to mount upon the high places that I may conquer by His song," and similarly the Vulgate makes the subscription part of the Psalm, a change not warranted by the Hebrew text. We prefer the translation of our English and German Bibles, a translation which adds more than mere plausibility to the presumption that Habakkuk was a Levite, one of the musicians (2 Chron. 29:25-28), perhaps one of the chorus leaders.

V. 16 ff. This closing paragraph "opens to our eyes the inmost soul of the prophet. In the midst of deepest anguish he manfully determines to rejoice, since even in the revelation of God's punitive judgment upon Judah and the enemies the manifestation of divine salvation flashes forth victoriously. — This prospect of deliverance rouses the prophet to heavenly joy, which transports him far beyond the still impending day of tribulation into the times of Messiah." (Delitzsch, *Zeitschrift für Lutherische Theologie u. Kirche,* 1842, p. 31.)

The vision granted to Habakkuk had left him deeply agitated. His innermost parts trembled with fear and forebodings. His lips quivered. His very bones seemed to have dissolved. He "trembled in himself," rather, "under himself." His feet would no longer support him. He was ready to collapse. (Cp. Dan. 8:17, 18, 27; 10:7-10, 15-19.) It was, however, not only the awe-inspiring vision that had frightened him. He names another reason: "that I might rest," etc. (Gr. N.); literally, that I will have to wait quietly for the day of tribulation, when the enemy will invade Judah. Yet, though deeply disappointed at the postponement of the deliverance, the fact that in God's own time divine deliverance will unfailingly come gives him strength to wait. And he not only prays that God would revive His work in the midst of the years (v. 2) — he also rejoices because of the assurance of God's salvation!

Vv. 17, 18. Fig tree, vine, olive; fields, flocks of sheep, herds of cattle; a double triad of things on which not only the prosperity, but the very life of the nation depended, may fail and be cut off. Destruction, poverty, destitution, desolation, may cover, like a shroud, the land where milk and honey had flowed (Deut. 8:7-9; 11:9-15). "Yet," nevertheless (cp. Ps. 73:23 ff.), I will rejoice in the Lord (v. 18). Twice the prophet calls the God of his salvation Jehovah. His God is I AM THAT I AM (Ex. 3:14), eternal, a God whose salvation is not measured in terms of yesterday or today. His salvation is not restricted to people fortunate enough to live after Calvary's victory; it includes all men from Adam and Eve onward to the end of time. And therefore Habakkuk, living more than 600 years before the Redeemer's advent, is as sure of his personal salvation, "my salvation," as if it had already been accomplished. God's covenant of peace shall not be removed (Is. 54:10); the redemption of the Anointed is an eternal redemption, retroactive in its effects (Heb. 9:12-15; ch. 11; Rom. 4:1-25; Gal. 3:6-18). Jehovah and His eternal salvation is the prophet's strength (v. 19), upholding him in the storm and stress of the times. Jehovah makes the feet of the prophet, which had begun to tremble and falter

(v. 16), once more "like hinds' feet," swift and sure (cp. 2 Sam. 22:34-43; Ps. 18:34 ff.), eager to pursue his way through all trials and obstacles, confident that the Lord will make him "to walk upon mine high places" (cp. Deut. 32:13; 33:29; 2 Sam. 22:34; Ps. 18:34). The high places, the hills, dominating the surrounding country, were usually strongly fortified, and their possession was essential to the possession and defense of the land. Once more Habakkuk is sure that the Church of God, of which he is a member by faith in the Redeemer, shall not be vanquished by the enemies. Rather it shall go on in its conquest of the world for the Lord and His Anointed.

On this note of joyous confidence ends this remarkable psalm. It was written not only as a private memorial of his conflicting emotions, but also as an encouragement for his fellow believers who were harassed by misgivings similar to his own.

"To the chief singer," etc. (See Gr. N. p. 351.)

ZEPHANIAH

I. Introduction, V. 1

1 The word of the LORD, which came to Zephaniah, the son of Cushi, the son of Gedaliah, the son of Amariah, the son of Hizkiah, in the days of Josiah, the son of Amon, king of Judah.

V. 1. The same introductory formula is found Hos. 1:1; Joel 1:1; Micah 1:1. The prophet declares at the very outset that what is to follow is the word of Jehovah, spoken by man. This is the only instance in which the genealogy of a prophet is traced to the fourth generation. Therefore it has been generally supposed that Hizkiah here is king Hezekiah, the attribute "king" being omitted because he was so well known. That is a very weak argument. Why, then, should the attribute "king of Judah" be added to Josiah, the son of Amon, who was the king at Zephaniah's time? The rule is that wherever a king is introduced for the first time, the attribute is added. (Cp. Prov. 25:1; Is. 1:1; 6:1; 7:1; Jer. 1:2 f.; Hos. 1:1; Amos 1:1, etc.) Zephaniah's royal descent cannot be proved.

II. Universal Judgment, Ch. 1:2—3:8

A. Judgment upon Earth and Sky and Sea, Ch. 1:2, 3

2 In ruinous destruction I will sweep everything off the face of the earth, 3 is the oracle of the LORD. I will sweep away man and beast; I will sweep away the birds of the sky, and the fish of the sea, and the ruins together with the wicked; and I will cut off mankind from the face of the earth, is the oracle of the LORD.

Grammatical Notes

V. 2. "Utterly consume." אָסֵף, the absolute infinitive of אָסַף, gather up, destroy, is connected with אָסֵף, Hiph. of סוּף, to make an end, sweep away, annihilate. The addition of the absolute infinitive of the same or a synonymous verb serves to intensify the action expressed (Gen. 2:17; Judg. 1:28; Amos 9:8; Jer. 30:11. G.-K. 113 n).

V. 2. With horrifying abruptness the Lord begins His proclamation of universal judgment. He will "utterly consume" (Gr. N.), in a complete and final sweeping away, every living being from earth and sky and sea, a destruction even more extensive than that of the

354

Deluge (Gen. 7:21 ff.). During the Deluge the divine ordinances of family and government continued within the ark, but they will be abolished on Judgment Day.

V. 3. "Stumbling blocks," literally, ruins. The term here and in Is. 3:6 (cp. v. 8) describes the ruined state of every social and political institution, whether of divine or human origin. Sinful man from the very beginning has rebelled against the sovereignty of the Lord and Ruler of the universe (Gen. 3:5, 22; 4:23 f.; 6:3-7; 11:3 ff.). Every divine institution for man's welfare, matrimony (Gen. 2:18-25), government (Rom. 13:1-7), has been defiled and crippled by human sin and wickedness. Every human civilization, the product of sinful man, for that very reason carries within itself the germ of decay and death. When it has run its tragic downward course (cp. Rom. 1:18-32), it will collapse and bury beneath its ruins all that in proud self-exaltation had relied on it as the salvation of the nation and the world. The prophet speaks here primarily of the Final Judgment, the final collapse at the end of time. Yet the collapse of every past civilization — Egypt, Assyria, Babylon, Greece, Rome — was for that particular nation the judgment of the Day of the Lord, total destruction, eternal death (Deut. 32:22). At the same time it is a warning herald announcing the coming of the Lord's Day of final judgment of all the earth.

"I will cut off man," adam, "from off the land," adamah. This play on words is a reminder of the story of the creation and fall of man. Formed of the dust of the ground, adamah (Gen. 2:7), man, adam, was dependent on the ground, adamah, cursed for his sake (Gen. 3:17), for the food necessary for sustaining his life until he would return to the ground, adamah, from which he was taken (Gen. 3:19). Sinful man shall be cut off from the land he had defiled by his sin. Sin is self-destruction.

This is not merely the well-founded warning of a man able to read the handwriting on the wall. It is the oracle of Jehovah, the Ruler of the universe!

B. Judgment upon Judah, Ch. 1:4—2:3

1. Its cause, 1:4-7

4 And I will stretch out My hand against Judah and against all the inhabitants of Jerusalem; and I will cut off from this place the remnant of Baal, the name of the Chemarim 5 together with the priests; and those who worshiped the host of heaven on the roofs, and those who worshiped and were swearing allegiance to the LORD while they 6 were swearing by their king; and those who have turned back from

355

the LORD; and those who did not seek the LORD nor inquired for Him. Silence before the Lord LORD! For the Day of the LORD is near, for the LORD has prepared a sacrifice; He has consecrated His guests.

7

Grammatical Notes

V. 5. "Swear by the LORD" — "by Malcham." In the first clause the preposition is לְ, swearing allegiance to one (cp. 2 Chron. 15:14; Is. 19:18; 45:23 b); in the second clause it is בְּ, swear by one's name (Is. 45:23 a; Joshua 2:12); also as a confessional act (Deut. 6:13; 10:20; Is. 48:1).

V. 6. "Sought" is the stronger term, occurring only as Piel, the intensive conjugation; while Qal = inquire, ask.

V. 7. "Bid His guests." Bid, הִקְדִּישׁ, to sanctify, consecrate, of God's placing into His service an object (1 Kings 9:3, 7; 2 Chron. 7:16, 20), or a person (Num. 3:13; 8:17), or setting them aside for a certain purpose; hence: appointing them, e. g., for slaughter (Jer. 12:3); here, as His instruments of destruction. — "Guests," literally, those that are called for some purpose; here, to consume Judah.

V. 4. The Lord now names a number of representative nations on whom His wrath shall be poured out. He begins with Judah, blest and honored more highly than any other nation (Deut. 4:7 f., 32 ff.; Rom. 9:4 f.); first also in its ungrateful and contemptuous rejection of its Covenant God and His Law and Gospel. Neither Judah, the nation of which Shiloh was to stem (Gen. 49:10), nor Jerusalem, the city which God has chosen as His own abode (Ps. 9:11; 78:68; 135:21), shall escape the judgments of the Lord. In spite of their boasting (Jer. 7:4, 10) they shall be swept away by the wrath of God. That same mighty and outstretched hand which had brought them out of the land of bondage to the Land of Promise (Deut. 26:8) will be stretched out against Judah and Jerusalem and all their inhabitants in order to make the whole land a desolate waste (cp. Jer. 21:5 ff.). God's chosen people had turned away from the Fountain of living waters and hewed out broken cisterns that can hold no water (Jer. 2:13). The Lord names five classes of idolatry of which Judah had become guilty. There is above all Baalism. Baal (= Lord) is the best-known West-Asiatic deity, and Baalism is often used as a synonym of idolatry in general. There were almost as many forms of Baalism as there were nations, and various functions were ascribed to these Baals. Cp. Jer. 11:13; Judg. 8:33 (Baal-berith, lord of the covenant); Num. 25:3, 5 (Baal-Peor); 2 Kings 1:2 f., 6 (Baalzebub, lord of flies). Originally Baal seems to have been a personification of the sun, since several Tell el 'Amarna letters speak of "Baal of heaven." (Koenig, *Geschichte der alttestamentlichen Religion*, p. 295, 1.) Baal was also the god of

356

fertility, and his festivals were connected with immoral practices, "sacred" prostitution, etc. (Cp. Hos. 4:12-19; Amos 2:7 f.) *Chemarim* among the Syrians and Canaanites was an honorable title for their priests. Here and 2 Kings 23:5 and Hos. 10:5 it probably denotes the non-Levitical priests, Jewish or heathen, officiating at the high places and heathen sanctuaries. Luther calls them derisively "Pfaffen," a term originally used as an honorable designation of the priests. These non-Levitical priests, however, as well as the idolatrous Levitical priests, and even the heathen priests were still called "priests." (Cp. 1 Kings 12:31 f.; 13:33; 2 Kings 10:19; 11:18; 16:11-16.) Whether called by heathen or Jewish terms, all idolatrous and syncretistic priests will be cut off. The "remnant" of Baal, its last traces, will be destroyed, the very name *chemarim* no longer used. This judgment began with Josiah's reformation a few years later than this prophecy. (Cp. 2 Kings 23:4-24.) During the seventy years of the Exile, Judah was a desert and waste country (Lev. 26:30-35, 43; 2 Chron. 36:21; Jer. 25:10 f.); no Baalism, no *chemarim,* no priests. And after the return to Jerusalem, the practice of idolatry was a thing of the past, the name *chemarim* forgotten, and only Levitical priests were permitted to officiate as the Lord's servants in the Temple (Neh. 7:63-65; 13:28-31).

V. 5. Another form of idolatry was the worship of the "host of heaven," sun, moon, and stars, Sabaism in its various forms. Baal was regarded as the sun god. Beside his altars were erected "groves" (Ex. 34:13; Deut. 7:5; Judg. 3:7, etc.), tree trunks, representing Asherah, the female deity associated with Baal. She was regarded as the moon goddess, perhaps one of the various forms of Ashtaroth (Judg. 2:13; 10:6; 1 Sam. 7:3 f., etc.), known in Assyria as Ishtar, the goddess of the planet Venus, the deity of love and of war. In western Asia she was known as Ashtarte, the goddess of love and fertility, as the name indicates (cp. "increase," Deut. 7:13; 28:4, 18, 51, the translation for the Hebrew word Ashteroth = fertility). Star worship may have been one of the forms of idolatry of which Terah, Abraham's father, was guilty, since it was one of the essential forms of the Babylonian and the Assyrian religion. (See Joshua 24:2.) Star worship was one of the sins causing the collapse of the Northern Kingdom (2 Kings 17:16). It was introduced in Judah by Ahaz and Manasseh (2 Kings 21:3, 5; 23:4 f., 11 f.; Jer. 8:2; 19:3 ff.; cp. "queen of heaven," Jer. 7:18; 44:17 ff.). It was frequently practiced on roofs, where in the cool of the morning and evening people gathered for conversation, meditation, prayer (Deut. 22:8; 1 Sam. 9:25; 2 Sam. 11:2; Acts 10:9). Here the stars could be seen better than in the narrow streets, and one felt closer to them.

"And them that worship" — "by" the Lord (Gr. N.), swear allegiance to Him while swearing also by Malcham, literally, their king, their Melech, also called Milcom (1 Kings 11:5, 33; 2 Kings 23:13; Molech, Lev. 18:21; 20:2-5, etc., LXX: Moloch). He was the chief idol of the Ammonites, to whom human sacrifices were offered (Jer. 9:5; 32:35; 2 Kings 16:3; 21:6). The Jews sought to combine Jehovah's and Molech's worship in a unionistic, syncretistic religion, an abomination to the Lord. (Cp. Baal and Jehovah, 1 Kings 18:21.) The modern counterpart of such syncretism is lodgery with its religion of "deeds, not creeds," the opinion that differences in religion do not matter so long as one seeks to live right.

V. 6 names two more classes of idolaters, those who are turned "back," away, from the Lord, had deliberately forsaken Him after having followed Him, apostates; and finally those who had never "sought" (Gr. N.) the Lord, or had not even taken the trouble to ask for Him, perfectly satisfied to go through life without giving God and His will and word any consideration. — All these various forms of idolatry are mortal sins.

V. 7. "Hold thy peace!" = Hush! Silence! (Cp. Hab. 2:20 b; Zech. 2:13.) "At the presence," literally, before the face; "the Lord God," literally, the Lord Jehovah. Jehovah is the Covenant God. As such He is Lord, the supreme God, who has the right to demand what He will, and the power to enforce His will. Hush! Silence before Him! This is a call to the people of Judah to cease every manner of opposition to God's word and will, to bow down in submissive obedience, in unconditional surrender, in loving service, to their Covenant God. "For the Day of the LORD is at hand." Its proximity is the strongest possible motive for ceasing their idolatry and returning in true repentance to their Lord and God. It is a matter of life and death! For the Lord has prepared a sacrifice; He has "bidden" (Gr. N.), appointed, His "guests." The Lord speaks here in terms well known to the Jews, taken from the legislation on the sacrificial meals they were permitted to celebrate in the courts of the Temple. They brought a clean animal, laid their hands upon it, transferring their guilt to the sacrificial animal, which was then slain. Certain parts were given to the officiating priest, while the remaining meat was to be eaten in a joyous family festival to which other guests were invited. Cp. Lev. 3:13 (transfer of sin); ch. 7:11-21; 2 Chron. 35:5-13 (festival meal); 1 Sam. 9:13, 22; 16:5; 2 Chron. 30:17 ff.; Is. 13:3; Jer. 22:17 (invitation and consecration of guests). The point, however, which the Lord stresses here is His command that the sacrificial animal be consumed completely within two days; if any meat was left after that period, it was to be destroyed (Lev. 7:15-18). To such a sacrifice, the slaying and destruction of the guilty victim, God had compared His judgment of destruction threatened to His enemies. Cp. Is. 34:6 (Edom); Jer. 46:10 (Egypt); Ezek. 39:17-24 (God and Magog). Israel had sunk to the level of the Gentiles and would be completely destroyed by the Lord, who had already bidden, consecrated, appointed His guests, His called ones, His instruments of destruction. (Cp. Deut. 28:49 ff.; Jer. 1:11-16.)

2. The extent of Judah's destruction, 1:8-13

8 And it shall come to pass on the day of the LORD's sacrifice that I will punish the princes and the kings' sons, and all that are clothed 9 in foreign garb. And I will punish on this day everyone that leaps over the threshold, filling the home of their Lord with violence and 10 fraud. And there will be on this day, it is the oracle of the LORD, a noise of shouting from the Fish Gate, and a yelling from the New City, and a great crash from the 11 hills. Howl, O inhabitants of the Mortar, for all the tradespeople shall be undone, all that lift up 12 silver shall be cut off. And it shall come to pass at this time that I will search Jerusalem with lamps, and I will punish the men that are lying on their lees, that are saying within their hearts, No good does the LORD do, nor does He do evil. 13 And their riches shall become a spoil and their houses desolation. They shall build houses and not dwell in them, and they shall plant vineyards and not drink of their wine.

Grammatical Notes

V. 9. "Threshold." מִפְתָּן, occurring also in 1 Sam. 5:4 f.; Ezek. 9:3; 10:4,18; 46:2; 47:1, in every instance denotes the threshold of a sanctuary, never that of a private home. — "Masters," *adonim* for the above reason not the masters of a private home, but the lords of the temples, the idols, called *baalim,* lords (v. 4), be they idols or men (Deut. 10:17; Ps. 95:3; 136:3; Rev. 17:14; 19:16).

V. 11. "Bear silver." נְטֵיל, derived from נָטַל, to lift up (Is. 40:15; 63:9), to lift up silver into their bags, or onto the scales to weigh it, or off them to give it to some person. The verb is also used in the sense of lay upon, place upon (Lam. 3:28), hence נֵטֶל, burden (Prov. 27:3). נְטֵיל may be either a passive formation, loaded down with silver, or an active form, bearing, lifting, handling silver, merchants and bankers.

V. 12. "Settled," קָפָא = to become firm, be condensed, coagulate; used of the waters of the Red Sea becoming firm, like walls (Ex. 15:8), "congealed" (Ex. 14:22).

V. 8. Neither rank nor riches nor social prestige will safeguard the sinful Jews against God's judgment. The civic leaders are named first.

"Princes," a term denoting the officers of the king's court, his personal advisers (1 Kings 4:2; 9:23; Jer. 36:12; Hos. 8:10), his representatives (1 Kings 20:14; 2 Kings 10:1), judges and magistrates (Is. 1:23; 3:4; Jer. 24:1), the aristocracy (Jer. 4:9; Hos. 3:4). They were the chief oppressors of the people. On their punishment, see 2 Kings 24:14 f., 25:18-26; Jer. 24:1, chs. 39—44. The king is not named because he was spared the agony of seeing Jerusalem's destruction (2 Kings 22:18 ff.). The king's sons, who refused to walk in the footsteps of their pious father, learned by personal experience the truth of Jer. 2:19. On Jehoahaz, see 2 Kings 23:31 ff.; Jehoiakim, ch. 24:2; 2 Chron. 36:5 f.; Jer. 22:17-19; Jehoiachin, 2 Kings 24:15; Jer. 22:24 ff.; Zedekiah, 2 Kings 25:5-7; Jer. 52:6-11.

"Such as are clothed with strange, foreign, apparel." Particularly in their foreign relations the Jews were unwilling to be recognized by their manner of dress as the people of Jehovah. The Lord had regulated also the dress of His people to a certain extent (Num. 15:38 f.; Deut. 22:11 f.; Matt. 23:5). As the people of Judah had adopted the idols of the surrounding nations largely in the hope of gaining political or business advantages, so they adopted also their dress and were eager to parade the latest creations from the millinery and tailor shops of Babylon, Nineveh, Memphis. In the world and of the world! (See Is. 3:16-24.)

V. 9. "Leap on," rather, over, "the threshold" (Gr. N.). This is evidently a reference to a Philistine custom (1 Sam. 5:5) which the Lord names as an example of self-chosen piety, a worship in which superstitious, silly fear of an idol, whose miserable impotence had become so plainly manifest (1 Sam. 5:3, 4), was combined with stubborn refusal to accept the true God, whose power they had seen (ch. 5:3—6:18), and with flagrant transgression of His Law written in their hearts (cp. Rom. 1:18 ff.; 2:14 f.). One example of their transgressions is given: they "fill their masters' houses with violence and deceit," with ill-gotten gain obtained by oppression and fraud. Their masters (Gr. N.), either their idols or their superiors, whose servile henchmen they were. We are nowhere told that the custom of leaping over the threshold of the Temple was adopted in Judah by people or priests. The Lord means to tell His people, however, that their worship had sunk to the level of silly, superstitious, wicked pagan worship. With their lips indeed they honored Him, but their hearts were far removed (Is. 29:13; see also Is. 1:10-15; Jer. 7:8-10; Matt. 23:14 ff.). Their worship no longer was that demanded by the Lord (Deut. 6:5; 10:12;

30:6; Micah 6:8). It was a man-made religion, external, sanctimonious piety, a meticulous, almost superstitious, attention to outward rituals and ceremonies, while they were leading a life pleasing to their wicked, deceitful heart (Jer. 17:9), secretly and openly practicing the worship of money and power and carnal pleasure, and ruthlessly oppressing and defrauding their fellow men (Hab. 1:2 ff.; Jer. 5:23 ff.; 9:2 ff.). Yet they were fanatically confident that they could easily obtain God's favor by bringing sacrifices, even though they regarded the price to be paid to their God as exorbitant (Micah 5:6 f.). Silly, foolish, wicked worship!

V. 10. The judgment of God covers the entire city. "Fish Gate" (cp. Neh. 3:3; 12:39; 2 Chron. 33:14), somewhere in the northern wall, near which perhaps the fish markets offering fish from the Lake of Gennesaret were located. "Second" = the new city extending west and north from the Temple area. The exact extension of western Jerusalem after Solomon's time is unknown. Here Huldah, the prophetess, lived. See 2 Kings 22:14; 2 Chron. 34:22 (A. V., "college"; Luther, *andere Teil,* the second part). The entire city will be filled with the noise of cries, of pitiful howling and shrieking, intermingled with the triumphant shouts of slaying, plundering enemies; while from all the hills on which Jerusalem was built will resound the crash of houses and walls and palaces and the Temple, as they are being ruthlessly smashed.

V. 11. "Maktesh," "Mortar," very likely a name applied to the shallow valley, called Tyropoeon Valley, the Valley of the Dyers, separating the eastern from the western city. Here the merchants plied their trade. The prophet calls them Canaanites, the name of the pre-Israelitic inhabitants of the Westjordanland, who were eagerly engaged in trading and merchandizing. (Cp. Is. 23:8, "traffickers"; Job 41:6, "merchants," M. T., 40:30; Prov. 31:24; Zech. 14:21.) Instead of setting a good example to the Canaanites, shrewd, unscrupulous bargainers, the Israelites themselves became greedy, bargain-driving Shylocks. "Bear silver" (Gr. N.), denotes the bankers or merchants. Woe to them; they will be cut down; annihilated, cut off, utterly destroyed.

V. 12. He will "search Jerusalem with candles," diligently, thoroughly (Luke 15:8). There is no possibility of hiding from Him; not even the huge natural and artificial caves and tunnels, which honeycombed the hill on which Zion was built, will safeguard them from His avenging wrath. (Cp. Ps. 139:7 ff.; Amos 9:1 ff.) "Settled on their lees" (Gr. N.), rather, thickened, hardened. The fermented wine was left on the "lees," the solid matter which had settled to the bottom, for a while in order to acquire greater strength and better flavor. Before this "wine on the lees" (Is. 25:6) was used, it was strained to free it from its impurities, "refined" (Is. 25:6). Jeremiah compares Moab to wine "settled" on its lees, having remained in undisturbed possession of its land and having retained its national character. Zephaniah also uses this comparison, but uses a stronger term than "settled," a term meaning thickened, hardened. If wine remained too long on its lees, it turned into a syrupy, bitter, unpalatable liquid. Instead of cleansing itself of the dregs of sin by daily repentance, Judah had settled down on its dregs and impurities, until the lusts of its wicked flesh had completely permeated the good wine of sanctification and obedience to the Lord and had changed God's chosen people to a nation hardened in iniquity, equaling and surpassing the Gentiles in moral impurities, shameless vices, and self-satisfied lip service. It had become unpalatable to God, unfit for its purpose, ready to be poured away. One example of its hardness of heart, its perversion, is stated: they "say," are saying, the participle denoting habit, custom, "The LORD will not do good, neither will He do evil." He will not keep His threats nor His promises. That was placing Jehovah on the level with the idols of the heathen, degrading Him below that level, for no heathen nation so flagrantly dishonored its self-made gods.

V. 13. The Lord will prove that He is indeed the Lord God of heaven and earth. Their goods, their wealth, all that they possessed, will become the spoils of their enemies. Their houses great or small, huts or palaces, will be devastated. On v. 13 b cp. Deut. 28:30 b; Micah 6:15. So swiftly and unexpectedly will come the great Day of the Lord.

---

3. The proximity and inescapable horror of God's judgment, 1:14-18

14 Near at hand is the great Day of the LORD, near, and ahurrying swiftly. Hark! the Day of the LORD! The mighty man shall cry
15 bitterly there. A Day of wrath is that Day! A Day of anguish and distress! A Day of destruction and desolation! A Day of darkness and gloom! A Day of clouds and thun-
16 derclouds! A Day of trumpets and battle cries against the fortified cities and against the highest battlements! And I will anguish man-
17 kind so that they shall walk like the blind, for they have sinned against the LORD! And their blood shall be poured out like dust, and
18 their flesh like dung! Neither their silver nor their gold shall be able to deliver them on the Day of the LORD's wrath, and in the fire of His zeal shall all the earth be consumed; for a complete end, indeed a horrible one, shall He make of all the inhabitants of the earth.

V. 14. In this entire paragraph the Lord pronounces His judgment upon Judah in terms of His Final Judgment on the Last Day. In fact, the day of final destruction of any opponent of God, be that an individual, or a group, or an entire nation, is for that party or person the Day of the Lord, the Last Day, on which the sentence of everlasting rejection and eternal damnation is pronounced and executed upon him. Such individual "days," though occurring in time, are merely phases of the Final Judgment of the eternal, timeless God (Ps. 90:3; 2 Peter 3:8; cp. Obad. 15, p. 000).

That great Day is near! Near! Hasteth greatly! A very impressive climax. To Assyria it was far nearer than anyone could imagine, coming less than two decades later, in 612 B. C., when it was destroyed by the Medes and Babylonians. (Cp. Nah., chs. 2 and 3.) To apostate Jerusalem it came in 586 B. C., less than two generations later, to powerful Babylon in 539, less than a century later, a short time in its long history dating back to Nimrod's time. (Cp. Gen. 10:9-11.) Near, indeed, for all these nations; approaching also Judah with terrible swiftness. Already the ominous rumbling of the thunderstorm can be heard with ever-increasing distinctness. Every prophetic foretelling of this Day is a warning of coming ruin, spoken by Him whose word never fails. The ever-increasing wickedness, the stubborn persistence in idol worship in spite of all divine threats, the shameful crimes and vices crying to heaven for vengeance, are so many handwritings on the wall: Weighed and found wanting! Death is the wages of sin! Hark! Listen to these warnings! Prepare your hearts in sincere repentance before the storm breaks upon you in all its fury! For terrible, dreadful shall that Day be! So horrible that the mighty man, the warrior of many battles, accustomed to blood-curdling scenes and horrifying destruction, will shriek in abject terror at this unprecedented devastation.

V. 15. The opening words of this verse as rendered in the ancient Latin version, *Dies irae, dies illa* (Day of wrath, that day), form the basis of that great Latin hymn commonly attributed to Thomas de Celano (about 1190—1250), an assistant to Francis of Assisi. His hymn (No. 607 in *The Lutheran Hymnal*) has been translated into more languages than any other hymn. Zephaniah describes in vivid language the horrors of Judgment Day, the original Hebrew being even more impressive and awe-inspiring than any translation. Above all, that Day is a "Day of wrath," of overflowing, overpowering, crushing wrath (cp. v. 18; Is. 13:9, 13; Hos. 5:10), "trouble," straits, angina, suffocation, rendering man completely helpless; "distress," anguish;

the two words are combined in Job 15:24; "wasteness," storm, resulting "desolation," complete collapse. "Darkness and gloominess" cover the earth. (Cp. Joel 2:31; Matt. 24:29.) No star of hope is to be seen; only "clouds and thick darkness," the black thunderclouds, from which flash forth the lightning bolts of the Lord's fierce wrath.

V. 16. From all sides is heard the shrill sound of the trumpet. (Cp. Ex. 19:16-19; Jer. 4:5, 19, 21; Matt. 24:31; 1 Thess. 4:16; Heb. 12:18 f.) "Alarm," the war cry of the enemy armies, as they come on in ever-increasing numbers to carry out God's judgment on wicked Judah. Not one "fenced" city, literally, inaccessible, strongly fortified city, not the highest and strongest "tower," battlement, pinnacle, turret shall withstand the onrush of hostile warriors on that Day, the Day of the Lord's wrath!

V. 17. So distressed, hemmed in, anguished will men be that they shall stagger about helplessly like blind men. No escape for them, for they have sinned against the Lord, have missed the mark by following their own inclinations instead of walking on the paths so clearly outlined in God's Word. (Cp. Jer. 6:13-16; Rom. 1:21 ff.) Since they have left the Fountain of Life, their blood, which is the very life of man and which even God holds sacred (Gen. 9:4-6), shall be poured out as dust, and their flesh as the dung. God's noblest handiwork, corrupted by sin, is treated as a matter of no value, as a thing to be despised; as good riddance!

V. 18. Their money, the "almighty dollar," which bought immunity from punishment for them, will have lost its buying power, is woefully deflated. God is not a venal judge whose favor can be bought for silver, whose righteous anger can be appeased by gold (Ps. 50:9-13; Is. 1:10ff.; Jer. 7:8-15; Micah 6:6ff.; Acts 8:18-23). In the fire of God's fury the whole earth shall be consumed. "A speedy riddance" (Gr. N.), swift and terrible destruction, will be the fate of all the inhabitants of the earth. Again the judgment coming upon Jerusalem and Judah is described in terms of the Final Judgment of the Lord's Day. On v. 18 b see Lev. 26:32 ff.; 2 Kings 21:12-15; Jer. 24:8 ff.; 25:9 ff.

CHAPTER 2

4. Call to repentance, vv. 1-3

1 Cause yourselves to stoop! And
2 stoop, O nation unloving! Before the decree is accomplished — like chaff the Day sweeps onward! — before the fury of the LORD's anger come upon you; before the Day of the LORD's anger come upon
3 you! Seek the LORD, all you meek of the earth, who do His Law! Seek righteousness! Seek meekness! Perhaps you may be hidden on the Day of the LORD's anger!

Grammatical Notes

V. 1. "Gather yourselves together; yea, gather together." The original has only two words, הִתְקוֹשְׁשׁוּ וָקוֹשׁוּ. The verb is a denominative from קַשׁ = straw, stubble, chaff, and denotes "to gather stubble." Cp. the English terms, to berry, to nut, in the sense of seeking or gathering berries or nuts (Standard Dictionary). Qal and Hithpael occur only here, both imperatives. The Piel, in its intensive sense, occurs in Ex. 5:7 (with "straw"); v. 12 (with "stubble"); Num. 15:32 f.; 1 Kings 17:10 (with "sticks"). Hithpael here has the causative reflexive sense: to make or cause oneself to stoop. The word is never used in the sense of people gathering or assembling themselves. In all passages the idea of stooping to gather up an object from the ground, to gather by backbreaking work is indicated. — "Not desired." The verb in Qal and Niphal is used in the active sense, to long for, to desire (Qal: Ps. 17:12; Job 14:15; Niph.: Gen. 31:30; Ps. 84:3). The sense of "be ashamed," preferred by some, does not fit the other four passages.

V. 2. "Before." To the second and third בְּטֶרֶם, לֹא is added; an example of mingling of two constructions. A, before it bring forth; B, that it may not bring forth; C, before it may not bring forth. — "Pass," here, sweep onward with overwhelming swiftness (as in Num. 5:14; Ps. 38:5, A. V., 4), "gone over" (Jer. 23:5; Dan. 11:10, 40).

V. 3. "Meek," עָנָו, from עָנָה, to occupy or adopt a lowly position, be subordinate; in a moral sense, to subordinate oneself to the Lord's will; to regard oneself as His servant. (Cp. Ps. 10:17; 22:27; 25:9; Amos 2:7.)

V. 1. "Gather yourselves," etc. (Gr. N.), literally, cause yourselves to stoop, yea, stoop, as if you were gathering stubble, like poor beggars or slaves. Since man finds nothing so loathsome as to humble himself in the dust before the Lord, the prophet exhorts his fellow men to force their haughty, self-exalting flesh to stoop in true humility before the Covenant God. They are to be stubble gatherers, recognizing and acknowledging their wretched poverty (Rev. 3:17).

"O nation." The Hebrew term is that used for a Gentile nation that does not know God. (Cp. Eph. 2:12.) Proud Judah had sunk to the level of the heathen. "Not desired" (Gr. N.). Luther's translation *"feindselig,"* inimical, opposed, agrees better with the original "not desiring" (Gr. N.), not longing for God. Judah proudly imagined that it could get along just as well without God. Its worship was base hypocrisy. What the nation needed first of all was humble return and submission to its God.

V. 2. The urgent need of repentance. "Before the decree bring forth." The context requires to regard this as God's punitive decree. "The decree of God is spoken of as the mother of the event" *(The Bible Commentary).* (Cp. Job 15:35; Ps. 7:15; Is. 33:11, and our expression: the wish is father of the thought.) The decree, long ago announced

(Deut. 28:15 ff.), is now rushing on to its enactment. "Before the day pass as the chaff" is best regarded as a parenthesis: "Like chaff the day sweeps onward!" The prophet makes use of an experience very familiar and disagreeable to the Jews, when at threshing time a sudden gust of wind overwhelms all in the neighborhood with a cloud of chaff. "Pass" (Gr. N.), here used in the sense of sweep onward, overwhelm suddenly, swiftly. A twofold warning to repent is added, lest the fierce anger of the Lord come upon them, the second clause describing this fierce anger as that of the Lord's Day, final, unappealable, immutable.

V. 3. This warning is addressed to all Jews, particularly to the "meek of the earth" (Gr. N.). This does not denote the proletariat, the working people, the socially oppressed; but the meek and humble among rich and poor. It describes those who acknowledge God's justice in sending His judgments and who humbly cling to His undeserved mercy in promising salvation through the coming Redeemer (Job 1:21; 2:10; 13:15; 19:25-27; 42:1-9; Acts 21:10-14; 2 Cor. 12:7-10). "Have wrought His judgment." They are obedient to His norm, the norm of His saving Gospel, making that the sole hope of their salvation. They also follow the norm of His Law, making that the sole rule of their lives. And since their best efforts in both endeavors do not reach perfection, the prophet calls on them that have by God's grace been endowed with spiritual life to continue to seek the Lord, who is gracious (Ex. 34:6); to seek righteousness, that of the Gospel by growing in faith, and that of the Law by growing in sanctification and good works. "Seek meekness," cast away every trace of self-righteousness and pride; walk meekly, humbly, in self-effacement, with your God. (Cp. 1 Cor. 15:9 f.; Gal. 2:20 f.; 6:14; Phil. 3:4-15.)

"It may be," here, as in Gen. 16:2; Is. 37:4; Lam. 3:29 and context, vv. 26-32; Amos 5:15; an expression of a humble yet confident petition, confessing the prophet's own powerlessness and unworthiness, yet his trust that by God's grace his admonition would not be altogether in vain. "Hid" from God's wrath. (Cp. Ps. 17:8; 27:5.)

C. God's Judgment upon the Gentile Nations, Vv. 4-15

The Lord's universal judgment is now announced as it shall come to each of the individual nations in God's appointed time. Four nations surrounding Judah are named: on the west, Philistia; on the east, Moab and Ammon; on the south, Ethiopia; on the north, Assyria. In the very center of the territory visited by the Lord's judgments lies

Judah. It will escape only if it ceases to adopt the idolatrous, immoral ways and customs of these Gentile nations and heeds the divine warning expressed vv. 1-3.

1. God's judgment upon Philistia, vv. 4-7

4 Surely, Gaza shall become forsaken and Ashkelon desolation. Ashdod! — at noontime they shall expel her;
5 and Ekron shall be uprooted. Woe unto the inhabitants of the seacoast, the nation of the Cherethites! The word of the LORD is against you, O Canaan, land of the Philistines! I will destroy you, so that you will
6 have no inhabitants. The sea coast shall become pasture land, caves for shepherds, and folds for flocks.
7 And the seacoast will belong to the remnant of the house of Judah. They shall feed on them. In the houses of Ashkelon they shall lie down at evening. For the LORD, their God, shall visit them and restore their fortune.

Grammatical Notes

V. 4. "Gaza," etc. Note the play on Gaza — *azubah*, "forsaken," the accent in both words on the last syllable; also Ekron — *te'aker*, "rooted up."

V. 5. "Coast," חֶבֶל = rope, cord; measuring cord; what is assigned by measuring, allotted portion, district; Deut. 3:4, 13, "region"; v. 14, "coasts"; Joshua 19:9, "portion"; Ps. 16:6, "lines."

V. 6. "Cottages." כְּרֹת occurs only here; the meaning is disputed. Probably derived from כָּרָה, to dig; hence, diggings, pit, cistern. We prefer to render it cave; natural, dug by nature, or artificial, man-made, used by shepherds and their flocks as a shelter at night or in stormy weather. LXX reads: Crete shall be a pasture, etc.

V. 7. "Lie down," primarily has the connotation of safety, satisfaction (Gen. 29:2; Is. 11:6 f.; Ezek. 34:14).

Vv. 4 ff. are directed against Philistia. The Philistines had settled on the lowlands of the Mediterranean coast as early as the time of Abraham (Gen. 20:1 ff.; 21:22-34; 26:1 ff.). They were a Hamitic nation, coming to Canaan from Caphtor (cp. Gen. 10:6, 13 f.), very likely Crete. Cherethites (v. 5) is either a second name of the Philistines or the name of a brother nation. (Cp. 1 Sam. 30:14; Ezek. 25:16.) The early history of the Philistines is still shrouded in darkness. They carried on an extensive commerce so that the land of Canaan was known far and wide as the land of the Philistines, the modern Palestine. Usually five "chief cities" of Philistia are named (Joshua 13:3; Judg. 3:3; 1 Sam. 6:4, 16-18). Here and in Amos 1:6-8 Gath is omitted, probably because it had not sufficiently recovered from its destruction by Uzziah (2 Chron. 26:6) to regain its rank. Gaza, the southernmost of the four cities named by Zephaniah, lay a few miles inland; Ashkelon, near the seashore; Ekron, some distance northeast of Ashdod,

367

exact site uncertain. Time and again these cities were destroyed during the many wars that ravaged Palestine in the centuries following this prophecy. Pharaoh Necho devastated Philistia (Jer. 47:1-7); Alexander the Great depopulated Gaza and repeopled it from the neighborhood (Arrian, *Anabasis* II, 27). Later, Philistia became a Syrian province and in the Maccabean wars was raided and ravaged repeatedly by the Jews (1 Macc. 5:68; 10:67-89; 11:60 ff.; 13:43 ff.). About 65 B. C. Pompey incorporated Ashdod and Gaza as free cities in the Roman province of Syria. Today Gaza, Ashdod, and Ashkelon are flourishing cities. During the first century Philistia was Christianized (Acts 8:40; 9:32 ff.), and for centuries it was the scene of vigorous Christian activity, until Islam took over.

V. 4. "Gaza shall be forsaken ... Ekron, rooted up" (Gr. N.). "At the noon day." Usually the invading armies rested during the hot noon hours. An attack at noontime had the purpose of surprising the unwary enemy. (Cp. Jer. 6:4 f.; 15:8; 1 Kings 20:16 and context, vv. 13-21.) Ashdod shall suddenly, unexpectedly, be captured and "driven out." (Cp. Ex. 23:29 ff.; 33:2.)

V. 5. "Coast" (Gr. N.), territory or district allotted to someone, so also v. 6 f. "Cherethites." See above, v. 4 ff. "The word of the LORD is against you," literally, upon you. Resting heavily on them is the curse now pronounced on them. For this reason their land is called Canaan, in reminiscence of the accursed son of Ham (Gen. 9:25). The whole nation shall be destroyed so that no Philistine shall dwell any more in the land. The nation has disappeared without a trace.

Vv. 6, 7. Instead of a mercantile, belligerent people inhabiting the land, seeking to heap up riches for themselves and to increase their own power, there "shall be dwellings and cottages for shepherds and folds for flocks." "Dwellings," the Hebrew term denotes primarily the temporary resting places or settlements of nomads and shepherds, and often acquires the sense of pasture, meadow. "Cottages" (Gr. N.), most probably caves, natural or artificial, in which shepherds and sheep sought shelter at night or in stormy weather. And here these terms are to be taken not in a merely physical sense, but in a nobler, spiritual sense (v. 7). The territory of the former inveterate enemy will be conquered by the "remnant of the house of Judah," the believing children of God, the Church of God's elect (Is. 10:20-22; 37:4, 32; Obad. 19; Micah 2:12; 5:6-8; Rom. 2:28 f.; 9:27 ff.). This "remnant" shall be composed of shepherds (cp. John 21:15 ff.; Acts 20:17, 28 ff.; 1 Peter 5:2 ff.) and sheep (John 10:2-30). They shall "feed," pasture, on the fields formerly occupied by the enemies of the Church; lie down (Gr. N.) without fear, in perfect peace with their God, safe and secure under His protection. What a gracious visitation by the Covenant God to His downtrodden people! What a wonderful change of their former condition! On the fulfillment see remarks on v. 4 ff., pp. 367 f.

---

2. God's judgment upon Moab and Ammon, vv. 8-11

8 I have heard the taunts of Moab and the revilings of the children of Ammon, who have taunted My people and arrogated to themselves authority over their territory.

9 Therefore as I live, is the oracle of the LORD of Hosts, the God of Israel, Moab shall become like Sodom, and the children of Ammon like Gomorrah, the possession of nettles, and salt pits, and perpetual desolation. The remnant of My people shall pillage them, and the remainder of My nation shall possess them. 10 This shall be their reward for their arrogance; for they have taunted and arrogated to themselves authority over the people of the LORD of Hosts. 11 The LORD will prove Himself terrible against them, for He will cause all the gods of the earth to waste away; and all the coastlands of the earth shall worship Him, each from his own place.

Grammatical Notes

V. 9. "Breeding," מִמְשַׁק, only here; possibly possession; the verb does not occur. בֶּן־מֶשֶׁק occurs Gen. 15:2; translated by Leupold, *Exp. of Genesis*, "son of possession" = my prospective heir; *The Complete Bible*, "my heir"; so also Keil-Delitzsch. A land becomes the heir, the heritage, the possession of nettles when it is overgrown by them.

V. 11. "Isles," אִיִּים, denotes the coastlands, bounded by the sea = continents; or surrounded by the sea = islands, irrespective of their size.

Vv. 8, 9. Moab and Ammon were brother nations, descendants of Lot (Gen. 19:30-38). They were noted for their proud arrogance (v. 10; cp. Is. 16:6; 25:10 f.; Jer. 48:11, 29 f.), their inhuman cruelty (Amos 1:13—2:1; 1 Kings 11:7; Jer. 7:31; 2 Kings 3:27). On their enmity against Israel see Num. 22:1-6; 25:1-8; Judg. 3:12 ff.; 2 Kings 3:4 ff.; 2 Chron. 20:1 ff.; Ezek. 25:8 (Moab); Judg. 11:4-33; 1 Sam. 11:1-11; 2 Sam. 10:1-14; 2 Chron. 20:1 ff.; Neh. 2:10, 19; 4:3-23; Jer. 40:14 (Ammon). "Magnified themselves," vaunted themselves, sought to domineer God's people; by open warfare or infiltration sought to regain possession of the land which the Lord had taken from them and given to His people. They rebelled against the Lord of Hosts, the Ruler of the universe, by harassing and attacking His chosen people. Descendants of mothers who had committed Sodomitic incest, they were to meet the fate of Sodom and Gomorrah, utter destruction

369

(v. 9). "Breeding" (Gr. N.), literally, possession. The whole land shall be overgrown with nettles, thorns, thistles, be possessed by them, a symbol of desolation (Prov. 24:31; Is. 34:13; Hos. 9:6; 10:8, etc.). "Salt pits," again a reminder of the curse resting upon Sodom and Gomorrah, covered by the salty waters of the Dead Sea. At its south-western end stretches from north to south a salt hill, five miles long, three miles wide, known as Jebel Usdum, Mountain of Sodom. Salt also was strewn on the foundation of a city as a token of irretrievable ruin (Judg. 9:45). Barren, desolate country is called salt land (Deut. 29:23; Job 39:6, marginal reading; Jer. 17:6). "The residue," *she'erit,* same word as rendered "remnant" in v. 7, the believing Jews. "Remnant," *yeter,* is used in the same sense here, and also Micah 5:2. The believing remnant, the Church of God, shall "spoil" Moab and Ammon, conquer their land and riches, and possess them. The *Westminster Historical Atlas* informs us: "Christianity had a great expansion in Transjordan in the early centuries. Prominent in this period were Gerasa, where the ruins of many splendid churches have been excavated and studied, and Medeba, where a marvelous mosaic map of Palestine has been found in the floor of an ancient church" (p. 60 b). Medeba at the time of Zephaniah belonged to Moab, while Gerasa, one of the Roman cities of the Decapolis, was situated on territory occupied by the Ammonites in the seventh century B. C.

Vv. 10, 11. Once more their besetting sin is named, their arrogant pride. They had had their day of grace; they had rejected the Lord, His Word, His Law, His Gospel. Proudly, stubbornly they clung to their man-made gods. Now there shall come upon them the terrible wrath of God (v. 11). The Lord will "famish" all the gods of the earth, among them the idols of Moab and Ammon. These gods, well fed by the multitudes of sacrifices, including the sons and daughters of the worshipers (see remarks on ch. 1:5), will famish, waste away as by consumption. The fate of the gods is the fate of their worshipers. Wherever the Gospel is preached and accepted, the thrones of man-made gods totter and fall. Their former worshipers bow down in grateful adoration before the God of their salvation. From all the isles (Gr. N.), the coastlands and islands, great and small, prayers shall ascend to the Lord God. Men of every nation (Rev. 14:6 f.) will glorify the God and Father of our Lord Jesus, "everyone from his place." No need of journeying to Jerusalem, for the true Jerusalem, the Church of God, comes to them wherever they are (Heb. 12:22 f.; John 4:21; Is. 2:3). But he that believeth not shall be damned.

3. God's judgment against the Cushites, v. 12

12 You also, O Cushites! Pierced by My sword are they!

V. 12. The Lord addresses the Cushites. They are to listen attentively. Suddenly the Lord turns to all the world. All nations are to take note of His judgment upon this powerful nation and let it serve as a warning in order to escape like punishment.

"Ethiopians," as "Cushites" is most frequently translated by LXX, were descendants of Cush, the son of Ham (Gen. 10:6). They settled in the south and southwest of Egypt. Ezekiel designates Syene, the modern Aswan, or Assuan, at the first cataract, about 530 miles south of Alexandria, as the southern boundary of Egypt (Ezek. 29:10; 30:6, "from the 'tower' [*migdol*] of Syene," literally, from Migdol — in the extreme north of Egypt — to Syene). Cush therefore included what is now known as the Eastern, or Egyptian, Sudan, together with Ethiopia, Somaliland, and Eritrea. Zephaniah speaks of rivers of Cush (3:10, cp. Is. 18:1), referring to the White and the Blue Nile and their many tributaries. Herodotus writes: "Ethiopia lies south and west of Arabia at the end of the world. . . . Its people are of great size and beauty, and long-lived" (Her. III, 20, 23, 114). (Cp. Is. 18:2, "scattered and peeled," literally, tall and sleek. *The Complete Bible*.) In the days of Hezekiah of Judah and Hoshea of Israel, Cushite kings, *Shabaka,* called *So* (2 Kings 17:4), *Shabataka,* and *Taharka,* called *Tirhaka* (2 Kings 19:9; Is. 37:9), ruled Egypt for a number of decades, until Tirhaka was decisively defeated by the Assyrian king Esarhaddon ca. 670 B. C. Asa had defeated the huge army of Zerah, a Cushite king threatening the very life of Judah (2 Chron. 14:9-13).

Against these southern enemies, Ethiopians and Egyptians, this brief statement is directed, the Lord Himself addressing them: "Ye shall be slain by My sword." The Lord is the sovereign Ruler of the world and of the destiny of every individual nation. He can and will destroy all enemies of His Church, no matter how powerful they may be (Ps. 46). The Gospel came to Ethiopia through the eunuch of Candace (Acts 8:26 ff.). Two captive Christians, Aidisius and Frumentius, established the Christian Church about A. D. 320. The latter was consecrated the first archbishop of Ethiopia by Athanasius of Alexandria ca. 330.

4. God's judgment upon Assyria, vv. 13-15

13 He will stretch out His hand against the north and destroy Assyria and make Nineveh desolate, arid as the 14 wilderness. And flocks shall lie down in her midst, all kinds of beasts in hordes. Pelicans as well

as hedgehogs shall roost in her capitals. A voice shall sing in the windows. Destruction on the threshold! For her cedarwork is 15 laid bare. This is the exultant city that sits at ease, that says in her heart, "I! and there is none else!" How will she become desolation, a resting place for animals! Everyone passing by will hiss and shake his hand.

Grammatical Notes

V. 14. "The beasts of the nations." חַיְתוֹ. חַיְתוֹ־גוֹי is the ancient form of the construct. It occurs in poetic and exalted speech (Gen. 1:24; Ps. 50:10; 79:2; 104:11, 20; Is. 56:9; Zeph. 2:14; בְּנוֹ, son of, Num. 23:18; 24:3, 15; מַעְיְנוֹ, Ps. 114:8). The genitive "of the nations" is appositional: the beasts, a nation, a horde. — "Cormorant" is a large, web-footed, aquatic bird, very voracious; also called "shag." The Hebrew קָאַת is rendered "pelican" by the LXX. The pelican is listed among the unclean birds in Lev. 11:18 and Deut. 14:17; while in Ps. 102:6 (A. V., 7) and Is. 34:11 it is described as inhabiting desolate places. "Bittern," a translation adopted by Hitzig and Cheyne, is generally rendered "hedgehog," so LXX. The Asiatic hedgehog is a short-tailed, spiny, insectivorous animal, named here, as in Is. 14:23 and 34:11, as dwelling in wastelands.

Vv. 13, 14. The prophet now speaks of God in the third person. From the extreme south his eyes sweep to the far north. Assyria is frequently called the enemy from the north. The wide desert lay between Israel and Assyria, and all attacks by Assyria came from the north via the Fertile Crescent. The Lord, who had stretched out His hand against Pharaoh and his host (Ex. 14 and 15), will destroy the rival of Egypt, Nineveh, the great city (Gen. 10:10-12), which dominated the world for almost 500 years, 1100—612. He will change it into a desolate, dry wilderness. Where once rose the mansions of the rich, the temples of their gods, the palaces of their kings, the storehouses filled with loot from many countries, there flocks of sheep shall find their resting place (v. 14). "All the beasts of the nations" (Gr. N.): the city teeming with people shall be the meeting place of hordes of wild animals. "Cormorant" (Gr. N.), rather, pelican. "Bittern" (Gr. N.), the hedgehog shall lodge, roost, "in the upper lintels," the elaborately carved capitals of the massive pillars supporting the roofs. Some of these pillars may have remained standing, affording a nesting place for pelicans; others crashed to the ground, and hedgehogs dug their burrows among them. The palaces of the nabobs, the proud rulers of the world, the majestic temples of their gods — now a hiding place for hedgehogs! The broad river on whose waters merchants came from afar with their wares, is now visited only by pelicans on their quest for food! What an ironical reversal! "Their

voice," rather, a voice. The sighing, moaning sound of the wind blowing through the wide open window spaces is compared to the chanting of a dirge over fallen Nineveh (cp. Hab. 2:11). Desolation, ruin,
like a grim specter, occupies the debris-covered thresholds of the
dwellings of rich and poor, men and gods. "For He," the one and only
true and holy God, shall uncover, lay bare, the cedarwork, the elaborate panelings covering the walls and ceilings, and expose them to
the ravages of storm and rain. From top to bottom all is ruin,
desolation.

V. 15. Nineveh had rejoiced, tumultuously, boisterously celebrated its triumphs. In careless, self-satisfied security it regarded itself
as invincible. "I! None other beside me!" had been her proud challenge to all the world, to Israel, the people of God, to the Lord Himself! The Lord's answer? "How is she become a desolation," ruin!
A resting place for animals; an object of scorn and malicious contempt
for all that pass by. The very site of Nineveh, covered by sand, was
forgotten for centuries! (Cp. Nah. 2 and 3.)

CHAPTER 3

D. God's Judgment upon Judah Repeated, Vv. 1-7

1 Woe to the rebellious and polluted
2 one, the city of oppression! She
has listened to no voice; she has
accepted no discipline. In the
LORD she has not trusted; to God
3 she has not drawn near. Her
princes in her midst are roaring
lions; her judges, evening wolves
that leave not a bone for the morn-
4 ing. Her prophets are wanton and
treacherous persons. Her priests
profane that which is holy; they do
5 violence to the Law. The LORD is
righteous in their midst. He does
not commit perversity. Morning by
morning He brings His judgments
to light without fail. Yet the perverted people know no shame!
6 I have cut off nations, ruined their
battlements. I have laid waste their
roads so that no one passes by on
them. Their cities are destroyed, so
that there is no man, so that there
7 is no inhabitant. I said, Surely you
will fear Me. You will accept correction — so that her dwelling place
might not be cut off in accordance
with what I have decreed against
her. Yet eagerly they corrupted all
their doings.

Grammatical Notes

V. 1. "Filthy and polluted." "Filthy" is
the Qal part. fem. of מֹרְאָ, a secondary
form of מָרָה, to be rebellious. "Polluted" is Niphal part. fem. of גָּאַל, to be
unclean, polluted (Is. 59:3; Lam. 4:14);
the Pual occurs Ezra 2:62; Neh. 7:64;
Mal. 1:7, 12.
V. 3. "They gnaw not." The verb occurs here, Num. 24:8; Ezek. 23:34,
"break." It denotes the breaking and
crushing of the bones; greedy, complete
destruction. The Hebrew perfect here
denotes the act as completed. — "In the
morning," לְ, may mean "in" (Gen.
8:11, "in the evening"; Gen. 49:27, "at
night") or "until" (Deut. 16:4; 1 Sam.

13:8, A. V.: "according to"). If one prefers "in," the sense would be that the
gnawing was no longer carried on in
the morning, because then there was
nothing left to gnaw.

V. 4. "Light." Part. Qal of פֹּחֵז = to
bubble over, be wanton, unbridled
(Judg. 9:4); the noun forms occur in
Jer. 23:32, "wanton lies," and Gen. 49:4,
of Reuben's sin, which made him unfit

for leadership, the right of the first-
born.

V. 7. "Howsoever I punished." כֹּל is the
adverbial accusative, denoting manner,
relation, etc. (G.-K. 118 m — r.) "Punished," here = appoint, ordain (2 Chron.
36:23; Ezra 1:2; Job 34:13; 36:23);
hence: according to all I had appointed
to them, viz., if they transgressed My
commandments (Deut. 28:16 ff.).

V. 1. Having pronounced His judgment on the countries surrounding Judah, the Covenant God once more turns to Judah in order
to call the apostates to repentance and encourage the faithful remnant.
Jerusalem (Ps. 78:68 f.; 132:13 f.) had sunk to the level of her
heathen neighbors. In one of the severest indictments recorded in
Scripture the Lord charges her with having become filthy (Gr. N.),
literally, rebellious, defiant, mutinous, against her Lord; polluted, contaminated by bloody guilt, sins crying to heaven for vengeance;
oppressing. (Cp. Hab. 1:2 ff.)

V. 2. In three short, piercing statements the Lord describes the
woeful wickedness of Jerusalem. "She obeyed not the voice," rather,
"a voice," my voice, absolutely refused to listen to any warning,
human or divine. "Correction," whether in the form of gentle rebuke,
loving admonition, or severest punishments, was rejected. Jehovah,
who had been her faithful Covenant God and Protector throughout
the centuries, was regarded as unworthy of her trust. Her people
did not draw near to Him, either in their prayer or in their sacrifice
(Is. 29:13).

Vv. 3, 4. Judah's civic and spiritual leaders excelled in wickedness. "Princes," civic officials in general, are like roaring lions, lusting
for new victims. The "judges," magistrates, are like evening wolves
that go out on their raids under cover of darkness and greedily gulp
down their prey, crushing the very bones until nothing is left. Under
the pretense of law and justice they mercilessly fleece their victims
and never are satisfied, always hungry for more gain (Amos 2:6-8;
Matt. 23:14, 25). The prophets (v. 4), the many self-styled messengers
of God (Jer. 23:9 ff.), are "light" (Gr. N.), frivolous, irresponsible,
unfit for leadership (Micah 2:11; 3:5; Jer. 6:13 b, 14), "treacherous,"
deceiving the people (Jer. 28:1-17; 29:21-23). The priests profaned the
sanctuary (1 Sam. 2:12-36). They did violence to the Law which they

were to teach to the people and the proper observance of which they were to safeguard (Lev. 10:11; Deut. 31:9 ff.; 33:8; Mal. 2:7 ff.). Instead, they twisted it to suit their own advantage and permitted and sanctioned such shameful wickedness as described in Jer. 7:8-11. They manipulated the Law of God chiefly for the purpose of filling their purses and paunches.

V. 5. In the midst of this people the Lord of unchanging righteousness dwells. He is guilty of no iniquity, no perverseness, no faithlessness, in keeping His covenant (Deut. 32:4). Every morning, day by day, He brings forth His "judgment," the "norm" of Jehovah, the Lord of righteousness and justice, and of eternal grace and mercy. And therefore His norm is one of never-relaxing holiness and of mercy new every morning. In the daily morning and evening sacrifice (Ex. 29:38-43) the sacrificial lamb, slain for sinful man, revealed God's wrath against the guilty sinner who had broken His norm, His Law; the need of man's redemption; the vicarious atonement to be accepted by faith in the Redeemer, revealed in the norm of the Gospel. Yet the perverse people know no shame (Is. 26:10); they regarded His very grace as a license for wickedness (Jer. 7:4-11).

Vv. 6, 7. Judah had seen many an example of God's judgment against nations transgressing His Law. Entire nations, including their sister nation Israel, had been cut off, extirpated. Such judgments should have caused Judah to fear God (v. 7). That had been one of the purposes of these judgments, a warning to the people of Judah "to receive," accept, "instruction," to learn the lesson intended for them, to turn from their wickedness (Jer. 3:6-10). Then their dwelling, Jerusalem, would not be cut off, destroyed, "howsoever I punish them" (Gr. N.), rather, according to all I have appointed, or decreed, against her in such threats as Lev. 26:14 ff.; Deut. 28:16 ff. None of these threats would be fulfilled if Judah would return in true repentance to the Lord. But, instead, "they rose early," became only the more eager in corrupting all their doings, deliberately doing what was corrupt, foul in itself, offensive to God, death-dealing to themselves.

---

5. Wait in patient trust for God's Day! V. 8

8 Therefore wait for Me, is the oracle of the LORD till the day when I shall arise to the prey. For Mine is the right to assemble nations, to gather kingdoms, in order to pour out My wrath upon them, the full fury of My anger. For in the fire of My zeal shall all the earth be consumed.

V. 8. "Wait ye upon Me!" Believers are often assailed by doubts as to God's justice when they see the wicked prosper and flourish (Ps. 73; Jer. 12; Hab. 1: 2 ff.). The Lord asks His believing followers patiently, trustingly to look for His help. In His own time He will arise, like a hunter rising up to seize his victim caught in the net. It is His determination, literally, His inalienable right, to assemble all the nations and kingdoms. (Cp. Joel 4: 2, 12, A. V., 3: 2, 12.) Even in slaying His opponents He exercises His right and privilege as the Judge of the world in order to deliver His oppressed Church. Again this judgment in time is regarded as merely a phase of that last Judgment Day when all the world will be consumed by fire. At the same time every overthrow of the enemies of God's people shall be a day of salvation for His people, foreshadowing the era of the New Testament salvation and the spreading of God's Church to the ends of the world. That is the final and comforting thought of Zephaniah's prophecy (vv. 9-20).

III. The Universality of God's Grace Embracing Jew and Gentile, Vv. 9-20

A. Gentiles and Jews United into One Holy Church, Vv. 9-13

9 For then I will turn to the nations cleansed lips, so that all of them will call upon the name of the LORD to serve Him with one ac-
10 cord. From beyond the rivers of Ethiopia will they bring My worshipers, the daughter of My dis-
11 persed, as My offering. On that day you will not be ashamed of any of your deeds whereby you have trespassed against Me, for then I will remove from your midst your haughty rejoicers, and you shall nevermore exalt yourselves again
12 on My holy mountain. And I will leave in your midst a humble and lowly people, and they shall trust
13 in the name of the LORD. The remnant of Israel will not do wrong, nor will they speak lies, and there will not be found in their mouth a tongue of deceit; for they shall feed and lie down, and no one shall disturb them.

Grammatical Notes

V. 9. "Turn a pure language." Turn, הֲפֹךְ, is used in the sense of changing the nature of an object (Ex. 10:19), turned the east wind (v. 13) into west wind; 1 Sam. 10:9, God "gave," turned (his heart) into another heart; here, changed the impure lips into pure lips. Lips = language (Gen. 11:1, 6, 7, 9, etc.). — "Consent," literally, shoulder, the upper part of the back, on which burdens were carried (Gen. 21:14; 24:15, 45; 49:15).

V. 11. "Rejoice in thy pride," עַלִּיזֵי גַּאֲוָתֵךְ. The pronominal suffix is added to the genitive describing an attribute, as in "the mountain of My holiness" = My holy mountain; here, the rejoicers in thy pride = thy proud rejoicers. — "Because of," בְּ, here in its local sense: on, upon.

V. 9. "For" states another reason for patient, hopeful trust in the Lord. Not only will all opponents of God's Church meet with their well-deserved punishment; the Church of God will also grow and flourish to an extent unprecedented in the centuries of its existence. The Lord will turn to the nations a pure language. No longer shall His Kingdom of Grace be confined to one small nation, whose territory at that time had dwindled to about 5,000 square miles. From distant Ethiopia (see ch. 2:12), at that time regarded as the end of the world, would His worshipers come to a Kingdom covering almost 40,000 times more territory than little Judah. It will be world-wide. This vast territory will not be conquered by bloody war machinery, but in a peaceful manner. The Lord will turn to nations a pure language (Gr. N.). As the lips of Isaiah, the sinful member of a sinful people, had been purified by the fiery coal from the altar typifying the Cross of Calvary, so the Lord will change the impure lips of Gentile nations by the preaching of this Cross. The lips, the mouth, speak out of the abundance of the heart, that desperately wicked heart (Jer. 17:9), harboring only evil continually (Mark 7:21), and contaminating every desire, thought, word, and deed of man. This heart the Lord purifies, renews (Jer. 31:33 f.; Ezek. 36:25-27; 47:1-12; Heb. 10:22; 1 Peter 1:22; 3:21; Acts 15:7-9), so that they all with one accord glorify God, even the Father of our Lord Jesus Christ (Rom. 15:6,9). And this will be no mere lip service, but "all will serve Him with one consent" (Gr. N.). All will put their shoulder to His service in joyful gratitude for His salvation. This new heart and life is not due to any self-preparation on the part of the Gentiles. God turns to them pure lips, God creates a new heart by His almighty grace (2 Cor. 4:6; Eph. 1:19 f.). He implants the knowledge of the Lord in their hearts (Hos. 2:20 b; John 17:3) and fills their lips with a new song (Ps. 40:3) and makes them able and willing to yield their members as instruments of righteousness to God (Rom. 6:13).

V. 10. Worshipers is regarded by A. V. as the subject, offerings as the object. In favor of this construction it is said that "daughter of My dispersed" must refer to the scattered Jews. (Cp. Ezek. 11:16; 12:15; 20:23, etc.) They shall return to Jerusalem, be converted to Christianity. Millennialists regard this as a prophecy of the physical return of the Jews. Yet also the Gentiles are called "scattered abroad," "aliens afar off," "going astray" (John 10:16; 11:52; Eph. 2:12-19; 1 Peter 2:25; cp. Is. 42:1-7; 49:22; 60:3-9; 66:18 ff.). The converted Gentiles carry on mission work among Gentiles and Jews throughout the world and so bring God's elect children, scattered throughout all lands, to the Jerusalem of the New Testament, the Church of Christ, as a thankoffering in gratitude for their own conversion. On this idea cp. Rom. 15:16; Phil. 2:17, Paul "offering" the converted Romans and Philippians, Jews and Gentiles, to God.

Vv. 11, 12. In that day, the New Testament era, the Church shall not be ashamed of all its doings. "Transgressed." The chief sin of the Old Testament people of God was their transgression, rebellion, apostasy from God. In the New Testament all "that rejoice in thy pride" (Gr. N.), that proudly rejoice in their own righteousness, that are haughty "because of" (Gr. N.), rather, on My holy mountain, shall be removed. Not only self-righteousness, but also every form of pride, such as boasting of one's Christian parentage, of the fact that one is baptized, confirmed, has joined the church, and making this external fact the basis of one's pride and assurance of salvation, excludes from God's Church. (See Is. 1:10 ff.; Jer. 7:2 ff.; Rom. 2:17 ff.; 2 Tim. 3:5.) If such people ever were members of the true Church of Christ, the Lord, who knoweth His own (2 Tim. 2:19), no longer acknowledges them as His own. Unless they return, they are stricken forever from the Lord's roster. In the New Testament Church there will be only an "afflicted" people (v. 12), bowed down, humbled by the knowledge of their own sinfulness and unworthiness (Luke 15:21; 18:13; 1 Tim. 1:15); "poor," having nothing to offer (Rom. 7:18). They put their whole trust in the "name of the Lord," in His revelation, in His Word, which assures them that He, the holy and just God, is at the same time the Lord of unchanging mercy and never-ending grace (Ex. 34:6, 7 a; 1 Tim. 1:15 f.). These humble, trusting believers He will "leave," cause to remain, in the midst of the mass of church members as the "remnant of Israel" (v. 13; cp. Is. 10:22 f.; Rom. 9:6-33; 11:1-7). They are what they are by the grace of God alone (1 Cor. 15:10).

V. 13. This "remnant shall not do iniquity," etc. The prophet does not teach perfectionism. To understand these words correctly we must consider that he lists here only mortal sins, which destroy faith. "Iniquity" is perverseness (Is. 59:3), crookedness; see "unjust," Zeph. 3:5; "speak lies," a "deceitful tongue," hypocrisy, all are mortal sins, condemned by the Lord (Matt. 23:2-35; Gal. 5:20 f.). In the second place, the verbs employed by the inspired prophet in v. 13 all are imperfects, which tense denotes reiteration. He is speaking here not of occasional lapses, but of a life of ever-repeated mortal sins which kill faith and trust in God's Word. Members of God's Church do not on every occasion practice these or similar sins, as unconverted heathen

378

do (Eph. 2:1-3; 1 Peter 4:1-5). They wage a daily warfare against sin (Rom. 7:14-25; 1 Cor. 9:24-27; Eph. 4:17 ff.). In waging this warfare they do not trust in their own strength, but in the power supplied by the Lord. "For they shall feed," etc. The Lord states the reason why the members of His holy Church lead a holy and godly life, as Paul calls it in Titus 2:12. "They feed and lie down" on the green pastures of God's Word and Sacraments, a pasture prepared by their Shepherd. His words are spirit and are life (John 6:63). By this Word they were regenerated (1 Peter 1:23); in this Word they find strength to grow in knowledge, to walk worthy of the Lord unto all pleasing (Col. 1:9ff.; Eph. 6:11 ff.).

B. Joyous Activity on Earth and in Heaven, Vv. 14-20

14 Sing loud, O daughter of Zion! Shout, O Israel! Be joyous and jubilant with all the heart, O
15 daughter of Jerusalem! The LORD has removed your judgments; He has cast out your enemy. The King of Israel, the LORD, is in your midst, you shall see no evil any
16 more! On that day it shall be said to Jerusalem, Fear not, O Zion! Let
17 not your hands be slack! The LORD, your God, is in the midst of you, a mighty Man who will help. He will rejoice over you with joy. He will be silent in His love. He will exult over you with shouting.
18 I will assemble those that are sorrowing for the festival gatherings. Of you they are! A burden upon
19 them is the shame. Behold, at that time I will deal with all that maltreat you; and I will deliver her that halts, and her that is driven out I will gather. And I will make them praised and renowned in
20 every land of their shame. At that time I will bring you home, at the very time that I gather you. For I will make you renowned and praised among all the nations of the earth, when I shall change your fortune before your eyes, is the oracle of the LORD.

Grammatical Notes

V. 15. "Cast out." Pi. of פָּנָה, to turn, here has the sense of "turn out," clear away, as dirt and rubbish are cleared away in housecleaning (Gen. 24:31; Lev. 14:36, "empty").

V. 17. "Rest." Both Qal of חָרַשׁ (Ps. 35:22, etc.) and Hiphil (Gen. 24:21 and more than 20 times) denote to be silent. There is no reason for changing the word to "renew" or for other emendations. It is a bold but very effective anthropomorphism describing the profoundness of God's joy.

V. 19. "Undo." עָשָׂה with the preposition אֵת is used here in the sense of "deal with." (See Jer. 21:2; Ezek. 17:17; 22:14; 23:25, 29.)

V. 14. Three honorable names are given to the Church of God: Daughter of Zion (Ps. 2:6; 48:2; Is. 1:8), Israel (Gen. 32:28), Daughter of Jerusalem (Ps. 135:21; 137:5 f.). The daughter of Zion is to sing as did the women who came out to meet the returning victor (1 Sam.

18:6 f.). Israel, the conqueror of God and man (Gen. 32:28), shall shout as the victors rejoice over their defeated enemies (1 Sam. 17:52). Jerusalem is to be glad and rejoice "with all the heart," with joy flowing from the very seat of life, true, sincere, living joy.

V. 15. The motivation for such joy. Judah's judgments in every sense of the term are removed; her condemnations and punishments canceled, her guilt pardoned, her indictment quashed. All her enemies, as many and varied as they may be, are "cast out" (Gr. N.) as rubbish is cast out of a home. And all this not by the edict of a mere man, the efforts of a human ruler. The Lord has done it. The King of Israel, even Jehovah, is in the midst of His Church; invisibly in the Temple during the Old Covenant; visibly walking among His people as the Lord Our Righteousness when the fullness of time was come; now sitting at the right hand of God, filling all in all (Eph. 1:20-23). He is with His Church always, even unto the end of the world (Matt. 18:20; 28:20), and in His Kingdom of Glory forevermore (Rev. 21:3). No evil, no real harm shall come to His Church, His elect. Sing and rejoice, ye blessed of the Lord! (Matt. 5:3-12; John 10:27 ff.; Rom. 8:28 ff.)

Vv. 16, 17. The joy of a believer is often dimmed and in danger of being destroyed by fear. Fear and joy are opposites. Therefore God tells His Church, "Fear thou not!" Fear also seriously interferes with a believer's joyous service of his God. Therefore the Lord tells His Church, "Let not thine hands be slack." Let nothing keep you from gladly doing My will. This will of God has a twofold aspect. God demands that the regenerated believer, endowed with spiritual powers, make proper use of these new powers (Lev. 19:2; 20:7 f.; Deut. 6:4 f.; Rom. 6; Titus 2:12, etc.). Also, they are to bring the joy they have experienced to their fellow men (Gen. 12:3; Deut. 6:7; Is. 40:9; 52:17; Matt. 28:19, etc.). There is to be no abatement in the believers' daily fight against sin, daily struggle for perfection; no yielding to discouragement because of constant failure to reach the high goal, nor to the whisperings of their flesh that such strenuous efforts were not necessary (Rom. 7:18-24; 1 Cor. 9:24—10:13; Heb. 12:1 ff.). There is to be no abatement in the believer's missionary zeal because of small gains, "prohibitive" costs, etc. The almighty God is at their side (v. 17) to help them in their struggle for personal sanctification (Phil. 1:6; 1 Cor. 1:8 f.; 10:13) and to prosper their missionary efforts (Matt. 28:20). Fear thou not, O Jerusalem! Let not thine hands be slack, O Zion!

"He will rejoice over thee with joy," etc. Another powerful motive for every believer to discard all fear and be joyously active in the service of his God. God rejoices not only over every repenting sinner (Luke 15: 7, 10); He rejoices also as He sees the Church and her individual members joyfully serving Him. As He sees their godly life (Titus 2: 17 ff.); as He sees their feet shod with the preparation of the Gospel, ready and eager to preach it near and far, He rejoices over them with joy! That new life is the fruit of the suffering and death of His own Son. For this the Son suffered the agonies of hell (Matt. 27: 46)! His work was not in vain. Now He sees His former enemies serving Him in holiness and good works, and joy so overwhelming fills His heart that, humanly speaking, He cannot give adequate expression to it. "He will rest in His love" (Gr. N.). Silently He contemplates His beloved Church as human beings are stricken dumb with overwhelming joy. And then there pours from His heart and lips such joyous shouting that the heaven of heavens echoes and re-echoes with His jubilation, His glad singing. If the Triune God so rejoices over His Church at work, ought the Church ever permit her hands to be slack?

Vv. 18-20. The closing words of Zephaniah's message are directed particularly to the believers living in the dark decades preceding Jerusalem's fall, during the horrors of the siege, and the long years of captivity at Babylon. There many sorrowed bitterly for the "solemn assembly," the festivals on which by divine command the nation was to assemble at the Temple (Ex. 23: 14-17). The destruction of God's house seemed to them the incontrovertible evidence that God had forsaken them (Lam. 1: 2 ff.; 2: 1 ff.). Now they learned by bitter experience the truth of the Lord's word: Jer. 2: 19. In order to save them from utter despair the Lord assures the repentant, sorrowing believers (Jer. 3: 22 ff.; Dan. 9: 4 ff.) that He still acknowledges them as members of His Church. "They are of thee!" (Cp. Ezek. 11: 16.) They are the good figs (Jer. 25: 3 ff.; 29: 10 ff.), unforgotten of Him (Is. 49: 15-17). "To whom the reproach of it was as a burden": All the taunting reproaches heaped upon them by their enemies and their own conscience, the shame of their sin, of their captivity, all this lay upon them as a heavy burden. Yet, though they are bowed down in shame and agony as is a woman forsaken and grieved, the Lord of constant kindness will have mercy on His betrothed spouse, the mother and her children alike (Is. 54: 5 ff.). "At that time" (v. 19), in the New Testament era, He will "undo" (Gr. N.), will deal with, all that afflict His Church. "He will save her that halteth." (Cp. Gen. 32: 25, 31 and remarks on Micah 4: 6 f., p. 267, which latter passage is quoted here by Zephaniah.) The New Testament will be the era of full salvation, when Satan's head will have been bruised (Gen. 3:15) and an ever-lasting salvation procured. This salvation is retroactive (Heb. 9:15). Therefore already the Old Testament believers could call the Suffering Servant (Is. 53) "the LORD *Our* Righteousness" (Jer. 23:6). In Him the repentant Israelites found pardon for their sins, and for His sake God would fulfill His promise given particularly to Israel (Deut. 30:1-5) that He would deliver them from exile if they would return to Him in repentant faith. In the New Testament this specific Old Covenant promise has ceased, since Israel is no longer the special covenant people of God (1 Thess. 2:16; Gal. 3 and 4; Eph. 2:1-12; Col. 2:1-23).

"I will get them praise and fame." This also was fulfilled in the promised Messiah and His work. Jesus, the God-Man, was the son of a Jewish virgin who traced her lineage back to David, the Jewish king, and to Judah, the tribal father of the Jews. What glory has come to the Jewish nation through this Jesus! To the end of days and in eternity the precious privilege of the Jewish nation will remain: that of them, as concerning the flesh, Christ came, who is over all, God blessed forever! (Rom. 9:5.) Salvation is of the Jews! (John 4:22.) A Jew is the Savior of the world! To a Jew is given a name above all other names (Phil. 2:9-11; Eph. 1:20-23). A Jew shall come at the Last Day to raise the dead (1 Thess. 4:16 f.). A Jew will sit on the throne of God as the Judge of all the world, and this Jew shall decide forever the fate of every human being (Matt. 25:31 ff.; 2 Cor. 5:10). To a Jew, the God-Man sitting with the Father and the Holy Spirit on the throne of everlasting glory, will be sung that ever new song in which all the children of God and all the host of heaven will join in a grand chorus: Rev. 5:6-14. Can greater glory, greater praise be imagined than that given to Christ, the Jew, the son of a Jewish mother, the noblest scion of the tribe of Judah?

In order to strengthen and comfort His people sorrowing in exile, the Lord repeats His promise (v. 20) and affixes His seal to this pledge and to all the prophecies of His messenger with the final solemn affirmation: "It is the oracle of the LORD!"

H A G G A I

Historical Background of the Era of Haggai and Zechariah

The Babylonian Exile, foretold already by Isaiah in the days of Hezekiah (Is. 39:6), God's punishment upon His rebellious people (Jer. 25:3-12), had run its course of seventy years (Jer. 25:11 f.). Cyrus the Great, ascending the Persian throne in 559 B.C., annexed the powerful kingdom of the Medes, rapidly extended his realm north-westward to the Caspian, Black, and Aegean Seas, and in 539 conquered the mighty city of Babylon, proud mistress of the world. By divine direction (Is. 44:24—45:7; Ezra 1:1 ff.) Cyrus issued the decree permitting the Jews to return to their homeland and rebuild the Lord's Temple, 536 B.C. This decree was in keeping with his policy to return the captive peoples and their gods to their homelands. (Cp. his decree, Barton, *Archaeology*, p. 483 f.) Not all the Jews in Babylonia availed themselves of this opportunity, fewer than 50,000, a small number (cp. 2 Sam. 24:9); those "whose spirit God had raised" (Ezra 1:5). They settled in Jerusalem and the surrounding cities (1:2 f.; 2:1-70). The leaders of this group were Jeshua, also called Joshua, the high priest, and Zerubbabel, the son of Shealtiel (3:2). The latter is also called Sheshbazzar while he was in Babylon (1:8, 11) and in a letter addressed to Darius (5:14, 16); hence this is evidently his Babylonian name. On Hebrews receiving also a Babylonian name cp. Dan. 1:6 f.; Esther 2:7. The governor appointed by Cyrus over Judah and Jerusalem and who led the returning Jews to Jerusalem is called Sheshbazzar (Ezra 1:11; 5:14,16), Zerubbabel (2:2; 3:2, 8; 4:3; 5:2); the man laying the foundation of the Temple is called Zerubbabel (3:8 ff.; 5:2), Sheshbazzar (5:16). Hence the two names denote the same person.

The first sight of the Holy City must have been a keen disappointment to the returning Jews. There was nothing left of the glory of the city once the object of Israel's jubilant hymns of praise. (Cp. Pss. 46, 48, 84, 87, 122.) Its proud walls now heaps of rubble (cp. Neh.

2:13 ff.); its gates burnt; its Temple a pile of blackened stones, rubbish, and ashes; its streets overgrown with weeds. Yet willingly they set to work and gave "after their ability" both money and labor (Ezra 2:68 f.; 3:7). On the first day of the seventh month (September-October) they had cleaned away enough rubbish to place the altar of burnt offerings on its base, so that the daily sacrifices could again be offered (Ezra 3:1 ff.). The Festival of Tabernacles was celebrated (3:4); and in the second month (April-May) of the next year (535 B. C.) the foundation of the Temple was laid (3:8). This happy occasion began with joyous hymns of thanksgiving by the priests and Levites, while all the people shouted with joy. Once more they would have a large Temple whose dimensions equaled in most respects those of Solomon's Temple. (Cp. Ezra 6:3 f. with 1 Kings 6:2 ff.; 2 Chron. 3:3 ff.) But the festival spirit of joy was suddenly dampened by the bitter weeping and loud lamentations of the old men who had seen the splendor and glory of Solomon's Temple. Their tears were not tears of sorrow and repentance over the sin and apostasy which had caused the destruction of the Temple. They lamented the loss of the outward glory, the rich ornamentations, which simply were out of question in Zerubbabel's time. They completely forgot that the presence of God, His grace and blessing, could be enjoyed in the new Temple as well as the old and that the Lord was greater than His dwelling. To make such a public display of sorrow over a transient matter was in itself wrong and could serve no good purpose. These tears only dampened the joy and enthusiasm of the people, discouraged them. When opposition arose, they only too readily regarded that as a good excuse to cease work entirely. Gradually they became used to worshiping amidst ruins and rubbish and for fifteen years, 535 to 520 B. C., the desire to rebuild God's house had died almost completely. Under such discouraging circumstances Haggai began his work, in which he was assisted two months later by Zechariah. Their combined testimony proved so effective that immediately building operations were begun (Hag. 1:14 f.), and were not interrupted even by Tatnai's investigation (Ezra 5:1-5), which resulted in a royal decree by Darius granting permission to continue the erection of the Temple on the lines decreed by Cyrus (Ezra 6:1-4) and guaranteeing financial aid (6:4 b-9) and protection against efforts to foil the work (v. 11 f.).

Chronology of Haggai and Zechariah

(The Hebrew months run from new moon to new moon)

Darius' Regnal Year	Year B. C.	Month	Day		
2	520	6 Sept./Oct.	1	Hag. 1:1-11	Haggai rouses the people into activity
			24	Hag. 1:12-15	The people begin to build
		7 Oct./Nov.	1	Hag. 2:1-9	The latter glory of God's Temple
		8 Nov./Dec.	?	Zech. 1:1-6	Zechariah begins to prophesy
		9 Dec./Jan.	24	Hag. 2:10-19	God will begin to bless
				Hag. 2:20-23	Messiah's kingdom established after overthrow of world powers
	519	11 Feb./March	24	Zech. 1:7—6:8	Zechariah's night visions
				Zech. 6:9-15	The crowning of Joshua prefiguring the Messiah's royal priesthood
4	518	9 Dec./Jan.	4	Zech. 7, 8	Repentance urged; blessing promised
6	516	12 March/April	3	Ezra 6:15	Dedication of Temple
		?	?	Zech. 9—14	After dedication of Temple

Building God's Temple

CHAPTER 1

I. The Prophet Urges the Sluggish People to Finish the Building of the Temple, Vv. 1-15

A. The Prophet's Reproof, Vv. 1-11

1 In the second year of Darius, the king, in the sixth month, on the first day of the month, the word of the LORD came through Haggai, the prophet, to Zerubbabel, the son of Shealtiel, governor of Judah, and to Joshua, the son of Jehozadak, 2 the high priest, saying: Thus speaks the LORD of Hosts, saying, This people say, It is not the time to come, the time to build the house 3 of the LORD. Then the word of the LORD came through Haggai, the 4 prophet, saying, Is it the time for

385

you yourselves to live in your paneled houses while this house is in 5 ruins? And now, thus says the LORD of Hosts, Give careful consideration to what is happening to 6 you! You have sown much, but reaped little; you ate, and were not satisfied; you drank, but not your fill; you clothed yourself, but did not get warm; and the wage earner earns wages into a bag full of holes. 7 Thus says the LORD of Hosts: Give careful consideration to your way! 8 Go up to the mountain, and bring lumber, and build the house, and I will be pleased with it and will glorify Myself, says the LORD.

9 You looked for plenty, and, behold, it had become little! You brought it home, and I blew it away! For what reason? is the oracle of the LORD. Because of My house, which is in ruins, and you are hurrying, everyone to his own 10 house. Therefore the heavens have withheld dew on your account, and the earth withheld its products. 11 And I have called a drought upon the land, and on the mountains, and on the grain, and on the wine, and on the oil, and on everything that the ground produces, and upon man, and upon beasts, and upon all the labor of their hands.

Grammatical Notes

V. 1. "By Haggai," בְּיַד by the hand, the instrumentality. (Cp. Num. 15:23; Joshua 22:9; 1 Kings 12:15; Jer. 37:2; 50:1.)

V. 2. "This people say." The Hebrew perfect describes the ever-repeated excuse as one complete act. — "The time is not come." The Masoretic text demands the translation: It is not the time to come, the time to build, etc. Haggai pictures vividly the hurried, confused manner in which the excuses were offered. On "come," see v. 14, "they came." There is no need to change the pointing.

V. 5. "Consider," literally, "set your heart upon." The heart is the seat of life, of intellect, emotion, and will (cp. Prov. 4:23). Direct your whole heart and all its capacities upon your "ways," here and v. 7, the way on which one is led, what happens to one, how onۿ fares, gets on. (Cp. Ps. 37:5; Job 3:23; Is. 40:27; Jer. 10:23.)

V. 8. "I will be glorified," the Niphal here not passive, but reflexive, I will glorify Myself (cp. Ex. 14:4, 17, 18; Ezek. 28:22; 39:13).

V. 9. "Ye looked for much." The absolute infinitive describes the constantly repeated looking forward in expectation of plenty; literally, there was "a turning forward." — "Unto his own house." לְ here = with reference to, in the interest of. (Cp. Gen. 19:21; 42:9, "of them"; Lev. 14:54-56; Joshua 22:28, "for.")

V. 10. "Over you" may quite properly be translated "on your account," "for your sakes." (Cp. Gen. 20:3, "for the woman"; Jer. 1:16, "touching"; 4:28, "for this"; 52:3, "through.") — "Is stayed," not passive, but active, "stays," withholds, construed with מִן = withholds from (giving) dew; with the accusative (v. 10 b).

V. 1. On the historical background, see pp. 383 f. The original ardent zeal of the returned exiles had soon flagged. The civic and spiritual leaders of the Jews, who were responsible for the spiritual welfare of the theocratic commonwealth, had permitted such neglect to continue for fifteen years, apparently without a serious attempt to remedy the situation. Haggai addresses these leaders first. Zerubbabel was the governor, the *pechah,* of Judah, a term used in translation of the Persian *satrap* (Ezra 8:36; Neh. 2:7, 9; 3:7, etc.), the civic and military ruler of one of the many provinces into which the huge Persian Empire had been divided. Joshua, consistently so called in the books of Haggai and Zechariah, is just as consistently called Jeshua in Ezra and Nehemiah. He is called the "high priest," a term found already in pre-Exilic times (Lev. 21:10; Num. 35:25, 28; Joshua 20:6). These two men had been honored by the Lord to be the first leaders of the liberated Jews. They are the first to hear His reproof for having neglected the very purpose for which God had constituted them leaders.

V. 2. From the very outset Haggai emphatically announces that he is now not proclaiming his personal views and convictions, although he would have had the full right to express them also, just as every member of God's Church has the God-given right and duty to warn privately and publicly against prevailing sins. Yet here Haggai speaks as the special messenger of one far greater than himself and the rulers of the Jews, the Lord Jehovah. He is not only the Covenant God of Israel (Ex. 19:5 f.), now a rather small nation; He is the Lord of Hosts (v. 2), the omnipotent Ruler of the universe. He, whose kingdom ruleth over all, has prepared His throne in heaven. Before Him stand the innumerable hosts of angels, excelling in strength, ever ready to do His command (Ps. 103:19-21). On earth, all the vast armies, together with their leaders, are under His command and can do no more than the Lord of Hosts (Ps. 46:7, 11) permits them to do. He sends them as the messengers of His wrath to make desolation in the earth, and He, if He sees fit, makes wars to cease unto the ends of the earth. (Ps. 46:8 f.; cp. Is. 10:5-15; Jer. 1:14-16; 18:1-11; 25:8-38; 28:1-22.) At a time when the Jews were under the sovereignty of Gentile rulers, it was of special significance that the prophets called attention to the fact that even these rulers were subject to the Lord of Hosts (Haggai no fewer than 13 times, Zechariah close to 40 times). It was the Lord of Hosts who had so shaped the history of the world's nations that Cyrus had become the world emperor, the instrument to carry out the Lord's will as foretold two centuries before by Isaiah (ch. 44:24—45:25; Ezra 1:1-4). The Lord of Hosts had raised the spirit of the returning exiles to go up to build the house of the Lord in Jerusalem (Ezra 1:5). The future of Israel, all the blessings promised to God's people could and would be realized only by this Lord of Hosts. Why, then, commit so great a wickedness as to refuse to obey His will?

The ever-ready excuse of the people was that the time to build the house of the Lord had not yet come. They could not possibly afford to build the Temple so long as hard times continued. The Lord addressed this first word chiefly to the leaders, Zerubbabel and Joshua (v. 1). Instead of rousing the people to action, instead of pointing out to them the groundlessness, the folly of their complaints, they had permitted building operations to cease for fifteen years. Have you leaders lost your sense of responsibility?

Vv. 3, 4. Since the leaders have done nothing, the word of the Lord comes by (Gr. N.), through, Haggai directly to the people. The Lord lays bare the shallowness of their excuses (v. 4): No time to build the Lord's house, while it is time for yourselves to dwell in "ceiled" houses, beautiful homes, the walls of which were ceiled, paneled, with expensive kinds of wood? The Hebrew term for "ceiled" occurs only in connection with the building of the Temple (1 Kings 6:9; 7:3, 7, "covered"; 6:15, "ceiling") and of Jehoiakim's magnificent palace (Jer. 22:14, "ceiled") and here. Such expensive homes were naturally furnished with every conceivable convenience, comfort, and luxury. Such people could not plead poverty! It was selfishness pure and simple. "You yourselves," their personal comfort, was their chief concern, while the house of the Lord lay waste! Their heathen neighbors had, in obedience to their human ruler's command, liberally supplied them with silver and gold and other gifts (Ezra 1:4, 6), but they, the people of God, would do nothing for the house of the Lord, were satisfied to worship among ruins while they dwelt in luxurious homes. Shameful selfishness!

Vv. 5, 6. The Lord is still their Covenant God, intent on their eternal welfare. He asks them to give their sincere and careful attention to their conduct during the past years. "Consider your ways!" (Gr. N.) Ought you to continue on your chosen path? Did your refusal to give your money for the Lord's house pay any dividends? What benefit has your catering to your own selfish interests gained for you? We must read v. 6 in the light of vv. 10, 11. Their hopes for rich harvests from their plentiful sowings were rudely shattered. They did not have enough food and drink to satisfy their hunger and thirst; not enough clothing to keep themselves warm! Even if they earned wages, the prices for the necessities of life were so exorbitant that the money earned seemed to have been put into a bag "with holes," literally, a pierced, punctured bag. (Cp. Lev. 26:20.)

Vv. 7, 8. Again the exhortation to consider their ways. The Lord points out the better way (v. 8): "Go up to the mountain"= Lebanon

388

(cp. Ezra 3:7), bring the wood needed for the building of My house, and complete it! Then I will take pleasure in it, while now it is a disgrace to My holy name. And then "I will be glorified" (Gr. N.), rather, I will glorify Myself. I will prove that I can keep My covenant promises to bless My obedient people as well as I have fulfilled My covenant threats (Lev. 26:14 ff.; Deut. 28:15 ff.).

Vv. 9-11. Once more the Lord recalls to their mind His judgments because of their neglect to build His Temple, and again His language closely approximates that of the original covenant (cp. Lev. 26:19, 20, 26; Deut. 28:16-18, 22 b, 23, 38-42). "Ye looked for much" (Gr. N.). At every seedtime their hopes turned forward to a rich harvest, only to be foiled time and again. On what they brought home the Lord blew, and it was gone like chaff before the wind. Why this depression? Because the Lord's house was still in ruins, while all their time and energy were spent on their own houses (Gr. N.). Therefore (v. 10 f.) the Lord sent His judgments which He had threatened to send to His disobedient people (Lev. 26:19 f.; Deut. 28:23 f.). And all this on their own account! (See Gr. N. on "over you," v. 10.) That was the fruit of their stubborn refusal to do their duty.

B. The Result of Haggai's Reproof, Vv. 12-15

12 And Zerubbabel, the son of Shealtiel, and Joshua, the son of Jehozadak, the high priest, and all the rest of the people obeyed the voice of the LORD, their God, and the words of Haggai the prophet, as the LORD, their God, had sent him; and the people feared before the LORD. 13 Then Haggai, the messenger of the LORD in the message of the LORD, spoke to the people, saying, I am with you, is the oracle of the LORD. 14 And the LORD aroused the spirit of Zerubbabel, the son of Shealtiel, the governor of Judah, and the spirit of Joshua, the son of Jehozadak, the high priest, and the spirit of all the rest of the people, so that they came and went to work on the house of the LORD of Hosts, 15 their God, on the twenty-fourth day of the sixth month of the second year of Darius the king.

Grammatical Notes

V. 14. "Stirred up." The strong ¹ denotes the stirring up as the result of Haggai's speech. "And so the Lord stirred up."

Vv. 12-15. Haggai had not resorted to high-flowing oratory. The people could not fail to understand his unvarnished exposé of their neglect and his simple declaration of God's will addressed to leaders and people alike. And all were deeply moved. Here was a prophet, a messenger of the Lord. They realized that their gracious deliverance from the Exile did not grant them license to do as they pleased, that they had shamefully neglected their duty in failing to build the Temple. Fear, holy awe, filled their hearts: that fear which, coupled with love, is the daughter of faith and the beginning of true wisdom. This fear expelled their self-complacent negligence toward God's will. They humbled themselves under the mighty hand of God. And the God of grace (Is. 57:15) at once revived their drooping spirits through the selfsame prophet who had laid down the law to them.

Note the emphasis on the fact that also as the Gospel preacher Haggai was the Lord's messenger, bringing an announcement as encouraging as it was brief and to the point: "I am with you, saith the LORD!" (Cp. 2 Chron. 15:2.) And again this brief word proved its life-giving power. Through it the Lord "stirred up" (Gr. N.) the spirit of leaders and people alike. Now they found time to come and build (cp. v. 2). After having carefully planned the undertaking, they began actual building operations on the twenty-fourth day of the sixth month, twenty-three days after Haggai had begun to speak to them.

CHAPTER 2

II. The Latter Glory of God's House, an Encouragement to the Builders, Vv. 1-9

1 In the seventh month, on the twenty-first day of the month, the word of the LORD came through
2 Haggai, the prophet, saying, Say now to Zerubbabel, the son of Shealtiel, the governor of Judah, and to Joshua, the son of Jehozadak, the high priest, and to the rest
3 of the people, saying: Who is left among you that saw this house in its former glory? And how do you now see it? Is it not as nothing in
4 your eyes? Yet now, take courage, O Zerubbabel! is the oracle of the LORD, and take courage, O Joshua, son of Jehozadak, the high priest! And take courage, all you people of the land, is the oracle of the LORD, and get to work! For I am with you, is the oracle of the LORD
5 of Hosts. The word which I have covenanted with you when you came forth from Egypt, and My Spirit is standing in your midst.
6 Fear not! For thus says the LORD of Hosts, Once more, in a little while, I will shake the heavens and the earth and the sea and the dry
7 land! And I will shake all the nations and the chosen of all the nations will come, and I will fill this house with glory, says the
8 LORD of Hosts. Mine is the silver, and Mine the gold, is the oracle of
9 the LORD of Hosts. The latter glory of this house shall be greater than the former, says the LORD of Hosts, and in this place will I give peace, is the oracle of the LORD of Hosts.

Grammatical Notes

V. 6. "Yet once." עוֹד here = addition, repetition. (Cp. Gen. 4:25; 8:21; 9:11; 24:20; again, more.) — "Once," אַחַת, fem. form used adverbially, once, one only time (Ex. 30:10; Lev. 16:34; 2 Kings 4:35. LXX = ἔτι ἅπαξ. Cp. Heb. 12:26f.).

—"A little while," a short time (Ruth 2:7; Is. 10:25; 29:17; Jer. 51:33).

V. 7. "The desire of all nations." חֶמְדָּה, from חָמַד, to desire, long for, covet (Ex. 20:17; Deut. 5:18; Joshua 7:21). The verb closely approaches the sense of choosing, since one usually chooses what one desires or cherishes; so Is. 53:2, "desire Him," so as to choose Him; Is. 44:9, the participle, "delectable things," which they chose as their gods (cp. selected, select; choice, chosen). The noun = desirability, delight (cp. 2 Chron. 21:20, without being "desired," an object of desire). With a construct preceding = objects of desire, "pleasant land," desired, choice (Jer. 3:19); "pleasant furniture," choice, selected (Nah. 2:10, A. V., 9); "pleasant land," choice, chosen (Zech. 7:14). In the construct form the noun occurs only three times, here, 1 Sam. 9:20 (the most desirable, precious thing in Israel = the kingship over God's own chosen nation), and Dan. 11:37 (the most precious thing in women = the purpose for which they were created; cp. Gen. 1:27; 2:18-25). In our passage it denotes the choicest thing in or among the nations, those whom God had chosen as His own

(Eph. 1:3-14; 2:11-22; Rom. 8:28-39; 1 Peter 1:1-5) to become members of His holy Church. (Cp. Heb. 12:22-24.) *Chemdat* is collective, denoting the whole number as a unit; the plural predicate בָּאוּ refers to every one of the individuals, as they come to the Church of God. The perfect describes the act of coming, which extends through the centuries as a completed act. The timeless God (Ps. 90:4; 2 Peter 3:8) already sees them all, from first to last, as having come. Collective nouns, even fem., frequently take a plural masc. predicate, either preceding (1 Sam. 17:46; Ps. 33:8; Amos 1:8) or following (Gen. 41:57; 48:6; 1 Sam. 2:33. G.-K. 145 e). Hence the LXX translation τὰ ἐκλεκτά need not indicate an originally different pointing, חֲמֻדֹת, particularly since the Greek neuter is quite frequently used of persons (singular, Heb. 7:7; Acts 26:7; plural, 1 Cor. 1:27. See Robertson, *A Grammar*, pp. 709, 763). LXX favors our translation, the elect, chosen. — "And I will fill." The accent above the Hebrew verb is placed over the ultimate syllable, hence the waw is consecutive. (Cp. remarks on Hos. 2:19, A. V., 17, p. 33. G.-K. 112 a.)

Vv. 1-3. Three and one-half weeks had passed since work at the Temple had been renewed. The last day of the Festival of Tabernacles (Lev. 23:34 ff.) had arrived. This usually joyous festival week had been rather a sad one. The year's harvest had been a dismal failure (Hag. 1:10 f.; 2:16 ff.). To build the Temple in such hard times seemed a hopeless undertaking. Moreover, some of the older people who had seen the glory of the former Temple again discouraged (cp. Ezra 3:12) the congregation by their disparaging remarks. That, of course, served only to increase the spirit of frustration which had seized the people. Their complaints were altogether unfair. They forgot that the prevailing conditions differed completely from the unusually prosperous days of Solomon (2 Chron. 9:9-27). They forgot that David and his people had amassed a huge amount of precious metals and stones (1 Chron. 29:1-9). They forgot that they themselves had done nothing to make the building of Solomon's Temple possible; they had inherited it from their forefathers. They forgot that they and their forefathers had forfeited their right to God's Temple by their wickedness (Jer. 7:8 ff.) and that they had helped to bring on the prevailing hard times by their own iniquities (Hag. 1:2 ff.). How unreasonable are the complaints of God's children, unwilling to do what the Lord demands! Yet how seriously will such complaints hamper the work so necessary for the growth of God's kingdom!

In order to show them the folly and sinfulness of their complaints, the Lord identifies the house they were now building with the Temple of Solomon (v. 3). He does not draw a distinction between two houses essentially different. He knows of only *one house*, this house. It is the same house, the only difference being in point of glory. And this difference in glory does not affect the essence, but merely the outward appearance, the lack of profusion of external embellishments. This house is one with Solomon's Temple in being acknowledged by the Lord as His house, the place of His abode, His grace, His salvation. Even the absence of the Ark of the Covenant does not essentially change this house. In this house He takes pleasure. Even in its waste state it is His house (ch. 1:9); and it is a shame that His people and their leaders have permitted it to lie in ruins for fifteen years and, now that it is beginning to rise out of its ruins, to make disparaging comparisons referring only to externals.

Vv. 4, 5. First of all Haggai is to address the leaders, whose duty it was to do all in their power to carry the work to a successful finish. They were to be strong, prove that they were worthy of the leadership divinely entrusted to them. Yet the leaders alone could not complete the job. Therefore Haggai is commanded to lay his finger on the chief sore spot, the unreasonable complaints which were the result of their unwillingness to do the Lord's work and resulted only in undermining what willingness was to be found among the people. All the people without exception were to be strong and work, labor, instead of foolishly complaining. Haggai adds a marvelous promise, "I am with you, says the LORD of Hosts." The mighty Ruler of the universe is on their side (Gen. 18:14; Num. 11:23; Jer. 32:17, 27). He will aid them, strengthen them, give them success. And He is satisfied with a house of less beauty. Here He will dwell and reveal Himself and His grace, all His blessings "according to the word" of the Sinaitic Covenant (v. 5; Ex. 19:5 f.; 24:1-18). Almost a millennium had passed since the establishment of this covenant. Generations had come and gone, but His covenant remained unchanged. Every generation had heard the

Aaronic blessing (Num. 6:22 ff.), which would again be spoken twice daily in the house they were building, assuring them of God's grace, blessing, protection, and peace. His Spirit (Gen. 1:2), the same Spirit the Lord had poured on Moses (Num. 11:17), on the seventy assistants (Num. 11:25), on Joshua (Num. 27:18), on Saul (1 Sam. 10:6, 10), on David (1 Sam. 16:13), still "remaineth among you," literally, stands firm, immovable! It is the eternal, unchanging Spirit of I AM THAT I AM. (Here we have a clear testimony to the eternity and deity of the Holy Spirit.) Why should they fear? Why hesitate to build so glorious a house? Why let externals deprive them of the joy in the things really worthwhile, the eternal realities freely offered and given to them in this house? Fear ye not!

Vv. 6, 7. "I will shake." "Shake" is the term used to denote the political and social disturbances and subversions brought about by Babylon (Is. 14:16 f.). Ezekiel uses it to describe God's overthrow of Gog (Ezek. 38:14-23, "shaking," "shake," vv. 19, 20). The humbling of proud Egypt by the ten plagues (Ex. 7—12; cp. 12:33) and the destruction of Pharaoh's army in the Red Sea (Ex. 14:21-31) are described in Ps. 68:7 f. as a shaking of the earth, heaven, and Sinai (cp. Ps. 77:15-20). Moses states that the Exodus and its accompanying miracles caused the surrounding nations to "be afraid"; to be gripped by "sorrow," agony, to "be amazed," "tremble," "melt away," be stricken with "fear" and "dread"; seven synonyms of being shaken (Ex. 15:14-16). This trembling and fear continued for decades (Joshua 2:9-11; 5:1) and centuries (1 Sam. 4:6-8). The Lord indeed had shaken heaven and earth, sea and dry land, to effect the deliverance of His people from the bondage of Egypt. In a similar manner the overthrow of Babylon preceding the deliverance of Israel from exile is described as a shaking of heaven and earth (Is. 13:1-22, see v. 13 and cp. vv. 10, 19; Jer. 50:46, cp. vv. 2 f., 9-16, 21-32, 35-45; also ch. 51:29, cp. vv. 1-28, 30-58). These two deliverances are the greatest in the Old Covenant (Jer. 16:14 f.; 23:7 f.), and both are prophetic types of the N. T. deliverance, which also made them possible.

The Lord of Hosts, however, speaks here not of past "shakings," subversions. He, the Ruler of the universe, reveals His plans for the future. "Yet once" (Gr. N.), once more "it is a little while," within a short time, "I will shake," etc. This shaking is defined as being not a physical shaking of heaven and earth and sea by earthquakes and windstorms. It will be a shaking of all nations, defined more closely in v. 22 as the complete overthrow and destruction of the thrones and the strength of the kingdoms of the heathen, the nations of the world. This cannot refer to the revolution occurring after the suicide of Cambyses, the son of Cyrus, who had ruled 530—522 B. C. A pretender claiming to be Smerdes, the younger brother of Cambyses, had sought to establish himself on the Persian throne. Also Babylon, Media, Armenia, and other provinces had revolted against the Persian rule. Yet Darius I Hystaspis defeated and slew the pretender and quickly suppressed the other rebellions. All this happened before Haggai spoke his prophecy. Darius ascended the throne in 522, Haggai spoke in 520. Two months later Haggai repeated his prophecy (ch. 2:10, 20 ff.), and again two months later the angelic riders sent by the Lord to walk to and fro through the earth reported back that "all the earth sitteth still and is at rest" (Zech. 1:11). There is therefore no foundation for the opinion that these revolutions had "stirred in Haggai and Zechariah the chimeric hope that their God was going to restore the kingdom of David under his descendant Zerubbabel (ch. 2:23; Zech. 6, where, however, in v. 11 Joshua has been substituted for Zerubbabel after the imprisonment or death of the latter had made the realization of this prophecy impossible)." (Pfeiffer, *Introd. to O. T.*, p. 602 f. Similarly, Eissfeldt, *Einleitung in das A. T.*, pp. 476, 484; Bewer, *Literature of the O. T.*, p. 240; Sellin, *Zwoelfprophetenbuch*, pp. 448, 522; *Expositor's Bible*, etc.) See also notes on Zech. 6:11, pp. 438 f. The Lord through His prophet foretells that era of constant warfare, of revolutions and counterrevolutions that characterize the last five centuries preceding the Christian era. The first ominous tremor of upheaval came only two decades after Haggai's prophecy. The Ionian Greeks, who had established settlements on the western shore of Asia Minor during the ninth and tenth centuries B. C., had been made tributary to Persia by Cyrus the Great about 540 B. C., but rebelled against Darius the Great in 501 B. C. This led to the ill-fated campaign of the latter against Greece, where he was ignominiously defeated at Marathon, 490 B. C. His son and successor, Xerxes, invaded Greece with an army of 1,800,000 men and a huge navy. The navy was scattered to the winds at Salamis, 480; the army suffered a loss of 20,000 men at Thermopylae and was defeated the next year at Plataea with a loss of almost 300,000 men. A reassembled navy was destroyed at Mycale on the western shore of Asia Minor in 479 B. C. These successive defeats destroyed forever all thoughts of renewing the contest on the part of the Persians. Now the gradual collapse of the mighty empire began, until Alexander the Great put an end to its power by his victories at the river Granicus, 334 B. C., at Issus, 332, at Arbela, 331. After his death several rivals for world sovereignty, particularly Syria and Egypt, wasted their power in bloody battle and internecine warfare, until Rome became the mistress of the world. "The Roman power was acknowledged in a series of provinces, protectorates, and client states which ringed the Mediterranean and made it indeed what the Romans like to call it, *Mare Nostrum* ("Our Sea"). (*Westminster Hist. Atlas*, p. 77 A.)

Yet all these "shakings of the nations" served God's purpose. They prepared the way for the spread of Messiah's kingdom, beginning at Jerusalem and extending unto the uttermost parts of the earth (Acts 1:8; Luke 24:47). Alexander's conquests served to spread Greek culture throughout the then known world and to make Greek the universal language. Rome's world-wide wars made imperative the building of an extensive road system, on which marched the legions of Rome and which were used as trade roads for innumerable caravans and as a safe means of travel for the people. The Mediterranean Sea was constantly traversed by large and small vessels, and travel by sea was a comparatively safe and pleasant means of communication between distant countries, linking them more closely. The *Pax Romana,* Roman peace, guaranteed safety and protection to Roman citizens throughout the length and breadth of the empire. (Cp. Acts 16:35-40; 22:25-30; 23:10-35; 24:6-12; 28:16 ff.; 30 f.)

This shaking of the nations precedes another noteworthy event in the history of God's Church: "The desire of all nations shall come." "The desire" (Gr. N.) cannot refer to Christ as the Desire of nations, since the predicate is plural. The term denotes here the choice, the chosen, the elect out of all nations, those Gentiles whom God has from eternity foreknown and predestinated, and whom in time He calls and justifies and will finally glorify (Rom. 8:29; Col. 3:12; 1 Thess. 1:4; 1 Peter 1:2; 5:13). "And I will fill." The Hebrew "and" (Gr. N.) here denotes an intensifying consequence, and so, in consequence of what has been stated, as the result of the coming of the elect Gentiles, "I will fill," etc. The glory of this house, which some of you regard as nothing (v. 3), will become so great that it will far excel even the former glory in the days from Solomon to the Exile (v. 9). In the Old Testament, God's Temple was built of stone and wood and metal, dead material, however precious. God's temple in the New Testament is built up of living stones, fitly framed together to be a habitation of God through the Spirit (Eph. 1:19-22; 1 Peter 2:4-8). In the Old Covenant, God's dwelling place was con-

395

fined to one nation, the people of Israel; in the New Covenant it will include members of every nation and kindred and tongue and people (Rev. 14:6; Matt. 28:19; Mark 16:15; Acts 1:8). In the Old Testament the nation whom God had chosen to be a peculiar treasure to Him (Ex. 19:5, 6; Amos 3:2 a), in whose midst He dwelt (Ex. 25:8; 29:45f.), was composed of believers and unbelievers (Ps. 95:7-11; 1 Cor. 10:1-5). The glory of the New Testament temple, or Church, of God is that it is a holy Church, all its members washed, all sanctified, all justified in the name of the Lord Jesus and by the Spirit of God (1 Cor. 6:11), a communion of saints. Other items of this greater glory are the difference of types and reality, prophecy and fulfillment (Col. 2:16 f.), of nonage and bondage, and full manhood and liberty (Gal. 4:1 ff.), of royal priesthood by representation (Ex. 28:1 ff.; Deut. 17:8-15), and universal (1 Peter 2:9; Rev. 1:6; 5:10; see also Heb. 7—10). Truly, a glorious Church (Eph. 5:25b-27), "filled with glory," every stone of which proclaims the glory of God's omnipotent grace (Eph. 1:11-20; 2:4-10) and which will reach its full perfection in the world to come as the Church Triumphant without spot or wrinkle, holy without blemish (Rev. 20 and 21).

V. 8. The Lord takes up another matter that disturbed the people, that of insufficient funds. I know, He seems to say, that you need money and that the times are not prosperous. Yet that lack should not stop the building of My house! Mine is the silver, all the silver, and all the gold there is in the world. I can, and I will (see v. 18 f.) supply the necessary funds by placing silver and gold into your pockets just as easily as I can take it out of your pockets by sending hard times. (See ch. 1:9-11; 2:16 f.) And I can and will create the willingness in your hearts to use My silver and gold for the building of My house. He, the mighty Ruler of the universe, had already moved the rulers of this world, Cyrus and Darius, to give liberally and even lavishly for this purpose (Ezra 1:2-11; 6:1-12). And He now proceeds to create such willingness in His people by a glorious promise (v. 9), by revealing the real cause of the prevailing depression (v. 16 f.), foretelling His blessing (v. 18 f.), repeating His prophecy of v. 6 f., adding another promise to Zerubbabel (vv. 20-23).

V. 9. On "latter" and "former" see notes on "latter days," Hos. 3:5, p. 40. "This latter house." Our Bible has followed the rendering of the Latin and Syriac versions, which has been adopted by most earlier interpreters, including Luther. According to this translation the greater glory of the latter house consists in the fact that Christ, greater than Solomon, preached in the latter, or second, Temple, the

Temple of Zerubbabel. Yet the Temple in which Christ preached was no longer "this latter house." Herod the Great had during a long period of years not merely repaired the Temple of Zerubbabel, but had torn down one part after the other of the old Temple and replaced each part by new buildings. He had also greatly enlarged the Temple area. The Temple in Christ's time differed from that of Zerubbabel to an even greater extent than the latter differed from Solomon's Temple. The correct translation of the phrase is: "the latter glory of this house." V. 3, which speaks of the first glory of *this* house, is conclusive proof that Haggai knows of only one house, whose glory varies. The glory of God's dwelling place among His people shall in the latter days far exceed the first glory of His Temple in the days of Solomon. See notes on this verse, pp. 392 f.

"In this place" = this house, My dwelling place, "will I give peace." God's peace is not merely an external peace and prosperity. The peace granted to God's people, freely offered in His holy Christian Church, is that peace of heart and conscience found only in Him who is the Prince of Peace (Is. 9:6). This peace was offered already in the Old Testament in God's holy Gospel, particularly in the Aaronic blessing (Num. 6:24-26), which according to Jewish tradition was spoken by the priest at the daily morning and evening sacrifice. (Cp. on this peace Is. 26:3, 12; 53:5; 54:10, 12; Micah 5:5, etc.) This peace Christ designates as the fruit of His vicarious suffering and death (John 14:27; 16:33; 20:19, 26; cp. Rom. 5:1-3; Eph. 2:14-17; Phil. 4:7, etc.). This peace is here guaranteed by the Lord of Hosts, the Ruler of the universe. While the O. T. believers looked forward to the coming of the Prince of Peace, the New Testament points to the Cross of Calvary: It is finished! God was in Christ, reconciling the world unto Himself (2 Cor. 5:19 ff.). The Hebrew imperfect "give" denotes the ever-recurring granting of peace during the life of the individual and the duration of the Church.

Such, in the light of the New Testament, is the greater glory of that house of God which the Jews were building many centuries before the New Testament was ushered in. Such a glorious prospect was indeed a powerful incentive in the work of building the Lord's house, and to do this work wholeheartedly, to cease their negligence, their disobedience, which was really the underlying cause of the hard times they were experiencing, while willing obedience to God's will would be rewarded by Him with material blessing in keeping with His covenant promise (Lev. 26:3 ff.; Deut. 28:1-14).

III. God Promises His Penitent People Immediate Blessings, Vv. 10-19

10 On the twenty-fourth of the ninth month of the second year of Darius came the word of the LORD by
11 Haggai, the prophet, saying, Thus says the LORD of Hosts, Ask the priests now for instruction, saying,
12 If a man carrying holy flesh in the skirt of his garment and with his skirt will touch bread, or pottage, or wine, or oil, or any kind of food, will it become holy? And the priests answered and said, No!
13 Then said Haggai, If one who is unclean by a corpse would touch any of these things, would it be unclean? And the priests answered and said, It will be unclean. Then Haggai answered and said, So is this people, and so
14 is this nation before Me, is the oracle of the LORD, and so is all the work of their hands and what they offer there. It is unclean.

15 And now, pray, pay close attention! From this day and onward, before you laid stone upon stone in the
16 Temple of the LORD; before these things happened, when one came to a heap of twenty measures, there were ten; when one came to the wine vat to draw fifty measures,
17 there were twenty. I smote you with blight and with mildew and with hail, all the products of your hands. Yet not one of you turned to Me, is the oracle of the LORD.
18 Now, pray, pay close attention! From this day forward from the twenty-fourth day of the ninth month, from the day that the foundation of the LORD's Temple was
19 laid, pay attention! Is the seed yet in the granary? And the vine and pomegranate and olive tree have not yet borne! From this day on will I bless you!

Grammatical Notes

V. 12. "If." הֵן, behold! quite frequently introduces a conditional clause, "if" (Ex. 8:22; Jer. 3:1; Is. 54:15; Job 12:14, etc.).

V. 13. "Unclean by a dead body," טְמֵא־נֶפֶשׁ, not unclean in soul, but unclean because of a dead body (Lev. 22:4); also with לְ (Num. 5:2; 9:6f.,10).

V. 15. "Consider," literally, set your heart, your mind, your attention on a matter. "Upward," מַעְלָה, what is above, upward (1 Sam. 9:2); of age (Num. 1:20); time, either forward (1 Sam. 16:13) or towards the past, backward, as here and in v. 18, the time of looking backward. "From before," מִטֶּרֶם, literally, from the nonexistence of laying stone upon stone, from the time that stone was not laid upon stone, i. e., that the building was not carried on. In v. 18 the time of looking backward begins on the twenty-fourth day and

extends to לְמִן הַיּוֹם, to the day on which the foundation of the Temple was laid. לְ in לְמִן designates the starting point from which מִן is to be reckoned, מִן being used in various meanings. (Cp. Job 36:3; 39:29; Is. 7:17; 37:26, etc. G.-B. sub מִן, 7 c.)

V. 16. "Since those days were," מִהְיוֹתָם, from their being, or coming into existence. The suffix is best regarded a plural neuter = things, circumstances, matters, since these circumstances obtained. — "Out of the press." פּוּרָה occurs also Is. 63:3, where it denotes the winepress. Here it may denote the measure usually obtained from one filling of the press. The sense is clear. Coming to the winepress, looking for fifty winepressfuls, he had only twenty.

V. 17. "Ye turned not to Me," אֶתְכֶם אֵלַי

אֵין. אֵין =nonexistence, followed usually by a nominative. G.-K., however, lists a dozen passages in which אֵת more or less emphasizes the noun before which it is placed, in the sense of "with respect to you," "as far as you are concerned." (Num. 3:46, "for those"; 5:10, "hallowed things"; 35:6; Judg. 20:44-46; 2 Chron. 31:17; Neh. 9:19, 34; Ezek. 17:21; 20:16; 35:10; 44:3; Dan. 9:13. G.-K. 117 m.) The rendering of LXX, "and you did not return to Me," is, like that of A.V., an interpretation rather than a literal translation. Literally: not, as far as you are concerned, to Me! V. 18. "Even from," see Gr. N. on v. 15.

Vv. 10, 11. It seems that even this marvelous promise (vv. 6-9) had failed to stir the people to wholehearted energy and enthusiasm. God had sent another prophet, Zechariah, a few weeks later. His first word (Zech. 1:2-6) had been a stern warning against misbelief and stubborn refusal to do the Lord's will. See p. 407. Yet a month later, God found it necessary once more to warn His people against the same sin through His spokesman Haggai. He does that in a very impressive manner. Since the people did not respond properly to Haggai's Gospel promise (vv. 6-9), they are to hear from the divinely appointed teachers of the Law, the priests (Lev. 10:8 ff.; Deut. 17:8 ff.; 33:8 ff.; Mal. 2:7), what the God of unwavering holiness thought of people who refused to obey His will joyfully. Haggai was to propose two questions to the priests and apply their answer to the people.

Vv. 12, 13. "If" (Gr. N.) "one bear holy flesh," the flesh of sacrificial animals (cp. Jer. 11:15), "in the skirt of his garment" — literally, in the wing, the border, or corner, of his garment; others, in the fold at the breast — would such flesh automatically impart its holiness to anything it touches, such as bread or pottage (Gen. 25:29, 34), etc.? The answer by the priests is an emphatic No. Another question (v. 13): If one that is "unclean by a dead body" (Gr. N.; Lev. 21:1, 11; Num. 6:6-11; 19:11 ff.) touch anything, will that object be unclean? The answer is, It shall be unclean.

V. 14. The application. "So is this people," the covenant people, "and this nation," the term usually applied to Gentiles, aliens and strangers from the covenants of promise because of their lack of faith and love and obedience to God. Every work of such a people or nation is unclean, coming from an unclean, uncircumcised heart. And no sacrifice offered by such people can make them acceptable, for all their offerings are unclean, because they are offered by a people refusing to obey the Lord wholeheartedly. Disobedience, rebellion against God's will in any matter, is as the sin of witchcraft (1 Sam. 15:22 f.).

Vv. 15-17. "Consider" (Gr. N.), set your hearts, pay close attention! "From this day" and "upward" (Gr. N.) = backward. "This day" is defined as the time before a stone was laid upon a stone in the Temple of the Lord, before the work of the rebuilding of the Temple had begun three months ago (Hag. 1:15). From this day they were to look backward to the years during which the work begun in 536 (Ezra 3:1-15) had ceased (Ezra 4:24). "Since those days were" (v. 16, Gr. N.), since these conditions existed, since you were remiss in your duty, your hopes for good harvests, on which prosperity depended, were blasted. A "heap," a stack of sheaves from which you calculated to thresh twenty measures, yielded only ten. "Out of the press" (Gr. N.). When you had counted on fifty *purahs* of grape juice to be taken from the "pressfat" (A. V.) (the vat into which the juice flowed from the winepress, where the grapes were trodden out by the feet of the vintagers), there were only twenty, less than half. Why? (V. 17.) The reason had already been given in ch. 1:9 ff., and still earlier in Deut. 28:38 ff. It is here repeated in the words of an older prophet, Amos (ch. 4:9, p. 155). "Yet ye turned not to Me!" (Gr. N.) They persisted in their stubborn refusal to do that work for which primarily the Lord had brought them back to their homeland from Babylon (Ezra 1:6).

Vv. 18, 19. "Consider," "upward" (Gr. N. on v. 15). "From this day" is defined as the 24th day of the ninth month, the day on which he spoke this message. "Upward," here as in v. 15, backward, consider the period "even from" (Gr. N.), starting from, since, the laying of the foundation of the Temple. Consider, pay close attention to that time of harvest failures (vv. 16, 17). And then look into your barns! (V. 19.) Is the "seed," the product of your harvest, the grain, yet in your barn? The natural answer is No! It has been consumed or used for sowing. If we answer Yes! then the prospect for a good harvest is very doubtful, the past years considered. And your vineyards and orchards, look at them! They have not yet borne! and all your skill, all your efforts, cannot cause one seed corn to sprout, cannot produce one sheaf of grain, one cluster of grapes, one pomegranate, one olive, unless I give My blessing! And that is what I am going to do: From this day I will bless you! This is a promise wholly unmerited! The people had for a long period of years absolutely refused to obey God's command to build the Temple. And even now they were not any too willing to carry on. And yet the God of infinite grace and mercy (Ex. 34:6) is ready to pour out His blessings to them. Who, indeed, is a God like unto the Lord? (Micah 7:18 ff.)

IV. Zerubbabel Encouraged: The Present Earthly Kingdoms Shall Collapse in Preparation for God's Messianic Kingdom, Vv. 20-23

20 Then the word of the LORD came a second time to Haggai on the twenty-fourth of the month, saying,
21 Say to Zerubbabel, the governor of Judah, as follows, I am about to shake the heavens and the earth,
22 and I will overturn the throne of the kingdoms, and I will destroy the power of the kingdoms of the Gentiles, and I will overturn char-iots and their riders, and horses and their riders will come down,
23 each by the sword of another. On that day, is the oracle of the LORD, I will take you, Zerubbabel, the son of Shealtiel, My servant, is the oracle of the LORD, and I will make you as a signet ring, for you have I chosen, is the oracle of the LORD of Hosts.

Vv. 20-23. For the second time on the same day (cp. v. 10), the word of the Lord came to Haggai in order to repeat the promise (v. 6) given two months earlier (v. 1), and explain it very definitely as an internecine warfare of the nations opposed to God and His Church (vv. 21, 22; see pp. 401 f.). And now a special promise was added for the encouragement of Zerubbabel, the faithful leader of God's people. "In that day" (v. 23), throughout that long era of crashing empires and toppling thrones, until the elect of all Gentiles (v. 7) shall come in great numbers from the ends of the earth (Gen. 28:14), the Lord, the World Ruler, will make, establish, Zerubbabel as a "signet." The signet, or seal, was a precious stone on which was engraved (cp. Ex. 28:11, 21, 36) either the name or some identifying emblem of the owner. The signet was impressed on the soft clay tablets (Job 38:14), on which business or legal or other important matters were inscribed, and then allowed to harden. If papyrus or parchment was used, the seal was imprinted on wax or clay discs affixed to the documents. This seal verified the document as an authentic declaration or manifest of the persons affixing their seal. (Cp. 1 Kings 21:8; Neh. 9:38; 10:1; Esther 3:12; 8:8, 10; Jer. 32:10-14, 44; Dan. 6:17.) For this reason the signet was highly cherished and carefully guarded against any possible loss, by being worn on the finger (Jer. 22:24) or carried on a cord fastened round the neck (cp. Gen. 38:18, where "bracelet," literally, is the cord, Hebrew, *pateel,* to which the signet was attached), hence near the heart (Cant. 8:6); or it was fastened to the arm (Cant. 8:6). The Lord honored faithful Zerubbabel not only by calling him "My servant" (cp. Num. 12:7; Joshua 1:1, 2, 7, Moses); He also established him as a signet, as a seal guaranteeing to His people the fulfillment of God's promise given to David (2 Sam. 7:12-16). As such he was "chosen," not by the people, nor by the powerful emperor Cyrus (cp. Ezra 1:8-11). This petty prince of Judah (Ezra 1:8), a small impoverished nation under foreign dominion, was honored by the supreme Ruler of the world and His Church, the Lord of Hosts, to be a prominent link in that illustrious chain of ancestors (Matt. 1:1ff., 6ff., 12; Luke 3:23ff., 27), extending from King David to Jesus Christ, the God-Man, King of Kings, and Lord of Lords (Rev. 17:14; 19:16; cp. Eph. 1:20f.; Phil. 2:9ff.). In the face of all opposition, in the midst of catastrophic political changes, the kingdom promised to David and the scepter assured to Judah would continue till Shiloh come, the Prince of Peace, whose kingdom is an everlasting kingdom. With the reassurance of this blessed promise Haggai closes his book.

ZECHARIAH

The Prophet of Hope and Encouragement
in Troublous Times

Introductory Remarks

1. Zechariah's Personality

Zechariah = Jehovah remembers. The prophet's name is also the theme of his message. He proclaims to his people Jehovah as their Covenant God, who remembers forever His covenant established with Israel on Mount Sinai. As the eternal Lord of unalterable holiness and justice He remembers forever His holy Law and is satisfied with nothing less than wholehearted, loving obedience to all its demands (Ex. 20: 3-5; Lev. 19: 18; Deut. 6: 5 ff.; Matt. 22: 36 ff.). Yet this same Holy One (Is. 40: 25) of absolute justice and righteousness is also the God of never-changing grace and mercy, who never forgets His promise and never forsakes His chosen children (Ex. 34: 6, 7a; Ps. 103; Is. 54: 7-10). By the Lord's command and inspiration (ch. 1: 1; cp. remarks on Hos. 1: 1, p. 17) Zechariah preached to his people God's Law, in order to make them conscious of their wickedness, and God's Gospel, which alone could turn them back to the Lord to serve Him in loving obedience (John 6: 63; 1 Peter 1: 23 ff.).

Zechariah was the son of Berechiah, the grandson of Iddo (ch. 1: 1-7). "The prophet" refers not to Iddo, but to "Zechariah *ben* Berechiah *ben* Iddo," the full name of the prophet. Ezra calls him the son (Hebrew, *ben*) of Iddo (Ezra 5: 1), who was the "chief," or head, of one of the priestly families returning with Zerubbabel (Neh. 12: 1-47). Evidently Zechariah's father, Berechiah, died before Iddo, so that Zechariah succeeded Iddo as head of his family (see Neh. 12: 12-16). This undoubtedly is the reason why Ezra in his purely historical record (Ezra 5: 1) calls Zechariah the "son" of the more illustrious grandfather. Compare Laban, Nahor's grandson (Gen. 22: 20-23; 28: 2-5), called the son of Nahor (Gen. 29: 5). See also 2 Kings 9: 14-20 (Jehu); 22: 2 (Josiah); 2 Chron. 17: 3; 28: 1; Neh. 12: 22, 23, etc. In establishing his personality in the heading of his book (ch. 1:1) and in his first prophecy (ch. 1:7 f.) Zechariah gives the exact genealogical information.

The last dated prophecy in the book was spoken in the fourth year of Darius, 519 B. C. (ch. 7:1). We do not know how long Zechariah continued his activity. Neh. 12:16, 26 is sometimes adduced to prove that he was still active in the days of Nehemiah (445—433 B. C.), hence more than one hundred years old. While this is not impossible, it cannot be proved from Neh. 12:26, which refers to the Levites named in vv. 22-25, not to the priests in the days of Joiakim (v. 12), the son of Jeshua, the high priest (v. 10; cp. Zech. 3:1; 6:11; Ezra 3:2, 8, 9), whose successors in the office of high priest are named in Neh. 12:10 ff.

Since Zechariah was a priest and the head of his family, he naturally takes a keen interest in the Levitical ritual and the restoration of the Temple.

2. Authorship of Chapters 9 to 14

For more than 2,000 years Zechariah was universally regarded as the author of the entire book. Hugo Grotius, one of the forerunners of rationalism, in 1644, the year before his death, declared chs. 9 to 14 to be post-Exilic and post-Zecharian. A decade later, an Englishman, J. Mede, regarded Jeremiah as the author of chs. 9 to 11 because of Zech. 11:12 f., compared with Matt. 27:9 f.; see p. 470. This theory was adopted by a number of English scholars, Whiston, Kidder, and others. A century later (1784), B. G. Fluegge, a pastor in Hamburg, declared chs. 9 to 14 to be pre-Exilic, and a year later Archbishop Newcome dated chs. 9 to 11 shortly before 722, and chs. 12 to 14 shortly before 685. L. Berthold (1774—1822), professor at Erlangen, sought to prove that chs. 9 to 11 were written by Zechariah, the son of Jeberechiah (Is. 8:2), in the days of Isaiah. This theory was adopted by Ewald, Hitzig, and others (see Sellin, *Zwoelfprophetenbuch*, p. 540). In 1881, Bernhard Stade, professor of theology at Giessen, sought to prove that chs. 9 to 14 were the work of an author writing 300—280 B. C. His theory was adopted with minor changes by Budde, Cornill, Hoelscher, and hesitantly by Wellhausen. Nowack suggested two to four authors. Rubinkam, who discovered no fewer than eight different authors, 9:1-10; 9:11-17; 10; 11; 12; 13:1-6; 13:7-9; 14, placed the composition of the book, as did Marti and Duhm, in the Maccabean era, 166—160 B.C.; Kuehnen, Baudissin, and Steuernagel regarded chs. 9 to 11 as a pre-Exilic writing revamped in the Greek era, 331—160; chs. 12 to 14 as post-Exilic; Sellin, chs. 9 to 11 as written by a contemporary of Hosea or Isaiah; chs. 12 and 13, by a contemporary of Jeremiah; ch. 14, as a post-Exilic apocalyptic addition. Later Sellin changed his mind: chs. 9 to 14 were written by an apocalyptic author of the third or second century B. C., who posed as a pre-Exilic prophet; the entire section might have been written 150—140 B. C. Sellin adds: "Once more, however, it must be emphasized that here every chronological fixation rests on very slim evidence *(an sehr duennen Faeden haengt)*." *(Einleitung,* p.123; *Zwoelfprophetenbuch,* p. 543.) Pfeiffer, who dates the book in the third century B. C., says: "A date later than about 200 B. C. is precluded by the fact that Sirach knew the book of 'The Twelve Prophets' substantially in its present form (Ecclus. 49:10), and it is difficult to see how Zech. 9—14 could have been added later to a volume of canonical Scriptures." (Pfeiffer, *Introduction,* p. 612.) So each succeeding theory refutes its predecessor while failing to establish its own claims.

Objections Answered

1. Different content: chs. 1 to 8, visions; while chs. 9 to 14, prophecies, no visions. Yet that certainly is no valid argument against unity of authorship. Amos' visions are found only in the last chapters of his book, chs. 7 to 9; yet that fact does not conflict with the unity of authorship. Moreover, Zech. 7 and 8 in Part I no longer record visions, while in Part II, ch. 11:4-17 presents a vision, cp. pp. 467 ff.

2. Chronological difficulties. The Greeks (Javan, Ionians) are named as enemies of Israel in ch. 9:13; hence the book cannot be dated prior to the Alexandrian era, 300—200. Yet there is no reason to assume that the Ionians were unknown to the Jews of Zechariah's time, 525—475. Moses names them in his table of nations (Gen. 10:2,4; cp. 1 Chron. 5:7). Ionians had colonized the western coastlands of Asia Minor as early as the tenth century B. C. Already in Joel's and Obadiah's days they had bought and sold Jewish captives (Joel 3:6; Obad. 20, pp. 130, 206).

3. Differences in language and style. What differences there are may well be explained by the different content. Pusey refers to an examination of three of Milton's poems by Prof. Stanley Leathes, from which it appears that in "L' Allegro" Milton employs about 450 different words, in "Il Penseroso," 578, in "Lycidas," 725. Yet of the 450 different words in "L' Allegro" 325 do not occur in "Il Penseroso," and 315 not in "Lycidas," yet Milton's authorship of the three poems is undoubted. (Pusey, *Minor Prophets,* p. 505, note q.)

4. "One who denies salvation to the Samaritans as harshly as Zechariah did in chs. 5, 7, 8, certainly cannot a few years later include these Samaritans in his promises of salvation, chs. 9 and 10." (Sellin, *Zwoelfprophetenbuch,* p. 540.) Yet Sellin fails to prove that chs. 5, 7, and 8 are directed particularly against the Samaritans, and, secondly, he ignores the essential difference between Law and Gospel. The same prophet wrote Jer. 48:1-46 (curse) and v. 47 (salvation); ch. 49:1-5 and v. 6; vv. 34-38 and v. 39; Obad. vv. 1-16 and vv. 17-21; the same apostle wrote Gal. 1:8, 9 and 3:26 ff.

5. The author of Part I uses introductory phrases (1:1 f.; 3:1; 4:1; 5:1) which do not occur in Part II. Yet the same usage is observed by Hosea. Cp. chs. 1—3 (1:1 f., 4, 9; 2:13 b, 16, 21; 3:1) and chs. 4—14.

6. "The obscure historical allusions and apocalyptic eschatology of Zech. 9—14, contrasting sharply with the clear historical background of Zech. 1—8, make it impossible to attribute these chapters to Zechariah." (Pfeiffer, *Introduction,* p. 607.) We can see no reason why the Lord may not have chosen the same man to write clear history and apocalyptic eschatology. Moreover, these so-called obscure historical allusions remain obscure only if one refers them to the contemporaneous history of the author and seeks to identify them with occurrences

between 450 and 150 B. C. As a matter of fact, Zechariah here does not refer to past or contemporaneous historical events, but prophesies the history of the Messianic era, of the New Testament Church, in terms of Old Testament times, as the exposition will show.

Other objections will be answered in the exposition. On the other hand, there are many evidences of the unity of the entire book. In both sections we meet with the same priestly background (ch. 3:1-8; 6:11, 15; 9:15; 14:16-21), the same stressing of the importance of the forgiveness of sins (3:1; 13:1), the same universality of salvation (2:14 ff., A. V., 10 ff.; 6:15; 8:21 ff.; 9:9 ff.; 14:16 ff.), the same confidence of divine mission (2:9; 4:9; 6:15; 11:11), the same Messiah and His royal priesthood (6:9-15; 9:9 ff.; 11:12 f.; 12:10-13; 14:9, 16 ff.). — A number of expressions and phrases, some of them of rare occurrence, are found in both sections: "passed through nor returned" (7:14; 9:8) occurs besides only in Ex. 32:27; Ezek. 35:7. *Metsulah*, Zech. 1:8, "bottom"; 10:11, "deep," occurs only 11 times more. "Eyes of Jehovah" = His providence, in 3:9; 4:10; 9:1, 8; 12:4; the habitual designation of the whole by its component parts: 1:12; 2:12, Jerusalem and cities of Judah; 1:14, 17, Jerusalem and Zion; 1:19, Judah, Israel, and Jerusalem; 3:7, house and courts; 3:10, vine and fig tree; see also ch. 9:5, 6, 10, 13, 17; 10:4, 6 f.; 11:2 f., 16 f.; 12:12-14; 14:10, 12.

There is not the slightest reason to reject the ancient tradition of the Jewish Synagog and the Christian Church, which regard Zechariah as the writer of the book bearing his name.

PART I

The Glory of God's Kingdom and the Destruction of All Enemies

Chapters 1—8

CHAPTER 1

A. Introduction. Call to Obedience, Vv. 1-6

1 In the eighth month in the second year of Darius the word of the LORD came to Zechariah, the son of Berechiah, the son of Iddo, the
2 prophet, saying, The LORD was
3 very angry with your fathers. And you shall say to them, Thus says the LORD of Hosts, Return to Me, is the oracle of the LORD of Hosts, then I will return to you, says the
4 LORD of Hosts. Be not like your fathers to whom the former prophets called, saying, Thus says the LORD of Hosts, Turn now from your wicked ways and from your wicked deeds! But they did not listen and paid no attention to Me,
5 is the oracle of the LORD. Your fathers, where are they? And the prophets, will they live forever?
6 Yet did not My words and My statutes which I commanded to My servants, the prophets, overtake your fathers? Then they turned and said, As the LORD of Hosts purposed to do to us according to our ways and according to our deeds, so has He dealt with us.

Grammatical Notes

V. 3. "I will turn." The Hebrew imperfect denotes here the ever-renewed action, progressive action.

V. 6. "Take hold." The Hebrew word denotes to reach or overtake one who has gone away or fled (Gen. 31:25; 44:4, 6; Ex. 14:9; 15:9, etc.); used metaphorically of blessing (Deut. 28:2; Is. 59:9); of curse (Ps. 69:25; Deut. 28:15, 45).

V. 1. Two months after Haggai had been called into his prophetic office, and only a few weeks after the Jews had again begun to rebuild the Temple (Hag. 1:1-15), another prophet was sent by the Lord to supplement and continue Haggai's work. On Zechariah's personality see pp. 403 f.; on general background, p. 383 ff. The very first message proved that he was suitably named Zechariah = the Lord remembers. It is a solemn word of warning from the Lord who remembers His holy Law (ch. 1:2, 4-6), yet does not forget His gracious promise (v. 3).

Vv. 2-4. The Lord recalls to the mind of the Jews the seventy years of His sore displeasure during the Babylonian Captivity, in which the fathers of the present generation had suffered the well-deserved punishment of their own and their fathers' sins. The Lord finally had fulfilled His threat (Ex. 20:5; Lev. 26:14 ff.; Deut. 28:15-68). This manifestation of God's displeasure was still very vivid in the memory of the Jews who had returned only fifteen years before. The lesson of the Exile and God's avenging justice ought never to be forgotten. Yet the Searcher of hearts (Jer. 17:9) sees the beginning of the rebellious spirit of the fathers in the refusal of the present generation to build the Temple and to give it their wholehearted support. This is in His eyes walking on evil ways, not hearing nor hearkening to the Lord, the Covenant God (v. 4). He is Jehovah, the Lord of Hosts, the almighty Ruler of the world, able to fulfill His threats, as He had cast them out of their land; yet just as able to keep His promises, as He had proved by bringing them back to their homeland (cp. Deut. 30:1-5). No enemy so powerful, I am stronger; no obstacle so great, I can remove it. Only turn to Me, and I will turn (Gr. N.) to you (v. 3) with all the riches of My grace! Be not disobedient to My Law, nor distrustful of My Gospel promises, lest you perish as did your fathers!

Vv. 5, 6. Where are your fathers, they who refused to hear Me (Jer. 6:16 f.), who continually boasted (Jer. 5:12 f.; 7:4-10 f.)? Where are they? Dead, and buried with the wicked in their death as they had joined the wicked in their life. And the prophets who warned them have not lived forever; they no longer personally speak to you. But My words (v. 6), spoken by their prophets as My mouths (Jer. 15:19), have proved that they are, like Me, spirit and life (John 6:63). Did they not "take hold"? (Gr. N.) God's words and "statutes," edicts, decrees, firm and unwavering, were like policemen, following the footsteps of your fathers, finally catching up with them and delivering them over to imprisonment and death. Sitting at the rivers of Babylon, they wept bitter tears of sorrow when they remembered

Zion (Ps. 137:1) lying in ruins because of their wickedness. Yet when despair threatened to overwhelm them, the memory of God's promises also became alive, and these, like divine messengers of grace, overtook them, caught them in their embrace, and with their tidings of peace soothed their aching hearts. Their sorrow did not remain or become a sorrow of the world, grim despair working death, but was a godly sorrow working repentance unto salvation, fruitful unto good works (cp. 2 Cor. 7:9 ff.). They submitted to the mighty hand of God and confessed (v. 6 b). And they had experienced the faithfulness of God's promises. They had been delivered at the exact time foretold by Him (Jer. 25:12; 29:10). To this God of truth (Is. 65:16), who always performs His word, whether threat or promise, they should turn, willingly continue in the work demanded by Him, gladly, confidently complete the building of His house.

The next revelation was received three months later. Doubtless, says Luther, the prophet in the meantime continued to repeat both the warning and the promise, adding examples of both judgment and help of God from the history of Israel, as it is customary in preaching.

B. Eight Night Visions. Ch. 1:7—6:15

1. The first vision: The Man among the myrtle trees, ch. 1:7-17

7 On the twenty-fourth day of the eleventh month, that is, the month Shebat, in the second year of Darius, the word of the LORD came to Zechariah, the son of Berechiah, the son of Iddo, the 8 prophet, saying, I saw in the night, and, lo, a Man riding on a red horse, and He was standing among the myrtle trees which were in the bottom, and behind Him were horses, red, sorrel, and white. 9 Then I said, What are these, my lord? And the angel that talked to me said, I will show you what they 10 are. Then the Man standing among the myrtle trees answered and said, These are whom the LORD has 11 sent to patrol the earth. Then they reported to the Angel of the LORD, standing among the myrtle trees, and said, We have patrolled the earth, and, lo, the whole earth is 12 quietly sitting and resting. Then the Angel of the LORD answered and said, O LORD of Hosts, how long wilt Thou not take pity upon Jerusalem and the cities of Judah, against which Thou hast been angry 13 these seventy years? Then the LORD spoke to the angel that talked to me kind words, comfort- 14 ing words. So the angel that talked to me said to me, Proclaim, saying, Thus says the LORD of Hosts, I am fervently zealous for the welfare of 15 Jerusalem and of Zion! And I am very angry at the proudly unconcerned nations which, when I was angry a little, helped to turn it into 16 disaster. Therefore thus says the LORD, I have returned to Jerusalem in mercy. My house shall be built in it, is the oracle of the LORD of Hosts, and a measuring line shall be stretched over Jeru- 17 salem. Again proclaim, saying, Thus says the LORD of Hosts, Again shall My cities overflow with prosperity, and the LORD shall again comfort Zion, and again choose Jerusalem.

408

Grammatical Notes

V. 8. "Bottom." The Hebrew word occurs here and ten times more in the sense of depth, deep places: of the sea (Ex. 15:5; Jonah 2:4; Micah 7:19; Ps. 68:23, A. V., 22; 107:24; Job 41:23, A. V., 31; Neh. 9:11); of a river (Zech. 10:11); a swamp (Ps. 69:3, 16, A. V., 2, 15); of the nether world (Ps. 88:7, A. V., 6). Invariably it symbolically denotes horrible, inescapable agony; hopelessness.

V. 9. "O my lord." The pointing demands a reference to the angel, *adoni*, not to the Lord, *Adonai*.

V. 10. "Walk to and fro," here = an exploratory journey (Gen. 13:17), a reconnaissance expedition (Joshua 18:4, 8).

The Angel of the Lord, Ch. 1:11

The Angel of the Lord appears first in the age of the patriarchs, then throughout the history of Israel, in the age of Moses, of the Judges, of David, of Elijah, in the visions of Zechariah, and in the prophecy of Malachi, as the Angel of the Covenant. Who is this Angel of the Lord? A careful study of the passages will make it evident that He is the Second Person of the Trinity, the Son of God before His incarnation. There ought to be no doubt that He is One with Jehovah. The Lord very definitely identifies the Angel of the Lord, or as He is also called, the Angel of God, with Himself. He promises Israel to send an Angel before them, to keep them and bring them safely to Canaan, and definitely identifies this Angel or Messenger with Himself: My name is in Him (Ex. 23:20 f.). That name which He Himself had called His own, His name forever (Ex. 3:14 f.), that name, His glory, which He will not give to another (Is. 42:8), is in the Angel, inherent in His very nature and being, He is Jehovah. Therefore He calls Him the Angel of His presence (Is. 63:9), literally, of His face. (Cp. Ex. 23:20-23; 32:34; 33:14.) They who look upon the Angel, look upon Jehovah; in the presence of this Angel Jehovah is present. (Cp. Num. 6:25-27.) The Lord calls this Angel God, Lord, Jehovah (Gen. 16:7-11, cp. v. 13; 32:28, cp. Hos. 12:4 f.; Ex. 3:2-15; 13:21, cp. 14:19; Num. 20:16; Judg. 6:12-16).

The Angel of God identifies Himself with God, the Lord, Jehovah. Speaking to Jacob (Gen. 31:11), He calls Himself the God of Bethel (v. 13; cp. ch. 28:10-22). He attributes to Himself the Lord's oath, His covenant, His deliverance from Egypt, His conquest of Canaan, the fulfillment of the Lord's promises (Judg. 2:1-3; Joshua 5:13—6:2). He accepts sacrifices offered to God (Judg. 6:17-24; 13:3-23).

Hagar recognizes in Him the Lord, Jehovah, and calls Him God (Gen. 16:7, 9, 11, 13 f.). So does Abraham (Gen. 22:11, 14), Jacob (Gen. 48:15 f.), Zechariah (ch. 3:1 f.).

Yet this Angel of the Lord, who is I AM THAT I AM (Ex. 3:2-14), is just as truly Jehovah's Messenger, His Angel sent by the Lord. Though One with Jehovah in the undivided and indivisible unity of God's Essence and Being, He is a second person. He is Jehovah sent by Jehovah as Jehovah's Messenger. We have here the same unsearchable mystery of the unity in Essence and the duality of Persons to which Christ refers in the New Testament when He says, I and the Father are One (John 10:30; cp. 14:9; 17:11, 21 f.), while just as clearly He states that the Father has sent Him into the world (John 17:18, 23, 25) and that He is coming to the Father (v. 11; cp. John 3:16 f.; 5:17-23; 8:16-18; 16:28, etc.).

This Angel of the Lord is the Covenant Angel, or, as Malachi (ch. 3:1) calls Him, the Messenger of the Covenant. As such He revealed Himself from the time of the patriarchs. He appeared for the first time after the Lord in a solemn manner had confirmed His covenant with Abraham, that covenant which included not only the possession of Canaan (Gen. 15:18-21), but also the promise of the Seed of Abraham (Gen. 12:1 ff.; 13:15 ff.; 15:4, 5), faith in whom is counted for righteousness (ch. 15:6). The Angel of the Lord manifested Himself at His very first appearance as the Messenger of the Covenant by exhorting and comforting a member of this covenant, Hagar, whom Sarah had given to Abraham to be his wife (Gen. 16:3-16). This Angel repeated and confirmed unto Abraham with a solemn oath the Messianic blessing of the covenant (Gen. 22:15-19). Again this Angel renewed the covenant promise to Jacob (Gen. 28:11-22) and kept it throughout

Jacob's lifetime (Gen. 48:15 f.). He appeared to Moses to establish His covenant with Israel (Ex. 3:2-22). He led the people on their journey to the Promised Land (Ex. 14:19 ff.; 23:20 ff.; Is. 63:9) and identified Himself to them as the Author of this covenant (Judg. 2:1-3). Time and again He came to the aid of His covenant people (Judg. 5:23; 6:11 ff.; 13:3 ff.), of Elijah (1 Kings 19:7; 2 Kings 1:3, 15; 1 Chron. 21:15-30. Cp. also Ps. 34:7; 35:5 f.). After the Exile it was the Angel of the Lord who pleaded for the covenant people (Zech. 1:11 ff.), who absolved Joshua and confirmed the high-priestly office of the Old Covenant as a type of the New Testament priesthood of all believers (Zech. 3:1-10). Malachi calls this Messenger of the Covenant "the LORD coming to His temple," the Church of the New Covenant, as the long-expected Redeemer, the Refiner of His people, the Judge of the world, the Messenger of the New Covenant, who by His work gave to the Old Covenant whatever power of forgiveness, life and salvation it possessed.

V. 7. The people had evidently obeyed the word of God's second spokesman and had, after a temporary lull (Hag. 1:2 ff.), again with renewed zeal taken up the work of rebuilding the Temple. In the next prophetic revelation granted to Zechariah we meet with no more rebukes and reprimands, but with words of encouragement and blessing, promises of salvation and glorification (ch. 1:7—6:15). The prophet is very exact in stating not only the month and day of the marvelous visions he was privileged to see, but once more he states also his full name, his genealogy, his office, and the fact that it was the Lord's word which came to him. He does this in order to assure his people and his future readers of the authoritativeness and reliability of his message. For this reason he calls the visions he saw (v. 8) the "word of the LORD" (v. 7), just as the oral revelation (vv. 2-6) is called by this term (v. 1). Whether perceived by the ear or the eye, Zechariah's prophetic message is the word, the revelation of God.

V. 8. "I saw by night" of the twenty-fourth day named v. 7. According to Jewish custom the day was reckoned from sunset to sunset (Gen. 1:5; Lev. 23:32); hence the night of the twenty-fourth day was the night preceding the sunrise of that day. In this night the prophet was shown a series of remarkable visions, forecasting in audio-visual revelation the glory of Messiah's kingdom and the destruction of all opposing forces. These visions were to serve as a powerful incentive to complete the building of the Lord's house with joyous enthusiasm. The visions came to the prophet during the night, but not in the form of dreams, as, e. g., in Gen. 28:12, 16; 37:5 ff., 9 ff.; 40:5 ff.; 41:1 ff.; Dan. 2:1 ff.; 7:1 ff. In fact, when Zechariah became exhausted by the visions and fell asleep, the angel roused him from his stupor to full wakefulness and alertness. In a miraculous manner the Lord caused His prophet to see and hear what did not reflect his own thoughts, was not a creation of his own mind, but what was brought to his attention

410

from without. He saw visions whose meaning and purpose he did not always understand, as he frankly confesses twelve times (ch. 1:9, 19, 21; 2:2; 4:4, 5, 11, 12, 13; 5:6, 10; 6:4). He saw, because his eyes were opened by the Lord to see what he could not have seen with his natural vision.

There is a close logical coherence and progress between the individual visions, particularly between 2 and 3, 4 and 5, 6 and 7, 8 and 1. In the first vision we hear of the preparatory steps for the following activities; the second vision prophesies the destruction of all opposing forces; the third, the building of Jerusalem; the fourth, the justification of the high priest; the fifth, the strengthening of the high priest by the Lord's Spirit; the sixth and seventh, the removal of the curse and all wickedness from the Church; the eighth returns to the first and shows God's armies sent forth on their work of salvation.

"In the bottom" (Gr. N.). The Hebrew term from the first time it occurs to the last is used metaphorically to designate deep distress, physical, mental, and spiritual agony, or all of these combined. This sense suits the situation here also. This world, the abode of the Church Militant, is for the Church collectively and its members individually a place of trials and tribulations (Is. 54:11 a; John 15:20 f.; 16:2, 22 a, 33 b; Acts 14:22). But the Lord has planted the Church as a myrtle grove in the accursed earth (Gen. 3:17; 5:29). The myrtle is a beautiful ornamental tree, 15 to 20 feet high, with small glossy green leaves and delicate fragrant white flowers. It grows wild in Palestine and was also cultivated in gardens and parks (Is. 41:19; 55:13). It is the age-old symbol of joy and peace (Is. 55:13). Its flowers were worn by brides, its branches used in constructing the booths erected for the joyous harvest festival, the Feast of Tabernacles (Neh. 8:15). Queen Esther's Jewish name was Hadassah, myrtle (Esther 2:7). — Among these myrtles the prophet sees a man riding a red horse. Behind him was a troop of horsemen, whose leader he was. There is no mention made of chariots, as in ch. 6:1 ff. Only horses are mentioned, their colors stated, and since the colors are in plural form, there must have been a number of horses of each color. That these horses were not riderless is evident from vv. 9, 10. These riders were not human messengers, but angels, God's messengers, often appearing in human form, standing before God, awaiting His commands (Ps. 103:20 f.; 104:4), always ready to minister to God's children, individually, and to His Church, collectively. (Heb. 1:14. Cp. Gen. 19:1, 15ff.; 28:12; 32:1; 1 Kings 19:5, 7; 2 Kings 6:15 ff.; Ps. 91:11; Matt. 18:10, etc.)

411

The fact that the colors of the horses are so definitely named, while the riders are not directly mentioned, lends strong probability to the symbolic nature of these colors. Red, here the dark red of blood, is naturally symbolic of bloodshed and war (Is. 63:2 f.; Rev. 6:4; 19:13 ff.). White is the color of victory and joy (Rev. 6:2; 19:11, 16). The meaning of "speckled" is uncertain; some — sorrel, bright yellowish red, symbolizing fire; others identify it with "grisled" (ch. 6:3), spotted, dappled, and regard it as symbolizing famine, or other plagues accompanying war.

V. 9. The prophet did not understand the purpose of the riders nor the meaning of the colors. He asks, O my lord (Gr. N.), what are these? This question evidently is addressed to the angel who immediately answers it, called "the angel that talked with me," or "communed with me" (v. 14). This angel, the interpreting angel, also appears in ch. 1:13 f.; 2:1-4 (A. V., 1:18-21); 2:7 (A. V. v. 3); 4:1, 2, 4 ff., 11-14; 5:2 ff., 5-8, 10 f.; 6:4, 5, 8. He answers the prophet's questions (1:9; 2:1, 4; 4:4-7, 11-14; 5:6-11; 6:4 ff.), is addressed by the Lord (1:13), reveals God's communication to the prophet (1:14-17), transmits an angel's word to the prophet (2:7-17, A. V., 3-13), calls the prophet's attention to new visions (3:1; 4:2; 5:2-5), explains visions (5:3 f.), wakes the prophet (4:1). While he does not inform the prophet on the meaning of the colors, he tells him, I will show thee, cause you to see, to understand "what these be."

Vv. 10-12. The prophet is now privileged to become an ear- and eyewitness of their duties. The leader of the troop informs him: These are they whom the Lord has sent to walk to and fro through the earth (Gr. N.). They are a reconnaissance troop sent out by the Lord Himself. They have returned from their mission and are ready to report to their Supreme Commander, who is now introduced, the Angel of the Lord (p. 409) (v. 11). While the Lord had sent them, they made no mistake in reporting to the Angel of the Lord, since the Lord Himself had said, My name is in Him (Ex. 23:21), He and I are One. Their observations on their journey through the various countries have convinced them that all the earth sitteth still and is at rest. This state of affairs was bound to be a keen disappointment to the Jews. Four months before, in the seventh month, and again in the ninth month, Haggai had told them that within a little while the Lord would shake heaven and earth prior to the coming of the nations into Messiah's kingdom. Now they are to learn that this little while was not, as the Jews had hoped, a matter of a few days, or months, or even years. There was little or no evidence of so great an upheaval in the near future as foretold by Haggai. The Angel of the Lord, of course, knew of it, since He Himself had so decreed it in the council of the Trinity. Yet He realized that this turn of affairs would be a sore disappointment for the small band of returned exiles, whose hope for a speedy increase of numbers, roused by Haggai's words, would be crushed. He, the Redeeming Angel (Gen. 48: 16; Ex. 14: 19; Ps. 34: 7, 22; Is. 63: 9), has compassion on that little flock still pining under the rule of foreign kings. That lowly Church (Is. 54: 11 a) is the Church He loves, the apple of His eye (Deut. 32: 10; Zech. 2: 8). To this Church He had given the promise of Is. 54: 5-17. This is the Church for which in the fullness of the time He will come as its Redeemer (Gal. 4: 4 f.), to make it a glorious Church (Hag. 2: 7, 9; Eph. 5: 25 ff.). Therefore He, the divine Intercessor and Mediator (Zech. 3: 4 f.; John 17: 6 ff.; Rom. 8: 34; 1 John 2: 1; Heb. 7: 25; 9: 24), in a prayer very similar to that of Habakkuk (Hab. 3: 2), brings the pleadings of His people to the throne of Jehovah, uniting with them His own (v. 12). In words so often used by His harassed people, He cries out, O Lord of Hosts, how long? (Cp. Ps. 6: 3; 90: 13; 94: 3 f.; Jer. 4: 21; 12: 4.) How long wilt Thou withdraw Thy mercies from Jerusalem and Judah, against whom Thou hast had "indignation"? a very strong term = rage, vehement anger. "These threescore and ten years" refer not to the seventy years of the Exile, 605—536 (Dan. 1: 1 ff.), but to the seventy years beginning with the destruction of the city, the burning of the Temple, the depopulation and desolation of Judah, 586 B. C. (Cp. 2 Chron. 36: 17-21; Is. 64: 9-12.) In 520 Judah had not yet recovered from this longest and severest period of ruin in its history. While pleading for mercy, the Angel of the Lord is sure that His prayer, the prayer of Him in whom is Jehovah's name, will be heard. (Cp. John 11: 42.)

V. 13. The Lord immediately answers. He does not, however, address the Angel of the Lord, since He knows the answer. The Lord speaks to the interpreting angel who is to transmit the answer to the prophet, who in turn will serve as God's spokesman to the people. The Lord spoke "good," kind, gracious words, such as were by their very nature "comfortable," literally, words of comforts, the plural denoting abundance, comfort in every need and sorrow. The essence of these words is summarized by the interpreting angel.

Vv. 14-17. Twice the prophet is told to "cry" (vv. 14, 17) with a loud voice, so that all may hear, a voice of conviction, that all may be convinced. Five times he is told to assure the people that his message is not the wishful thinking of mortal man, but the word of the Lord, the I AM THAT I AM (Ex. 3:14), the Covenant God of Israel. Three times he is reminded that the Covenant God of that small colony is the Lord of Hosts, the Ruler of the world, having inexhaustible resources at His disposal to carry out His pledge. And what a pledge it is! "I am jealous," etc. (v. 14), eagerly zealous. He will make His people the object of His deepest concern. Far from being pleased with the cruel treatment they had suffered from their enemies, He is "very sore displeased" (v. 15), furiously enraged (Is. 10:25 f.) against the heathen "that are at ease," that now enjoy peace and security, and attribute it to their own power and statesmanship (Is. 47:5-11). "I was but a little displeased" (cp. Is. 54:7, 8, "a small moment," "a little wrath"; Is. 10:25, "a very little while"). If seventy years of desolation is only a little displeasure, what will be the fate of the enemies when the full fury of God's wrath shall be unleashed against them! The Gentiles "helped forward the affliction," literally, assisted toward evil. They had done their utmost to make the Lord's chastisements — which were to teach His people to put their trust in God, not in man or idols (Is. 10:20 f.; Jer. 3:22-25) — an unendurable evil (Is. 10:5-19, 24). Therefore the anger of the Lord now turns against the heathen, while His full mercies will be restored to Jerusalem.

V. 16. "I am returned." The Hebrew tense (perfect) here denotes an accomplished fact whose blessings will continue indefinitely. He has returned to Jerusalem and will remain there "with mercies," the plural of abundance. The chief mercies are immediately announced. "My house shall be built in it." Jerusalem again will be honored by harboring in its midst the house God had chosen as His dwelling place (Ex. 25:8; 29:42 ff.; 40:33 ff.), the place of His revelation (Num. 7:89), of propitiation (Lev. 1:1 ff.). He, the Lord of Hosts, the Ruler of the world, had moved the heart of Tatnai, the Persian governor, not to order the building stopped (Ezra 5:3 ff.), and the heart of the world emperor Darius to grant to the Jews financial and moral support and full liberty to practice their religion (Ezra 6:1 ff.). See also the decree of Artaxerxes Longimanus (465—425 B. C.), issued 458 (Ezra 7:1-26). Also the walls of the city were later rebuilt by Nehemiah (Neh. 1—6) and the city repopulated (Neh. 7—11), 445 B. C. The Lord indeed returned to Jerusalem with mercies.

V. 17. Another message is transmitted to the prophet by the interpreting angel (cp. v. 14), to be proclaimed with loud and joyous voice. "My cities," the cities of the World Ruler, the Lord of Hosts, Israel's

Covenant God, shall "yet," again, "be spread abroad," rather, over-flow, "through prosperity," literally, with good things, choice blessings. In particular, Zion-Jerusalem, which lamented (Lam. 1—5), shall be comforted in a manner possible only to the Lord (2 Cor. 1:2 ff.; Is. 51:3, 12; 66:13) and shall again be chosen as the Lord's own dwelling place, where He would abide among His people, where His incarnate Son would be presented in the Temple (Luke 2:22 ff.), where as a young boy He would cause learned doctors to marvel at His understanding (Luke 2:42 ff.), from which He would drive the money-changers (John 2:13), where He would preach (John 5:17 ff.; 7:14 ff.; 8:1 ff.; 10:1 ff.), perform miracles (John 5:1 ff.; 9:1 ff.), and which He would enter as King of Israel, who was to procure eternal salvation for all mankind (John 12:12 ff.). Here the first fruits of the Gentile world would find in Him their Jesus (John 12:20 ff.). From Jerusalem the Church of God, the Zion-Jerusalem of the New Testament (Gal. 4:26; Heb. 12:22 f.), would spread forth to the uttermost parts of the earth (Luke 24:48; Acts 1:8). Good tidings of great joy indeed for that little flock of faithful followers of the Lord and His prophets, and a powerful inducement to build His Temple!

CHAPTER 2 (A. V., Ch. 1:18—2:13)

2. The second vision: The four horns and four carpenters, ch. 2:1-4
(A. V., 1:18-21)

1 (A. V., 1:18) I lifted my eyes and looked, and, lo, four horns.
2 (1:19) Then I said to the angel that talked to me, What are these? And he said, These are the horns which scatter Judah and Israel and
3 (1:20) Jerusalem. Then the LORD showed me four blacksmiths.
4 (1:21) And I said, What are these coming to do? And He said, These are the horns which scatter Judah, so that not a man has raised his head; and these have come to terrify them, to cast down the horns of the nations lifting their horn against the land of Judah to scatter it.

Grammatical Notes

V. 2 (A. V., 1:19). "Have scattered." The Hebrew perfect denotes the action in its completion, even though it still continued and will continue in future. We translate by present tense. (Cp. Ps. 1:1, three perfects; 10:3; 119:40, etc.)

Vv. 1, 2 (A. V., 1:18, 19). Insuperable obstacles, enemies from without — hostile nations, Satan — and from within — sin and wicked-ness — seemed to make the fulfillment of God's glorious promise im-possible. The next visions describe the defeat and destruction of every force opposing the Church of God and the glorious growth and expan-sion of God's kingdom (ch. 2—6:8).

415

After a brief interval of meditation the prophet again lifts his eyes and sees another strange vision: four horns. We are not told whether these horns were attached to some object or floated in the air. Nor is there any indication that they were iron horns. (Cp. 2 Chron. 18:10.) Horns are symbols of strength and power. (Cp. Deut. 33:17; 1 Sam. 2:1-10; Ps. 18:2; Amos 3:14; 6:13; Micah 4:13.) Four is the number of completeness. (Cp. Prov. 30:15, 18, 21, 29; Is. 11:12; Ezek. 1:5-18; 14:21, etc.) It is useless to speculate which special nations are included in this number; it embraces all nations that have opposed and will oppose the Church of God. In answer to the prophet's question (v. 2, A. V., 1:19) the interpreting angel (cp. 1:9) informs him that they represent the nations (no number is stated!) that have scattered (Gr. N.), rather, scatter Judah, a reference to the cruel custom of deporting entire cities and nations to foreign countries. Judah is the tribal name, Israel, the honorable name of the nation chosen by the Lord (Gen. 32:24-30); and Jerusalem, the seat of God's dwelling; a climax indicating the wickedness of the enemy who opposed and sought to destroy not merely a sister nation, but God's people, Jehovah's own city, a blasphemous crime. (Cp. Ps. 2:1 ff.; 74:2 ff.; 83:1 ff.)

V. 3, 4 (A. V., 1:20, 21). The Lord showed, caused His prophet to see, four "carpenters." The Hebrew term denotes an artisan, a craftsman, working with wood or stone or metal. Again the prophet fails to understand their purposes (v. 4, A. V., 1:21). The interpreting angel tells him once more that the horns are the scatterers, who had done their work so well that no man dared to lift up his head. The Jews were captives in a land whose rulers brooked no opposition, tolerated no disobedience. The history of God's Church is replete with cruel oppression, bloody persecution by its opponents (Judg. 6:2-6; 1 Sam. 13:5, 6, 17-22; Heb. 11:36 ff.), the bloody persecutions by imperial and papal Rome. But for every oppressor there is a destroyer, four horns, four carpenters, the latter coming to "fray" the former, to terrify them, to change their insolent tyranny into abject fear, and cast down "the horns of the Gentiles," the plural signifying all resources of the nations that "lifted up their horn," dominated the land of Judah to scatter, destroy it. There is no oppressor of God's Church so proud, so boastful, so strong but God is stronger! Assyria, Babylon, Persia, Rome — where are they? The Lord's "carpenters," His chosen instruments, have "frayed" and destroyed them. The Church will remain victorious until God will finally and forever end all opposition (Ps. 2:5, 9; Rev. 20:8-10).

416

3. The third vision: The man with the measuring line, ch. 2:5-17 (A. V., 1-13)

5 (A. V., 1) And I raised my eyes and looked. And, lo, a man with a measuring tape in his hand.

6 (2) So I said, Where are you going? And he said to me, To measure Jerusalem, to see what shall be its breadth and its length.

7 (3) And, lo, the angel that talked to me went forward, and another angel went forth to meet him.

8 (4) And he said to him, Run and tell this young man, saying, As unwalled towns shall Jerusalem remain because of the large number of men and animals in the midst

9 (5) of her. And I Myself will be unto her, is the oracle of the LORD, a wall of fire round about, and her glory will I be in the midst of her.

10 (6) Ho! Ho! Flee from the Northland, is the oracle of the LORD, for like the four winds of heaven I will spread you, is the oracle of the

11 (7) LORD. Ho! O Zion! Escape, you that dwell with the daughter

12 (8) of Babylon! For thus says the LORD of Hosts, After the glory He hath sent Me to the nations that have plundered you; for he that touches you touches the apple of

13 (9) His eye. For, lo, I will wave My hand over them, and they shall be a plunder to those serving them. And you shall know that the LORD

14 (10) has sent Me. Rejoice and be glad, O daughter of Zion, for, lo, I am coming and will dwell in your midst, is the oracle of the LORD.

15 (11) And many nations shall join themselves with the LORD on that day, and they shall be My people, and I shall dwell in their midst; and you shall know that the LORD of Hosts has sent Me to you.

16 (12) And the LORD will take possession of Judah as His portion in the Holy Land and will again

17 (13) choose Jerusalem. Silence! all flesh, before the LORD, for He rouses Himself from His holy dwelling.

Grammatical Notes

V. 8 (A. V., 4). "Be inhabited." The Hebrew term = to sit, of a city's location (Num. 21:5); of a palace (Jer. 30:18); to throne (1 Sam. 4:4; Ps. 9:5, A. V., 4). — "Towns without walls." The Hebrew term denotes the open country in contrast to the walled cities. (Cp. Ezek. 38:11; Esther 9:19, where the term is defined.)

V. 10 (6). "Spread you abroad." שָׁרַשׁ here is commonly translated "scattered" and referred to the Exile. Neither Qal nor Piel occurs in this sense. The Piel occurs here, also Ps. 143:6; Is. 1:15; 25:11; 65:2; Jer. 4:31; Lam. 1:17; always "to spread," and Ps. 68:15, A. V., 14. In the last passage A. V. translates "scattered." The correct translation: When the Lord "spreads" kings, rulers, leaders in it, in His Church, "it snows on Tsalmon," the shady, dark, mountain = darkness becomes light. Hence this verse cannot be used to prove Exilic or pre-Exilic authorship of the book of Zechariah.

Vv. 5-9 (A. V., 1-5). The prophet sees a man with a measuring tape in his hands. In eager curiosity he asks, Where are you going? (V. 6, A. V., 2.) The prophet is not merely an idle spectator, but is deeply interested in the visions shown to him by the Lord. The man tells him that he is about to measure the width and length of Jerusalem. Now the interpreting angel leaves Zechariah, but neither the

417

direction nor his purpose is stated. There is no stereotyped form of the manner in which Zechariah obtains his information, but a truly remarkable variation. (See ch. 1:9, 10, 11, 12, 13-17; 2:1, 3-4; 5:1, 2, 5-11.)

While the interpreting angel is on the way, another angel meets him and tells him to run and speak to "this young man" (vv. 7, 8, A. V., 3, 4). This phrase does not refer to the man with the measuring line, who is to be told that Jerusalem is to remain an unwalled city and that therefore he is not to measure its extent. The angel is not speaking here of the physical Jerusalem. The walls of Jerusalem, though destroyed, could be measured, and were repaired and rebuilt later by Nehemiah under God's direction and blessing (Neh. ch. 1 ff.), and parts of these walls stand to this day. The angel speaks of the spiritual Jerusalem, the New Testament Church. This one shall "be inhabited" (Gr. N.), rather, sit, throne, as towns without walls (Gr. N.), as open country, the wide-open spaces. It shall have such a "multitude of men and cattle" (cp. Jonah 4:14) that no walls could possibly compass them. (See Matt. 28:19, "all nations"; Mark 16:15, "all the world"; Luke 24:47; Acts 1:8.) "Cattle" here represents all the possessions, the wealth of the city. The Church of God does not need any wall of stone or metal. The Lord Himself (v. 9, A. V., 5) will be like a wall of fire (cp. 2 Kings 6:17) round about His Church so that no power of man or Satan can overthrow it (Ps. 2; Zech. 12:2 ff.; 14:3 ff.; Matt. 16:18; Rev. 20:8-10).

"I will be the glory in the midst of her." Says the Son of God, Jehovah Our Righteousness, "I am with you alway" (Matt. 28:20). As He dwelt among His people visibly, so to the end of the world He remains in Word and Sacraments with His Church. This inseparable presence of the Lord Jehovah, the greatest glory imaginable to the human mind, shall be the crowning splendor of the city of God and all its inhabitants, whether gathered in majestic cathedrals or in humble shacks and dark foxholes. (Cp. Matt. 18:20.)

V. 10 (6). "The land of the north" = the standing term for Assyria and Babylon (Jer. 1:14 f.; 3:18; 6:22; Zeph. 2:13) as the most powerful opponents of God's chosen people, symbolizing all enemies of the Church throughout the world to the end of time. God's people are to flee from the land of the north. Why? "For I have spread you abroad (Gr. N.) as the four winds of the heaven." Here the Lord explains the phrase "inhabited as towns without walls" (v. 8, A. V., 4). No longer a special land shall be assigned to the people of God in the

New Testament era. As the Lord spreads the four winds over the entire world, so He will spread His Church by sending His Gospel messengers into all the world. Even in God's own land of Canaan (Ex. 25: 8; 2 Chron. 7: 20; Jer. 2:7; 16: 18) they were surrounded by ungodly heathen and were warned against closely associating with them lest they be seduced to like wickedness and like them be rejected by the Lord (Lev. 18: 1-5, 24-30). In the New Testament era God's people are scattered over all the earth. They live among the godless, wicked people of this world, symbolized by Babylon, and therefore they must be especially careful to flee from Babylon and its wicked ways. Cp. 2 Cor. 6: 14-18, quoting Is. 48: 20; 52: 11, the world in general; and Rev. 18: 4-24, papal Rome. During the Old Testament era this was the standing invitation to all Jews scattered in foreign countries to do what the 42,000 Jews had done under Zerubbabel, to return to the Land of Promise, the Lord's land, where the danger of seduction to idolatry and apostasy was not so great as in heathen surroundings.

V. 11 (7). Deliver thyself, escape, O Zion, that dwellest with (Gr. N.) the "daughter" = the people (cp. Is. 1: 8; Ps. 137: 8; Jer. 46: 19, 24) of Babylon. Even while living among the Babylonians, they should escape its wickedness, lest they perish with it. In the world, not of it (John 17: 11, 14-16). Such escape is possible through the power of the Lord.

Vv. 12, 13 (8, 9). The Messenger sent by the Lord, His Angel, is very definitely called "the LORD of Hosts," the World Ruler. He speaks with the full authority of His Godhead. He is sent "after the glory" (cp. Ex. 14: 4, "honored") = His promise to protect His chosen people against their enemies (Lev. 26: 7 f.; Deut. 28: 7; Matt. 16: 18). This glory the Angel is to win back from the nations which "spoiled," despoiled, plundered Israel and boasted that the Lord was unable to keep His promise (Is. 10: 5-15; 36: 14-20; Ezek. 36: 19-23). The Lord regarded their cruel oppression of His people as a violation of His majesty. His chosen nation (Ex. 19: 5, 6) was as dear to Him as the apple of His eye (Gr. N.), a very sensitive organ, carefully guarded against any harm (Deut. 32: 10; Ps. 17: 8). Any harm done to them irritates Him, provokes His just wrath as if it had been done to Himself personally. (Cp. Acts 9: 4; Matt. 25: 40-45.) Egypt had felt His wrath (Ex. 3—15); proud Nineveh had been wiped out (Nah. 1—3; pp. 293—312); Babylon had fallen (p. 383). So every nation and every individual opposing the Lord's Church will be shattered by

419

the Lord. When He shakes His hand (v. 13, A. V., 9), which formed the earth (Ps. 95:5) and makes the mountains smoke (Ps. 104:32), the proud masters will become servants; the presumptuous rulers, abject slaves. So will the glory of the Lord and His Angel as the Ruler of the world and the Protector of His Church become manifest and be gratefully praised by all His people and acknowledged with bitter resentment and horrified fear by His enemies (Ex. 14:25; 15:14 ff.; Joshua 2:9 ff.; 1 Sam. 4:6 ff.; Rev. 6:15-17).

V. 14 (10). God's people, now under foreign dominion, are still the daughter of Zion, the mount chosen by Him (Ps. 78:68 f.; 132:13 f.). He comes and will dwell in the midst of them. He had dwelt in the Tabernacle (Ex. 25:8, 21 f.), in Solomon's Temple (1 Kings 8:10 f.). So He will dwell in the house now being erected by them. In the New Testament, when the Lord of Hosts will come in the person of the incarnate Son, He will dwell visibly among His people (John 1:14). With His Church He will dwell invisibly but actually (Matt. 28:20) to the end of time, and eternally in glory (Rev. 21:3). Sing and rejoice, O little flock!

V. 15 (11). "Many nations," etc., repeats the promise so often repeated in the Old Testament (Gen. 18:18; 22:18; 28:14; 49:14; Ps. 2:7 ff.; 72:8 ff.; Is. 60:3 ff., etc.). "I will dwell," etc., repeats v. 10 b; "and thou shalt know," etc., the assurance of v. 9, last clause.

V. 16 (12). In this manner the Lord will take possession (Gr. N.) of the true Judah (cp. Rom. 2:28), the Church, as His portion, as His precious heritage (cp. Ps. 94:5; Jer. 12:7-9; Joel 2:17; 3:2; Micah 7:14, 18). "In the holy land." Wherever God reveals Himself, there is the holy land (Ex. 3:5). In the New Testament this land is not restricted to Judah and Jerusalem. He creates holy land and holy homes wherever He is in the midst of His believers, be it millions of them, or only two or three (Matt. 18:20), or only one individual believer, a husband, wife, son, daughter, servant, laborer, in whose heart He dwells (John 14:16-20). Again Jerusalem shall be chosen of Him (Gal. 4:26; Heb. 12:22 f.).

V. 17 (13). Silence, all flesh, before the Lord (Hab. 2:20; Zeph. 1:7); for He is raised up, rouses Himself, arises out of His holy habitation. He is getting ready to fulfill His promises. Do not rebel against Him. Quietly, joyously do His work. Do not become impatient! He will come in His own time, not a minute late! (Cp. 1 Peter 4:12-19; 2 Peter 3:8 ff.)

CHAPTER 3

4. The fourth vision: Joshua, the high priest, and Satan standing before the Angel of the Lord

1 And he showed me Joshua, the high priest, standing before the Angel of the LORD, and Satan, standing at
2 his right hand, to oppose him. And the LORD said to Satan, The LORD rebuke you, O Satan! The LORD that hath chosen Jerusalem, rebuke you! Is not this one a brand
3 plucked from the fire? Now Joshua was clothed in filthy garments as he was standing before the Angel.
4 And He answered and said to those standing before Him, Remove the filthy garments from him! Then He said to him, See, I have taken your guilt away from you, and have
5 clothed you with festal garments. So I said, Let them place a clean turban on his head! And they placed the clean turban on his head and clothed him in garments, and the Angel of the LORD was stand-
6 ing by. Then the Angel of the

LORD solemnly assured Joshua,
7 saying, Thus says the LORD of Hosts, If you will walk in My ways and observe My ordinances, then you shall also judge My house and guard My courts, and I will give you right of way among these
8 standing here. Hear now, Joshua, the high priest, you and your friends who are sitting in your presence, for they are men of por-tent; and, lo, I am about to bring
9 My Servant, the Branch. For, lo, the stone which I have set before Joshua! On one stone seven eyes! Lo, I am engraving its inscription, is the oracle of the LORD of Hosts, and I will remove the guilt of this
10 land in one day. On that day, is the oracle of the LORD of Hosts, every-one shall invite his friend under the vine and under the fig tree.

Grammatical Notes

V. 1. "Resist," שָׂטַן, to antagonize, op-pose (Ps. 38:21; 71:13; 109:4, 20, 29). The noun is used of an opponent in battle (1 Sam. 29:4; 1 Kings 5:18; 11:14-23, 25), in court (Ps. 109:6). Cp. Satan, "ac-cuser," "accused" (Rev. 12:9, 10).

V. 3. "Filthy," literally, rendered filthy by excrements (Deut. 23:14, "unclean thing," cp. v. 13; Ezek. 4:12; Is. 36:12, Q'ri); the filthiness of vomit (Is. 28:8); a symbol of guilt here (Is. 4:4; Prov. 30:12).

V. 4. "Change of garment," literally, a garment that is put off, taken off, before going to work, hence precious, costly, beautiful garments, "for glory and for beauty" (Ex. 28:2), "changeable suits" (Is. 3:22).

V. 5. "Mitre," צָנִיף, the turbanlike head-dress of the king (Is. 62:3, "diadem"); of rich, honorable men (Job 29:14, "diadem"); of rich women (Is. 3:23,

"hoods"). Here a synonym of *mits-nephet*, the usual term for the priestly headdress (Ex. 28:4, 37, 39; 29:6; 39:28, 31, etc.), which in turn is used of the royal diadem (Ezek. 21:31). Both offices are united in the Messiah (Ps. 110). — "They clothed him"; the imperfect here denotes the progressive action until it is completed.

V. 8. "Branch," *zemach*, never denotes an individual branch or twig of a tree, but invariably an individual growth or sprout. (Cp. Gen. 19:25; Ps. 65:11; Is. 4:2; 61:11; Ezek. 16:7; Hos. 8:7; Jer. 23:5; 33:15; Zech. 6:12.)

V. 9. "Upon — shall be seven eyes." Not: seven eyes are engraved on the stone, but are directed upon the one stone. (Cp. Job 24:23; Ps. 32:8 without a verb; with אֶל, Ps. 33:18; 34:16 without verb; שִׂים עַל, Gen. 44:21; Jer. 39:12; 40:4.)

V. 1. "Among all the visions of Zechariah this might be called the most beautiful one, for it leads us into the very center of our holy Christian faith" (L. Fuerbringer, *Synodalbericht des Nord-Wisconsin-Distrikts*, 1918, p. 20). Joshua, also called Jeshua, the high priest (Ezra 3: 2, 8 f.; 5: 2 ff.; Hag. 1: 1, 14; 2: 2, 4), was seen "standing before" the Angel. The servants and officers of the king stood before the king, who sat on his throne, in order to consult with him and then carry out his orders. (Cp. Gen. 41: 46; 1 Sam. 16: 21 f.; Jer. 40: 10; 52: 12; Dan. 1: 5.) The term is also used of the priests serving the Lord in the sanctuary (Deut. 10: 8; Judg. 20: 28; Ps. 134: 1). The high priest was the representative not only of the priesthood, but also of the entire nation (Ex. 28: 1, 9-12; 29 f.; Lev. 16: 15 f., 20-22, 34; Heb. 5: 1-3). The Angel of the Lord (see p. 409) appears here as the One to whom the sacrifices and prayers of God's people are to be offered, who is the Lord Our Righteousness (Jer. 23: 6). Joshua stands here as the divinely appointed mediator between God and man. At the right hand of the high priest stands Satan, the adversary, opponent, accuser (Job 1: 6-8, 12; 2: 1-4, 6-9), "to resist him" (Gr. N.), to oppose, accuse him. That is Satan's characteristic trait. Cp. Rev. 12: 10, where the participial form "accusing" (A. V., "which accused") denotes habitual, unceasing activity. One example of such never-ceasing accusations is presented in this vision. Satan challenges Joshua's right to appear as mediator before God, since he is a sinner, unworthy to stand in the presence of God, according to God's own statement (Deut. 27: 26; Jer. 11: 3 f., etc.). Satan is quite sure of gaining his point. How can the holy God change His own judgment of damnation, repeated time and again? With brazen shamelessness he appears before God (cp. Job 1: 6 ff.; 2: 1 ff.) and arrogantly places himself at the right hand of Joshua (Ps. 109: 6) in order to advance his charges. Was not the high priest clothed in filthy (Gr. N.), evil-smelling garments? (V. 3.) Were not these clothes the irrefutable evidence that Joshua was a sinner (Is. 64: 6) and therefore utterly unqualified for his office? Satan was ready to challenge the Lord's own institution for the forgiveness of sin, to deny the right of God to pardon the sinner. He seeks to overthrow the Throne of Grace, so hateful to him, and to turn it into a seat of judgment and condemnation. With one fell stroke he hopes to obtain even the child of God as his victim and fellow prisoner in the flames of hell.

Vv. 2, 3. Before Satan can utter a word, the Angel of the Lord foils his wicked scheme. "The LORD rebuke thee." The Angel of Jehovah speaks of Jehovah. There is plurality of persons in the

indivisible essence of I AM THAT I AM. "Rebuke" = scold, reprimand (Gen. 37:10; Jer. 29:27; Is. 17:13). — "That hath chosen Jerusalem." The Lord repeats and confirms His promise of ch. 1:17; 2:16
(A. V., 12). The Lord had chosen Jerusalem, and He owes to no one
any apology or explanation of His reasons (Ex. 33:19 b). And as
for Joshua, is he not a brand plucked out of the fire? "Fire" refers
to the Exile, which seemed to be the hopeless end, the final destruction
of Jerusalem and the nation. Compare their agonized cry in Jer. 14:19;
Lam. 1:12-17; 3:1-18. Yet the Lord had proved the truth of Jeremiah's
word (Lam. 3:22 ff., 31 ff.) and of His own promise (Jer. 25:11 f.;
29:10 ff.). He had delivered His people from their captivity, had
plucked them out of the fire that threatened to consume them. One
of these brands snatched out of the conflagration was Joshua, the high
priest. He was one of those whose spirit God had raised, had made
willing to return to Jerusalem (Ezra 1:5), who had accepted the
promised Messiah as the Lord his Righteousness, one of the elect
citizens of Jerusalem, the city which God had chosen. Though he,
like Isaiah, was a sinful man (v. 3; Is. 6:5; 64:6), yet he could rejoice
with Isaiah: Is. 61:10. The Angel of the Lord proves that by His action.

V. 4. The Angel of the Lord commands the angels standing before
Him as His servants to remove Joshua's filthy garments and at once
explains this symbolic act by His full absolution, the declaration that
every trace of iniquity, of guilt, has been taken away by Him, and
by His assurance that He will clothe Joshua with "change of raiment"
(Gr. N.), with festal garments, a reference to the "holy garments for
glory and beauty" (Ex. 28:2 ff.), to be worn by the high priest
whenever he served in the Temple (Ex. 28:3, 29, 38, 40-43). Having
justified Joshua, the Angel of the Lord retains him in his office
notwithstanding the charges of Satan and the fact that these charges
to a certain extent were true. What Satan could not understand and
what passes all human comprehension is the fact so clearly taught
here that the God of absolute holiness, justice, and righteousness is
at the same time the God of unalterable and everlasting grace, forgiving iniquity, trespasses, and sin, without relinquishing the least iota
of His holiness.

V. 5. The prophet is intensely interested in the gowning of the
high priest and cannot curb his eagerness to see him completely robed.
He cries out, "Let them set a fair mitre upon his head!" This mitre
(Gr. N.), or turban, was the crowning headgear of the high priest,
made of "white linen," byssus, either cotton or linen of finest quality.

423

On the turban was fastened a plate of pure gold with the inscription "Holiness to the LORD" (cp. Ex. 28:4, 36-39; 29:6; 39:28-31; Lev. 8:9; 16:4). Zechariah's appeal was neither reproved nor ignored. Since it agreed with God's ordinance, it was carried out to the letter. A "fair," literally, "clean," turban was placed on Joshua's head, and so they "clothed him" (Gr. N.), finished his robing. And all the while the Angel of the Lord "stood by," rather, was standing, "ordering and approving the rite as the Lord of the Temple, and honoring it by His presence." (C. V. Michaelis, quoted by Hengstenberg.)

We have here a beautiful Old Testament illustration of the truth so clearly revealed in Holy Writ that God's promise of grace and glory is valid even though spoken by a man of unclean lips. (Cp. Num. 6:23-27: ye shall bless, v. 23; I will bless, v. 27. Lev. 4:13-21: the congregation's sin, v. 16; the priest's sacrifice, vv. 15-21 a; God's forgiveness, v. 21 b. Vv. 22-26: the ruler's sin forgiven by the priest's sacrifice; vv. 27-35: the sin of any one of the people. Cp. also Matt. 9:8; 18:18; John 20:21 ff.)

We must not overlook the fact that the high priest represented the entire sinful nation (Ex. 28:1; Heb. 5:1). His absolution and reacceptance includes that of the nation as the kingdom of priests and a holy nation (Ex. 19:6).

Vv. 6, 7. "Protested," here = solemnly testified, asserted. "Walk in My ways" (v. 7), observe My commandments governing your life, lead a life of personal holiness. "Keep My charge" is also used in this general sense, e. g., in Gen. 26:5; Lev. 18:30; 22:9; but here may refer particularly to official duties. (Cp. Lev. 8:35; Num. 1:53; 3:7 f., 28, 32.) "Judge My house" = be the ruler and judge of all affairs pertaining to the Temple service; high priest not only in name, but also in deed. "Keep My courts," guard them against being desecrated by ungodliness and frivolity. Service in God's Church is the best reward and highest honor the Lord can bestow on human beings. "Places to walk." See note on "journey," Jonah 3:3, p. 233. "Stand by," are standing, the angels standing before Him, ready to serve Him (v. 4 f.; Ps. 103:20 f.; Matt. 18:10). While the high priest was permitted to enter the Most Holy Place only once a year, and then only under certain conditions (Lev. 16:1 ff.), the Angel of the Lord here promises that a time was coming when the high priest and his assistants together with the entire congregation here represented by them would have access not only to the Most Holy Place, but even to the very throne of God; a time when all believers, young and old, would have paths among the angels, the boldness to enter into the holiest by the blood of Jesus (Heb. 10:19) and would no longer need any human priest or mediator (John 16:23-27).

V. 8. The Lord includes Joshua's fellow priests in His message. "That sit before thee," a phrase denoting the relation of colleagues to their presiding chairman, of servants to their superior, here of the priests as assistants to the high priest, performing their duties under his training and supervision. (Cp. 2 Kings 4:38; Ezek. 8:1.) On the change from the second to the third person vv. 8, 9, cp. Ezek. 28:22; Hos. 2:6-23; Zeph. 2:12. They are men "wondered at," literally, men of portent, of omen, of significant, symbolical import. In building the Temple they were not merely officials of a human king, carrying out the edicts of two mighty potentates (Ezra 1:2 ff.; 6:3 ff.; 7:11 ff.); they were not only servants of the Lord of Hosts, the Ruler of the world, building His sanctuary (Hag. 1:2, 8 ff.). Theirs was an infinitely higher honor. They were "men of portent." The Hebrew term is used of men rousing the attention of the people to a coming event by their strange, symbolical names (Is. 8:1-4, 18) or actions (Is. 20:3 and context; Ezek. 12:6, 11 and context; 24:24, 27; cp. vv. 15-18). Joshua, the high priest, and his fellow priests are to be types prefiguring the New Testament High Priest (Ps. 110:4; Heb. 5:6, 10; chs. 7—10) and the New Testament royal priesthood (1 Peter 2:5, 9; Rev. 1:6; 5:10; 20:6). "For, behold" states the reason why Joshua and his fellows are such omens, types. They foreshadow the eternal Priest (Ps. 110:4), who will by His vicarious obedience and suffering obtain full forgiveness, the garments of righteousness and salvation for mankind (Heb. 7—10). He is here called the Lord's Servant because of His willing, patient, perfect obedience to His Father (Ps. 40:6-8; Is. 42:1 ff.; 49:1-5; 52:13 ff.; 53:1 ff.), the "Branch" (Gr. N.), or Sprout, God's Branch (Is. 4:2; Jer. 23:5; Zech. 6:12), "because the Lord caused Him to sprout, implanted this Sprout in a mysterious manner into mankind. Hence this name points to the miraculous origin of the Messiah and to the mystery of His person" (G. Stoeckhardt, *Kommentar,* on Is. 4:2).

V. 9. "For" adds another reason why Joshua and the other priests are to pay close attention. They are to direct their eyes to the stone which the Lord Himself has laid before Joshua. This stone is deserving of their close observation, for on this one stone "shall be seven eyes" (Gr. N.), directed on them in loving care. The eyes regarding this stone are the eyes of the Lord, as ch. 4:10 directly states. The work on this stone is not yet completed; the Lord declares that He will "engrave the graving thereof"; will beautify it. This stone does not

425

symbolize the Messiah, for He was still to come, while the stone is already placed before Joshua. Joshua had been told that he was to judge the house of the Lord and keep His courts (v. 7). Now he is given another honorable charge. He is to be not only the caretaker and ruler of the visible Temple, but of that invisible, spiritual temple, the Church, represented by the stone which is the object of God's loving attention. He is to be a laborer together with God (cp. 1 Cor. 3:9 ff.), working as God's servant in building His eternal Kingdom of Grace and Glory. The engraving of the stone, its beauty and glory, it owes entirely to the Angel of the Lord, the Messiah (Eph. 5:25b-27), who assures the prophet that He will remove the iniquity of that land "in one day," on that great Day of Atonement (cp. Lev. 16), when Christ offered up Himself (Heb. 7:26 ff.).

V. 10. In that day, the glorious day of the New Testament, the justified members of God's Church, enjoying peace with God, will share their joy with their fellow believers and urge one another to rejoice and sing with them, to taste and see that the Lord is good! (Ps. 34:8.)

CHAPTER 4

5. The fifth vision: The golden candlestick and the two olive trees

1 Then the angel who talked with me returned and roused me like a man
2 roused out of his sleep and said to me, What do you see? And I said, I see, and, lo, a candlestick all of gold and its bowl at the top of it, and its seven lamps on it and seven pipes for each of the lamps at its
3 top. And there are two olive trees at its side, one on the right of the
4 bowl and one on its left. So I spoke again to the angel who talked with me, saying, What are these, my
5 lord? Then the angel who talked with me answered and said to me, Do you not know what these are?
6 And I said, No, my lord. So he replied and said to me as follows, This is the word of the LORD to Zerubbabel, saying, Not by might, nor by power, but by My Spirit,
7 says the LORD of Hosts. Who are you, O great mountain? Before Zerubbabel you shall become a plain! And he shall bring forth the topstone with shoutings, Grace! Grace

8 to it! And the word of the LORD
9 came to me, saying, The hands of Zerubbabel have laid the foundations of this house, and his hands shall complete it! And you shall know that the LORD of Hosts has
10 sent me to you. For all who have despised the day of small things shall rejoice and see the plummet in the hand of Zerubbabel. These seven, they are the eyes of the LORD ranging over all the earth.
11 Then I answered and said to him, What are these two olive trees at the right hand of the candlestick
12 and on its left? And I asked a second time and said to him, What are the two olive branches which are at the side of the golden pipes pouring out from themselves the
13 gold? Then he said to me, Do you not know what these are? And
14 I said, No, my lord! Then he said, These are the two anointed ones standing before the Lord of the whole earth.

426

Grammatical Notes

V. 2. "Bowl." גֻּלָּה is to be pointed גֻּלָּה, as in v. 3; it is derived from a stem = to roll, hence a round vessel or bowl. — "Seven pipes," מוּצָקוֹת, from a stem = to pour or empty out, hence feeder pipes. "Seven" here distributive. There is no hard and fast rule in the manner of expressing the distributive use of numerals; it is done either by simple repetition of the numerals (Gen. 7:9, 15), or by לְ following the numeral (Deut. 1:23), or by repetition of the numeral and the addition of לְ (Num. 13:2; Is. 6:2), or by joining by "and" two numerals preceded by plurals (2 Sam. 21:20, literally, "the fingers of his hands and the fingers [toes] of his feet, six and six, twenty-four the number"). Here Zechariah joins the two numerals by "and" and adds לְ with the plural; seven pipes to each of the lamps; supplying a steady and ample amount of oil.

V. 10. "Who hath despised." The interrogative is here used in the sense of an indefinite pronoun, whoever. (Cp. Ex. 24:14; 32:26; Judg. 7:3; Is. 50:8,10; Hos. 14:10, etc.) — "Plummet," literally, "the stone, lead." Stone = weight. (Cp. 5:8.) Occasionally a noun determined by the article is more closely defined by another noun so determined placed in apposition. (Cp. Ex. 39:17, the chains, the gold = the golden chains; 2 Kings 16:14, the altar, the brass [bronze], the bronze altar; cp. v. 17; Jer. 32:12, etc.) Here the leaden weight used as a plummet.

V. 12. "Branches," literally, ears. The two branches full of olives are compared to ears filled with kernels of grain, hence, bunches, or clusters. — "Emptying out," pouring out, used of sacks (Gen. 42:35); of rain (Eccl. 11:3; Mal. 3:10). The idea of abundance is strengthened by the participial form, denoting constant action. — "Pipes," a different word from that of v. 2. It occurs only here; probably related to *tsinnor*, waterfall, waterspout (Ps. 42:8); "gutter" (2 Sam. 5:8), the channel or subterranean passage leading from the Kidron Valley into the city. Here, the channels or pipes leading from the clusters of olives to the bowl (v. 3), conveying the oil as it poured out directly from the clusters of olives.

V. 14. "Anointed ones," literally, sons of oil. As the son has inherited certain qualities from the father, which rule him and govern his actions, so the expression son of death, of Belial = wickedness, etc., is used to denote a quality, or condition, which rules him or stands in some relation to him. (Cp. Deut. 13:14; 1 Sam. 20:31; Is. 5:1; Jonah 4:10, p. 238, Gr. N.) Sons of oil = men possessed, ruled, by the Spirit, symbolized by the oil.

Vv. 1-3. The prophet had seen the first four visions while fully awake. He had been a deeply interested observer. But, like Daniel, he was human. The intense strain on his physical and mental powers had exhausted him so that he had fallen into a stuporlike sleep. (Cp. Dan. 8:17 f.; 10:8-10.) While he was asleep, the angel seems to have left him, but then returned to rouse him as a man is wakened out of sleep. Only when fully awake was the prophet ready for the next vision. This time the angel calls the prophet's attention to the next vision by asking him, What seest thou? (V. 2.) The prophet assures him that he is alert and sees a golden candlestick, or candelabrum, to which seven lamps are attached. In the Holy Place of the Tabernacle a seven-branched golden candelabrum was placed on the south side (Ex. 40:24). Its lamps were trimmed and filled with pure olive oil every morning and lighted every evening by the high priest, to burn during the night (Ex. 25:31ff.; 27:20f.; 30:7,8; 37:17ff.; 40:4, 24; Lev. 24:2-4). In Solomon's Temple ten candelabra were placed (1 Kings 7:49). The candelabrum symbolized the Church, God's people (Rev. 1:20), who are to send out light into the darkness of the world surrounding them, by preaching and living the Word of God Ps. 119:105; Prov. 6:23; cp. Matt. 5:14 ff.; Phil. 2:15 f.; 1 Peter 2: 9-12). — Though similar to the golden candlestick in the Tabernacle (A), Zechariah's candlestick (B) differed materially from the former. 1) A was filled daily with a fresh supply of oil; B had a bowl (Gr. N.), a round vessel, from which the oil was supplied to the lamps. 2) A had only branches, or arms, extending to the seven lamps; in B each of these "arms" was made up of seven pipes constantly feeding the oil to the lamps. 3) A's oil was supplied by the people (Ex. 27:20; Lev. 24:2); B was fed directly by two olive trees, one standing on the right side of the bowl, the other on the left (v. 3).

Vv. 4-7. The prophet does not understand the vision and is enlightened by the interpreting angel. This vision expresses a general truth, which Zerubbabel is to apply to himself and his work (v. 6). The two Hebrew words for "might" and "power" denote inner strength, but the latter far more frequently than the former denotes also the means or manifestations of strength. Here both are included: inherent power, courageous bravery, fortitude, as well as manpower, large numbers of soldiers, riches, leaders, well co-ordinated organizations, good financial systems, etc. The Lord's work, the building of His Temple, the inner growth, the expansion of His Church cannot be properly carried out by mere external means. Human strength and wisdom alone will fail. My Spirit must do it! On God's Spirit see Gen. 1:2, Creator Spirit; with sevenfold gifts of grace, see Is. 11:1 f.; Num. 11:17, 25-29; 24:2; Judg. 3:10; 6:34; Ezra 1:5; Ps. 51:12; resting on the Messiah, Ps. 45:7; condemning the wicked, Gen. 6:3. This Spirit is able to overcome all obstacles (v. 7). No matter how mountain-high the difficulties may loom, the Spirit will make them a plain before Zerubbabel, on which no unscalable heights shall make progress impossible. Every seeming impossibility will become an opportunity through the Spirit's power. In due time Zerubbabel will bring forth the headstone, the top or crowning stone, finishing the work begun when the foundation stone was laid. Then glad shoutings will be heard, Grace, grace unto it! Let God's grace rest lovingly upon this stone, this building, this Church represented by the Temple.

Vv. 8, 9. Once more the prophet receives a comforting revelation in the form of a twofold promise such as only the Ruler of the world can fulfill, whose almighty hand sends success or failure (Ps. 127:1, 2) and who alone allots to every man his span of life (Ps. 31:16, A. V., 15; 139:16; Job 14:5). The work which seemed so impossible to many will be finished, and Zerubbabel, who began it, will live to complete it (v. 9). By this twofold fulfillment the divine mission of the speaker, the Messenger sent by the Lord, would be gloriously vindicated. "Thou shalt know," the nation as such; "sent Me unto you," plural, to all believers. The completion of the Temple under such adverse circumstances would be the incontrovertible proof that the Angel of the Lord, Jehovah their Righteousness (Jer. 23:6), was on their side. We have here a clear reference to the three persons constituting Jehovah, I AM THAT I AM: the Lord of Hosts, His Spirit, His Messenger. Every year of increasing extension of the New Testament temple, the Church, ought to strengthen our conviction that this work is not by human might, nor by human power, but by the invincible power of the Spirit of the Lord of Hosts, who has sent His Messenger in the person of the God-Man.

V. 10. "For who hath despised" (Gr. N.). The glorious consummation of the building shall put to shame all those who despise the day of small things (Ezra 3:12 f.; Hag. 2:3). Unbelief, grumbling, weeping, will be changed to joyous hymns of gratitude and praise of God's grace and power. "The plummet" (Gr. N.), used to place the stones in proper alignment, shall be seen in the hand of Zerubbabel, as he inserts the capstone in its place, an occasion for special services of thanksgiving on the order of our cornerstone laying. This stone symbolized the Church of God (ch. 3:9). On this stone were centered the seven eyes of the Covenant God (3:9). This stone, the Church it symbolized, is the object of His loving care; the Church, the stone, is under constant observation of His eyes, which run to and fro in the whole earth (Ps. 11:4-7; 33:13-22), protecting His people against all the forces of Satan (Matt. 16:18). Therefore be of good cheer! The Lord is with you! Continue your task until it is completed!

Vv. 11-14. The prophet asks for information on the nature and purpose of the two olive trees; but before the angel answers, Zechariah makes his question more specific. He names an item not mentioned

429

before (v. 12). On each tree there is a particular "branch" (Gr. N.), a bunch, or cluster, of olives which "empty" (Gr. N.), or pour out from themselves in a never-ceasing stream the "gold," as the oil is called because of its color and its precious symbolism. This oil flows through two golden "pipes" (Gr. N.) leading to the bowl of the candelabrum (vv. 2, 3) and is conveyed from there to each of the seven lamps by seven pipes leading to each lamp (v. 2). He is told that they symbolize the two "anointed ones" (Gr. N.) (v. 14), literally, sons of oil, "standing by," literally, over, since the ruler sits and the servants stand before him, over him. "The Lord," Hebrew, *adon,* one who has authoritative power, over the whole earth, the World Ruler. These two anointed servants are quite evidently the two leaders, civic and ecclesiastic, of Judah. Priests and kings were the only "anointed ones"; priests (Ex. 28:41; 30:29; 40:12-16); kings (1 Sam. 15:1, 17; 16:3, 12, 13, etc.). Oil is a symbol of the Holy Spirit (1 Sam. 10:1, 6, 9f.; 16:13f.; Ps. 45:7; Is. 61:1ff.; Luke 4:18; Acts 4:27; 10:38; 1 John 2:20, 27). Again Joshua and Zerubbabel come into consideration here only in their official capacity as representatives of that nation chosen by God as a royal priesthood, a kingdom of priests (Ex. 19:5, 6). As such they have the honor of standing before the World Ruler as His servants. As such they also are types of the Messiah (ch. 3:8), men wondered at, p. 425. The Messiah, like Melchizedek (Gen. 14:18 ff.; Ps. 110:4; Heb. 5—7), combined these two offices in His person. Through Him all believers of the New Testament are priests and kings before God, from the baptized infant in the cradle (cp. Ps. 8:3; Matt. 18:1 ff.; 21:18) to the highest leader in the Church or state (1 Peter 2:5, 9; Rev. 1:6; 5:10; 20:6). These royal priests God uses as His channels through which the gold, the precious oil, His Holy Spirit with His gifts, is conveyed to their fellow men by the preaching of the Gospel to all nations (1 Peter 2:9; Matt. 28:19 f.; Mark 16:15 f.; cp. Acts 2:14, 40, 41; 3:12 ff.; 4:4, 31 ff.; 8:4 ff.; 11:19 ff.).

CHAPTER 5
6. The sixth vision: The flying roll, vv. 1-4

1 Then again I raised my eyes and looked, and, lo, a flying scroll!

2 And he said to me, What do you see? And I said, I see a flying scroll, the length of which is twenty cubits and its width ten cubits.

3 Then he said to me, This is the curse going forth upon the whole land, and every thief will be swept away from here in accordance with it, and everyone that sweareth will be swept away from here according to it. I have released it, is the oracle of the LORD of Hosts, and it shall enter the house of the thief and into the house of him who swears falsely by My name, and it shall settle in the midst of his house and shall consume it, both its timbers and its stones.

4

Grammatical Notes

V. 3. "Whole earth," the whole land, here the land of Judah (also v. 6), the Holy Land, from which sin is to be removed. — "Cut off." The Hebrew word is נִקָּה = to be clean, pure. Similarly, the English "purge," which may mean to cleanse, to remove dirt, or to remove like dirt, to put out, sweep out; the Piel of the Hebrew word is used also in the sense of "sweep away" (cp. Is. 3:26, "desolate" = sweep away). — "As on this side," "as on that side." מִזֶּה, מִזֶּה, may be used in this sense. (See Ex. 17:12; 32:15; Num. 22:24; Ezek. 2:9, 10; 47:17.) Yet the two words are never so widely separated as they are here. Hengstenberg, Keil, and others regard this as a reference to the two tables of God's Law (the first table comprising the first three, the second, the last seven Commandments) and refer to Ex. 32:15. However, the latter passage does not say that each of the two tables was written on one stone; nor does Zechariah say that the one side of the scroll covers only the sins against one of the two tables. God issues no special curse against the transgressors of one table and another special curse against such as sin against the second table. His Law is one, and His curse is the same against transgressions directed specifically against God and sins neglecting love toward the neighbor. We prefer the translation "from here," "from this place." (Cp. Gen. 37:17, "hence"; Jer. 2:37, "from him," rather, "from here.") — "According to it," כָּמוֹהָ; the fem. suffix refers either to the curse (אָלָה, fem.) written on the roll, or to the roll (מְגִלָּה, fem.), on which the curse was written.

Ch. 3 had symbolized the forgiveness freely granted to sinful Joshua as the representative of God's people. Ch. 4 had pictured the granting of the Holy Spirit by means of justified and sanctified men, and the glorious dignity of their work in building God's Temple. In ch. 5 another important truth is taught. The Lord of infinite grace remains forever the Lord of unchanging holiness and justice, who will punish wickedness and insist on its removal from His Church. This truth is symbolized in two visions, both of which present imagery so strange as to be almost uncanny.

Vv. 1-4. The prophet sees a roll, or scroll, flying in mid-air. In ancient times books were written on long sheets or rolls made of papyrus, a sort of paper made of the pith of the papyrus plant, the paper reed. The pith was cut into strips, several layers of which were laid crosswise and pressed or glued together to form the writing paper of the ancients. Sometimes both sides were used (Ezek. 2:9 f.; Rev. 5:1). Comparatively few books were written on leather or parchment, which was too expensive for ordinary use. The scroll seen by Zechariah was not sealed (Rev. 5:1), but open so that all might read it. It represented God's curse on "the whole earth" (Gr. N.) (v. 3), rather, the land of Israel; the curse pronounced on the wicked, impenitent

431

Jews who called themselves God's people; curses proclaimed centuries before (cp. Lev. 26:14 ff.; Deut. 28:15-68; 29:18-29; 32:15 ff.), curses repeated by all the spokesmen of God. Two sins are mentioned: stealing, representing all violations of the rights of one's fellow man; and swearing, representing all sins directed specifically against God and His holy name. One of the chief sins against God is contempt of His Gospel. (Cp. Ps. 2:2-12; Prov. 1:22-33; 8:32-36, Wisdom, the Son of God, Eternal Life, speaking; Matt. 12:31 f.; Mark 16:16; Heb. 6:6.) "Cut off" (Gr. N.) = removed, swept away. — "As on this side" (Gr. N.) = from here, from the land of Jehovah, the Church of God. On such removal or sweeping away cp. Acts 8:21, "neither part nor lot"; 1 Cor. 5:2, 5, 9-13. — "According to it" (Gr. N.), in keeping with the curse written on the scroll. God's curse is not a mere threat, a passing outburst of passion soon forgotten. It will be fulfilled in due time (v. 4). The curse shall enter the house of the wicked, impenitent sinner and remain there, so that all he thinks, or speaks, or does, is accursed (Deut. 28:16-20). Like an unquenchable fire this curse will consume such a house with the timber thereof, its woodwork, and even its stones. All will be consumed completely, finally, eternally. This is the same lesson inculcated by the Lord when He caused His glory to pass before Moses and proclaimed His name Jehovah, the Lord of infinite grace, but who will by no means clear the guilty, the impenitent sinner (Ex. 34:6 f.).

---

7. The seventh vision: The woman in the ephah, vv. 5-11

5 Then the angel that spoke to me
6 went forth and said to me, Raise your eyes and look, what this coming forth may be. So I said, What is it? And he said, This is the
7 ephah going forth. Then he said, This is their figure in all the land. And, lo, a round cover of lead was lifted up, and there was one woman
8 sitting inside the ephah. And he said, This is Wickedness, and cast her back into the ephah and cast the stone of lead on its opening.
9 Then I raised my eyes and looked, and, behold, two women came forth with wind in their wings, and they had wings like the wings of storks, and they lifted up the ephah be-
10 tween earth and heaven. And I said to the angel that talked to me, Where are they bringing the
11 ephah? And he said to me, To build her a house in the land of Shinar, and it will be firmly established, and she will be brought to rest there upon her proper base.

Grammatical Notes

V. 6. "An ephah that goeth forth," rather, the ephah that proceeds, spreads. See its definition in v. 8. — "Their resemblance," literally, "eye." עין is frequently used in the sense of likeness, appearance. See Lev. 13:55; Num. 11:7; Ezek. 1:4, 7, 16, 22, 27 = "color," in parallelism to "likeness," דמות, vv. 10, 13, 16, etc.; and "appearance," mar'eh, vv. 5, 13, 14, 16; 1 Sam. 16:7, "outward appearance," Dan. 10:6. — "All the earth," the land, Judah (cp. v. 3).

V. 7. "Talent of lead." כִּכָּר = circle, the encircling territory (Gen. 13:10 ff.; Neh. 12:28); something round (Ex. 29:23; 1 Sam. 2:36); so here, a round lead, a leaden cover or lid.

V. 8. "Weight," literally, "stone"; here = weight (cp. Gr. N. on 4:10).

V. 11. "Established," Hoph. of כּוּן, to be firm; Hoph., to be firmly established

(1 Kings 2:45; Ps. 93:2). — "Set," Hoph. of נוּחַ, to rest; Hoph., to be brought to rest, dwell safely and securely, without disturbance. — "Base" is a noun derived from the same stem as "established." It is used to denote the ten-wheeled bases on which were mounted the lavers in the Temple (1 Kings 7:27–39; Jer. 52:17, 20). Here, a base or pedestal, on which the ephah was placed to be worshiped.

Vv. 5, 6. While Zechariah's mind was still occupied with the strange vision he had seen, the interpreting angel once more approaches him (cp. 4:1), rouses him from his meditation, and tells him to direct his attention to "what is this that goeth forth." Zechariah asks, What is it? (V. 6.) The angel informs him, This is the (Gr. N.) ephah that goeth forth. The precise sense of this statement was not grasped by the prophet, and therefore the angel adds a second explanatory word: This is "their resemblance" (Gr. N.), the people's appearance, their likeness, through all the "earth," rather, "land," Judah. An ephah was a measure about equivalent to our bushel and here denotes the container or basket holding a bushel. As is evident from v. 7, it signifies here a large container having the shape of a bushel basket or barrel large enough to hold a woman. The term is a symbol of trade, commerce. The Lord demands a just ephah, full measure, integrity and honesty in selling and buying in all business and judicial transactions (Lev. 19:35 f.; Deut. 25:14 f.; Ezek. 45:9 ff.; Micah 6:10-15). This honesty was beginning to disappear from their markets and their judgment halls. Already the pre-Exilic prophets had charged their generations with being "Canaanites," merchants, intent only on gain and personal profit (Hos. 12:8, A. V., 7; Zeph. 1:11; Amos 8:4 ff.; Micah 6:10 ff.). The Lord sees not only the root of this evil in their hearts. He sees throughout the land ever-increasing proofs of this mercenary spirit, of selfish, hard-hearted, grasping greed. (Cp. Hag. 1:2, 4, 9; Zech. 8:10, 16.) He presents to His prophet the nation as it appears to the holy God, so that the prophet may in turn warn his fellow Jews before it is too late.

Vv. 7, 8. As the ephah comes closer, the prophet sees a "talent of lead" (Gr. N.), a round leaden lid on the ephah, being lifted up from within, and there appears before his astonished eyes a woman endeavoring to escape from the basket. And now the prophet is finally told what "this" is that he had seen go forth (v. 5). "This," repeated three times in vv. 5, 6, and twice in vv. 7, 8, is the "wickedness" (v. 8), godlessness, rebellion against God and His Law and His Gospel (Ps. 36:1 ff.; 2:1-3). A woman is chosen as the symbol of wickedness because of the alluring, captivating, deceptive power of sin. (Cp. Judg. 14:15 ff.; 16:5-20; Prov. 2:16-19; 7:7 ff.; 9:13 ff.) Wickedness by its very nature is not willing to be caged, confined to narrow limits. It longs for liberty to roam about at will. Yet in spite of her violent efforts to gain her liberty, the woman is hurled back into her prison, and the "weight," literally, the stone, such as were used to cover large openings (cp. Gen. 29:2 f.; John 11:38, 41) "of lead" was replaced over the opening end of the ephah.

Vv. 9-11. The vision does not end with the imprisonment of wickedness. That is only the means to an end. The prophet sees two more women appearing, having huge wings like the wings of a stork. They lift up the ephah with its occupant and fly away between heaven and earth. What is their goal? asks the prophet and receives the answer, "To build it," rather, her, for the woman, wickedness, a house in the land of Shinar. Shinar (Gen. 10:10; 11:2; 14:1, 9) was from its earliest days, shortly after the Flood, a land of open rebellion against God (Gen. 11:1-9, the tower of Babel). Throughout Scripture it is symbolic of wickedness and opposition against God and His Church (Ps. 137:8; Is. 13 and 14; 48:14, 20; Jer. 50 and 51; Rev. 14:8; 16:19; 17:5; 18:2, 10, 21). The land of Merathaim, double defiance, is the proper place for sin, not the Holy Land. Of course, Shinar, Babylon, does not come into consideration here as a physical city, but as the symbol of Satan's kingdom of wickedness. There a house shall be built for wickedness, and firmly founded, established (Gr. N.); there she shall be set (Gr. N.), made to rest upon her own base (Gr. N.) to be adored and worshiped and served with an eagerness and devotion which puts to shame many a one claiming membership in God's Church.

Such a warning against wickedness was not out of place or ill-timed in the days of Zechariah. Wickedness had again attempted to raise its head in God's Holy Land. Judah's lack of enthusiasm in building the Temple, the actual stoppage of work for fifteen years, was disobedience, rebellion, refusal to do God's will, was an attempt of wickedness to regain possession and rule over the nation. The Holy

Land is for holy people. While even the justified and sanctified believers have need of daily forgiveness, wickedness, manifest rebellion against God, cannot be tolerated in God's holy Church, the communion of saints. It must be removed by removing the wicked man or men (Matt. 18:15-20; 1 Cor. 5:9-13). This is the lesson to be learned by the Church to the end of time from the strange vision recorded here.

CHAPTER 6

8. The eighth vision: The four chariots, vv. 1-8

1 Then I raised my eyes again and looked, and, lo, four chariots were coming from between the two mountains, and the mountains were
2 mountains of bronze. In the first chariot were red horses, and in the
3 second chariot, black horses, and in the third chariot, white horses, and in the fourth chariot, dappled
4 horses, stallions. So I answered and said to the angel that talked to me,
5 What are these, my lord? And the angel answered and said to me, These are four spirits of heaven going forth after standing before
6 the Lord of all the earth. The one with the black horses, these are proceeding to the Northland, and the white will proceed behind them, and the dappled will proceed to the
7 Southland. And the stallions started out and were eager to go to patrol the earth. So He said, Go! Patrol the earth! And they began to patrol
8 the earth. And He cried out to me and spoke to me, saying, Look! They are proceeding to the Northland. They will satisfy My anger against the Northland.

Grammatical Notes

V. 1. "Brass," an alloy of copper and zinc, was unknown to the ancients. נְחֹשֶׁת = either copper or bronze, an alloy of copper and tin.

V. 3. Grisled = grizzly; בְּרֻדִּים occurs only here, v. 6, and Gen. 31:10, 12, where it means "speckled," "spotted." — "And bay"; "and" is added by the translators. "Bay." אֲמֻצִּים, from a root = to be strong, courageous, in Gen. 25:23 and some forty times more. (Cp. the nouns אֹמֶץ in Job 17:9; אַמְצָה in Zech. 12:5; the adjective אַמִּיץ in 2 Sam. 15:12; Is. 28:2; 40:26; Amos 2:16; Job 9:4, 19.) It is a synonym of אַבִּיר = strong, valiant, which often denotes bulls (Ps. 22:12; 50:13; Is. 34:7) or stallions (Jer. 8:16; 47:3; 50:11). In this latter sense, steed, stallion, war horse, the term

amuzzim is used here. Cp. God's description of the war horse in Job 39:19-25. Others who feel that a color is intended here regard it as a variant of חָמוּץ, "sharp," brilliant red (Is. 63:1), but as Keil observes, there is no provable instance of ח being softened to א; while the idea of strength is commonly connected with the root amaz. — Susim is joined to beruddim by merkha, a conjunctive accent; the phrase is separated from amuzzim by tiphchah, one of the stronger accents. The M. T., therefore, refers "strong ones" not only to the speckled horses, but also to the four teams, all of which were strong war horses, able to endure the hardships of warfare.

V. 5. "Spirits." רוּחוֹת is a term denoting winds and spirits, both of which are connected, e. g., Ps. 104:4; Zech. 5:9; Rev. 7:1, since both are servants, messengers of the Lord.

V. 7. Note the change of gender: the command, "Get you hence!" is masculine; the predicate, "so they walked," feminine, denoting the spirits symbolized by the horses and chariots.

V. 8. "Quieted My spirit." Spirit, רוּחַ, here = anger (cp. Judg. 8:3; Prov. 16:32; Eccl. 10:4). Quiet the spirit = appease the anger (cp. Ezek. 16:42; 24:13).

This vision points back to and links the series of visions with the first night vision (ch. 1:7 ff.), completing the circle.

Vv. 1-3. Many interpreters place the scene of this vision in the Kidron Valley and regard the two mountains as Zion and Olivet. The Kidron Valley is a deep cleft running between Jerusalem and the Mount of Olives, where the valley is about 300 feet lower than the summit of the Temple hill. Somewhat south of its juncture with the Valley of Hinnom it becomes narrower and its slopes steeper as it turns southeast to the northwestern shore of the Salt Sea, 1,275 feet below sea level, some 3,850 feet below the Temple. If the vision is based on the topography of Jerusalem, the two mountains may be either Zion and Olivet or the steep cliffs near Hinnom. Yet the definite article before "two mountains" in the original may merely refer to the two mountains appearing in the vision. In any case the hills here are symbolic, as indicated by the statement that they were "of brass" (Gr. N.), copper or bronze, the strongest metal known to ancients. (Cp. Jer. 1:18.) These indestructible mountains form the gate towers guarding the entrance to the palace of the Supreme Ruler of the universe. The prophet sees four chariots, four being the number of completeness. (Cp. 1:18, 20; 2:6.) Whether the drivers here are identical with the riders of 1:8 ff. is an idle question. Their mission is an entirely different one. They are to carry out God's judgments upon the enemies of His Church. Of the colors (vv. 2, 3), only two are like those of 1:8, red and white. Black and grisled horses do not appear in ch. 1; while "speckled," 1:8, does not occur here. Black symbolizes famine with all its horrors. (Cp. Rev. 6:5.) Grisled (Gr. N.), rather, speckled, spotted, may be a synonym of "speckled," 1:8; or it may denote either larger or smaller spots or blotches. These "grisled" horses may well correspond to the pale horse of Rev. 6:8, carrying one whose name was Death and Hell, having power to kill with sword and hunger and death and with the beasts of the earth. (Cp. Jer. 15:2 f.) As "pale," χλωρός (Rev. 6:8), denotes the yellowish green, ashy pale color of sickness and death, so the speckles or spots here may denote the blotchy skin accompanying undernourishment and starvation or resulting from the worried fear and anxious fore-bodings of what the next day or hour may bring. (Cp. Luke 21:25 f.; Dan. 5:1-7, 22-30.) "And bay horses" (Gr. N.); "and" is not added in the Hebrew text. "Bay," not a color, but strong, courageous horses, war horses, stallions, steeds. (Cp. Job 39:19-25.) The term refers to the four spans.

Vv. 4-6. These horses "in the chariot" = hitched to it, together with the chariots and drivers symbolize the four "spirits" (Gr. N.) of the heavens (v. 5). Winds and spirits (the Hebrew term denotes both) are messengers of God, willing to carry out His commands speedily (Ps. 103:20 f.; 104:4; Heb. 1:7, 14; Rev. 7:1). — "Which go forth" (Gr. N.), are in the act of proceeding, "from standing before the Lord," as servants stand before their master awaiting his command. The black horses (v. 6) and their chariot are ready to "go forth" (Gr. N.) to the North Country, the Assyrian-Babylonian world power. The white "go," are ready to go after them to make the victory over these inveterate enemies of God's people and their complete defeat doubly sure. The grisled "go," are ready to go to the South Country, Edom (Obad. 18) and Egypt, the age-old enemies of Israel to the south. The East and West are not named, because no danger threat-ened the Israelites of Zechariah's time from these directions. Babylon in the north and Egypt in the south, for centuries the most powerful empires, are deprived of all their riches and power. The granaries of the world are reduced to misery, starvation, and death. Their doom pictures that of all nations seeking to destroy the Church and dethrone its King (Ps. 2). The red horses in the first chariot (v. 2) are not mentioned again. We do not know why; probably because the war and bloodshed they symbolize are included in the plagues symbolized by the other chariots. We have here a symbolic vision, not a detailed historic description of the actual events.

Vv. 7, 8. The angel's message to the prophet ends with v. 6. Now the prophet resumes the narrative. As he looks, "the bay," the steeds, or stallions, "went forth" (Gr. N.), began to go forth, eagerly seeking to start out on their mission, "that they might walk to and fro through the earth"! The earth, the world known to Zechariah's age, comprised the two world empires, Assyria-Babylonia, now ruled by the Persians, and Egypt. Now the prophet hears a voice, "Get you hence!" "Go!" Spurred on by this command, the horses at once start out on their punitive expedition. As the prophet sees them rushing past, he hears a voice crying to him above the rattling of the chariots (v. 8). It is the voice of Jehovah, speaking of Himself in the first person. The chariots going toward the north have quieted (Gr. N.), will satisfy, calm My spirit, appease My wrath, by allotting to My enemies the full measure of their well-deserved punishment.

C. The Crowning of Joshua, Vv. 9-15

9 Then the word of the LORD came
10 to me saying, Take from the exiles, from Heldai and from Tobiah and from Jedaiah; and go yourself on this day, and go to the house of Josiah, the son of Zephaniah, where they have arrived from Bab-
11 ylon. And take silver and gold and make a crown, and place it on the head of Joshua, the son of Jehoz-
12 adak, the high priest. And say to him, Thus says the LORD of Hosts, Behold a Man, Branch is His name! He shall branch out from His lowliness, and He shall build the temple
13 of the LORD. And He shall build the temple of the LORD, and He shall bear glory, and shall sit and rule on His throne; and He shall be a Priest upon His throne, and counsel of peace shall be between the
14 two of them. And the crown shall be for Helem and for Tobiah and for Jedaiah, and for the kindness of the son of Zephaniah, as a memorial in the temple of the LORD.
15 And such as are afar off will come and build in the temple of the LORD, and you shall know that the LORD of Hosts has sent Me to you. And it shall come to pass. if you will truly listen to the voice of the LORD, your God!

Grammatical Notes

V. 11. "Crown." עֲטָרוֹת, the plural construed with singular, v. 14; hence not two or more crowns, but one composed of several circlets.

V. 12. "Out of his place," מִתַּחְתָּיו, from below him, beneath him, from lowly places.

V. 14. "To Hen." לְחֵן, here not a proper name, but a common noun, kindliness, favor, hospitality (cp. Prov. 12:10; Zech. 4:7; 12:10), for the kindly hospitality of the son of Zephaniah.

Vv. 9-13. "The captivity" = the exiles at Babylon; they had sent a gift of silver and gold to Jerusalem by a delegation of three men, Heldai, Tobiah, and Jedaiah. The exiles had heard that the work of restoring the Temple had been resumed and were willing to support the work by sending financial aid. This action pleased the Lord, and He showed His approval in a very remarkable manner. He tells Zechariah to go, personally, and at once, on the same day of their arrival, to the house of Josiah, where they had found lodging. From the offering of the Jews at Babylon he was to make "crowns" (Gr. N.) (v. 11), a crown composed of several circlets of silver and gold, and place this crown on the head of Joshua, the high priest. (Cp. Hag. 1:14; 2:2-4; Zech. 3:1 ff.) This, of course, was a purely symbolic,

438

prophetic act. (Cp. vv. 12, 13.) Joshua was not to be pronounced king of Jerusalem. Such a transference of the royal crown from the tribe of Judah and the house of David to the tribe of Levi would have been not only obnoxious to the Jews, but also have voided all the promises of the Lord to the tribe of Judah (Gen. 49:10 ff.) and to the house of David (2 Sam. 7:12 ff.). — The Lord would have contradicted Himself; or the prophet, the high priest, and the governor would have been guilty of a despicable, blasphemous deception. Modern liberal scholars change the text by substituting "Zerubbabel, the son of Shealtiel, the governor," for "Joshua," etc. (See J. M. P. Smith in *The Complete Bible,* p. 873.) They have invented the fable that Haggai and Zechariah regarded Zerubbabel as the promised Messiah. (Cp. p. 394.) The Lord Himself reveals the interpretation of this symbolic act (v. 12). Behold, a Man whose name is Branch! This is a clear reference to former prophecies (Is. 4:2; Jer. 23:5), which were already repeated in Zech. 3:8. (See Gr. N., p. 421, and remarks, p. 425.) "And He shall grow up," branch forth, "out of His place," from beneath Himself (Gr. N.), from lowliness and humbleness. He shall build the temple of the Lord; the Hebrew tense (perfect) here denotes the act in its completion. In v. 13 the same prophecy is repeated with a slight change, the imperfect instead of the perfect denoting the gradual building of Messiah's temple, the Church of the New Testament throughout the centuries. "He shall bear the glory," the article is omitted, glory as glory, excellence, splendor, majesty (Ps. 96:6; 104:1; Heb. 3:3). On the fulfillment see Eph. 1:20 ff.; Phil. 2:9 ff.; Rev. 5:6-14; 14:1 ff.; 19:11-16. In such supreme majesty He shall act and rule upon His throne as Lord of lords; a Priest upon His throne. In Him the two highest offices in Israel shall be united, royalty and priesthood. (Cp. Ps. 110.) No longer will there be any conflict between royalty and priesthood, one opposing the other. (Cp. 1 Kings 2:22-27; 13:1 ff.; 14:1-16; 16:1 ff.; ch. 17 ff.) In Christ both offices are united in one person and are in perfect harmony in carrying out the work for which the Son of God became man, the establishment of a kingdom of unending peace by the vicarious sacrifice of Himself and the protection of this kingdom against all its enemies. The Messianic interpretation as fulfilled in Christ is the only one doing justice to this marvelous prophecy, the only one in keeping with the words and facts. This was a promise given to the little flock of Jews to strengthen their faith in the promised Messiah, the priestly King, the royal Priest.

Vv. 14, 15. After the crown had been placed on the head of the high priest in a symbolic act, it was removed and placed into the Temple; not merely as a constant reminder of this precious revelation, but as a lasting memorial to the three men and the Jews at Babylon, whose representatives they were, and also to serve as such a memorial "to Hen" (Gr. N.), literally, to the kindness, the friendly hospitality, of the son of Zephaniah, Josiah (v. 10). What the Savior promised Mary centuries later (Matt. 26:10 ff.; Mark 14:6-9; cp. also Matt. 10:40 ff.; Mark 9:41) is granted to Josiah as a wonderful reward for his brotherly kindheartedness in placing his home at the disposal of the delegates. From distant countries (v. 15) people shall come. (Cp. Is. 49:6 ff., 17-23; chs. 60, 61, 62; Acts 2:9 ff.) They all shall build in the Temple; they shall all work and labor and pray for the extension and glorification of God's Church. "And then ye shall know," etc. The history of the Christian Church, its very existence and continuation, especially its constant growth and extension, is the irrefutable proof of the divine mission of the prophet and the eternal truth of His Word, the Word of the living God, that the work of the Church is God's work (Acts 4:13, 16) and that all who oppose it are fighting against God (Acts 5:38, 39). All this shall come to pass if they willingly and eagerly obey the will of God to build the Temple. This does not mean that the fulfillment of God's promise is dependent on the obedience and endeavor of man. It is an encouragement to go on with their work, which is so glorious a work and brings such rich rewards, in which they will share only if they will obey the word of the Lord.

D. The Justice and Mercy of the World Ruler as Incentives to Obedient Service

CHAPTER 7

1. Not selfishness, but godliness is demanded by the just and holy God. Therefore obey His word in loving trust

1 In the fourth year of Darius, the king, the word of the LORD came to Zechariah on the fourth of the
2 ninth month, in Chisleu. Bethel sent Sharezer and Regem-Melek and his men to entreat the LORD,
3 saying to the priests who were at the house of the LORD of Hosts and to the prophets, Shall I weep in the fifth month with fasting as I have done these many years?

4 Then the word of the LORD of
5 Hosts came to me saying, Speak to all the people of the land and to the priests thus: When you fasted and mourned in the fifth and seventh months, these seventy years, did you fast so strictly for Me, for
6 Me Myself? And when you are eating, and when you are drinking, are not you the eaters and you
7 yourselves the drinkers? Should

you not hear the words which the LORD proclaimed through the former prophets, while Jerusalem was inhabited and prosperous and her cities round about her, and the Southland and the Shephelah were 8 inhabited? And the word of the LORD came to Zechariah, saying, 9 Thus says the LORD of Hosts, Judge true judgments, and practice mercy and compassion toward one 10 another. And do not oppress widows and orphans, aliens and needy, and let none of you imagine evil in his heart against his brother. 11 But they refused to give heed and presented a rebellious shoulder, and dulled their ears so that they could

12 not hear, and made their hearts like adamant so that they could not hear the Law and the words which the LORD of Hosts sent by His Spirit through the former prophets. Therefore great wrath came from the LORD of Hosts. 13 And so it came to pass, that as they had not heard when He called, so they called, and I did not hear, says 14 the LORD of Hosts. And I whirled them away among all the nations whom they had not known, and the land was desolate after them, so that no one passed through, and no one returned. And they made the pleasant land desolate.

Grammatical Notes

V. 1. Chisleu, rather, Chislev, is the Assyrian name for the ninth month, December/January.

V. 2. "Unto the house of God." Beth-El is never used to denote the Temple. Wherever "the house of God" occurs in A. V., it is invariably the translation of Beth-ha-Elohim. Zechariah uses Beth-Jehovah, house of the Lord, exclusively (ch. 7:3; 8:9; 11:13; 14:20 f.). Bethel is not the accusative of direction, "unto the house"; it is the subject of the sentence and construed here, as in Amos 5:5 b, as a masculine (G.-K. 122 b). — "To pray before the LORD," literally, to make soft, lenient, favorable, always with "the face of"; used with man as the object: Ps. 45:13 (A. V., 12), "entreat thy face" (marginal reading); Job 11:19 b, "make suit"; Prov. 19:6; with God as object, implore His grace: Ex. 32:11, "besought"; 1 Sam. 13:12, "made supplication"; Zech. 8:21; Mal. 1:9, etc.

V. 3. "Separating." The Hebrew term denotes primarily separation, then consecration (Hos. 9:10). Since the Nazarites, separated, consecrated people, were obliged to refrain from certain foods (Num. 6:2-21; Judg. 13:5,7; Amos 2:11 f.), the word acquired the sense of abstaining (Lev. 22:2) and here = fasting, the original sense of consecrating oneself not being entirely lost. By fasting they hoped to be regarded as God's consecrated, favored people.

V. 7. "Should you not hear the words," literally, "Not the words" is an aposiopesis, certain words being omitted. "Do you not know the words?" or "Have you not heard the words?" (G.-K. 117 l.)

V. 11. "Shoulder," כָּתֵף (Ex. 28:12; Num. 7:9; Judg. 16:3, etc.). — "Pulled away," turning away, the participle denoting habitual, stubborn revolting (Deut. 21:18; Prov. 7:11; Jer. 6:28).

Vv. 1-3. Almost two years had passed since the events narrated in chs. 1—6. The building of the Temple was progressing favorably. The inquiry of the Persian governor as to the authority for building the Temple had not stopped the work, but had resulted in the discovery

441

of the original decree of Cyrus and in the issuance of a decree by Artaxerxes guaranteeing religious liberty to the Jews, protecting them against interference, and granting them liberal support (Ezra 5:1 to 6:14). Now an occasion arose which the Lord used to give a needed lesson to His people on the fourth day of the ninth month, Chisleu, December/January. "Unto the house of God" (Gr. N.) (v. 2), rather, Bethel, the well-known city about ten miles north of Jerusalem (Gen. 28:19; 1 Kings 12:29; Ezra 2:28), had sent Sharezer, an Assyrian name (2 Kings 19:37; Jer. 39:3, 13), and Regem-Melek (cp. 1 Chron. 2:47) with his men to "pray before the Lord" (Gr. N.), to entreat Him to give them instruction. Their question pertained to a matter of ritual, and they approached the priests, who were to watch over these matters (Lev. 11:9-11), and the prophets as spokesmen of God (v. 3). "Should I weep," mourn. They speak as representatives in the name of the community. "Separating myself" (Gr. N.), refrain from food, fast. The fifth month was the month in which Jerusalem and the Temple had been burnt and the walls torn down (2 Kings 25:8 ff.; Jer. 52:12). In v. 5 another fast is mentioned occurring in the seventh month, not the divinely appointed fast on the Day of Atonement (Lev. 16:29, 31), but a special fast day instituted (according to tradition on the third day of the month) in commemoration of the murder of Gedaliah (Jer. 41:1 ff.), which resulted in the end of the Jewish commonwealth in the Land of Promise for 70 years. In ch. 8:19 two more fast days are named, that of the fourth month, in which the walls of Jerusalem had been breached, 586 B. C. (Jer. 52:6), and that of the tenth month, when the siege of Jerusalem had begun, 588 B. C. (2 Kings 25:1; Jer. 52:4). Since the restoration of the Temple was rapidly approaching its completion, the question naturally arose whether these fasts were still to be observed. "These so many years," the seventy years of exile (v. 5; cp. Ps. 137). Opinions differed, hence the delegation.

Vv. 4-7. The Lord answers their question, commanding Zechariah to speak the word of the Lord of Hosts not only to the delegates, but also to the people of the land, including the priests (v. 5). His first words are words of sharp rebuke. The Searcher of hearts saw the germ of self-satisfied, hypocritical work-righteousness sprouting in the hearts of the people. The root of self-righteousness, like that of idolatry, is self-service, placing one's own efforts, one's own pleasure or pride, above the service of God and complete submission to His will, His Law and His Gospel. This self-righteousness, unless nipped in the bud, would prove even more ruinous to the nation than the coarse idolatry of which the fathers had been guilty. (Cp. Matt. 23; 1 Thess. 2: 16.)

"Did ye at all fast unto Me?" (V. 5.) The fasting of most of the people in exile had not been a fasting pleasing to the Lord. (Cp. Is. 58: 3-11.) Their weeping had not been a mourning in sorrow for their transgression of God's Law and their repudiation of His Gospel. They had mourned chiefly for their personal distress, for the loss of their homes, their country, for their captivity in a foreign land. Or it had been a fasting and lamentation in the hope of thereby atoning for their sins and gaining God's favor. (Cp. Is. 58: 3.) Theirs had been a self-appointed, self-interested, self-righteous, self-satisfied fasting and mourning; not godly sorrow working repentance to salvation, but a sorrow of the world, of their flesh, working death (2 Cor. 7:10; Jer. 14:12). And when they were eating and drinking (v. 6), their feasting was just as selfish as their fasting. They were concerned only with satisfying their craving for food and drink with little or no thought of the Giver of all good gifts or the least consideration for their needy neighbors.

"Should ye not hear the words" (Gr. N.) (v. 7). The prophet leaves the statement incomplete; the A. V. has supplied the predicate. The Jews are referred to the ancient prophecies spoken while Jerusalem "was inhabited," rather, was sitting, throning like a princess (Lam. 1:1), and in prosperity, peaceful, safe and secure, undisturbed, surrounded by scores of cities, like a mother surrounded by her daughters. And the Southland, extending to Beersheba, and the Plain, the Shephelah, the fertile slopes, extending from the hill country westward to the Sea, were still populated. These former prophets beginning with Moses had warned their people against disloyalty to the Lord and had foretold God's judgments. These words spoken centuries ago were still the living Word of the living God (Is. 40:8; 1 Peter 1:25). Age did not affect their pertinence nor change their power (Is. 8:20; Luke 16:29; John 5:39). They applied to the Jews of 520 B. C. as they had applied to the people to whom they had been spoken centuries before and apply with like force in the twentieth century and to the end of time (Matt. 24:35; John 6:63).

Vv. 8-14. Again the word of the Lord came to Zechariah. Neither here nor in ch. 8:1 is the time stated, very likely on the same day (v. 1), or at least while the delegation was still at Jerusalem. The Lord repeats the age-old yet ever timely and always needful demand of justice and mercy (v. 9). These attributes characterize Him (Ex.

34: 6, 7), and His people should be like Him. "Execute true judgment,"
literally, Judge judgment of truth. Establish and observe norms and
laws in full keeping with the model presented in His holy Law;
show "mercy" = loving-kindness, and "compassions," heartfelt pity, at
all times (note the plural!). Refrain from oppressing widows and
orphans, strangers and poor (v. 10), the four classes who usually were
the victims of sharpers and Shylocks and therefore objects of God's
special care. (Cp. Lev. 19: 10, 33 f.; Deut. 14: 29; 15: 11; 16: 11, 14;
24: 12 ff.; Is. 1: 17; 3: 15; Amos 5: 11 ff.; 8: 4 ff.; Micah 3: 2 ff.; 6: 10 ff.;
Ezek. 22: 7, 27-29.) Let not the faintest imagination of evil, of wickedness, such as a man might conceive against his fellow man, arise in
your heart, the starting point of your thoughts, speech, and actions.
Remember it is your brother (Deut. 15: 7-15) whom you are to love
as your own self (Lev. 19: 18). That is the lesson the Lord of Hosts
taught through His prophets sent by His Spirit to the former generations. They refused to listen (v. 11), they "pulled away" their shoulder
(Gr. N.), literally, gave their shoulder, their support, to stubborn
refusal (Neh. 9: 29), like an ox refusing to be yoked; the exact opposite
of Zeph. 3:9, "one consent," literally, one shoulder. They "stopped,"
made heavy, hardened their ears, closed them against all admonitions.
Their hearts they made as an "adamant" stone (v. 12). The English
term is derived from a Greek root = to be untamed, unconquerable,
and denotes impenetrable hardness. The Hebrew term *shamir* =
thorn (Is. 5: 6; 7: 23 ff.; 9: 17, etc.), then, a sharp point, very likely
a diamond, used for engraving (Jer. 17: 1; Ezek. 3: 9). In the latter
passage it is said to be harder than flint, and Zechariah here uses it
in the same sense. Therefore the "great wrath" threatened in Lev.
26: 14 ff. and Deut. 28: 15 ff. came upon them. God fulfilled His word:
Prov. 1: 24-33; Jer. 14: 11-18. On v. 14 cp. Deut. 28: 64 f.; 2 Chron. 36: 21.
So they had laid desolate the "pleasant land," the land of desire
(Jer. 3: 19; Ps. 137: 1 ff.).

CHAPTER 8

2. The Lord of Mercy is ready to prosper your labor. Therefore build His Temple!

1 The word of the LORD of Hosts
2 came, saying, Thus says the LORD
of Hosts, With zealous eagerness
I am interested in the welfare of
Zion, and with burning fervor I am
3 zealous for her. Thus says the
LORD, I will return to Zion and
dwell in the midst of Jerusalem,

and Jerusalem shall be called the
City of Faithfulness, and the mountain of the LORD of Hosts, the holy
4 mountain. Thus says the LORD of
Hosts, Again aged men and women
shall dwell in the squares of Jerusalem, each with his staff in his
5 hand because of old age. And the

squares of the city shall be filled with boys and girls playing in her
6 squares. Thus says the LORD of Hosts, If it seem too wonderful in the eyes of the remnant of this people in those days, shall it seem too wonderful also in My eyes? is the
7 oracle of the LORD of Hosts. Thus says the LORD of Hosts, Lo, I will deliver My people from the land of the East and from the land of the
8 setting sun, and I will bring them, and they shall dwell in the midst of Jerusalem; they shall be My people, and I Myself shall be their God in truth and in righteousness.
9 Thus says the LORD of Hosts, Strengthen your hands, you who are hearing in these days these words from the mouths of the prophets which spoke on the day when the foundation was laid of the house of the LORD of Hosts, the
10 Temple, that it might be built. For before these days men's wages were nonexistent, and there were no wages for beasts, and there was no peace from the oppressor, neither for him that went out nor for him that came, and I set every man one
11 against another. But now I shall not be as in the former days to the remnant of this people, is the
12 oracle of the LORD of Hosts. For the seed of peace, the vine, shall yield its fruit, and the earth shall yield her product, and the heavens shall give their dew, and I will make the remnant of this people
13 possess all these things. And it shall come to pass that as you have been a curse among the nations, O house of Judah and house of Israel, so I will deliver you, and you shall be a blessing. Fear not!

14 Strengthen your hands! For thus says the LORD of Hosts, As I planned to do harm to you when your fathers provoked Me to anger, says the LORD of Hosts, and I did
15 not relent, so likewise I have planned in these days to do good to Jerusalem and to the house of
16 Judah. Fear not! These are the things that you must do: Speak truth one with another; in your gates judge in keeping with truth
17 and the promotion of peace. And let no one imagine evil in his heart against his neighbor, and do not love perjury; for all these are things I hate, is the oracle of the
18 LORD. And the word of the LORD of Hosts came to me, saying,
19 Thus says the LORD of Hosts, The fast of the fourth month, and the fast of the fifth, and the fast of the seventh, and the fast of the tenth, shall become to the house of Judah joy and gladness and happy festivals. But love truth and peace!
20 Thus says the LORD of Hosts, It shall yet come to pass that peoples shall come and citizens of many
21 cities, and the citizens shall come one to another, saying, Let us hurry to go to propitiate the LORD and to seek the LORD of Hosts. I will
22 go! I also! So many peoples will come and great nations, to seek the LORD of Hosts in Jerusalem and
23 to propitiate the LORD. Thus says the LORD of Hosts, In those days it shall be that ten men of all languages of the nations shall take hold, and they shall take hold of the skirt of a Jewish man, saying, We will go with you, for we have heard that God is with you.

Grammatical Notes

V. 2. "I was jealous," see Joel 2:18, Gr. N., pp. 122 f. — "With great fury," חֵמָה = warmth, fervor, the heat of anger and fury (Gen. 27:44; Deut. 29:20 f.; Nah. 1:2). His zeal for Judah is by its very nature one of fury against the enemies of His chosen people.

V. 4. "Streets," also v. 5 = רְחֹבוֹת, see Amos 5:16, Gr. N., p. 160.

V. 10. "Affliction," צַר = either distress, oppression (Ps. 4:2; 18:7, etc.), or oppressor, adversary (Gen. 14:20; Num. 10:9, etc.). Here the context seems to favor oppressor.

445

V. 12. "The seed shall prosper." Targum, Peshito, "the seed will be safe"; similarly Klostermann, Sellin, and others. Others change the text to read, I will sow peace = prosperity; LXX, "Yea, rather, I will present peace." Hengstenberg's translation, The seed of peace, the vine, shall give her fruit, regards "the vine" as an explanatory apposition to "the seed of peace." This translation does not change the text, is grammatically incontestable, and renders a sense suitable to the context. The grapevine is a well-known symbol of peace and prosperity (1 Kings 4:25; Micah 4:4; Zech. 3:10); or it may be called "the seed," or offspring, plant (cp. Job 39:12; Jer. 2:21; 1 Sam. 8:15) of peace, because it can prosper only in times of peace, while war is destructive of vineyards and vines (Jer. 5:17; Lev. 26:16).

V. 19. "Cheerful," טוֹב, here = happy, joyous. (Cp. 1 Sam. 25:8; Esther 8:17; 9:19, 22; Prov. 15:15.) — "Feasts." The Hebrew term denotes an appointment (Judg. 20:38), appointed meetings (Lam. 1:15; 1 Sam. 20:35), or appointed seasons and festivals (Lev. 23:2; Jer. 8:7; Hos. 9:5; 12:10).

Vv. 1-5. The Lord of Hosts is speaking. Seventeen times, in addition to the six times in ch. 7, the people are assured that it is the Ruler of the universe, of the world, of His Church who speaks. If God be for us, who can be against us? (Cp. Ps. 27:1; 118:6; Rom. 8:31.) "I was jealous" (Gr. N.) (v. 2), I will be zealous = zealously active, "with great jealousy," with great and eager zeal; "with great fury" (Gr. N.), with great warmth, with burning fervor. The Lord of Hosts had been "a little displeased" (ch. 1:15 b) with His people. They had been exiled and their land devastated. Now He will return to Zion (v. 3) in the fullness of His grace (ch. 1:16). He will once more establish His dwelling place, His Temple, in their midst (cp. Ex. 25:8; 29:43 ff.), as a symbol of His spiritual dwelling within their hearts (Jer. 31:33; Ezek. 36:26 f.; John 14:23; 2 Cor. 6:16). Jerusalem, the unfaithful city (Is. 1:21 ff.), shall be a city of truth and faithfulness in consequence of His justifying and sanctifying presence (Is. 1:25; 4:4 f.). The mountain of the Lord, which had been a heap of ruins, shall again be the holy mountain, where the Holy One will sit in the majesty of His unchanging justice and mercy (Is. 40:21-25; Ex. 34: 5 ff.). In fulfillment of His promise (Deut. 30:1-5) the city shall be rebuilt and repopulated. No longer shall death in the form of war and pestilence slay the old people and young children, usually the first to fall victims to the ravages of war (Jer. 7:32; 9:17-22). "In the streets" (Gr. N.) (vv. 4, 5) of the city, its open, parklike spaces, where in times of war the soldiers camped, old men and women shall again, supported by their staffs, walk in peace and safety, while the parks will resound with joyous laughter of young boys and girls playing their happy games undisturbed by the shouts of foreign warriors.

V. 6. The "remnant" (cp. the residue, v. 11 f.) are God's elect (Is. 1:9; Rom. 9:29; 11:4 ff.). "In these days" (Gr. N.), the days of fulfillment. So great will be the change that even those who shall live to see it shall be like them that dream (Ps. 126:1), shall not be able to understand how so great a change is possible. Their fondest expectations shall be far, far surpassed. Yet it is not too marvelous in the eyes of Jehovah, the World Ruler, the omnipotent Lord. It is He that will do the seemingly impossible. That is the next thought.

Vv. 7, 8. "I will save." The participial form denotes the continuous performance of the act. Throughout the ages He will save, deliver, His people from the east and the west. (Cp. Gen. 28:14; Is. 49:8-12; 60:1-22.) They shall return to Jerusalem (v. 8), many of them to physical Jerusalem, as long as the Old Covenant continued, in which Jerusalem was His chosen city, but all to spiritual Jerusalem, the Church of God spread throughout the world (Gal. 4:26; Heb. 12:22 f.). And throughout the Old and New Testaments and in eternity the remnant, the despised and persecuted people chosen by the Lord, will be His people and He their God. "In truth and in righteousness," refers to both, people and God. The people will cling to God in faithful trust and willing obedience, and God will faithfully and righteously, keeping every detail, fulfill His promises.

Vv. 9, 10. The practical application of the promise, vv. 2-8. The people are to keep on with unflagging zeal to build the Temple. Seventeen years had passed since the foundation of the house of God had been laid (Ezra 3:10). The Jews had been released from exile by the decree of Cyrus not merely in order to lay a foundation, but to build the Temple (Ezra 1:5). The chief of the fathers had freely offered a large sum to build the house (Ezra 2:68 f.). Still the Jews were in constant need of being told by the divinely appointed prophets Haggai and Zechariah the same message: Build! From the day the foundation was laid they had been dissatisfied, unwilling (Ezra 3:12 f.; Hag. 1:3 f., 9 b; 2:3; Zech. 5:3, 6 ff.). The Lord had severely punished the laggards. He had sent hard times (v. 10; Hag. 1:6-11; 2:15), "affliction" (Gr. N.), enemies oppressing them from without (Ezra 4:4 ff.) and from within, creating dissensions, strife, leading to violence, cruelty, oppression, and other outrages, such as are named in Zech. 7:10. Therefore let your hands be strong and build My house!

Vv. 11-17. Now the Lord is willing to change these sad conditions. He does so for the sake of the "residue" (v. 11), the "remnant" (v. 12), of His people, His elect. (Cp. Luke 18:7; Matt. 24:22; Gen. 18:26-32.)

"The seed shall be prosperous" (Gr. N.), rather, the seed of peace, the vine, shall give her fruit. Harvest failures shall be changed to plenty (v. 12), the curse, to salvation, so that they shall become a blessing to others (v. 13; Gen. 12:2, 3; Zech. 8:13), the Lord's counsel of punishment to a counsel of welldoing (vv. 14, 15; cp. Jer. 18:6-8). In vv. 16, 17 the repetition of God's demands (ch. 7:9, 10) are flanked by the command to speak the truth, to be honest, upright, faithful in dealing with the neighbor, and to give due honor to God's holy name.

Vv. 18, 19. The Lord now answers the question asked by the delegation in ch. 7:3. On the four fasts, see remarks on 7:3, p. 442. These fast days shall be changed to days of joyous gladness, "cheerful" (Gr. N.), merry festival times and gatherings (Gr. N.) (v. 19). The Lord means to say, Only keep My commandments, love truth and peace, and let fasting take care of itself. "I will do so much good to Jerusalem that all afflictions which caused you to choose and keep such fastings will be completely forgotten, that the recurrence of these days will be to you an occasion for joy and gay festivities, for the city and the Temple, whose destruction you bewailed, shall stand again in their glory" (Luther, St. L., XIV, 1903). On fasting and weeping turned to joy, see Ps. 126; Is. 35:10; John 16:20, 22.

Vv. 20-23 state another reason for such joy: the conversion of the heathen. "People," the plural, nations, "shall come"; the Hebrew imperfect describes the progressive coming throughout the New Testament era. These converts from one city will in turn go to their neighboring cities (v. 21) and invite their fellow men to hurry while it is day (John 9:4) to implore the Lord in heartfelt prayer, to seek Him where He is to be found, in Jerusalem, the Church of God, where He reveals Himself (Ex. 25:22; 30:6, 36; Ps. 46:4; 84:1 ff.; Is. 8:20; 28:16) in the assembly of the faithful in Word and Sacrament (Matt. 18:20; 28:19, 20). They will encourage others by their own example. I will go also, I myself! This invitation will not be in vain (vv. 22, 23). And so evident will be the change in the lives of these converts that from all nations will arise the Macedonian cry, "Come over . . . and help us!" (Acts 16:9.) On "Jew" cp. John 4:22; Luke 24:47; Acts 1:8; Rom. 2:26-29; 1 Peter 2:9; 1 Thess. 1:5-10. The history of the New Testament Church is the record of the fulfillment of this prophecy.

PART II
Messianic Prophecies

Chapters 9—14

CHAPTER 9

A. The Messiah's Advent

1. All enemies shall perish; the Church will endure, vv. 1-8

1 An oracle, the word of the LORD against the land of Hadrach, and Damascus is its goal. For the LORD has an eye on mankind and
2 all the tribes of Israel; and also on Hamath, which borders on it, on Tyre and Sidon, for it is very wise.
3 And Tyre has built a stronghold for herself and has heaped up silver like dust and fine gold as the mud
4 of the streets. Lo, the LORD will dispossess her and smite her power into the sea, and she shall be consumed with fire. Ashkelon shall see
5 and be afraid; Gaza also, and shall be in great anguish; also Ekron, for her confidence has been put to shame; and the king shall perish
6 from Gaza, and Ashkelon shall no longer sit on her throne. And a mongrel people shall dwell in Ashdod, and so I shall cut down the
7 pride of the Philistines. And I will take his blood from his mouth and his abominations from between his teeth; and he also shall be a remnant unto our God, and he shall be like a prince in Judah, and Ekron
8 like the Jebusite. Then I will encamp in defense of My house against an army, against him that passes over and against him that returns, so that no oppressor shall any more pass over him; for now I have seen with My eyes.

Grammatical Notes

V. 1. "The burden of the word of the LORD." "At the end of the Book of the Minor Prophets the editors have collected anonymous oracles in three parts, each of which is entitled, 'An Oracle': Zech. 9:1; 12:1; Mal. 1:1." (Pfeiffer, *Introduction*, p. 607.) Though this view has been widely adopted, it is as unwarranted as Sellin's substituting "Oracle of Zechariah" as the superscription. Zechariah uses this form of introducing a new division of his book. He had used other forms in 1:1, 7, 18; 4:1; 7:1; 8:1. He is not bound to any stereotyped form. — "When the eyes of man." "When," כִּי, is causal as in Gen. 5:24; Is. 2:3, 6, 22, etc. "Toward the LORD," לְ here that of possession, to Jehovah belongs, He has. (Cp. Ps. 50:10; 74:16; 89:12, A. V., 11; Ezek. 29:3, 9.) Jehovah has an eye "of man."

The genitive here is objective, an eye directed toward man. See Obad. 10, "violence of thy brother," directed toward him; Amos 8:10, "the mourning of an only son," mourning over him; Gen. 3:24, "way of the tree," toward the tree; Gen. 18:20 f., "cry" or "rumor of Sodom," cry concerning Sodom. At no time are the eyes of all the world directed toward Jehovah, but at all times His eyes are directed upon the world and particularly upon Israel, His own people. (Cp. Ps. 33:13-19; Prov. 15:3; Jer. 32:19 ff.)

V. 2. "Also shall border." The Hebrew is an abbreviated relative clause, the relative being omitted. (Cp. Ex. 4:13; Job 29:12; Mal. 2:16. G.-K. 155 n.)

V. 6. "Bastard," מַמְזֵר, occurs only here and Deut. 23:3 (A. V., 2), where it denotes a class of people not permitted to

449

enter the congregation of the Lord. LXX translates Deut. 23:3 ἐκ πόρνης, the offspring of a harlot; Zech. 9:6, ἀλλογενεῖς, sprung from another race, an alien. Jewish writers vary in defining the term. Philo: a child born of an adulterous wife, a licentious woman, or a professional prostitute; Hillel: a child of adultery; Rabbinical tradition: a child born of contact between Jew and heathen, within or without wedlock. This latter definition seems to suit our passage better: not pure-blooded Ashdodians, but children of mixed blood.

V. 8. "Because of the army." צָבָה, מִצָּבָה, a variant form of צָבָא, with מִן, here in sense of because, on account of, as in Ex. 15:23; Is. 6:4; 53:5, etc. The army is the enemy army invading Judah.

Vv. 1, 2. "Burden," see Nah. 1:1, pp. 293 f. The oracle foretells the fate of a number of Syrian and Phoenician cities, north and northwest of Israel, representing the enemies of God's people in the Old and New Testaments. Hadrach, for centuries a puzzling historical problem, has now been definitely identified with Khatarika mentioned in the annals of Assyrian kings as an Aramaean country near Damascus and Hamath, against which Assyria campaigned in 772, 755, and 733 B. C. (Rogers, *Cuneiform Parallels*, pp. 232 f.; 315.) Though the city seems to have been destroyed in the eighth century B. C., the land may have retained its name, or the prophet names it here, like Assyria, Nineveh (Zech. 10:10 f.), destroyed 612, and Babylon (Zech. 2:7), conquered 539, as one of the nations typical of all enemies of God's Church throughout the ages. Other cities included in the oracle are named vv. 1-6. "Rest" = here in sense of resting place, goal. (Cp. Num. 10:33; Deut. 12:9.) The cities named v. 1ff. are the goal where the prophecy shall find its fulfillment. Great or small, every power rising up against God's kingdom shall be destroyed. On Damascus, see Amos 1:3 ff., p. 141; also Jer. 49:23 ff. "When" the eyes, etc., rather, for, because, the eyes of the Lord, etc. (Gr. N.). God's eyes here = God's providence directed upon all men (Ps. 33:13 ff.; Prov. 15:3), and especially upon Israel (Deut. 11:12; 1 Kings 9:3). God's providence so shapes the affairs of mankind that they must serve the welfare of His Church, the apple of His eye (Zech. 2:8; cp. Rom. 8:28). Often the punitive judgments of God upon the enemies are at the same time deliverances for His people. (Cp. Ex. 12:27; 14:13, 19 f., 25, 30; 15:1 f.) Quite evidently Zechariah here had in mind Jer. 32:19 f., as Hengstenberg suggests. There is a striking similarity in thought and phraseology. On "Hamath" (v. 2), see Amos 6:2, p. 169. "Also shall border" (Gr. N.) is a relative clause: which borders on it.

"Tyrus and Zidon" (v. 2) were the chief cities of Phoenicia. Tyre's "antiquity was of old" (Is. 23:7). Sidon was the grandson of

Ham (Gen. 10:6, 15, 19), and it seems that Sidon was founded before Tyre, which later outstripped its sister city, 20 miles south. The boast of the priests to Herodotus on his visit to Tyre that the city was 2,300 years old (Herodotus, *Hist.* 2, 44) seems to have been an exaggeration. "Though," rather, "for," states the reason for God's judgment. On its wisdom, cp. 1 Kings 5:6, 17, 18; 7:13-46; 2 Chron. 2:7-9; Ezek. 27:8; 28:4, 5, 7, 12, 17. Yet its very wisdom was the cause of its destruction. It was not founded on the fear of God, nor was its purpose the glory of Jehovah. It sought its own glorification.

V. 3. In Ezekiel's time the city stood partly on the shore, partly on a rocky island about a half mile offshore. Tyre, the Hebrew *Tsor,* rock, built herself a *matsor,* rockwork, walls of solid stone rising high and houses and palaces of equal height, because of the limited space, about 150 acres, offered by the island. So strongly was Tyre fortified that Sennacherib (704—681), Esarhaddon (680—669), Ashurbanipal (668—625), and Shalmaneser (605—552) had vainly sought to conquer it. Nebuchadnezzar (605—562) besieged it for thirteen years (585—572), "served a great service, yet had he no wages" (Ezek. 29:18). His siege, though weakening Tyre's power, seems to have ended in a truce. Tyre went on to "heap up silver as the dust and fine gold as the mire of the streets." (Cp. 1 Kings 10:27.) These immense riches came to Tyre through its world-wide commerce. Situated on one of the few harbors of the eastern shore of the Mediterranean Sea, it was one of the chief centers of trade, where East and West met to exchange their goods. "From its ports ships trafficked up the Nile, along the shores of the Black Sea, among Tyrian colonies on the North African coast, and in Sicily, Sardinia, and southern France. Spain was a market for them. The merchants from these shores worked tin mines in British Cornwall and built depots in the Scilly Islands and the Isle of Wight." (H. E. Fosdick, *A Pilgrimage to Palestine,* p. 211.) (Cp. 1 Kings 9:26 ff.; 10:11; Is. 23; Ezek. 27 and 28.)

V. 4. Proud Tyre had to learn the lesson of Prov. 11:2; 16:18. "Behold!" What seemed impossible the Lord will do when His hour has come. "Cast her out," dispossess her. He will smite, strike down her "power," all that combined to give her the exalted position so long enjoyed. Her fortifications, her military and commercial navy, her riches, her palaces, her wisdom, her culture — all will be smitten into the sea, devoured by a fire kindled by the Lord against which even the mighty waters of the sea were of no avail. This smiting began when Alexander the Great on his triumphant march to India

451

built a mole to the island and with the aid of the Phoenician navy conquered and sacked the city after a seven months' siege (332 B. C.). Even from this severe blow Tyre recovered. In the early Christian era Tyre again was an important city (Luke 10:13 f.; Acts 12:20; 21:3, 7). In the fourth century after Christ a large Christian cathedral was built, replacing a former church building (Eusebius, *Ch. Hist.*, X, IV, 37—45). Church councils were held there in 335 and 518. For a while the Crusaders held possession of the city, but finally the Saracens destroyed it, 1291, and it never recovered from this devastation. Of Tyre, Fosdick writes, "We walked through the poor and shrunken town and stood on the jetty of its choked-up harbor, to see a few fishing smacks where once rode the navies of the world. Then we returned to the mainland beach, to sit in meditation on Ezekiel's prophecy about Tyre, so improbable at the time and yet so obviously come true: 'It shall be a place for the spreading of nets in the midst of the sea' " (Ezek. 26:5). (Op. cit., p. 210.)

The political relations between Phoenicia and Israel were as a rule peaceful, largely because Phoenicia depended on Israel for its grain, olive oil, and other foodstuffs (1 Kings 5:9-11; Ezra 3:7; Ezek. 27:17; Acts 12:20). Yet this friendly relation aided in spreading Phoenician idolatry in Israel, the worship of Baal and Ashtaroth with all its immorality. (Cp. Judg. 2:11, 13; 3:5-7; 1 Kings 11:5; 16:30 ff.; 18:18-22; 19:18; 2 Kings 17:16 f., and the many prophecies against Baalism.) This seduction of God's people was another reason why God sent His judgments upon proud Tyre.

Vv. 5, 6. The prophet now turns to the inveterate enemy of Israel, Philistia. On the four cities named, cp. notes on Amos 1:6-8, pp. 141 f. The predicates distributed among the subjects really refer to all the subjects and describe the fear, the sorrow, the disappointment which shall grip all Philistines at the news of the fall of Tyre. Their "expectation," their confident hope of retaining their power and independence and national purity, will be thoroughly disappointed. No longer will they remain royal cities. Alexander either slew or deposed the kings he had defeated and replaced them with governors of his own. Some of the cities became depopulated, small, unimportant towns, or were inhabited by "bastards" (Gr. N.) (v. 6), mongrel, mixed people, no longer purebred Philistines. Hengstenberg translates *Gesindel*, rabble. So the pride of the Philistines, their love of independence and their intense nationalism, was "cut off," destroyed.

V. 7. While Israel was forbidden to drink blood or eat raw or

452

half-raw meat (Lev. 3:17; 7:26 f.; 17:10-14), the Philistines knew of no such restrictions in their homes or in their sanctuaries. The Lord will stop this practice. "Abominations" here = the heathen sacrificial meals, which are here called abominations because the idols in whose honor they were celebrated were an abomination to the Lord (1 Kings 11:5-7; Jer. 7:30; 13:27; 32:34). Yet even among these age-old enemies of God and His people there shall be "he that remaineth," a remnant, elect, chosen of the Lord (Is. 1:9; 10:22 f.; Rom. 9:23 ff.; 11:4 ff.), "for our God," the Lord's own, members of His household of saints (Eph. 2:11-22). And they shall not merely be bond servants. They shall be as a governor, an *alluph,* the term used for Edom's "dukes," rulers, kings (Gen. 36:15-30, 40-43); here of the honor to be bestowed upon the converted Philistines, representing the Gentiles joining the Christian Church, the royal priesthood of God (1 Peter 2:9; Rev. 1:6). "Jebusite," the name of the original inhabitants of Jerusalem, formerly called Jebus (Joshua 18:28; Judg. 19:10). The Jebusites had taunted David, but were conquered by him and incorporated in Israel, amalgamated with God's people (2 Sam. 5:6 ff.; 24:16, 18-24). We have here a prophecy similar to Ps. 87:4. For the fulfillment see Acts 8:40; 9:32-43, Christian congregations in former Philistine cities.

V. 8. "Encamp" = surround like a mighty army "about Mine house," literally, for, in defense of. (Cp. Ps. 34:8, A. V., 7; 35:5, 6; 2 Kings 6:17.) "Because of the army" (Gr. N.). There will always be relentless enemies of God's Church, who "pass by," pass over, ruthlessly overrun God's people and return time and again in frenzied efforts to finish their work of destruction, no matter how often they have been repelled. (Cp. Is. 51:23; 52:1 f.) Assyria succeeded in devastating the Northern Kingdom (2 Kings 15:19-29; 17:1-41), Babylonia, the Southern Kingdom (2 Kings 25:1 ff). When the Jews returned from the Babylonian Captivity, they did not regain their independence. They were subject to the Persian monarchy, to the Macedonians, Syrians, Seleucidans, Romans. Never again will the twelve tribes of Israel regain national independence, never again as a united nation be God's chosen people, as Israel was acknowledged by the Lord (Ex. 19:5, 6). In the New Testament era God's Church, the Church of God's elect, composed of believing Jews and Gentiles, will never be overcome by her opponents. No oppressor shall pass through them, overcome them any more. Even the gates of hell (Matt. 16:18; Eph. 6:12) shall not prevail against God's Church. From every attack the Church of God's elect comes forth more than a conqueror through Him that loved His Church (Rom. 8:35-39;

Eph. 6: 10-18). Jehovah and His Angel camp round about her, protect her, deliver her. Neither heathen Rome with its bloody persecutions, nor papal Rome with its "deceivableness of unrighteousness" (2 Thess. 2:10), nor rationalism, nor liberalistic modernism has succeeded to destroy the Church of God, nor will they ever succeed (Zech. 14; Rev. 20:7-10). What an encouragement for that small group of returned exiles! They were God's people, members of God's Church, which would have a future glory far surpassing that of Israel in its days of greatest splendor; a Church outlasting the centuries of time, indestructible by any power on earth or in hell, safe under Jehovah, its Protector, its King.

---

2. Thy King, O Zion, cometh unto thee, v. 9

9 Rejoice greatly, O daughter of Zion! Shout with joy, O daughter of Jerusalem! Behold, your King is coming to you! Righteous and One Delivered is He; lowly, and riding upon a young ass, the foal of an ass.

Grammatical Notes

V. 9. "Having salvation." Marginal reading, "saving Himself." נוֹשָׁע, the Niphal occurs twenty-one times, never in active sense, to save, deliver; nor in reflexive, save oneself; always passive. The A. V. translates once, "be safe" (Ps. 119:117); here, "having salvation"; nine times, "be saved." The last is the only correct translation and suits the context. See exposition. — "Lowly," עָנִי, may mean of low rank, or humble, not necessarily poor. The Hebrew term denotes one who has no land of his own, having for some reason lost his patrimony allotted to his forefathers (Joshua 13—21; 1 Kings 21:3). In this allotment each family received a portion large enough to prevent poverty, for the Lord would bless them if they would obey His Word (Deut. 15:4, 5). Yet for various reasons, sickness, drought, locusts, incompetence, oppression, "the poor would never cease from the land" (Deut. 15:11), and therefore various laws were given to alleviate their poverty (Ex. 22:25 ff.; 23:11; Lev. 19:10 f.; 23:22; Deut. 15:11 ff.; 24:12 ff.). עָנִי occurs about 75 times, and in all but three passages (Is. 25:6; Zeph. 3:12; Zech. 9:9) LXX translates it "poor," πτωχός, or a synonym; in these three passages πραΰς, humble, lowly. Matthew adopted the LXX rendering in Matt. 21:5, since that suited the context. Yet the original Hebrew term always = poor, needy. In a number of passages the M. T. wavers between ani, poor, and anaw, humble: K'tib has anaw, Q'ri, ani (Is. 32:7; Amos 8:4; Ps. 9:19, A. V., 18, "poor"); K'tib, ani; Q'ri, anaw (Prov. 14:21). Yet the K'tib need not be changed in any of these passages nor in any of the passages listed by G.-B. for a possible "humble" as translation for ani. — "Ass," חֲמוֹר, always = the male ass, except 2 Sam. 19:27 (A. V., 26). "And the foal," "and" here explanatory: "namely." (Cp. 1 Sam. 17:40; Jer. 17:11; Amos 3:11; 4:10.) "The foal of an ass," literally, "of she-asses," the plural of species. (Cp. Gen. 37:13; Judg. 14:15; Cant. 2:9.) LXX translates, having mounted a ὑποζύγιον, an animal under the yoke, a beast of burden (Matt. 21:5), "the foal of an ass," literally, the son of an animal under the yoke.

V. 9. "Rejoice," exult, leap for joy; "shout," cry out. Both verbs emphasize the intensity of irrepressible joy, that manifests itself not only in leaping, but also in loud proclamation of the good tidings of great joy. (Cp. 2 Sam. 6:16; Acts 3:8 f.; 4:20.) "Thy King." The Messiah is in a special sense Zion's King, the King of the Jews; a descendant of Israel, of the tribe of Judah, of the royal house of David, who had established Zion, Jerusalem, the royal city. The long-expected, eagerly desired (Gen. 4:1; 5:29; 49:18; Ps. 14:7) King cometh, is coming. The Hebrew tense, imperfect, vividly describes Him as He is on His way. "Unto thee," for you, for your deliverance, your salvation, your protection. (Cp. Is. 9:6, "unto us" = for us.) "He is just," righteous, that righteous Servant (Is. 53:9, 11), that righteous Branch (Jer. 23:5; Matt. 3:17; 17:5; Heb. 7:26; 1 John 2:1), whose judgments are always right (Is. 11:3 f.). This righteous King is the Lord Our Righteousness (Jer. 23:5 f.), who procured a perfect righteousness for mankind by placing Himself under the Law (Gal. 4:4 f.), in order to fulfill its every demand (Matt. 5:17 f.), taking upon Himself the sin of man (Is. 53:6, 10, 12; John 1:29) and its penalty (Is. 53:3 ff.; 2 Cor. 5:21; Gal. 3:13). "Having salvation" (Gr. N.), literally, being saved, unfailingly delivered. So He is already presented in the word of prophecy. See Is. 53:8; Ps. 22, where He, forsaken of God, cries to God for deliverance (vv. 1, 2, 8, 11-21), confesses that from His mother's womb He depended on God's aid (v. 9 f.), and in answer to His prayer is delivered (vv. 21b-25). See also Matt. 26:38 ff.; Luke 12:50; 22:41 ff.; 23:46; John 11:41 f.; 12:27 ff.; Heb. 5:7-9. Even though He was forsaken of God for a little while, He was delivered from the depths of hell, was crowned with honor and glory in answer to His prayer (Heb. 2:9 f.). "Lowly" (Gr. N.), rather, poor. (Cp. Luke 2:7; Matt. 8:20; 2 Cor. 8:9.) The ass and her colt were borrowed. He was supported by the gifts of loving women whom He had cured (Luke 8:2 f.). This self-chosen poverty of Him who was the Lord of Glory (1 Cor. 2:8) was at the same time the incontrovertible evidence of His self-humiliation. He comes not at the head of a mighty army, riding in royal splendor on a sumptuously decorated war horse. He rides on an ass, and this ass is described as the foal of an ass (Gr. N.). Since the time of David and particularly of Solomon (1 Kings 4:26 ff.; 10:26-29; 18:5; 22:4, etc.) horses became the animals of royalty and military power, while asses were used as beasts of burden. The Messiah comes on such a lowly animal, and not on a full-grown, powerful animal. He rides on a colt, a foal, a young, untrained, unbroken animal, still running with its mother (Mark 11:2).

His chariot is humility! Yet, though not arrayed in splendor, He still makes death surrender. The weak and timid find how meek He is and kind!

---

3. The establishment and extension of Messiah's Kingdom of Peace, vv. 10-17

10 Then will I cut off the chariot from Ephraim and the horse from Jerusalem; and the battle bow shall be cut off. And He shall proclaim peace to the nations, and His rule shall be from sea to sea, and from the River to the ends of the earth.
11 You also — because of the blood of your covenant I will send forth your captives from the pit in which
12 there is no water. Return to the stronghold, you prisoners of hope! Even this day I am announcing that I will restore double to you!
13 For I will bend Judah for Me as a bow. I will fill it with Ephraim. And I will stir up your sons, O Zion, against your sons, O Greece, and I will make you like the sword of
14 a mighty one. Then shall the LORD be manifested over them and His arrow shall go forth as lightning, and the Lord LORD will blow the trumpet and will march forth in
15 the storms of the south. The LORD of Hosts will shield them, and they shall devour and shall trample on the sling stones; and they shall drink and be intoxicated as with wine and shall be filled like sacrificial bowls, like the corners of
16 the altars. And the LORD, their God, shall deliver them on that day as the flock of His people; for they shall be like stones of a diadem that lift themselves like a banner
17 over His land. For how great is His goodness! How great His beauty! Grain will nourish His young men, and new wine the maidens.

Grammatical Notes

V. 10. "River," וְהָר here = the River Euphrates. (Cp. Jer. 2:18; Ps. 72:8; Micah 7:12.)

V. 12. "Stronghold." בִּצָּרוֹן, only here, a noun form from Piel of בָּצַר, to be inaccessible, strong, safe, Piel = intensive, something strong, whither no enemy can come. On ending וֹן see G.-K. 85 w.

V. 13. "Greece," יָוָן (Gen. 10:2, 4; 1 Chron. 1:5, 7; Is. 66:19; Joel 4:6), the Ionians, or Greeks, descendants of Javan, a son of Japheth, who settled in Asia Minor; hence all Greeks. (See Dan. 8:21; 10:20.)

V. 15. "Subdue with sling stones"; strike with, subdue; same word as in Micah 7:19, trample under foot, disregard, treat with contempt. "Sling stones," stones hurled from a sling. — "Bowls," the sacrificial bowls, or basins (Ex. 27:3; 38:3; Num. 4:14), in which the blood of the sacrificial animals was caught up and then sprinkled against the altar (Lev. 1:5) by pouring the blood against the corners of the altar "in such a manner that with two sprinklings all the four sides of the altar were wetted. Mishnah, Sebachim, v. 4 ff.; and Rashi on Lev. 1:5." (Keil.)

V. 16. "Lifted up as an ensign," Hithp. of נָסַס, occurring only here and in Ps. 60:6 (A. V., 5), "a banner . . . displayed."

V. 10. Ephraim and Jerusalem shall no longer be separate kingdoms, often warring against each other (2 Sam. 20:1 ff.; 1 Kings

12:16 ff.; 14:30; 15:7, 17 ff.). They shall be reunited "in those days" (Jer. 3:18), the days of Messiah, as God's Israel. (See also Hos. 1:10 f.) Horses, chariots, battle bows, regarded as essential for the defense and enlargement of their kingdoms, shall be cut off. Zion's King needs them neither for defense nor offense (Zech. 4:6). "He shall speak." He rules by His Word (John 8:26-53; 18:37). And He speaks not dire threats of condemnation, He proclaims peace (Micah 5:5; Ps. 72:7; Is. 9:10), a message addressed not only to Israel, but to "the heathen" as well, the vast mass of humanity. Though He has no other weapon but His Word, His Gospel, folly and a stumbling block to Jews and Gentiles (1 Cor. 1:23), yet His Word is spirit and life (John 6:63), a power of God unto salvation (Rom. 1:16 f.; 1 Cor. 1:18 ff.; 2 Cor. 10:4 f.). By this Gospel His kingdom shall spread from sea to sea (Ps. 72:8), not only from the Mediterranean to the Salt Sea, but beginning at the Mediterranean and going westward also to the Atlantic, the Arctic and the Antarctic, the Pacific, and back to the Mediterranean. "From the River" (Gr. N.), the Euphrates, named as the eastern boundary of the Promised Land (Gen. 15:18; Deut. 1:7; 11:24; 2 Sam. 8:3, etc.). Messiah's kingdom extends eastward to the ends of the earth. "Jesus shall reign where'er the sun does his successive journeys run." (Cp. ch. 2:4.)

Vv. 11, 12. In extending the boundaries of His kingdom, King Messiah will not overlook His covenant people. "The blood of thy covenant" = the covenant established on Sinai (Ex. 19:5, 6) and ratified by blood (Ex. 24:5-8), foreshadowing the atoning blood of Christ (Heb. 9:18-26; 1 John 1:7), retroactive (Heb. 9:14 f.), because it was the blood of the eternal Son of God (Acts 20:28; Heb. 1:3 ff.). This blood, to be offered centuries later, was already in the Old Testament the sole and only, yet immovable, basis for God's gracious preservation and deliverance of His people "out of the pit wherein is no water." From such a pit there was hope of delivery (cp. Gen. 37:21-28; Jer. 38:6-13), while in a pit filled with water death by drowning was inevitable. The "pit" here is the prison into which sin and Satan had brought them and held them captive, God's wrath, temporal and eternal punishment. The Babylonian Exile had been for them such a pit, a penalty for their apostasy (Jer. 25:1-11). From this pit they had been delivered by the Lord, who had kept His covenant promise (Deut. 30:1-5). Now Satan was trying to imprison them in the pit of disappointment, discouragement, unbelief (Hag. 2:3; Zech. 4:7-10). The Lord assures them that He is ready to deliver them

(v. 12). Only they are to turn to the Stronghold (Gr. N.), the Rock and Fortress. (See Ps. 61:2 f.; Prov. 18:10; Is. 26:4, "Rock of Ages," marginal note; cp. Is. 51:12-14.) Having such an omnipotent Refuge, they are indeed prisoners "of hope." "Even today," at a time when there seems no possible prospect of ever regaining their former glory, when they are harassed by fightings without and fears within (2 Cor. 7:5), the Lord declares that He will render double unto them. Their trials shall not be fatal, nor shall they last forever. (Cp. 1 Cor. 10:13; 2 Cor. 1:3-10; 4:8-18; Phil. 2:25-28.) There is a glorious future awaiting His people. Not only will they be given the full inheritance of children, but each shall also receive double. See Is. 40:2; 61:7, the share of the first-born, who received a portion twice as large as that of any other son (Deut. 21:17; cp. Heb. 12:23). Turn to this Stronghold, ye prisoners of hope!

V. 13. In a bold metaphor the Lord compares Himself to a warrior using Judah as His bow, Ephraim as His arrow. He explains this figurative speech. He will raise up, stir up, the sons of Zion, His beloved children, His Church, in a holy warfare against the sons of Greece (Gr. N.). Two centuries later the conquests of Alexander the Great had spread Greek culture and the Greek language throughout the world, and in the early Christian Church Jews and Greeks were united into one body, the latter representing the Gentile world. (Cp. Acts 6:1; 10:1—11:26; Rom. 1:14, 16; Eph. 2:11-22; see also John 12:20 ff., certain Greeks coming to see Jesus, the first fruits of the Gentile world.) So the Lord will make the Church, like the sword of a mighty man, His instrument in conquering the Gentile world for Messiah's Kingdom of Peace (Matt. 28:18-20).

V. 14. So signal shall be the victories gained by the Church that the very magnitude of her success shall prove that the Lord is with her. He is over His people as the General leading His troops according to His plans. He endows them with His strength so that they are His arrows going forth as lightning, swiftly, surely, victoriously. The Lord with His trumpet, His holy Word (cp. Amos 1:2), urges them on, encourages and strengthens them whenever they slow down, become discouraged. So He "with whirlwinds of the south," which, like the east wind (Ezek. 17:10; Hos. 13:15; Jonah 4:8), blow from the desert with deadly fury, sets out against the strongholds of Satan. No enemy can stop His triumphant march (2 Cor. 2:12-16).

V. 15. "Defend" = cover like a shield. (Cp. Ps. 46; Is. 43:1 ff.; 51:7 ff.) He protects them in danger. (Cp. 2 Cor. 6:1-10; 11:23—12:10.)

In the strength of the Lord (Eph. 6:10) they shall "devour." Perhaps the prophet had in mind Balaam's prophecy (Num. 23:24; cp. Micah 5:8 f.). "Subdue with sling stones" (Gr. N.), literally, tread under foot, disregard, despise sling stones, representing every method of attack used by the enemies. (See Heb. 11:33 f.; Rom. 8:35 ff.; Acts 5:41; 16:22-25; 20:22 ff.) "They shall drink," as lions drink the blood of their victims (Num. 23:24 b). This signifies the complete victory, the conquest of former enemies of Christ, who now willingly surrender to Christ (2 Cor. 10:5). "Make a noise as through wine." Intoxicated with joy over their glorious victories, they sing and shout glad hymns of praise glorifying the Lord, their King. "Filled like bowls, and as the corners of the altar." The bowls are the sacrificial bowls filled with the blood of the sacrifices, which was then dashed against the corners of the altar of burnt offering (Lev. 1:5, 11; 3:2, 8, 13). The warfare of the Church against Satan's kingdom, her mission work, the Gentiles gained for Christ, are sacrifices, offerings brought to God by His people in gratitude for His Gospel grace (Rom. 15:16). "Through the preaching of the Gospel the Holy Ghost is given, and by this Holy Ghost the hearts of men are sanctified, renewed, converted to God, given to God, brought to Him as a sacrificial offering" (Stoeckhardt, *Roemerbrief,* p. 627 f.).

Vv. 16, 17. The Lord shall save them "in that day," throughout the New Testament era, because they are the flock of His people, His chosen children, His elect, who will not perish (John 10:27-30). He will honor and glorify them. They shall be as stones of a crown, precious gems in the royal diadem of their King, His Church (Is. 62:3). Lifted up as an ensign (Gr. N.), as a banner, upon His land, His Church throughout the world points out to all mankind the way to salvation. "For" (v. 17) motivates the last statement. How great is His goodness, His kindness (Ps. 25:7; 27:13; Is. 63:7) as expressed in His blessings (Jer. 31:12-14; Hos. 3:5), and His beauty as revealed in His Son, the beautiful Savior (Ps. 45:2; Cant. 1:16; 5:10 ff.), a beauty reflected in His bride, the Church (Ps. 45:9 ff.; Cant. 1:8 ff.; 4:1 ff.)! One example of His kindness and of the beauty of His redeeming work is named. He causes corn and wine to grow, to make young men and maids cheerful, happy; gives them the bread and wine of His Gospel (Is. 55:1 ff.; Jer. 31:12 ff.), without which fair virgins and young men faint and die for hunger and thirst (Amos 8:11-13). The joy and peace passing all understanding, which dwells in Christian hearts and homes revealing the kindness and beauty of the Lord, is a marvelous inducement for the despairing world to join the Church of Christ, the King of Peace.

Most commentators refer Zech. 9:10 ff. to the war of the Maccabeans against the Seleucidan oppressors; some exclusively, others partly to the Maccabean wars, partly to the times of the expansion of the New Testament Church. Yet, beginning with v. 9, the prophet speaks of King Messiah coming to establish His New Testament kingdom. Moreover, the Maccabean wars ended with the subjection of Judah to Rome, with whom Judas Maccabeus had sought a league of amity and confederacy (1 Macc. 8:17 ff.). Rome came and remained, and Judah became a Roman province.

CHAPTER 10

B. Jehovah Alone Is to Be Trusted, for He Alone Can Bless

1. The Lord exhorts His people to pray for rain and promises to send it, vv. 1, 2

1 Ask of Jehovah rain at the time of the latter rain! Jehovah is the Creator of lightnings, and He will give showers of rain to them; to every-
2 one vegetation on the field. For the *teraphim* speak falsehood, and the soothsayers see a lie and speak dreams of deceit. They comfort in vain! Therefore they move on like a flock, they are oppressed, because there is no shepherd.

Grammatical Notes

V. 1. "Bright clouds." חֲזִיז, of unknown root, only here and Job 28:26; 38:25. A. V. in both passages, "lightning of thunder," literally, "of voices," i. e., the thunderbolts, lightning flashes, the forerunners, heralds, of rain. Cp. Ps. 135:7, "lightnings for," לְ, "the rain"; Jer. 10:13, "lightnings with," rather, for, לְ, "the rain." The LXX, φαντασίας, appearances, pomp, display (cp. Acts 25:23, "pomp"), the majestic display of lightning, fireworks, at the approach of a rainstorm; the Syriac Peshito, "the drops"; Targum, "winds."

V. 2. "Have spoken." The perfects here do not refer to the past, but denote an action which, beginning in the past, continues in the present. (Cp. Ps. 10:11; 143:6; Is. 52:7; G.-K. 106 g.) In vv. 3, 4 the perfects are prophetic, as is evident from v. 5 ff.

V. 1. In a marvelous manner the Lord demonstrates His eternal goodness and beauty (ch. 9:17) by inviting His people to pray for gifts He alone can give. (Cp. 1 Kings 3:5.) Such a gift is rain, the "early," that is, the autumnal rain, so essential for the sprouting of the newly sown grain, and the "latter," or spring rain, equally necessary for the proper maturing of the crops. Without the rains the crops were sure to fail (Deut. 11:10-17). As the withholding of these rains was a sign of God's displeasure (Jer. 5:24 f.; Amos 4:7 f.; Hos. 2:8 f.),

460

so the sending of these rains in their proper season and measure was a token of His grace and favor, and at the same time of His willingness to fulfill all His covenant promises, material and spiritual (Hos. 2: 21-23; Joel 2: 21-32; Is. 30: 23-26). "Bright clouds" (Gr. N.), lightning, accompanying the thunderstorms; "grass," vegetation, herbage. (Cp. Gen. 1: 11 f., "herb" in distinction to "grass.")

V. 2. "Idols," here = *teraphim,* house gods (Gen. 31: 19, 34 f.; 1 Sam. 15: 23; 19: 13, 16; Hos. 3: 4), consulted as oracles (Ezek. 21: 26). This reference to idolatry and "diviners," false prophets, has been regarded as proving the pre-Exilic authorship of either the entire book or at least of chs. 9—14, since after the Exile idolaters and false prophets were no longer found among the Jews. Yet at all times the deceitful and desperately wicked heart of man (Jer. 17: 9) is inclined to idolatry and superstition. Moreover, the returned exiles were children of their fathers, many of whom had served false gods in Babylon (Jer. 16: 13). In pre-Exilic times the worship of Israel had frequently been syncretistic, combining the worship of Baal (1 Kings 18: 21) or the *teraphim* (Judg. 17: 3-5; 18: 3-6, 13-26) with that of Jehovah. So in some of the homes of the returned Jews, *teraphim,* household gods, strictly forbidden (Ex. 20: 4 f.), may have been consulted, and other superstitious customs may have been practiced. How many superstitions have been handed down for generations in Christian homes! Malachi, prophesying only a few decades later, mentions sorcerers (Mal. 3: 5), and Nehemiah names a false prophet who sought to deceive him (Neh. 6: 10-12). The Searcher of hearts saw the danger threatening His people and warned them against the folly of their fathers, lest they would be judged in like manner. The stern warnings of Zechariah and Malachi were instrumental in thoroughly eradicating idolatrous and superstitious tendencies and practices still existing. "For" states the reason why the Jews are to ask the Lord for help in need. All other "helpers" are helpless. In contrast to the Lord of goodness and beauty the idols "have spoken" (Gr. N.) "vanity," nothingness; their oracles of peace are without the slightest foundation. The "diviners," soothsayers, fortunetellers, are liars; the dreams they tell are dreams of falsehood, deceit. Their comfort is vain, literally, wind, breath, which dissipates as quickly as it issues. (Cp. Jer. 27: 9 f.; 29: 8; Ezek. 13: 22; 22: 28.) Therefore all that resort for help to these vain comforters "went" (Gr. N.), literally, will go their way, roam about, be troubled in distress, because there is no shepherd. Soothsayers, false prophets are ravening wolves in sheep's clothing (Matt. 7: 15).

The Lord of infallible truth had revealed the glorious future of His Church, of which that small group of His children, subject to foreign rulers, were members. What willingness, what holy joy, what burning zeal this marvelous prospect should have awakened in their hearts and made manifest in their actions!

---

2. The Church's equipment for world-wide extension of Messiah's kingdom, vv. 3-12

3 Against the shepherds My wrath is kindled, and the leaders I will punish. For the LORD of Hosts will visit His flock, the house of Judah, and will make them His stately 4 horse in battle. From them the Cornerstone; from them the peg; from them the battle bow; from them shall come forth every over- 5 lord, all together. And they shall be like valiant men, trampling down the mud of the streets in battle. And they shall fight, for the LORD is with them; and they shall put to shame those that ride on 6 horses. And I will strengthen the house of Judah, and the house of Joseph will I deliver, and I will make them dwell, for I have compassion on them so that they shall be as if I had not rejected them, for I am Jehovah, their God. I will 7 hear them. Then Ephraim shall be as a mighty man, and their heart shall rejoice as with wine. Also their children shall see and rejoice;

their heart shall exult in the 8 LORD. I will hiss for them and assemble them, for I have redeemed them, and they shall increase as 9 they have increased. I will sow them among the nations, and in faraway places shall they remember Me, and together with their children they shall live and return. 10 I will also bring them back from the land of Egypt, and from Assyria I will gather them and bring them back to the land of Gilead and Lebanon, till no more room 11 shall be found for them. And He shall pass through the sea of affliction and smite the waves in the sea, and all the depths of the Nile shall dry up, and the pride of Assyria shall be brought low, and the 12 rod of Egypt shall depart. I will make them strong in the LORD, and they shall walk in the name of the LORD, is the oracle of the LORD.

Grammatical Notes

V. 3. "Punished," "visited"; פָּקַד used of God's visit to punish His enemies and to save His people. The perf. = future, prophetic.

V. 4. "Out of him" refers to "house of Judah," and proves that Judah is the Lord's stately battle horse. — "Corner," the pinnacle (Zeph. 1:16; 3:6), the corner, of a street (Prov. 7:8, 12), of a house (Job 1:16); here metaphorically, *totum pro parte,* the cornerstone, referring to the leaders as the cornerstones of the community (Judg. 20:2; 1 Sam.

14:38, "chief"; Is. 19:13, "stay"). — "Oppressor," נֹגֵשׂ, is one who insists on the fulfillment of a certain obligation. The verb occurs, e. g., Deut. 15:2, 3 in the meaning of "exacting," demanding payment of borrowed money, sinful against needy brother (v. 2); permitted in the case of a foreigner (v. 3); in Is. 58:3, "exact all your labors," insist on fulfillment of tasks, proper on week days, sinful on the Sabbath; in Ex. 3:7; 5:10, 13 f., "taskmasters," not sinful for them to demand a day's work from slaves, but wicked to make excessive demands and maltreat the laborers; in 2 Kings 23:35 and Dan. 11:20, the collector of revenue or taxes, not necessarily an oppressor. (Cp. Rom. 13:5 ff.) Zechariah uses the term in the good sense; see exposition.

V. 5. "In the mire." לְ is used here to denote the manner in which an action is carried out or a person is treated, *hunc in modum,* tread down like mud, as if they were mire. (Cp. Amos 4:10,

"after the manner"; Is. 10:24, 26; Gen. 1:26, 27; 5:1, "in the image, likeness.")
V. 10. "Place shall not be found," the Hebrew word here as in Joshua 17:16, and Qal in Num. 11:22; Judg. 21:14 = to suffice, be sufficient.

V. 11. "River," יְאֹר, denotes the Nile, whether it has the article, as in Gen. 41:1-3; Is. 19:8, etc., or not, as in Is. 19:7; 23:3; Amos 8:8; 9:5; only in Dan. 12:5-7 = Tigris.

V. 3. God's anger blazes forth against the shepherds; He will "punish" (Gr. N.), visit, the goats, the leaders of the flock (Jer. 50:8); here, the leaders of the nations (Is. 14:9; Ezek. 34:17). The context, v. 4 f., proves that foreign rulers are meant, all such kings of the earth as set themselves against King Messiah and His kingdom. The Lord of Hosts, Jehovah, the Covenant God, who is at the same time the Ruler of the universe, comes on a visit of glorification for His people. He will make the house of Judah, that little flock (Is. 54:6, 11), His goodly horse in battle, His stately, glorious, victorious battle steed. This is explained in vv. 4-12. He will fully equip His people for the work of building and expanding His Church.

V. 4. "Out of him" (Gr. N.), from Judah shall come forth the Corner, the Messiah to be born at Bethlehem of Judea (Micah 5:2; Luke 2:4), who together with the apostles and prophets forms the foundation of God's Church (Is. 28:16; Eph. 2:20; Matt. 16:18). Out of Judah, the Church of God, comes forth the nail, literally, the pegs fastened on the walls on which clothes, etc. were hung (Is. 22:23, 25; Ezek. 15:3), and on which the families depended for keeping their clothes in good order. Others regard it as the tent peg (Ex. 27:19; 38:20, 31, 39 f.; Is. 54:2, 31) to which the ropes were fastened that held the tent in proper position. The sense is not changed. From the Church will proceed men on whom the Church can depend for support, for leadership, for advice, for work to be done decently and in order (1 Cor. 12:4 ff.; 14:40; Eph. 4:8 ff.). "Battle bow," such as fight the battles of the Lord at home and abroad, faithful pastors, teachers, fathers, mothers, missionaries and their converts, who will spread the Gospel. "Every oppressor" (Gr. N.) denotes an exactor who insists on the fulfillment of all duties demanded by the Head of the Church (Matt. 28:20), who insists on purity of doctrine (Rom. 16:17 f.; Titus 3:10 f.), on the practice of church discipline (Matt. 18:15; 1 Cor. 4:21;

5:4, 5, 13; 2 Cor. 10:3-6; 13:3-10; 2 Thess. 3:1-16). See the Pastoral Letters to Timothy and Titus.

V. 5. "Tread down in the mire" (Gr. N.). As soldiers trample through mud and mire, as their bespattered uniforms as well as their blood-stained clothes (Zech. 9:15) proclaim their valiant bravery, so the soldiers of the Lord go onward. Disregarding inconveniences, disappointments, death, they go on to do their duty. (See Acts 4:18 ff.; 5:25 ff., 41 f.; 14:19 ff.; 16:19 ff.; 20:18 ff.; 2 Cor. 11:23-30.) They fight not in their own strength, but in the power of the Lord, who is with them, so that even the riders on horses, the most powerful and most feared part of the enemy's army, shall be confounded, put to shame.

V. 6. The predicates belonging to both subjects are distributed between the two subjects. "Bring them again to place them," literally, I will cause them to sit, to throne in honor, safety, and security; not because of their worthiness, but because I have mercy on them, they are more than conquerors, for the Lord has chosen them in His grace (Rom. 8:28-39). They shall be as though He had not rejected them. (The same word occurs in Ps. 43:2; 44:10, 24, A. V., 9, 23; 74:1.) Jehovah is their Covenant God, who will hear them and answer the prayer of those who obey His gracious invitation (v. 1).

V. 7. Vv. 7-12 are particularly, though not exclusively, directed to the Northern Kingdom. The ten tribes had been deported from their land, their royal city Samaria destroyed, their territory populated by foreigners, so that it became a semipagan land (2 Kings 15—17). Very few Israelites had returned with Zerubbabel. It seemed as if God had forever rejected Ephraim = the Northern Kingdom, Israel. Yet God had not forgotten His people. Even though He had given Israel a bill of divorce (Jer. 3:6-8), He remembered her (Jer. 3:12 ff.). Israel shall be reunited with Judah in the days of the Messiah. (Cp. Hos. 1:10 f.; 2:23.) According to the Holy Spirit's interpretation in the New Testament (Rom. 9:24 ff.; 1 Peter 2:9 f.), the paganized Israelites include not only the descendants of the ten tribes deported 722 B. C., but represent also the Gentiles, those countless numbers of heathen converts who through faith in the Savior of Jews and Gentiles become the Israel of the New Testament (Rom. 2:28 f.; 3:29 f.; Gal. 3:7-9, 26-29; 6:16; Heb. 12:22 f.). Like Judah (v. 5), they will be mighty soldiers of the Lord. Their heart also shall rejoice as through wine. Joyfully, exultingly, they shall serve their Lord, together with their children. Generation upon generation shall see and taste the goodness and beauty of the Lord (ch. 9:17; 1 Peter 1:8; 2:3; Ps. 34:8; Phil. 4:4).

V. 8. "I will hiss," whistle, for them, as a beekeeper calls the bees to the hives. "For them" = Judah and the house of Joseph (v. 6), Ephraim (v. 7), and the Gentiles represented by Ephraim, all shall be gathered into one swarm. Through the preaching of the Gospel (Luke 10:16) the Lord calls them into His Church on earth, the vestibule of their eternal home in heaven. They are His redeemed people, purchased by the vicarious suffering of His Servant (Is. 53). They shall increase, as they have increased. (Cp. Ex. 1:7, 12.)

V. 9. "Sow them" does not denote scattering them as in the Exile. Already Hosea spoke of a sowing of Israel "to the Lord" (ch. 2:23), in His interest. (Cp. Jer. 31:27.) Zechariah also speaks of a blessing. There, far away from the Promised Land, they shall remember the Lord. On hearing His call (v. 8), they together with their children shall live, obtain new spiritual life, faith in the Lord and His Messenger. (Cp. John 17:3.) So they shall turn back to the Lord, their Covenant God.

V. 10. Since the Lord has in mind particularly Ephraim, He names Egypt as the oppressor and enemy of His people, because there all the twelve tribes had been held in bondage for 430 years (Ex. 12:40), and Assyria, because the Assyrians had deported the ten tribes. Therefore He promises return to Gilead, the Eastjordanland, and Lebanon, the northern section of Westjordanland, both of which had constituted the homeland of the ten tribes. Ephraim is at the same time the representative of all Gentiles (cp. v. 7). So large is the number of God's children among Judah, Israel, and the Gentiles (cp. also Jer. 3:17 f.) that "place shall not be found for them" (Gr. N.). The Holy Land would be far too small to offer all a home. The homeland of God's Church extends to the ends of the earth (ch. 9:10). We have here New Testament realities described in terms of the Old Testament, which the Jews of Zechariah's time could understand, while the fulfillment brought a glory far greater than they had hoped for and expected. Compare the questions of the disciples revealing their false conception of Messiah's kingdom in Matt. 16:21 ff.; 17:10 ff.; 20:20 ff.; Luke 9:45; 18:34 f.; 24:21; Acts 1:6.

V. 11. "With affliction" (Gr. N.), rather, sea of affliction. The Church will never be without affliction (John 16:33; Acts 14:22). Yet the Ruler of wind and waves is the Leader of His Church. (Cp. Ps. 65:8, A. V., 7; 93:2-4.) He shall smite the waves as He smote the waves of the Red Sea (Ex. 14:21 ff.) and dry up the waters of the "River" (Gr. N.), the Nile, as He had dried up the waters of

Jordan (Joshua 3:14 ff.). He will lead His people safely through every sea of affliction. While the smiting of the waters served to save His people, the drying up of the waters of the Nile will turn Egypt into a desert land. Proud Assyria and haughty Egypt shall be ruined; all enemies of the Church be judged, condemned.

V. 12. The Lord will give strength to His people, strength in the Lord (Eph. 6:10; cp. Is. 45:24; Jer. 16:19), strength that makes them more than conquerors (Rom. 8:37; 1 John 5:4).

"In His name," as He has revealed Himself in His holy Word and by His mighty deeds, they "walk up and down." The Hebrew term is the same used in Gen. 5:24; 17:1; 24:40; 2 Kings 20:3; Is. 38:3, etc.; to cause oneself to walk, the sincere and continued desire to walk worthy of the name of their Lord, according to His will, in keeping with His commandments. The Lord who has created this desire by His Gospel, will also supply the strength to constantly resist temptations of Satan, the world, and their own flesh (2 Cor. 3:5; Phil. 2:13). So they walk as children of God, in His company, on His ways, the paths chosen by Him to lead them to their eternal home (Is. 35:8-10).

CHAPTER 11

C. The Destruction of Jerusalem Because of Her Rejection of the Good Shepherd

1. The approach of the enemy, vv. 1-3

1 Open your doors, O Lebanon, that fire may consume your cedars!
2 Wail, O cypress, for the cedar is fallen, for the mighty ones are destroyed. Wail, O oaks of Bashan, for the impenetrable forest is fallen! Hark! the wailing of the shepherds, for their glory is destroyed.
3 Hark! the roaring of lions, for the jungle of Jordan is ruined!

Grammatical Notes

V. 2. "Vintage," בָּצוּר, from a root, Niphal = to be inaccessible (Job 42:2), impossible (Gen. 11:6); Piel = causative (Is. 22:10; Jer. 51:53). The participial adj. בָּצוּר is used of inaccessibly high or steep walls (Deut. 28:32; Is. 2:15; Jer. 15:20), of well-fortified cities (Deut. 1:28; 9:1, etc.), here of an impenetrable forest. K'tib בָּצוּר, Q'ri בָּצִיר, occurs only here.

V. 3. "Pride of Jordan"; the phrase occurs here, and, translated "swelling of Jordan," in Jer. 12:5; 49:19; 50:44. It denotes, literally, highness, excellence, glory, used here of the lush, junglelike vegetation on both banks of the Jordan.

Vv. 1-3. In a remarkable vision the prophet hears the voice of the Lord threatening complete destruction to Lebanon, the mountain range north of the Westjordanland, and to Bashan (v. 2), the northern section of Eastjordanland, and to the "pride" (Gr. N.) (v. 3), the junglelike thickets on the banks of the Jordan River. Rugged Lebanon (v. 1) with its majestic forests is told to open its doors, to give access to the hosts of enemies advancing against the Holy Land. Its stately "firs," rather, cypress trees, and its magnificent cedars will be hewn down and used for bulwarks and other war machinery. (Cp. Deut. 20:19 f.) What is left after the hewers had finished their job will be burnt with fire, so that Lebanon's thickets will no longer impede the march of the enemy forces. (Cp. 2 Kings 19:23; Is. 14:8.) Bashan (v. 2) will meet with like destruction. Its "forest of the vintage" (Gr. N.), literally, the impenetrable forests of oak trees, are laid low, so that the enemies can proceed unhindered on their campaign. Its rich pasture lands, offering lush feeding grounds to immense flocks, are laid waste (v. 3), their glory turned into devastation, the happy chants of the shepherds changed into dismal howls and wailings. Even the junglelike thickets on the banks of the Jordan, where lions raised their young and from which they made their forages into the surrounding country, are spoiled, laid waste. A ruthless enemy who knows no pity, who delights in destruction, murder, cruel oppression, is advancing against Judah and Jerusalem. As the vultures gather from afar round about the carcass, so the enemy forces are seen gathering about Jerusalem (Job 39:30; Heb. 1:8; Matt. 24:28).

Since the context refers to the days of the Messiah (v. 12 ff.), the reference is to the siege and destruction of Jerusalem and the devastation of the entire land by the armies of Rome A. D. 70 and 71. The Jewish nation will be rejected by the Lord because of its rejection of its Lord and His Shepherd (vv. 4-14).

---

2. The prophet symbolizes the Good Shepherd, His rejection by the people, and God's rejection of the nation, vv. 4-14

4 Thus said the LORD, my God, Shepherd the flock of slaughter,
5 whose purchasers slay them without feeling guilty; and they that sell them say, Bless the LORD, for I am getting rich! And their own shepherds? Not one pities them!
6 For I no longer pity the inhabitants of the land, is the oracle of the LORD. And, behold! I Myself am delivering them, everyone into the hand of his neighbor and into the hand of his king. They shall lay waste the land, and I will not de-
7 liver out of their hand. So I shepherded the flock of slaughter, hence the most miserable of the flock. And I took for myself two rods; the one I called Beauty, and the other I called Bands; and so I shep-
8 herded the flock. Then I put to death the three shepherds in one month, and I became impatient with them, and they also loathed me.
9 So I said, I will not be your Shepherd! What is to die, will die! And

467

what is to be cut off, will be cut off! And the surviving women, each woman will eat the flesh of her 10 neighbor! And then I took my staff Beauty and broke it in order to change my covenant which I had 11 made with all the nations. And it was broken in that very day, and thus the poorest of the flock, such as were heeding me, came to realize that this was the word of Je- 12 hovah. And I said to them, If it seem good to you, give me my wages, and if not, let it go! So they weighed out my wage, thirty pieces 13 of silver; and the LORD told me, Throw it to the potter, the precious price at which I was priced by them! And I took the thirty pieces of silver and threw them into the house of the LORD to the potter. 14 Then I broke my second staff, Bands, that I might break the brotherhood between Judah and Israel.

Grammatical Notes

V. 5. "Hold themselves not guilty." On this sense of *asham* cp. Hos. 4:15.

V. 7. "I will feed." The strong ן demands the translation, And so, then, I fed, began to shepherd. — "Even you," לָכֵן. G.-B. lists as one of the usages of this term "what may be concluded from a given fact" (Job 34:25; 42:3). The term occurs also in Is. 61:7, A. V., "therefore"; so also R. S. V., Koenig, Pieper. LXX connects the term with the following word and translates "to Canaan"; similarly Symmachus and Lucian. Kittel, *Bibl. Hebr.*, recommends to read "to the Canaanites of the flock," i. e., the sheep dealers or merchants. We retain the meaning "therefore," on that account. — "Poor of the flock." Not infrequently a construct adjective acquires the sense of a superlative, the poorest of the flock. (See Judg. 5:29; Job 30:6; Is. 14:30; 19:11, etc. G.-K. 133 h.) — "Beauty," from a root = to be lovely, pleasant, sweet (2 Sam. 1:26; Ps. 141:6; Prov. 2:10, etc.). The noun occurs in Prov. 3:17; 15:26; 16:24; Ps. 27:4; 90:17. These passages will help towards a fuller understanding of the present one. "Bands," from a root = to bind, pledge (Ex. 22:25; Deut. 24:6, 17; Ezek. 18:16, etc.). Here, the participial plural is used as an abstract noun, a binding union, confederacy. (Cp. v. 14, "brotherhood.")

V. 8. "Three shepherds." Who are they? Pfeiffer says that "Ch. 11:4-17 and 13:7-9 allude to historical events in the immediate past easily recognized by the prophet's contemporaries, but entirely unknown to us." (*Introduction*, p. 608.) Eissfeldt: "Ch. 11:4-17; 13:7-9 present quite definite references to definite contemporary historical events and conditions, but not sufficiently unmistakable to render their exact dating possible." (*Einleitung*, p. 488.) Most modern commentators are not so reserved in expressing their opinion. Ewald assigned the passage to the rapid succession of Zechariah, Shallum, and Menahem (2 Kings 15:10-17). Marti, Duhm, and others: the three shepherds are the wicked high priests Lysimachus, Jason, and Menelaus; the good shepherd is pious Onias IV; the foolish shepherd is the latter's successor, Alcimus (163 to 160 B. C.). (See 1 Macc. 7:5-25; 9:54-57.) But Onias did not remove the high priests. Sellin (*Zwoelfprophetenbuch*, 1930, p. 564): "The good shepherd is Onias III (ca. 199—175 B. C.) of 2 Macc. 3:1; 4:1-38, who expelled three temple officials and tax collectors, Simon, Menelaus, and Lysimachus. (Cp. Josephus, *Wars* I, 1.) The foolish shepherd is Menelaus, who instigated the murder of Onias and was put to death in a disgracing manner (2 Macc. 13:3-8). Sellin dates ch. 11:4—13:9

about 154—140 B. C. and is in doubt whether the writer's intention is to record history or eschatology, facts experienced or still to be looked for. He finally decides on an apocalyptic presentation of contemporary events (p. 561). We know that this is divinely inspired prophecy (1 Peter 1:10 ff.). — "My soul loathed." Soul, נֶפֶשׁ, never stands merely for the personal pronoun, but always denotes the heart and soul interest in, or impulse toward, an act. "Loathed," תִּקְצָר, literally, to become short (Prov. 10:27; Is. 28:20); with "soul" or "spirit," רוּחַ, to become impatient. (Cp. Num. 21:4; Judg. 10:16; 16:16; Micah 2:7; Job 21:4.)

V. 9. "That that dieth." The Hebrew feminine here is collective (G.-K. 122s). "Let it die," "be cut off"; "Let the rest eat." The Hebrew forms are jussives announcing facts decreed by the Lord in punishment of their unbelief.

V. 12. "Weighed thirty pieces of silver." Before coined money came into use after the Exile (cp. dram, or daric, the Persian coin, Ezra 2:69; 8:27; Neh. 7:70 f.), rings or bars of silver were used for money. Cp. Gen. 17:12 f., "bought with money," literally, a purchase by silver; Gen. 23:9, 13, 15 f., "money" = silver, keseph. This silver was weighed, שָׁקַל, on a scale (Gen. 23:16), and hence the unit of weight was called a shekel, a piece of silver worth about 55 cents. — Note the play on words in vv. 12, 13; yishqelu, hashlikehu, wa'ashlik. They weighed; cast it away! I cast; and again, hayeqar yaqarti, the price I was priced.

V. 13. "Cast it unto the potter!" These words have proved a puzzle particularly to interpreters who refused to accept the interpretation of the New Testament (Matt. 27:3-10). Many regarded the words as a common expression of contempt: Cast it to the dogs, the hang-man. Others adopt the translation of the Targum and Peshito, "to the treasury," and change yotser to otsar. Septuagint and Symmachus render it, "to the smelting oven" = to the smelter. Torrey refers to a passage in Herodotus (III, 96), stating that Darius I (521—486 B. C.) smelted the silver and gold received as tribute money and molded it into bars, from which he cut whatever money he happened to need. Torrey suggests that this custom was adopted by the Temple officials, who instituted a smeltery in the Temple. Eissfeldt in Forschungen und Fortschritte, May 1, 1937, adopted this suggestion. Torrey had referred to Ex. 32:4 in order to prove that this custom of smelting the metal offerings was an ancient one in Israel. Yet "graving tool," cheret, is not "smelting form" (Gussform). Cheret, derived from charat, to dig or cut into, engrave, denotes the engraver's tool, chisel, stylus. Cp. Is. 8:1, where it denotes the product of engraving = letters, scripts. Cp. also charit, pocket, money bag, purse (2 Kings 5:23; Is. 3:22); chartom, the sacred scribe or sage, Koenig: Griffelfuehrer, wielder of the stylus, pencil (Gen. 41:8; Dan. 2:2, 10). Eissfeldt also refers to 2 Kings 12:5-17 and 2 Kings 22:3-6. Yet the latter passage says nothing of a smelting furnace in the Temple and in 2 Kings 12:5-17 wayyatsuru (v. 10) is correctly translated "put up in bags." Cp. 2 Kings 5:23, "bound," tied, where "smelting" is impossible. Hence the king's scribe and the high priest tied the money they found in the chest into bags, then counted it and paid the laborers. There was no need of smelting the money. The individual worshipers gave relatively small amounts, which could readily be paid out to the workmen. We can see no reason to change the sense of יוֹצֵר, "potter," to "smelter"; and Matt. 27:3 ff. compels us to accept the former translation.

Note on Matt. 27:9 — Jeremiah or Zechariah?

The Holy Ghost, speaking through Matthew, did not make a mistake, did not confuse the two prophets. Matthew here states that a word of Scripture was fulfilled by the purchase of a potter's field for the thirty pieces of silver paid as the price of the Messiah. Zechariah says nothing of the purchase of a field nor of his appointment to buy a field. But Jeremiah, who says nothing of the betrayal, does state that the Lord "appointed him" (Matt. 27:10) to buy a field (Jer. 32:6-8). He was to buy this field as a solemn guarantee by the Lord Himself that fields and vineyards would again be bought and sold in the land (vv. 15, 43 f.). The prophet had regarded that as impossible, but the Lord assured him that nothing is too hard for Him (v. 27). That potter's field would not and could not have been bought by the chief priests if the threefold divine assurance (Jer. 32:15, 43 f.) had not been fulfilled. This potter's field was one of the fields the omniscient Lord (Acts 15:18) had in mind when He spoke to Jeremiah. On the other hand, Jeremiah says nothing of another circumstance closely connected with the purchase of this potter's field, that it was to be bought for the thirty pieces of silver, the price of Him that was valued (Matt. 27:9), nor that this money would be cast into the Temple (Matt. 27:5). These details were added by Zechariah. Matthew combines both prophecies and names Jeremiah, because he was the major prophet and had foretold what Matthew particularly intended to stress, the purchase of the field. So Matthew, in ch. 21:5, combines two prophecies spoken by two different prophets, Isaiah (ch. 62:11) and Zechariah (ch. 9:9), and ascribes the prophecy not to "prophets," but to "*the* prophet," the well-known prophet. Mark 1:2, according to the best Greek texts, ascribes prophecies spoken by Malachi (ch. 3:1) and by Isaiah (ch. 40:3) to one prophet, Isaiah. The Minor Prophets, though frequently quoted in the New Testament, are rarely quoted in the name of their writers. Only three prophets are named: Hosea once (Rom. 9:25), Joel once (Acts 2:16), and Jonah in the parallel passages Matt. 12:29 ff. and Luke 11:29 f.

Vv. 4, 5 are directed to the prophet, who calls the Lord "my God." The prophet's heart is attached in true loyalty to Jehovah, whose will he delights to do (Ps. 40:8). As Zechariah had been honored to be the recipient of the marvelous night visions (ch. 1:7—6:8), so here in a similar vision he is to see himself symbolizing the Messiah, the true Shepherd (John 10:11, 14; Heb. 13:20), in whose person Jehovah Himself will visit and deliver His sheep (Ezek. 34:11 ff.). "Feed," be the shepherd of the flock, the nation chosen by the Lord as His own (Ex. 19:5 f.; Deut. 4:32 ff.; Amos 3:2), as the sheep of His flock (Ps. 80:1; 95:7; 100:3; Jer. 23:1; Ezek. 34:6-31). "The flock of slaughter," appointed for slaughter, not because of an eternal decree of destruction and damnation, but because their wicked leaders "slay," literally, strangle them (v. 5), particularly at the time of Messiah's sojourn on earth, of which era this chapter speaks. "Possessors," "they that sell," "shepherds." The three terms do not necessarily distinguish three classes of rulers. Each term rather describes all the leaders of the people; spiritual leaders, such as the priests and Levites (Lev. 10:11; Deut. 17:9; 31:9; 2 Chron. 15:3; 17:8 ff.; Mal. 2:1-8), prophets (1 Sam. 3:9-21; 7:3-15; Jer. 1:7-19; 25:2 ff.), the various civic officers, national and local kings, magistrates, etc., who as officials in a church-state had the solemn duty to guard not only the material but also all the spiritual welfare of their subjects (Deut. 17:18 ff.; Joshua 1:7 f.; 24:1-27; 2 Kings 18:3 ff.; chs. 22 and 23; 2 Chron. 17: 3-10). In the days of Messiah the leaders of the nation had shamefully neglected their duties. The participial forms of the three Hebrew terms describe their habitual activities. Whether they are buying, or selling, or shepherding the sheep, they are not concerned about the welfare of the flock or the individual, but only and always about their own gain. They regard their subjects as chattels, to be bought or sold at will. Neither in buying, in their endeavor to enlarge their realm, nor in selling, getting rid of people not to their liking, nor even in shepherding (cp. Matt. 15:3 ff.; 16:12; 23:15), do they seek the eternal welfare of the souls entrusted to their care. Their sole aim is to fill their purse and their belly, to gain personal or political advantage. No matter what crimes they commit, they "hold themselves not guilty" (Gr. N.); they feel no compunctions; unashamed they continued their tactics. In base hypcrisy they even thank God for granting them riches and honors, while they unmercifully fleece the sheep (Matt. 23:1 ff.).

V. 6. "For" states the reason why the prophet is to feed this flock, so that at least the remnant, the "poor of the flock" (v. 7), might be saved. The sheep have deserved no better treatment. Instead of joining the true prophets of God in their opposition to wickedness, they willingly believe the promises of peace and plenty so lavishly proclaimed by the political and religious leaders, and adopt their wicked ways. Like priest, like people; like prince, like subjects. (Cp. Matt. 23:37 f.; 27:20-25; Luke 19:41-44.) Since rulers and people had rejected the Lord and His Messenger of grace (John 1:16), there was left for them only the pitiless wrath of the holy God (Deut. 32: 18-25; Prov. 1:20-32). The Jews, rejected by the Lord, were "delivered everyone into his neighbors' hands." They had preferred a murderer to their divinely appointed Shepherd, and therefore the Lord surrendered them to their fellow Jews, the leaders of the various factions, bands of gangsters bitterly opposing one another. These constant battles among themselves weakened the nation and finally delivered them "into the hand of their king." They would not have this man Jesus to rule over them (Luke 19:14); they would have no king but Caesar (John 19:15). Therefore God delivered them into the hands of their self-chosen king, the Roman emperor; and Roman soldiers carried out the destruction foretold, chs. 11—13. Jews and Romans combined to smite the land, and God sent no deliverer. That was the final judgment upon Judah as a nation. (See 1 Thess. 2:16, foretold already Is. 6:1-13; 65:1-14; cp. Acts 28:23-28; Rom. 9:22-33; 11:7 ff.) Yet before this final judgment was carried out, the Lord in a marvelous manifestation of His love (Jer. 31:3; John 3:16) sent His own Son (cp. Matt. 21:37) in a last effort to bring the wayward nation back into His fold. This is foretold v. 7, where in a remarkable prophetic vision Zechariah sees himself taking the role of the Good Shepherd.

V. 7. "And I will feed" (Gr. N.), rather, So I began to feed, to be a shepherd to the flock of slaughter, "even you" (Gr. N.). In that wicked nation there were still many of God's elect, here called the poorest of the flock. They clung to the Lord and His Word and sought by word and example to call their fellow men to repentance. Yet they reaped only contempt, hatred, persecution, oppression for their efforts. (Cp. John 7:45-52; 9:24-41.) For the sake of these He became the Shepherd of the flock. (Cp. Gen. 18:23 ff.; Is. 1:9; 1 Kings 19:15-21.) The wicked shepherds had neglected and oppressed these poor sheep; so the faithful Shepherd regards it as His sacred duty to shepherd them with special care. He takes "unto" Himself, for the efficacious performance of His office, two staffs. The staff was an essential part of a shepherd's equipment. With his staff he led the sheep, kept them from straying, pulled them back from danger, or out of crevices or pits into which they had fallen, protected them against wild animals or thieves. One of the staffs He called Beauty (Gr. N.), Grace, Loving-kindness, Friendliness. This grace was evidenced by the covenant He had made with "all the peoples," all nations (v. 10), not to hurt or harm His chosen nation (Ex. 19:4-6; Deut. 32:8-14; 33:26-29; Zech. 1:14-21; 2:5, 8 ff.). The other staff He called Bands (Gr. N.), Binding, Confederacy, Union. This staff signified "the brotherhood between Judah and Israel" (v. 14), the national unity which had been broken by Jeroboam's rebellion (1 Kings 12:19), but had been re-established to some extent after the return from the Exile. Jesus, the Governor to rule over God's people Israel (Matt. 2:6), sought to reunite the lost sheep of the house of Israel. He preached not only in Judah and Jerusalem, but also in Samaria (John 4:7-42), and particularly in Galilee (Matt. 4:12-25), and even to Gentiles (cp. Matt. 4:25), in Decapolis with a largely heathen population (John 12:20 ff.), in order that not only Judah and Israel, but together with them the Gentiles also might be united into one fold under one Shepherd (John 10:15 f.; 11:51 f.). Having taken these two staffs, the Messiah, typified by Zechariah, began His work, which is summarized

472

in vv. 8-11, not, however, in chronological sequence, but in a panorama-like vision.

V. 8. The first item mentioned is the removal of three shepherds in one month (Gr. N.), a comparatively short time. The three shepherds are the three well-known classes of leaders: kings, or civic rulers, priests, and prophets, three groups frequently named by the divinely inspired writers, and particularly by Jeremiah, in various combinations. (Cp. Jer. 1:18; 2:26; 5:31; 26:7-11, etc.) "Kings" and "princes" comprehend all civic rulers; priests, the administrators of the Temple service; prophets, functioning as God's messengers to both classes and to the people. The three offices were divinely instituted, kings and civil rulers (Deut. 17:14 ff.; 1 Sam. 10:1; 16:1-13), priests and Levites (Ex. 28:1 ff.; Num. 8:6 ff.), prophets (Num. 11:25; 12:6; Jer. 1:5; 25:4; 1 Peter 1:10 ff.; Heb. 1:1). The Jews continued in their stubborn refusal to accept Jesus as their Messiah (Matt. 27: 15-26, 62 ff.; Acts 4:1 ff.; 5:17 ff.; 6:8 ff.). Cp. also their persistent opposition to Paul (Acts 13:45—28:29). Finally, they were rejected as a nation by the Lord (1 Thess. 2:15 f.) and never again as a nation had their own divinely appointed kings, or priests, or prophets. On the complete abolition of the Levitical priesthood see Heb. 7—10. Cp. also 1 Peter. 2:5, 9; Rev. 1:6.

"My soul loathed them." The soul is the seat of feelings and emotions. As the Lord in the days of Jeremiah became "weary of repenting" of the evil He had threatened (Jer. 15:6), so the Good Shepherd became weary (Gr. N.), lost patience, with the wicked people and their wicked leaders. That weariness was not unjustified. When Jesus began His public office, the people had enthusiastically proclaimed Him as the Messiah. They regarded Him as their bread king, their political liberator (John 6:14 ff., 26 f., 60 ff.). When He taught them the true nature of His kingdom, they lost their enthusiasm (John 6:26-71) and abhorred Him, turned away from Him, against Him in disgust and bitter hate.

V. 9. The Shepherd, symbolized by the prophet, will no longer "feed," shepherd them. He withdraws His grace and patience, surrenders them to their enemies. The three clauses, "let" etc., are jussives. They shall die, shall be cut off by their enemies. The rest, who were not slain by the foreign armies, shall eat everyone the flesh of another. This is not to be restricted to cannibalism, although Josephus tells of a mother slaying and eating her own child (*History of the Jewish War*, VI, 3. 4). It refers to the bloody battles fought

473

by the various opposing factions among the Jews, each faction seeking to gain the leadership. These quarrels, of course, only served to weaken the nation. The Shepherd's refusal to feed the flock any longer is symbolized by His cutting asunder His staff Beauty (v. 10); the internal dissensions, by His breaking His staff Bands (v. 14).

Vv. 10, 11. Zechariah explains the breaking of his staff Beauty as the breaking of God's covenant with all people. (Cp. v. 6, p. 000.) He withdrew His grace from His former people and surrendered them to their enemies. Yet the stubbornly fanatic Jews could not and would not read the handwriting on the wall. Only the poor of the flock (v. 11, cp. v. 7), the believing remnant that "waited upon Him," which observed and studied and obeyed Him and His Word, knew, realized, recognized, that now was the time God's age-old threat (Deut. 32: 22-25) was about to be fulfilled. Most of the believers obeyed the warning of their gracious Savior (Matt. 24: 15, 16) and fled to Pella on the other side of Jordan, where they were spared the horrors of the siege and final capture of Jerusalem.

Vv. 12-14 point out the justice of God's judgment. It came in punishment of their heinous ingratitude and contemptuous treatment of the Good Shepherd. The prophet asks for his price, the wages due a faithful shepherd. This wage is to be given willingly or not at all. With devilish ingenuity they found a way of disobeying both commands. They offer him a wage, and at the same time they add ignominious insult to their rejection of him. Meticulously they weigh out thirty pieces of silver (Gr. N.), the exact sum stipulated in God's Law as payment to the owner of a slave gored to death by an ox (Ex. 21: 32). Thirty shekels, a little more than sixteen dollars. Their faithful Shepherd, symbolized by Zechariah, Jehovah their Righteousness (Jer. 23: 6), worth no more to them than the price of a lowly slave! (Cp. Acts 3: 15; 1 Cor. 2: 8.) The insult offered to His Messenger is regarded by Jehovah as an insult to Himself, for He is One with this Messenger, in whom is the name, the essence of Jehovah (Ex. 23: 20, 21). "The goodly price" etc., literally, the magnificence of the value at which I was valued by them! In the symbolic vision the people pay this miserable wage to the prophet; in the fulfillment the representatives of the people pay the money to the traitor (Matt. 26: 15). Yet in both cases the utter contempt in which Jesus was held by His enemies and by His former apostle is indicated as clearly as by their preferring a murderer to the Messiah (Matt. 27: 17-26). "Cast it unto the potter!" (Gr. N.) says the Lord (v. 13), and the prophet in the vision cast it to the potter in the house of the Lord.

There was indeed no potter in the actual Temple; yet neither the Lord nor the prophet made a mistake. True, until their fulfillment no one knew the hidden meaning of this command and this action, just as no one knew the hidden meaning of Ex. 12:46 until its fulfillment (John 19:36). The omniscient Ruler of history (Is. 46:10; Acts 15:18) foretells what would happen more than 550 years later. The very same thirty pieces of silver paid out to Judas by the chief priests for delivering Jesus to them (Matt. 26:15) were cast into the house of the Lord by the traitor (Matt. 27:5), and the chief priests took these very same silver pieces and gave them to the potter from whom they bought a field to bury strangers in (vv. 6, 7). On the seeming substitution of Jeremiah for Zechariah see Special Note on Matt. 27:9, Jeremiah or Zechariah? p. 470.

V. 14. On "Bands" see v. 7, p. 468, v. 9, p. 474.

---

3. The foolish shepherd, vv. 15-17

15 Then the LORD said to me: Furthermore, take to yourself the equipment of a foolish shepherd.
16 For, lo, I am about to raise up a shepherd in the land: He will not search for that which is hidden; that which is going astray he will not seek; what is wounded he will not heal; what is standing he will not strengthen. But the flesh of the well-fed he will eat and tear
17 them to pieces. Woe to the idol shepherd who forsakes the flock! The sword upon his arm and his right eye! His arm shall utterly wither and his right eye be totally blinded!

Grammatical Notes

V. 15. "Yet." עוֹד, here = in addition, moreover, furthermore (Gen. 18:29; 37:9; Ex. 3:15; 2 Kings 4:6). — "Foolish," from a stem = to be in the front, first, in leading position. The adjective occurs ca. 23 times, the noun *iwwelet* more than 20 times. It designates the self-satisfied fool, who always demands first honors, leadership, irrespective of his qualifications. His will is his law, and others are to accept it as such. (See Prov. 1:7; 12:15 f.; 14:9, 24; 15:5; 20:3; 27:22.)

V. 16. "Young," נַעַר, a young person, from infancy (Ex. 2:6) to the period of manhood, including all who are not yet able to take on the full responsibility of a given profession, hence, inexperienced (Judg. 8:20; 1 Sam. 17:33; 1 Kings 3:7; Jer. 1:6). Since the term is never used of animals, many interpreters derive it from a root נָעַר = to shake, shake loose (Ex. 14:27, A. V., "overthrew"; Ps. 136:15; Is. 33:9, 15; 52:2) and translate "scattered." We prefer the A. V. "young," inexperienced, since the prophet has in mind not animals, but people. — "Feed" *yekalkel* = Pi. of כּוּל, to measure (Is. 14:12); measure out, provide for, supply with food (Gen. 45:11; 50:21; 1 Kings 17:4, 9); support, guard against falling (Ps. 55:23, A. V., 22). — "Tear in pieces," פָּרַק, to tear off (Gen. 27:40; Lam. 5:8); Pi., intensive (Ex. 32:2; 1 Kings 19:11). — "Claws," פַּרְסָה = hoof (Ex. 10:26; Lev. 11:3-7, 26, etc.). The plural usually פְּרָסוֹת. Therefore Sellin's suggestion is acceptable,

475

that פֶּרֶס here is the Aramaean *peras,*
"piece," for the Hebrew *perez.* (Cp.
Dan. 5:28, division, piece.) Hence, he
tears off their pieces, tears them in
pieces. Either translation denotes wanton cruelty, unfeeling, bestial covetousness.

V. 17. "Idol." אֱלִיל occurs in this sense
sixteen times (Lev. 19:4; 26:1; Is. 2:8,
18, 20; 10:10 f.; 19:13; 31:7; Ezek. 30:13;
Hab. 2:18; Ps. 96:5; 97:7; 1 Chron.

16:26). G.-B. lists for the sense of
"worthless," "futile," only Job 13:14
(A. V., "of no value"), where "idol"
would not be unsuitable. Cp. v. 7 ff.;
Jer. 14:14, "of nought," where K'tib =
elul, which does not occur elsewhere in
this sense. G.-B. adds the note: "Possibly the word originally denoted idols,
gods, but acquired the sense of futile,
vanity, in Hebrew." The odds seem to
be in favor of "idol," which is very
suitable here.

Vv. 15-17. "Yet," "foolish" (Gr. N.). The foolish shepherd is
usually regarded as symbolizing the wicked leaders among the Jews
during the last centuries of the pre-Christian era and up to the
destruction of Jerusalem A. D. 70. Yet the prophet had spoken of
these "shepherds" in the plural (see vv. 5, 8, 12), just as Jeremiah
and Ezekiel had spoken of many false prophets and wicked leaders
(Jer. 23:1, 2, 9-32; Ezek. 34:1-6). Note also the change of number and
gender in the original of v. 16, indicating plurality referring to the
sheep. On the contrary, every reference to the foolish shepherd is
in the singular and masculine; even so every reference to the Good
Shepherd, Christ, symbolized by Zechariah, is masculine and singular.
This fact, together with the remarkable agreement of vv. 15-17 with
2 Thess. 2, compels this writer to regard the foolish shepherd as the
counterpart of the Good Shepherd, as the Antichrist, the man of sin,
the son of perdition, the Wicked One, as St. Paul calls him (2 Thess.
2:3, 8), the head of the Roman Papacy. In just punitive judgment
upon His apostate Church the Lord will raise up a foolishly wicked,
wickedly foolish (Gr. N.) shepherd, again symbolized by Zechariah
(v. 16). "The instruments of a shepherd," his equipment, consisted
chiefly of the staff, the shepherd's bag or scrip, in which food and
stones were placed, a sling. (Cp. 1 Sam. 17:40, 43; Ps. 23:4.) The
slovenly, dirty appearance of the equipment revealed the slovenly,
careless character of the shepherd. "In the land," here, as in v. 6;
12:12, the Holy Land, the Church. This foolish, wicked shepherd
will not visit, look about in search for (cp. 1 Sam. 20:6, "miss")
"those that be cut off" = are hidden, those who for various reasons
remain in the background, are quiet and unobtrusive, or who have
strayed from the herd and are in danger, hidden in some crevice or pit.
In contrast to the Good Shepherd (Luke 15:4-7), the foolish shepherd
is unconcerned for their welfare. Mr. Rich must be visited. Mr. Un-

known — what's the use? The "young" = inexperienced (Gr. N.), that need training (Prov. 22:6) he does not solicitously seek (same word as 12:9). We think of the Dark Ages, the illiteracy and superstition in countries dominated by the Pope. "That is broken," wounded, heartbroken under the guilt of sin, he does not heal. He refers them not to the Savior, but to human mediators, to their own efforts. Luther is not the only one who experienced this misdirection. Those who are standing firm on the Rock, on Christ and His Word, the Pope does not "feed." He does not provide for their needs. He is not like the good scribe (Matt. 13:52). He does not seek to increase their Christian knowledge as he should. (Cp. Heb. 5:12-14; 1 Peter 2:2; 2 Peter 3:18; Eph. 4:14 f.) He rather will condemn and persecute those who dare to differ with him. We think of men like Wiclif, Huss, Savonarola, Luther, of the Inquisition, etc. But he shall eat the flesh of the fat and tear their claws in pieces (Gr. N.), squeeze the last penny out of the poor deluded people, and still claim to be the vicar of Christ.

The Lord pronounces His judgment upon the "idol" shepherd (Gr. N.) (v. 17), the foolish shepherd, again significantly, not of death, but the loss of his right arm, the seat of strength, and the blinding of his right eye, the symbol of seeing, perception, wisdom. The Pope was deprived of his power to a great extent by Luther's Reformation and the open Bible, the re-establishment of the Gospel of grace through the vicarious work of Christ. His right eye is blinded. He cannot see the truth. He remains the teacher of lies and deceptions, such as the doctrine of Mary's immaculate conception, 1854; of his own infallibility in his official definitions of doctrines pertaining to faith and morals, 1870; and in 1951, the declaration of Mary's bodily assumption into heaven. He remains the Antichrist until the end of time. (Cp. 2 Thess. 2:8.)

D. The New Testament Church, Chs. 12 and 13

CHAPTER 12

1. The Lord protects His Church and leads it on to victory, vv. 1-9

1 The prophecy, the word of the LORD concerning Israel; the oracle of the LORD who stretches out the heavens, and lays the foundations of the earth, and forms the spirit of 2 man within him. Lo, I am about to make Jerusalem a bowl of intoxication for all the people round about; and also against Judah shall the siege against Jerusalem be directed. 3 And it shall come to pass on that day that I will make Jerusalem a heavy stone for all peoples. All who will try to lift it will gash themselves severely. And all the nations of the earth will be gathered

4 against her. On that day, is the oracle of the LORD, I will smite every horse with confusion, and its rider with madness, but upon the house of Judah I will open My eyes, and smite every horse of the 5 peoples with blindness. Then the princes of Judah shall say to themselves, Strength for me are the inhabitants of Jerusalem in the LORD 6 of Hosts, their God. On that day I will make the princes of Judah like a pot of fire among kindling wood and like a flaming torch among sheaves, so that they shall consume to the right and to the left, all the peoples round about, while

Jerusalem shall still throne on her 7 place, in Jerusalem. And the LORD will deliver the tents of Judah first, in order that the splendor of the house of David and the splendor of the inhabitants of Jerusalem may not exceed that of 8 Judah. On that day the LORD will protect the inhabitants of Jerusalem, and the stumbler among them shall on that day be like David, and the house of David be like God, like the Angel of the 9 LORD before them. And it shall come to pass in that day that I will seek to destroy all the nations that come against Jerusalem.

Grammatical Notes

V. 2. "Cup of trembling." The Hebrew term *saph* here denotes not the threshold (Is. 6:4; Amos 9:1; Zeph. 2:14, etc.), but bowl, basin (Ex. 12:22; 2 Sam. 17:28; 1 Kings 7:50; Jer. 52:19).— "Shall be in the siege." In the Hebrew text two expressions are fused: הָיָה מָצוֹר עַל, there shall be a siege against, and הָיָה בְּמָצוֹר, it shall be in siege. בְּמָצוֹר, one shall be in siege. There is not the slightest indication in the context that Judah shall join the enemies in the siege against Jerusalem; on the contrary, Judah throughout the context here appears as the friend and ally of Jerusalem (vv. 4-7). The clause is correctly translated in A. V.

V. 3. "Burdensome stone," מַעֲמָסָה, from a root = to lift up, carry a load; hence a stone of lifting, to be lifted in order to test one's strength, a heavy stone. — "Burden themselves" = the participle of the verb עָמַס, that are lifting, trying to lift it. — "Cut in pieces," from a root = to cut into, make incisions. The Niphal with the absolute inf. = to cut oneself a cutting, wound severely.

V. 5. "Governors," *alluphim*, the tribal heads of the Edomites (Gen. 36:15-21, 29 f., 40-43; Ex. 15:15; 1 Chron. 1:15-54); here and ch. 9:7 of the tribal heads or princes of Judah, a usage peculiar to Zechariah.

V. 1. The word of the Lord for Israel is called a "burden." See Nah. 1:1 (Gr. N.), p. 293. Here the term evidently describes not a threat, but one of the most beautiful promises of the Lord. In the introductory words the Lord emphasizes the universality of His rule. The three verbs, stretch forth, lay, form, are participial forms in the original text, denoting characteristic, habitual action. Jehovah it was who stretched out the heavens and laid the foundations of the earth and who to the end of time upholds that vast canopy with its innumerable host of luminaries and still keeps firm the foundations created millenniums ago. Jehovah it is who not only formed the body of man, but also placed into this dust of dust (Gen. 3:19) "spirit," mind, reason, understanding, which enables him to become the lord of the earth (Gen. 1:28), able to delve deep into God's miracles in physical creation and in spiritual revelation, a miracle repeated as often as a human child is born (Job 10:8 ff.; Ps. 139:13 ff.). These miracles, observable every day, proclaim aloud to all mankind the glory of Jehovah, whose unsearchable wisdom and almighty power alone can perform these miracles. Shall there be anything too hard for Him? Jer. 32:17, 27 gives the answer. Though His promises may at times seem incredible, shall human doubt and unbelief and ridicule set a limit to Jehovah's power?

V. 2. A striking promise! Jerusalem, the small, despised town, just rising out of its seventy-year-old ruins, its walls still demolished, this city is to become "a cup of trembling" (Gr. N.) to all nations, even when all the kingdoms of the earth shall be arrayed against Judah and Jerusalem. "Shall be in the siege" (Gr. N.). Judah is the Holy Land, Jerusalem the Holy City, both chosen by the Lord as His dwelling place, both being types of the New Testament Church. Satan and his hosts regard this Church as a cup easily drained and cast away. This cup, however, shall prove to be a cup of trembling to them. They shall tremble with disappointment and helpless rage at their failure to destroy the Church, with fear and terror as they behold the judgments of God coming upon the enemies of His Church. Every enemy of the Church will in time and eternity experience the truth of this divine promise to His Church. God will not have the apple of His eye, His anointed ones, touched (Zech. 2:8; Ps. 105:15-38; 73:3-9, 16-28).

V. 3 expresses the same thought. The Church will be made "a burdensome stone" (Gr. N.), a heavy stone used by athletes, young and old, to test or prove or exercise their strength by lifting or throwing or rolling it. Any attempt to lift the Church off its sure foundation (Is. 28:16; Eph. 2:20 f.) in order to destroy it is doomed to utter failure. All that "burden themselves" (Gr. N.) with it, try to lift it, will not only weary themselves in vain; they will also be "cut in pieces" (Gr. N.), will wound themselves, destroy themselves. To destroy Christ's Church is as impossible as to destroy Him that sits at the right hand of God as the Head of the Church (Ps. 2:2 ff.; 110:1 ff.). "Though" = and. The Lord once more states the universal enmity of the nations against the Church. On the underlying idea cp. Is. 8:14; 28:16; Dan. 2:34 f., 44 f.; Luke 2:34 f.; Rom. 9:32 f.

V. 4 explains v. 3. The Lord Himself destroys the enemies of His

479

Church. "Horse." The cavalry and the chariots were the most formidable means of attack and are here named as a type of the entire machinery of war directed against the Church. The horses will be smitten with "astonishment," confusion. J. M. Powis Smith in *The Complete Bible* renders it well by "staggers," a disease characterized by vertigo, causing staggering movements and sometimes falling, because of a disorder of the brain and the spinal cord. "His rider with madness," insanity. They are deprived of their reason, of the power of strategic planning, by their insane fury, their fanatic hatred of the Lord and His Church. Already the ancient heathen had a proverb: Whom the gods would destroy they first drive mad. During all this time the Lord opens His eyes upon Judah in loving care (Jer. 31:3 ff.), manifesting His kind affection by protecting His Church in the midst of fiercest attacks, delivering her from her enemies, increasing her numbers, glorifying her. This fact is brought out in v. 5 ff., after it has been stated once more that every horse, every possible source of strength of the people, the nations united against the Church, will be smitten with blindness, rendered useless.

V. 5. The "governors" (Gr. N.) of Judah are the leaders of the Church. While the enemy forces become confused, bewildered, disappointed, the leaders of God's Church are confident of victory. They can rely on the faithful co-operation of Jerusalem's citizens, the members of the Church. Throughout the world Christian fathers, mothers, and children (Ps. 8:2; Matt. 21:15 f.) lift up holy hands for their leaders in their home congregation as well as for all those men whom God has placed at the head of the Church or on the battle front in the far-flung missionary outposts. They support them also by personal contributions of money (cp. Phil. 4:10-20) and by personal mission work (cp. Acts 8:1; 11:19 ff.). In this manner they become the strength of the leaders, not, of course, because of their own strength and wisdom, but because they have dwelling in them the strength of the Lord of Hosts, their God. (Cp. Is. 45:24; 49:5; Eph. 6:10 ff.; Phil. 4:13.)

V. 6. The Church of God under the able leadership of consecrated "governors," princes of faith, will spread like wildfire and conquer the world for King Messiah. Heathendom, idolatry, superstition shall be consumed by the glorious Gospel as is wood in a "hearth of fire," in a fire pot, as are dry sheaves by flaming fire. Jerusalem, the Holy City, the Church of God, shall no longer sit in the dust, but "shall be inhabited again," rather, still shall sit like a queen on her throne (cp. Zech. 6:13) and "in her own place," literally, "on that which is

480

under her" (cp. Gr. N. on Zech. 6:12, p. 438); and the place beneath, under the Church, is all the earth, the whole world (Ps. 72:6 ff.; Dan. 2:35, 44; Zech. 2:4-6; 9:10; Matt. 28:20).

V. 7. Usually the open country and small towns of Judah were the first to be taken by the enemy. (Cp. 2 Kings 8:13-17; 2 Chron. 32:1-10; Jer. 34:7.) The citizens of Jerusalem would likely look down on the rural population, exhibit a state of mind not altogether uncommon in our day. But though Jerusalem was strongly fortified, was the royal city, the city of God's Temple, yet Judah, the Holy Land outside the city limits, was to have the honor of being the first to be delivered, so that Jerusalem would have no occasion to look down upon Judah. The Messiah was born not at Jerusalem, but at Bethlehem; He did not grow up in Jerusalem, but in Nazareth; not Jerusalem, but Capernaum and Galilee were the center of His activity, with only occasional visits at Jerusalem. In the Christian Church there is to be no superiority of city over country, of capital city over others, of large congregations over gatherings of two or three (Matt. 18:20). Not locality or size, but Christ and His Word represent the true glory of congregations and churches.

V. 8. The Lord will not forget Jerusalem, His Church. He will defend it, cover it as with a shield, so that no enemy can destroy it. "He that is feeble," literally, that stumbles, is lame, shall be as David, the victorious youth (1 Sam. 17:32-53). Even the prayers of babes and sucklings shall be like a strong wall about the Church and homes (Ps. 8:2; Matt. 21:15, 16). "The house of David shall be as God," for out of this house came forth He who is the Mighty God, the Everlasting Father (Is. 9:6, 7), the Lord Our Righteousness (Jer. 23:5, 6). Note, again the Angel of the Lord is placed on the same level with God. The Church, its members and its leaders, shall be equipped with the strength of the Lord (Eph. 6:10; 2 Cor. 12:9 f.; Phil. 4:13; Rom. 8:37).

V. 9. "I will seek," will make it My object, My point, to destroy all the nations that come against Jerusalem. If God be for us, who can be against us? (Rom. 8:31.)

---

2. The outpouring of the Holy Ghost and repentant turning to the pierced Lord,
vv. 10-14

10 And I will pour out upon the house of David and upon the inhabitants of Jerusalem the Spirit of grace and supplications; and they shall look upon Me whom they have pierced, and shall lament for Him as the lamentations for an only child; and they shall weep bitterly for Him, the bitter weeping for the 11 firstborn. On that day there shall

481

be a great mourning in Jerusalem, like the lamentation at Hadad-Rimmon in the plains of Megiddo.
12 And the land shall mourn, each family by itself; the family of the house of David by itself, and their women by themselves; the family of the house of Nathan by itself,

and their women by themselves; 13 the family of the house of Levi by itself, and their women by themselves; the family of the house of Shimei by itself, and their women 14 by themselves. All the families remaining, each family by itself and their women by themselves.

Grammatical and Textual Notes

V. 10. "Supplications." The Hebrew term is derived from a root = "to be favorably inclined, gracious." Hiphil, "to ask for grace or favor, beseech" (Gen. 42:21; Esther 4:8; 8:3; Hos. 12:5, A. V., 4). — "Upon Me." Sellin: "The Masoretic reading אֵלַי [unto Me], which could only refer to Jehovah, is of course [natuerlich] impossible; for then we would have to find עָלַי in the next clause. — On the basis of LXX (Lucian) and John 19:37, which presuppose only אֲשֶׁר אֵלַי, the אֵת correctly has been regarded as a variant to אֵלַי, a poetic form of אֶל, found in Job 3:22; 5:26; 15:22; 29:19, a variant possible

since הִבִּיט may be construed with the accusative or with אֶל. — Hence אֵת is to be deleted and the clause to be translated, 'Upon Him whom they have pierced.'" (Zwoelfprophetenbuch, p. 574 f.) Yet all extant Hebrew manuscripts read אֵלַי. Rahlf's edition of LXX does not adopt Lucian's reading, does not even mention it, but reads πρὸς μέ, upon Me. And John 19:37 is not a literal quotation of Zech. 12:10, but an adaptation like Rev. 1:7. Sellin regards the pierced person as the shepherd referred to in 11:4-13; 13:7, Onias III; see pp. 467 f., 490. There is no need of changing the translation of the A. V.

Vv. 10-14 no longer speak of the defeat of the hostile nations, but of the streams of grace which Jehovah sheds on the Church of the New Testament. The day of Pentecost is foretold, which was to usher in the New Testament era (vv. 11-14) and on which the blessed fruits of Good Friday (v. 10 b) would begin to become publicly manifest.

V. 10. In the Old Covenant, kings (1 Sam. 10:1; 15:1, 17; 16: 1, 3, 16; 2 Sam. 20:19), priests (Ex. 40:12-15; 28:41), sometimes prophets (1 Kings 19:15 f.), were anointed. This anointing symbolized the gift of the Spirit of God. See Is. 61:1, where the Messiah says that His preaching of the Gospel was the result of His being anointed with the Spirit of the Lord God before He began His public ministry. (Cp. Acts 10:38; Matt. 3:16 f.; Mark 1:10, 14; Luke 3:22; John 1:32 f. See also 1 Sam. 10:6, 9-11, 26 f.; 11:6-15; 16:14-23; Zech. 4:11-14.) In the New Testament the Spirit of the Lord will be poured out not only on the houses of David and Levi, representing the kings and priests of Israel, but also on all "the inhabitants of Jerusalem," here, as in v. 1 ff., on the members of the Christian Church, hence on all believers, men and women, young and old (Joel 2:28 f.; Acts 2:16-38; 7:55; 8:14 ff.; 9:17, 31; 10:44 ff.), all being kings and priests before God (1 Peter 2:5, 9; Rev. 1:6). God will "pour," give not sparingly, but in full measure. The Holy Spirit with His gifts (cp. Is. 11:2) will fill the heart and soul of the believers, will permeate their entire nature. This Spirit is here called "the Spirit of grace and of supplications." Grace is divine loving-kindness, redeeming, justifying, sanctifying grace, procured for all mankind by the Messiah (Is. 53:11 f.; John 1:16 f.; 1 Cor. 1:30) and appropriated to believers by the Holy Spirit (Ps. 51:10 ff.; 143:10; Prov. 1:23; Ezek. 36:25 ff.; 1 Cor. 6:11). "Supplications" (Gr. N.), pleadings for grace, prayers, flowing from the experience and appreciation of God's grace. (Cp. Acts 9:11, "Behold, he prayeth.") Cherishing this grace as the greatest gift of God, the believer makes it the chief object of his prayers and approaches the Throne of Grace in childlike confidence, telling his Father all his sorrows and worries. This grace makes him sure that his Father will hear him and grant his prayer in the manner and at the time the Father's grace and wisdom chooses. Such prayer is taught by the Holy Spirit, who at the same time prays in and with the believer (Rom. 8:26 f.).

Now a remarkable statement is added. The Lord Jehovah speaks of Himself as having been pierced by men who shall look upon Him and shall mourn for Him. The word pierce = thrust through, occurs nine times of a thrust by a sword or spear (Num. 25:8; Judg. 9:54; 1 Sam. 31:4; 1 Chron. 10:4; Is. 13:15; Jer. 37:10, "wounded"; 51:4; Zech. 12:10; 13:3); it occurs once as pierced by pangs of hunger described as more painful than a sword thrust (Lam. 4:9). Jehovah, I AM THAT I AM, pierced by an instrument of death wielded by human beings! That is impossible, say many commentators and change the text (Gr. N.). Yet what human reason cannot understand is clearly stated here by Him who has created man's spirit (v. 1). And He demands that His creature bring into captivity every thought to the obedience of Christ (2 Cor. 10:5), whose Spirit testified beforehand the sufferings of Christ (1 Peter 1:11). This Spirit through His apostle reveals to us the actual fulfillment of this strange prophecy. More than 500 years later the Lord used a Roman soldier as the unwitting agent to fulfill this prophecy (John 19:34, 37). And the water and blood which flowed from the side of Him who was already dead (v. 33) proved beyond doubt that this Pierced One was the Prince of Life, Jehovah Our Righteousness (Jer. 23:6; Acts 3:15; 1 John 5:5-12, 20).— "Look upon *Me*," "mourn for *Him*" (Gr. N.). As Christ says, "I and the Father," distinguishing two persons, yet adding at once "are One" (John 10:30; cp. John 14:9 ff.). So here Jehovah speaks of the Messiah as of a different person who nevertheless is One with Him in the undivided and indivisible Essence of Jehovah. Cp. Deut. 32:39; Is. 48:12; I am He = Jehovah, the First and the Last. Yet He calls Himself the Messenger of the Lord God and His Spirit (v. 16). Indeed, without controversy great is the mystery not only of godliness (1 Tim. 3:16) but also of the Godhead, the sole Author of true godliness (Is. 40:18, 25).

Another great miracle: The same persons who had despised and rejected Him (Is. 53:3) had killed the Prince of Life (Acts 3:15; 1 Cor. 2:8), had brought about His piercing, now "look" upon Him whom they have pierced. "Look," here = look attentively, hopefully, trustingly. (See Num. 21:9, "beheld"; 1 Sam. 16:7, "look not"; Is. 8:22, "look"; 22:8, 11; 51:1, 2, etc.) As they realize the enormity of their sin, they mourn in bitter anguish for Him, as parents lament bitterly the death of an only child or a first-born son. This lamentation began on the same day they had pierced the Lord (Luke 23:47 f.) and will continue throughout the New Testament era, as the next verses state.

Vv. 11-14. The universality, continuity, and personality of repentance.

V. 11. "In that day," the age of Messiah's Kingdom of Grace. (See vv. 3, 4, 6, 8 f.) "In Jerusalem" (v. 11), the Holy City, "the land" (v. 12), the Holy Land, both names symbolizing, as in vv. 2, 5, 6, 7, the Christian Church, throughout which, as long as it continues on earth, the repentant mourning connected with the believing look toward Him who was pierced, shall continue. In point of bitterness and universality it is compared to that at Hadad-Rimmon in the Valley of Megiddon.

Hadad-Rimmon is the name of a Babylonian and Aramaean weather deity. (Cp. 2 Kings 5:18.) Both names were also personal names, Hadad (Gen. 36:35 f.; 1 Chron. 1:46 f.; 1 Kings 11:14-25), Edomites; Rimmon (= pomegranate, Num. 20:5; Deut. 8:18) is the name of several cities (Joshua 15:32; 1 Chron. 4:32; 6:62; Zech. 14:10), of a rock (Judg. 20:45-47). The idea that Hadad-Rimmon here refers to the worship of the Syrian deity whose cult was similar to that of Adonis, or Tammuz (Ezek. 8:14), is preposterous. No prophet of Jehovah would take such an abominable, immoral rite as an emblem of the Church's penitential mourning. There is no valid reason to doubt Jerome's statement that Hadad-Rimmon was a city near Jezreel in the plain of Megiddo, called Maximianopolis in his day. Modern archaeologists have identified it with Rummane, north of Nazareth, about 1½ miles northwest of Taanek. (See Map VIII, *Westminster Atlas*.)

At Megiddo, pious King Josiah was slain by Pharaoh Necho (2 Kings 23: 29 ff.; 2 Chron. 35: 20 ff.). He was the first king of Judah to fall in battle and leave his country at the mercy of foreign conquerors. (Cp. 2 Kings 23: 31-35; 24: 1 ff.; 2 Chron. 36: 1-7, 10-20.) His death was a catastrophic loss for Judah, for with him had passed away (2 Kings 22: 15-26) the last bulwark against the flood of wickedness which now swept through the land and carried it to its destruction. The entire nation lamented Josiah's death, and by official decree an annual day of mourning was appointed, still observed when the Book of Chronicles was written (2 Chron. 35: 24 f.). Hadad-Rimmon is named as the place or one of the places of such mourning perhaps because it afforded a view of the battlefield, or Josiah may have died here when, mortally wounded, he was being rushed to Jerusalem (2 Kings 23: 29 ff.; 2 Chron. 35: 22 ff.).

V. 12. "The land," the Holy Land, the Church, "every family apart," for itself. So the Israelites had pitched their tents in the wilderness round about the Tabernacle, the center of worship; and so they had marched on their journey to the Holy Land, "every one after their families" (Num. 2: 2, 34), yet one nation. So the prophet sees the Church "in that day," in the New Testament era, as the members of God's people mourn for the Pierced One. No family and no individual will be satisfied to have others mourn in their stead. There is no vicarious mourning or substitutionary repentance in God's Church. Zechariah names men more highly honored than any other Israelite: David, the ancestor of the royal house (2 Sam. 7: 12 f.), and Levi, the forefather of the priesthood (Ex. 32: 26-29; Deut. 33: 8-11). Yet side by side with them he names men, descendants of royalty and of Levitical parentage, yet men of whom nothing but their names are known, Nathan, a son of David, an ancestor of Zerubbabel (Luke 3: 27, 31), and Shimei, the grandson of Levi (Num. 3: 17 f.). As four men are named (vv. 12, 13), so four times their "wives," the women of each family, are mentioned. (Cp. 2 Chron. 35: 25, "singing men and singing women"; also Ex. 15: 20, 21; Judg. 11: 34, 38-40; 1 Sam. 18: 6 f.) In their prayers and supplications before the throne of God all believers are equal; none receives special privileges or priorities because of rank or influence or sex. Each man and each woman individually, and all alike, confess their sin and unworthiness. Their

485

sins have pierced and slain the Lord Jehovah. Every individual feels his own personal guilt; all alike look with the eyes of faith to the Pierced Lord for their salvation. On all alike and each one individually is poured out the Spirit of God; all alike are children of God, sons and daughters of Jehovah, kings and queens, priests and priestesses (1 Peter. 2: 5, 9). Lest anyone fear that by naming the four families (vv. 12, 13) his own family is excluded, the prophet adds v. 14: "all the families that remain, together with their women." All mankind needs the grace and salvation of the Lord; and this grace and salvation is universal, ready for all.

CHAPTER 13

3. Justification and sanctification of the Church, vv. 1-6

1 On that day there shall be a fountain opened for the house of David and for the inhabitants of Jerusalem for sin and uncleanness. And
2 it shall come to pass on that day, is the oracle of the LORD of Hosts, that I will cut off the names of the idols from the land, and they shall no longer be remembered. And I will drive also the prophets and the spirit of uncleanness out of the
3 land. So it shall come to pass that, if any one still prophesies, his father and his mother will say to him, You shall not live, for you have spoken lies in the name of the LORD. And his father and mother that begot him shall stab him while
4 he is prophesying. And it shall come to pass on that day that the prophets will be ashamed, each of his vision while he is prophesying, so that they will not put on a hairy
5 garment in order to deceive; but he will say, No prophet am I! A tiller of the soil am I! For a man
6 has bought me in my youth. And when someone says to him, What are these wounds between your hands? then he will say, Those with which I was wounded in the house of my friends.

Grammatical Notes

V. 1. "There shall be." יִהְיֶה, the imperfect denotes progressive duration, fresh waters every day, new mercies every morning (Lam. 3: 22 f.), throughout the era of "that day." — "Fountain," מָקוֹר, from a stem = to dig, denotes a natural spring that has been dug out for easier access to its waters, a reservoir, large or small, fed by a spring. — "Sin," from a root חָטָא = to miss the mark, fail to reach the goal (Qal. Prov. 8:36; 19:2; Job 5:24; Is. 65:20; Hi., Judg. 20:16), denotes sin as a missing of the goal, as coming short of full obedience to God's Law (cp. Deut. 22:26; James 2:10) with all its dreadful consequences (cp. Gen.

4:13; Prov. 8:36; Zech. 14:19). — "Uncleanness," נִדָּה, from a root נָדַד = to flee, chase away, abominate (Nah. 3:7; Ps. 31:12; Hos. 7:13) or נָדָה = to remove, repel, excommunicate (Amos 6:3; Is. 66:5), hence the noun = something repulsive, abominable, unclean, filthy (Lev. 15:19 f.; Ezek. 7:19 f.; Lam. 1:17; Ezra 9:11).

V. 2. "Unclean spirit." רוּחַ הַטֻּמְאָה, from a root טָמֵא = to be unclean, of Levitical uncleanness (Lev. 5:2; 11:24-40, etc.), moral defilement (Lev. 18:20, 23; Ezek. 22:3 f.; Micah 2:10, etc.). The leper's cry, "Unclean, unclean!" = טָמֵא (Lev.

13:45). The noun occurs frequently in Levitical legislation; practically a synonym of *niddah*.

V. 4. "Rough." שֵׂעָר = hair (Lev. 13:3 f., 10, 20-37; Cant. 4:1; 6:5). The adjective, *sa'ir*, occurs in Gen. 27:11, 23. "Garment," אַדֶּרֶת, from a root = to be great, splendid, hence "glory" (Zech. 11:3), "goodly" (Ezek. 17:8), denotes the Babylonian "mantle" (Joshua 7:21, 24), the royal "robe" (Jonah 3:6). The same combination occurs in Gen. 25:25: "hairy garment," garment of hair. It does not denote a pelt or skin (עוֹר, Gen. 3:21; 27:16; Lev. 4:11; 8:17, etc.), but a mantle, a cloak. "In a rabbinical discussion on Gen. 3:21, *Bereshith rabba*, end of ch. 20, garments woven from the hair of camels, rabbits, or goats are mentioned as distinguished from various kinds of pelts or skins. To obtain a somewhat softer material, sheep wool was added to camel's hair in varying proportions." (Theodor Zahn, *Evang. Matth.*, ch. 3:1-6, p. 129.) The only persons mentioned in the Bible as wearing such hairy garments are Elijah (2 Kings 1:8), his successor, Elisha (2 Kings 2:13 f.), and John the Baptist, the second Elijah (Mal. 4:5; Matt. 3:4; Mark 1:6).

V. 5. "Husbandman," אִישׁ עֹבֵד אֲדָמָה, a man serving as a slave of the soil, a farmer. "Taught me to keep cattle," הִקְנַנִי, from קָנָה, to acquire by purchase, Hiphil = to sell, give into possession; cp. מִקְנַת כָּסֶף, a slave obtained by money (Gen. 17:12 f., 23, 27; Ex. 12:44).

V. 6. "In thine hands," בֵּין = between; here, the area from one hand up the arm, across the breast and down the other hand. (Cp. "between the eyes" = the forehead, Ex. 13:9, 16; Deut. 6:8; 11:18; 14:1.) — "My friends." The Piel participle of אָהַב is used only of illicit lovers or friends, idols (Hos. 2:7-15), idolatrous allies (Ezek. 16:33-37; 23:5, 9, 22; Jer. 22:20-22; Lam. 1:19). Here either idolaters or wicked, immoral, dissolute associates, male and female.

V. 1. "In that day," the Messianic era, "there shall be" (Gr. N.) "a fountain" (Gr. N.), not a hidden wellspring, but one dug out, prepared by digging a pool or reservoir, so that people may have access to its refreshing waters. The term is never used of cisterns or stagnant pools. (Cp. the contrast, Jer. 2:13.) It always denotes a reservoir fed by a wellspring, whose waters are always fresh. Etymologically the term indicates a special preparation, abundant supply, accessibility. The idea of ample supply of fresh water is especially clear, e. g., Ps. 36:9; 68:26; Prov. 13:14; 18:4; Jer. 2:13; 9:1; 17:13. The idea of preparation, "digging," Jer. 9:1, where the prophet asks that his eyes be made into a fountain, since they were not sufficient to furnish enough tears for his woe.

This fountain was prepared, dug, by the Lord Our Righteousness when He cried: "It is finished!" (John 19:30.) By His vicarious suffering and death that fountain, filled with blood drawn from Immanuel's veins, was opened. True, already in the Old Testament the believer obtained forgiveness (Lev. 1:4, 9, 13; 2:2, 9; 16:16, 22-34; 2 Sam. 12:13; Ps. 32:5; Is. 1:18), but none of the rites and ceremonies instituted for this purpose had the power to forgive sins inherent in itself. They could grant remission only because of the retroactive power of the blood of the Eternal High Priest (Heb. 9:7-15). This fountain is "opened" (Gr. N.), made accessible to all men. No barriers are erected, no guards posted, no tollgates required, in order to discourage men or make it impossible to come to this fountain. As the promise of forgiveness and salvation already in the Old Testament was universal (Gen. 3:15; 12:3; 22:18; Is. 55:1, etc.), so the Lord has made His forgiveness available to all men in His Word (Matt. 9:2-6; 2 Cor. 5:18-21; 1 Peter 1:25), in Baptism (Matt. 28:19; Acts 2:38; 22:16; Titus 3:5,6; 1 Peter 3:21), in the Holy Supper (Matt. 26:27 f.).

In a special sense this fountain is opened to the "house of David and the inhabitants of Jerusalem," the Church of God and its leaders, irrespective of rank or riches or sex. (Cp. 12:12-14.) This fountain is here described as a special gift of God to His Church, as Luther so aptly says in his explanation of the Third Article: "In which Christian Church He daily and richly forgives all sins to me and all believers." Cp. 1 Tim. 4:10, "specially of those that believe," who already are enjoying through faith the fullness of forgiveness promised to, and procured for, all mankind.

"For sin and for uncleanness." "Sin" (Gr. N.), every missing of the mark from the slightest transgression in thought or desire (Ps. 19:12; 90:8), to the most horrible crime (Eph. 5:3-5; Gal. 5:19 ff.). "Uncleanness" describes these sins in their effect, as defiling man, rendering him repulsive to God, an abomination to Him. (Cp. Is. 64:6; Amos 5:21 f.) Yet for every missing of the mark and for every guilty stain there is cleansing, washing, forgiveness (Is. 1:18; 1 Cor. 6:9 ff.; Eph. 2:5 ff.; 1 John 1:7; 2:2). The terms "sin" and "uncleanness" remind of certain O. T. rites and ceremonies. "For sin," cp. the cleansing of the Levites (Num. 8:5-22) by the water of purifying (v. 7), literally, water of sin = for removal of sin, sprinkled upon them at their installation into office. "For uncleanness," cp. Num. 19:1-22. The ashes of a red heifer were mixed with the water to be used as a water of "separation" (vv. 9, 13, 20); literally, water of, or for, uncleanness (same word as in Zech. 13:1), cleansing from defilement incurred by touching a dead body (Num. 19:11-22).

Vv. 2, 3. A second gift of the Lord to His Church. Those whom He has justified by forgiving their sin He also sanctifies. Sin is the result of failing to love God above all things, placing the desire of one's own flesh, the pleasures and seeming advantages of sin above God's will. Therefore, in sanctifying man the Lord goes to the root of the matter by removing from man's heart every form of idolatry, from actual worship of wood and stone images to the most subtle form of serving sin or self. The very names of idols as objects of worship will be forgotten. These names are today of archaeological interest only to Christians; a reminder of heathen folly and super-stition. No child of God would think to call on Baal, or Jupiter, or Wodan, for help in time of trouble.

Another item of God's sanctification of the Church, in intimate connection with the removal of idolatry, is the abolition of false prophecy, false teaching. Zechariah does not, as, e. g., Sellin holds, foretell the complete cessation of all prophecy. There were prophets in the New Testament era. (Cp. Acts 2:17; 11:27; 13:1; 15:32; 19:6; 21:9 f.; 1 Cor. 11:4 f., etc.) Zechariah places the prophets he has in mind on the same line with idolaters and the unclean spirit. Their desire to prophesy even without divine commission, or their claim to such commission, was the evidence of their uncleanness (Gr. N.), of one who refuses to be purified from all selfishness and deceit. His own parents (v. 3), placing the obedience and love to God above their parental affection, would slay him as God has commanded (Deut. 13: 1-10; 18:20). Israel in the Old Testament was a church-state, in which the entire Mosaic Law of God with all its moral, ceremonial, social, and political requirements was the state Law, and every transgression of this Law in any of its demands was a crime against the state Law and to be punished by the state in the manner prescribed by the divine Law. In the New Testament the Church has no longer the right of capital punishment. Stubborn and impenitent sinners are to be excommunicated (Matt. 18:17), declared to be "as an heathen man" (Eph. 2:1, 5, 11 ff.), an even severer punishment than temporal death.

Vv. 4-6. So completely will false prophecy be in disrepute that the prophets themselves will be ashamed of their visions which they had proclaimed in their fanatic frenzy, during which they had slashed and mutilated their bodies with knives (v. 6; cp. 1 Kings 18:28). They will no longer wear a rough garment to deceive. The only prophet who according to the Biblical record wore a rough garment (Gr. N.), a cloak of camel's hair, is Elijah, who among the many prophets of his day (1 Kings 18:4, 13) was identified by his mantle (2 Kings 1:7 f.). Hence it could hardly have been the garment commonly worn by the prophets as a specifically prophetic garb. When Elijah ascended to heaven, his mantle fell from him and was taken by Elisha. This mantle caused the sons of the prophets to recognize in him the successor to

Elijah (2 Kings 2:9-15), just as his raiment of camel's hair served to identify John the Baptist as the second Elijah (Matt. 3:4; 11:14; Mal. 4:5). The false prophets of Zechariah's time, wearing a mantle of camel's hair, were aping Elijah, the great leader among Israel's prophets, posing as his successors. Aping the dress, the manners, the peculiarities of great men, does not make anyone their equal, but rather betrays his own meanness and insignificance.

Seeking to disassociate himself completely from the prophetic profession, the false prophet declares vehemently, Not a prophet am I! A husbandman am I! (v. 5), literally, a man serving as a slave of the soil. He could not possibly be a prophet, even if he were so inclined. From his early youth he has been a bond servant, sold into such menial service by a parent, or an owner of his enslaved parents, who could not pay his debt and was sold into slavery together with his family. (Cp. Gen. 14:14; 17:12, 23, "born in the house" = a slave; Ex. 21:2-6; Lev. 25:25 ff.; Jer. 34:8-16; Matt. 18:25.) As such a slave, all his time belonged to his master. How could he possibly be a prophet roaming about at will from city to city? Unconvinced, the inquisitive questioner asks, What about the wounds "in thine hands" (Gr. N.) (v. 6), on your arms and body? (Cp. 1 Kings 18:28.) Rather than confess himself a prophet, he professes to have received the wounds in some drunken brawl with his "friends" (Gr. N.), his dissolute associates. What a difference between these contemptible, cowardly deceivers and the man they tried to ape, the noble, courageous Elijah! (See 1 Kings 17:1 ff.; 18:1 ff., 17-40; 21:17-24; cp. also Jer. 26:1-16; 28:1-17.)

---

4. The Shepherd smitten, the sheep scattered and gathered, v. 7

7 Arise, O sword, against My Shepherd, and against the Man, My Associate! is the oracle of the LORD of Hosts. Smite the Shepherd, and the flock shall be scattered, and I will turn My hand back upon the little ones.

Grammatical Notes

V. 7. "And against." "And" here explanatory. (Cp. 1 Sam. 17:40, "even"; Amos 3:11, "even"; Ex. 24:12, "and a law" = namely; Ex. 25:12; Judg. 17:3; G.-K. 154 a, Note 1 b.) — "The man." גֶּבֶר denotes the male as the stronger sex (Ex. 10:11; 12:37; Judg. 5:30; Jer. 41:16, etc.). — "My Fellow," עֲמִיתִי, from עָמָה = עָמַם, to join, connect. (Cp. preposition עִם, "with"; adverb and preposition עֻמָּה, close to, at the side.) Ex. 25:27 and 28:27 have "over against"; Lev. 3:9, "hard by"; Ezek. 3:8, "against" = like, equal to. An עָמִית may be a "neighbor," one living nigh, near, next to another, or a friend united by bonds of friendship. (Cp. Lev. 19:15; 25:14 f., 17.) In Lev. 19:17 and 25:14 it is a synonym of "brother"; in Lev. 5:21 (A. V., 6:2), one so close to you that he trusts you implicitly. — "Turn his hand upon" (Ps. 81:5; Is. 1:25; Jer. 6:9; Ezek. 38:12; Amos 1:8). "The phrase means to make something or someone once more the object of one's attention" (Hengstenberg on Ezek. 38:12). Hence a *vox media*. Here, as Matt. 26:31 f. indicates, it denotes the loving care of the Lord.— "Little ones" = participle plural of a root = to be small, humble. Cp. Jer. 30:19; Job 14:21, in both passages the opposite of glorified, hence, overlooked, despised.

V. 7. As the prophet in disgust turns away from these miserable wretches, the Lord honors His faithful servant by granting him another vision of Him whose death will open the fountain of life (v. 1). He sees the Shepherd about to be pierced (ch. 12:10), smitten by the sword of divine judgment. The Lord summons the sword not in defense of the Shepherd, but to awake, rise up, against God's Shepherd, still acknowledged as such by the Lord who had appointed Him and who calls Him "My Shepherd." "And against the man." "And" (Gr. N.) here explanatory, defining more clearly the nature of this Shepherd. He is not a mere human shepherd. He is Jehovah's "Fellow" (Gr. N.), His Associate, close to, next to the Lord, as the Second Person in the Trinity, corresponding to Him, One with Him in essence (Prov. 8:30, "by" = at his side; Ex. 23:21; Jer. 23:6; John 10:30; 14:9-11). Jehovah, the Lord of Hosts, the World Ruler, pronounces the death sentence upon Him who like Him is Jehovah. "Smite," slay Him; same word as in Is. 53:4, because the Lord had laid on His "Fellow" the iniquity of us all (Is. 53:6, 8, 10, 12; 2 Cor. 5:19 ff.). The death sentence was pronounced by the enemies, whose sole purpose was to get rid of the man (John 11:46-50, 53); but it was the Lord who used these wicked men as His instruments in carrying out His eternal counsel of redemption (Is. 53:10-12; John 11:51 f.). Very significantly, however, the Lord addresses the sword, not the enemies as if He sanctioned their sinful act and their wicked purpose. He, the great, the mighty God, the Lord of Hosts — how wonderful, how unsearchable, how utterly past finding out are His counsels!

"The sheep shall be scattered." A clear prophecy of the offense taken by the disciples when Christ was smitten. So Christ Himself interprets these words (Matt. 26:31; Mark 14:27). They were fulfilled (see Matt. 26:56; Mark 14:50 ff.). Yet the Lord would not forsake the sheep. The Lord Himself, acting in and through the person of His "Fellow" (John 5:19 f., 30), will turn His hand upon (Gr. N.), come to the aid of the little ones (Gr. N.), His despondent, terrified disciples (Luke 24:4 f., 11, 17 ff., 37; John 20:2, 11 ff., 19, 26). These weaklings and deserters became the courageous, invincible heralds of the

491

Messiah's kingdom. Cp. Book of Acts. The history of the New Testament Church is the story of "little ones" doing unbelievably great things through the power of the Savior's might.

---

5. God's judgments either cleansing or consuming, vv. 8, 9

8 And it shall come to pass in the whole earth, is the oracle of the LORD, that two parts within it shall be cut off, and die, and the third part shall remain within her.
9 And I will bring the third part through the fire, and I will refine them as silver is refined and test them as gold is tested. They will call upon My name, and I Myself will answer them. I will say, This is My people, and they will say, Jehovah is my God!

Grammatical Notes

V. 8. "Two parts," פִּי־שְׁנַיִם, literally, two mouthfuls, portions, the right of the first-born, inheriting a portion double that of any other child (Deut. 21:17; 2 Kings 2:9). Death claims this right. — גָּוַע denotes the infirmity of old age, wasting away, one of the penalties of man's sin (cp. Gen. 25:8, 17; 35:29; 49:33); most frequently = death as divine judgment (Gen. 6:17; 7:21; Num. 16:26 ff.; 20:3; Joshua 22:20; Lam. 1:19, etc.).

Vv. 8, 9. Not all who are invited to the Kingdom enter it. "Two parts" (Gr. N.), two thirds, shall be cut off; not because they were predestinated to eternal damnation, for there is no such horrible decree. (Cp. Ezek. 33:11; 2 Cor. 5:18 ff.; 1 Tim. 2:4, 6; 2 Peter 3:9; 1 John 2:2.) They refuse to accept the Messiah as their Savior-Shepherd (Acts 2:13; 4:12; 13:45; 17:18, 32; 1 Cor. 1:18-31; 2 Thess. 1:8; Mark 16:16). "And die" (Gr. N.). Since they refuse to accept Christ as the Prince of Life, their whole life will be a wasting away, continuing in spiritual death, without Christ, without God, without hope in this world, until they are swallowed up by eternal death. "The third shall be left therein," the remnant (Is. 1:9; 10:20 ff.). They will be brought "through the fire" (v. 9) = tribulation, sorrow, sickness, persecution, poverty, even death. Yet the fire will not consume them. It is a fire sent by the Lord and controlled by Him and His good and gracious will. It will serve as a refining fire, purging them, as silver and gold are cleansed from dross. When finally they issue forth from the furnace on the Last Day, they shall be free from all imperfections (Eph. 5:27; 1 Peter 1:5 ff.). In the midst of the fire they will call on the Lord's name, and He will hear them. They are God's covenant people, and the Lord of unchanging grace is their Covenant God. (Cp. Ex. 19:6; 24:8; Jer. 30:22; 31:9, 33; Ezek. 37:27; Zech. 8:8.)

CHAPTER 14

E. The Coming of the Lord for Judgment and Salvation

1. Jerusalem ravished and rescued, vv. 1-7

1 Behold, a day is coming for the LORD when your spoil shall be
2 divided in your midst; and I will gather all the nations against Jerusalem for battle, and the city shall be taken, and the houses plundered, and the women ravished. And half the city shall go into exile, but the rest of the people shall not be cut off from the city.
3 Then the LORD shall go forth and war against these nations as on the day when He battles in the day of
4 warfare. And on this day His feet shall stand on the Mount of Olives, which faces Jerusalem on the east, and the Mount of Olives shall be split in two from east to west into a very large valley, and one half of the mountain shall move northward
5 and the other half southward. Then you shall flee to My mountain valley, for the mountain valley shall extend to Azal, and you shall flee as you fled from the earthquake in the days of Uzziah, king of Judah. And the LORD, my God, shall come! All His saints with Him!
6 And it shall come to pass on this day that there shall be no light,
7 the luminaries shall shrink. And it shall be a singular day — it is known to the Lord — neither day nor night; and it shall come to pass that at evening time it shall be light.

Grammatical Notes

V. 1. "The day of the Lord cometh," יוֹם בָּא לַיהוָה = A day comes for Jehovah. The M. T. correctly joins יוֹם to בָּא by Merkah. — "Spoil divided." The phrase usually denotes the division of the spoil of a city after its capture. (See Is. 9:2, A. V., 3; Amos 7:17; Micah 2:4.)

V. 2. "Residue," יֶתֶר, here as in Micah 5:2 (A. V., 3); Zeph. 2:9 = the elect, God's chosen people (cp. v. 16 and ch. 13:8).

V. 4. "Mount of Olives" is the central peak of a ridge extending about a mile from north to south, opposite Jerusalem and overtopping it, varying from ca. 2,400 feet to 2,715 feet. The Mount of Olives rises ca. 2,640 feet, while the Kidron Valley at its foot is about 2,275 feet above sea level. (Measurements made by Gust. Dalman, cp. his *Orte und Wege Jesu*, p. 224 f.) According to the *Westminster Historical Atlas*, Jerusalem is 2,593 feet above sea level, a descent of ca. 300 feet to the valley and an ascent of almost 400 feet to the top of Mount Olivet. This made escape to the east a very difficult task.

V. 5. "The valley of the mountains" = *ge harai*, My mountains, prepared by Jehovah, My mountain valley. — "Azal," cp. Beth-ezel, Micah 1:11. Beth is sometimes omitted in city names. Cp. Beth-Aven = Aven, Ezek. 30:17; Beth-Geder = Geder, 1 Chron. 2:51; Joshua 12:13; Beth-Nimrah = Nimrah, Num. 32:3, 36, etc.

V. 6. "Not clear nor dark." LXX, "There will be no light and cold and ice." Others, "There will be no light, but cold and ice." Since neither translation is acceptable, the opposite of light being not cold, but darkness, Kittel, *Bibl. Hebr.*, suggests to "read קוּר for אוֹר, cp. Gen. 8:22." There is no need for this change nor to read "and" cold, "and" ice with LXX. יְקָרוֹת is the feminine plural of the frequently recurring יָקָר = heavy, costly, precious, splendid, bright. Cp. Job 31:26, "the moon walking in brightness," splendor. The fem.

pl. is frequently used to denote abstract nouns. Cp. Gen. 42:7, 30, A. V., "roughly" = hard, harsh words; 2 Kings 25:28, A. V., "kindly" = good things or words; Ps. 16:6, "pleasant places" or things. (G.-K. 122 g.) Hence, bright, splendid things, luminaries, sun, moon, and stars. יִקְפָּאוּן, the K'tib is to be pointed *yiqqapheun*, the Q'ri demands *w'kippaon*, ice, frost, a word not occurring elsewhere. קָפָא occurs twice in Qal, in Ex. 15:8, "the depths were congealed," and in Zeph. 1:12, "settled," thickened, "on their lees," of wine becoming oily, turbid, full of sediment, syruplike; once in Hiphil, in Job 10:10, of milk curdling, solidifying, to form cheese. In every instance it denotes a drawing together, thickening, solidifying, losing some of the characteristic attributes or functions. Zechariah uses this term of the bright things, the luminaries drawing together, contracting themselves, losing their characteristic brightness, their functions of being light bearers. They cease to shine, grow dim, so that dusk, gloom, darkness takes the place of light on the earth. This suits the context and is in full keeping with the etymological meaning of the terms.

V. 7. "One day," אֶחָד, here = singular, unique, only one. (Cp. v. 9; Deut. 6:4; 2 Kings 19:15; Ezek. 7:5; Cant. 6:9.)

Vv. 1-5. "Behold" introduces another noteworthy period in the history of the New Testament Church. "The day of the LORD" (Gr. N.), rather, A day is, or comes, for the Lord. The Lord it is who brings on this day, He knows its purpose, its nature, its duration. He it is whose glory it must serve. (Cp. Ezek. 39:11-13; Is. 2:11, 17.) On this day Jehovah's justice and judgment as well as His grace and mercy (cp. Jehovah's name, Ex. 34:5-7) shall be manifested in a manner far surpassing human understanding. God's punitive justice also on that day begins at the house of God, His Church (1 Peter 4:17; Jer. 25:29; Ezek. 9:6). As He called the heathen nations to battle against Jerusalem (Jer. 1:11 f.), so He will turn over the Jerusalem of "that day," the New Testament Church, to the hostile bands under the leadership of Satan (v. 2), because she had left her first love and had become lukewarm (Rev. 2:4; 3:16). The enemy will take the city and divide her spoils (Gr. N.). The Church will be deprived of her most precious treasures, the purity of the Gospel of forgiveness through the all-sufficient merits of her Savior King. The houses are rifled, every home invaded and looted, the women ravished, all the horrible excesses of savage warfare will be inflicted on the Church. One half of the people are carried off into captivity as slaves of the enemy. Yet it will not be a complete annihilation of the city. There will be a residue (Gr. N. Cp. 1 Kings 19:18; Is. 1:9; 10:20 ff.). The little flock of God's chosen saints will not be cut off from the city. There will still remain a Church of God even in the day of Satan's triumphant conquest. On this day of God's judgment upon His

Church the Lord Himself will go forth to battle against the nations oppressing His Church (v. 3), and He will fight as only He, the Man of war, Jehovah is His name, can fight (Ex. 15:3; cp. Joshua 10:14, 42; 23:3; Judg. 4:15; 1 Sam. 7:10 ff.; 2 Kings 3:9-27; 2 Chron. 14:9 ff.; 20:15 ff.). A similar miracle He will perform in that day (v. 4). The feet of Him before whom the hills melt (Ps. 97:5; Micah 1:4) will rest on the Mount of Olives (Gr. N.), and the mountain will split apart from east to west, one section moving southward, the other toward the north. Thus a large valley will be formed. "And ye" (v. 5), the people of God living at the time the Church is being ravaged by the enemy, shall flee, seeking to escape the enemy, as the people had fled from the earthquake in the days of Uzziah, prophesied in Amos 1:1. "The valley of the mountains" (Gr. N.), rather, the valley of My mountains = My mountain valley, prepared by the Lord's cleaving the mount. There will be ample space for all refugees, "for" the valley of mountains will extend to Azal, the exact site of which is no longer known. It may best be identified with Beth-ezel (Micah 1:11. See Gr. N.). In this valley, prepared by the Lord as a refuge for His people, the Lord Himself will be present together with His "saints," His holy angels (cp. Deut. 33:2, 3; Matt. 25:31; Mark 8:38; Rev. 19:14), His servants carrying out His commands (Ps. 103:20 f.; 104:4; Matt. 18:10; Heb. 1:14). What a beautiful picture of the loving providence of the Lord of grace who finds ways and means to protect His Church even in its fiercest trials!

To which period in the history of the Church does this refer? It cannot refer to the destruction of Jerusalem by the Romans, for then no Jews remained in the city. Josephus writes of Jerusalem's destruction by Titus, A. D. 70: "The army had no more people to slay or to plunder because there remained none to be the objects of their fury." (*History of the Jewish War*, VII, 1, 1.) Emperor Hadrian (117—138), in order to prevent further rebellion of the Jews after Bar-Cochba's bloody revolt, rebuilt Jerusalem as a pagan city and forbade all Jews under pain of death to enter the city. It cannot refer to the persecution of the Church by imperial Rome, for the heathen Romans never took possession of the Church nor deprived it of its spiritual blessings. The blood of the martyrs became the seed of the Church. Nor can it refer to the attack by Gog and Magog in the last days of the earth (Rev. 20:8 ff.), for chapter 14, as we shall see, speaks of the entire period of the New Testament Church. See Interpretation. This prophecy announces the coming of "that man

of sin," the "wicked," described 2 Thess. 2, and is fulfilled in the Roman
Papacy. Antichrist established his throne in the temple of God, His
Church, claiming to be the vicar of Christ and usurping sovereignty
over all kingdoms, demanding obedience to all his official definitions
of doctrine. He rifled the houses, forbidding the laity to read the Bible
and only in certain countries permitting the reading of Bibles anno-
tated and sanctioned by the Church of Rome. "Women ravished."
We think of the unspeakable sins resulting from the papal institution
of monasticism and the celibacy of the priesthood. "Half of the city
captive." Only God knows how many have been influenced by the
papal substitution of human works for Christ's all-sufficient merits,
of saints for the One Mediator, Jesus Christ, by the papal anathema
upon the doctrine of justification solely by the imputing of Christ's
righteousness, or the forgiveness of sins. Only God knows how many
have been robbed of the saving faith and have placed their hope of
salvation on their own works or the merits of the saints, or have been
driven into despair of ever gaining salvation. Papal Rome extended
its power over "all nations" (v. 2). The Inquisition, courts for the
examination and punishment of "heretics" (and that term included
anyone who opposed the arrogant claims or false doctrines of the
Papacy), inaugurated by the bishops ca. 1163 and by the Pope in 1215,
was aided and abetted by civil governments, and spread from France
to Spain, northern and central Italy, Germany, the Netherlands, and
mercilessly imprisoned and cruelly tortured and killed untold thousands of victims during the next centuries. In England, the bones of
Wycliffe (died 1384, excommunicated 1415 by the Council of Con-
stance) were dug up in 1428, burnt, and their ashes thrown into the
Swift River. In Bohemia, John Huss was burnt alive at the stake
1415, and Jerome of Prague less than a year later. Tyndale, who
translated the Bible into English, was burnt at Antwerp 1536. These
martyrs are only a few of the thousands of men and women martyred
for no other reason than their opposition to the false claim of the
"Holy Father." Consult any standard encyclopedia or history of the
Middle Ages, and you will see the extent to which the nations were
dominated by the Papacy and how frequently the "ban" (= excommunication) and the "interdict" (= refusal of sacraments and religious service) were pronounced against individuals, cities, and entire
countries.

Vv. 6, 7 describe the conditions existing during these centuries
and are convincing proof that the Papacy is foretold in vv. 1-7. The
Papacy had succeeded in covering the bright lamp of God's Word

(Ps. 119:105; Prov. 6:23) with the soot of human opinions and errors; yet it had not succeeded in extinguishing it altogether. True, the light was not "clear nor dark" (Gr. N.), rather: "Not shall there be light, the luminaries shall be contracted, congealed = lose their brilliance. But even this day of darkness is a day known to the Lord, the Ruler of His Church, and He will overrule the wicked scheme of Satan to deprive the Church entirely of its light. The day will be "one day" (Gr. N.) (v. 7), a singular, unique day, "not day," not like the bright day of the apostolic era of Gospel brilliance, yet, by the marvelous grace of the Lord, neither the "night" of heathendom (Eph. 2:11 f.). Throughout the spiritual gloom of the Dark Ages the Lord of the Church provided sufficient light that His people could come to the saving knowledge of Jesus, their Redeemer. And when this day of semidarkness came to its close, it ended not in night. Contrary to the laws of nature (Gen. 8:22), "at evening time," at the time appointed for night to come, "it shall be light," the full, bright light of the Gospel, shall illumine the world. The Dark Ages were followed by the age of the Reformation; the Sun of Righteousness once more arose with healing in His wings (Mal. 4:2; Rev. 14:6-8; 2 Thess. 2:8).

---

2. Living waters from Jerusalem, vv. 8-11

8 And it shall come to pass on that day that living waters shall flow forth from Jerusalem, half of them to the Eastern Sea, and half toward the Western Sea. So shall it be in 9 summer and in winter. Then the LORD shall be King over all the earth. On that day the LORD shall 10 be One, and His name One. All the land shall be turned as into the Plain, from Geba to Rimmon south of Jerusalem. And she shall raise on high and throne on her place from the Gate of Benjamin to the place of the First Gate, to the Corner Gate, and the Tower of Hananeel to the King's wine 11 presses. And they shall live there, and no longer shall there be any cursed thing, but Jerusalem shall throne securely.

Grammatical Notes

V. 10. "Be turned," יִסֹּב, to turn oneself, here = to be changed (so Hiphil, 2 Kings 23:34; 24:17; 2 Chron. 36:4; Hophal, Num. 32:38). — "As a plain," the article demands the proper noun, the Arabah. — "Lifted up," רָאֲמָה, a variant to רָמָה. (G.-K. 72 p.) — "Inhabited," יָשְׁבָה, to sit, dwell, throne. (Cp. 1 Sam. 4:4; Ps. 80:2; Num. 21:15; Jer. 30:18.) — "The First Gate." הָרִאשׁוֹן = the first (Is. 41:4; 44:6; Ex. 40:2, 17, etc.); perhaps identical with the "Old Gate" (Neh. 3:6), rather, the gate of the "old" city; the first gate naturally is the oldest; or it may be the first gate west of the Temple. — "The Corner Gate," sha'ar happinnim, most likely identical with the sha'ar happinnah (2 Kings 14:13; 2 Chron. 26:9; Jer. 31:38).

V. 11. "Utter destruction." חָרֶם denotes the compulsory dedication, the enforced surrender to God and His punitive justice of a person (and all his possessions) who had obstinately refused to consecrate Himself willingly to the Lord, or of any object that had been placed into the service of idolatry. The Canaanite cities in the land given to Israel by the Lord (Gen. 12:6 f.; 15:18 ff.) were to be "utterly destroyed," all inhabitants slain (Deut. 2:34; 7:2; 20:17; Joshua 6:17 f.; 8:26; 10:1, 35-40; 11:11 f., 20 f.). This divine command was to prevent the seduction of Israel to the filthy immoralities of the Canaanites (Lev. 18:24 ff.; Deut. 20:16 ff.). In wars with other nations only the adult male population was to be slain, while the Israelites were allowed to keep the women, children, cattle, and other spoil for themselves (Deut. 20:13). In the campaign against Midian (Num. 31) the cities and fortresses were burnt (v. 10), all males and married women slain; girls, cattle, sheep, and other goods were taken as spoils (vv. 11, 17, 18). All metal objects were purified by fire and the water of separation (vv. 22, 23 a); other objects by this water. The spoil was to be divided into two parts, one for the army, the other for the people (v. 27). Both were to levy a tribute to the Lord (v. 28); the army's tribute to be assigned to the priesthood (v. 29), the people's tribute, to the Levites (v. 30; see also vv. 31, 54; Num. 18:14; Joshua 6:19; Ezek. 44:29). Any object thus devoted to the Lord became a *cherem,* "an accursed thing" to the rest of the people, and was not to be sold or redeemed (Lev. 27:28 f.); nor was it to become the property of, or be used by, any other person, but remain the exclusive property of the Lord and His sanctuary servants on pain of death (Deut. 13:16 ff.; Joshua 6:17 f.; 7:1-15).

V. 8. A brighter picture: Living waters, waters of life-giving power, issue from Jerusalem. This change began in the days of the apostles, who in obedience to Christ's command (Matt. 28:19 f.; Mark 16:15; Acts 1:8), beginning at Jerusalem, the seat of the Christian Church, preached the Gospel of Him who was pierced (Zech. 12:10. See also Acts 2:23 f.; 3:13 ff.; 4:10 ff.; 5:30 ff.; 13:27 ff.; 1 Cor. 1:23 f.; 2:2). So they brought the water of life to souls perishing with thirst. "The former sea" = the Eastern Sea, the Salt Sea (Ezek. 47:1-12). "The hinder sea," the Western Sea, behind one looking toward the east = the Mediterranean Sea, connected with the ocean. This Gospel is preached until East and West touch each other, the full length and breadth of the earth. "In summer," the season of heat and drought, when many rivers dried up, "and in winter," the season of rain and snow, filling the rivers to overflowing, "shall it be," the waters shall flow in inexhaustible volume. Even during the papal rule the Gospel was not entirely silenced; it remained a power of God unto salvation to many. And in the new earth the river of God's peace, life, and salvation will never cease to flow (Rev. 22:1 ff.).

V. 9. Another bright picture. Not only in little Judah, 45 by 50 miles, but even in all the earth as far as the Church extends, will the Lord be King. (Cp. Dan. 2:35, 44; Ps. 72:8 ff.) "One LORD,"

498

"one name." Human kings and kingdoms come and go; human laws and ordinances change; the Lord is and remains one, unchangeable, I AM THAT I AM (Ex. 3:14; Ps. 102:26 f.; Is. 44:6; 45:5, 18, 21 ff.). His name, His revelation of Himself and His good and gracious will, is ever the same; the same Bible in many languages, the same water of life. Here in time we see Him in His Word as through a glass, darkly, but in eternity, face to face, even as we are known (1 Cor. 13:12); yet it is our understanding of His Being and revelation that changes, not the Lord Himself or His name.

Vv. 10, 11. Still another strange, yet truly marvelous vision. Geba, on the northern boundary of Judah, five to six miles north of Jerusalem (Joshua 21:17; 2 Kings 23:8; Neh. 11:31). Rimmon, in the vicinity of Ziklag and Beersheba (Joshua 15:28; 19:1-7; Neh. 11:29), near the southern boundary of Simeon (1 Chron. 4:24, 28, 30, 32), whose territory was within that of Judah (Joshua 19:1-9). Judah, the Holy Land at Zechariah's time, was the hill country (Luke 1:39, 65), a country of hills and mountains. Yet from its southern limits to its northern boundary, the hill country round about Jerusalem "shall be turned as a plain" (Gr. N.), become like the Plain, the Arabah, the long valley through which the Jordan flows from the Sea of Gennesaret to the Gulf of Akabah. It shall become a huge steppe, or prairie, flat, level land, easily traversed. This is a prophecy which foretells in symbolical language the fulfillment in the New Testament era of Isaiah's remarkable vision (Is. 40:3 f.). Cp. Hymn 75, stanza 2, *The Lutheran Hymnal.*

> Prepare the way before Him!
> Make straight, make plain the way!
> The lowly valleys raising,
> The heights of pride abasing,
> His path all even lay!

The spirit of pride, of self-righteousness, of self-confident Pharisaism (Luke 18:11), will by God's almighty grace be humbled into willing submission to God's plan of salvation, changed to joyous acceptance of Jesus' blood and righteousness. The valley of doubt, fear, dejection, despondency, will be raised to confident hope and assurance of God's grace and life eternal (Rom. 5:1 ff.; 8:28-39; Heb. 11:1 ff.). All obstacles to Christ's kingdom entering into, and remaining in, the hearts of men will be removed by the Lord (Eph. 1:17 ff.; 2:10-22).

"And it" = Jerusalem, symbolizing the Church of God on earth and in heaven, shall be "lifted up" (Gr. N.), exalted, sublime. The Church built of living stones (Eph. 2:19; 1 Peter 2:5), the communion of saints, how high and exalted a position does she occupy in a believer's heart! "I love Thy Church, O God! . . . To her my cares and toils be given till toils and cares shall end!" And the Jerusalem above, that city fair and high, remains the object of the Christian's hope and desire (Heb. 13:14; Col. 3:1, 2; Phil. 1:23; Rev. 21). "Inhabited" (Gr. N.) = sit, dwell, throne, "in her place," on what has been placed beneath her (cp. ch. 6:12, Gr. N., p. 438) by divine decree, her eternal foundation, Christ, the immovable Rock (Is. 28:16; Matt. 16:18; Eph. 2:20). The boundaries of Jerusalem are described in terms indicating to the Jews of Zechariah's time that the city whose walls and houses were still lying in ruins would be rebuilt on the area it occupied before the Exile, symbolizing the building of the New Testament Church according to the plans of the eternal Lord of the Church. On the north side of the city a wall extended westward from the center of the Temple area to the Corner Gate (Gr. N.), on the site of the modern Jaffa Gate. Toward the center of this north wall lay the Benjamin Gate, very likely identical with the Ephraim Gate (2 Kings 14:13; Neh. 8:16). This gate was the main exit to Benjamin and Ephraim, north of Jerusalem. It may be the same gate called the Middle Gate (Jer. 39:3). The "First Gate" (Gr. N.) was eastward of the Benjamin Gate, either a gate close to the Temple or the ancient Jebusite city gate. The added words "the place of" seem to indicate that this gate had been completely destroyed 586 B. C. It may be identical with the Old Gate (Neh. 3:6). These three gates on the north side are named to indicate the extent of the city from east to west; from the central Benjamin Gate eastward to the First Gate and westward to the Corner Gate. Then follows the extent from north to south, from the Tower of Hananeel, in the northwest corner of the Temple area, southward to the king's wine presses, very likely in, or close to, the king's gardens on the slope of the Kidron Valley southwest of the city. Within these ancient boundaries of Jerusalem the city again shall be inhabited (Gr. N.), sit, throne (v. 11). Within this city men shall dwell. It shall again be filled to capacity with people. (Cp. Jer. 30:17-22; 33:6-13.) "No more utter destruction" (Gr. N.), no more objects of God's curse and damnation; for all the inhabitants of the New Testament Jerusalem, His holy Christian Church, are holy (1 Cor. 6:11; Eph. 2:19). "Safely inhabited." It shall sit, throne securely, protected by the Lord of the Church, endowed with His grace.

3. Eternal punishment for all enemies, everlasting blessings for all believers, vv. 12-19

12 And this shall be the plague with which the Lord will plague all the people who fight against Jerusalem: He will cause their flesh to rot while they are standing on their feet; and their eyes shall rot in their sockets, and their tongues
13 shall rot in their mouths. And it shall come to pass on that day that there will be a great panic from the LORD among them, and they will grasp one another's hand, and everyone's hand will be raised
14 against the other. And also Judah will fight in Jerusalem, and the wealth of all nations all around will be gathered, gold and silver and garments, in great abundance.
15 So also, like this plague, shall be the plague upon the horses, and the mules, and the camels, and the asses, and all the animals which
16 shall be in these camps. And it shall come to pass that everyone who is left of all the nations that come up against Jerusalem shall go up year after year to worship the King, the LORD of Hosts, and to celebrate the Feast of Tabernacles.
17 And it shall come to pass that whoever of the races of the earth shall not go up to Jerusalem to worship the King, the LORD of Hosts, there
18 shall be no rain upon them. And if the race of Egypt will not go up and will not come, then neither upon them (shall rain come)! There shall be the plague with which the LORD will plague the nations which do not go up to celebrate the Feast of Tabernacles.
19 This will be the sin of Egypt and the sin of all the nations which do not go up to celebrate the Feast of Tabernacles.

Grammatical Notes

V. 12. "Their flesh." From "their flesh" to "their tongue." The suffixes and predicates are singular to indicate that no one will be overlooked; all, individually and collectively, will be punished. "Their mouth" has the plural suffix. — "Consume away," קָקַק = to melt, be dissolved, pine away (Lev. 26:39; Ezek. 4:17); corrupt, rot (Ps. 38:6, A. V., 5).

V. 13. "Tumult," opposite of peace (Amos 3:9; 2 Chron. 15:5), feeling of discomfort, restlessness (Prov. 15:16), confusion, consternation (Deut. 7:23; 28:20; Is. 22:5; cp. Is. 2:19 ff.; Rev. 6:15 ff.)

V. 14. "At," בְ, here local, at, in; not "against," as frequently; on "in" see Ex. 17:8, "in Rephidim"; 2 Sam. 21:19, "in Gob"; v. 20, "in Gath."

V. 15. "Tents," the Hebrew term = camps.

V. 17. "Families," a term denoting various divisions, nations (Gen. 10:18, 20; Jer. 1:15), tribes (Judg. 13:2; 17:7), between tribes and households (Joshua 7:14; Zech. 12:12 ff.). — "Shall be no rain," גֶּשֶׁם the general term, including spring and fall rains; the article points to a special rain. See Interpretation.

V. 18. "That have no rain," וְלֹא עֲלֵיהֶם = Not upon them! The predicate is to be supplied from v. 17. "There shall be," etc., names the punishment.

V. 19. "Punishment," חַטָּאת = sin, missing of the mark. (See Gr. N. on "sin," ch. 13:1, p. 486.)

V. 12. The Lord Jehovah pronounces His sentence on all who fight against His Church, both individuals and nations. Their flesh (Gr. N.) shall rot while they are still standing on their feet. They are doomed to a living death, to sink ever deeper into spiritual darkness and ignorance. Their eyes shall rot (Gr. N.) in their sockets. Indeed, they shall be stricken with blindness (cp. John 9:37 ff.); their intellect, their way of looking at things, their entire mind, shall become foul, perverted; their tongue, their language, literature, art shall become lewd, filthy, putrid. (Cp. Is. 57:20; Rom. 1:21-32; 3:10-18.) That is the divine judgment for rebellion against God: the descent into the fathomless abyss of sin and its corrupting, corrosive influence. That is the fate of everyone refusing the Messiah, Jesus, and His redeeming, justifying, sanctifying blood (Zech. 13:1; Rom. 3:21 ff.; 1 Cor. 6:9-11). This living death, this rotting, reaches its climax in the lake burning with fire and brimstone (Is. 48:22; 66:24; Rev. 14:10 ff.; 20:10-15).

V. 13. A great "tumult" (Gr. N.), a paniclike confusion shall be sent among the hostile forces by the Lord. Like the enemies of God's people in the day of Gideon (Judg. 7:14), of Jonathan (1 Sam. 14: 13-20, "discomfiture" = same word translated "tumult" here), of Jehoshaphat (2 Chron. 20:22 ff.), these enemies shall war among themselves, while Jerusalem, the Church, remains unharmed. The history of the New Testament Church furnishes many an example. We think, e. g., of the Lord's twice using the Turks, the bitter enemies of the Christian Church, to frustrate the efforts of Charles V to suppress the Reformation, when he was forced to make peace with the Protestant princes, whose support he needed at Speyer, 1526, and at Augsburg, 1530. We think of the modern critics endeavoring to overthrow the divine authority and inspiration of the Bible, as one theory after the other is advanced with brazen assurance only to be refuted, ridiculed, discarded by other theories doomed to the same fate. Yet throughout the centuries the Bible has abided and will abide as the divinely inspired Word of God, the beacon light to eternal salvation.

V. 14. While disharmony, confusion, international warfare disturb and weaken the forces opposing Jerusalem, Judah shall fight "at Jerusalem" (Gr. N.), side by side with the inhabitants of the Holy City. In fact the Old Testament distinction between Judah and Jerusalem shall vanish in the New Testament. There will be no longer a Holy City more highly honored than the Holy Land. (Cp. Zech. 12:5, 7.) Judah will join Jerusalem, will fight in the city and with the city against the common enemy seeking to destroy the Church of God. Even though the visible Church is divided into many factions, the true Church, the invisible Church, is the one Holy Christian Church, the communion of saints, one in faith, in hope, in love (Eph. 4:3 ff.; 1 Cor. 12:12 f.). Side by side its members battle against the common foe;

side by side they gather the nations into communion with the Church of God. Paul, the greatest missionary; the Ziegenbalgs and Schwartzes, the Eliots and Brainerds, the Careys and Judsons, the thousands of other missionaries laboring faithfully under the most adverse conditions have made unceasing inroads upon the vast empire of Satan. From East to West, from North to South, the name of Jesus is known and glorified as the only Lord and Savior. The wealth once used only in serving self and sin and Satan, is now laid at the feet of Messiah to be used in spreading His Kingdom of Grace.

V. 15. While in foreign cities the women, children, and livestock were spared, in Jericho (Joshua 6: 17 f., 24), in the Canaanite cities (Deut. 20: 16), and in apostate Israelite cities (Deut. 13: 13 ff.) every living being was to be slain, the creatures suffering with guilty man (Rom. 8: 19 f.). The enemies of God's Church will finally be deprived of all their resources. When death and hell and with them all the enemies of God and His Church shall be cast into the lake of fire (Rev. 20: 14 f.), they shall no longer be able to attack God's Church or molest it (Rev. 21: 3 ff.). "Tents" (Gr. N.) = camps.

V. 16. "Everyone that is left" (cp. ch. 13: 8 f.), the believing remnant. Instead of going up against Jerusalem to destroy it, they come to worship, to prostrate themselves before the King Messiah in humble repentance and assured faith, vowing loyalty to Him, Jehovah, their Righteousness. In Christ they recognize the Lord of Hosts, the World Ruler. From year to year, throughout their lifetime, they keep the Feast of Tabernacles, in never-ceasing gratitude for all the blessings material and spiritual, temporal and eternal, which the Lord Christ showers down upon them. The Feast of Tabernacles was the festival of joyous thanksgiving and renewed avowal of grateful service (Lev. 23: 39 ff.; Deut. 16: 13 ff.; Neh. 8: 14 ff.).

Vv. 17-19. "Families" (Gr. N.), tribes, races, nations. Any people that will not come to Jerusalem to worship the Lord of Hosts as their Covenant God, "upon them shall be no rain" (Gr. N.), literally, the rain shall not be upon them. In contrast to "the plague" (v. 15 = living death, physical, spiritual, eternal death), the "rain," here with the definite article, denotes the blessing of God in its entirety (Prov. 1: 33; 4: 18; Phil. 2: 15), a life in which God's benediction (Num. 6: 23-27) is realized (Ps. 121). Rain is chosen as a symbol of God's blessing, because rain was a divine blessing, essential to Palestine, where the lack of rain meant lack of harvest, famine. Rain was granted in abundant measure as a token of His favor and blessing to His grateful, obedient people (Deut. 28:12; Hos. 2:21; Joel 2:23 ff.). The withholding of rain was a sign of divine displeasure (Deut. 11:17; 28:23 f.), a dreadful penalty. (Cp. Jer. 14:1-10; Joel 1:16-20.)

"Egypt" (v. 18) was the ancient enemy of God's people, Israel's first oppressor (Ex. 1—15); it was an enemy at David's time (1 Chron. 11:23); it protected Jeroboam rebelling against Solomon (1 Kings 11:26-40); Shishak (1 Kings 14:25 ff.). Necho slew Josiah (2 Kings 23:29), made Judah tributary (ch. 23:31 ff.), always incited Judah to rebel against Nebuchadnezzar without rendering any effective help (Is. 30:2 f.; Jer. 2:18, 36; 37:5-8; 46:17). "That have no rain" (Gr. N.), rather, "And neither on them," a very effective omission of the predicate readily supplied from v. 17. The threat of no rain might not seem so ominous to Egypt, since the fertility of that land depended almost entirely on irrigation and the annual overflowing of the Nile. (Cp. Deut. 11:10 ff.) It rarely rains in Egypt. Yet even the floods which made irrigation possible depended on the torrential rains in the region of the Upper Nile in Ethiopia and Nubia. If the Lord did not send these rains, there were no floods; and if such conditions continued, drought and crop failure and famine would be the inevitable result. (Cp. Gen. 43:1; 47:13 ff.) "There shall be the plague." Vv. 17, 18 had stated God's judgment negatively: No rain! No blessings! V. 18 b states the positive judgment as pronounced vv. 12, 15. The plague which shall come upon all enemies of Israel shall also come upon Egypt, if it refuses to acknowledge the God of Israel as the one and only God and Redeemer. There is no neutrality possible. Either accept or reject! (See Luke 11:23; Mark 16:16.)

This shall be the "punishment" (Gr. N.) (v. 19), literally, the sin, the missing of the mark and its dreadful consequences. He that sinneth against Me, fails to find Me, misses Me, wrongeth His own soul (Prov. 8:36; cp. v. 35, "findeth"). This will be the sin of Egypt and its inherent consequence for Egypt and every nation that refuses to worship the Lord by joining the Church. (Cp. John 16:8 ff.)

This is one of the concluding thoughts of Zechariah's book of prophecy: There is no salvation without the Messiah and outside His Church. Another concluding thought is added vv. 20, 21: In the Church there is perfect holiness, universal holiness.

---

4. All Jerusalem is Holiness to the Lord, vv. 20, 21

20 On that day there shall be upon the bells of the horses, "Holiness to the LORD," and the pots in the house of the Lord shall be as the sprinkling bowls before the altar. 21 And every pot in Jerusalem and

in Judah shall be Holiness unto the LORD of Hosts; and all that sacrifice shall come and take of them and shall boil in them. And on that day there shall be no longer a Canaanite in the house of the LORD.

Grammatical Notes

V. 20. "Pots" were used by the Israelites for boiling meat (Ex. 16:3; Ezek. 11:3, 7, 11; 24:3,6; Micah 3:3), water (Job 41:23; Jer. 1:13), often heated by means of dried nettles, "thorns" (Ps. 58:10; Eccl. 7:6). Washpots are mentioned in Ps. 60:10 and 108:10. In the sanctuary, pots were used for the altar service, the removal of ashes (Ex. 27:3; 38:3), boiling meat (1 Sam. 2:13,15; 2 Chron. 35:13). Pots are also mentioned in 1 Kings 7:45; 2 Kings 25:14; 2 Chron. 4:11,16; Jer. 52:18 f.— "Bowls," from a root = to sprinkle, a sprinkling bowl or basin (Ex. 27:3; 38:3; Num. 4:14; 7:13-85; 1 Kings 7:50; Jer. 52:19 cp. Zech. 9:15, p. 456).

Vv. 20, 21. "Bells," a reference to the age-old custom of placing tinkling bells on horses, etc. Cp. "Hear the sledges with the bells" (E. A. Poe, *The Bells*). Horses were one of the chief military resources, frequently the objects of human pride and trust (cp. 1 Kings 4:26; Is. 2:7 b; Jer. 4:13; 46:9, etc.) and for that reason became the objects of God's wrath (Micah 5:10; Zech. 9:10; 14:15). In v. 20 "horses" symbolize all the resources of the Church. In the New Testament era even the horses will bear on their bells the same inscription that was engraved on the golden band affixed to the miter of the high priest (Ex. 28:36), "Holiness to Jehovah." In other words, the Christian Church will sanctify all its resources by the Word of God and prayer (1 Tim. 4:3-5), by dedicating them prayerfully to the service of God and their fellow men, to the greater glory of God (1 Cor. 10:31). "The pots" (Gr. N.) "shall be like the bowls" (Gr. N.). In the Old Covenant there were various degrees of holiness. The bowls, the sprinkling or sacrificial bowls, in which the blood of the sacrificial animals was caught up to be sprinkled against the corners of the Altar of Burnt Offerings (Ex. 24:6; Lev. 1:5, 11; 3:2, 8, 13, etc.), were regarded as holier than the "pots" (Gr. N.). Another distinction refers to holy places. The cities of Israel were holy (Is. 64:10) because the Lord had chosen the entire land as His own (Lev. 25:23; Jer. 2:7; 16:18). Yet Jerusalem was holy in a special sense (Is. 48:2; 52:1) because there God dwelt in His holy Temple (Ps. 68:16; 79:1; 134:13 f.). In this Temple there were degrees of holiness; the Court, where the people gathered, was holy; but the Holy Place, to be entered only by the priests, was holier; and the holiest part was the Most Holy Place (Ex. 26:33 f.), where the Ark of the Covenant was placed and which was to be entered only by the high priest once

505

every year (Lev. 16:1 ff.). On the distinction between the holiness of the people, that of the Levites, the priests, and the high priest cp. Ex. 19:6; Deut. 7:6; 14:2 (people); Num. 3:14-41; 8:5-26 (Levites); Ex. 28:1, 4, 40 ff.; Lev. 9:22; Num. 6:23 ff.; 18:3 (priests); Ex. 28:2, 4-39; Lev. 16:1 ff. (high priest); see also Num. 16:1—18:32. Incense and oil for use by the priests was holy, not to be used or prepared by the people on pain of excommunication (Ex. 30:22-38). Certain foods and animals as well as certain actions and conditions (some of which were natural and quite unavoidable) rendered the Israelite unclean, excluding him from public worship and other intercourse with his fellow Israelites for the duration of such uncleanness (Lev. 11—15). All these distinctions shall be abolished in the New Testament Church. There will be no more "unclean" things (Matt. 15:10-20; Luke 11:41; Rom. 14:20; Col. 2:16-20; Titus 1:15). Every pot, not only in the Temple, but also in Jerusalem, the Holy City, and in Judah, the Holy Land, symbolizing the Christian Church, shall be holiness to the Lord of Hosts (v. 21). In the Church of the New Testament every "pot," every vessel, every tool, every instrument used in the service of the Lord to His glory, will be holy, the broom in the hand of the Christian housemaid as well as the scepter of a king; the pick and shovel of the miner as well as the pen of the preacher. "All they that come," etc. The members of the Christian Church no longer need what the believers in the Old Covenant needed, a mediating priesthood. They themselves will perform the functions which were the exclusive privilege of the priesthood. From the infant in the cradle, received by Baptism into union with the Triune God (Matt. 28:19), to the aged Simeons and Annas, young and old, men and women, all Christians without exception are included in such passages as Rom. 8:14 ff.; Gal. 3:26 ff.; 4:4 ff.; Eph. 2:18; 3:12; Heb. 4:16; 10:19 ff.

"The Canaanite" = the original inhabitants of the Holy Land. They were under the curse of God because of their abominations (Lev. 18:24 ff.). Israel was commanded to exterminate them (Deut. 7:1; 20:17), but failed to do so (Judg. 1:27, 33; 3:5; Obad. 20). In the New Testament Church, the communion of saints, of the elect children of God (Eph. 1:1-5; 1 Peter 1:2), there will be no more Canaanites. That Church consists entirely of believing, faithful children of God (1 Cor. 6:11).

"In that day" is repeated in the Hebrew text at the close of v. 21.

506

MALACHI

Introductory Remarks

Person and Name

We know nothing more about Malachi's personality than his book reveals. Neither the names of his parents nor that of his birthplace is stated; cp. Obadiah and Habakkuk. Even his name has been regarded as doubtful. The Targum Jonathan, an Aramaic paraphrase of the prophetic books, written during the fourth and the fifth Christian century, but representing a much older tradition, added to the words "by Malachi," ch. 1:1, the note, "whose name is called Ezra the scribe." The LXX translated the same phrase ἐν χειρὶ ἀγγέλου αὐτοῦ, by the hand of His angel (or messenger). Consequently a number of church fathers regarded the term Malachi as a mere appellative or title adopted by the prophet. Modern critics generally agree in the main with Pfeiffer's opinion that "the Book of 'Malachi' was originally anonymous and bore the same title as the two books Zechariah 9—11 and 12—14. — An editor added at the end of 1:1 the words 'by the hand of Malachi.'" (Pfeiffer, *Introduction to O. T.*, p. 612.) We cannot agree with this position. There are valid reasons to regard Malachi as the proper name of the prophet, not as a mere appellative.

The Second Book of Esdras, dating from the second century after Christ and presenting much material far older, lists the twelve Minor Prophets, naming as the last three books those of Aggaeus, Secharias, Malachias, *"qui et angelus Domini vocatus est* (who is also called the angel [messenger] of the Lord)." In the Vulgate, Second Esdras is listed as the "Fourth Book of Esdras" and placed after the Book of Revelation. (See "Biblia Sacra, Vulgatae editionis Sixti V," etc., ed. Hetzenauer, 1922, p. 1219.) The writer of Second Esdras regards Malachi as a proper name, the Greek and Latin form of which is Malachias, the Hebrew Malachiyah, the messenger of the Lord. This same Greek form appears in the superscription of our book in the LXX. Hence the LXX "His messenger" = the Lord's messenger, may be only a different form of Malkiyahu. Hebrew names ending in "yahu" or "yah" not infrequently drop these endings or shorten them to mere "i." Cp. Zacher, 1 Chron. 8:31, called Zechariah, ch. 9:37; Shema, 1 Chron. 5:8, called Shemaiah, 1 Chron. 5:4; Chelubai, 1 Chron.

507

2:9 = Caleb, 1 Chron. 2:18, 42. Haroeh = the one seeing, the seer, called Reaiah, "he saw the Lord," 1 Chron. 2:52; 4:2. Similarly "El," God, is omitted in Phalti, 1 Sam. 25:44, identical with Phaltiel, 2 Sam. 3:15. Cp. also the variant forms of Jehoiachin in Jer. 52:31; called Jeconiah, Jer. 24:1; 27:20; 29:2; Joiachin, Ezek. 1:2 (Hebrew text); Coniah, Hebrew: Coniahu, Jer. 22:24, 28; 37:1. James, Jim, Jimmy; Elisabeth, Elsa, Lizzie, Bessie, Beth, are modern parallels. We see no valid reason why Malachi should not be regarded as a proper name.

The Time

The edict of Darius (522—486), Ezra 6:6-12, which promised the funds for the building of the Temple and the maintenance of its service, had been reaffirmed by Artaxerxes (465—423), to Ezra in 457 (Ezra 7:12-26). Under Nehemiah, in the year 445, the Jews had agreed to pay or help pay for the support of the Temple and its service by a self-imposed annual tax of one third of a shekel of silver per person, and to bring the first fruits of the field, the first-born of their children, the firstlings of their herds and flocks and other offerings, and tithes for the support of the priests and Levites (Neh. 10:32-39). This agreement (Neh. 9:38—10:39) included a number of other reforms (10:30 f.): the cessation of mixed marriages, the strict observance of the Sabbath and the sabbatical year (Ex. 23:11; Lev. 25:4), and the promise to give up the pledge-taking which had been so harshly practiced (Neh. 5:2-13). Nehemiah had been recalled by the Persian king in 432. On his return he found that many of the abuses he had abolished were again practiced by the people (Neh. 13:1-31), all of which are also rebuked by Malachi. The only one not directly mentioned by him, the breaking of the Sabbath law (Neh. 13:15-22), is included in the general exhortation to keep the Law of Moses (Mal. 4:4).

These facts make it certain that Malachi was a contemporary of Nehemiah, that he aided Nehemiah in his reform, or supported him after his return, or on both occasions. His activity therefore extended from Nehemiah's arrival at Jerusalem 445 B. C. to sometime after the latter's absence, beginning 432.

With this timing agrees the fact that Malachi does not mention Haggai or Zechariah, nor is he mentioned by them; that the Temple and its service is fully restored; and the frequent reference to disrespect of the Temple and its service by priests and people (Mal. 1:6 ff., 12 f.; 2:9, 17; 3:5, 7 ff., 13 ff.).

Style

"The style of Malachi is more prosaic than that of the prophets generally — and his diction betrays marks of lateness. — 'In place of the rhetorical development of a subject, usual with the earlier prophets, there appears in Malachi a dialectic treatment by means of question and answer. We have here the first traces of that method of exposition which in the schools that arose about this time became ultimately the prevalent one.' (Koehler, *Malachi*, 1865, p. 26, after Ewald)" (Driver, *Lit. of O. T.*, 1912, p. 358). Bewer, *Lit. of O. T.*, p. 258, correctly states: "There is a freshness in the lively debates of the little book that makes it interesting reading. It is written in prose which sometimes has the rhythmic swing of poetry."

Throughout his book, Malachi, the spokesman of God, presents a remarkable picture of God's holiness and man's unholiness. We see here the Lord's unmerited, free grace and man's self-righteous demand of reward. We see divine patience in the face of human stubbornness; the Master's condescension and the servant's impudence. We behold the Creator's solicitude for the eternal welfare of His handiwork, and the creature's sullen dissatisfaction with his Maker's will and way. We observe the Judge's solemn warning of impending judgment and the blind, self-righteous sinner arrogantly demanding the coming of judgment. We see our God's perfect holiness and our own imperfections and guilt. In the same measure that we recognize our own sinfulness and wickedness, the mystery of divine love and the depths of Jehovah's grace become the more unfathomable, and the greater ought our gratitude grow toward Jehovah, our Covenant God through Jesus Christ, His Messenger, the Angel of the Covenant.

The Lord, the Father, Redeemer and Judge, Calls His People to Repentance

PART I

God Is the Father of Israel; Therefore Give Him the Father's Due: Fear, Love, Trust

Chapters 1 and 2

CHAPTER 1

A. The Love of the Lord of Hosts Toward His People, Vv. 1-5

1 An oracle, the word of the LORD
2 through Malachi. I have loved you, says the LORD. But you say, How hast Thou loved us: Was not Esau a brother of Jacob? is the oracle of
3 the LORD, Yet I loved Jacob. But Esau I hated, and I have made his mountains a waste and his heritage one for the jackals of the wilder-
4 ness. Because Esau says, We are shattered, but we shall rebuild the ruins, thus says the LORD of Hosts, Though they build, I will tear down! And they shall be called The Wicked Country, and The Nation Against Which the LORD
5 Shows His Wrath Forever. And your eyes shall see, and you shall say, The LORD is great beyond the boundary of Israel.

Grammatical Notes

V. 2. "I have loved you." The Hebrew perfect frequently denotes an action resulting in a state which may be of longer or shorter duration, according to the context. (Cp. Gen. 4:6, 9; 32:10.) Where the consequence of such action or the action itself continues into the present, we may render it by the present (Job 9:2; 10:13; Ps. 31:7; Amos 5:21, etc. G.-K. 106 g; Driver, *Tenses*, p. 16). This rule applies also to the second "loved," v. 1 c, and to "hated," v. 2.

V. 5. "Be magnified from." יִגְדַּל is never used as a passive, always = to be great, or manifest oneself as great. "From," מֵעַל, over, above, upon. (Cp. Gen. 1:7; Neh. 12:31, 37; Eccl. 5:7; Ezek. 1:25.)

Vv. 1, 2. "The burden," see note on Nah. 1:1, pp. 293 f. The entire book is an utterance coming as the word of Jehovah, the Covenant God. It is addressed to Israel (cp. Gen. 32:27 ff.), the covenant nation, now reduced to Judah. Malachi is merely the spokesman of God. Jehovah, the great Lover (Deut. 33:3; Jer. 31:3; Hos. 11:1; John 3:16; 1 John 4:8 ff.), begins His message with a solemn avowal of His love, as eternal and unchanging as He who calls Himself I AM THAT I AM (Ex. 3:14). "I have loved you" (Gr. N.) (v. 2) = I love you! Yet this amazing announcement of the God of truth meets with a cold reception. In shameful unbelief the people ask, "Wherein hast Thou

510

loved us?" Where is the evidence of Thy love? We cannot see it! This question reveals their shameful ingratitude, their absolute failure to realize and appreciate what the love and grace of God had done for them. This ingratitude was, as we shall see, rooted in their selfishness, the prevailing sin of post-Exilic Judaism, which finally led to their own rejection by the Lord. Pre-Exilic Israel from its earliest national history had been guilty of coarse idolatry. (Cp. Ex. 32:1 ff.; Num. 25:1 ff.; 2 Kings 17:7-17; Hos. 1:2; 4:12 ff.; Amos 2:8; 3:14; 5:25 f.; Is. 1:2-4; 2:8; Jer. 2:5-13, 23-28; 11:10-13.) After the Exile this coarse idolatry was practiced only rarely. Yet it was superseded by another form of idolatry just as hateful to the Lord and just as surely a transgression of the First Commandment, even more dangerous because it paraded under the guise of serving the true God. For worship of idols the Israelites substituted the worship of self. Ignoring the weightier matters of the Law, the love, and fear of, and trust in God, they were satisfied with a mere outward performance of such works as appealed to them. In this self-conceived and self-made righteousness they trusted and were bitterly disappointed and ready to charge God with failure to keep His promises of blessing and prosperity whenever God did not reward them as richly as they felt they deserved. In order to save His people from their dangerous delusion, the Lord in infinite patience and condescension answers their querulous question as a loving father seeks to convince his dissatisfied child.

"Was not Esau," etc. The original stresses the brotherhood more emphatically: Was not a brother Esau to Jacob? The Lord calls attention to facts well known to every Jew. Their ancestor Jacob had a twin brother, Esau. Both were by divine decree to be representatives of their respective posterity (Gen. 25:23). Both were descendants of men who according to God's promise were to be the forefathers of the Woman's Seed (Gen. 3:15), the Messiah (Gen. 12:3; 17:19, 21; 18:18; 22:18; 26:4). Yet the history of the two brothers and their descendants shows clearly that Jacob received far greater blessings as an individual and as the forefather of a nation than did Esau. Even though Esau was the first-born son (Gen. 25:25), the Lord had determined to give the right of the first-born (a double portion, cp. Deut. 21:16, 17; 2 Kings 2:9) to Jacob, the younger of the twins. Even though Esau was the favorite son of his father (Gen. 25:28) and Isaac had the firm intention to give the choicest blessing to him (ch. 27:1-4), God so shaped events that not Esau, but Jacob, received it. See Gen. 27:27 ff., 33, "and he shall be blest." Esau, indeed, had despised his birthright (Gen. 25:29 ff.). Yet Jacob was by no means a man whose righteousness had deserved a richer reward. He had become partner with Rebekah in deceiving aged Isaac in order to obtain the blessing by fraud. He himself later confesses his unworthiness (Gen. 32:10). Why, then, this manifest preference of Jacob? Because the Lord loved Jacob; because He will be gracious to whom He will be gracious in His free, unmerited grace (Ex. 33:19 b; cp. Deut. 4:37; 9:4-7; 10:15; 23:5). The unworthiness of the ancestor and his descendants may have been the reason why God here calls His people not by the highly honorable name of Judah (Gen. 49:8 ff.), nor Israel (Gen. 32:28), but Jacob, to recall to their mind the bitter yet true words of Gen. 27:36 ("supplanter" = deceiver); Hos. 12:4 (A. V., 3), p. 93. They were no better than their deceitful father Jacob. (Cp. Mal. 1:14; 2:10 f., 14 f.; 3:5, 7-9.) "Yet I loved Jacob." In His unsearchable wisdom and unfathomable grace He had so shaped events in the life of the two brothers and the two nations that it must have been apparent to all that Jacob was the recipient of blessings far richer than those granted to his brother. In order to drive home this truth to the self-righteous Jews, who doubted the Lord's word, He adds a surprisingly strange statement, "I hated Esau" (v. 3).

V. 3. These words have been a stumbling block to many. Some charge God with injustice, arbitrariness, sinful passion. Others make this passage a proof for their horrible doctrine of an eternal decree of reprobation. A closer study of God's words will show that neither interpretation is justified. God is not an arbitrary God. His ways are often unsearchable and past finding out (Rom. 11:33) just because they are not our thoughts and ways, but God's ways (Is. 55:9). The Lord Jehovah must not and cannot be judged by human standards of right and wrong (Is. 29:16; 45:9; Rom. 9:24). He is and remains I AM THAT I AM, the unalterably Holy One (Is. 40:18, 25, 28), who cannot be pressed into the mold of human mind (Deut. 32:4). Moreover, the Lord is speaking here not of absolute love embracing only one nation and of absolute hatred directed against another nation. Had He hated Esau absolutely, He would not have granted him so choice a blessing as he received (Gen. 27:39 f.), nor made him so powerful and prosperous a nation. (Cp. Obad. 3 ff., pp. 195 ff.) The Lord is addressing the self-righteous Jews, who failed to recognize and refused to acknowledge the love of God which had been granted to them in a far greater measure than to Esau. Here the word "hate" is not used in its absolute sense, as, e. g., in Ps. 5:5; 11:5; Jer. 12:8;

Hos. 9:15; but in the sense of less love, bestow less love, fewer favors on a person. (Cp. Gen. 29:30 f.; Deut. 21:15-17; Prov. 13:24; Luke 14:26; cp. also with its parallel Matt. 10:37, "loveth more.") Above all, God is not speaking here of a predestination of Jacob to eternal life and a reprobation of Esau unto eternal damnation. He is speaking of the unique position Jacob and his descendants occupied in the history of God's kingdom on earth. They, and no other nation, were chosen to be the ancestors of the Messiah; they were given privileges and blessings of a high nature, not given to the elder son of Isaac. (Cp. John 4:22; Rom. 3:2; 9:4, 5.) But this exalted position did not restrict salvation to Israel. From the first promise given in Paradise (Gen. 3:15) the promise of salvation was universal. (Cp. Gen. 12:3; 22:18; Is. 42:1 ff.; 49:6, etc.) Esau and his descendants are especially included (Jer. 49:11; Amos 9:12; Obad. 19, 21; cp. Mark 3:8).

V. 4. "Impoverished" = laid waste, ruined, occurs only here and in Jer. 5:17. This verse undoubtedly refers to the Nabataean invasion of Edom, which resulted in the expulsion of the Edomites and their migration to the desert country south of Judaea, known later as Idumaea (Mark 3:8; cp. Obad. 20, pp. 205 ff.). We cannot definitely decide whether the Hebrew term "laid waste" (v. 3) is to be translated as a present, past, or future. The Hebrew form may denote any of the three tenses. One fact is clear, the very fact the Lord seeks to drive home to the Jews. All attempts of the Edomites to rebuild and reoccupy their destroyed cities, whether undertaken in the present or future, will be unsuccessful. The Edomites never were able to regain their homeland, where the Nabataeans established a flourishing civilization lasting until ca. A. D. 100, when Rome took possession of the country. "In general the Nabataeans may be accounted one of the most remarkable peoples that have ever crossed the stage of history. Sprung swiftly out of the deserts of Arabia to a position of great power and affluence and glory, they were thrust back by the Romans even more swiftly into the limbo of history whence they came. While their turn lasted, the Nabataeans wrought greatly, developing overnight, almost, into builders of magnificent cities, unique in the history of the handiwork of man. They were tradesmen, and farmers, and engineers, and architects of great energy and skill. The ruins which they left behind them testify eloquently to the glory which was theirs." (N. Glueck, *The Other Side of the Jordan*, p. 200.) Yet just as surely they testify eloquently to the fulfillment of God's threat against Esau, his nation, and his country. For the last twelve centuries or longer

Edom has been a desolate waste. On the death of Edom as a nation see pp. 208 f.

The World Ruler, unto whom are known from eternity all His ways (Acts 15:18), here calls attention to the future history of Edom, which again would clearly demonstrate His preference of Jacob to Esau. The Jews had been allowed to return to their former homeland from Babylon to rebuild its cities and their Temple. Edom would never enjoy this privilege. Whatever they rebuilt would be again destroyed by the Lord. They would be known as the "border," the territory, "of wickedness," because of their bitter opposition to the Lord and His people, and on that account they would be recognized and called "the people against whom the Lord hath indignation," raging wrath, "forever." (Cp. Jer. 49:13-23.)

V. 5. The eyes of the self-righteous Jews will see the irrefutable evidence that the Lord had indeed loved their nation with a love far transcending that extended to their ancestor. Willingly, or grudgingly, they shall confess that the Lord will be "magnified from the border of Israel" (Gr. N.), rather, is great over, above the territory of Israel; great in majesty and power, but greater still in mercy and grace and love. Why not acknowledge this love now in grateful, loving service of their great Lover? Alas, He finds no joyous appreciation of His affection, no grateful return of love for love, but coldhearted contempt of His grace and ungrateful, self-righteous, grumbling dissatisfaction with His ways.

B. Priests and People Dishonor the Lord, Vv. 6-8

6 A son honors his father, and a servant his master. If I am a Father, where is My honor? And if I am a Master, where is My fear? says the LORD of Hosts to you, O priests, who despise My name. Yet you say, Wherein are we de-
7 spising Thy name? You are bringing to My altar polluted food! And you say, Wherein have we polluted Thee? In that you say, The table of the LORD is contemptible!
8 And when you bring the blind as an offering, that is not evil! And if you bring what is lame and sick, that is not evil! Pray, bring it to your governor, will he accept you or regard you graciously? says the LORD of Hosts.

Grammatical Notes

V. 6. "Honoreth." The imperfect, expressing progressive continuation, is frequently used to denote reiterated actions, implying what may be expected to occur time and again, as in Ps. 1:3-5: giveth, fade, doeth, maketh to prosper, driveth away, do not stand; Prov. 13:5; 26:14, etc. — "Master," אֲדוֹנִים, the majestic plural, to denote a king, as in 1 Kings 22:17; 2 Chron. 18:16; Is. 19:4; here of God = King, Lord, Master. (Cp. Deut. 10:17; Ps. 136:3.) — "Fear,"

מוֹרָא, never denotes the loving fear of a child, but dread, horror, terror. (Cp. Gen. 9:2, "fear," "dread"; Deut. 4:34, "great terrors"; 11:25, "fear," "dread"; 26:8, "terribleness"; 34:12, "terror"; Ps. 76:12, "that ought to be feared"; see v. 13; Is. 8:12, 13, "fear," "dread"; Ps. 10:18, "oppress," margin: "terrify.") It is a fear such as the Psalmist experienced at the contemplation of God's majestic revelation in His Word (Ps. 119:120), and Isaiah (Is. 6:1-5), and Habakkuk (Hab. 3:16).— Mal. 1:6, "fear" is "the object of fear," as, e.g., Ps. 76:11; Is. 8:12, 13.— "Despise My name," the participial form "despising" denotes continuous manifestation, a state of mind, a characteristic trait, etc. (G.-K. 116.) V. 7. "Polluted." Qal not used; Niph. = to be contaminated, as by blood (Is. 59:3; Lam. 4:14; Zeph. 3:1). Pi. = to contaminate. Pu., passive (cp. v. 12),

rejected as unqualified, unfit (Ezra 2:62; Neh. 7:64). V. 8. "If ye offer," the introductory clause of a conditional sentence; "if," כִּי, here = even if, as in Ps. 21:12; 37:24; Prov. 6:35; Hos. 13:15.— "Is it not evil?" We prefer to translate, It is not evil, not regarded as a wickedness. This brings out the wicked character of the people more forcefully. Deliberately they ignore God's Law. — "Governor," פֶּחָה, the modern pasha, the representative of the Persian king. (Cp. Ezra 8:36; Neh. 2:7; 5:14,18; Hag. 1:1,4; 2:2, 21.) This does not refer specifically to Nehemiah, but in general to any "governor." — "Accept thy person," thy face = grant you a cordial reception, welcome you. (Cp. Gen. 32:21, A.V., 20, "accept of me"; 2 Kings 3:14, "regard the presence"; Job 42:8; Prov. 6:35. See also Mal. 1:9, "regard your persons.")

Vv. 6, 7. "Honoreth" (Gr. N.). If a son is at all worthy of the name, he will always be ready to honor his father. Even a slave will honor his master, because the latter is his superior. Such honor is demanded by the natural law of God written in man's heart. This truth the Lord applies to Judah. God had again proved to them that He was in an outstanding manner their loving Father. Where, then, is My honor? And if I am indeed, as you call Me times without number, your Master (Gr. N.) — He uses the majestic plural = Lord — where is My fear? The term used for fear here never denotes the loving fear which prevents a child from grieving his father by disobedience. It rather denotes slavish fear, that dreads the punishment rather than the disobedience. The Lord does not ask, Where is the love you owe Me? He knows that He cannot look for love where honor and fear are lacking. Among the Jews He fails to find even slavish fear. Openly, in unabashed contempt, they transgress His holy Law; the Law of Him who is not a mere human father, not an earthly ruler without power to enforce His will. He is the Lord, the Covenant God, who in this covenant adopted Israel as His son, His first-born (Ex. 4:22), as the object of His special love. He is the Lord of Hosts, the Ruler of the universe, whose power is infinite. Him they neither honor nor fear! These words are addressed par-

515

ticularly to the priests, whom the Lord had loved and honored by making them the spiritual leaders of the people and the mediators between His people and Himself (Ex. 28—30). They thank Him by "despising" (Gr. N.), by becoming mockers, sneering at His name, at the revelation of His will. The Hebrew term denotes the habitual mockery such as only a perverse and crooked nation commits (Deut. 32:5 f.). Once more they challenge the truth of this charge: "Wherein have we despised Thy name?" Again the Lord proves His accusation. "Ye offer polluted bread upon Mine altar" (v. 7). It is the Lord's altar, not the priests'! He alone has the right to order what shall, and what shall not, be offered on His altar. Very definitely He had forbidden to bring animals with certain blemishes to His altar as burnt offerings (Lev. 1:3-10; 22:17-25). The priests had no authority to change the Lord's ordinances. Their duty was to teach these regulations to the people and insist on their conscientious observance. Yet they themselves ignored the clearly expressed will of the Lord by accepting from the people, and offering on the Lord's altar, "polluted bread" (Gr. N.). "Bread" here is the bread, or food, both animal and vegetable, produced by Israel and offered to God in any of the various kinds of sacrifices prescribed by Him. It is called God's "food," or bread (Lev. 3:11, 16; 21:6, 8, 17, 21 f.; 22:25; Num. 28:2, 24). "Polluted," contaminated, impure, because of a blemish, and therefore declared unacceptable by the Lord. (Cp. Lev. 22:17-25.) For the third time they repudiate the Lord's charge. They realize, as their question shows, that offering polluted bread on the Lord's altar is a pollution of the Lord Himself, but refuse to plead guilty of this wickedness. They are always right, the Lord invariably wrong. Once more the Lord convicts and condemns these self-righteous people. "In that ye say," etc. Even if they did not publicly use these exact words, their actions spoke louder than could any words that they regarded the Temple service not as an undeserved honor, but as a contemptible, miserable job. If they had realized the true dignity of their office, they would have obeyed His least command in grateful love and in holy awe have performed every detail of their duty in strict observance of His ordinances. Yet carelessly they disregarded the will of their Lord.

V. 8. "And if ye offer" (Gr. N.). "Ye" includes both the people and the priests. The people did not regard it as an evil, as a wickedness, to bring for sacrifice animals declared by the Lord as unqualified and unacceptable to Him, nor did the priests hesitate to accept such animals, so that it became quite the common custom. In bitter irony the Lord tells them to offer gifts of this nature to their governor (Gr. N.), the representative of their Persian king, in order to gain his favor. They did not dare to do that, knowing too well what would happen. Yet they brazenly offered polluted animals, forbidden, rejected by Him, to the Lord God of Hosts! Will He accept them? The answer is given in the next paragraph (vv. 9-14), a stern No!

C. The Lord Is Ready to Reject the People and the Priests, Vv. 9-14

9 And now, please, implore God that He may be gracious to us! While this is being done by your hands, will He for your sake be gracious?
10 Oh, that even there were one among you that would shut the doors so that there would be no more kindling of fire on My altar uselessly! I have no pleasure in you, says the LORD of Hosts, and I am not pleased with an offering
11 from your hands. For from the rising of the sun to its setting My name shall be great among the nations, and everywhere offerings shall be brought to My name, and a pure offering! For My name shall be great among the nations, says

12 the LORD of Hosts. And you yourselves are profaning it by saying, The table of the LORD is polluted together with its product; His food
13 is contemptible. And you say, Behold, what a wearisome work! And you sniff at it, says the LORD of Hosts. And you offer stolen goods, and lame, and sick, and you bring it as an offering! Shall I be pleased with it from your hands? says the
14 LORD. And cursed is the deceiver in whose flock there is a male, yet who vows and sacrifices to the LORD that which is blemished. For I am a great King, says the LORD of Hosts, and My name is feared among the nations.

Grammatical Notes

V. 9. "Beseech," חַלּוּ פָנִים, literally, to make weak, soften, soothe the face of God, soothe, appease Him, entreat His favor. — "This hath been by your means"; a circumstantial clause, "while this is being done by your hand." (G.-K. 156 d.) — "Regard your persons," מִכֶּם, here, because of you, issuing from you, on your account. (Cp. Ex. 6:9; 15:23; Is. 6:4; 53:4, etc.)

V. 10. The first "for nought" in italics is to be omitted. "An offering," מִנְחָה, here and v. 11 the general term for all sacrificial offerings, animal and vegetable. (Cp. Gen. 4:3-5; Judg. 6:18 f.; 1 Sam. 2:17; Is. 66:20; Zeph. 3:10.)

V. 11. "Incense." מָקְטָר, Hoph. participle of קְטַר, to smoke; Hiph., to cause to arise as smoke, to offer, used of animal and vegetable offerings (Lev. 1:9, 15-17; 2:2-16, etc.). Hoph., passive, that which is being offered. "Offered," literally, brought near, Hoph. of נגשׁ (Ex. 32:6; Amos 5:25; Mal. 1:8; 2:12; 3:3). The participle denotes habitual performance. "Fruit," נִיב, only here and in Is. 57:19, "fruit," product.

V. 13. "What a weariness," מַתְּלָאָה = מַה־תְּלָאָה, from a root = to be tired (Gen. 19:11; Ex. 7:18; Is. 1:14; 16:12, etc.). — "Torn," גָזוּל, taken by force or fraud, illegally gotten (Gen. 21:25; 31:31; Deut. 28:31; Micah 2:2).

517

V. 9. Ironically the prophet urges the wicked priests to try to appease God while they are offering polluted sacrifices and have no intention to change their wicked practice. "Will He regard your persons?" (Gr. N.), rather, Will He accept persons, become gracious unto us, on your account, for the sake of you and your sacrifices? Your sacrifices for us, your prayers for us, your entire mediatory work in our behalf is, as far as you are concerned, contaminated, polluted, unacceptable to the Lord, an abomination to Him! You would make the obtaining of God's grace and forgiveness impossible, unless indeed the Lord, regardless of your personal wickedness, would graciously forgive the sins of the penitent sinner, who brings his offering in complete personal compliance with God's will. But, then, why are we in need of your mediatorship? Does the Lord really need you? Listen to the word of the Lord!

V. 10. "Who is there," etc. (Gr. N.). "Even" adds a thought wholly unexpected, actually shocking to the Jews. Not only does the Lord disregard their offerings, He "even" wishes that someone among them would close the doors so that the entire Temple service, useless as it has been made by the wickedness of priests and people, might be stopped! This wish implies, of course, a threat. He is thoroughly disgusted with the prevailing manner of the Temple service. Even though many Jews were pleased to have such priests, the Lord of the Temple is not pleased with them and will not accept any offerings from hands such as theirs!

V. 11. The doors of the Temple were effectively and forever closed when the Roman armies destroyed it. The Temple was later replaced by a heathen temple. (See p. 495.) Judah had been rejected (Matt. 21:43; 23:37 ff.; Acts 13:45 ff.; 28:24 ff.; 1 Thess. 2:16). But the Lord was not the poorer for the lack of Jewish sacrifices, nor did His worship cease with the rejection of the Jews and the destruction of the Temple. "For" Gentiles would take the place of the Jewish nation as God's people. (Cp. 1 Peter 2:9 with Ex. 19:5, 6.) Looking into the future, the Lord of eternity (Ps. 90:4; 2 Peter 3:8) already sees, from east to west, entire nations magnifying His name. No longer will Jerusalem's Temple be the only sanctuary where His offerings are to be brought to Him to please Him (Deut. 12:5-14; 1 Kings 8:1-13). In every place, throughout the world, "incense shall be offered" (Gr. N.), sacrifices brought to His name. These sacrifices shall not be polluted (cp. v. 7), not brought by penny-pinching hands, or in a spirit of self-righteousness, of dissatisfaction, of greedy bargaining, giving little and demanding rich rewards. These sacrifices will be the offerings given by broken and contrite hearts (Ps. 51:17) in joyous gratitude for God's unmerited grace and in unselfish love of Him who loved them with an everlasting love (Jer. 31:3). Note the stress laid on Jehovah's name, His revelation in His Word, the only means to bring man to a knowledge of the Lord and His salvation. This name shall become great among the Gentiles. (Cp. Acts 8:30-39, "went on his way rejoicing"; 10:33-48; 11:20 ff.; 13:46 ff.; 15:30 f.; 16:14 f., 34.) So says the Lord of Hosts!

Vv. 12-14. This name, to be glorified by the heathen, is the same name revealed to Israel for centuries. But the priests (vv. 12, 13) and the people (v. 14) profaned this name. The priests said in their hearts, by their actions, and undoubtedly often in whining complaints, "The table of the Lord is polluted!" In Ezra 2:62 "polluted" denoted men whose claim to the priesthood could not be substantiated and who were therefore disqualified, rejected from this office. In Malachi's time the priests regarded this divinely instituted office, one of the greatest honors the Lord could bestow on sinful men, as a mean, paltry, poorly paying job. Far from possessing the humble spirit which later characterized the great apostle (1 Cor. 2:1-6; 3:5; 15:8 f.), they felt that they were shamefully underprivileged people. The "fruit" = the product, the gain, the living we get from our job, the "bread" = the food we receive for our service at the altar, how contemptible it is! What the people cannot sell, what they refuse to eat, all the sick and old and defective animals are palmed off on us, and the best parts, the fat, must be offered on the altar, while we get what is left! And what a weariness (v. 13) to stand all day long and be ready whenever someone feels like bringing his sacrifice, to slay it, and skin it, and gut it, and cut it up, a filthy, bloody job, and what do we get out of it? A few pieces of tough meat, unfit for food! Dissatisfied, they fault the Lord for conditions they themselves had brought about. The Lord tells these self-righteous, self-opinionated people that they were addressing complaints to the wrong party. Squarely He puts the blame where it properly belongs, on the shoulders of the faithless priests. He tells them that in glaring disrespect of the Lord's ordinances (Lev. 22:17 ff.) and in greedy, selfish desire to fill their stomach with food, they had permitted, and by such permission encouraged, the people to offer to God the cheapest possible price for His favor and blessing, which they felt He owed them. Instead of insisting on strict observance of God's restrictions, they had accepted the sick and lame and even "that which was torn" (Gr. N.), rather,

519

stolen, or gotten by fraud, and then brought "as an offering" (Gr. N.), as the offering which God had prescribed and to which He had attached His promise of forgiveness (Lev. 1:4-9, 13, 17; 2:2, 9). Shall God be satisfied with an offering which they themselves regarded as contemptible and the Lord had declared polluted, unfit? From such unworthy priests He refuses to accept any offering. They are ripe for judgment, for rejection from His presence.

Nor does the wickedness of the priests exonerate or even excuse the individual Jew offering polluted sacrifices. He pronounces His curse (v. 14) on the deceiver who has in his flock a male and instead vows and sacrifices a corrupt animal unto the Lord as a burnt offering. This particular perfidy stands for all similar deceptions and tricks whereby a self-righteous people sought to deceive the omniscient Lord (Jer. 17:10). People and priests alike are ready for God's curse and rejection.

The Lord has the right to demand the best, for He is a great King. This was a title claimed by the Persian kings. Compare the edict of Cyrus, in which he calls himself the king of the world, the great king, and applies the latter title, "great king," to his father, his grandfather, and great-grandfather (Rogers, *Cuneiform Parallels*, p. 382). King Cyrus' proclamation (Ezra 1:1-4) was honored by a later king, Darius (Ezra 5:1-12). The proclamation of the King of Kings, the World Ruler, was deliberately set aside by His appointed priests and His adopted people. Once more He calls attention to the fact that heathen despised by Israel will glorify and revere the great and dreadful name of the Lord. Gentiles will be adopted by grace; Israel, rejected for contempt of this grace!

CHAPTER 2

D. The Corrupt Priesthood, Vv. 1-9

1 And now, this command is for you,
2 O priests. If you will not obey and will not lay it to heart, to give honor to My name, says the LORD of Hosts, then I will send the curse among you, and I will curse your blessings, and I will indeed make it a curse, for none of you lay it to
3 heart. Behold, I will rebuke your seed, and I will scatter dung on your faces, the dung of your festivals, and you shall be carried to
4 it, and you shall know that I have sent this command to you, that My covenant was with Levi, says the
5 LORD of Hosts. My covenant was with him, life and peace, and I gave them to him that he might fear, and he feared Me and trembled at
6 My name. Instruction of truth was in his mouth, and no perversity was found in his lips. In peace and straightforwardness he walked with Me and turned many from iniquity.
7 For the lips of a priest preserve knowledge; and they seek instruction from his mouth, for he is the messenger of the LORD of Hosts.

8 But you have turned aside from the way and have made the Law a stumbling block for many. You have violated the covenant of Levi, 9 says the LORD of Hosts. So I My- self also have made you despised and abased before all the people inasmuch as you are not keeping My ways and are showing par- tiality in the Law.

Grammatical Notes

V. 2. "Yea, I have cursed them already," literally, "yea I have cursed it." The singular suffix "it" points to each in- dividual blessing of the many just men- tioned. LXX translates the plural "blessings" as a singular.

V. 3. "Corrupt." עֵר never denotes to corrupt, but to cry out aloud, rebuke, scold. God's rebuke keeps the seed from fulfilling its desire to sprout. (Cp. Hos. 2: 21 f., pp. 31 ff.) "One shall take."

"One" here indefinite, "one," someone, or "they," or it may be rendered by the passive, "you shall be carried to it."

V. 5. "For the fear," as an object of fear. (Cp. ch. 1: 6; see Gr. N. there.) "Was afraid," Niph. of a root = to be broken, downcast, frightened. (Cp. Is. 7: 8; 8: 9; 20: 5; Jer. 1: 17.)

V. 8. "Corrupted," שָׁחַתֶּם, Pi. = ruin, de- stroy (Gen. 13: 10; Is. 14: 20; Jer. 12: 10).

Vv. 1, 2. This prophecy is addressed particularly to the priests as a special divine commandment. (Cp. 1 Sam. 13: 13; 1 Kings 13: 21.) Besides the prophets and kings, the priests were divinely appointed leaders of the people. They were mediators between God and His people (Ex. 28: 1 ff.), the teachers of Israel (Lev. 10: 11; Deut. 33: 10; 2 Chron. 15: 3; Mal. 2: 7), a court of appeal (Deut. 19: 17 ff.). Their honorable position demanded a corresponding faithfulness in the per- formance of their varied duties. The Lord urges them to hear, to give wholehearted attention to His words, so that they might in the execu- tion of their duties give proper honor and glory to His name. They had failed to do that (ch. 1: 6 ff.). The Lord had promised the priests that their blessings would be God's blessings (Num. 6: 23-27). Since they refuse to obey Him, He will also change their blessings into a curse (v. 2). He has already begun to curse "them" (Gr. N.), every one of their blessings, whether they were repetitions of God's benediction or blessings of their own invention. (Cp. Jer. 4: 10; 6: 14; 8: 11.)

Vv. 3, 4. The Lord will "corrupt" (Gr. N.) their seed, literally, will rebuke, scold, threaten the seed for them. He will forbid the seed to sprout and grow and bear fruit for such disobedient priests. And the seed, unlike the priests, will obey His command. The priests will be punished where these selfish belly servants are most vulnerable; they will have nothing to fill their bellies. Their corruption smelled to high heaven (Amos 5: 21). Now God will spread the dung of their solemn feasts upon their faces. Their sanctimonious mien, their hypo-

521

critical piety will be turned into an abhorrent spectacle. Together "with it," that dung clinging to them, their reputation smeared by their own actions, they shall be taken away (Gr. N.), carried to the dung pile (cp. Is. 66:24), the proper place for such filthy people (Rev. 21:8; 22:15; Mal. 3:5). So shall they realize that He, Jehovah, had sent them this commandment (v. 4), had called them into the priesthood, here defined as the Lord's covenant with Levi. It was not an institution which they were free to twist and bend according to their own whims. It was the Lord's creation, which no one would dishonor and besmirch unpunished.

V. 5. His covenant with Levi was one of life and peace (cp. Num. 25:12 f.), one of God's means to create and nourish "life," spiritual life, eternal life, the possession and assurance of which would give true value to physical life, make it a joy to live, no matter what the outer circumstances might be. It was a means of granting that peace with God (Num. 6:26) which the Messiah was to procure for sinful people (Is. 53:5; cp. Is. 26:3-12; 32:17 ff.; 54:10-13; 55:12; 57:2-19; 66:12 ff.). "I gave them," the life and the peace of God, "to him," Levi, and in him to the priesthood, "for the fear," as an object of fear, dread (same word as in ch. 1:6; see Gr. N. there). The very thought of losing this high gift by disdain or carelessness was to horrify him, and the preservation of this covenant by faithfully attending to its varied duties was to be his daily anxious concern. (Cp. Ezra 7:10, 25-28; Is. 8:13; Phil. 2:12; 1 Peter 1:17; 1 Tim. 1:18 f.; 4:12-16; 2 Tim. 1:6 ff.; 2:15 f.) "Wherewith" is not found in the original. "He feared Me," in filial, loving fear, the beginning of wisdom. "He was afraid" (Gr. N.), always aware of the solemn obligation resting upon a sinful human being honored by His Creator and Redeemer to be His servant. (Cp. Gen. 39:9.) "Before My name," in view of God's holy name and revelation. (Cp. Ex. 3:5; 33:20 ff.; 34:8; 40:35; 1 Sam. 3:9 f.; 1 Kings 8:11; Heb. 2:20.)

V. 6. "Law" here = instruction, teaching (cp. Prov. 1:8; 13:14), particularly that given by the Lord in His Word (Is. 1:10; 2:3; 8:20). "Of truth," God's Word (Ps. 119:43, 142, 151; John 17:17; 2 Cor. 6:7). They taught not their own views, human theories and speculations, but the infallible, invariable truth the Lord had revealed in His Word. This they taught without addition or diminution, without fear or favor. "Iniquity," crookedness, twisting the Word to suit their fancy, was not found in their lips. They were reliable, trustworthy witnesses of God's will. They walked with God, ever remaining on the paths He had chosen for them, "in peace," in full harmony with Him. And His continued presence gave them peace. (Cp. Ex. 33:14; Is. 26:3.) The certainty that God was with them and they with Him made them unafraid. In the midst of antagonism the peace of God, passing all understanding, kept their hearts and minds calm and satisfied. "Equity," literally, what is straight, even, plain. They applied God's Word, Law and Gospel, rightly dividing the Word of truth (2 Tim. 2:15; Matt. 13:52), ever mindful of the Lord's word (Ezek. 33:1-9). And their faithful service was blessed by the Lord: they turned many away from iniquity, helping them to remain on the way of life, or to return to it, or to find it.

V. 7. "Knowledge," here as in Prov. 1:4; 2:6; Jer. 22:16; Hos. 4:6, the living and loving knowledge of God and His Word and will, a knowledge which the Lord alone can give (Ps. 94:10; Prov. 2:6) and of which the fear of the Lord is the indispensable requisite (Prov. 1:7; 9:10; Job 28:28; Ps. 111:10). This knowledge the lips of the priest are to keep, observe, guard as a precious treasure. As the divinely appointed teacher of God's people he shall teach God's Word, no more, no less. The repeated admonitions of the Lord addressed to the people in general (Deut. 4:2; 12:32; Prov. 30:6; cp. Rev. 22:18) certainly included the leaders, civic rulers (Deut. 17:18 ff.; Joshua 1:7 ff.), prophets (Jer. 1:7, 17; 23:25 ff.; 26:2), and are here applied to the priests. From their mouths the people are to seek the Law, instruction in God's Word. They were messengers of the Lord God of Hosts, a great honor which neither the priests nor the people are to forget or ignore.

Vv. 8, 9. The priests in Malachi's time did not measure up to this high standard. The Lord presents three charges against them. They have been unfaithful toward themselves. They have deliberately turned away from the way of salvation. They have caused the people to stumble at the Law. Laxity in applying the Law of God and partiality in its administration will naturally lead to contempt of the Law, to ever bolder transgressions and ever wider spread of illegal practices. Finally, the priests have "corrupted" (Gr. N.), destroyed, broken the Levitical covenant; they are covenant breakers, revolters against the Lord's charter with Levi. Such wickedness the Lord will not permit to remain unavenged (v. 9; cp. Ex. 21:23 ff.; Lev. 24:20). As they have despised the Lord, so He will make them despised and base, disreputable to the entire nation, in the same measure as they had refused to keep His way and had become guilty of partiality in applying the Law.

E. Marrying Heathen Wives Dishonors God's Covenant, Vv. 10-12

10 Have we not all one Father? Has not one God created us? Why, then, do we deal treacherously one with his brother, to desecrate the
11 covenant of our fathers? Judah deals treacherously, and abominations are committed in Israel and in Jerusalem, for Judah desecrates the sanctuary of the LORD, which He loves, and has married the
12 daughter of a foreign god. May the LORD cut off for the man that does this the watcher and the answering one from the tents of Jacob, and him who brings an offering to the LORD of Hosts.

Grammatical Notes

V. 10. "Profaning," לְחַלֵּל, from a root = to loosen, relax; to degrade, desecrate, make common, base.

V. 11. "Judah." Leah connected the name of her fourth son with a verb denoting giving of thanks, praising (Gen. 29:35; cp. Gen. 49:8, *yoduka,* "shall praise"). St. Paul may have alluded to this play on words in Rom. 2:29.

V. 12. "Will cut off, יַכְרֵת, jussive, expressing wish, desire, command; "the master and the scholar," עֵר וְעֹנֶה, evidently a proverbial expression in the form of combining two opposites in order to express totality. (Cp. "shut up or left," Deut. 32:36; "city-field," "basket and store" ["store" is "kneading trough"] Deut. 28:3, 5, 16, 17.) The exact meaning of the two terms used by Malachi can no longer be definitely determined. Targum and Syriac have "son and grandson," Jerome has "teacher and pupil," so A. V. and Luther; LXX has ἕως (reading עַד for עֵר) καὶ ταπεινωθῇ, until He also has humbled, abased them. Most interpreters render the phrase "watcher and answerer." עֵיר occurs in Dan. 4:10, 14, 20 (A. V., 13, 17, 23) as "watcher," the sentinel, to whose warning cry the people "answer," respond. Hence the phrase as used by Malachi may mean the entire body of people, the whole nation. — "Him that offereth an offering," מַגִּישׁ. The Hebrew term is used of the people (Ex. 32:6; Amos 5:25), of Moses (Lev. 8:14), of Gideon (Judg. 6:19), of priests (Lev. 2:8). Malachi uses it exclusively of priestly sacrifice (ch. 1:7; cp. v. 6, "priests"; 3:3, "sons of Levi"). Hence it is preferable to think of the sacrifice offered by the priests here also.

Vv. 10, 11. This passage is very frequently cited as a proof for the universal fatherhood of God and the universal brotherhood of man. The context forbids such an interpretation. If Malachi had regarded all mankind as children of the universal Father, he certainly would not and could not have used this universal brotherhood as an argument against the marriage of Jews to heathen women. The Lord does not regard these women as His daughters, but as "daughters of a strange god" (v. 11). As the offspring of a strange, foreign god they derived their character from their parent. They did not love and worship Jehovah in filial affection. They gave to an idol that honor which the Lord claims as His exclusive due (Is. 42:8; 48:11; Ex. 20:3 ff.). Moreover (v. 10), the Lord calls the intermarriage of Jews and heathen a "profaning (Gr. N.) the covenant of our fathers" = the Sinaitic Covenant. This was not a universal covenant, but a covenant with an individual nation chosen by the Lord to be a peculiar treasure to Him "above," separate from, "all other people" (Ex. 19:5; cp. Deut. 4:32-38; Ps. 147:20; Amos 3:1 ff.). In this covenant, accepted by Israel (Ex. 19:8; 24:3-8), the Lord adopted this nation as His own, acknowledging the Israelites as His children (Ex. 4:22; Is. 63:16; 64:8; Jer. 31:9; Hos. 1:10). "Has not one God created us" cannot therefore refer to their physical creation. That, of course, also was His work (Ps. 139:13 ff.; Job 10:8 ff.). Yet here he speaks of a creative act whereby He accepts human beings, born in sin and by nature His enemies, as His children and declares Himself their Father. (Cp. Ex. 4:22 f.; Deut. 14:1; 32:6; Ps. 103:13; Is. 1:2; 63:16; 64:8; Jer. 3:19; 31:9; Mal. 1:6; Rom. 8:14-17, 29; Gal. 3:26 f.; 4:4 ff.; 1 John 3:1 ff.) If this is true — and no Jew would deny it — "why do we" — the prophet includes himself! He is a member of that sinful nation — "why do we deal treacherously every man against his brother," one against another? That is a serious charge! But he adds an even graver charge. Their sin is not only a violation of brotherly love. It is a profanation of their Magna Charta, the covenant of their fathers, established not between man and man, but between man and his God, the Lord Jehovah. This desecration of a solemn covenant was committed, not by a heathen nation, but by a nation honored by the Lord in a special manner, Judah, Israel, Jerusalem. Judah (Gr. N.) (v. 11) was the name of their ancestor so highly honored that He was praised by his brothers. He alone of the twelve brothers had been chosen to become the father of the royal house of Israel, the ancestor of the Messiah (Gen. 49:8-12; Jer. 23:6). This Judah had turned traitor, was dealing treacherously! Israel (Gen. 32:28), the honorable name of the twelve tribes, of which Judah was now the only representative; Jerusalem, the city chosen by the Lord to be His habitation (Ps. 132:13 ff.), this Israel, this Jerusalem had committed an "abomination," a term used to describe pagan idolatry and immorality. (Cp. Ex. 8:26; Lev. 18:26; 20:13.) "The holiness" here not God's personal holiness, as the added "which He loves" shows. Israel, whom the Lord loved (cp. Mal. 1:1), had been given the blessed privilege to be a holy nation (Ex. 19:6), a holy people (Deut. 7:6; 14:2), holiness (Jer. 2:3), a sanctuary (Ps. 114:2), a holy seed = a seed of holiness, in whom the holiness of God, its Father, was to be reflected. Now Judah was guilty of profaning this holiness, of desecrating itself, lowering itself to the common level of unholy mankind. After having called attention to the wickedness of Judah's sin, the Lord finally names it: not blasphemy, murder, theft, but what had seemed to the people a harmless matter, marriage with heathen women. Such marriages were forbidden primarily because of the danger of seduction to idolatry (Ex. 34:11-16; Deut. 7:1-4). No Israelite was to marry a Canaanite woman, one of the original inhabitants of Canaan. Because of the constant danger of seduction, other heathen nations were later included in this prohibition. Cp. 1 Kings 11:1, where descendants of Esau and Lot (Edomites, Moabites, Ammonites) are added. Even wise King Solomon had been seduced to idolatry by his wives (1 Kings 11:1-11). On such marriages in Malachi's time cp. Ezra 9:1 ff.; Neh. 13:23-31.

V. 12 is a threat of total destruction to be visited upon Israel, the covenant nation (Ex. 19—40; Lev. 26:12; Deut. 4:5-8). "The master and the scholar" (Gr. N.), high and low, learned and unlearned, all alike, the entire nation shall be cut off from the "tabernacle" of Jacob, the visible emblem of God's covenant with His people. Already in Moses' time God had threatened to consume the people, total extinction of the covenant nation, averted only by Moses' plea, Ex. 32:1-14.

F. Divorce Is Hateful to God, Vv. 13-16

13 And this you are doing as a second sin: You cover with tears the altar of the LORD, with weeping and wailing, because there is no longer any turning to the offerings or favorable reception from your hands.
14 And you say, For what reason? Because the LORD is a witness between you and the wife of your youth, against whom you have been unfaithful, though she is your mate
15 and your covenanted wife. And the one has not done this, and he had a remnant of spirit! And what was that one seeking? God's (Promised) Seed! So take heed of yourselves, and let no one be unfaithful to the wife of his youth.
16 For I hate divorce, says the LORD, the God of Israel; and he covers his garment with wickedness, says the LORD of Hosts. But take heed of your spirit, and do not be unfaithful!

Grammatical Notes

V. 13. "Again," שֵׁנִית, here = a second thing, a second sin. — "Insomuch," מֵאֵין; the English adverb = in such wise, to such a degree. So a number of interpreters translate the Hebrew term and refer the weeping, etc., to that of the divorced women weepingly pleading with God to avenge them and on whose account the Lord refused the offerings of the guilty husbands. Yet there seems to be no warrant for this translation; the Hebrew term always = because there is not; here = the divorcing Jews weep because God no longer rewards their sacrifices. Cp. the plague named ch. 3:11.

V. 14. "Companion," חֲבֶרְתְּךָ, from a root = to bind, join, unite. (Cp. Gen.

526

2:24.) "The wife of thy covenant," the suffix belongs to the entire phrase, thy covenant wife.

V. 15. "Did he not make one," "make" = עָשָׂה, here in sense of "operate," conduct oneself, behave, act. (Cp. 1 Sam. 26:25; Ps. 22:32, A. V., 31 = act effectively; Ezra 10:14; Jer. 9:6, A. V., 7; 14:7; Dan. 8:24; 11:30.) "One," here = one only, single, alone. (Cp. Gen. 27:38; Deut. 6:4; Joshua 17:14, 17; 1 Kings 8:56; Zech. 3:9; 14:7, 9; Mal. 2:10.) The article is frequently omitted for the purpose of intensifying the root idea of the noun, in order to create the sensation of something great, extraordinary, exalted. (G.-K. 125 c.) Cp. Job 8:10, "words" remarkable for wisdom; Job 15:13, "words" remarkably wicked; Ps. 2:7, a decree, and what a decree! v. 12,

a Son, unique! Is. 28:2, a Mighty and Strong, of excelling might and strength; 31:8, three times, "a sword" = the all powerful, all-consuming sword of the Lord. Hence here, the one, the lone man, and what a lone man!

V. 16. "He hateth," שָׂנֵא, third person sing. Qal. The prophet states a fact, and then claims divine authority for this fact — "One covereth," etc. This may be an example of suppression of the demonstrative pronoun (G.-K. 155 n). Cp. Is. 41:24, literally, an abomination, it chooseth you; Ex. 4:13, send by, you will send; hence here, I hate, and him who covers. Or it may simply add the personal consequence of the sin, and (by doing that) he covers his garment with violence. The A. V. rendering cannot be upheld, rather, covers violence upon, over, his garment.

Vv. 13, 14. "Again" (Gr. N.). The Lord names a second instance of treacherous profanation of the divinely established covenant. (Cp. vv. 10 b, 11 a.) As in the previous charge, so here He names the sin only after pointing out its wickedness as indicated by its dire consequences. They "are covering the altar of the LORD," deluging it with tears, and weeping, and lamentation, "insomuch" (Gr. N.), rather, because it was a weeping caused by the Lord's refusal to reward or even regard their offerings and prayers. (Cp. Is. 1:10-15; 58:2-7.) Yet it was not the sorrow of penitent sinners bewailing their sins. These outbursts of woe and anguish were the complaints of untractable children, who in stubborn self-satisfaction demanded the Father's blessings and favors while refusing to give Him the love and obedience they owed to Him. Once more their stubborn self-righteousness manifests itself. "Wherefore?" they impudently ask (v. 14). Immediately the Lord tells them why His blessings are no longer forthcoming. He "hath been witness." The Lord, the Author of the state of matrimony, has heard their marital vow, in consequence of which He had joined them together as husband and wife in closest, most intimate union, a union which only death was to sever, a union in which the husband shall cleave to his wife (Gen. 2:24), cling in love and affection to the wife of his youth. Age is not to destroy or even to weaken marital love; it is to purify, solidify, deepen it. As the years

pass, husband and wife in ever higher degree are to become one
(Gen. 2: 24; Matt. 19: 5, 6; Eph. 5: 28 f.), united in mutual affectionate
love. That was no longer the common custom in Israel. Addressing
the husband, God charges him with having dealt treacherously with
his wife; he has played the traitor, has broken the solemn covenant
of marriage made in the sight of God. He has done this even though
she is his "companion" (Gr. N.), who has shared not only his joys,
but helped him to bear his sorrows. More than that, she is "the wife
of his covenant." With him she is a member of God's covenant people,
to whom has been given the promise of the Woman's Seed (Gen. 12: 3;
18: 18; Jer. 23: 5, 6). This divine covenant he has treacherously violated by divorcing his Jewish wife and marrying a heathen woman.
"He who annuls the distinction between an Israelite and a heathen
woman proves by this very action that he has already annihilated the
distinction between the God of Israel and the idols of the heathen,
that he has no longer the theocratic consciousness of God." (Hengstenberg, *Christologie* III, ed. 1835, p. 381.)

V. 15. The interpretation of this verse presents the most contro-
versial problem in Malachi's book (see Gr. N. on "make one"). After
all that has been said and written on this subject, we believe that
Luther's translation and interpretation of this verse is substantially
correct. According to him, the Lord here foresees and forestalls
another attempt of the Jews to justify their conduct, as they had
done in ch. 1: 2, 6, 7; 2: 14, 17; cp. 3: 7, 8, 13 ff. They might try to defend
their action by pointing to the example of their father Abraham,
whose offspring they boastingly declared to be. (Cp. Matt. 3: 8;
Luke 3: 8; John 8: 33, 39; 2 Cor. 11: 22.) Abraham took a foreign woman
as his wife, Hagar (Gen. 16: 3). Why should not Abraham's children
be permitted to do likewise? Abraham had repudiated Hagar (Gen.
21: 7-14). Why should not the Jews have the same liberty? The Lord
shows the irrelevancy of their appeal even before they had advanced it.
Luther also makes a very practical application. "It is disastrous to
follow all the deeds of the fathers without divine call, and equally
harmful to teach such a practice. One should rather imitate their
faith and their obedience to God's Word. We must observe what God
has commanded us to do, not what some other person does." (St. L.,
XIV, 2177 f.) — The objection raised by many that the Jews of
Malachi's time could not have understood this allusion without further
explanation is groundless. This is not the only passage in which
Abraham is called "one." (Cp. Is. 51: 2; Ezek. 33: 24, where "one,"
"alone," also refers to his singleness, his childlessness.) Abraham,

who was to be made a great nation, many nations (Gen. 12:2; 15:5; 17:4-6, 16; 18:8), was called when he was 75 years old and childless (Gen. 12:4), and Sarah, ten years younger (Gen. 17:17), was barren (11:30; 16:1 f.). Humanly speaking, there was no hope for a son and heir, and every passing year made the fulfillment of this promise, humanly speaking, the more impossible (ch. 15:2; 17:17; 18:11 f.; 21:7). In their intense desire to bring about the fulfillment they had resorted to various plans. (Cp. Gen. 15:2; 16:1-4, 16.) The promise was renewed when Abraham was 99 years old (17:1, 5). A year later Isaac was born (21:1-7). For 100 years Abraham was the one forefather of the promised Woman's Seed. For 25 years after he had received the promise Sarah remained childless. Abraham of all men was the great "lone man," the *echad,* in the history of Israel. This fact was not unknown to the Jews. Moses had recorded it very definitely and repeatedly. Isaiah had called attention to it (Is. 51:2). In Ezekiel's time the Jews based their vain hope of never losing possession of their homeland on the fact that they were many, while Abraham was "one," a single, childless man when he inherited the land (Ezek. 33:24). Such Jews as had forgotten this fact were reminded of it by the prophet's words.

"Yet had he" (Gr. N.) "residue of the spirit." The Lord speaks ironically. Abraham, the lone man, had more than a remnant of the spirit, a small portion of spirituality. He was a man of extraordinary spiritual strength, of powerful faith, unwavering trust, and unquestioning obedience to God's will. (Cp. Is. 51:1, 2; Rom. 4:16-22; Heb. 11:8-19.) He did not marry a foreign woman, as did the Jews of Malachi's time, to satisfy his carnal desire. He did it at the suggestion of his wife (Gen. 16:1-3) in an endeavor to seek "a godly seed," "a seed of God" (marginal reading), promised to him by the Lord. And he repudiated Hagar, not because he hated her, but because her son Ishmael was continually mocking Isaac (the frequentative participle) (Gen. 21:9) and persecuting him with his mockeries (Gal. 4:29). For the sake of the seed of God, Isaac, Abraham cast out Ishmael and his mother. "Therefore" do not seek to defend your marriage with heathen women and your dismissal of your covenant wives by pointing to Abraham, but take heed to your spirit, your spiritual life, your faith and love of God, lest by willful, persistent disobedience to His will, by your treacherous repudiation of your wives, you lose what spiritual life you still possess.

V. 16. The Lord hates (Gr. N.) "putting away," because the divorcer "covereth violence with his garment" (Gr. N.), rather, covers his garment with "violence." His divorce is like a filthy spot on his garment, his cloak, his reputation, stigmatizing him as guilty of "violence," atrocious wickedness, outrageous criminality, a sin which brought on the Deluge (Gen. 6:11, 13). So speaks the Lord of Hosts, the Ruler of the universe, the Judge Supreme. He adds a final warning appeal, repeating the warning of v. 15 b.

PART II

The Lord Will Come as the Redeemer and Judge; Therefore Prepare to Meet Him

Chapters 2:17—4:6 (M. T., 3:24)

A. The Occasion for This Prophecy, Ch. 2:17

17 You have wearied the LORD with your words! But you say, Wherein have we wearied Him? Because you say, Every evildoer is good in the eyes of the LORD, and He is pleased with them; or, Where is the Lord of Judgment?

Grammatical Notes

V. 17. "Good," טוב, here in the ethical sense, morally good, righteous, virtuous. (Cp. 1 Kings 3:9; Ps. 112:5; Prov. 12:2; 13:22; Eccl. 9:2.)

V. 17. "Ye have wearied." The Covenant God of unchanging holiness and infinite grace warns His dissatisfied people. Their past behavior has wearied Him. The Hebrew perfect describes the act in its completion. They have succeeded in making Jehovah tired of His people! He is ready to withdraw His blessings promised to a loving, God-fearing, obedient people (Lev. 26:3-13; Deut. 28:2-14), ready to carry out the curses He pronounced upon them if they refused to do His will (Lev. 26:14-38; Deut. 28:15-68). Blinded by their self-righteousness (cp. Matt. 23:16, 17, 19, 24, 26; John 9:39-41), they insolently ask, "Wherein have we wearied?" You certainly have no cause to be tired of such faithful servants as we are, who have meticulously observed Your Law! Again the Lord condescends to speak to these insolent fellows in a final effort to convince them of their wickedness and the danger of imminent rejection. He calls to their mind the blasphemous charges they had uttered against the Lord of holiness and justice. They had openly charged Him with being guilty of the same perversity He had so severely condemned (Is. 5:20), of regarding the wicked evildoers as "good" (Gr. N.), virtuous, pious people with whose person and whose actions He was well pleased. Some Jews not quite so outspoken had couched their complaints in milder words, "Where is the God of judgment?" Wherever the recognition of man's total depravity and unworthiness is absent or begins to wane, there in the same measure the realization of the unmerited grace of God becomes darkened. When God sends trials and sorrows, such people begin to charge Him with injustice. Why does He permit the wicked transgressors of His Law to live and enjoy life, while we, His obedient servants, must suffer hardships, poverty, shame? That is not the language of faith and trust in God; that is the language of self-righteousness, of doubt, of unbelief, of selfish pride. Puny man, the ephemeral creature, criticizing the eternal Jehovah, his Creator and Redeemer, simply because he cannot comprehend Him whose ways are past finding out (Ps. 36:6; Is. 40:28; 55:9). It is the same sin for which the Lord had pronounced His woe on the fathers of the Jews (Is. 5:20 ff.). Unbelief is a damnable sin, whether found in manifestly wicked scoffers or in the heart of professed believers (Is. 7:9 b; 2 Kings 17:14-18; Ps. 78:21 ff., 32 f.; 106:24 f.). Both classes had wearied the Lord; both are on the point of being rejected. Yet the Lord has no pleasure in the death of the wicked. Once more He addresses and warns His dissatisfied, rebellious people in an urgent plea, For why will ye die, O house of Israel? Turn ye from your evil ways, and live! (Ezek. 33:11.)

CHAPTER 3

B. The Lord Will Come Surely and Suddenly! V. 1

1 Behold, I will send My messenger, and he shall prepare the way before Me. And suddenly shall come to His temple the Lord whom you are seeking and the Messenger of the Covenant in whom you delight. Behold, He is coming! says the LORD of Hosts.

Grammatical Notes

V. 1. "Behold, I will send," etc. "He shall come." Behold! הִנֵּה, with the participle does not necessarily indicate the immediate fulfillment of the prophecy. (Cp. 1 Kings 13:2; 16:3; Is. 7:14; 13:17; Jer. 1:15; 30:10; 31:8; 49:35; 50:9,18,41; Zech. 9:9.) "It asserts forcefully and suggestively the certainty of the approach" (Driver, *Tenses*, p. 196, par. 135,3). — "Suddenly," פִּתְאֹם, is never used to denote immediacy; it always means unexpectedly, regardless of the lapse of time (Joshua 10:9; 11:7; Num. 12:4; Ps. 64:5,8, A. V., 4,7; Prov. 3:25; 6:15; Is. 47:11; Jer. 4:20, etc.). — "Lord," אָדוֹן, one vested with power, authority, commanding respect. (Cp. Gen. 23:6,11, 18; 40:1,7; 42:10,30,33, etc.) The majestic plural is often used of God; the singular with article, denoting the one supreme Lord. (Cp. Ex. 23:17; 34:23; Is. 1:24; 3:1; 10:16,33; Micah 4:13; Zech. 4:14; 6:5, etc.)

531

V. 1. The self-righteous Jews had charged the Lord with in-justice and had clamored for the manifestation of His judgment. The Lord answers this charge as only the Lord of unalterable justice and unchanging mercy can answer it (Ex. 34: 6 f.). He reveals once more His holiness, which demands perfect holiness in His people because He is holy (Lev. 11: 44; 19: 2; 20: 7). At the same time He manifests His long-suffering, His patience, His forbearing grace and mercy by seeking to win back to childlike love and fear these selfish, stubborn, grumbling people, ready for rejection.

"Behold, I will send" (Gr. N.); the speaker is the Lord of Hosts. His promises are assured facts (Num. 23: 19; Ps. 33: 9). "My mes-senger," My angel, My herald, sent not only to announce the Lord's coming, but also to "prepare the way before Me" (Is. 40: 3). The High and Lofty One dwells only with those who are of a contrite and humble spirit (Is. 57: 15); therefore the preparation of the way consists in the removal of all stumbling blocks (Is. 57: 14; cp. 62: 10). All self-righteousness and proud reliance on one's own goodness, all unbelief and doubt, all crookedness and perversity must be removed. This is a work impossible to man (Jer. 17: 9; 31: 18; Lam. 5: 21). But the Lord will send His messenger to prepare the way before the Lord by His message. There ought to be no doubt as to the identity of this messenger. All four evangelists unite in declaring that Is. 40: 3 was fulfilled in the person of John the Baptist (Matt. 3: 3; 11: 7-10; Mark 1: 3; Luke 3: 4; John 1: 23). Malachi furthermore calls this messenger the second Elijah (ch. 3: 23, A. V., 4: 5), and we have the testimony of God's angel (Luke 1: 16 f.) and of the Son of God, whose Spirit moved the prophets (1 Peter 1: 11), that John the Baptist was the second Elijah (Matt. 11: 12-15). Christ bewails the fact that the unbelieving Jews did not "receive," believe, this fact, or obey the Baptist's penitential call (cp. Matt. 17: 10-13). Hence "messenger" here cannot be regarded as a collective term, including all prophets and preachers preparing the way for Christ. We have here a very specific prophecy fulfilled in the mission of John the Baptist. Nor does the fact that in Mal. 2: 7 "the priest" is collective, i. e., the priesthood as represented by Levi, permit the generalization of the future herald. Ch. 2: 7 speaks of a past fact, a divine institution which had existed for centuries, while ch. 3: 1 speaks of a messenger to come in the future, who is definitely identified by Christ and the divinely inspired evan-gelists as John the Baptist, the special herald of the Lord. On his message see Matt. 3: 2, 7-12; Mark 1: 4-8; Luke 3: 7-18; John 1: 6-8,

19-36; 3:22-36. Law and Gospel! This messenger of the Lord of Hosts shall prepare the way, not for an earthly ruler, but "before Me," Jehovah Sabaoth. Yet Jehovah, speaking of Himself in the first person, announcing His advent, suddenly speaks of Him whose way shall be prepared, in the third person, "The Lord shall come"; *adon* (Gr. N.), same word as ch. 1:6, "master," "ruler," one vested with authority and power. The article designates Him as the Supreme Ruler. He is that Son of David whom David called his Lord, *adon*, sitting at the right hand of the Lord Jehovah (Ps. 110:1; cp. Matt. 22:42-45), who as the eternal royal High Priest (Ps. 110:4) is Jehovah Our Righteousness (Jer. 23:5 f.). Yet He is not a second Lord. Though a second person, He is One with Jehovah in one indivisible essence and being (Ex. 23:20 f.; John 10:30; 14:9 ff.). When this Lord comes, Jehovah comes.

"To His temple." The Temple built by Solomon and rebuilt by Zerubbabel was Jehovah's dwelling place (1 Kings 8:11; Hag. 1:9, 14; Mal. 1:7, 10; 2:13; cp. Ex. 25:8; 40:34 f.). This Temple prefigured the New Testament temple of God, His holy Christian Church. (Cp. Ezek. 37:26 f.; 43:7.) The dwelling of God among people with His Word makes them His temple. (Cp. Ex. 25:8; Lev. 26:12; Ezek. 11:16 [Israel in exile; "little" = for a little while]; Matt. 16:17 f.; 18:18-20; 1 Cor. 3:9-17; 2 Cor. 6:16 ff.; Eph. 2:19 ff.; 1 Peter 2:4 f.; Heb. 12:22 ff.) The Lord's coming to His temple must not be restricted to Christ's presentation in the Temple (Luke 2:22 f.) or to His visits to the Temple (Luke 2:41 ff.; 20:6 ff.; John 2:13; 5:1 ff.; 7:14 ff., etc.). These were only some of the manifestations of His having come to His Church (John 1:11-15).

"Suddenly" (Gr. N.), unexpectedly. How suddenly and unexpectedly came the announcement of the forerunner's birth (Luke 1:5-22), of the Messiah's birth (Luke 1:26-38; 2:8 ff.; Matt. 1:18-25; 2:1-8)! How unexpected the voice in the wilderness (Luke 3:2 ff.), the public appearance of the Messiah (Luke 3:21 ff.; John 1:10 f., 29 ff., 46 ff.; 2:18; 6:41 ff.; 7:40-53)! All in exact fulfillment of Malachi's prophecy.

"The Messenger of the Covenant." See "The Angel of the Lord," pp. 409 f.; the Son of God before His incarnation. "Whom ye seek," "whom ye delight in." Throughout the Old Testament era there had been large numbers of believing children of God, who in eager longing awaited the coming of the Woman's Seed. (Cp. Gen. 4:1; 5:29; 15:1-6; 49:18; 1 Sam. 2:10; Ps. 14:7; Is. 9:6 f., etc.) Here, however, the Lord addresses people who for a great part were self-righteous pharisees and thoroughly dissatisfied with God's judgment. They looked for a Messiah who would properly reward their piety, would grant them the blessings they had deserved, would punish their enemies and oppressors, and make Israel once more a prosperous, powerful nation, ruler over the hated Gentiles. In such vain hopes of reward the people would be sorely disappointed. Their clamoring for the coming of the God of judgment would be answered in a manner altogether unexpected. (Cp. John 2: 13 ff.; Matt. 21—23; Luke 13: 34 f.; ch. 20.) But the patient and waiting believers would not be disappointed. "Behold, He shall come!" Jehovah, the World Ruler, repeats His promise to make assurance doubly sure. The long era of waiting for the advent of the Messiah was nearing its end. Nine tenths of the 4,000 years of longing had passed; only one tenth remained, a comparatively short time. Then the Messenger of the Covenant shall come for the salvation of mankind, especially of His believing flock (1 Tim. 4: 10). This is brought out in the next paragraph.

C. The Lord Will Come as the Sanctifier and Judge, Vv. 2-6

2 And who can endure the day of His coming? Who can stand when He appears? For He shall be like a refiner's fire, and as the lye of the fuller. 3 And He shall sit like a refiner and cleanser of silver, and He shall cleanse the children of Levi and refine them as gold and as silver so that they shall be such as bring offerings to the LORD in righteousness. 4 And the offering of Judah and Jerusalem shall be pleasing to the LORD as in the days of old and the years gone by. 5 And I will come to you for judgment. And I will be a swift witness against the sorcerers, and against the adulterers, and against those that swear falsely, and that rob the wages of the hired laborer, and defraud the widow and the orphan, and defraud the alien, and do not fear Me, says the LORD of Hosts. 6 For I, the LORD, change not! And you, the children of Jacob, have not perished.

Grammatical Notes

V. 2. "Soap," בֹּרִית, lye, alkali, particularly vegetable alkali, potash, obtained by leaching the ashes of plants. Occurs only here and Jer. 2: 22. "Fuller," literally, "washer," cleaner; כָּבַס, to knead, massage; the cleaner massaged the clothes by treading, trampling on them.

V. 5. "Swift," the participle of a verb = to hasten, hurry (Gen. 18: 6; Nah. 2: 6, A. V., 5; Is. 49: 17, etc.). The participial form denotes a habitual, characteristic quality.

Vv. 2, 3. In this paragraph the Lord through His prophet makes a practical application of His wonderfully mysterious name Jehovah as defined by Himself (Ex. 34: 6 f.). Jehovah, merciful and gracious, is at the same time the Lord of unalterable holiness who will by no means clear the guilty. The covenant of Jehovah, while revealing the abundant goodness of the God who forgives iniquity and transgression and sin, remains the covenant of the God of truth, who will fulfill not only His promises but also with like exactness His most horrible threats. Jehovah's judgments, while those of a long-suffering, divinely patient and forbearing Lord, yet remain unalterably just. While His loving-kindness extends to all sinners, yet for those who persistently refuse to accept His grace there is no more mercy (Zeph. 1:18; Heb. 10:27). The unalterably just and merciful Lord warns His people, "Who may abide the day of His coming?" Are they ready to meet the God of judgment whose coming they so importunately demanded in ch. 2:17? Shall they remain unharmed when He appears? He is like fire which burns whatever it touches, like "soap" (Gr. N.), lye, which eats deep into the tissues. And this fire burns, this lye consumes what the sinner so dearly loves, not only flagrant transgressions of God's Law but just as surely all self-righteous works. He comes to refine silver (v. 3). Are they silver? Or has their silver turned to dross? (Cp. Is. 1:22.) Are they like flinty rock, on which neither His Law nor His Gospel has made any impression? Are their works of which they boast no longer the outflow of a loving, grateful heart rejoicing in God's grace, but the product of a servile wage-seeking spirit? Will not the Lord's Covenant Angel come to break them to pieces like a hammer that shatters the rock (Jer. 23:29)? Yet the refiner comes not only to burn, the fuller not only to consume. He comes chiefly to refine, to purify. He is ready to give them a new heart, to take away the stony heart out of their flesh and give them a heart of flesh. He will put His Spirit in them (Ezek. 36:26 f.; Jer. 31:33 f.). The divine Fuller clothes them with garments washed in His own blood, robes of righteousness (Is. 61:10). He implants in their hearts the precious silver and gold of faith in the Redeemer (1 Peter 1:7). And He continues His work of purifying and refining as long as they live. The Hebrew participial form for "refiner" and "purifier" describes His work as going on continually throughout the believer's life. This is necessary, since the believer's flesh ceaselessly battles against the new spiritual life. Daily the Refiner purges away the dross and takes away all tin. Even if this tin may seem like precious silver to the believer, it remains tin. No matter how highly polished, it is worthless dross, and as such is removed by the Purifier, the Searcher of hearts. Though painful (cp. Rom. 6:16-21;

7:5-25; 8:1 ff.; Gal. 5:13-26), it is a necessary, a blessed work, for which the believer will in time and eternity thank his Refiner, made of God unto us wisdom, righteousness, sanctification, and redemption (1 Cor. 1:30).

The Refiner is called the Purifier of the sons of Levi. The priesthood had been instrumental in seducing the people (ch. 1:6 ff., 10 f.; 2:1-9). After their purification they shall once more be God's instruments in turning many away from iniquity (2:6 b) so that the sacrifices brought by the people and offered by the priests at the Lord's altar will again be in every respect "offerings in righteousness," meeting every requirement of the Lord. They will be brought by the people in a spirit of humble repentance and sincere gratitude, and offered by the priests in holy awe and proper awareness of the high responsibility of their sacred office.

V. 4. Such offerings will not be offensive to the Lord (ch. 1: 6-10, 14; Is. 1:10 ff.; Amos 5:21 f.). They shall be what the Lord had intended all sacrifices to be, a sweet savor unto Him (Gen. 4:3-8; 8:20 f.; Lev. 1:9, 17), to be accepted by Him, to make atonement for the offerer (Lev. 1:4). "Days of old," former years, such as the days of the patriarchs and the early Levitical priests (Mal. 2:4 ff.), of Joshua (Joshua 5:7-12), of Samuel (1 Sam. 7:3-17), Hezekiah (2 Chron. 30—33), Josiah (chs. 34 and 35). — In the New Testament Church, foreseen here by Malachi, there is no special priesthood; every believer is a royal priest (1 Peter 2:5, 9). Being washed, sanctified, justified (1 Cor. 6:11), they offer sacrifices acceptable to God (Phil. 4:18; cp. Rom. 12:1 f.; Heb. 13:15 f.). The spotless perfection of Christ's offering Himself cleanses away, as does fuller's soap, every spot and blemish from their persons and their offerings.

V. 5. Malachi warns his people against the fatal mistake of offering gifts to God without first offering themselves a living sacrifice to Him. The Cleanser and Purifier of sinners comes also as the Judge. Every believer needs this warning. The Jews at Malachi's time were no longer guilty of worshiping dead idols. Yet they were in great danger of becoming slaves of the flesh. Compare the sins enumerated here with the "works of the flesh" listed Rom. 13:13 f.; 1 Cor. 6:9 ff.; Gal. 5:19 ff. Not only self-righteous Pharisaism was raising its ugly head, but also Sadduceeism and its carnal lusts were gradually ensnaring them in their seductive net. (Cp. Ps. 9:15; Prov. 5:22.) And sorcery, witchcraft (Ex. 7:11; 22:17; Deut. 18:10; 2 Chron. 33:6; Micah 5:11), adultery (Ex. 20:14; Hos. 3:1; 4:13 f.), false swearing, perjury (Lev. 5:4; 19:12; Jer. 5:2; Zech. 5:4; 8:17), cruel oppression, and "turning aside," bending, twisting, distorting the right of aliens, foreigners dwelling in Israel, often having no influential friends to protect them and therefore at the mercy of greedy oppressors (Deut. 24:14; Prov. 18:5; Amos 4:1; 5:12; Zech. 7:10). And finally is named the wellspring of all these shameful crimes, the lack of the fear of the Lord. As long as this fear is lacking, no one is immune against any sin. The Lord will be a "swift" (Gr. N.), a hurrying, speedy, witness. His all-seeing eyes behold all the ways, all the sins of men (Ps. 90:8; Jer. 32:19); and He, the Lord of Hosts, the Ruler and Judge of the world, will pronounce and execute His judgment upon all these workers of iniquity. (Cp. Matt. 23.)

V. 6 states the reason for vv. 2-5. He is the Lord Jehovah, I AM THAT I AM. He changes not (Deut. 33:27; Prov. 8:22 ff.; Ps. 90:1 f.; 102:26 f.; Is. 40:28; 43:13; 57:15; Jer. 10:10). He cannot be satisfied with less than perfect holiness (Lev. 11:44 f.; 20:7, 26; Deut. 7:6). Therefore He will be a swift witness against all transgressors of His Law. Yet this unalterable holiness and justice does not cancel or even interfere with His unchanging grace and mercy. This grace is free grace, unmerited love and mercy, based solely on the all-sufficient merits of His appointed Servant (Is. 53:4-12). It is a grace which becomes the grander by the fact that it is intended for all sinners, even the greatest not being excepted (Rom. 5:20 f.). Because of this unchanging grace "the sons of Jacob are not consumed" (Gr. N.) by the unalterable holiness of God. The Jews are called "sons of Jacob" because they bore the likeness of their father. Like him (Gen. 27:1-36), they had been guilty of deceit and treachery toward God and man (Mal. 1:14; 2:10-16; cp. Jer. 3:7-11). Yet they were sons of a man whom God had graciously chosen even before his birth to be the ancestor of the promised Redeemer (Gen. 25:23; 27:28 f.; 28:3 f., 12 ff.; 32:26 f.; 35:10 ff.). The Lord by sufferings and heartaches and hardships had taught Jacob to realize his own wickedness and unworthiness and to lean wholly on God's unmerited grace and mercy (Gen. 32:9 ff.; 48:15 f., 21; 49:10 ff., 18, 29-33). So the sons of Jacob, passing through many a trial, the judgments of the ever holy God, shall not be consumed. This chastening Lord is the God of unchanging grace. His grace makes it possible that their sorrow will become a godly sorrow working repentance unto salvation (vv. 2-4; cp. 2 Cor. 7:10 f.; Heb. 12:15-18).

D. God's Call to Repentance and Obedience and Promise of Rich Blessings, Vv. 7-12

7 Since the days of your fathers you have strayed away from My statutes and have not kept them. Return to Me, and I will return to you! says the LORD of Hosts. Yet you say, Why shall we return?
8 Shall a man rob God? Yet you have robbed Me! But you say, Wherein have we robbed You? In the tithes and the heave offering.
9 With a curse are you cursed! And Me are you robbing! The entire
10 nation! Bring your entire tithe to the treasury that there may be provision in My house! And test Me, I pray, in this matter, says the LORD of Hosts, whether I will not open for you the windows of heaven and pour out for you a blessing
11 beyond measure! And I will rebuke for you the devourer that he shall not destroy for you the products of the earth and that the vine in the field shall not be unfruitful,
12 says the LORD of Hosts. And all the nations shall call you blessed, for you shall be a land of delight, says the LORD of Hosts.

Grammatical Notes

V. 7. "Ordinances," from a stem = cut, engrave, define, denotes a clearly defined, firmly established custom, law, ordinance, statute. Used of divine decrees, unwavering in their demands (Ex. 12:24; 18:16; Deut. 4:5, 8, 14; Jer. 3:36).

V. 8. "Rob," קָבַע, occurs only here and Prov. 22:23, where the context demands "rob." Delitzsch quotes a number of passages from the Midrashim (Jewish exegetical writings dating from the second to the tenth century after Christ), in which the word is explained as the colloquial term for "rob." (Delitzsch, *Sprueche Salomos,* 1873, p. 362, Note 2.) The LXX read or changed to עָקַב, "to grasp the heel" and translates: εἰ πτερνιεῖ, "shall a man heel," grasp the heel = deceive; a reference to Gen. 25:26 f.; 27:35 f. Kittel, *Biblia Hebraica,* suggests as a probable reading הֲיַעְקֹב: Shall a man deceive God? Sellin adds "Jacob" = a deceiver, before "even this whole nation" (v. 9). There is no need of such a change or addition.

V. 10. "Not be room enough to receive it," literally, until there is no דַּי = measure, no more possibility to measure the abundance. (Cp. Gen. 41:49.)

V. 11. "Devourer." The Hebrew term is the participle of אָכַל, to eat. This is the only time the term is used to denote the locust or grasshopper, although the verb is used three times by Joel to denote the ravages caused by the voracious locusts (Joel 1:4, "hath eaten").— "Cast her fruit, תְּשַׁכֵּל, to become childless, Pi. and Hiph. = to make barren, to suffer a miscarriage; here used of premature production, of unripe, undeveloped fruit falling to the ground. (Cp. Gen. 31:38; Ex. 23:26; Job 21:10; Hos. 9:14.)

V. 12. "Ye shall be," the personal pronoun is added in order to emphasize you, you yourselves. (Cp. 2 Sam. 12:28; 17:15; 22:18; Eccl. 2:1, 11, 15.) — "A delightsome land." The nation is called by the name of the land; cp. America = the people of America.

V. 7. The Lord impresses upon the self-righteous Jews the bitter truth that they would have deserved to be consumed by His wrath had it not been for His unchanging grace. The entire history of Israel is the record of ever-recurring departing from, and rebellion against, God's "ordinances" (Gr. N.), His unchanging laws and regulations for His covenant people, broken by them only forty days after their solemn proclamation (Ex. 24:18; 32:1-9, 15-19; cp. Deut. 9:6-24; 31:27-29; also the Books of Judges, of Samuel, and of Kings). They had deserved to be rejected as covenant breakers, yet even now the Lord is not yet ready to cast off His people. He pleads with them, "Return," etc. Their answer to this gracious invitation proves how completely their self-righteousness had blinded them as to their spiritual condition. They see no need of return to God. Their spiritual pride is as impudent as ever. Patiently the Lord counters their question with another question in order to show them the urgent need of repentance.

Vv. 8, 9. Shall a man rob God? (Gr. N.) A citizen stealing from his government by refusing to pay his share of the taxes is fined and jailed and avoided by his fellow citizens as a chiseler, a despicable thief. Yet here is an entire nation (v. 9 b) of robbers, defrauding not merely a human government, but robbing even God. Can anything be meaner, more despicable? Mortal men, sinners, who had been chosen as God's own people, made kings and priests (Ex. 19:5 f.), enriched by treasures incorruptible (Luke 12:32; 1 Peter 1:3 ff.; Col. 3:1 ff.) — these people steal from their heavenly Father, their Creator, Preserver, Redeemer! Indignantly the people deny the charge of robbery. They demand proof, as if His word were not to be trusted. The Lord immediately answers their request. They rob Him in refusing to pay the tithes and offerings demanded by Him. (On tithes see Lev. 27:30-33; Num. 18:21-28; later legislations, Deut. 12:5-18; 14:22-29; 26:12-14; see also 2 Chron. 31:5, 12, 19; Neh. 12:44; Matt. 23:23; Luke 18:12; Heb. 7:5-8. On offerings, cp. Lev. 1—7; 12—15; 23 and 24.) These tithes and offerings were to be given willingly as the evidence of their love and gratitude to the Giver of all good and perfect gifts. Already God has pronounced and sent His curse upon this ungrateful nation of robbers (v. 9, cp. v. 10 f.), who not only violated the rights of their fellow Jews, their brethren and sisters (ch. 2:10 f.), but also shamelessly robbed their God! Is Malachi out of date? Are there no such robbers to be found in the churches of our day?

V. 10. The Lord challenges His people. If they bring all their tithes into His storehouse, the Temple treasury (cp. 2 Chron. 31:11 ff.; Neh. 10:38 f.; 12:44; 13:12), so that there may be meat, food, in His house (cp. ch. 1:12, p. 519), then He is willing to be proved, tested.

He will open the windows of heaven (cp. Gen. 7:11; 8:2; 2 Kings 7:2, 19; Is. 24:18) and pour out a veritable deluge of blessings that there shall not be room enough to receive it (Gr. N.), that no one can measure the divine gifts. (Cp. Gen. 41:49; Hos. 2:21 f.)

Vv. 11, 12. "Rebuke," scold, threaten, for the purpose of turning someone away, preventing him from doing harm (Ps. 9:6, A. V., 5; 68:31, A. V., 30; Nah. 1:4; Zech. 3:2). The "devourer" (Gr. N.), here the locust, on which see Joel 1:4, pp. 113 ff. "Cast her fruit" (Gr. N.), drop it before it is fully matured, caused by blight, drought, insects, etc. So bountifully will the Lord bless the repentant Jews that all nations shall call them blessed (v. 12), for "you" (Gr. N.), you yourselves, shall be a land of delight, to which the nations round about shall come to join in its blessings. (Cp. Is. 2:3, 4; 60:3-14; 62:1-4, 10-12; Jer. 3:17; Matt. 5:16; 1 Peter 2:12; 3:1-4.)

E. The Unbelieving Jews Charge God with Injustice; the Believers Repent and Are Accepted by the Lord, Vv. 13-18

13 You have used harsh words against Me, says the LORD. Yet you say, What have we said against You? 14 You say, It is useless to serve God! And what gain have we for having kept His charges and have walked in mourning before the LORD of 15 Hosts? And now we ourselves must call the arrogant blessed; the evildoers are firmly established; even when they tempt God, they 16 get by! Then they that feared the LORD spoke to one another. But the LORD gave heed and heard them; and a book of remembrance was written before Him concerning those who fear the LORD and keep 17 in mind His name. And they shall be to Me, is the oracle of the LORD of Hosts, on the day on which I shall go into action, a possession; and I shall spare them as a man spares his son who has 18 served him. Then you shall again see the difference between the just and the wicked, between God's servant and one that does not serve Him.

Grammatical Notes

V. 13. "Have been stout," חָזְקוּ, are hard, harsh; used only here of strong, offensive language. — "Spoken so much," the Niph. of דָּבַר denotes to speak to one another, converse. (Cp. v. 16; Ps. 119:23; Ezek. 33:30.)

V. 15. "And now," וְעַתָּה, literally, at the time, here denotes the result of former circumstances, under these circumstances. (Cp. Gen. 11:6; 12:19; Ps. 2:10, etc.) — "Proud," זֵדִים, from a root = to boil, cook (Gen. 25:29), to boil over in anger, pride, or cruelty. (Cp. Ex. 18:11; 21:14; Deut. 1:43; Neh. 9:16, 29.) The noun is used in Is. 13:11; Jer. 43:2; Ps. 19:13 a; 119:21 a, 51, 69, 78, 85, 122; Prov. 21:24. A study of these passages will reveal these "proud" men as self-willed, malicious, unprincipled, turbulent, "seething" spirits. — "Yea—yea," גַּם—גַּם, the Latin et—et; each statement adds something to the preceding one; also, also; as well as; both—and. — "Tempt," בָּחַן, same word as "prove,"

v. 10; a blasphemous perversion of God's challenge, v. 10.

V. 16. "Spake often"; see Gr. N. on v. 13, "spoken so much."

V. 17. "Make up," עָשָׂה, here = to act, go into action, do successfully; see Gr. N. on Mal. 2:15, p. 527. "My jewels," סְגֻלָּה, a possession exclusively one's own. (Cp. Ex. 19:5; Deut. 7:6; 14:2; 26:18; Ps. 135:4; 1 Chron. 29:3.) "Jewels" (A. V.), rather, "possession" is the object of "they shall be Mine," literally, "to Me." — "Spare," "spareth," חָמַל, here = "to have pity, compassion" (Ex. 2:6; Joel 2:18, etc.).

V. 18. "Return" here denotes repetition, "again." (Cp. Gen. 26:18; 30:31; Deut. 23:14; Hos. 2:11; 11:9, etc.)

V. 13. The Lord had promised blessings such as He alone can grant (ch. 3:10-12). Yet even this evidence of His love of Jacob (ch. 1:2) is ignored by the stubborn, self-righteous Jews. The Lord charges them with uttering "stout words" (Gr. N.), hard, harsh, offensive language, against Him. They immediately resented the charge. "Spoken so much" (Gr. N.), rather, spoken to one another, conversed. Once more God is mistaken! They are not guilty! The omniscient Lord now quotes their very words.

Vv. 14, 15. "Vain," an unprofitable business, is the service of a God who demands so much and gives so little in return. We fasted, and wept, and mourned, and lamented, and walked in sackcloth, and sat in ashes. (Cp. Is. 3:24; 15:3; Luke 10:13; 18:12.) And what is our reward? What do we get for our labor? Look at the "proud," impudent, haughty sinners who transgress every law of God and man. "And now" (Gr. N.), under these circumstances, we must call them happy (v. 15). "Yea" (Gr. N.), also, indeed, even. They are even "set up," built, they prosper in spite of their wickedness, and all that "tempt" (Gr. N.) God, all that have the courage to test God by deliberately transgressing, ignoring His commandments, are even delivered, escape punishment. And what do we get if we test God, as He has asked us to do (v. 10)? We fail to see His blessing! They repeat their blasphemous charge of ch. 2:17 b. God's repeated pleadings, His promises as well as His threats have fallen on deaf ears and unbelieving, impenitent hearts.

V. 16. As there were 7,000 in Israel at Ahab's time (1 Kings 19:18), so there were also in Malachi's age believing children of God, who loved and feared Him. Seeing the general hypocrisy and wickedness, they "spoke often" (see Gr. N. on "spoken so much," v. 13), they conversed among themselves. "One to another" is added to emphasize their eagerness not to overlook anyone who needed a word of admonition, warning, comfort. (Cp. Acts 2:42; 1 Cor. 7:11ff.;

Eph. 6:18 ff.; Heb. 10:24 f.) The Lord took great interest in their work. He "hearkened," paid attention, and "heard," listened to their conversations. "A book of remembrance was written before Him." Cp. the Persian custom in Ezra 4:15; 6:1 f.; Esther 2:23; 6:1 ("records" = the feminine plural of the same word rendered "remembrance" here). The same custom was common in Israel and Judah (1 Kings 11:41; 14:29, etc.). On God's "book" see Ex. 32:32; Ps. 56:8; 69:28; 139:16; Ezek. 13:9; Dan. 7:10; Rev. 13:8; 20:12-15. The faithful Jews are here assured that God will forget neither them nor their good works. (Cp. Matt. 10:41 ff.; 25:35 ff.; Mark 9:41; Rev. 14:13.) "Thought upon" = esteem, revere. "His name," His revelation of Himself, His Word. (Cp. ch. 1:6.)

V. 17. He will acknowledge them as His own on the day when He shall "make up His jewels" (Gr. N.), when He shall make "an adoption," shall publicly declare and acknowledge them as His own particular people. He will do this when He "will spare them" (Gr. N.), when He will again manifest His pity and compassion by His temporal and spiritual blessings. (Cp. v. 10 ff.) This promise refers particularly to the New Testament era, and in full perfection to the life that is to come. (Cp. Matt. 10:32; 25:31-40; Luke 18:29; 1 John 3:2; Rev. 3:5, 12, 21.)

V. 18. "Return" (Gr. N.). Then again shall they see, realize, that after all God had not forgotten His own in days of poverty and affliction, or preferred the wicked to His faithful children.

F. Final Threat, Promises, and Admonitions, Ch. 3:19-24
(A. V., 4:1-6)

19 (A. V., 4:1) For, behold, the Day shall come, burning like an oven, and all the arrogant and every evildoer shall be stubble and the coming Day shall burn them up, says the LORD of Hosts, who will leave to them neither root nor branch.

20 (4:2) Then there shall rise for you who fear My name, the Sun of Righteousness with healing in His wings; and you shall go out and leap like calves of the stall.

21 (4:3) And you shall tread down the wicked, for they shall be dust under the soles of your feet, on the Day I shall go into action, says the

22 (4:4) LORD of Hosts. Remember the Law of Moses, My servant, which I commanded him on Horeb for all Israel as statutes and judg-

23 (4:5) ments. Lo, I will send to you Elijah the prophet, before the Day of the LORD shall come, the

24 (4:6) great and fearful one; and he shall turn the hearts of the fathers to the children and the hearts of the children to their fathers, lest I come and smite the land with a curse.

Addendum by Masoretes: Lo, I will send to you Elijah the prophet, before the Day of the LORD shall come, the great and fearful one.

Grammatical Notes

V. 20 (A. V., 4:2). "Sun." שֶׁמֶשׁ is construed as masculine in Gen. 19:23; 28:11; Joshua 10:12 f.; Joel 3:4, etc.; and as feminine in Gen. 15:17; Ex. 22:3; Deut. 24:15; Ps. 104:22; 2 Kings 23:4, etc. Here = fem., cp. זָרְחָה, she rises; כְּנָפֶיהָ, her wings; either because the sun is regarded as serving mankind (G.-K. 122 o) or because the fem. צְדָקָה, righteousness, determined the choice of the gender. — "Arise." "LXX translates ἀνατελεῖ; and Zacharias' 'Dayspring,' Luke 1:78, ἀνατολή, evidently refers to our passage, just as he had already quoted and later again refers to the same chapter of Malachi, Luke 1: 17, 76" (Theodor Zahn, *Das Evangelium des Lucas*, p. 119.) "Grow up." פּוּשׁ occurs only here, in Jer. 50:11, and Hab. 1:8; in the last passage it denotes the prancing, rearing, leaping of a battle horse; in Jer. 50:11 and here, the joyful leaping, gamboling, frolicking of calves.

V. 21 (4:3). "Tread down," עָסַס, only here = to press, tread, as the grapes in the wine press. The noun = the new wine freshly pressed (Is. 49:26; Joel 1:5; 4:18; Amos 9:13). — "Do," here in absolute sense, to act, do successfully. Cp. Gr. N. on Mal. 2:15, p. 527.

V. 22 (4:4). "Statutes and commandments," a second accusative to "command," hence "with" is to be omitted. Statutes, חֹק, from a verb = to cut, engrave. Laws engraved on stone are thereby recognized as binding decrees, "statutes." Generally speaking, these statutes prohibit actions not sinful in themselves, but illegal and therefore sinful, because they are contrary to divinely prescribed manner or order of procedure. Cp. the laws prescribing the nature, time, manner of offering sacrifices and other instructions concerning the sanctuary in Ex. 25:1—34:26, excepting 34:21; Lev. 1—16 (Kyle, *The Problem of the Pentateuch*, p. 20 ff.). "Judgments," מִשְׁפָּטִים, "judgings," decisions of judges, which had come to be recognized to be just and equitable and thus accepted as common law. "The promulgating of them with the authority of God made them the laws of God" (Kyle, op. cit., p. 16. Cp. Ex. 21: 1—23:19; Lev. 19:11-18; Num. 31:9-26). The two terms combined denote the entire corpus iuris of Israel as divinely appointed, as God's *Torah* = instruction, on their proper religious, political, social, and family conduct and relations.

V. 24 (4:6). "Turn — to." עַל here = אֶל; cp. the same phrase in various senses: return unto dust (Job 34:15), return to his vomit (Prov. 26:11), return to the earth, return unto God (Eccl. 12:7).

V. 19 (A. V., 4:1). "For" supplies the reason for 3:18. "Behold!" the Lord of Hosts (v. 1 b), the World Ruler and Israel's Covenant God, whose threats will be as surely fulfilled as His promises (Num. 23:19; Ps. 33:9, 11), calls the attention of the people, the righteous, the wicked, the dissatisfied grumblers, to the Day that cometh, the Day of final and everlasting judgment. Cp. Is. 13:9; Jer. 47:4; 50:27; Joel 2:31; Zeph. 1:14 ff.; notes on Obad. 15, pp. 203—205.) On that Day the Lord will manifest the difference between the righteous and the wicked. All the "proud," whom the Jews had called happy, and the "wicked," who seemed to prosper and enjoy deliverance from all evil

543

(ch. 3:15), shall be like "stubble," the worthless stubs that remain after the wheat has been cut and gathered into the garners. Like stubble consumed in a roaring furnace (cp. Matt. 6:30), they will be cast into the lake of unquenchable fire (Matt. 25:41; Mark 9:43 f.; cp. Is. 66:24; Rev. 20:9-15). "Neither root nor branch" (cp. Hos. 8:7 b; 9:16). This Day shall come for the unbelievers when the Lord shall call them out of this world. The sentence of all who die in unbelief and rebellion against God is unalterably determined on the day of their death (Prov. 11:7) and frequently is manifested already in their lifetime (Ps. 7:14 ff.; 37:15,17; Prov. 14:34; 24:16; 28:1). This warning is addressed not only to the ungodly; it includes also the grumblers. If they persist in their carping criticism of the Lord's justice, they will meet with the same fate prepared for the wicked. Hypocrisy is wickedness covering itself with the cloak of righteousness, more displeasing to the Lord than manifest ungodliness (Jer. 3:10 f.).

V. 20 (4:2). "Fear My name," His revelation, His Word; the believing children of God. (See ch. 3:16.) The Lord will unfailingly keep His promises to His children. All His promises rest on the first promise given to fallen mankind in Paradise (Gen. 3:15). Though almost four thousand years had passed, the Lord eternal had not forgotten His promise. It will be fulfilled in due time.

The promised Messiah is called the Sun (Gr. N.). Balaam had called Him the Star out of Jacob (Num. 24:17), Isaiah, a Great Light (Is. 9:2), the Light of the Gentiles (ch. 42:6; 49:6). It remained for the last prophet to present Him as the Sun, the Great Light to rule the day of the New Testament. (Cp. Gen. 1:16.) "Sun of Righteousness." He was called the Lord Our Righteousness (Jer. 23:6). In Him righteousness is personified. The Branch of David is Righteousness Incarnate, not only because of His personal righteousness (Is. 53: 9b, 11b; Jer. 23:5) but also because of that vicarious righteousness procured by Him who fulfilled the Law as our Substitute (Gal. 4:4 f.). He took upon Himself not only the penalty of our sin (Is. 53:5, 7) but also the guilt, the iniquity of mankind (Is. 53:6, 8, 10-12). "Arise" (Gr. N.). "Wings." (Cp. Ps. 139:9.) The rays of the rising sun are compared to wings, which spread from hill to hill with marvelous swiftness, chasing away darkness, bringing life and joy to all the earth. "Healing." On the wings of a hospital airship comes healing to the sick and wounded on the bloody battlefield. No more welcome sight to the suffering, tormented, dying soldiers! So to the suffering, dying world comes the Lord Our Righteousness, the Physician of our

sin-sick soul (Ps. 41:4; 103:3; 107:20; 147:3; Is. 57:18 f.; 61:1 ff.).
While He is the Propitiation for the sins of the world (1 John 2:2),
He is in a special sense the Savior of them that believe (1 Tim. 4:10),
that fear His name, for they alone possess and enjoy the healing
brought to them in the Gospel. They have in Him that peace passing
all understanding, that peace of heart and mind and conscience which
comforts them in the darkest hour of sorrow and forsakes them not
even in the valley of the shadow of death (Is. 25:1-8; 26:19 ff.). In the
light of this Sun they shall go forth to their daily tasks in this world
of sin and temptation and trials; and they shall "grow up" (Gr. N.),
leap with joy, gambol, frolic, "as calves of the stall." They are not
like sheep compelled to look for their scanty food on parched desert
ground. They are carefully fed in the "stalls," special feeding com-
partments, where they receive the best of food. They have the Word
of God, the Sacraments, their Bible, their devotional books, the
communion with their fellow men (Col. 3:16; Heb. 10:22-25), so that
they can go forth joyfully in exuberant vitality and strength. (Cp.
Is. 35:10; 55:12 f.; Jer. 33:11; Neh. 8:10-18; Matt. 5:10 ff.; Acts 5:41;
16:25; Rom. 5:1-3; 2 Cor. 6:4 ff.; 1 John 5:4.)

V. 21 (4:3). The wicked! Will they not oppose and oppress,
alarm and harm the believers? Let not such thoughts disturb you,
says the Lord. They have been reduced to ashes (v. 1) by the furious
fire of My wrath; and you, believing My word, shall regard them
as ashes. The Sun of Righteousness will endow the believers with joy
and with strength that disdain the furious wrath of the world. They
"shall tread them down" (Gr. N.), not in their own strength (Rom.
7:18), but because the Lord is with them. He shall "do" (Gr. N.),
perform, perfect, what they cannot accomplish (Jer. 1:8, 17 ff.; 9:23 f.;
Phil. 4:12; Rom. 8:35 ff.; 2 Tim. 4:6, 7, 16-18; Heb. 11:32-38). In the
strength of their Savior, healed by His righteousness from sin and
guilt, from fear and cowardice, they shall go forth joyously, cou-
rageously; sheep for the slaughter, yet more than conquerors.

V. 22 (4:4). In order to be acknowledged as the Lord's covenant
people and be blessed accordingly, the Jews are admonished to
remember the Law of Moses. (Cp. Num. 15:39; Joshua 1:7 f.; Ps.
103:18; 119:1-176.) Moses is called "My servant," an honorable title.
(Cp. Num. 12:7; Deut. 34:5-12; Joshua 1:1, 2, 7.) This Law was given
to Israel as its national Law at Horeb, the mountain of God (Ex. 3:
1, 12; 17:6; Deut. 1:2, 6, 19), in the Desert of Sinai (Ex. 19:1 f.),
hence also called Mount Sinai (Ex. 19:11; 24:16, etc.). This "Law,"

instruction, regulating the entire religious, political, social, and family life, included not only the Moral Law, binding on all mankind; it embraced also a large number of "statutes and commandments" (Gr. N.), customs, rites, regulations, given specifically to the Israelites, to distinguish them from all other nations. (Cp. Lev. 1—7, 11; Deut. 4: 5-8, 20; 33: 26 ff.) Like the Moral Law, these ceremonial and political laws were enacted by the Lord as an integral part of His covenant with Israel. To neglect these laws was a mortal sin for the Israelite (Ex. 30: 19 ff.; Lev. 10: 1-7; Num. 15: 33-36; 18: 22, 32; Jer. 17: 27). Only in the New Testament were these ceremonial and political laws abrogated. (Cp. Acts 10, 11, 15; Gal. 1—5; Col. 2: 8-23.)

A question: Would Malachi, the spokesman of God, have said that the Law of Moses had been commanded by the Lord to His servant Moses at Horeb if a large number of these statutes had never been enacted by Moses, but had originated in the minds of priests and scribes living many centuries after Moses? Perish the thought!

Vv. 23, 24 (4: 5, 6). The promise of the herald and way-preparer for the Messiah (ch. 3: 1) is repeated, and he is called Elijah, 1 Kings 17 ff. Ch. 3: 1 pictured him as the forerunner of the Messiah at His first advent. Here he is to prepare the people for the second advent. The Purifier of His people (ch. 3: 3) is also the Judge (3: 2, 5). As so frequently in prophecy, the coming of Christ into the flesh and His coming unto judgment are here seen in one grand, panoramic view. (See note on Day of the Lord, p. 203; cp. also 2 Thess. 2: 2 f.; 1 Peter 4: 7; James 5: 8 f.; Rev. 3: 20; 22: 20; to be read in the light of 2 Peter 3: 8.) In preparing the people for the first advent, by preaching Law and Gospel, the forerunner prepared them also for His second advent, the great and dreadful Day of the Lord (Zeph. 1: 14 ff.). This preparation is described as "turning the heart" (Gr. N.) (A. V., 4: 6). It is not a mere outward change of attitude, but a change of the heart, for that alone is acceptable to God (Deut. 4: 9, 29; 6: 5; 10: 12, 16). Frequently the ancient times and ways (Mal. 2: 5 f.; 3: 4; Deut. 32: 7; Ps. 77: 5; 143: 5; Is. 8: 20; Jer. 6: 16; 18: 15) and the men and women, the fathers and mothers are presented as ideal, exemplary. (Cp. Gen. 18: 17 ff.; Deut. 6: 6 f.; Prov. 10: 1; 13: 1; 31: 1 f.) Malachi pictures the pious ancestors as rejoicing over the faith and piety of their posterity, as turning in joyful love to their children, whom they see walking in the truth as they had received the commandment from the Lord. (Cp. 2 John 4.) And He will turn the heart of the children to the fathers. The children will no longer seek to be different, more

546

up-to-date, more liberal and broad-minded than their forebears. They will gladly follow them in their childlike faith and trust and submission to God's Word and will. (Cp. Prov. 6:20-24.) They will follow in the footsteps of faithful Moses (Num. 12:7), of Jacob (Gen. 32:26), of David in his trust (Ps. 23) and in his frank confession of sins (Ps. 51), of Josiah (2 Kings 23:25; cp. Heb. 11:1 ff.). Such repentance is necessary, "lest I come and smite the earth with a curse," with complete destruction. (See Gr. N. on Zech. 14:11, pp. 497 f.) "Earth," here = land, the land of Canaan, now Israel's land (Joel 1:2; Jer. 1:14; 3:2; Ps. 37:3; 44:3, etc.). If Israel takes on the character of the Canaanites, it will together with the land share the curse that came upon the Canaanites (Lev. 18:27-30; Deut. 12:28-32).

As did Isaiah, Malachi closes his book with a reference to everlasting damnation in a final appeal to his people to forsake their wickedness and in sincere repentance to return to the Lord, their Covenant God. Compare Paul's last words addressed to the Jews at Rome (Acts 28:24-29).

To the last, the last prophet of the Old Testament points out to all sinners the need of repentance and faith in the promised Redeemer, the Angel of the Covenant, the Sun of Righteousness. This promise connects the Old Testament, the time of prophecy and hopeful waiting, with the time of fulfillment and joyous realization, the era of the Gospel of Jesus Christ (Mark 1:1 f.; Luke 1:13-17; Matt. 13:16 f.; Acts 2:14-47).

The Masoretes repeated v. 23 after v. 24, and the LXX reversed the order of the last two verses in order to have the last book of the Bible close, not with a curse, but a blessing. That is not the way for unbelief to escape the curse. None but Jesus saves! (Acts 4:12; 10:43.)

Topical Index

A

AARON, the Lord's messenger, 278 transl. v. 4
Aaronic blessing, 393
Abraham, his segregation, 526 f., 528 f.; the lone man, 528 f.; man of spirit, 529; his marriage to Hagar does not justify marriage of Jews to Gentiles, 528 f.
Achmeta, edict of Cyrus found at, 422
Adam, first covenant breaker, 60
Adon, defined, 531 Gr. N., 533
Adonai, defined, 183
Adullam, cave, 252
Afflictions, God saves from, 465 f.
Ages, Dark, Middle Ages, 494 ff.
Ahab, king of Israel, 7, 22 f., 210
Ahaz, king of Judah, 7
Akabah, gulf, 12, 194
Alexander the Great, 8; his conquests prepare the way for the rapid spread of the Gospel, 395
Alliances, without divine permission sinful for Israel, 28 f.; fatal, 26 ff., 54
Altars, to be erected only at God's command, 51; altar at Jerusalem rebuilt after the Exile, 384
Amanah, river at Damascus, 141
Amaziah, opposes Amos; punished, 177 f.
Ammon, Ammonites, their sin and penalty, 131, 133, 143; judgment, 366, 369
Amorites, their land given to Israel, 147
Amos, personality, 136; quotes Joel and Obadiah, 113; foretells fate of Israel and surrounding countries, 138 ff.; eloquent style, 138; gripping climax, 138—145; opposed by Amaziah, 177 f.
Angel of the Lord, 408 ff.; Ruler of the world, 419; defends Joshua, 421 ff.; rebukes Satan, 422 ff.; commands angels, 423; prophesies, 424; pleads for Jerusalem, 408, 413, 421 ff., 429, 481
Angels (created), 408—438, 495
Anointed ones, defined, 427 Gr. N. v. 14
Anointing of kings, priests, prophets, a divine means of giving them the Holy Spirit and enabling them to fulfill the duties of their office, 482
Antichrist, the Roman papacy oppressing the Church, 495 ff.; God saves the Church, 497
Antipater, an Idumean, governor in Judah, cruel ruler, father of Herod the Great, 209
Aphra, city in Judah, destroyed, 251
Apostates, 358; apostate children return to God, 33

Apple tree, 116
Arabah = wilderness on the eastern shore of the Dead Sea, 174
Aramaic forms, not necessarily a mark of post-Exilic authorship, 219 f.
Asa, king of Judah, 7, 118
Asherah, female deity associated with Baal; the Syrian form of Ashtarte, goddess of love and fertility, 357
Asherim, statues and figurines made of clay, wood, or stone, representing Asherah, 357; found in large numbers throughout Palestine, 15
Ashtarte, or Astarte, Assyrian goddess of love and fertility, Venus, 15, 357; see also *Groves*
Ashur = Assyria, 3 f.
Ashurbanipal, 4
Ashur-nasirpal II, 4
Ass, 454 Gr. N., 455, Messiah to ride on foal of an ass, 455
Assemble, the Lord assembles scattered Israel, 257; lame and blind, 267; calls Israel to assemble at Temple, 122; the enemies for destruction, 133 f.; Philistines and Egyptians around Samaria, 152
Assembly, solemn, at Temple, 381
Assyria, see also *Nineveh*; its history, 3, power, 314 f., wickedness, 306—308, cruelty, 221, 303; introduced system of deportation and repopulation with foreigners, 303; symbolic of enemies of God's Church, 418; Israel vainly sought their help, 66, 70 f.; Israel deported to, 91, 167, 296
Astarte, see *Ashtarte*
Azal, 493, 495 = Beth Ezel

B

BAAL, Canaanite idol, cut off, 355
Baalism, 15, 22, 39; various forms of, 356 f.; futile, 69; wicked, 50—52, 248; destroyed by the Lord, 33, 355 f.
Babes, prayers of, support Church, 481
Babylon, 4 ff., 407
Babylonian Captivity, 407
Babylonian exiles sent silver and gold for Temple, 438
Balaam, 278
Balak, 278
Bands, see *Beauty and Bands*
Banqueting, riotous, 170
Bashan, 287; laid waste, 467
Bastard, 449 f. Gr. N. v. 6, 452
Battle customs of Assyrians, Babylonians, and Medes, 304

549

Gate, Fish, 361

Gates, city, 161; of Jerusalem, names of, 361, 500

Gath, Philistine city, 169; its transgression and punishment, 169, 250

Gaza, Philistine city, 141 f., 367 f., 449

Gentiles, converted, convert Jews, 377 f., both united in Christian Church, 376 f.

Gentleness, God's, 89

Gibeah, 52, 75, 83

Gilead, 210, 287

Gilgal, seat of calf worship, 75, 77, 156; its hypocrisy, 156; stubbornness, 156; punished, 157 f.

God, His anger surpassed by His love, 90 f.; adored by His Church, 20; attributes not conflicting, 91: blesses His Church, 20; blessed by His children, 10; calls to repentance, 538; Captain of Salvation, 92; changes sorrow to hope, 540; charged with injustice, 540; chastisements accomplish their purpose, 29; conversion His work, 33 f.; His faithfulness, 24 f., 99; encourages Hosea to pray, 55; Father of believers, 109, 524; Gentiles will honor Him, 518; His goodness defined, 298; encourages man to come to Him, 40; His Gospel and Law, 105; His grace, 483; holiness unchanging; His jealousy defined, 294 Gr. N., 296; His kingdom a glorious one, 406 ff.; His law has a salutary purpose, 105; burden to unbelievers, 539; obedience rewarded, 539 f. His love for the Church a righteous love, 91 f.; proved by blessings, 109; for Judah, 60; foiled by their wickedness, 60; His loving-kindness, defined, 35, 58 f., His mercy, 290; His name, profaned by priests, 519; God permits wicked to rule; why? 318 f.; His promises reliable, 35; the only Savior, 103; tramples sin underfoot, 291; woos Israel, 32

Gomer, Hosea's marriage to, symbolic of God's marriage to Israel, 18 ff.

Gospel, often placed side by side with God's Law, 105

Gourd, Jonah's, 238 Gr. N., 241 ff.

Governors = leaders of the Church, 478 Gr. N., 480; confident of victory, 480; supported by prayers and contributions of believers, 480

Grace, defined, 427, 483; day of, ends, 167

Grandson, at times called son, 403

Grasshopper, the Lord makes, 175

Greed, 151, 161 f.

H

HABAKKUK, personality, 313; date, 313 f., 316; language, 317; dialog with God, 317 ff.; complaints, 323 ff.; God's answer, 328 f.; a vision granted, 329; prayer in adoration of God's way, 341—351; finally rejoices in midst of tribulations, 352 f.

Hadad Rimmon, lamentation at, 484 f.

Hadrach, in Syria = Khatarika, 450

Hagar, Abraham's marriage to Hagar does not justify marriage of Jews to Gentiles, 529

Haggai, historical background, 383 f.; exhorts Jews to finish building of Temple, 384; chronology of his activity, 385

Hamath, 169, 450

Hardening oneself, 47, 444, hardened sinners finally surrendered to their doom, 47 f.

Hazael, king of Syria, 7

Healing, 544 f.

Heart, the seat of life in its various forms, 46, 62, 63, 66, 76, 79 Gr. N., 81, 91, 102, 305, 377, 462; hardened, 444; Israel to change the hardness of their hearts, 444; God, the Searcher of the heart, 334

Heathen, marriage to, forbidden to Jews, 528; heathen nations = foreign nations surrounding Israel, 122; enemies of God and His Church punished, 414; Gospel preached to heathen, 457; converted by it, 235, 264, 277, 448; gathered into Church, 503; worship the Lord, 307; magnify His name, 518 f.

Heaven, heavens, the horizon, 345 f.; give their dew, 445 transl. v. 12; locusts more than stars of, 307; tremble, 120; signs in, 129; host of heavens, star worship, 357; heaven of heavens, 185; God's throne in, 185, 387; heavens are steps to His throne in heaven, 185; third heaven, 185; pleas of creatures relayed to, 36; winds of = spirits, 435 Gr. N., 437; symbolizing spread of Gospel, 418 f.

Hedgehog, translated "bittern" by A. V., 372 Gr. N.

Hell, its horrors, 103 f.; Lord conquers it, 104

Hen, not a personal name, but the Hebrew term for kindness, hospitality, 440

Herod the Great rebuilt the Temple, 397

Hezekiah, delivered from Assyrians, 23

High places, hills, sites of idolatrous worship, 82, 158, 177, 248, 261, 353; a delusion, 82

T

TABERNACLE, defined, 94 Gr. N. v. 10 (9); the Assyrian-Babylonian idol Sakkut, or Sikkut, 164 Gr. N.

Tabernacles, Feast of, 94 f. Gr. N. 10 (9), after Exile, 384, continuous in New Testament, 503

Table of the Lord = altar and Temple service; what the Lord offered as food or wages for such service seemed contemptible to the priests, 516, 519

Tables = tablets, Habakkuk to write his vision on tablets, placards, to be put up in the Temple, 328 transl. and Gr. N. v. 2, 330

Tabor, Mount, in Westjordanland, 50 f.

Tarshish = Tartessus in Spain, 221

Taught, Ephraim is as an heifer that is taught to thresh, 84

Taunt, enemies take up a taunting song against Chaldeans, 333 transl. v. 6, 334 ff.

Teach, priests of Jerusalem teach for hire, 259 transl. v. 11, 261; God will teach believers of His ways, 264

Teacher, Christ the Teacher of the righteousness He has procured for all mankind, 126

Tekoa, city of Judah, 137, site, 137, home of Amos, a herdsman, 137, called to be God's prophet, 138

Teman, grandson of Esau, 194; one of the chief cities of Edom, 194; land of Edom called Teman, 194; to be destroyed by fire, 142 transl. v. 12

Tempest, sent by the Lord, 224, 227, quieted, 227 f., Jonah saved from its fury, 231

Temple, porch of = portico, 122, to be smitten, 183 f.; Phoenicians and Philistines ransack Solomon's Temple, 201; in ruins during Exile, 383 f., rebuilding begun, 384, work stopped, 384 f., resumed after Haggai's and Zechariah's admonitions, 384—390, 396 f., work again ceased for seventeen years, 447, finally completed, 508; future glory of Temple, 390—397; the Branch, Messiah, shall build His Temple, God's Church, 439; converted Gentiles help build Church, 440

Tents of Cushan and Midian afflicted, 346, of Judah, delivered first, 481

Teraphim, household idols, 461

Thebes = No Amon in southern Egypt, 309 f.

Three and four, defined, 140, compare 140—144, translations

Thresh, Damascus threshed Gilead with threshing instruments of iron, 141

Threshing floor, the Lord gathers oppressors of Judah like sheaves upon, 268; Israel's threshing floors scenes of immoralities, 73

Threshold, priests of Dagon leap over, 360

Tiglath-Pileser, name of several Assyrian rulers, 2, 4, 7, 8

Times, signs of, neglected by Israel, 150 f.

Tithes, willingly given, rewarded, 539 f.; grudgingly given, or self-righteously offered, sinful, displeasing to God, 156

Toi, king of Hamath, 6

Training, God's love in, 89

Trample, God tramples sin underfoot, 291

Transgression = revolt, rebellion, 140

Trinity in Unity, Jehovah's, revealed, 429

Trumpet, 52, 68, 118, 144, 150, 364, 458

Turban, 421, 423

Types, to be distinguished from figures, 88

Tyre, history, 450 ff.; opposes Judah, 112; its treachery and penalty, 142; destroyed, 450 ff.

Tyropean Valley, 263 (Josephus calls it the Cheesemakers' Valley)

U

UNBELIEF, defiles, 91 ff., 399; ruinous, 29 ff., 39, 42 ff., 47 f., 69 f., 399 f., 501 f.; cannot overthrow truth, 502 f.

Unclean, Levitically, 73, 398

Uncleanness, Levitical, 486 Gr. N. v. 2, 488

Ur, 166

Uzziah, king, 9, 12, 136 transl. v. 1, 214, 495

V

VALLEY of the Mountain, 493 Gr. N. v. 5

Vision, a method of divine instruction, defined, 193 f.; Obadiah's vision, 193 ff.; Nahum's prophecy called a vision, 293; vision, divine, will surely be fulfilled, 328; God's prophetic promise, 330 f.; visions of false prophets put to shame, 260; false prophets ashamed of their visions, 260; young men shall see visions, 128; Zechariah's night visions, 408 ff.

Vitality of nations sapped by use of contraceptives and other efforts to prevent birth, 78

W

WALK, after God, 92; with God = in His ways, 111, 150, 264, 266, in the name of the Lord, 466; humbly with God, 281; believers walk safely even in distress, 351 ff.; in peace and equity, 522 f.; with angels to God's throne, 424; need of walking uprightly, 256; Israel refuses to walk with God, 256, 281; follows human ordinances, 53; wicked cannot walk with God, 149; heathen walk in ways of idols, 266; Israel, in counsels of Omri and Ahab, 281 transl. v. 16, 282; wicked walk like blind men, 364; walking wind-bags, 256; horses of reconnoiterers walk through the earth, 412, 437; locusts, like an army, 120; walking with God essential to salvation, 148 Gr. N. v. 3, 149 f.; failure to walk with God fatal, 150

Warnings, God's, rejected by Israel, 174

Weak shall become strong, 491 f.

Wealth, abuse of, 169

Why? Habakkuk asks, 323 ff.; receives answers which cause renewed whys, 328 ff.

Wicked, why are nations helpless against wicked oppressors? 326; God withdraws His Word from, 181 f.; why do they flourish? 318 f., 324 f.; God does not prefer them to the faithful, 542; are destroyed, 58—64, 135, 281, 299 f., 309, 312, 349, 354—359, 537, 543—545; Edom called a wicked country, to be punished, 208 f., 513 f.; wicked scales = scales used by wicked people, 282, in house of wicked, wicked treasures, procured by wickedness, are found, 282; Israel's wicked practices call for punishment, 281, 51 ff., 58—66

Wickedness, Samaria's, 58—64; Bethel's sanctuary wickedness of wickedness, 86; Israel plowed, 86, perishes, 86; Israel's, symbolized by woman in ephah carried away, 433 f.; wickedness of priests no excuse for people, 515—517; wickedness general in the world, 162; not to be tolerated in the Church, 434 f.

Wife, Hosea's, a harlot, 18 ff.; Israel no longer God's wife, 27; Jacob compelled to work for, 99; Amaziah's wife to become unfaithful to him, 178; Jewish wife divorced by husband, in order to marry a heathen wife, 527 f.

Wild beast, God shall tear Israel like a wild beast, 102

Wilderness = steppe, prairie land; proper noun, the Arabah, the Jordan Valley, 147, through which God led Israel, 147, Israel's idolatry in, 165; brook of, probably Arnon, 174; Israel turned into, 28; led into, 32; wilderness becomes a vineyard, 32, in which Israel shall sing, 33; Edom to be waste for dragons of, 513; Nineveh to become dry as a wilderness, 372; locusts turn land into a, 119

Wind, sowing, reaping whirlwind, 69 f.; God creates wind, 224; winds obey their Creator, 224, 242; believers spread as far as winds of heaven, 418 f.

Windbag, walking, 256

Wine, God's gift, abused, 26 transl. v. 10 (8), 28 f.; "left on lees," defined, 362; without wine, no morning or evening sacrifices, 116; libations of wine in strict keeping with God's Law not possible in Exile, 73; wine of Lebanon renowned, 110; wine relays pleadings of nation to Lord, 36; wicked cry to God only for wine, 66; forbidden to Nazarites, but wicked Israelites forced them to drink, 147; impenitent Israelites shall not drink the wine promised by rich harvest, 386 transl. v. 11, 389, 281 transl. v. 15; rich oppressors drink wine obtained by extortion of their poor fellow men, 146, 162, drink out of ritual bowls, 171, give wine to their neighbors in order to enslave them, 338; wine takes away the heart, 46; new wine may intoxicate, 46; strong wine, 46 Gr. N. v. 18, 46; drowns conscience, 63

Wine press, immoralities committed there, 73

Wings, a picture of swiftness of destruction, 48; women having wings carry an ephah, 432 transl. v. 9; Sun of Righteousness rises with healing in His wings, 544 f.

Winter house smitten, 153; in winter and summer living waters proceed from Jerusalem, the Church, 498

Wisdom, man of, shall see, understand, 281 Gr. N. v. 9, 282

Woman, Hosea told to marry harlotrous, 18, and retain her, 36 transl. v. 1, 37 Gr. N. v. 1, 38; in ephah, 433, emblem of wickedness, carried to Shinar, Satan's kingdom, 434

Women of God's people evicted by oppressors, 256; Nineveh to become like defenseless women, 310; women ravished, 494, 496